TRANSPORTATION SYSTEM STUDIES AND POLICY ANALYSIS

Edited by

S. SRIRAMAN

Walchand Hirachand Professor of Transport Economics

Department of Economics

University of Mumbai

Himalaya Publishing House

MUMBAI	DELHI	NAGPUR	BENGALURU	HYDERABAD	BHUBANESWAR
CHENNAI	PUNE	INDORE	AHMEDABAD	LUCKNOW	ERNAKULAM

FIRST EDITION : 2010

PUBLISHED BY : Mrs. Meena Pandey
for **HIMALAYA PUBLISHING HOUSE PVT. LTD.**
"Ramdoot", Dr. Bhalerao Marg, Girgaon, **Mumbai-400004**
☎ 23860170 • 23863863 • Fax: 022-23877178
Email: himpub@vsnl.com
Website: www.himpub.com

BRANCH OFFICES

Delhi : "Pooja Apartments", 4-B, Murari Lal Street, Ansari Road, Darya Ganj, **New Delhi-110 002**. ☎ 23270392 • 23278631 • Fax: 011-23256286

Nagpur : Kundanlal Chandak Industrial Estate, Ghat Road, **Nagpur-440018** ☎ 2738731 • 3296733 • Telefax: 0712-2721215

Bengaluru : No. 16/1 (Old 12/1), 1st Floor, Next to Hotel Highlands, Madhava Nagar, Race Course Road, **Bangalore-560001.** ☎ 22281541 • 22385461 • Fax: 080-22286611

Hyderabad : No. 3-4-184, Lingampally, Beside Raghavendra Swamy Matham, Kachiguda, **Hyderabad-500027**, ☎ 040-65501745 • 09848130433

Chennai : No. 85/50, Bazullah Road, T-Nagar, **Chennai-600017**. ☎ 044-28144004 • 28144005

Pune : No. 527, "Laksha Apartment", 1st Floor, Mehunpura, Shaniwarpeth, Near Prabhat Theatre, **Pune-411030** ☎ 020-24496323 • 24496333

Lucknow : Jai Baba Bhavan, Near Dr. Sanjiv Awasthi, Church Road, Kurshi Road, Aliganj, **Lucknow-226024** ☎ 9305302158, 9415349385, 9389593752

Ahmedabad : 114, Shail, 1st Floor, Opp. Madhusudan House, C.G. Road, Navrangpura, **Ahmedabad-380009.** ☎ 079-26560126 • 09327324149, 09314679413

Ernakulam : No. 39/104A, Laxmi Apt., Karickamuri Cross Road, Ernakulam, **Cochin-622011.** ☎ 0484-2378012 • 2378016. 09344199799

Bhubaneswar : 5, Station Square, Bhubaneshwar, Orissa-751001. 9861046007.

Indore : Kesardeep Avenue Extension, 73, Narayan Bagh, Flat No. 302, IIIrd Floor, Near Humpty Dumpty School, Narayan Bagh, **Indore (M.P.)** 99301386468

DTP by : Sudhakar Shetty (HPH Pvt. Ltd., Mumbai)

Printed by : Esquire Printers, Worli, **Mumbai.**

PREFACE

Transportation systems are our means of gaining access to people, places, and things. Accordingly, there are a major component of the infrastructure of every economy. The phenomenal growth in transportation activities in the past five decades or so has given rise to a host of problems which forms the basis for corrective policy measures. Conferences, Seminars, Workshops, etc. have always attempted to provide a forum for interaction between experts from a particular sector, policymakers and the academicians. The outcomes of such academic events have quite often influenced decision-makers in framing an appropriate policy framework. The second International Conference on Transportation System Studies (ICOTSS) organised in January 2008 by the Walchand Hirachand Unit in Transport Economics, Department of Economics, University of Mumbai under the aegis of the Association for Transport Development in India (a registered body of transport professionals in India) which was exclusively devoted to transportation system studies with the broad theme being **"Emerging Challenges in Transport"** could be considered to be one in such a series of events.

At the conference, more than a hundred presentations were made over a period of three days which included around seventy research papers. This book which is being presented to you which has been edited by me contains thirty-two papers selected from among these research papers. These papers have been classified into the following five sub-themes/areas:

- Transport Modelling.
- Transportation Accessibility.
- Urban Transport.
- Ports and Shipping.
- Policy Issues.

Under "Transport Modelling", we have six papers some of them deal with theoretical issues in transport modelling with suggested applications while others attempt to empirically verify their hypothesis. One paper specifically deals with the issue of lack of data in empirical modelling and the use of appropriate techniques to generate useful data from the existing data base. On the sub-theme of "Transport Accessibility", there are four papers three of which focus exclusively on urban accessibility issues while the fourth looks at the problem of inaccessibility of hilly regions of the Himalayas in India. The "Urban Transport" sub-theme set of papers has examined a variety of issues such as the continuing role of urban bus undertakings, use of Omni-buses as a complementary mode, the emerging significance of information systems in decision-making in the context of road transport, the impact on the environmental situation and also the role of telecommunication in reducing transport requirements. There are three papers related to "Ports and Shipping" one of which focuses exclusively on the role of containerisation in the context of India's trade competitiveness. The other two papers deal with the impact of ports on the respective local hinterlands with an emphasis on effective inland connectivity. The final set of papers coming under the sub-theme "Policy Issues" cover a wide range of policy-related issues including governance and implementation. While competition is emphasised for effective performance, it has been pointed out that the privatisation has not been really the answer to many problems. On the other hand, an effective policy implementation framework even within the public sector sphere could take care of some of the issues especially at the ground level.

The publication has been long overdue — delayed by a year at least. I apologise to the authors of all the papers for this delay which was due to both official and personal pressure. To the authors, I offer my sincere thanks for the trouble they took in preparing first rate papers for presentation at ICOTSS-2008 and then revising these for publication. I must also thank all those who have helped me in this venture. Thanks are due specifically to Manisha Karne, Jerome Monteiro, Vidya Mohite for the very useful assistance in the editing. To Nitin Ghag and Mahendra Parihar, I owe thanks for the backoffice efforts. My special thanks are due to my dear friend V.G. Kalyankar who hastened the process of the publication. I take this opportunity to express my gratitude to Shri K.N. Pandey and his team from Himalaya Publishing House, Mumbai for their efforts in bringing out this publication.

S. SRIRAMAN

Walchand Hirachand
Professor of Transport Economics,
Department of Economics,
University of Mumbai, Mumbai.

March 2, 2010

LIST OF CONTRIBUTORS (IN ORDER OF PAPERS)

Akshaya Kumar Sen
Housing and Urban Development Corporation (HUDCO), New Delhi.
akshaya_sen@hotmail.com

Geetam Tiwari
Department of Civil Engineering, IIT, Delhi.
geetamt@gmail.com

V. Upadhyay
Department of Humanities and Social Sciences, IIT, Delhi.
upadhyay@hss.iitd.ac.in

Madhuri Jain
Faculty of Science, Dayalbagh Educational Institute, Dayalbagh, Agra.
madhulikajain32@yahoo.com

A. K. Sinha
Dayalbagh Educational Institute, Dayalbagh, Agra.
dbei@sancharnet.in

Arti Saxena
Women's Polytechnique, Dayalbagh, Agra.
artisaxenadayalbagh@yahoo.com

Preetvanti Singh
Dayalbagh Educational Institute, Dayalbagh, Agra.
preetvantisingh@gmail.com

P.K. Saxena
Department of Mechanical Engineering, Dayalbagh Educational Institute, Dayalbagh, Agra.
premkumarsaxena@yahoo.com

K. Ramachandra Rao
Department of Civil Engineering, IIT, Delhi.
rrkalaga@iitd.ac.in

A.M. Jain
Ex-Research Scholar, Department of Civil Engineering, IIT, Delhi.

V. Sayal
(Ex-B.Tech Student), Department of Civil Engineering, IIT, Delhi.

M. S. Mir
Department of Civil Engineering, National Institute of Technology, Srinagar.
shafi@nitsri.net

K. V. K. Rao
Department, of Civil Engineering, IIT, Bombay, Mumbai.
kvkrao@civil.iitb.ac.in

J. D. Hunt
Professor, Transportation Engineering and Planning,
Department of Civil Engineering,
University of Calgary, Calgary Alberta, Canada.
jdhunt@ucalgary.ca

Sudhir K. Sinha
Ex-Research Scholar, Inter-disciplinary Programme on Industrial
Engineering and Operations Research, IIT, Bombay, Mumbai.
sk9599@yahoo.com

N. Rangaraj
Inter-Disciplinary Programme on Industrial Engineering and Operations Research,
IIT, Bombay, Mumbai.
narayan.rangaraj@iitb.ac.in

N. Hemachandra
Inter-disciplinary Programme on Industrial Engineering and
Operations Research, IIT, Bombay, Mumbai.
nh@iitb.ac.in

Debabrata Datta
Ashutosh College, University of Calcutta.
d.debabrata@gmail.com

Christo Venter
Department of Civil and Bio-systems Engineering,
University of Pretoria, Pretoria, South Africa.
christo.venter@up.ac.za

Rinki Sarkar
Independent Infrastructure Consultant, New Delhi.
rinkisarkar@gmail.com

M.R. Tagore
Systra MVA Consulting (India) Private Limited, Mumbai.
moduga@rediffmail.com

Mridula Krishna
Consulting Engineering Services (I) Pvt. Ltd., Mumbai.
cesmb@vsnl.com

Sanjay Gupta
Department of Transport Planning, School of Planning and Architecture, New Delhi.
s.gupta@spa.ac.in

Amit Bhatt
New Delhi.
amitb4u@yahoo.com

P. S. Kamble
Department of Economics, Shivaji University, Kolhapur.
pskamble2007@rediffmail.com

Arif Elhag Aydrous
Alneelian University, Khartoum, Sudan.
aydrousdr@yahoo.com

N. Ramasaamy
Central Institute of Road Transport, Pune.
nrswaamy@yahoo.com

Smruti Bulsari
Department of Business and Industrial Management,
Veer Narmad South Gujarat University, Surat-395 007.
bsmruti@hotmail.com

Kshama Puntambekar
Department of Architecture and Planning MANIT Bhopal (MP).
kshamapuntambekar@yahoo.com

Ashutosh Sharma
Department of Architecture and Planning, Dean (Admin.) MANIT Bhopal, (MP) India.
ashutoshbpl7@yahoo.co.in

G. Raghuram
Indian Institute of Management, Ahmedabad.
graghu@iimahd.ernet.in

Rachna Gangwar
Indian Institute of Management, Ahmedabad.
rachna@iimahd.ernet.in

Jeronimo G.R. Monteiro
Department of Economics, University of Mumbai.
jgrm@rediffmail.com

P. Anbalagan
Department of Economics, Presidency College, Chennai - 5.
pvanbalagan@yahoo.co.in

Ashima Goyal
Indira Gandhi Institute of Development Research, Mumbai.
ashima@igidr.ac.in

T.V. Ramanayya
Indian Institute of Management, Bangalore.
tvr@iimb.ernet.in

G. Ramesh
Indian Institute of Management, Bangalore.
rameshg@iimb.ernet.in

Anand Venkatesh
Institute of Rural Management, Anand.
anand.eco@gmail.com

Tuba Modassir
Aditya Bhagat, Sampada Dev
Pratik Nowlakhe, Shashikant Ganti
Ex-students of Goa Institute of Management (GIM), Goa.

S. Sriraman
Department of Economics, University of Mumbai.
sriraman@economics.mu.ac.in

Manisha Karne
Department of Economics, University of Mumbai.
Manisha.karne@gmail.com

Vidya Mohite
Department of Economics, University of Mumbai, Mumbai.
vidyamoh2000@yahoo.co.in

L.G. Burange
Department of Economics, University of Mumbai.
lgburange@gmail.com

Shruti Yamini
Department of Economics, University of Mumbai, Mumbai.
shrutiyamini@gmail.com

Kayitha Ravinder
Central Road Research Institute, New Delhi.
krrcrri@gmail.com

S. Velmurugan
Central Road Research Institute, New Delhi.
vms_04@yahoo.co.in

S. Gangopadhyay
Central Road Research Institute, New Delhi.
sgp.crri@nic.in

M.K. Datar
IDBI Bank, Mumbai.
mkdatar@gmail.com

G.A. Tadas
IDBI Gilts Ltd., Mumbai.
Ga.tadas@idbigilts.com

Sanjay K. Singh
Indian Institute of Management, Lucknow.
sanjay@iiml.ac.in

M. Ravibabu
Rail India Technical and Economic Services Limited, Gurgaon, Haryana.
ravibabumanchala@gmail.com

R. Badri Narayan
Centre for Railway Information Systems, New Delhi.
rbadrinarayan@hotmail.com

Sudakshina Gupta
Dept. of Economics, Ramakrishna Sarada Mission, Vivekananda Vidyabhavan, Kolkata.
sudakshinagupta@yahoo.co.in

Dinesh S. Hegde
National Institute of Industrial Engineering (NITIE), Mumbai.
dshegde@nitie.edu; dshegde108@gmail.com

Lakshmikanth Hari
National Institute of Industrial Engineering (NITIE), Mumbai.
hlkanth@nitie.edu

Ramakrishna Nallathiga
Centre for Good Governance, Hyderabad.
ramanallathiga@yahoo.co.uk

CONTENTS

1

LABOUR-LEISURE CHOICE AND URBAN TRANSPORT PRICING REFORMS — A CASE OF DELHI

Akshaya Kumar Sen
Geetam Tiwari
V. Upadhyay

ABSTRACT

There is a growing interest in the use of transport pricing and taxation to solve transport problems, mainly, of congestion, air pollution, accidents and noise. This paper makes an attempt to capture transport tax reforms in the presence of labour-leisure choice and endogenous value of time in a multiple trip purpose passenger transport market within a partial equilibrium framework. The model developed in this paper addresses precisely four research questions, viz. (i) How important is the endogenous labour supply in determining optimal transport pricing? (ii) What are optimal tax rates in the presence of labour-leisure choice? (iii) How important is the strict complementarity assumption between commuting transport and labour supply for the optimal tax results?, and (iv) How significant is the issue of relative taxation of different trip purposes? It is suggested that relaxing strict complementarity assumption enables one to determine unique optimal tax rates for commuting transport, non-commuting transport and labour supply. It is also found that for a given labour tax rate, commuting trips should be taxed less than non-commuting trips, the more complementary commuting is with labour. The numerical model finds that the introduction of a differentiated transport tax system for a given level of labour tax leads to a welfare gain of 9.42 per cent of generalised income (as compared to the reference situation), an increase in labour supply by 47 per cent, a traffic volume reduction of 22 per cent and increased peak period speed of over 22 per cent thereby reducing congestion conditions considerably in Delhi. Thus, introducing optimal differentiated transport prices with the labour supply function in the consumer's preference function leads to a net welfare increase. The extent of welfare increase, however, depends upon distortions in the labour market.

1. INTRODUCTION

The problem of urban transport, in general, and traffic congestion, in particular, is worsening day by day with growing population, real income and labour force participation rate. Economic literature suggests that one way of approaching the problem is optimal transport pricing to reduce congestion externalities by making road users pay for driving in the peak periods. This means that optimal prices should include all resource costs and external costs. External costs associated with increasing transport demand have generated substantial research on optimal externality taxes and optimal tax reform in the urban transport sector. It is no wonder, therefore, that urban transport reforms currently attract a lot of attention in academic and policy-making circles.

There are many theoretical models in the transport literature (e.g., Ochelen and Proost (1996); and Proost and Van Dender (2001), Sen (2006)) which are mainly concerned with inter-related transport markets only and do not consider any interaction with the labour market for solving transport problems. These models also assume restrictive assumptions like strict complementarity between commuting to work trips and labour supply, constant value of time and single trip purpose.

This paper relaxes the restrictive assumptions mentioned above and builds a partial equilibrium model which captures transport tax reforms in the presence of labour-leisure choice and endogenous value of time in a multiple trip purpose passenger car transport market. The paper examines the additional role played by endogenous labour supply and endogenous value of time in determining optimal transport pricing in the presence of externalities. This model, therefore, extends the traditional theoretical models (e.g., TRENEN-URBAN[1], TRAP-BASIC[2]) in the following three directions:

(*a*) Endogenous labour supply is the consumer utility function. In models like TRAP-BASIC & TRENEN-URBAN labour supply is fixed. It is recognised in the literature that both the effects of marginal value of labour time and the marginal value of leisure need to be taken into account in designing appropriate transport pricing policy (see Abrego and Whally, 1998). In a second-best world where distortionary labour taxes exist, it is important to include the labour market in the analysis of optimal transport pricing reforms. (Parry and Bento, 2001, Van Dender, 2001, Calthrop, 2001).

(*b*) The value of time is introduced as an endogenous factor into the model. The TRAP-BASIC model explicitly assumes that the value of time is constant and the model does not distinguish between different trip purposes such as commuting and non-commuting trips. However, it is recognised in the literature (see Jara Diaz, 2000) that the value of marginal time saving differs between commuting trips, non-commuting trips and leisure. The use of endogenous values of time is especially relevant for the analysis of optimal tax models and in studying tax reform exercises in the transport sector, where the prevalence of congestion externalities may require relatively large adjustments in prices. The model developed in this paper captures this important aspect while determining optimal transport taxes.

(*c*) The assumption regarding strict complementarity between commuting and labour supply is relaxed. Given the importance of interaction between the transport market and the labour market, the paper introduces labour supply into the model in a more flexible way than in the literature.

Many (general equilibrium) models impose strict complementarity between commuting and labour supply while considering labour supply in their models (see Parry and Bento, 2001, Van Dender, 2001, Calthrop, 2001). The main reason for relaxing this assumption is that when labour supply changes take the form of a fixed number of workers supplying extra hours per day, there are very different implications for congestion levels than when workers decide to work an extra day per week or non-workers are induced into the workforce (Calthrop, 2001). When there is a strict complementarity between commuting transport and labour supply and commuting is the only trip purpose, a tax on commuting transport is basically a tax on labour supply. It is realised that strict complementarity between commuting transport and labour supply is not realistic, especially with multiple trip purposes. This leads to the indeterminacy of optimal taxes for transport and labour supply. It is recognised that with multiple trip purposes, the differences in the complementarity in trip purposes to leisure matter for the optimal taxes. Since this model has different trip purposes, it recognises that there will be some degree of complementarity between commuting and labour supply but not perfect complementarity. When one relaxes this strict complementarity between commuting transport and labour supply, one will be able to determine optimal taxes for commuting transport, non-commuting transport and optimal labour tax.

The model, developed in this paper, addresses the following questions:

(*i*) How important is the endogenous labour supply in determining optimal transport pricing?

(*ii*) What are optimal tax rates in the presence of labour-leisure choice?

(*iii*) How significant is the issue of relative taxation of different trip purposes?

(*iv*) How important is the strict complementarity assumption for the results?

The paper is structured as follows. Section 2 presents the theoretical model of consumer choice with multiple trip purposes and the government welfare maximisation problem in a partial equilibrium framework. In this section the optimal tax rules for commuting trips, non-commuting trips and labour are derived. The paper also deals with the issue of relative taxation of different trip purposes in this section. The theoretical predictions of the model are tested through a numerical model applied to the Delhi Urban Agglomeration in Section 3 and Section 4 provides the concluding remarks.

2. THE THEORETICAL MODEL

In order to derive the optimal tax structure in the presence of externalities, the section proceeds as follows:

2.1 Model Components and Consumer Optimum

The paper uses a simple model of the urban transport sector with multiple trip purposes, describing preferences by a single representative consumer's utility function. It assumes that utility is a function not only of commodities but also of the time allocated to them. The consumer's preferences are represented in the following utility function:

$$MaxU = u(q_{0,}\ q_1, q_2, L, N, T_1, T_2) \qquad \text{... (1)}$$

Subject to the following constraints:

$$(i)\quad q_0 + p_1 q_1 + p_2 q_2 = w(1 - t_L)L + \bar{y} \qquad [\lambda]$$
$$(ii)\quad L + N + T_1 + T_2 = \bar{T} \qquad [\mu] \qquad \dots (2)$$
$$(iii)\quad T_1 \geq aq_1 \qquad [\gamma_1]$$
$$(iv)\quad T_2 \geq aq_2 \qquad [\gamma_2]$$

where q_0 = composite (non-transport) commodity with price normalised at one, q_1 = non-commuting transport goods; q_2 = commuting transport goods (journey-to-work); L = labour time; N = leisure, T_1 = time spent on non-commuting transport; T_2 = time spent on commuting transport; aq_1 = minimum time required for non-commuting transport; aq_2 = minimum time required for commuting transport; y = exogenous income (lump sum transfer from the government); t_L = tax rate on labour (wages are normalised to 1 without loss of generality) and $\bar{T}$ = Total time endowment. p_1 and p_2 are respective transport prices per trip for non-commuting and commuting. These prices are consumer prices which consist of pre-tax prices or producer prices plus the taxes (i.e., $p_i = rc + t_i$, producer price= rc).

Constraint (*i*) is the representative consumer's budget constraint. The budget constraint states that spending on transport and other goods should be equal to the sum of labour income net of tax and the government transfer. Constraint (*ii*) is the consumer's total time resource constraint where is the total time endowment. Total time endowment is allocated across labour time (L), leisure time (*N*) and time spent on non-commuting and commuting transport goods (T_1 + T_2). Constraints (*iii*) and (*iv*) stand for the time allocation or consumption constraints where 'a' may be interpreted as technologically determined minimum amount of time required to consume one unit of q_i, which is a function of the level of congestion.

The literature suggests that the time consumption constraint will be binding for nearly all households in certain activities, like transport, due to the nature of these activities (De Serpa, 1971). Therefore, it is assumed that these constraints are binding for all transport activities. This implies that, value of time saving in these activities is non-zero. One can increase welfare by transferring time from transport to leisure.

In order to proceed further on the development of the model, a number of simplifications and assumptions are made. They are as follows:

1. All transport activities have been broadly classified into two trip purposes: commuting trips (going to work) and non-commuting trips (all other transport activities, e.g., leisure trips, shopping, going to school, cinema, etc.).
2. Commuting transport is assumed to be highly complementary to labour supply (but not strictly complementary) and non-commuting transport is assumed to be complementary to leisure.
3. Only the peak transport market has been considered for the theoretical model.
4. For simplicity, it is assumed that there is only one transport mode (car).
5. The resource cost of a car trip is equal across trip purposes. Taxes are allowed to differ across trip purposes.

6. It is assumed that commuting and non-commuting transport use the same congestible road network and therefore, jointly determine travel time, a = average travel time on a road = $F(nq_1 + nq_2)$, where $F(\bullet)$ is the congestion function and 'n' is number of road users.
7. All transport modes contribute to congestion. The contribution may differ between modes but not between trip motives.
8. The representation of the supply side is as simple as possible. Producers are profit maximisers in an environment of perfect competition under constant returns to scale.

2.1.1 First-order Conditions

The consumer's problem of efficiently allocating his money and time resources may be expressed as the maximisation of the Lagrange function given below:

$$\begin{aligned}\Im &= u(q_0, q_1, q_2, L, N, T_1, T_2) + \lambda\{[w(1-t_L)]L + \bar{y} - q_0 - p_1q_1 - p_2q_2\} \\ &\quad + \mu\{\overline{T} - L - N - T_1 - T_2\} + \gamma_1\{T_1 - aq_1\} + \gamma_2\{T_2 - aq_2\} \qquad \text{... (3)}\end{aligned}$$

where the Lagrange multiplier, λ, μ, > 0 represent shadow variables for marginal utility of money income and marginal utility of time respectively. γ_1, γ_2 > 0 represent marginal utilities of decreasing time requirements of non-commuting and commuting transport activities respectively.

The optimisation process yields the following first order conditions

$$\begin{aligned}u_0 &= \lambda \\ u_1 &= \lambda p_1 + \gamma_1 a \\ u_2 &= \lambda p_2 + \gamma_2 a \\ u_L &= \mu - \lambda[w(1-t_L)] \rightarrow \mu = u_L + \lambda[w(1-t_L)] \qquad \text{... (4)} \\ u_N &= \mu \\ u_{T_1} &= \mu - \gamma_1 \rightarrow \gamma_1 = \mu - u_{T_1} \\ u_{T_2} &= \mu - \gamma_2 \rightarrow \gamma_2 = \mu - u_{T_2}\end{aligned}$$

Substituting the values of μ in γ_1, γ_2, values of γ_1, γ_2, in u_1, u_2 and rearranging the above, the first order conditions can be written as given below:

$$\begin{aligned}u_0 &= \lambda \\ u_1 &= \lambda\left(p_1 + \left[(w(1-t_L)) + \left(\frac{u_L}{\lambda} - \frac{u_{T_1}}{\lambda}\right)\right]a\right) \\ u_2 &= \lambda\left(p_2 + \left[(w(1-t_L)) + \left(\frac{u_L}{\lambda} - \frac{u_{T_2}}{\lambda}\right)\right]a\right) \qquad \text{... (5)} \\ u_N &= u_L + \lambda[w(1-t_L)] \\ u_L &= \mu - \lambda[w(1-t_L)]\end{aligned}$$

Two important components of the above first order conditions are values of time and generalised prices. The next two sub-sections discuss these components.

2.1.2 The Value of Time and the Value of Saving Time

The cost of travel time can be regarded as having two distinct elements: an opportunity cost reflecting the value of the activity one would otherwise be engaged in and a disutility element reflecting the characteristics of the journey itself as experienced by the traveller including waiting time, walking, discomfort, etc. Studies of the value of time (VOT) generally distinguish between travel for business and working purposes as opposed to travel for non-working purposes. Following the literature on value of time (Deserpa, 1971, Jara-Diaz, 2000), one obtains the marginal value of time from the system of first order conditions (5) as follows:

$$V.O.T._N = \frac{u_N}{u_0} = \frac{\mu}{\lambda} = \frac{u_L + \lambda[w(1-t_L)]}{\lambda} = \left[w(1-t_L) + \frac{u_L}{\lambda}\right] \quad \dots (6)$$

(value of time as a resource which is also called v.o.t. of leisure)

$$V.O.T._1 = \frac{\gamma_1}{\lambda} = \left[\frac{\mu}{\lambda} - \frac{u_{T_1}}{\lambda}\right] = \left[w(1-t_L) + \left(\frac{u_L}{\lambda} - \frac{u_{T_1}}{\lambda}\right)\right] \quad \dots (7)$$

(value of marginal time saving in non-commuting)

$$V.O.T._2 = \frac{\gamma_2}{\lambda} = \left[\frac{\mu}{\lambda} - \frac{u_{T_2}}{\lambda}\right] = \left[w(1-t_L) + \left(\frac{u_L}{\lambda} - \frac{u_{T_2}}{\lambda}\right)\right] \quad \dots (8)$$

(value of marginal time saving in commuting)

The value of time can be interpreted as the net real wage per time unit, corrected for the marginal (dis-) utilities of labour supply and travel. Since the generalised price method is used in this model, it is assumed that marginal (dis-)utilities of labour supply and travel are constant in the reference period. It is further assumed that the welfare difference from spending one unit of time in transport rather than in labour $\left(\frac{u_L}{\lambda} - \frac{u_{T_i}}{\lambda}\right)$ is constant.

2.1.3 Generalised Prices

Generalised price plays an important role in the model because the time needed to complete a journey will be endogenous in the model as this depends on the level of congestion on the transport mode used. In the model, the demand functions are defined as a function of the generalised price of transport. The generalised price of transport consists of money price (e.g., the expenditures for the use of a car, p_i) plus the time cost (the time necessary for the trip times the value of time of that mode). For instance, in this transport model, if commuting transport is q_2, the monetary cost of which is p_2, the generalised price of commuting transport is:

$$GP_2 = p_2 + \left[\frac{\partial u}{\partial q_2} \Big/ \frac{\partial u}{\partial y}\right] a = p_2 + [V.O.T.]a \quad \text{where V.O.T.} = \left[w(1-t_L) + \left(\frac{u_L}{\lambda} - \frac{u_{T_2}}{\lambda}\right)\right] \quad ...(9)$$

It is known from consumer theory that in equilibrium, the ratio of marginal utilities of the two goods should be equal to the ratio of their prices for a consumer optimum. Since this model uses 'generalised prices' in stead of 'money prices', it is assumed that the same condition also holds for generalised prices, i.e.,

$$\frac{MU_i}{MU_j} = \frac{GP_i}{GP_j}$$

$$\frac{u_1}{u_0} = \frac{MU_1}{MU_0} = \frac{GP_1}{GP_0}; \quad \frac{u_2}{u_0} = \frac{MU_2}{MU_0} = \frac{GP_2}{GP_0}; \quad \frac{u_N}{u_0} = \frac{MU_N}{MU_0} = \frac{GP_N}{GP_0}$$

Since it is assumed that the generalised price of q_0 is normalised to 1, this implies:

$$GP_1 = \frac{u_1}{\lambda} = p_1 + \frac{\gamma_1}{\lambda} a = p_1 + \left[w(1-t_L) + \left(\frac{u_L}{\lambda} - \frac{u_{T_1}}{\lambda}\right)\right] a$$

$$GP_2 = \frac{u_2}{\lambda} = p_2 + \frac{\gamma_2}{\lambda} a = p_2 + \left[w(1-t_L) + \left(\frac{u_L}{\lambda} - \frac{u_{T_2}}{\lambda}\right)\right] a \quad ... (10)$$

$$GP_N = \frac{\mu}{\lambda} = \left[w(1-t_L) + \frac{u_L}{\lambda}\right]$$

$$GP_L = \left[\frac{\mu}{\lambda} - w(1-t_L)\right] = \frac{u_L}{\lambda}$$

$$GY = \left[w(1-t_L)\bar{T} + \bar{y}\right]$$

As stated earlier, the model developed in this paper uses Generalised Prices for the optimisation of the consumer utility function where time is not an argument of the utility function. The above first order conditions enable us to transform the original optimisation problem (1) into the following optimisation problem (11), the solution of which gives the same first order conditions as defined in system (5).

$$Max. U = u(q_0, q_1, q_2, L, N) \quad ... (11)$$

Subject to the following generalised budget constraint:

$$q_0 + GP_1 q_1 + GP_2 q_2 + GP_L L + GP_N N = GY$$

The first order conditions are:

$$q_0 + \left[p_1 + \left\{w(1-t_L) + \left(\frac{u_L}{\lambda} - \frac{u_{T_1}}{\lambda}\right)\right\} a\right] q_1 + \left[p_2 + \left\{w(1-t_L) + \left(\frac{u_L}{\lambda} - \frac{u_{T_2}}{\lambda}\right)\right\} a\right] q_2 + \left[w(1-t_L) + \frac{u_L}{\lambda}\right] N$$

$$+ \left[\frac{u_L}{\lambda}\right] L = [w(1-t_L)]\bar{T} + \bar{y} \quad [\varsigma] \quad ... (12)$$

where $\varsigma > 0$ represents the shadow variable for the marginal utility of generalised income. Each consumer's total generalised income consists of net wage and an exogenous component. The consumer's optimisation problem (11) implies that the first-order conditions for the above generalised budget constraint must hold at given prices, taxes and exogenous congestion level.

2.2 The Indirect Utility Function

The above first order conditions enable us to write the ***indirect utility function*** 'V' (the optimal value for the utility function (11)) as a function of vector of generalised prices, and generalised income as follows:

$$V = \begin{bmatrix} \left[p_1 + \left\{w(1-t_L) + \left(\frac{u_L}{\lambda} - \frac{u_{T_1}}{\lambda}\right)\right\}a\right]; \left[p_2 + \left\{(w(1-t_L) + \left(\frac{u_L}{\lambda} - \frac{u_{T_2}}{\lambda}\right)\right\}a\right]; \left[w(1-t_L) + \frac{u_L}{\lambda}\right]; \\ \frac{u_L}{\lambda}; \left[w(1-t_L)\overline{T} + \overline{y}\right] \end{bmatrix} \quad \text{...(13)}$$

where

$GP_i = p_i + v.o.t._i.a = p_i + \left[w(1-t_L) + \left(\frac{u_L}{\lambda} - \frac{u_{T_i}}{\lambda}\right)\right]a$ and value of time (VOT) is mode and trip specific (i.e., different value of time according to trip purposes). However, the value of time will change between equilibria, as functions of wage rate (w) and tax rate on labour(t_L). This is correct only if marginal utility of income [λ], marginal disutility of labour(u_L/λ) and marginal utility of travel time are constants. It is assumed that (U_L/λ) and $\frac{UT_i}{\lambda}$ remain constant at the level of reference equilibrium. That means it is assumed that the welfare difference from spending one unit of time in transport rather than in labour $\left(\frac{u_L}{\lambda} - \frac{u_{T_i}}{\lambda}\right)$ is constant.

2.3 The Government's Welfare Maximisation Problem

The government's problem is to maximise consumer welfare (given by the indirect utility function above), subject to a government revenue constraint as given below:

$$\underset{t_1, t_2, t_L}{Maximise} : \frac{1}{\lambda_r}[V] \quad \text{... (14)}$$

where

l_r = Marginal utility of income in the reference equilibrium; and

$$V = \begin{bmatrix} \left[p_1 + \left\{w(1-t_L) + \left(\frac{u_L}{\lambda} - \frac{u_{T_1}}{\lambda}\right)\right\}a\right]; \left[p_2 + \left\{(w(1-t_L) + \left(\frac{u_L}{\lambda} - \frac{u_{T_2}}{\lambda}\right)\right\}a\right]; \left[w(1-t_L) + \frac{u_L}{\lambda}\right]; \\ \frac{u_L}{\lambda}; \left[w(1-t_L)\overline{T} + \overline{y}\right] \end{bmatrix}$$

subject to the following government revenue constraint.

$$\sum (t_i q_i + t_L L) = S \tag{15}$$

Here the indirect utility function for a single representative consumer is maximised, taking the total flow of traffic ('n' individuals) into account.

The indirect utility function thus derived is assumed to have standard properties of differentiability and to be negatively related to the prices (inclusive of taxes) and positively related to exogenous disposable income. The government revenue constraint stipulates that the available tax instruments must be used to finance an exogenous revenue requirement 'S'. Given a certain target of tax revenue 'S' , the solution of above problem is a vector of indirect taxes (t_1, t_2, t_L) that minimises the impact on consumer's utility. The Lagrangian below (16) produces the optimal conditions.

$$\Im = \max_{t_1, t_2, t_L} \frac{1}{\lambda_r} v \begin{bmatrix} [p_1 + \{w(1-t_L) + (\frac{u_L}{\lambda} - \frac{u_{T_1}}{\lambda})\}a];\ [p_2 + \{(w(1-t_L) + (\frac{u_L}{\lambda} - \frac{u_{T_2}}{\lambda})\}a];\ [w(1-t_L) + \frac{u_L}{\lambda}]; \\ \frac{u_L}{\lambda};\ [w(1-t_L)\bar{T} + \bar{y}\ ] \end{bmatrix}$$

$$+ \eta[t_1 q_1 + t_2 q_2 + t_L L - S] - [ec_1.nq_1 + ec_2.nq_2] \qquad \ldots (16)$$

η is shadow value of revenue constraint. The terms in the last bracket are the marginal external costs other than congestion costs which can be a function of any of the variables in the model. For simplicity they are taken as constant per vehicle-km of non-commuting and commuting trips.

Decomposing consumer prices into producer prices plus taxes, $p_i = rc_i + t_i$, in the above Lagrangian, one can derive the first-order conditions which will give the following optimality conditions with respect to t_1, t_2 and t_L.

$$\frac{\partial \Im}{\partial t_1} = \frac{1}{\lambda_r}\frac{\partial v}{\partial t_1} + \eta \frac{\partial REV}{\partial t_1} - \frac{\partial EC}{\partial t_1}$$

$$= \frac{1}{\lambda_r}\frac{\partial v}{\partial GP_1}\left[\frac{\partial GP_1}{\partial p_1} + \frac{\partial GP_1}{\partial a_1}\cdot\frac{da}{dt_1}\right] + \frac{1}{\lambda_r}\frac{\partial v}{\partial GP_2}\left[\frac{\partial GP_2}{\partial p_1} + \frac{\partial GP_2}{\partial a_2}\cdot\frac{da}{dt_1}\right]$$

$$- \eta\left[q_1 + t_1\frac{dq_1}{dt_1} + t_2\frac{dq_2}{dt_1} + t_L\frac{dL}{dt_1}\right] - \left[n.ec_1\cdot\frac{dq_1}{dt_1} + n\cdot ec_2\cdot\frac{dq_2}{dt_1}\right] = 0 \qquad \ldots (17)$$

$$\frac{\partial \Im}{\partial t_2} = \frac{1}{\lambda_r}\frac{\partial v}{\partial t_2} + \eta \frac{\partial REV}{\partial t_2} - \frac{\partial EC}{\partial t_2}$$

$$= \frac{1}{\lambda_r}\frac{\partial v}{\partial GP_1}\left[\frac{\partial GP_1}{\partial p_2} + \frac{\partial GP_1}{\partial a}\cdot\frac{da}{dt_2}\right] + \frac{1}{\lambda_r}\frac{\partial v}{\partial GP_2}\left[\frac{\partial GP_2}{\partial p_2} + \frac{\partial GP_2}{\partial a}\cdot\frac{da}{dt_2}\right] \qquad \ldots (18)$$

$$- \eta\left[q_2 + t_1\frac{dq_1}{dt_2} + t_2\frac{dq_2}{dt_2} + t_L\frac{dL}{dt_2}\right] - \left[n.ec_1\cdot\frac{dq_1}{dt_2} + n.ec_2\cdot\frac{dq_2}{dt_2}\right] = 0$$

$$\frac{\partial \Im}{\partial t_L} = \left(\begin{aligned} & \frac{1}{\lambda_r}\frac{\partial v}{\partial GP_1}\left[\frac{\partial GP_1}{\partial t_L} + \frac{\partial GP_1}{\partial a}\cdot\frac{da}{dt_L}\right] + \frac{1}{\lambda_r}\frac{\partial v}{\partial GP_2}\left[\frac{\partial GP_2}{\partial t_L} + \frac{\partial GP_2}{\partial a}\cdot\frac{da}{dt_L}\right] \\ & + \frac{1}{\lambda_r}\frac{\partial v}{\partial GP_N}\left[\frac{\partial GP_N}{\partial t_L} + \frac{\partial GP_N}{\partial a}\cdot\frac{da}{dt_L}\right] + \frac{1}{\lambda_r}\frac{\partial v}{\partial GP_L}\cdot\frac{\partial GP_L}{\partial t_L} + \frac{1}{\lambda_r}\frac{\partial v}{\partial GY}\cdot\frac{\partial GY}{\partial t_L} \end{aligned} \right) \quad \text{... (19)}$$

$$+\eta\left[q_L + t_1\frac{dq_1}{dt_L} + t_2\frac{dq_2}{dt_L} + t_L\frac{dL}{dt_L}\right] - \left[n.ec_1\cdot\frac{dq_1}{dt_L} + n.ec_2\cdot\frac{dq_2}{dt_L}\right] = 0$$

Using Roy's rule and after some rearranging, one can write the government's maximisation problem as a function of the three tax instruments available: t_1,t_2 and t_L as in equations (20-22):

$$(t_1 - mec)\frac{\partial q_1}{\partial t_1} + (t_2 - mec)\frac{\partial q_2}{\partial t_1} + t_L\frac{\partial L}{\partial t_1} = \left(\frac{1 - \eta\lambda_r/\lambda}{\eta\lambda_r/\lambda}\right) q_1 \quad (20)$$

$$(t_1 - mec)\frac{\partial q_1}{\partial t_2} + (t_2 - mec)\frac{\partial q_2}{\partial t_2} + t_L\frac{\partial L}{\partial t_2} = \left(\frac{1 - \eta\lambda_r/\lambda}{\eta\lambda_r/\lambda}\right) q_2 \quad (21)$$

$$(t_1 - mec)\frac{\partial q_1}{\partial t_L} + (t_2 - mec)\frac{\partial q_2}{\partial t_L} + t_L\frac{\partial L}{\partial t_L} = \left(\frac{1 - \eta\lambda_r/\lambda}{\eta\lambda_r/\lambda}\right) \mathrm{L} \quad (22)$$

where λ is the marginal private utility of income, λ_r is the marginal utility of income in the reference equilibrium and η is the marginal cost of raising an additional unit of government revenue. The term (λ_r/λ) is an approximation term with a value close to 1. '*mec*' is the total marginal external cost of road use and given by equation (23):

$$mec = \left(\begin{aligned} & \left[\frac{\lambda}{\eta\lambda_r}\xi a'n(q_1 Z_1 + q_2 Z_2)\right] + \left[\frac{ec_1}{\eta}\left[n + \xi a'n\left(\frac{\partial q_1}{\partial GP_1}Z_1 + \frac{\partial q_1}{\partial GP_2}Z_2\right)\right] + \frac{ec_2}{\eta}\xi a'n\left(\frac{\partial q_2}{\partial GP_1}Z_1 + \frac{\partial q_2}{\partial GP_2}Z_2\right)\right] \\ & -\left[t_1\xi a'n\left(\frac{\partial q_1}{\partial GP_1}Z_1 + \frac{\partial q_1}{\partial GP_2}Z_2\right) + t_2\xi a'n\left(\frac{\partial q_2}{\partial GP_1}Z_1 + \frac{\partial q_2}{\partial GP_2}Z_2\right) + t_L\xi a'n\left(\frac{\partial L}{\partial GP_1}Z_1 + \frac{\partial L}{\partial GP_2}Z_2\right)\right] \end{aligned} \right) \quad \text{...(23)}$$

where '*n*' is number of transport users. Z_1 and Z_2 are the values of time associated with non-commuting and commuting trips respectively. x is the congestion feedback effect and is given by:

$$\frac{1}{\left(1 - a'n\frac{\partial q_1}{\partial a} - a'n\frac{\partial q_2}{\partial a}\right)} \quad \text{... [24]}$$

The total marginal external costs *(mec)* defined in (23) is the ***net social Pigouvian tax*** which consists of broadly three components. The terms in first bracket of (23) $\left\{\frac{\lambda}{\eta\lambda_r}\xi a'n(q_1 Z_1 + q_2 Z_2)\right\}$ is the marginal external congestion cost due to change in the price of transport goods and consists of the value of time losses for all transport users. This is the pure Pigouvian tax weighted by the ratio of private marginal utility of income and marginal cost of raising an additional unit of government revenue.

The second component

$$\left[\frac{ec_1}{\eta}\left[n + \xi a'n\left(\frac{\partial q_1}{\partial GP_1}Z_1 + \frac{\partial q_1}{\partial GP_2}Z_2\right)\right] + \frac{ec_2}{\eta}\xi a'n\left(\frac{\partial q_2}{\partial GP_1}Z_1 + \frac{\partial q_2}{\partial GP_2}Z_2\right)\right]$$

reflects the full effect on external costs other than congestion (e.g. pollution) due to price or tax changes. The third component

$$\left[t_1\xi a'n\left(\frac{\partial q_1}{\partial GP_1}Z_1 + \frac{\partial q_1}{\partial GP_2}Z_2\right) + t_2\xi a'n\left(\frac{\partial q_2}{\partial GP_1}Z_1 + \frac{\partial q_2}{\partial GP_2}Z_2\right) + t_L\xi a'n\left(\frac{\partial L}{\partial GP_1}Z_1 + \frac{\partial L}{\partial GP_2}Z_2\right)\right]$$

shows the total effect of change in the demand for transport good due to change in the price of that good on the government revenue constraint via congestion function. This is the derivation of revenue constraint with respect to t_1, t_2, and t_L. This component represents induced tax revenue when the level of congestion changes.

All the above three components combined together give the total *Marginal External Cost (MEC)* of road use. When there is no feedback effect from the externality on tax revenue, then the net social marginal Pigouvian tax consists of only the first two components of the above expression. Of course, when there are no externalities present (i.e. *mec=0)*, then the above first order conditions reduce to the standard first order conditions to the optimal tax problem of the Atkinson & Stiglitz type.

2.4 Optimal Tax Rules

For simplicity of derivation and interpretation of optimal tax expressions the first order conditions given in equations (20-22) can be expressed in the form of uncompensated own- and cross-price elasticities as shown in the system of equations (25-27). The price elasticities show the change in congestion level via change in the demand for transport goods caused by their price changes. As can be seen from the system of equations (25-27), transport taxes t_1, t_2 contain three similar components: the Ramsey component, the Pigouvian component and the trip interaction component. Equation (27) for labour tax rate (t_L/p_L) does not contain the Pigouvian component. This is due to the "additivity property" of the indirect tax structure: net Pigouvian tax only enters the expression for the indirect tax of the externality-generating good. Since labour supply as such does not generate congestion, there is, therefore, no Pigouvian component in that equation.

$$\frac{t_1}{p_1} = \underbrace{\left(\frac{1 - \eta\lambda_r / \lambda}{\eta\lambda_r / \lambda} \right) \frac{1}{\varepsilon_{11}}}_{\text{Ramsey component}} - \underbrace{\frac{1}{p_1} \left[\frac{\varepsilon_{21}}{\varepsilon_{11}} \frac{q_2}{q_1} (t_2 - mec) + \frac{\varepsilon_{L1}}{\varepsilon_{11}} \frac{L}{q_1} t_L \right]}_{\text{Trip interaction component}} + \underbrace{\frac{1}{p_1} mec}_{\text{Pigouvian component}} \quad \ldots (25)$$

$$\frac{t_2}{p_2} = \underbrace{\left(\frac{1 - \eta\lambda_r / \lambda}{\eta\lambda_r / \lambda} \right) \frac{1}{\varepsilon_{22}}}_{\text{Ramsey component}} - \underbrace{\frac{1}{p_2} \left[\frac{\varepsilon_{12}}{\varepsilon_{22}} \frac{q_1}{q_2} (t_1 - mec) + \frac{\varepsilon_{L2}}{\varepsilon_{22}} \frac{L}{q_2} t_L \right]}_{\text{Trip interaction component}} + \underbrace{\frac{1}{p_2} mec}_{\text{Pigouvian component}} \quad \ldots (26)$$

$$\frac{t_L}{p_L} = \underbrace{\left(\frac{1 - \eta\lambda_r / \lambda}{\eta\lambda_r / \lambda} \right) \frac{1}{\varepsilon_{LL}}}_{\text{Ramsey component}} - \underbrace{\frac{1}{p_L} \left[\frac{\varepsilon_{1L}}{\varepsilon_{LL}} \frac{q_1}{L} (t_1 - mec) + \frac{\varepsilon_{2L}}{\varepsilon_{LL}} \frac{q_2}{L} (t_2 - mec) \right]}_{\text{Trip interaction component}} \quad \ldots (27)$$

The Ramsey component of the above equations reflects the revenue raising function of the tax. As can be seen, it is inversely related to the own price elasticity of the taxed good and positively related to the marginal cost of public funds (η). It follows, therefore, that the Ramsey component is positive (negative) as long as the uncompensated own price elasticity of the taxed good is negative and marginal cost of public funds (MCPF) greater (less) than one.

The Pigouvian component is the net social Pigouvian tax which internalises the total marginal external cost of road use caused by the taxed good. This component is decreasing in the MCPF, i.e., net Pigouvian tax falls as MCPF rises. This implies that as the MCPF increases, the externality part of the optimal tax decreases below the pure Pigouvian component and the Ramsey component increases. In other words, the optimal tax system focuses more on generating revenues (Ramsey component) and less on internalising externalities.

The third component is the trip interaction component which shows the deviation between taxes and marginal external costs on the other transport markets. It captures the interactions between taxes in the presence of price distortions on other transport markets. When there are no price distortions, then those deviations are zero, implying the trip interaction component drops out from the tax expression.

2.4.1 Optimal Tax for Non-commuting Trips

This sub-section derives optimal tax rate for non-commuting trips when labour tax is optimal and also for a given level of labour tax rate, under different assumptions regarding cross-price effects between the taxed goods.

Assume that the uncompensated price elasticites between non-commuting and commuting trips and between non-commuting and labour supply are zero. Then the optimal non-commuting tax rate can be derived from (25) as:

$$\frac{t_1}{p_1}=\left(\frac{1-\eta\lambda_r/\lambda}{\eta\lambda_r/\lambda}\right)\frac{1}{\varepsilon_{11}}+\frac{1}{p_1}mec \quad \text{... (28)}$$

This is the familiar Ramsey inverse elasticities rule which says that when there are no cross-price effects between the taxed goods, the proportional rates of tax should be inversely related to the price elasticity of demand of the good on which they are levied. This means there is no deviation between prices and marginal social costs in the commuting trips. The optimal non-commuting tax rate hence only contains the Ramsey component and the Pigouvian component.

If one assumes non-zero cross-price effects between commuting and non-commuting while assuming as before the zero cross price effects between non-commuting and labour supply and commuting and labour supply, one gets the following expression for optimal tax rate for non-commuting trips:

$$\frac{t_1}{p_1}=\left(\frac{1-\eta\lambda_r/\lambda}{\eta\lambda_r/\lambda}\right)\left[\frac{\varepsilon_{22}}{\varepsilon_{11}\varepsilon_{22}-\varepsilon_{12}\varepsilon_{21}}-\frac{\varepsilon_{21}}{\varepsilon_{11}\varepsilon_{22}-\varepsilon_{12}\varepsilon_{21}}\cdot\frac{p_2q_2}{p_1q_1}\right]+\frac{1}{p_1}mec \quad \text{... (29)}$$

It can be seen from equation (29) that the first component of the Ramsey weight is decreasing in the own price elasticity of non-commuting trips and in the cross-price elasticities with respect to commuting trips. It is increasing in the own price elasticity of commuting trips. Since commuting and non-commuting trips are substitutes, the second component of the weight increases the Ramsey element of the optimal tax on non-commuting trips.

To interpret equation (29) it is assumed that the own price elasticities are negative, uncompensated cross-price elasticities are positive for substitutes and negative for complements and that the own price effects are larger than cross-price effects. Then the first component in right hand side of (29) is negative and second is positive. The overall Ramsey term, which takes into account the trip interaction effects, is positive, given that the MCPF is positive. This implies the trip interaction component is critical in the determination of the optimal tax structure.

Now assume that the cross-price effects between non-commuting and commuting are zero but there exist non-zero cross-price effects between non-commuting and labour supply. In this case, the optimal non-commuting tax equation would be the one given as below:

$$\frac{t_1}{p_1}=\left(\frac{1-\eta\lambda_r/\lambda}{\eta\lambda_r/\lambda}\right)\left[\frac{\varepsilon_{LL}}{\varepsilon_{11}\varepsilon_{LL}-\varepsilon_{L1}\varepsilon_{1L}}-\frac{\varepsilon_{L1}}{\varepsilon_{11}\varepsilon_{LL}-\varepsilon_{L1}\varepsilon_{1L}}\cdot\frac{p_LL}{p_1q_1}\right]+\frac{1}{p_1}mec \quad \text{... (30)}$$

As before, the Ramsey weight is decreasing in the own price elasticity of non-commuting trips and in the cross-price elasticities with respect to labour. It is increasing in the own price elasticity of labour. But in the second component it is increasing in the cross-price elasticities with respect to labour. Assuming the signs of the own- and cross-price elasticities remain the same as before and non-commuting and labour are substitutes, it can be seen that the first component of the Ramsey weight is negative and the second is positive. Since the second is subtracted from the first, the overall Ramsey term is positive if the MCPF is positive. Since, the Ramsey term is positive, non-commuting should be taxed, even if there are no externalities.

Assume now that *labour tax rate is fixed* ($\bar{t}_L$). For a given level of labour tax rate and assuming no cross-effects between commuting and non-commuting transport, the optimal non-commuting transport tax rate can be derived from equation (25), where now it is assumed that t_L is fixed. Then one can have:

$$\frac{t_1}{p_1} = \left(\frac{1-\eta\lambda_r/\lambda}{\eta\lambda_r/\lambda}\right)\frac{1}{\varepsilon_{11}} - \frac{1}{p_1}\left[\frac{\varepsilon_{L1}}{\varepsilon_{11}}\cdot\frac{L}{q_1}.\bar{t}_L\right] + \frac{1}{p_1}mec \quad \text{... (31)}$$

It can be seen that the optimal tax expression (31) for a given labour tax rate has three components, i.e. Ramsey component, labour supply interaction component and the Pigou component respectively. This equation shows that when the labour tax rate is fixed, the optimal non-commuting transport tax rate is determined by the cross-effect between labour supply and non-commuting transport, .i.e. and the own price elasticity of non-commuting transport (ε_{11}). The main difference between equations (30) and (31) is that in (31) the labour tax is fixed and hence, sub-optimal. There is, therefore, no role for own price elasticity of labour supply (ε_{LL}) and cross effect of wage rate on non-commuting (ε_{1L}) in equation (31).

2.4.2 Optimal Tax for Commuting Trips

If one assumes that the cross-price effects are same as those in case of non-commuting trips discussed above (28), then the optimal tax for commuting trips looks like the one given in expression (32).

$$\frac{t_2}{p_2} = \left(\frac{1-\eta\lambda_r/\lambda}{\eta\lambda_r/\lambda}\right)\frac{1}{\varepsilon_{22}} + \frac{1}{p_2}mec \quad \text{... (32)}$$

The interpretation is the same as in the case of non-commuting trips (inverse elasticity rule of Ramsey term). However, if one relaxes the assumption by allowing for non-zero cross price elasticities between commuting and non-commuting while retaining all other assumptions made in case of non-commuting trips, the optimal tax expression for commuting trips can be defined as in (33) which has similar interpretation as in case of non-commuting trips given in (29).

$$\frac{t_2}{p_2} = \left(\frac{1-\eta\lambda_r/\lambda}{\eta\lambda_r/\lambda}\right)\left[\frac{\varepsilon_{11}}{\varepsilon_{11}\varepsilon_{22}-\varepsilon_{12}\varepsilon_{21}} - \frac{\varepsilon_{12}}{\varepsilon_{11}\varepsilon_{22}-\varepsilon_{12}\varepsilon_{21}}\cdot\frac{p_1q_1}{p_2q_2}\right] + \frac{1}{p_2}mec \quad \text{... (33)}$$

As was the case with non-commuting trips, here also the first component in right hand side of (33) is negative and second is positive. The overall Ramsey term, which takes into account the trip interaction effects, is positive, given that the MCPF is positive. This implies that trip interaction component is critical in determination of optimal tax structure.

However, in reality, commuting transport and labour supply are related in a complementary way. It has been assumed in this model that this relationship is highly complementary, though, not strictly complementary. So now assume that the cross-price effects between non-commuting and commuting transport are zero but there exist non-zero cross-price effects between commuting and labour supply. In this case, the optimal commuting transport tax expression is defined by equation (34).

$$\frac{t_2}{p_2} = \left(\frac{1 - \eta\lambda_r/\lambda}{\eta\lambda_r/\lambda} \right) \left[\frac{\varepsilon_{LL}}{\varepsilon_{LL}\varepsilon_{22} - \varepsilon_{L2}\varepsilon_{2L}} - \frac{\varepsilon_{L2}}{\varepsilon_{LL}\varepsilon_{22} - \varepsilon_{L2}\varepsilon_{2L}} \cdot \frac{p_L L}{p_2 q_2} \right] + \frac{1}{p_2} mec \quad \ldots (34)$$

In (34) the Ramsey weight is decreasing in the own price elasticity of commuting trips and in the cross-price elasticities with respect to labour. It is increasing in the own price elasticity of labour. But in the second component it is increasing in the cross-price elasticities with respect to labour. Assuming commuting and labour are complements, it can be seen that the first component of the Ramsey weight is negative and the second is also negative. Since the second is subtracted from the first, the overall sign of the Ramsey weight for commuting transport depends upon the magnitudes of the elasticities. For example, if the absolute value of ε_{LL} greater than that of ε_{L2}, other things remaining same, it implies the Ramsey weight for commuting transport is negative. Given the positive MCPF, the overall Ramsey term is positive indicating, in this particular case, commuting transport should be taxed irrespective of external costs.

If one further relaxes the assumptions and allow for the non-zero relationship between commuting and labour supply and commuting and non-commuting (while continuing to assume no cross-price effects between non-commuting trips and labour supply), the optimal tax rate for commuting transport is as follows:

$$\frac{t_2}{p_2} = \left(\frac{1 - \eta\lambda_r/\lambda}{\eta\lambda_r/\lambda} \right) \left[\begin{array}{l} \dfrac{\varepsilon_{11}\varepsilon_{LL}}{\varepsilon_{11}\varepsilon_{22}\varepsilon_{LL} - \varepsilon_{12}\varepsilon_{21}\varepsilon_{LL} - \varepsilon_{11}\varepsilon_{2L}\varepsilon_{L2}} - \dfrac{\varepsilon_{12}\varepsilon_{LL}}{\varepsilon_{11}\varepsilon_{22}\varepsilon_{LL} - \varepsilon_{12}\varepsilon_{21}\varepsilon_{LL} - \varepsilon_{11}\varepsilon_{2L}\varepsilon_{L2}} \\ \cdot \dfrac{p_1 q_1}{p_2 q_2} - \dfrac{\varepsilon_{11}\varepsilon_{L2}}{\varepsilon_{11}\varepsilon_{22}\varepsilon_{LL} - \varepsilon_{12}\varepsilon_{21}\varepsilon_{LL} - \varepsilon_{11}\varepsilon_{2L}\varepsilon_{L2}} \dfrac{p_L L}{p_2 q_2} \end{array} \right] + \frac{1}{p_2} mec$$

$$\ldots (35)$$

The weight of the Ramsey term consists of three components. Under usual assumptions with respect to own- and cross- price elasticities, it can be seen that the first component is negative, the second one is positive and the third component is negative. The overall weight of the Ramsey term is negative or positive depending upon the weight in absolute terms of the three components which depends upon the degree of complementarity and substitutability among the three goods. If the weight is negative and the MCPF is positive, then the overall Ramsey term is positive and vice versa.

Now assume that *labour tax rate is fixed* ($\bar{t}_L$). For a given level of labour tax rate, and assuming zero cross-effects between commuting and non-commuting transport, the optimal commuting transport tax rate can be derived from equation (26), where now it is assumed that t_L is fixed. Then one can have:

$$\frac{t_2}{p_2} = \left(\frac{1-\eta\lambda_r/\lambda}{\eta\lambda_r/\lambda}\right)\frac{1}{\varepsilon_{22}} - \frac{1}{p_2}\left[\frac{\varepsilon_{L2}}{\varepsilon_{22}}\cdot\frac{L}{q_2}\cdot\bar{t}_L\right] + \frac{1}{p_2}mec \quad \text{... (36)}$$

Expression (36) shows that when the labour tax rate is fixed, the optimal commuting transport tax rate is determined by the cross-effect between labour supply and commuting transport, *i.e.*, and the own price elasticity of commuting transport (ε_{22}). The main difference between equations (34) and (36) is that in (36) the labour tax is fixed and hence, sub-optimal. There is, therefore, no role for own price elasticity of labour supply (ε_{LL}) and cross effect of wage rate on commuting (ε_{2L}) in equation (36) as was the case with non-commuting transport tax rate defined in (31).

2.4.3 Optimal Tax for Labour

When there is no constraint on labour tax, meaning labour tax rate can be flexible and determined optimally, then substituting the optimal tax expressions (30) and (34) into the first order condition for labour tax (27) one gets the following expression for optimal labour tax rate. Let R_1 and R_2 denote the Ramsey weights for the non-commuting and commuting taxes.

$$\frac{t_L}{p_L} = \left(\frac{1-\eta\lambda_r/\lambda}{\eta\lambda_r/\lambda}\right)\left[\frac{1}{\varepsilon_{LL}} - \frac{\varepsilon_{1L}}{\varepsilon_{LL}}\frac{p_1q_1}{p_LL}R_1 - \frac{\varepsilon_{2L}}{\varepsilon_{LL}}\frac{p_2q_2}{p_LL}R_2\right] \quad \text{... (37)}$$

where

$$R_1 = \left[\frac{\varepsilon_{LL}}{\varepsilon_{11}\varepsilon_{LL} - \varepsilon_{L1}\varepsilon_{1L}} - \frac{\varepsilon_{L1}}{\varepsilon_{11}\varepsilon_{LL} - \varepsilon_{L1}\varepsilon_{1L}}\cdot\frac{p_LL}{p_1q_1}\right]$$

$$R_2 = \left[\frac{\varepsilon_{LL}}{\varepsilon_{LL}\varepsilon_{22} - \varepsilon_{L2}\varepsilon_{2L}} - \frac{\varepsilon_{L2}}{\varepsilon_{LL}\varepsilon_{22} - \varepsilon_{L2}\varepsilon_{2L}}\cdot\frac{p_LL}{p_2q_2}\right]$$

Assuming labour supply has no cross-price effect with commuting transport and non-commuting, i.e., $\varepsilon_{2L} = 0, \varepsilon_{1L} = 0$, the optimal labour tax rate would then simply be a Ramsey component as given below:

$$\frac{t_L}{p_L} = \left(\frac{1-\eta\lambda_r/\lambda}{\eta\lambda_r/\lambda}\right)\frac{1}{\varepsilon_{LL}} \quad \text{... (38)}$$

Equation (38) shows the optimal labour tax only contains the Ramsey term and it is inversely related to the own price elasticity of labour and positively related to the marginal cost of public funds. It follows, therefore, that the Ramsey component is positive (negative) as long as the uncompensated own price elasticity of labour is negative and MCPF greater (less) than one.

If there are no cross-price effects between non-commuting and labour supply but non-zero cross-effects between commuting transport and labour supply, one gets the following expression for optimal labour tax rate from equation (37).

$$\frac{t_L}{p_L} = \left(\frac{1 - \eta\lambda_r/\lambda}{\eta\lambda_r/\lambda} \right) \left[\frac{1}{\varepsilon_{LL}} - \frac{p_2 q_2}{p_L L} \frac{\varepsilon_{2L}}{\varepsilon_{LL}} R_2 \right] \quad \text{... (39)}$$

Equation (39) establishes the following relationship between labour supply elasticities and Ramsey term weight for commuting taxes.

$$\varepsilon_{2L} = \frac{p_L L}{R_2 . p_2 q_2} + \frac{t_L/p_L}{\left(\frac{1 - \eta\lambda_r/\lambda}{\eta\lambda_r/\lambda} \right)} \quad \text{... (40)}$$

when there is no labour tax, then, $\varepsilon_{2L} = \frac{p_L L}{R_2 . p_2 q_2} \quad \varepsilon_{2L} < \varepsilon_{LL}$

Equation (40) shows that the Ramsey weight of the commuting transport tax (R_2) is inversely related to the cross-price elasticity of labour supply. Since it is assumed that commuting transport is highly complementary to labour supply, it means a higher cross-price elasticity of labour supply implies demand for commuting trips will be less and hence less revenue raising through commuting transport tax. This implies when the tax discourages labour supply more then commuting should be taxed less.

In the special case, when commuting transport and labour supply are perfectly complementary, then equation (40) becomes the one similar to the one derived in Van Dender (2001):

$$\varepsilon_{LL} = \frac{p_L L}{R_2 . p_2 q_2} + \frac{t_L/p_L}{\left(\frac{1 - \eta\lambda_r/\lambda}{\eta\lambda_r/\lambda} \right)} \quad \text{... (41)}$$

A higher elasticity of labour supply implies less revenue-raising through commuting transport tax. In this case of strict complementarity between labour supply and commuting transport, the optimal commuting tax depends on the prevailing labour tax rate. When the labour tax rate is low, commuting transport tax becomes relatively high. On the other extreme case, as in Mayeres and Proost (1997), where there is no distinction between commuting and non-commuting trips, this relationship disappears and commuting and non-commuting are taxed at a uniform rate.

If one now assumes positive cross-price effects between non-commuting transport and labour supply but zero cross-price effects between commuting and labour supply, then the optimal labour tax expression can be written be as follows:

$$\frac{t_L}{p_L} = \left(\frac{1-\eta\lambda_r/\lambda}{\eta\lambda_r/\lambda}\right)\left[\frac{1}{\varepsilon_{LL}} - \frac{p_1 q_1}{p_L L}\frac{\varepsilon_{1L}}{\varepsilon_{LL}} R_1\right] \quad \text{... (42)}$$

Equation (42) establishes the following relationship between labour supply elasticities and Ramsey term weight for non-commuting taxes.

$$\varepsilon_{1L} = \frac{p_L L}{R_1 . p_1 q_1} + \frac{t_L/p_L}{\left(\frac{1-\eta\lambda_r/\lambda}{\eta\lambda_r/\lambda}\right)} \quad \text{... (43)}$$

If there is no labour tax, then $\varepsilon_{1L} = \frac{p_L L}{R_1 . p_1 q_1}$.

Equation (43) shows that the Ramsey weight of the non-commuting transport tax (R1) is inversely related to the cross-price elasticity of labour supply. It is well-known that the Ramsey component crucially depends on the relative complementarity of the taxed good with respect to (untaxed) leisure, in the sense that tax rates on relative complements to leisure are relatively high. Since by assumption non-commuting transport is a relative complement to leisure and a relative substitute to labour, it means a higher cross-price elasticity of labour supply with non-commuting transport implies demand for non-commuting transport will be more when labour tax increases and hence more revenue raising through non-commuting transport tax. Relatively higher tax rate on non-commuting transport is, therefore, expected.

2.5 Relative Taxation of Different Trip Purposes for a Given Labour Tax Rate

For a given level of labour tax rate ($\bar{t}_L$)and assuming no cross-price effects between taxed transport goods, the optimal tax expressions for commuting and non-commuting transport are given in the equations (31) and (36) above. To know which of the two transport taxes should be taxed more, one needs to know the relative tax expression as defined below:

$$\frac{t_1/p_1}{t_2/p_2} = \frac{\left(\frac{1-\eta\lambda_r/\lambda}{\eta\lambda_r/\lambda}\right)\frac{1}{\varepsilon_{11}} - \frac{1}{p_1}\left[\frac{\varepsilon_{L1}}{\varepsilon_{11}}.\frac{L}{q_1}.\bar{t}_L\right] + \frac{1}{p_1}mec}{\left(\frac{1-\eta\lambda_r/\lambda}{\eta\lambda_r/\lambda}\right)\frac{1}{\varepsilon_{22}} - \frac{1}{p_2}\left[\frac{\varepsilon_{L2}}{\varepsilon_{22}}.\frac{L}{q_2}.\bar{t}_L\right] + \frac{1}{p_2}mec} \quad \text{... (44)}$$

Relative taxation depends upon own price elasticities, i.e., ε_{11} and ε_{22} cross-price relationship of commuting and non-commuting transports with labour, i.e., ε_{L1} and ε_{L2}. Equation (44) says that if both commuting and non-commuting transport stand in the same relation to labour, then they should be taxed according to their own price elasticities, ceteris paribus. However, by assumption non-commuting transport is a relative substitute and commuting transport is relatively complementary with labour. In the above expression when commuting and labour supply is more complementary, it means the absolute value of ε_{L2} becomes larger. The denominator of (44) becomes smaller which means the left hand side of the expression (tax ratio) becomes larger. This implies, $t_1/p_1 > t_2/p_2$ *i.e.*, non-commuting transport should be taxed more than commuting transport, when commuting trips are more complementary with labour supply. This result can also be obtained from the relationship between labour supply and non-commuting. Assume that non-commuting is a better substitute for labour. Then ε_{L1} will be positive and the absolute value of ε_{L1} will be larger. All other terms remaining same, the numerator of equation (44) will increase which means higher value for the left hand side of the expression (i.e., tax ratio), indicating again that non-commuting transport should be taxed more than commuting transport.

However, this result cannot be true always. The reverse could be true in some cases. Relative tax rates also depend upon the own price elasticities ε_{11} and ε_{22}. Tax literature suggests that the good which is more price elastic should be taxed less. If one assumes non-commuting trips more price elastic than commuting trips and cross- price effects ε_{L1} & ε_{L2} counter balances each other, then, ceteris paribus, $t_1/p_1 < t_2/p_2$, i.e., non-commuting transport could be taxed less than commuting transport in this case. The relative tax rates, therefore, depend upon the relative magnitudes and counter balancing effects of different elasticities.

3. EMPIRICAL APPLICATION OF THE MODEL

3.1 Consumer's Direct Utility Function — The Utility Tree

The theoretical model and optimal tax rates which have been developed in section 2 need to be put into practice by using a more elaborate numerical model involving different transport modes and multiple trip purposes to find out the validity and implications for tax levels.

The paper assumes that the direct utility function of a representative consumer is a weakly separable utility function of the following form:

$$U = [u_1(q_2, L), u_2(q_0, q_1, N)] \qquad \text{... (45)}$$

where q_0 = composite (non-transport) commodity with price normalised at one, q_1 = non-commuting transport goods; q_2 = commuting transport goods (journey-to-work); L = labour time; N = leisure. u_1 and u_2 are weakly separable utility function.

The above direct utility function 'U' of each consumer is a *nested utility function*[3] with 6 levels ($L = 0,\ldots,5$) defined over the quantities of different commodities (transport and non-transport commodities). Figure 1 shows the utility tree describing the commodity groups and the hierarchical structure of the tree. The use of sub-utility functions for each level in the tree rests on the assumption that preferences on each level can be defined independently of quantities on other levels.

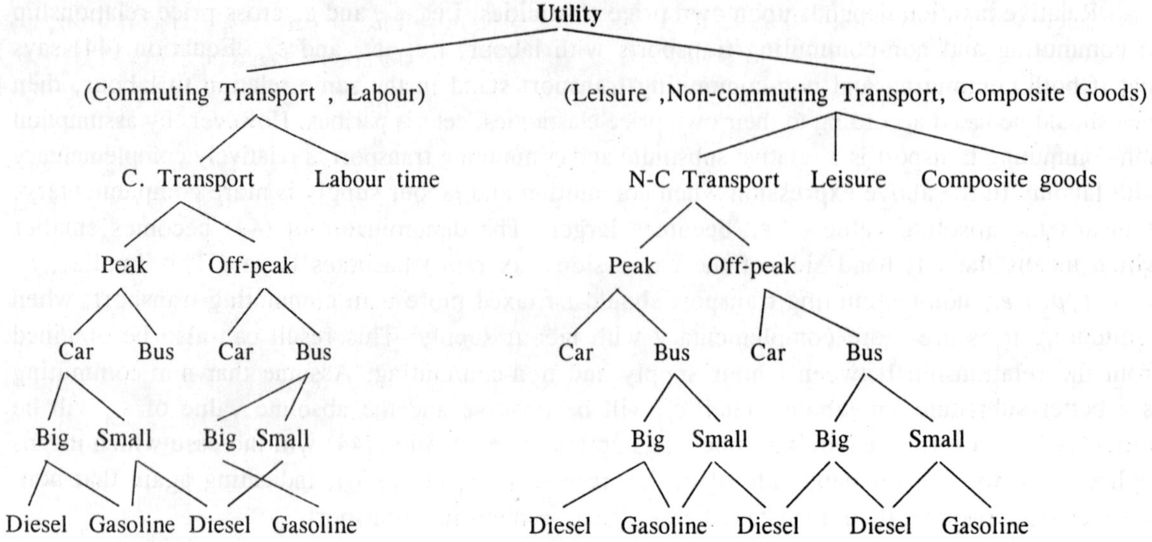

Fig. 1: Nested Utility Tree with Labour Supply

At the highest level (**L = 0**) of the tree, the utility component is a CES type of the function (Keller-1976). CES has the following form in the case of 2 goods q_1 & q_2.

$$U = \left[\alpha . q_1^{\frac{1}{\sigma_1}} . q_1^{\frac{\sigma_1 - 1}{\sigma_1}} + (1-\alpha) . q_2^{\frac{1}{\sigma_1}} . q_2^{\frac{\sigma_1-1}{\sigma_1}} \right]^{\frac{\sigma_1}{\sigma_1 - 1}} \qquad \text{... (46)}$$

$$\text{Price Index} = PU = \left[\alpha . q_1 \cdot p . q_1^{1-\sigma_1} + (1-\alpha) \cdot q_2 \cdot p \cdot q_2^{1-\sigma_1} \right]^{\frac{1}{1-\sigma_1}} \qquad \text{... (47)}$$

Price elasticities:

$$\varepsilon_{ii} = - w_i - \sigma w_j \; (i, j = 1, 2; \; i \neq j) \qquad \text{... (48)}$$

$$\varepsilon_{ij} = w_j \, (\sigma - 1) \, (i, j = 1, 2; \; i \neq j) \qquad \text{... (49)}$$

with $w_i = p_i q_i / m$ (share)

The income elasticity for a CES function equals one, so one has homothetic preferences or constant returns to scale in utility production. Therefore, the composition of the budget is independent of total income and of total utility. The price elasticities are dependent on budget shares and the constant elasticity of substitution.[4]

At level $L = 0$, the consumers allocate their resources between commuting transport and labour supply on the one hand and all other goods which includes non-commuting, leisure and other composite goods, on the other hand. A higher value of the elasticity of substitution(σ) at level $L = 0$ will make the relationship between commuting transport and all other goods (leisure, non-commuting and composite goods) highly substitutes (σ > 1). All other utility components ($L = 1,...,5$) are specified as linear homogeneous Modified Constant Elasticity of Substitution (MCES) functions of the associated utility components at the next level, following Keller, (1976).

The **separability** which follows from the specification of 'U' means that goods on a branch of the tree will react identically to price changes for all goods on other branches. For instance, when commuting transport gets cheaper, the demand for leisure, non-commuting transport and composite goods reacts in the same way. When the price of commuting transport becomes cheaper, the demand for it will increase and the demand for its substitutes like non-commuting and leisure will decrease. When commuting is a substitute for leisure, it is also a substitute for non-commuting transport and composite goods. The relationship between goods in 2 branches depends on the elasticity of substitution(σ). The specification also implies that a change in the price of a transport mode in the off-peak period will affect all transport modes in the peak period in the same way. For example, the change in the price of car transport in peak period will affect the changes in the demand for car and bus transport in the off-peak in the same way. In other words, the consumer chooses first whether, he wants to travel in the peak or in the off-peak and then selects his transport mode, the vehicle type, etc.

In the model, it is assumed that there is no strict complementarity between labour supply and commuting to work. The restrictive assumption of strict complementarity has been done away with. In reality, an individual is likely to enjoy some 'flexibility' (e.g. s/he can take a second job; s/he can work at home; s/he can move his residence closer to his workplace). This paper, therefore, relaxes the assumption of strict complementarity and consider CES function of q_2 and L.

The model, therefore, treats the complementarity between labour and commuting as not strict (i.e., $\sigma \neq 0$) but highly complimentary ($\sigma > 0$). This is done by choosing a higher value of the elasticity of substitution (σ) at level L=0 such that commuting transport and all other goods (leisure, non-commuting and composite goods) are highly substitutes ($\sigma > 1$) and a lower value of the elasticity of substitution ($0 < \sigma < .5$) at level L=1 such that leisure, the non-commuting transport and composite goods are highly complimentary with each other.

At level **L = 1**, the group of commuting transport and labour time is a MCES function of commuting transport and labour time that has complementary relationship between them. All other commodities are a MCES function of non-commuting transport, leisure and composite goods. In order to make these three branches complimentary, one needs to choose a low value of s. At the level **L = 2**, the utility index of commuting and non-commuting transport are MCES functions of peak and off-peak transport. This means that price changes of off-peak transport will affect peak car and peak bus transport through the same channel. At the level **L = 3**, in each period (peak and off-peak), commuting and non-commuting transport are MCES functions of transport by different modes (cars and buses). At the level **L = 4**, car transport is a MCES function of transport by different car sizes (big or small). At the level **L = 5**, car transport is a MCES function of transport by different car types (Diesel, Gasoline).

3.2 Calibration of the Model

After defining the model through a nested utility tree, the next step is to calibrate the model. Calibration requires that the entire model specification should be capable of generating a benchmark equilibrium observation as a model solution. This model consists of a nested CES structure for consumer demand for transport. Empirical data on demand, prices, speeds, etc. are used to calculate the unknown parameters of the theoretical model, assuming that these data represent so-called benchmark equilibrium. In the calibration, the benchmark equilibrium situation is taken to be the one in the Delhi urban agglomeration in 2005, a choice which is motivated primarily by data availability. To completely determine parameter values, information is needed on substitution elasticities. The substitution elasticities determine the curvature of indifference curves; the benchmark data define their position. The benchmark data and the substitution elasticities define the other model parameters. Once the model has been calibrated, it can be used to generate counterfactual equilibria, by simulation or by optimisation. The model developed here is an optimisation model: counter factual equilibria are social welfare maxima, given constraints on policy instruments.

3.3 Calibration Results

The model is calibrated to a Delhi Urban Agglomeration (DUA) dataset using a congestion function derived through a speed-flow relationship. The congestion function is linear, with a free flow speed of 45 km/h, peak traffic speed of 24 km/h and off-peak traffic speed of 40 km/h. The average value of time, as implied by the calibration, is Rs. 50.84/hour for car travel and Rs. 17.11 for bus travel.

The total number of persons residing in DUA in 2005 is 12.90 million, of which 4.54 million supply 8 hours of labour per day. The length of the working day is fixed. A representative individual supplies 1.84 hours of labour per day as per the estimation. The gross wage rate is Rs. 46.80/hour. With an average labour tax of 20%, the net daily labour income per representative individual is Rs. 37.44/hour.

As per the available data from RITES (primary survey, 2001), commuting trips (going to work) account for 25% of the total number of trips. Leisure trips accounts for the remaining 75% of trips consisting of education trips of 22% return to home trips of 49% and others trips of 4%. It is estimated that the modal split for commuting transport is 38.5% car trips and 61.5% bus trips. The paper assumes the same modal share for leisure trips.

In the CES function, the combination of elasticities of substitution with prices and quantities determine price elasticities. The values of the elasticities of substitution used for the optimisation equilibrium and the resulting compensated price elasticties more or less conform to those found in the literature. As can be seen from Table 1 the own price elasticity of labour supply is 0.67, which is in line with the literature. For example, it lies in between the values of 0.35 and 1.09, used by Parry and Bento (2001) and Mayeres (1999) respectively. The own price elasticity of demand for commuting trips is determined by the labour supply elasticity. It is lower for commuting trips than for non-commuting trips. In addition, the parameters are chosen such that the cross-price elasticities between transport modes is larger for commuting trips than for non-commuting trips. The underlying assumption is that the availability of public transport modes is larger for commuting trips than for leisure trips, because of differences in the spatial distribution of origins and destinations.

Table 1: Elasticities of Substitution and Compensated Own- and Cross-Price Elasticities

Elasticities of Substitution*	
Commuting Transport – Other Commodities	0.6
Commuting Transport – Labour Supply	0.2
Non-commuting Transport – Leisure	0.2
Compensated Own – Price Elasticities**	
Labour supply (E_{LL})	– 0.67
Leisure (E_{NN})	– 0.49
Peak Commuting Car Transport (E_{22})	– 0.43
Peak Non-Commuting Car Transport (E_{11})	– 0.44
Compensated Cross – Price Elasticities**	
Labour – Commuting Transport (E_{L2})	– 0.47
Labour – Non-commuting Transport (E_{L1})	0.71
Leisure – Non-commuting Transport (E_{N1})	– 0.29
Peak Car Commuting – Bus Commuting	0.13
Peak Bus Commuting – Car Commuting	0.45
Peak Car Non-commuting – Bus non-Commuting	0.01
Peak Bus Non-commuting – Car non-Commuting	0.32

*Source: * Own assumptions based on literature (De Borger et. al. 1993).*
** Computed in the Calibration Model.

3.3.1 Optimal Differentiated Transport Taxes (*for a given level of labour tax*)

For a given level of labour tax, Table 2 gives the optimal transport taxes for commuting and non-commuting trips for a small gasoline car and for public transport characterised by bus. As can be seen from Table 2, in the optimal situation taxes increases for all modes for commuting trips and non-commuting trips compared to the reference situation and differentiated tax rate leads to more tax for non-commuting trips than for commuting trips as was predicted by the theoretical model. This is the case for both peak and off-peak periods. For public transport too commuting trips should be taxed less than non-commuting in both peak and off-peak periods. The results also indicate that the public transport should not be subsidised. The above results proved the theoretical finding that in the presence of distortionary taxes on labour supply, an optimal tax system would set lower taxes on commuting trips than on non-commuting trips, the more complementary commuting is with labour.

Table 2: Taxes in Reference Situation and Optimal Differentiated Taxes (Rs./pkm)

Reference Situation	***Commuting***	***Non-commuting***
Pk.car.sm.gs	1.74	1.74
Off-pk.car.sm.gs	1.47	1.47
Pk.bus	0.01	0.01
Off-peak bus	0.02	0.02
Welfare	3766.94	
Consumer Surplus (Rs. million)	292.44	
External Costs (Rs. million)	5.52	
Traffic Volume (million/pkm)	65.48	
Optimal Pricing		
Pk.car.sm.gs	9.99	13.50
Off-pk.car.sm.gs	5.85	8.34

Pk.bus	1.55	2.18
Off-peak bus	1.26	1.85
Welfare	4121.95	(9.42% increase over R.F.)
Consumer Surplus (Rs. million)	319.85	
External Costs (Rs. million)	4.06	(26.45% decrease over R.F.)
Traffic Volume (million/pkm)	51.00	(22.00% decrease over R.F.)

Source: Numerical Model Output.

Since the principal standard for policy assessment is overall welfare level of a given economic equilibrium, one can see from the Table 2 that the introduction of differentiated transport tax system for a given level of labour tax leads to a welfare gain of 9.42 per cent of generalised income, as compared to the reference situation. Further, external costs of air pollution, noise and accidents decrease by Rs.1.46 million per day, a decrease of 26.43 per cent. The change in congestion condition is reflected in the overall decrease of traffic volume by 22 per cent and increase in peak period speed of car by also 22 per cent, though, off-peak speed does not increase significantly (1.35 per cent). Further, the per day labour supply has increased from 2 hours/day in the reference situation to 2.94 hours/day in the optimal policy, an increase of 47%, on account of differential taxation of commuting and non-commuting trips. The detailed volume effect and effect of optimal policy on labour supply are given in Table 3.

Table 3: Effect of Differentiated Taxation on Traffic Volume and Labour Supply

	Reference Situation		*Optimal Situation*	
	Commuting (Million pkm)	*Non-commuting (Million pkm)*	*Commuting (Million pkm)*	*Non-commuting (Million pkm)*
Peak Private	3.51	10.35	2.72	7.66
Peak public	5.60	16.55	4.62	12.95
Total Peak	9.11	26.90	7.34	20.61
Off-Peak Private	2.87	8.47	2.67	7.51
Off-Peak public	4.59	13.54	3.40	9.47
Total Off-Peak	7.46	22.01	6.07	16.98
Total Volume	16.57	48.91	13.41	37.59
Labour Supply (hrs./day)	2.00	2.94		

Source: Numerical Model Output.

As is evident from Table 3, there is a reduction in both peak and off-peak traffic volume in the optimal policy scenario over the reference situation. Though, the volume of commuting trips decreased from 16.57 million pkm per day to 13.41 million pkm (a reduction of 19%), its share in total traffic increased from 25% in the reference situation to 26. 30% in the optimal policy due to increase in labour supply. The labour supply has increased by 47% in the optimal policy over the reference situation. This has a positive revenue effect on the government. The tax revenue from labour supply has increased from Rs. 265.31 million per day in the reference situation to Rs. 312.24 million per day in the optimal policy, an increase of 17.7% over the reference scenario. Thus, as a conclusion, introducing optimal differentiated transport prices with labour supply function in the consumers preference function leads to a net welfare increase along with increases in the labour supply and reduction in both peak and off-peak traffic volume thereby, reducing congestion. The extent of welfare increase, however, depends upon the distortions in the labour market.

4. CONCLUSIONS

This paper develops a theoretical model, which attempts to captures transport tax reforms in the presence of labour-leisure choice and endogenous value of time in a multiple trip purpose passenger transport market.

The theoretical model and optimal tax rates developed in this paper were tested empirically by using a numerical model involving different transport modes and multiple trip purposes to find out the validity and implications for tax levels. The paper found that in the optimal situation taxes increases for all modes for commuting trips and non-commuting trips compared to the reference situation and differentiated tax rate led to more tax for non-commuting trips than for commuting trips as was predicted by the theoretical model. This was the case for both peak and off-peak periods. For public transport too commuting trips should be taxed less than non-commuting in both peak and off-peak periods. The paper also found that the introduction of differentiated transport tax system for a given level of labour tax led to a welfare gain of 9.42 percent of generalised income, an increase in labour supply by 47%, a traffic volume reduction of 22% and increased peak period speed of over 22%. The results also indicated that the public transport should not be subsidised. The above results proved the theoretical finding that in the presence of distortionary taxes on labour supply, an optimal tax system would set lower taxes on commuting trips than on non-commuting trips, the more complementary commuting is with labour.

Notes:

1. TRENEN-URBAN model developed at CES, KULeuven (Proost & Van Dender 2001).
2. TRAP-BASIC model developed by Sen (2006).
3. A nested structure means that the utility of the representative consumer has a tree structure: welfare depends upon some aggregates that each can be subdivided in lower level aggregates until the level of the goods reached. The main advantage (or disadvantage) of a tree structure is that substitution possibilities between goods are strongly structured so that less behavioural information needs to be collected.
4. Constant elasticity of substitution is a crucial parameter in the utility tree. This means that the degree of substitution between commodities does not depend on the relative levels of consumption.

REFERENCES

Abrego, L. and Whally, J. (1998), The Non-Environmental Consequences of Environmental Damage, *paper presented at the NBER Meeting*, August.

Calthrop, E., (2001), Subsidising Commuting, in Essays in Urban Transport Economics, *Ph.D Thesis* Nr. 151, Faculteit ETEW, KULeuven., pp-141-170.

De Borger, B., Mayeres, I., Proost, S. & Wouters, S. (1993), Social Cost Pricing of Urban Passenger Transport-With an Illustration for Belgium, *CES Discussion Paper*, KULeuven.

DeSerpa, A.C. (1971), A Theory of the Economics of Time, *The Economic Journal*, Vol. 81, pp. 828-845.

Jara-Diaz, S.R. (2000), Allocation and Value of Travel-time Savings, in: D.A. Hensher and K.J. Button, (eds.) *Handbook of Transport Modelling*, Handbooks in Transport, Vol. 1, Pergamon-Elsevier, 303-319.

Keller, W.J. (1976), A Nested CES-Type Utility Function and Its Demand and Price-Index Functions, *European Economic Review*, Vol.,7, pp. 175-186.

Mayeres, I. (1999), The Control of Transport Externalities: A General Equilibrium Analysis, *Ph.d Thesis nr 126*, Faculteit ETEW, KULeuven,

Mayeres, I., and Proost, S. (1997), Optimal Tax Rules for Congestion Type of Externalities, *Scandinavian Journal of Economics*, Vol. 99, pp. 261-279.

Ochelen, S., and Proost, S. (1996), Internalisation of transport externalities by a local government, Paper presented at *NBER Workshop on Public Policy and the Environment,* Cambridge, July.

Parry, I. and Bento, A. (2001), Revenue Recycling and the Welfare Effects of Road Pricing, *Scandinavian Journal of Economics*, Vol. 103, pp. 645-672.

Proost, S. and Van Dender, K. (2001), The Welfare Impacts of Alternative Policies to Address Atmospheric Pollution in Urban Road Transport, *Regional Science & Urban Economics*, Vol. 31, No.4, pp. 383-412.

RITES Ltd. (2001), Primary Survey, Rail India Technical and Economic Services Limited, Gurgaon, Haryana.

Sen, Akshaya K. (2006), Optimal Pricing of Urban Road Transport — A Case of Delhi, *Ph.D Thesis* (unpublished), Indian Institute of Technology, Delhi.

Van Dender, K. (2001), Aspects of Congestion Pricing for Urban Transport, *Ph.D Thesis nr. 149*, Faculteit ETEW, KULeuven, Belgium.

2

STRATEGIC PLANNING FOR DELHI METRO RAIL

Madhuri Jain
A. K. Sinha
Arti Saxena
Preetvanti Singh
P. K. Saxena

ABSTRACT

The transport situation in most Indian metropolitan cities is rapidly deteriorating because of increasing travel demand and inadequate transportation facilities. Despite huge investments in road infrastructure and plans for land use and transport development, all cities face problems of congestion, traffic accidents and air pollution which continue to grow. Stifling commuter congestion in the major Indian city of Delhi has become an economic liability. Delhi metro has been planned to reduce congestion on Delhi roads and augment current public transport facilities which is primarily bus based. Thus, an effective strategic for policy planning is required for a healthy transportation system in Delhi. In this paper, an attempt has been made to develop a Strategic Planning (SP) Model for effective strategic planning of Delhi Metro using a Multi-Criteria Decision Making Methodology (MCDM) involving Fuzzy Hierarchy Process (FHP). The developed SP Model is a package of strategic policies and techniques which concentrates on measures directed at the alleviation of symptoms of transportation problems of Delhi. The philosophy of the model ensures the development of effective decision making strategies to generate a wide spectrum of options for transportation system planners and managers.

1. INTRODUCTION

Mobility is a pre-requisite for today's highly developed societies. In striving for economic and social progress, they place ever newer and greater demands on systems for information, control, and management solutions in the transport sector that promote mobility of the individual and of society as a whole. The quality of life in metropolitan areas depends to a great extent on the ability to ensure the smooth flow of traffic. With rapid urbanisation, the pressure on transportation systems has increased in most cities in India. The inadequate transport system of cities, accompanied a comprehensive urban transport management strategies is promoting the use of private individual transport. Delhi is one of the fast growing metropolitan areas in India with a population of 13 million as reported in the Census of India Report for the year 2001 and facing acute problems of transportation. During the last two decades, there has been an exponential growth in the vehicular population in the metropolis of Delhi- the total number of registered motor vehicles has crossed the 4 million mark, which is more than the combined number of vehicles in the other three metros of India viz., Mumbai, Chennai and Kolkata. This results in acute congestion, inordinate delays, serious accidents, high-energy consumption particularly of fossil fuels, and intense pollution of the environment, slower vehicular speeds, increase in road accidents and fuel wastage.

Delhi Metro Rail provides multiple benefits: reduction in air pollution, time saving to passengers, reduction in accidents, reduction in traffic congestion and fuel savings. Advani and Tiwari [2005] analyzed the feasibility of mass transport systems like MRTS and BRTS in Indian cities, which were dominated by two wheelers, para transit modes and bicycles. Cichy [1996] explained ways to transform a static fixed rail system serving radial travel patterns into a new dynamic demand responsive system. Mohan and Tiwari [1999] discussed issues concerning public transport, safety and the environment. Advani and Tiwari [2006] analyzed the methodology and arguments used to justify MRTS/LRT systems and also presented the evaluation of Delhi metro in terms of capacity, travel time and accessibility to the system and evaluation indices reflecting commuter's perspective. Sibal [1996] studied the available funding sources for urban mass transit projects in the developing countries and suggested an approach to urban transport financing under the socio-economic conditions prevalent in India. Kumar [2006] analyzed the impact of the Metro rail in Bangalore. Badami [2006] described the existing railway load, its actual design capacity and discussed idea of the capacity proposed under the Mumbai Metro Master Plan (MMMP). Sarna [1990] reviewed the traffic and transportation problems of Delhi and suggested the need for modification of the urban transportation planning process, keeping in view the socio-economic environment prevailing in the country. Banerjee and Satsangi [1986] developed a methodology for forecasting the demand for various modes of transport of the Delhi Urban Area. Al-Hemali and Jantan [2003] explored the potential of management science tool, namely AHP to be used as a tool for strategic decision-making, and discussed how this decision tool could be made more systematic. Strategic Planning is an ongoing event kept in the foreground to be seen, used as a guide and revised as change is noted in the environment. It is meant for selecting and stabilizing central objectives in a metropolitan city development, with wide agreement among responsible actors in the pursuit of them in the development process.

Proper management of a transportation system poses a challenge for the decision maker to select an alternative based on multiple and often conflicting criteria that necessitate the use of decision support aid. The MCDM Methodologies works on the premise that decision-making of complex problems can be handled by structuring the complex problem into a simple and comprehensible hierarchical structure. Cheong et. al. [2008] developed a fuzzy multicriteria decision-making tool that was equipped with analytical hierarchy process framework to help the users in semi-structured and unstructured decision-making tasks. Dagdeviren and Yuksel [2008] studied the work safety issue through the fuzzy Analytic Hierarchy Process (AHP) approach which allowed both multi-criteria and simultaneous evaluation to determine the level of Faulty Behavior Risk (FBR) in work systems. Samaras, Matsatsinis and Zopounidis [2008] described a multicriteria decision support system which aimed at presenting an evaluation of the Athens Stock Exchange (ASE) stocks, on the basis of fundamental analysis. Nasiri and Huang [2008] proposed a Fuzzy Multiple Attribute Analysis (FMAA) approach for the environmental performance assessment of waste recycling programs.

The primary objective of this paper is to present a new methodology the Fuzzy Hierarchy Process (FHP) to guide decision-making under vagueness type uncertainty. A model is also developed for Strategic Planning of Delhi Metro Rail (DMR) using FHP Methodology. FHP considers complex and unstructured decisions, which can handle both tangible and intangible factors; and also considers the concept of risk attitude and associated confidence of a decision maker on the estimates of pair wise comparisons.

2. FUZZY LOGIC THEORY

Fuzzy logic is a superset of conventional logic that has been extended to handle the concept of partial truth. In contrast to Classical Logic, which is only equipped to deal with completely true and completely false situations, Fuzzy Logic aims at providing a body of concepts and techniques for dealing with modes of reasoning which are approximate rather than exact.

2.1 Fuzzy Set Theory

Zadeh [1965] demonstrated a method of dealing with vague and approximate situations when classes of object which may not be compartmentalised into watertight sections are identified. Zadeh called such sets "Fuzzy"; and defined them as those sets ".....which have a continuum of grades of membership (μ_A) ranging between zero and one."

Relaxing the constraint of membership for any object- from the two element set {0, 1} in the case of Crisp sets to any value from the unit interval [0, 1] in Fuzzy Sets -provides one with an effective means of modeling situations, which are known approximately and possess an inherent vagueness. This generalisation of the axiomatic structure of Conventional Set Theory provides us with a parallel and infinitely more powerful theory called The Fuzzy Set Theory.

2.2 Fuzzy Numbers

A recent endeavour of mathematicians is to express numbers in an approximate manner and to carry out computations on them using Fuzzy arithmetic. A fuzzy number means a number that is a special fuzzy subset of real numbers. The membership function (μ_A) of a Fuzzy Number is a continuous mapping from R to a closed interval [0, 1] having the following characteristics:

1. $\mu_A(x) = 0$ for all $x \varepsilon (-\infty, \alpha) \cup (\delta, \infty)$;
2. $\mu_A(x)$ is monotonically increasing in $[\alpha, \beta]$ and monotonically decreasing in $[\gamma, \delta]$;
3. $\mu_A(x) = 1$ for all $x \varepsilon [\beta, \gamma]$.

Different shapes of fuzzy numbers are possible (e.g. bell, triangular, trapezoidal, Gaussian, etc.). In order to simplify the implementation, Triangular Fuzzy Numbers (TFNs) are used in this paper. TFN is represented by three points (*a, b, c*) on the universe of discourse (scale X on which criterion is defined), representing the minimum, most likely, and values, respectively. Some commonly used fuzzy arithmetic operations on the TFN are shown below in Table1 where $A = (a_1, a_2, a_3)$ and $B = (b_1, b_2, b_3)$:

Table 1: Fuzzy Arithmetic Operations

Operators	*Formulae*	*Results*
Summation	A + B	$(a_1 + b_1, a_2 + b_2, a_3 + b_3)$
Subtraction	A − B	$(a_1 - b_1, a_2 - b_2, a_3 - b_3)$
Multiplication	A × B	$(a_1 \times b_1, a_2 \times b_2, a_3 \times b_3)$
Division	A/B	$(a_1/b_1, a_2/b_2, a_3/b_3)$
Scalar Product	Q × B	$(Q \times b_1, Q \times b_2, Q \times b_3)$

A fuzzy number M on R is to be a triangular fuzzy number if its membership function $\mu_M(x): R \rightarrow [0,1]$ is equal to

$$\mu_M(x) = \begin{bmatrix} \dfrac{x}{\chi-\beta} - \dfrac{\beta}{\chi-\beta}, & x \in [\beta,\chi] \\ \dfrac{x}{\chi-\delta} - \dfrac{\delta}{\chi-\delta}, & x \in [\chi,\delta] \\ \\ 0, & \textit{otherwise} \end{bmatrix}$$

where $\beta \leq \chi \leq \delta$, and δ stand for lower and upper value of the support of respectively and χ for the modal value. The triangular fuzzy number can be denoted by (β, χ, δ).

3. THE COMPUTATIONAL ALGORITHM

Step 1. Goal and problem formulation by 6 members of Decision-Making Group.

Step 2. Selection of IR (Interdisciplinary Respondent) Group of 60 participants and Expert (EP) Group of 14 Experts.

Step 3. Generation of CDP by Expert Group to meet the Goal.

Step 4. Cluster formation of CDP by Decision Maker into a responsible set of mutually exclusive and encompassing "i" Multi-Futuristic Decision Parameters (MFDPs).

Step 5. Design and development of Modified Delphi Questionnaire (MDQ).

Step 6. These MFDPs were rated and ranked by the IR Group using a 10 point scale, where 10 is most important and 1 is least important for all the levels

L (L = 1, 2 ...,10).

Step 7. Triangular fuzzy decision numbers (TFDN) were established by the Decision Maker using fuzzy arithmetic for each level.

$$\tilde{m}_j = \left(\beta_j, \chi_j, \delta_j\right)$$

where $\beta_j \le \chi_j \le \delta_j$

and $\beta_j = \min\left(M_{ijk}\right)$

$$\chi_j = \frac{\sum_{k=1}^{n} M_{ijk}}{n}$$

$$\tau_j = \max\left(M_{ijk}\right)$$

where M_{ijk} represents judgment of IR Group member k regarding the relative importance of MFDPs.

Step 8. Calculate the ∝-cut to get the crisp interval for all levels. The value of ∝ indicates the Decision Maker degree of decision-making confidence in their subjective evaluations. By defining the interval of decision-making confidence level μ the triangular fuzzy decision numbers can be characterised as:

$$\forall \alpha \in [0,1]$$

$$C_\alpha = \left[\phi^\alpha{}_j, \theta^\alpha{}_j\right] = \left[\left(\chi_j - \beta_j\right)\alpha + \beta_j,\ -\left(\delta_j - \chi_j\right)\alpha + \delta_j\right]$$

Step 9. Acquire crisp decision scores for all levels. The risk tolerance of the Decision Maker is calculated for the IR Group by

$$\left(S_{m_j}{}^\alpha\right)^r = \left[r\phi^\alpha{}_j + (1-r)\theta^\alpha{}_j\right]$$

Step 10. Obtain the priority weights Y_i by sorting the scores for each level in descending order.

Step 11. The relative criterion weights (w'_{ij}) were calculated for all levels using.

$$w'_{ij} = \left\{ \begin{array}{ll} 0, & i > j \\ \dfrac{Y_j \times 100}{Y_i}, & i \le j \end{array} \right\}$$

Step 12. Calculate the matrix F' (Calibrated Judgment Matrix) from the calculated w'_{ij} weights using the calibrating table for all levels.

Step 13. Construct a Fuzzy Pair wise-Comparison Questionnaire (FPCQ) to be filled by the Expert Group.

Step 14. Rate and rank the questionnaire using 9-point Fuzzy Pairwise Comparison Scale.(given in Table 2).

Table 2: Fuzzy Pair-wise Comparison Scale

Input Crisp Value	*Description*	*Fuzzified Value*
$\tilde{1}$	Equal importance	(1,1,1) if diagonal (1,1,3) otherwise
$\tilde{3}$	Week dominance	(3–ζ, 3, 3+ζ)
$\tilde{5}$	Strong dominance	(5–ζ, 5, 5+ζ)
$\tilde{7}$	Demonstrated dominance	(7–ζ, 7, 7+ζ)
$\tilde{9}$	Absolute dominance	(9–ζ, 9, 9+ζ)
$\tilde{2}, \tilde{4}, \tilde{6}, \tilde{8}$	Intermediate Value	(x–1, x, x+1) x=2, 4, 6, 8

$0 \le \zeta \le$ and ζ is fuzzification factor.

Step 15. Establish triangular fuzzy decision numbers for each level (from the feedback of the Expert Group)

$$\tilde{e}_{ij} = (\eta_{ij}, \rho_{ij}, \varphi_{ij})$$

where $\eta_{ij} \le \rho_{ij} \le \varphi_{ij}$

$$\eta_{ij} = \min(E_{ijk})$$

$$\rho_{ij} = \frac{\sum_{k=1}^{n} E_{ijk}}{n}$$

$$\varphi_{ij} = \max(E_{ijk})$$

where E_{ijk} represents judgment of Experts regarding the relative importance of MFDPs.

Step 16. Construct the aggregate fuzzy Pair-wise Comparison matrix.

$$\tilde{A}' = \begin{bmatrix} 1 & \tilde{a}_{12} & \tilde{a}_{13} \ldots\ldots\ldots \tilde{a}_{1n} \\ \vdots & 1 & \vdots \quad \ldots\ldots\ldots\ldots \\ \vdots & \vdots & \vdots \quad \ldots\ldots\ldots\ldots \\ \vdots & \vdots & \vdots \quad \ldots\ldots\ldots\ldots \\ \tilde{a}_{n1} & \tilde{a}_{n2} & \ldots\ldots\ldots\ldots 1 \end{bmatrix}$$

where $\tilde{a}_{ij} = (\eta_{ij}, \rho_{ij}, \varphi_{ij})$, and $\tilde{a}_{ij} = 1$, if i is equal to j.

Step 17. Calculate ∝-cut to get the crisp interval. Solving fuzzy eigen value: A fuzzy eigen value, $\tilde{\lambda}$ is a fuzzy number solution to

$$\tilde{A}' \; \tilde{x} = \tilde{\lambda} \; \tilde{x}$$

Where $\tilde{A}$ is n × n fuzzy matrix containing fuzzy number $\tilde{a}_{ij}$ and $\tilde{x}$ is a non-zero n×1, fuzzy vector containing fuzzy number $\tilde{x}_i$. To perform fuzzy multiplications and additions by using the interval arithmetic and ∝-cut, the equation $\tilde{A}'\ \tilde{x} = \tilde{\lambda}\ \tilde{x}$ is equivalent to

$$\left[a_{i1\eta}^{\alpha} x_{1\eta}^{\alpha},\ a_{i1\varphi}^{\alpha}\ x_{1\varphi}^{\alpha}\right] \oplus \cdots \oplus \left[a_{in\eta}^{\alpha} x_{n\eta}^{\alpha},\ a_{in\varphi}^{\alpha}\ x_{n\varphi}^{\alpha}\right] = \left[\lambda x_{i\eta}^{\alpha},\ \lambda x_{i\varphi}^{\alpha}\right]$$

where $\tilde{A}' = \left[\tilde{a}_{ij}\right],\ \tilde{x} = (\tilde{x}_1, \ldots\ldots \tilde{x}_n)$

$$\tilde{a}_{ij}^{\alpha} = \left[a_{ij\eta}^{\alpha},\ a_{ij\varphi}^{\alpha}\right],\ \tilde{x}_i^{\alpha} = \left(\tilde{x}_{i\eta}^{\alpha}, \tilde{x}_{i\varphi}^{\alpha}\right),\ \tilde{\lambda}^{\alpha} = \left[\lambda_{\eta}^{\alpha},\ \lambda_{\varphi}^{\alpha}\right]$$

For $0 < \alpha \le 1$ and all i, j, where $i=1\ldots n$ and $j=1\ldots n$.

Degree of satisfaction for the judgment matrix $\tilde{A}'$ is estimated by the index of optimism μ. The higher value of index μ indicates the higher degree of optimism. The index of optimism is a linear convex combination defined as

$$\tilde{a}_{ij}^{\alpha} = \mu a_{ij\varphi}^{\alpha} + (1-\mu)\, a_{ij\eta}^{\alpha} \qquad \forall \mu \in [0,\ 1]$$

Step 18. Construct the μ-cut fuzzy comparison matrices for all levels

$$\tilde{A}'^{\alpha} = \begin{bmatrix} 1 & \tilde{a}_{12}^{\alpha} & \tilde{a}_{13}^{\alpha} \ldots\ldots\ldots \tilde{a}_{1n}^{\alpha} \\ \vdots & 1 & \vdots \quad \ldots\ldots\ldots\ldots \\ \vdots & \vdots & \vdots \quad \ldots\ldots\ldots\ldots \\ \vdots & \vdots & \vdots \quad \ldots\ldots\ldots\ldots \\ \tilde{a}_{n1}^{\alpha} & \tilde{a}_{n2}^{\alpha} & \ldots\ldots\ldots\ldots 1 \end{bmatrix}$$

Step 19. Acquire crisp decision matrix T for all levels using:

$$T = \left(H_{ij}^{\alpha}\right)^{r} = \left[r a_{ij\eta}^{\alpha} + (1-r)\, a_{ij\varphi}^{\alpha}\right] \qquad 0 \le r \le 1, \qquad 0 \le \alpha \le 1$$

Step 20. Calculate the matrix U (Average Relative Judgment Matrix) for all levels

Step 21. Calculate the decision weights for each level using step 17 of MCFDM.

Step 22. The Overall Judgment Priority Weights $\left(W_i^{J_L}\right)$ are calculated for all levels.

4. The SP Model

The developed SP (Strategic Planning) Model incorporates the best of formal, incremental and systematic paradigms and accounts for dynamic interaction among the MFDP of the Delhi Metro Management Program, proceeding logically from current decision plan through performance criteria to alternative Scenarios or mixes of Action Plan. The development steps are as follows:

Step 1. Goal formulation by 6 members of Decision Making Group. The Goal of this research study was to calculate the Judgment Priority Weights $\left(W_i^{J_L}\right)$ for Strategic Planning of Delhi Metro Rail.

Step 2. Selection of IR Group consisting of 60 participants and EP Group of 14 Experts was selected by Decision Making Group.

Step 3. In this study 138 MFDPs were generated, which were decomposed into a hierarchy of 6 Levels.

Step 4. The MDQ was used by IR group to rate and rank the MFDPs using a 10 point scale, where 10 is most important and 1 is least important for all the 6 levels

Step 5. Triangular fuzzy decision numbers (TFDN) were established by the Decision Maker using fuzzy arithmetic for each level as $\tilde{m}_j = \left(\beta_j, \chi_j, \delta_j\right)$.

Step 6. ∝-cut was calculated to get the crisp interval for all levels and the crisp decision scores for all levels were acquired.. The risk tolerance of Decision Maker is calculated for IR Group by

$$\left(S_{m_j}{}^{\alpha}\right)^r = \left[r\phi^{\alpha}{}_j + (1-r)\theta^{\alpha}{}_j\right]$$

Step 7. The priority weights Y_i were obtained by arranging the $\left(S_{m_j}{}^{\alpha}\right)^r$ scores for each level in descending order.

Step 8. The relative criterion weights ($w_{ij}^{'}$) were calculated for all levels using.

$$w_{ij}^{'} = \begin{Bmatrix} 0, & i > j \\ \dfrac{Y_j \times 100}{Y_i}, & i \le j \end{Bmatrix}$$

Step 9. The matrix F' was computed from the calculated $w_{ij}^{'}$ weights using the calibrating table for all levels.

Step 10. FPCQ was used for pairwise comparison of the MFDPs using 9-point fuzzy Pairwise Comparison scale.

Step 11. Establish triangular fuzzy decision numbers $\tilde{e}_{ij} = \left(\eta_{ij}, \rho_{ij}, \varphi_{ij}\right)$ for each level from the feedback of Expert Group

Step 12. Construct the aggregate fuzzy Pair-wise Comparison matrix $\tilde{A}'$.

Step 13. Construct the ∝-cut fuzzy comparison matrices for all levels.

Step 14. Acquire crisp decision matrix T for all levels using

$$T = \left(H_{ij}^{\alpha}\right)^r = \left[ra_{ij\eta}^{\alpha} + (1-r)a_{ij\varphi}^{\alpha}\right] \qquad 0 \le r \le 1, \qquad 0 \le \alpha \le 1$$

Step 15. Calculate the matrix U (Average Relative Judgment Matrix) for all levels

Step 16: The Overall Judgment Priority Weights $\left(W_i^{J_L}\right)$ were calculated for all levels.

5. GENERATION OF $\left(W_i^{J_L}\right)$

The research study was completed within 5 months. The Parameter Preference Series (PPS) is illustrated in Figure 1 below.

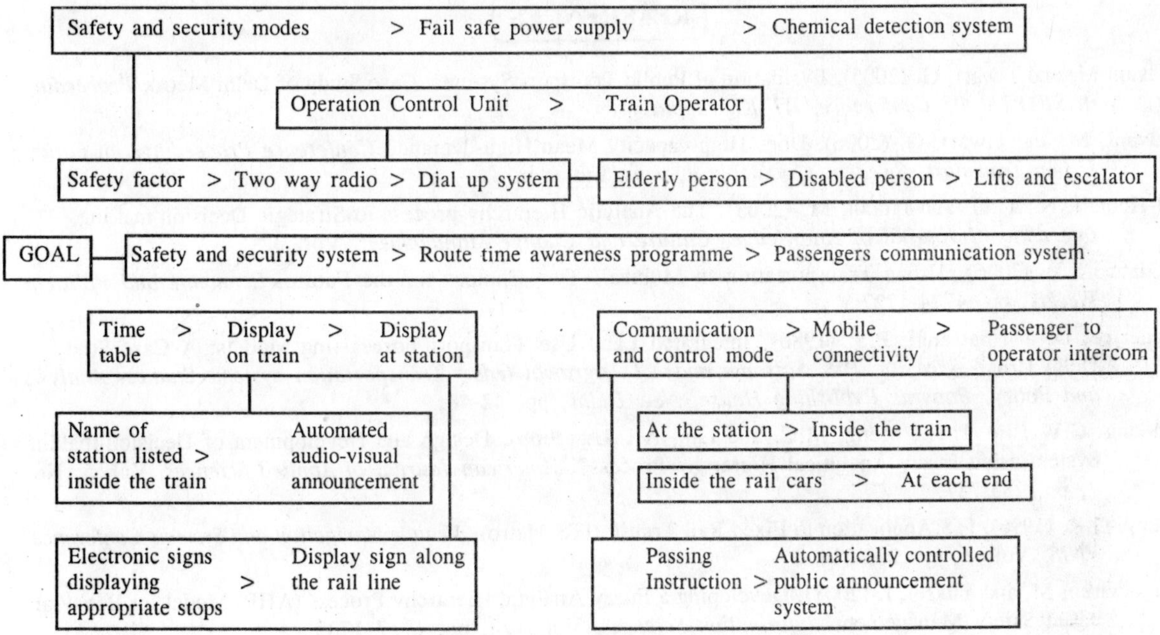

Fig. 1: Parametric Preference Series

The generated $(W_i^{J_L})$ demonstrate that:

- To ensure the safety and security of the passengers the Metro Rail should be equipped with new technology based Safety and Security System ($W_i^{J_L}$: 0.469). Safety and security system should comprise Safety Factor ($W_i^{J_L}$: 0.330), Two Way Radio ($W_i^{J_L}$: 0.103) and Dial up System ($W_i^{J_L}$: 0.034) which may be accessible by all the passengers including disabled person and elderly persons.
- Passengers should be made aware of the route and the schedule of a Metro train by the Route Time Awareness Programme ($W_i^{J_L}$: 0.198). This program should include Time Table ($W_i^{J_L}$: 0.105), Display the Route/Time on Train ($W_i^{J_L}$: 0.053) and Display the Route/Time at Station ($W_i^{J_L}$: 0.027).
- To provide safety of the passengers, effective Passenger Communication System ($W_i^{J_L}$: 0.161) should be provided in the Metro Rail, through various Communication and Control Modes ($W_i^{J_L}$: 0.070), like Mobile Connectivity ($W_i^{J_L}$: 0.038), Passengers to Operator Intercom ($W_i^{J_L}$: 0.022) etc.

6. CONCLUSIONS

The developed Methodology FDHP will help to guide in decision-making and strengthen the comprehensive and reasonableness of the decision-making process under uncertainty. The SP Model will contribute to solve complex decision problems by structuring a hierarchy of criteria. The output of the Model for Delhi transportation reveals continuing intelligence about the performance of the transportation system the identification, formulation and finances of project, as well as traffic management, facility management and maintenance programs.

REFERENCES

Advani M,.and Tiwari, G. (2005), Evaluation of Public Transport Systems: Case Study of Delhi Metro, *Proceeding in START-2005 Conference, IIT Kharagpur*.

Advani, M. and Tiwari, G. (2006), Does High-capacity Mean High-demand? *Conference Proceedings on Future Urban Transport, Sweden*. (Available at www.iitd.ac.in).

Al-Hemali, N. A. O. and Jantan, M. (2003), The Analytic Hierarchy process to Strategic Decision-making, *The International Journal of Knowledge, Culture and Change Management*, Vol. 3.

Badami, S.P. (2006), Urban Transportation in Mumbai: Two Choices for the Future, *Economic and Political Weekly*, pp. 4724-4727.

Banerjee, D. and Satsangi, P.S. (1986), Integrated Land Use Transport Forecasting Models: A Case Study of Delhi Urban Area, *In: P.S. Satsangi and A.L. Agrawal (eds.) Transportation Systems Studies: Analysis and Policy, Papyrus Publishing House, New Delhi*, pp. 42-48.

Cheong, C.W., Jie, L.H., Meng, M.C. and Lan, A.L.U. (2008), Design and Development of Decision-making System using Fuzzy Analytical Hierarchy Process", *American Journal of Applied Sciences*, Vol. 5, No. 7, pp. 783-787.

Cichy, G.R. (1996), ITS Application to Fixed Rail Transit (ITS Metro), *Vehicle Navigation and Systems Conference, VNIS*, Vol. 7, pp. 205-214.

Dagdeviren, M. and Yuksel, I. (2008), Developing a Fuzzy Analytic Hierarchy Process (AHP) Model for Behavior-based Safety Management, *Information Sciences*, Vol. 178, pp. 1717–1733.

Ferson, S. and Hajagos, J.G. (2004), Arithmetic with Uncertain Numbers: Rigorous and (often) Best Possible Answers, *Reliab Eng Syst Safe*, Vol. 85, pp. 135–152.

Jain, M., Saxena, A., Singh, P. and Saxena, P.K. *Generation of MFDPs for Evaluation of Delhi Metro Rail*, Working Paper WP 3010, Faculty of Science, Dayalbagh Educational Institution, Agra.

Klir, G.J. and Yuan, B., (1995), *Fuzzy Sets and Fuzzy Logic: Theory and Applications*, Prentice Hall International, Upper Saddle River, New Jersey, U.S.

Kumar, S. H. (2006), Impact of Metro Rail on Bangalore, *Foresight*, a Journal from St. Joseph's College of Commerce, Bangalore, Vol. 3, No. 3.

Mohan, D. and Tiwari, G. (1999), Sustainable Transport Systems Linkages between Environmental Issues, Public Transport, Non-motorized Transport and Safety, *Economic and Political Weekly*, Vol. XXXIV, No. 25, pp. 1580-1596.

Nasiri, F. and Huang, G. (2008), A Fuzzy Decision- aid Model for Environmental Performance Assessment in Waste Recycling, *Environmental Modelling & Software*, Vol. 23, pp. 677-689.

Samaras, G.D., Matsatsinis, N.F.and Zopounidis, C. (2008), A Multicriteria DSS for Stock Evaluation using Fundamental Analysis, *European Journal of Operational Research*, Vol. 187, pp. 1380–1401.

Sarna, A.C., (1990), Traffic and Transportation Problems of Indian Cities — A Review", *in P.S. Satsangi and A.L. Aggarwal (eds.) Transportation System Studies: Analysis and Policy, Papyrus Publishing House, New Delhi*, 213-219.

Sibal, V.K., (1996), Financing Urban Mass Transit Projects in India: with a special referenced to the Proposed Delhi MRTS, *Transports Urbains dans les pays en Developpement, actes de la conference*, Vol. 1, pp. 11.161-11.170.

Singh, P. and Saxena, P.K., (1999), Futuristic Decision Priorities to Eradicate Tribal Oncological Population by the year 2020 AD", *Advances in Biosciences*, Vol. 18, No. 1, pp.15-22.

Zadeh, L., (1965), Fuzzy sets, *Information Control,* Vol. 8, pp. 338-353.

3

DISCRETE CHOICE MODELLING FOR INTERCITY AIR TRAVEL IN INDIA

K. Ramachandra Rao
A. M. Jain
V. Sayal

ABSTRACT

A discrete choice model for intercity air travel demand is developed with the purpose of forecasting the behaviour of individuals regarding their preference choice. The model has been calibrated using data collected at the domestic terminal of Delhi's International Airport, incorporating trip related and socio-economic data of the individual. The model is developed using the software BIOGEME for calibration purposes. The model incorporates different variables during the calibration out of which airfare and flight frequency turn out to be the significant ones in the choice decisions of the individual.

1. INTRODUCTION

Demand forecasting for a mode, a route, time, and choice is a central issue in transportation planning, which affects strategic areas such as pricing, scheduling, frequency setting, and other managerial activities. Such forecasting has at its core the econometric modeling of choice behaviour of passenger within specific categories of choice set and services.

In the current scenario of high growth in the domestic air travel sector, a variety of choices exist before the traveller. Airlines have also geared up for competition. In this complex scenario strategic decisions would have to rely on some sound forecasting tools, which would help to estimate demand reasonably well. There are a number of attributes that can measure air travel choices and hence, the demand. To consider these choices and be able to replicate the travel behaviour, discrete choice models would be of great use. It is useful to model individual passenger choices, as opposed to aggregate demand forecasting, since individual passengers tend to be heterogeneous in terms of both the variables that drive their choice behaviour and the relative importance of these variables in the selection of their choice.

Discrete choices models are categories of disaggregate travel demand models, which incorporate individual behaviour (Ben-Akiva and Lerman, 1985; Train, 2003). These models have advantages in terms of explaining why individuals makes a particular choice, transferability to different points of time and geographic location due to their causal nature, understand the behaviour, efficient data use, and when properly specified gives unbiased estimates (Koppleman and Bhat, 2006). The decision maker in each situation is the individual, group or institution, which has the responsibility to make the decision at hand. In the present case, it is the air-traveller who has to choose among various cost and schedule alternatives. The alternatives in a choice process are characterised by a set of attribute values. Attributes may be generic or alternative-specific. In the present case, the attributes could be flight frequency, cost of air-ticket, income of passenger, vehicle ownership and dummy variables for gender and age. In order to establish which of these variables are useful in describing the traveller's choice, discrete choice models could be useful. Further, data collection at the point of departure would reveal the traveller's preferences.

This paper is organised as follows. In Section 2, the description of the choice decision process with the underlying attributes is given. Section 3 presents the questionnaire designed for this purpose and the case study related details. Section 4 discusses the details of the application of the software BIOGEME (Bierlaire, 2007), for obtaining the parameter estimates of the model. While Section 5 provides the results, Section 6 presents the conclusions of the study.

2. DISCRETE CHOICE MODEL

A discrete choice model predicts a decision made by an individual (choice of mode, choice of route, etc.) as a function of any number of variables, including factors that describe facility improvement or policy change. The model can be used to estimate the total number of people who change their behavior in response to an action (for example, motorized vehicle or non motorized vehicle drive). The logit function is a common mathematical form used in discrete choice modeling. (Ben–Akiva and Lerman, 1985). The model generally includes characteristics of the individual (e.g., age, gender, and income) and relative attributes of competing choices (e.g., cost and time etc). It also might include environmental factors, personal attitudes, or other factors, which are thought to influence the choice in question. The model is developed from a data set containing individual trip decisions, characteristics of alternative choices for the trip, geographical characteristics, and characteristics of the individual.

The estimated coefficients (or weights for each factor) can be used to derive elasticities. Elasticities indicate the percent change in the variable being predicted (i.e., probability of choosing a mode) for a given change in one of the independent variables, holding the other variables constant. While transferring elasticities to real world situations involves a number of assumptions, the elasticities may be used to estimate the change in users as a function of a given change in a facility or policy variable.

2.1 Assumptions

Discrete choice models assume that choices made by individuals can be predicted based on a limited set of quantifiable factors and that people are essentially rational decision-makers who seek to make choices that maximise their utility. Furthermore, the relationship between the underlying factors and the probability of the individual choosing a particular alternative is assumed to bear a particular functional form (i.e., a logit function).

2.2 Utility Theory

Utility is an indicator of value to an individual. Utility can be thought of being derived from the attributes of alternatives. An individual will select the alternative from his/her set of alternatives that maximises his/her utility. That is to say alternative 'i' is chosen from a choice set C, if

$$U(X_i) \geq U(X_j), \text{ for all } j \in C$$

Utility is decomposed into two major components:

$$U_{it} = V_{it} + \varepsilon_{it}$$

where

U_{it} is the true utility of the alternative i to the decision maker t

V_{it} is the deterministic or observable portion of this utility

ε_{it} is the random portion of the utility, which is unknown to the analyst

The mathematical form of a discrete choice model is determined by the assumptions made regarding the error components of the utility function for each alternative. Various discrete choice models are:

- Binary Logit
- Binary Probit
- Multinomial Logit model (MNL)
- Nested Logit model (NL)
- Other Cross-nested Logit Models

The MNL structure has been widely used for both urban and intercity mode choice models due to its simple mathematical form and ease of estimation (Bhat, 1997), but it has been widely criticised for its IIA (Independence of Irrelevant Alternatives) property. This along with the nested logit model was used for discrete choice analysis in this study.

There could be many choice combinations that are relevant as choices in an air-travel scenario and that could be evaluated for travel demand through this analysis. For example: full Supply – low Cost, Indian – Foreign Airlines. But these choices would not be as discrete in the minds of passengers while making a decision on an air-trip. But time and cost of flight are the basic factors which will always affect the decision-making of air-travelers; hence, these are used as pertinent parameters to formulate the choice set.

3. DESIGN OF SURVEY QUESTIONNAIRE FOR DATA COLLECTION

Data is an essential component of any modeling exercise. It is also an expensive activity. So careful design and planning of survey instruments and procedures is essential to reduce costs and increase the effectiveness of data to be collected. Further, survey data affects the models that transportation planners develop. Any error in the data will create errors in models, and often these errors can become far more serious for the model than what appears in the data. It is important to minimise survey and data error in order that data of adequate quality are produced for modeling purposes. (Stopher, 2000).

3.1 Intercept Surveys

Intercept surveys were undertaken for the purpose of this study. Intercept surveys are self-administered questionnaires that are distributed to travellers when they are at bus terminals, railway stations or airports. In the present case, the survey was conducted for passengers in the visitor areas of the airport.

The reasons for using intercept survey instead of any other survey methodology are:

- Its ability to target specific routes, customer segments, etc.
- It gives better information (accuracy, reliability, detail) from respondents.
- The response rate is high compared to the other survey techniques.

Discrete choice models are developed from data sets containing individual trip decisions, including characteristics of the individual and of alternative choices for the trip. Two types of data, revealed-preference and stated-preference, are generally used, as described below:

(1) 'Revealed-preference'(RP) data (or data on actual behaviour): This may be collected from a travel survey, which determines characteristics of a trip (origin and destination, mode, travel time, etc.) as well as characteristics of the individual and other influencing factors. Observations on trip decisions by 1,000 to 3,000 people are required. (Horowitz et al., 1985).

(2) 'Stated-preference' (SP) data: To collect this type of data, respondents are asked to identify the choices they would make under various scenarios. For example, different combinations of the relative trip time, cost, and presence of airlines would be presented, and for each combination, the respondent would choose any particular option.

The SP technique of collecting data is capable of evaluating a wide range of factors that may or may not yet exist. However, it has at least three significant drawbacks:

(1) Respondents are frequently overly optimistic when responding to hypothetical questions (Hunt and Abraham, 1997). For example, asking people "if they would prefer one airline or price, given factor X" will significantly overestimate the actual number of people who will switch to airline if factor X is provided. This problem can be largely overcome through the design of survey questions that force people to make tradeoffs between attributes, and by relating their responses to similar tradeoffs to their actual behaviour.

(2) Respondents must imagine what their choices would be like rather than experiencing them directly, and they may not accurately be able to judge their response to a situation that they have not encountered. Thus, the hypothetical situation sometimes creates confusion in the minds of individual decision maker. Visual simulation techniques such as those used by Wilbur Smith Associates (1996) can partially although, not completely overcome this drawback.

(3) The range of factors to be evaluated must be kept simple and phrased in terms that people can conceptualize them. For example, people may be able to predict their choice to walk given the 'presence or absence of a sidewalk', but not as a specific function of sidewalk design, street crossing types, and other factors that make up the pedestrian environment.

Finally, respondents may say what they think the interviewer wants to hear rather than expressing their true opinion. This problem may vary depending on the methodology used to implement the survey and the ways in which the survey questions are phrased. Thus, the survey technique is required to handle the situation which very much depends upon the modeler's judicious wisdom as well as the method used for parameter estimation.

3.2 Developing Questionnaire — Survey Goals

Planning an intercept survey involves first and foremost consideration of the survey goals. The purpose behind this survey design is travel demand modeling. Figure 1 shows a schematic diagram of the relationships between the survey purposes (i.e., travel modeling), research questions and survey questions.

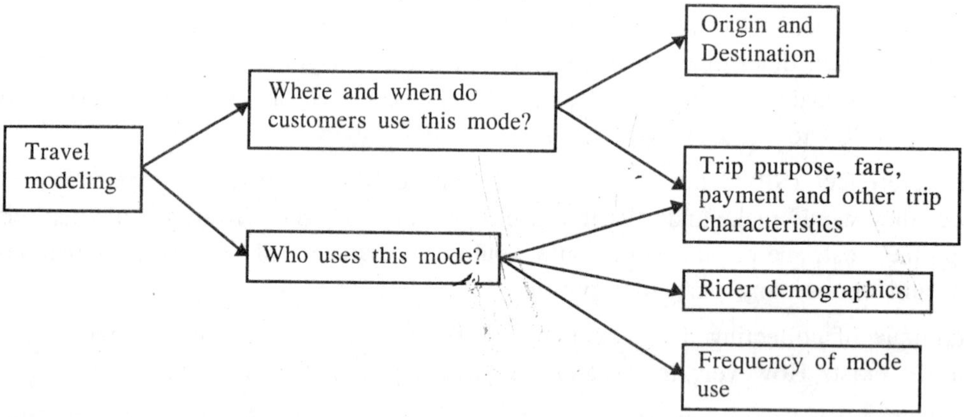

Fig. 1: Type of Questions for Travel Demand Modeling

3.3 Types of Survey Questions

Intercept surveys include a short introduction that explains the purpose and use of the survey and request the recipient to complete the questionnaire. Five types of survey questions are:

(1) Origin and Destination (O&D): Origin and destination questions generally pertain to ask the commuter about their locations for each trip. In the present case for air-travel between Delhi (origin) to different location (Destination) which is given by the passenger (viz. Mumbai, Kolkatta, Luknow, Ranchi, Chennai, Hyderabad, Bhopal. Chennai, Banglore, Gauhati, Agra, etc)

(2)Trip Purpose and other trip characteristics: Trip purpose is sought in terms of O&D activities. Other trip characteristics include estimating the Access and Egress time as well as the mode used by the person during access and egress. The actual fare paid by the passenger as well as the time of booking the ticket is also asked in order to capture the trend of the booking in the different Origin and Destination pairs. They are also asked about the class by which they are travelling.

(3) Rider Demographics: Demographic questions cover topics such as Gender, Age, Household Income and Household size. In the present case, different types of vehicles used by household are also recorded, to use it as a proxy for income.

(4) Frequency of transit use: Frequency of transit use shows the degree to which riders are regular versus occasional users or first time users.

5. Quality of Service: Different passengers are asked for their opinion in connection with the service quality, which is considered important, and related to the safety, punctuality as well as the availability of ticket at affordable price and the ease by which the ticket is procured by individual from different sources.

3.4 Administering the designed survey and data collection

Data for the survey was collected by means of the survey instruments: an interviewer-administered self-completion questionnaires which were given to the individual respondent and to help them in case they wanted any clarification in filling the same. The aim of the questionnaire was to collect sufficient information regarding their trip, socio-demographic characteristics as well as their preferences for non-chosen alternative.

3.4.1 Questionnaire

The questionnaire comprised of different questions related to travel and socio-economic characteristics of commuters. The questions were objective type with options provided for most of the questions. The questionnaire served to cover all the variables used in analysis.

3.4.2 Survey

Survey was done in the Departure Hall of Terminal 1B and 1A of Indira Gandhi International Airport, Delhi. The timing of survey was between 5.00 A.M. in the morning and 12.00 midnight. Survey was a random sampling survey. Some passengers chose to fill up the survey forms for themselves, and few of them were interviewed and the interviewer filled up forms.

4. BIOGEME SOFTWARE

BIerlaire **O**ptimisation toolbox for **GE**v **M**odel **E**stimation (BIOGEME) is a freeware designed for the development of research in context of discrete choice models. The software uses Maximum Likelihood Estimation and is used for estimation of Generalised Extreme Value (GEV) Model.

4.1 Inputs and Outputs

Inputs to the software are a modified model file, data-text files of recorded observations in a predefined format, and parameter file. Output from biogeme is a HTML document with all the constants, estimated utility function parameters, (nest parameters, in case of Nested Logit (NL) model) alongwith standard errors and t-statistics.

4.2 Variables and assumptions in model

Initial variables taken in the utility function were: Vehicle Ownership Index (VOI), Airfare, Out of vehicle Travel Time (OVTT) and Flight Frequency. Out of these VOI and OVTT got excluded from analysis due to important t values.

Variables finally included in regression and their estimates reported are: Airfare, Flight Frequency. The estimation was done for the multinomial logit model and for the nested logit model.

4.2.1 Assumptions

(a)Availability of Choices: The availability of all choices was assumed to be true, except in the case of those choices where the flight frequency was zero. In those cases, the availability of choices was taken to be zero.

(b)Weights to Observations: The only consideration regarding the weights was that their sum should equal the number of observations. Weights to all observations were assumed to be unity for an unbiased analysis.

5. RESULTS AND DISCUSSION

5.1 MNL model for Flight Time Schedule

The dataset described here are the trips from Delhi to five major Cities like Mumbai, Kolkata, Bangalore, and Chennai & Hyderabad, which will be stated as Category I Route in this section. The data sample consists of 1330 observations. The trips are having their time schedule divided into three sections as described below:

Morning Time Schedule : 5.00 am to 10.00 am

Afternoon Time Schedule : 10.00 am to 5.00 pm

Evening Time Schedule : 5.00 pm to 12.00 am

The findings of the analysis fitting the MNL models for the time schedule choice are described below.

Model 1

The data sample is estimated using the BIOGEME software for Multinomial Logit Model. The estimation dataset contains information on airfare, flight frequency and income and purpose of the trips as dummy variables. It also matters what choice of flight time they place for their purpose of trips. Table 1 gives the overall picture of the model. Each variable and its statistical significance are given in Table 2.

Table 1: Model Characteristics — Model 1

Model	*Multinomial Logit*
Number of estimated parameters:	15
Number of observations:	1330
Number of individuals:	1330
Null log-likelihood:	–1461.154
Init log-likelihood:	–1461.154
Final log-likelihood:	–1191.111
Likelihood ratio test:	540.087
Rho-square:	0.185
Adjusted rho-square:	0.175

Table 2: MNL Estimation Results for Flight Time Schedule - Model 1

	Model-1	
Variables	*Estimated Value*	*t-stat*
No. of Observations	1330	
Airfare	–0.431	–12.93
Flight Frequency		
Morning	0.215	2.5
Afternoon	0	
Evening	0.317	4.16
Income		
Morning	0.00124	3.62
Afternoon	0	
Evening	0.000775	3.1
Trip Purpose — Dummy variables		
Work Trip		
Morning	0.604	0.91
Afternoon	0	
Evening	0.34	0.73
Resident Trip		
Morning	–0.13	–0.2
Afternoon	0	
Evening	0.932	2.01
Leisure Trip		
Morning	0.353	0.51
Afternoon	0	
Evening	0.44	0.88
VFR Trip*		
Morning	0.185	0.27
Afternoon	0	
Evening	0.382	0.77

Constants		
Morning	-2.86	-3.93
Afternoon	0	
Evening	-1.71	-3.41
Log-Likelihood at Zero	-1461.154	
Log-Likelihood at Convergence	-1191.111	
Likelihood Ratio Test	540.087	
Rho-Square w.r.t Zero	0.185	
Adjusted Rho-Square w.r.t Zero	0.175	

* Visiting Friends & Relatives.

Model 2

In addition to the above Model-1, a minor improvement has made in terms of Airfare to arrive at a better goodness of fit. The generic variable, which is Airfare, is divided by respective destination's Air Distance. The model characteristics are shown in Table 3 and each variable and its statistical significance are given in Table 4.

Table 3: Model Characteristics – Model 2

Model	*Multinomial Logit*
Number of estimated parameters	15
Number of observations	1330
Number of individuals	1330
Null log-likelihood	-1461.154
Init log-likelihood	-1461.154
Final log-likelihood	-1188.603
Likelihood ratio test	545.103
Rho-square	0.187
Adjusted rho-square	0.176

The estimation process revealed significant effects for Airfare, Flight Frequency and Income, which are important variables for understanding the travel behaviour. The model also includes purpose of the trip as dummy variables for all the categories of the time. The results indicate that airfare is a sensitive factor for the travellers. When comparing both the models, Model 2 is performing better than Model 1 in terms of goodness of fit measures.

5.2 MNL model for Trip Purpose

The estimation dataset described here are the trips from Delhi to five major Cities like Mumbai, Kolkata, Bangalore, Chennai and Hyderabad which is stated as Category I Route in this section. The data sample consists of 1330 observations. The choice is classified according to their purpose of trips described as below:

- Work
- Resident
- Leisure
- VFR — Visiting Friends and Relatives

The choices mentioned above are quite an important factor for understanding the behaviour of travel. The trip purpose choice enables to understand the value of airfare placed by an individual during his/her trip. The findings of the analysis fitting the MNL models for the Trip purpose choice are described below (Table 5 & 6).

Table 4: MNL Results for Flight Time Schedule — Model 2

Variables	*Model -2*	
	Estimated Value	*t-stat*
No. of Observations	1330	
Airfare	–0.592	–12.97
Flight Frequency		
Morning	0.183	2.13
Afternoon	0	
Evening	0.326	4.24
Income		
Morning	0.00126	3.62
Afternoon	0	
Evening	0.000798	3.19
Trip Purpose — Dummy Variables		
Work Trip		
Morning	0.635	0.96
Afternoon	0	
Evening	0.38	0.83
Resident Trip		
Morning	–0.103	–0.16
Afternoon	0	
Evening	0.959	2.08
Leisure Trip		
Morning	0.366	0.53
Afternoon	0	
Evening	0.483	0.97
VFR Trip*		
Morning	0.213	0.31
Afternoon	0	
Evening	0.414	0.84
Constants		
Morning	–2.82	–3.89
Afternoon	0	
Evening	–1.76	–3.51
Log-Likelihood at Zero	–1461.154	
Log-Likelihood at Convergence	–1188.603	
Likelihood Ratio Test	545.103	
Rho-Square w.r.t Zero	0.187	
Adjusted Rho-Square w.r.t Zero	0.176	

* Visiting Friends & Relatives.

Model 3

The data sample is estimated using the BIOGEME software for Multinomial Logit Model. The estimation dataset contains information on airfare and flight frequency. Table 5 gives the overall picture of the model. Each variable and its statistical significance are given in Table 6.

Table 5: Model Characteristics - Model 3

Model	*Multinomial Logit*
Number of estimated parameters	7
Number of observations	1330
Number of individuals	1330
Null log-likelihood	-1843.772
Init log-likelihood	-1843.772
Final log-likelihood	-1440.902
Likelihood ratio test	805.739
Rho-square	0.219
Adjusted rho-square	0.215

Table 6: MNL Results for Trip Purpose - Model 3

Variables	*Model 3*	
	Estimated Value	*t-stat*
No. of Observations	1330	
Airfare	-0.297	-8.79
Flight Frequency		
Work	0	
Resident	0.0329	0.51
Leisure	0.324	2.74
VFR*	0.0891	0.83
Constants		
Work	0	
Resident	-0.148	-1.31
Leisure	-2.38	-10.45
VFR*	-1.7	-9.04
Log-Likelihood at Zero	-1843.772	
Log-Likelihood at Convergence	-1440.902	
Likelihood Ratio Test	805.739	
Rho-Square w.r.t Zero	0.219	
Adjusted Rho-Square w.r.t Zero	0.215	

* Visiting Friends & Relatives.

Model 4

In addition to the above Model-3, a minor improvement has made in terms of Airfare to arrive at a better goodness of fit in this choice also. The generic variable Airfare is divided by respective, to their destination origin air distance. The model characteristics are shown in Table 7 and each variable and its statistical significance are given in Table 8.

Table 7: Model Characteristics — Model 4

Model	*Multinomial Logit*
Number of estimated parameters	7
Number of observations	1330
Number of individuals	1330
Null log-likelihood	-1843.772
Init log-likelihood	-1843.772

Final log-likelihood	–1425.507
Likelihood ratio test	836.528
Rho-square	0.227
Adjusted rho-square	0.223

Table 8: MNL Results for Trip Purpose — Model-4

Variables	*Model-4*	
	Estimated Value	***t-stat***
No. of Observations	1330	
Airfare		
	–0.461	–10.1
Flight Frequency		
Work	0	
Resident	0.0271	0.41
Leisure	0.336	2.83
VFR*	0.101	0.94
Constants		
Work	0	
Resident	–0.149	–1.31
Leisure	–2.39	–10.48
VFR*	–1.71	–9.09
Log-Likelihood at Zero	–1843.772	
Log-Likelihood at Convergence	–1425.507	
Likelihood Ratio Test	836.528	
Rho-Square w.r.t Zero	0.227	
Adjusted Rho-Square w.r.t Zero	0.223	

* Visiting Friends & Relatives.

The estimation process revealed significant effect for Airfare and Flight Frequency, which are important variables for understanding the travel behaviour. The model somehow showed insignificant effect for income, which was later, removed. The results indicate that airfare is a sensitive factor for the travellers choosing for their particular purpose. When comparing both the models, Model 4 is performing better than Model 3 in terms of goodness of fit measures.

6. CONCLUSIONS

The objective of the study was to examine and develop a service quality measurement technique that incorporates key service quality attributes. The models were developed for intercity passenger travel choice based on two broad criteria: time of travel; and purpose of travel. Both these models have shown a good correlation with airfare and flight frequency. Moreover, among these two models, the one with trip purpose choice yielded better parameter and goodness of fit estimates. However, if scenario building is to be done, then stated preference (SP) techniques would be useful. This technique (SP) incorporates the qualitative attributes like reliability (On Time Performance) and the leg room space needs of an individual alongwith the attributes like frequency variation, price change, and the loyalty for the air carrier.

REFERENCES

Ben-Akiva, M. and Lerman, S.R. (1985), *Discrete Choice Analysis*, The MIT Press, Cambridge, USA.

Bhat, C.R. (1997), An Endogenous Segmentation Mode Choice Model with an Application to Intercity Travel, *Transportation Science*. Vol. 31, pp. 34-48.

Bierlaire, M. (2007), *An Introduction to BIOGEME (version 1.5)*, Transport and Mobility Laboratory, Ecole Polytechnique Fédérale de Lausanne, Switzerland.

Hensher, D.A., Rose, J.M. and Greene, W.M, (2005), *Applied Choice Analysis -A Primer*, Cambridge University Press, Cambridge, UK.

Horowitz, J.L., Koppelman, F.S. and Lerman, S.R. (1986), A *Self-instructing Course in Disaggregate Mode Choice Modeling*. Prepared for the Urban Mass Transit Administration (now Federal Transit Administration), Washington, DC.

Hunt, J.D. and J.E. Abraham. (1997), *Influences on Bicycle Use*, Transportation Research Board Annual Meeting.

Koppleman, F.S. and Bhat, C. (2006), *A Self-instructing Course in Mode Choice Modeling: Multinomial and Nested Logit Models*, U.S. Department of Transportation.

Sayal, V. (2007), *Intercity Travel Demand Forecasting for Air Travel*, Unpublished B.Tech Project Report, Department of Civil Engineering, Indian Institute of Technology Delhi.

Schaller, B. (2005), *On-board and Intercept Transit Survey Techniques*, Transit Cooperative Research Program Synthesis 63, Transportation Research Board, Washington, D.C.

Stopher, P.R. (2000), Survey and Sampling Strategies in Hensher, D.A. and Button, K.J. (eds), *Handbook of Transport Modeling*, Elsevier Science, UK.

Train, K.E. (2003), *Discrete Choice Methods with Simulation*, Cambridge University Press, Cambridge, UK

Wilbur Smith Associates (1996), *Non-Motorized Access to Transit: Final Report*. Prepared for Regional Transportation Authority, Chicago.

4

DATA SOLUTIONS FOR DEVELOPING A SPACE DEVELOPMENT MODEL OF A DEVELOPING METROPOLITAN REGION

M. S. Mir
K. V. K. Rao
J. D. Hunt

ABSTRACT

The objective of this paper is to present a technique/procedure for generating the unavailable data from the readily available data, in a developing countries' context for the development of a space development model for Mumbai Metropolitan Region (MMR) in India. There is no direct information available about the existing space quantities in a zone, maximum allowable person densities, floor-space rent values and also transport disutilities. This information needs to be synthesized from the available data. The paper explains techniques of generating this information by making use of the readily available data. It is concluded that, although, all the data may not be available for the development of a space development model in a study region the model can be developed using the procedure explained in this paper. It is further asserted that this technique of generation of non-available data is very useful in the context of developing countries and that it is a useful method of making best use of the little available data.

1. INTRODUCTION

The greatest difficulty in developing a space development (SD) model for an urban region of any developing country is the lack of an adequate statistical data base. Inadequacy, non-availability, and unreliability of spatial information, are handicaps in developing an SD model in these countries. Given the heterogeneity in the regional setup, it is difficult, time consuming and expensive to collect data which puts constraints on data collection surveys (Dezhbakhsh, 2005). That is why Leontief (1971) calls for a sharp increase in resources allocated to data collection and its maintenance. The aim of this paper is to present a technique/procedure for generating the unavailable data from the readily available data, in the context of a developing countries', for the development of a space development model. The paper is the outcome of the initial work done to develop a space development model for Mumbai Metropolitan Region (MMR), in India. The formulation adopted for the development of space development model is that defined in PECAS (Production, Exchange and Consumption Allocation System) framework. The frame work considers, essentially, two types of space developments taking place on a land category in an urban region. It includes the demolition and redevelopment of the existing space as well as the development of new space, taking place from one point in time to the next (Hunt and Ibrahim, 2003; Hunt and Ibrahim, 2005; Abraham and Hunt, 2005). Any time period for a model forecast can be considered but one year is a proper time step to give a quick response of land developers.

There is no direct information about existing space quantities in a zone, maximum allowable person densities, floor-space rent values and transport disutilities (travel times and travel distances). This information needs to be synthesized from the available data. In all, seven floor space types were considered for the development of a space development model for MMR and their floor space types include flats/apartments, independent house and slums in residential category as well as commercial office, commercial non-office, industrial and public/institutional in non-household category. Logit allocation models were used to calculate the redevelopment of the existing space types into one or more permitted space types, depending upon the existing development controls and regulations. New development of space types were also worked out with the help of logit allocation models. The utility functions used in these Multinomial Logit (MNL) models include the variables as mentioned above. There was need to calibrate these models so that the sensitivities of these influencing variables is determined and the models can be used in a computer programme to compute the quantities of floor space types for future points in time.

2. SPACE DEVELOPMENT MODEL

The space development model of a region gives forecasts of the space quantities of different types at various points in time in the future. This space quantity forecast was obtained at the zonal level and so that, a detailed land use of the study region is obtained. The SD model for MMR was set-up taking into consideration the existing land types, existing space categories and the various development plans that have been made from time to time. The MMR has been divided into 1030 internal Traffic Analysis (TA)/Land Use (LU) zones (MMRDA, 2005b). Use has been made of the data supplied by MMRDA about the zonal areas under existing land uses, built-up area in each zone and the areas zoned for development under development plans. The zoning rules were collected mainly from Draft Regional Plan, 1996-2011 (MMRDA, 1996a&b). The space rents were collected from various real estates sites like real estate Mumbai (Real estate Mumbai, 2005), Ready Reckoners like stamp duty ready reckoner (Kumar et al., 2005) and property news material published in various news papers (Mumbai property times) and magazines (India Today, 2007) . Information about the proportion of land under slums in various parts of MMR has been collected from SRA for MCGM (SRA, 2005) and different municipalities of MMR. This has been used to work out the zonal slum populations and hence, spaces. Some field surveys have also been done to get on the spot information about the characteristics of various space and land categories in the study area. Based on the available information (MMRDA, 2005a;

MMRDA, 1996a & b) the various land categories and space types defined for the development of the SD module for MMR are given in Table 1.

Table 1: Land Categories with Corresponding Possible Permissible/ Acknowledged Space Types Defined for MMR

S. No.	Land Category	Possible Permissible/Acknowledged Space Type
1.	Zoned Residential Land	Flats/Apartments Independent house Slum
2.	Zoned Commercial Office Land	Commercial office Public/Institutional(educational institutes, entertainment/tourism, public places etc) Slum
3.	Zoned Commercial Non-office Land	Commercial non-office (Shops, etc) Public/Institutional (educational Institutes, entertainment/tourism, public places etc) Slum
4.	Zoned Industrial Land (industrial, truck terminal)	Industrial(Manufacturing industry, warehouse, film industry etc.) Slum
5.	Zoned Public/Institutional Land	Public/Institutional(educational institutes, entertainment/tourism, public places etc.) Slum
6.	Zoned Green (recreation, forest, agriculture)	Slums
7.	Zoned Transport (road, rail, port, airport)	Slums
8.	Zoned Other (coastal wetland, salt pans, water bodies etc)	Slums

3. FLOOR SPACE TRANSFORMATIONS AND NEW DEVELOPMENTS

The formulation adopted for the development of space development model is that defined in PECAS (Production, Exchange and Consumption Allocation System) framework. The framework, like in MEPLAN and TRANUS models, considers two types of space developments taking place on a land category in an urban region which includes the demolition and redevelopment of the existing space as well as the development of new space, taking place from one point in time to the next. Any time period for model forecast can be considered but one year is a proper time step to give a quick response of land developers.

3.1 Space Development Factors and Logit Allocations

Based on literature, expert opinion and taking a practical point of view, it was found that the floor-space rents existing in various zones, the proportion of existing space quantities, the travel times from main CBD of the region and the minimum path distances from the nearest railway stations were the prime factors responsible for enticing developers for development and redevelopment of space. There are two logit allocations involved in the model development. One logit expression allocates the existing space for each space type, for a particular land category, among the possible new space types. This is shown below:

$$TS_{i,k,j} = S_{i,k}\left(\frac{e^{UT_{i,k,j}}}{\sum_j \left(e^{UT_{i,k,j}}\right)}\right) \quad \dots (1)$$

with

$$UT_{i,k,j} = \alpha'\left(P_j - PB_j\right) + \theta'\left(PA_j - PBA_j\right) + \mu'\left(R_{j,k}\right)^{\pi t} + \phi'(TTCB_j) + \sigma'(TDNR_j) + \beta'_{i,j} + \gamma'_{i,j} \quad \dots (2)$$

and

$$R_{j,k} = \frac{S_{j,k}}{\sum_{j\varepsilon J(k)} S_{j,k}} \quad \dots (3)$$

where,

$TS_{i,k,j}$ = quantity of space of type *i* on land type *k* that is transformed by redevelopment into space of type *j* (m2)

$S_{i,k}$ = quantity of space of type *i* on land of type *k* (m^2)

i,j = index for space type; I,J = the set of all space types

k = index for land category; K = the set of all land categories

$I(k)$ = set of space types whose development is permitted or acknowledged with land type *k* according to the zoning rules for the zone z

$TS_{i,k,j}$ = quantity of space of type *i* transforming to space of type *j* in land category *k*

α' = zonal price parameter for space transformation allocation

P_j = zonal price (rent) for space type *j* *(Rs/ m^2/year)*

PB_j = zonal base price (rent) for space type *j* *(Rs/ m^2/year)*

θ' = modelwide price parameter for space transformation allocation

PA_j = model-wide average price (rent) for space type *j* *(Rs/ m^2/year)*

PBA_j = model-wide average base price (rent) for space type *j* *(Rs/ m^2/year)*

μ' = inertia multiplicative term for space transformation allocation

$R_{j,k}$ = existing proportion of space type *j* in land category k

$S_{j,k}$ = quantity of space of type *j* on land of type *k* (m^2)

π' = inertia power term for space transformation allocation

ϕ' = zonal travel time parameter for space transformation allocation

$TTCB_j$ = Minimum travel time of j zone from main CBD, min

σ^t = zonal travel distace parameter for space transformation allocation

$TDNR_j$ = Minimum travel distance of j zone from nearest railway station, km

$\beta^t_{i,j}$ = transition constant for permitted transformation from space type i to space type j

$\gamma^t_{i,j}$ = transition constant for acknowledged transformation from space type i to space type j

The second logit expression allocates the total available Floor Area Ratio (FAR) each space i type in a land category k among the set of possible new types $i \varepsilon DI(i)$. This allocation quantity is required to compute the quantity of new space development in a zone of the study region. The logit expression used is as shown below:

$$DQ_{i,k} = Q_k \left(\frac{e^{UD_{i,k}}}{\sum_i \left(e^{UD_{i,k}} \right)} \right) \quad \dots (4)$$

with

$$UD_{i,k} = \alpha^d (P_i - PB_i)/W_{i,k} + \theta^d (PA_i - PBA_i)/W_{i,k} + \mu^d (R_{i,k})^{\pi d} + \phi^d (TTCB_i) + \sigma^d (TDNR_i) + \beta^d{}_{i,k} + \gamma^d{}_{i,k} \quad \dots (5)$$

and $$R_{i,k} = \frac{(W_{i,k} * XS_{i,k})}{M_k} \quad \dots (6a)$$

It is for all the permitted and acknowledged space types i for land type k

$R_{i,k} = \dfrac{Q_k}{M_k}$ for the 'no use' type (i.e. for $i=0$) ... (6b)

Where,

$DQ_{i,k}$ = share of available FAR on land type k that is allocated to space type i

Q_k = total available FAR for land type k

α^d = zonal price parameter for space development allocation

θ^d = modelwide price parameter for space development allocation

μ^d = inertia multiplicative term for space development allocation

π^d = inertia power term for space development allocation

$\beta^d{}_{i,k}$ = allocation constant for permitted development of space type i for land type k

$\gamma^d{}_{i,k}$ = allocation constant for acknowledged development of space type i for land type k

$W_{i,k}$ = FAR reduction factor for space of type i on land of type k *(ranges from 0 to 1)*

$XS_{j,k}$ = updated (interim) quantity of space of type j on land type k after considering redevelopment (m^2)

M_K = maximum permitted FAR for space of all types combined on land of type k

The data on zonal areas (1030 zones) under existing land uses, built-up area in each zone and the areas zoned for development under development plans was available from MMRDA. There is no direct information about the existing space quantities in a zone, maximum allowable person densities and floor-space rent values. This information needed to be synthesized from the available data.

4. SPACE GENERATION

The available data, from MMRDA was in terms of quantities of various land types which includes residential and commercial, industrial, institutional and public land, green, transport and others. Same built-up land for all zones was available, space quantities for each type of space was calculated.

Densities that were considered in generating various space types are given below:

(*i*) Residential density

(*ii*) Office density on commercial land

(*iii*) Non-office density on commercial land

(*iv*) Industrial density

(*v*) Institutional and public land density

4.1 Density Checks on Land Categories

Population and Employment densities are found to be very high in some of the zones. These high density zones on various land types were identified. The high densities needed to be smoothened by redistributing the areas among various land types by following certain rules so that, total area in a zone will not change. The rules followed were:

(*i*) If residential density is high, then some portion of green land can be considered as residential land so that, the total residential land can bring down that high residential density to a reasonable density value.

(*ii*) If commercial office or non- office densities are high, then some portion of residential land can be considered as commercial land so that, the total commercial land can bring down that high commercial office or non-office density to a reasonable density value.

(*iii*) If industrial density is high, then some portion of transport land can be considered as industrial land so that, the total industrial land can bring down that high industrial density to a reasonable density value.

(*iv*) If institutional and public land density is high, then some portion of transport or industrial or commercial land can be considered as institutional and public land so that, the total institutional and public land can bring down that high institutional and public density to a reasonable density value.

The various types of constructions housing various space types were surveyed in MMR and the densities and the FSI values calculated for each of these space types. While smoothening the density values, the maximum density criteria were fixed referring to these calculated values. The buildings in Hiranandani Gardens, faculty and other family quarters in IIT Bombay, various slum settlements and rehabilitation buildings in Mumbai, Office complexes in IIT Bombay and Bandra Kurla Complex were surveyed and the maximum density criteria and maximum and existing FSI values for various space types were reviewed. An example of calculations made for space type slum is shown in Table 2. This calculation is based on the diagram shown in Fig 1.

Table 2: Person Density and FSI Calculations for Space Type — Slum

Parcel Area (ha)	0.0014
Gross Land Area (ha)	0.0016
Building Footprint Area (sqm)	14
Building Floors	1.05
Units per Floor	1
Common Area Proportion on Floor	0
Persons per Unit	5.5
Total Units in Building	1.05
Gross Space per Unit, including common areas (sqm)	14
Net Space per Unit (sqm)	14
Gross Space per Person, including common areas (sqm)	2.55
Net Space per Person (sqm)	2.55
Total Space in Building, including common areas (sqm)	14.7
Total Persons in Building	5.78
Net Footprint Ratio (Building Footprint/Parcel Area)	1
Net Floor Area Ratio (Total Space in Building/Parcel Area)	**1.05**
Net Person Density (Total Persons in Building/Parcel Area) (persons/sqkm)	**412500**
Net Unit Density (Total Units/Parcel Area) (units/ha)	750
Gross Footprint Ratio (Building Footprint/Gross Land Area)	87.5
Gross Floor Area Ratio (Total Space in Building/Gross Land Area)	**0.92**
Gross Person Density (Total Persons in Building/Gross Land Area) (persons/sqkm)	**360938**
Gross Unit Density (Total Units/Gross Land Area)(units/ha)	656.3

4.2 Floor-space Information

(a) Residential Space

Residential floor-space was categorised into 3 types. These are:

(*i*) Flat/Apartment

(*ii*) Independent House

(*iii*) Slum

The criteria considered for generating residential floor-space is that (in a house) there will be certain amount of space commonly used by all the persons in the house and certain amount of space is meant for his/her personnel use. The formulae used in generating residential space, based on average space-use, are given below:

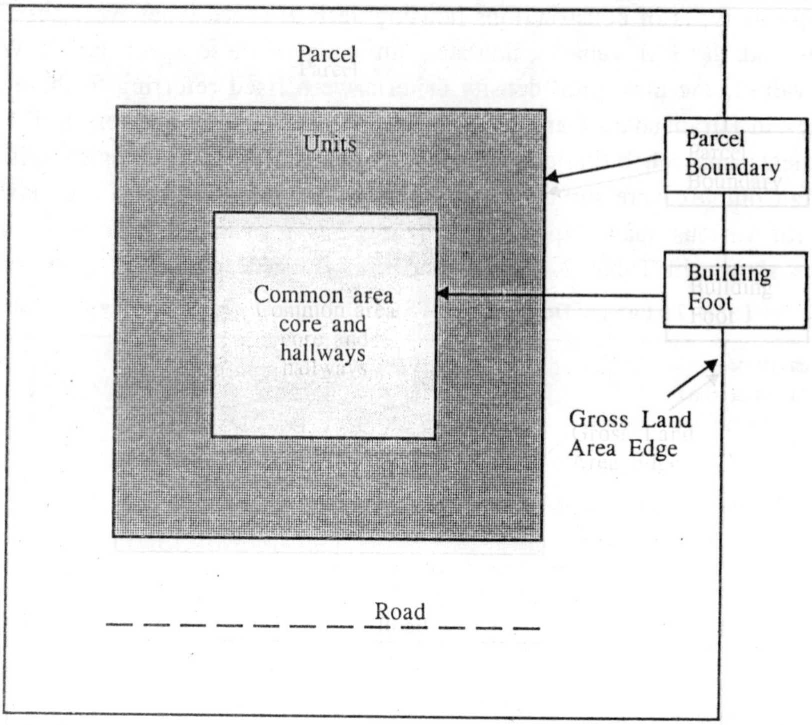

Fig. 1: Building Plan with Surrounding Transport Facilities

(*i*) Flat/Apartment = (10.43)*n ... (7a)

(*ii*) Independent House = (21.11)*n ... (7b)

(*iii*) Slum = (2.55)*n ... (7c)

Where n = population in the zone

Average space-use was calculated considering the average FAR in the zone. It was physically observed that the criteria on which these calculations are based are reasonable. At the same time, average household size was calculated and found to be appropriate. Few zones were found to have very less average household size and few zones were found to have very high average household size. These zones were adjusted by redistributing the population among each other in such a way that total population across all the zones remains same.

(b) Commercial Office Space

Firstly the inverse of office density on commercial land was calculated and these values were in terms of square meters utilized by an employee based on an FSI of one. A maximum FSI of 10 for each employee in an office is a reasonable assumption made for generating office space. The variation in square meter per employee based on FSI of 1 is observed across all the zones. Assuming that these values will vary from a minimum to a maximum with respect to a range of FSI of 10 to 0.4, a plot is made with sqm per employee based on FSI of one on x-axis and considering the range of FSI of 10 to 0.4 on y-axis. An equation is fitted to that curve

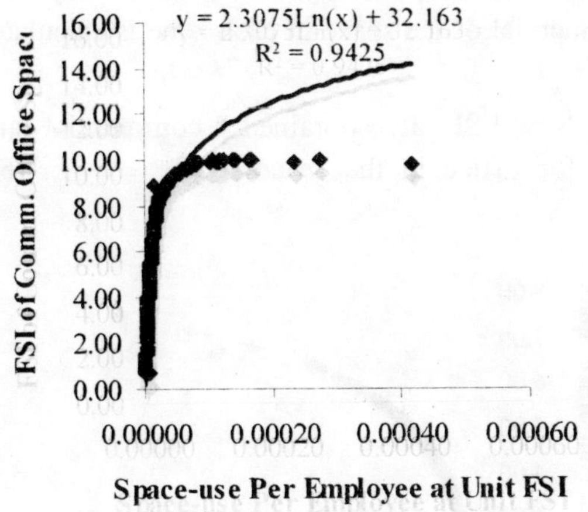

Fig. 2a: FSI Variation of Commercial Office Space Vs Space-use from Survey Data

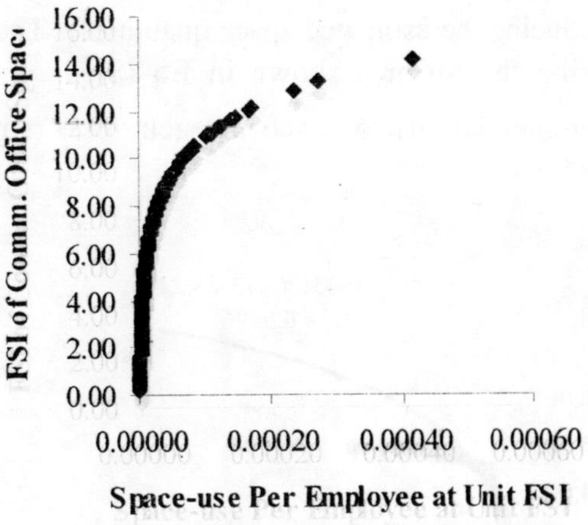

Fig. 2b: FSI Estimates of Commercial Office Space, Generated Using Logarithmic Function

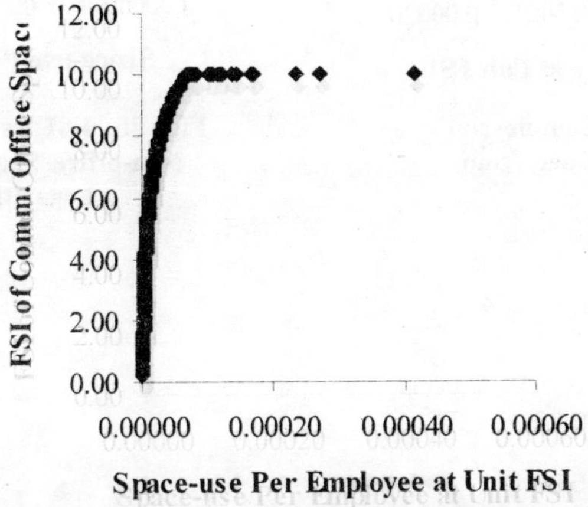

Fig. 2c: FSI Estimates of Commercial Office Space, Generated Using Logarithmic Function, and restricting Maximum FSI to 10.00

so that, by knowing the value of square meter occupied by an employee in a zone, the value of new FSI considered on y-axis, can be calculated. From the survey data that was collected it was observed that considering a logarithmic variation of space-use with respect to FSI values is a better proposition than considering this variation as linear, polynomial or exponential. Fitting a logarithmic equation to the data gave desirable results. Fig 2 shows the variation of FSI values of commercial office space with respect to commercial office space-use per employee at unit FSI and also the variation trend. Fitting a logarithmic equation to the data gives R^2 value of 0.9425 which is quite appropriate. The plot of the FSI values generated from the above logarithmic equation is given in Fig 2. But since we have to restrict the FSI values of commercial office space to 10.00, the generated FSI values exceeding this value in some zones is to be restricted. The plot with all FSI values less than or equal to 10.00 is shown in Fig 2c. Restricting the FSI values makes a difference of just 2.67% in terms of overall space quantity of the study area (by reducing the estimated space quantities). Then commercial office space in each zone is calculated by using the formula shown in Eq (8):

Commercial office space in each zone (sqm) = New FSI value obtained * commercial land for office in that zone * 10^6 ... (8)

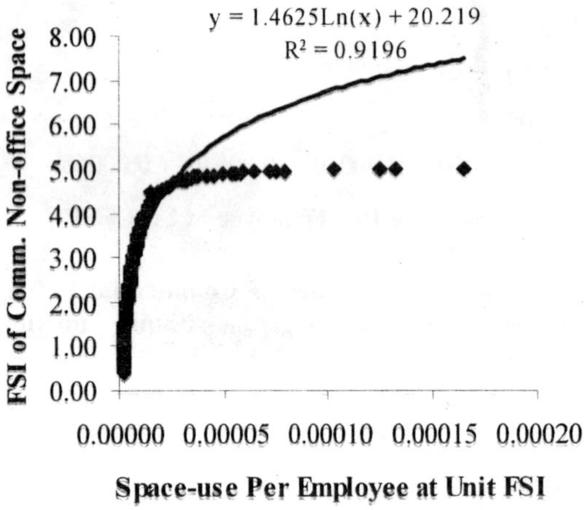

Fig. 3a: FSI Variation of Commercial Non-office Space Vs Space-use from Survey Data

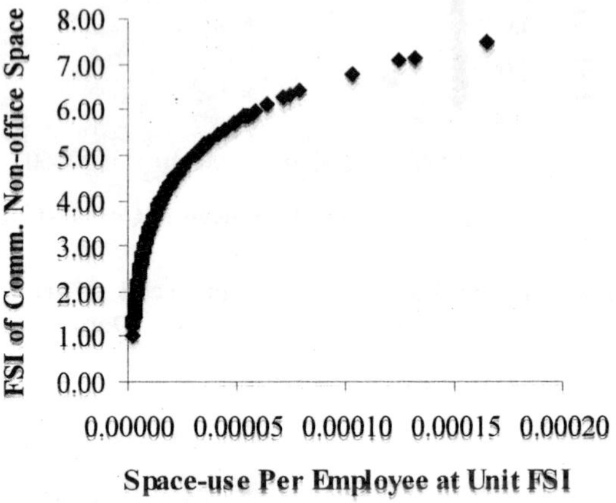

Fig. 3b: FSI Estimates of Commercial Non-office Space, Generated Using Logarithmic Function

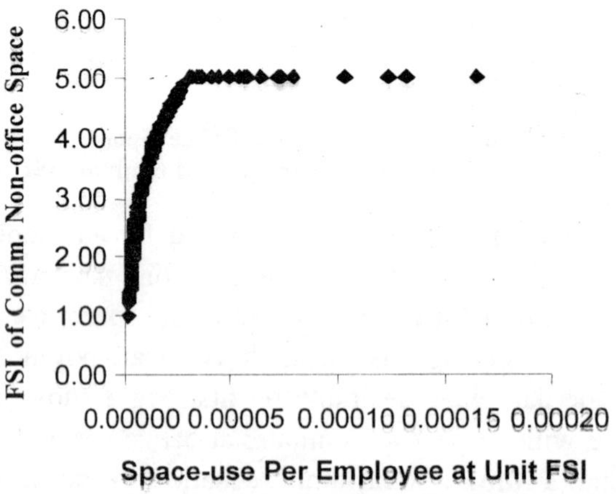

Fig. 3c: FSI Estimates of Commercial Non-office Space, Generated Using Logarithmic Function, and restricting Maximum FSI to 5.00

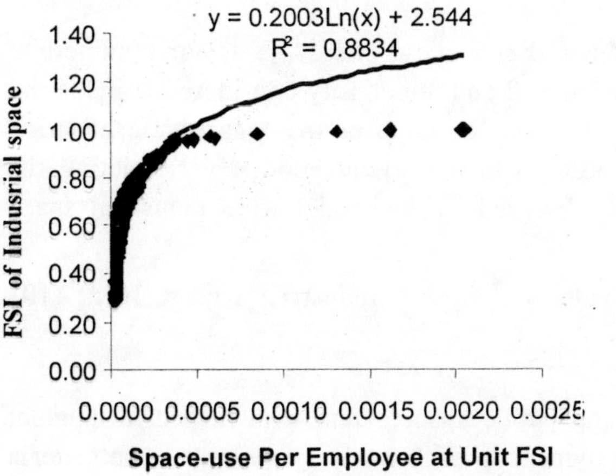

Fig. 4a: FSI Variation of Industrial Space Vs Space-use from Survey Data

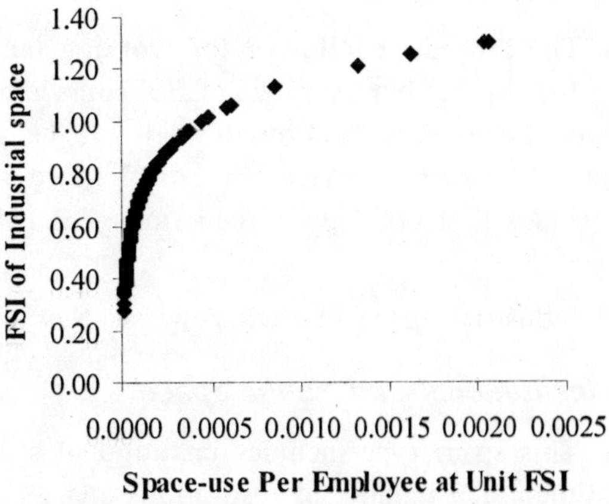

Fig. 4b: FSI Estimates of Industrial Space, Generated Using Logarithmic Function

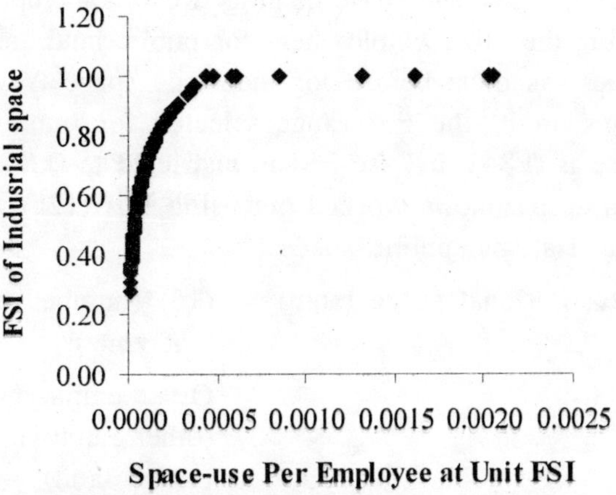

Figure 4c: FSI Estimates of Industrial Space, Generated Using Logarithmic Function, and restricting Maximum FSI to 1.00

(c) Commercial Non-office Space

The procedure followed was the same as for commercial office space, but the range of FSI considered was 5 to 0.4 and the density considered was non-office density for commercial land. Figs 3a through 3c show plots for commercial non-office space, as shown earlier for commercial office space. Restricting the FSI values makes a difference of 6.58% in terms of over-all space quantity of the study area (by reducing the estimated space quantities). Again the commercial non-office space in each zone is calculated by using the formula shown in Eq (9):

Commercial non- office space in each zone (sqm) = New FSI value obtained * commercial land for non-office in that zone * 10^6 ... (9)

(d) Industrial Space

The procedure followed for working out industrial space was the same as for commercial non-office space, but the range of FSI considered is 1 to 0.2 and the density considered is industrial density. From Figs 4a through 4c it can be seen that the R^2 value of the logarithmic equation fitted to the survey data of industrial space is 0.8834, which is quite good. By restricting the FSI values to 1.00, only a reduction of 2.13% is observed in the model wide industrial space quantity.

Industrial space in each zone = New FSI value obtained * industrial land * 10^6... (10)

(e) Institutional and Public Space

This space type includes institutional space and public space. Data with respect to student enrollment and number of institutions and its employment in each zone is available. The criteria considered for generating institutional space was same as for residential space i.e., in an institution there will be certain amount of space commonly used by all the students and certain amount of space available individually. The formula used in generating institutional space, based on average space-use, is given in Eq (11). The space quantity for other employment on public land is worked out by first estimating the other employment for public land and then determining the new non-commercial FSI values, as done before for industrial space type. Based on field data and the subsequent calculations on it, the FSI range selected for public-use space is 0.29 to 0.86. The R^2 value in this case is 0.842 and the FSI is restricted to 0.86. The space for public use and total space quantity in each zone is worked out using Eqs (12a), (12b) & (13). Figures 5a-c shown the plots for industrial and public space.

Institutional space (sqm) = (15)*(number of students enrolled in that zone) ... (11)

Other employment for public land = (other employment for institutional and public land) – (institutional employment) ... (12a)

Space for other employment on public land (sqm) = (new non-commercial FSI values) * (other employment for public land) ... (12b)

Total institutional and public space in a zone (sqm) = (institutional space) + (space for other employment on public land) ... (13)

5. PRICE/RENTAL INFORMATION

(a) Zonal Current Price/Rental Information

Purchase prices per square feet of floor-space for different areas across MMR are collected from various sources like ready reckoners (Kumar et al., 2005), property magazines and real

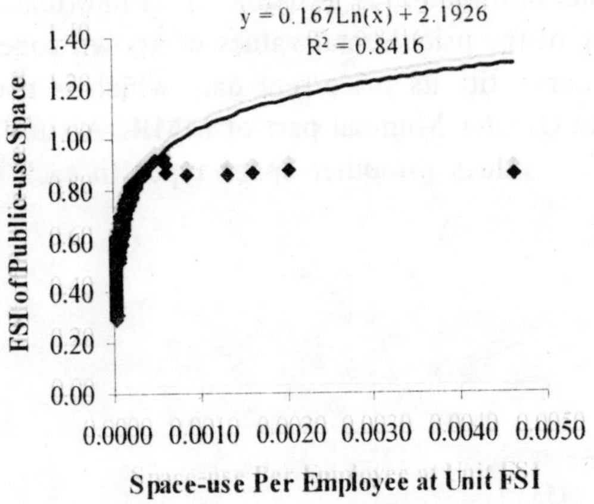

Fig. 5a: FSI Variation of Public Space Vs Space-use from Survey Data

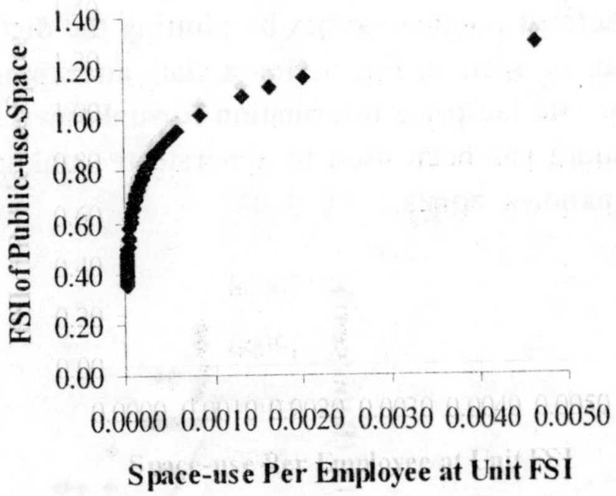

Fig. 5b: FSI Estimates of Public Space, Generated Using Logarithmic Function

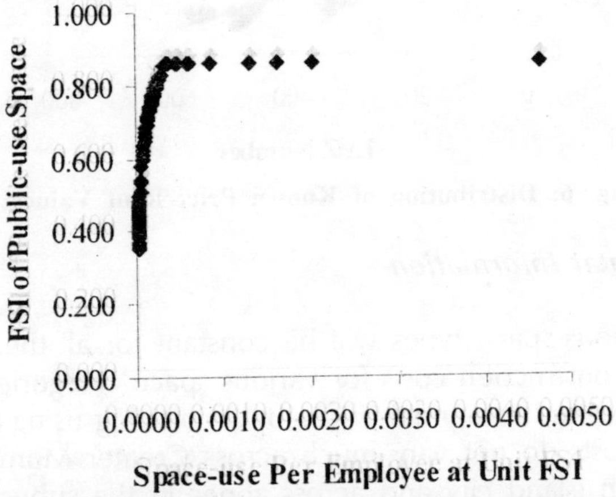

Fig. 5c: FSI Estimates of Public Space, Generated Using Logarithmic Function, and restricting Maximum FSI to 0.86

estate sites through internet (realestatemumbai.com). These purchase prices are converted to monthly rents by amortizing using the formula given in Eq (14). Monthly rentals are calculated by assuming an annual interest rate of *8%* and *40* years of mortgage.

$$R = P\frac{i(1+i)^n}{\left[(1+i)^n - 1\right]} \qquad \text{... (14)}$$

$R =$ rent paid per month

$P =$ Purchase Price

$i =$ interest rate per month = *(1/12)* th of annual interest

$n =$ period in months

Some zones fall in areas about which no price/rental information is available. This information is generated for these zones by plotting the distribution of the price/rental values of known zones. As can be seen in Fig 6, for a flat, an exponential curve fits its price/rent data which is used to generate the price information for unknown zones in Greater Mumbai part of MMR. A similar procedure has been used to generate the unknown price values for other space types in each of the unknown zones.

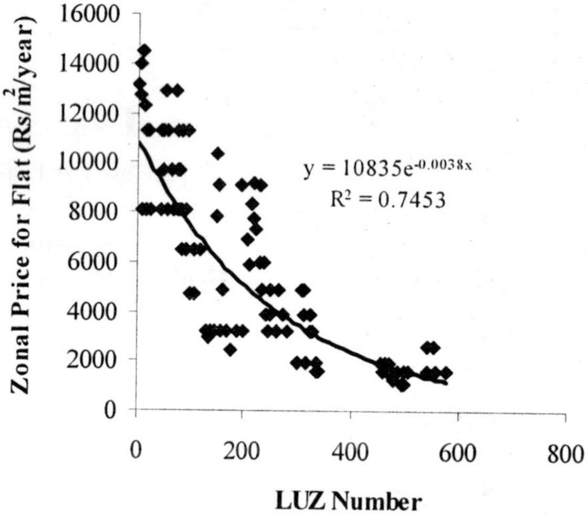

Fig. 6: Distribution of Known Price/Rent Values

(b) Zonal Base Price/Rental Information

Base price values for various space types will be constant for all the zones. The stamp duty ready reckoners give the construction costs for various space categories (Kumar, 2005). These construction costs are converted to annual prices by amortizing using the formula given in Eq (14). Since construction costs do not vary much across Greater Mumbai, so these values do not change across zones in island city and across zones in the suburban part.

(c) Model-wide Average Current and Base Rent/Price

Model-wide average current price is calculated by finding the average current price of all zones weighted by the existing space quantities in each zone. Price is the weighted average value of space and rent in terms of space across all the zones.

$$PA = \frac{s_1 r_1 + s_2 r_2 + \dots + s_n r_n}{s_1 + s_2 + \dots + s_n} \qquad \dots (15)$$

where:

$PA =$ model-wide average price for a particular space type

$s_1, s_2, \dots\dots\dots, s_n$ = quantities of existing space available in various zones

$r_1, r_2, \dots\dots\dots, r_n$ = rent values of that particular space in various zones

$n =$ number of zones

For all the space types, model-wide average price is calculated and these values are constant across all the zones.

Model-wide average base price/rent values are also calculated the same way, by finding the weighted average of the zonal base prices.

6. TRANSPORT DIS-UTILITIES
(Minimum Travel Times from Main CBD and Minimum Travel Distances from Nearest Railway Station)

Like every metropolitan/planning region which has a Central Business District (CBD), MMR also has zone number 08 as its main CBD. It has been observed that the transport accessibility (in terms of minimum travel time) of the zones to this main CBD has a strong influence on space changes that are taking place in the study region. This travel time from the zones has been worked out in GIS using TransCAD software. The routing toolbox of the software has the shortest path toolbox within it which can be used to find the shortest path between two points in the study region by overlaying a multimodal route network layer over a zonal map layer of MMR. The minimum travel time gets displayed on the screen.

Likewise, the travel distance from the nearest railway station has also been found to influence the attractiveness of a zone for development. The same procedure, as above, is used to find the travel distances of all the zones from their nearest railway stations, which is also displayed on the screen.

7. CONCLUSIONS

Though, all the data may not be available for the development of a space development model in a study region, the SD model can be developed using the procedure explained in this paper. It is asserted that this technique of generation of non-available data is very useful in a developing country context and that it gives a method of making best use of the little data that is available.

REFERENCES

Abraham, J.E. and Hunt, J.D. (2005), The Random Utility Theory Foundations of PECAS, *10th International Conference of the Hong Kong Society for Transportation Studies (HKSTS 2005)*, Hong Kong, December.

Dezhbakhsh, H. (2005), The Political Economy of Statistical Evidence: Economic Data Problems in Developing Countries and their Impact on Empirical Research. in: Ayogu, M. D. and Ross, D.(eds) *Development Dilemmas: The Methods and Political Ethics of Growth*, pp.80-102, Routledge, Taylor and Francis Group, London.

Hunt, J.D. and Abraham, J.E. (2005), Design and Implementation of PECAS: A Generalised System for Allocating Economic Production, Exchange and Consumption Quantities, in Lee-Gosselin, M.and Doherty, S., *Integrated Land-Use and Transportation Models, Behavioural Foundations,* Elsevier Science,

Hunt, J.D. and Abraham, J.E. (2003), Design And Application Of The PECAS Land Use Modelling System, *8th International Conference on Computers in Urban Planning and Urban Management (CUPUM)*, Sendai, Japan.

India Today (2007), Buyer's Guide To Homes in Mumbai, India Today Group, Mumbai, India, .

Kumar, S. and Gupta, S. (2005), Stamp duty Ready Reckoner and Market Value of Flats in Mumbai, The Architects Publishing Corporation of India, Malad (East), Mumbai, India.

Leontief, W. (1971), Theoretical Assumptions and Nonobserved Facts, *American Economic Review,* Vol.61, No.1, pp.1-7.

MMRDA (1996a), Development Control , Chapter-14, Draft Regional Plan of MMR: 1996-2011, Planning Division, MMRDA http://www.mmrdamumbai.org/ (accessed in Mumbai on 18-10-2006).

MMRDA (1996b), Development Control Regulations for MMR. Chapter-15, Draft Regional Plan of MMR: 1996-2011, Planning Division, MMRDA, http://www.mmrdamumbai.org/ (accessed in Mumbai on 18-10-2006).

MMRDA (2005a), *Report on MMR Land Use* (MUTP) through LEA International Ltd. Canada and LEA Associates South Asia Pvt. Ltd, India, December.

MMRDA (2005b), Report on Household Survey Preliminaries: Sampling Framework, Questionnaire Design and Survey Methodology, Volume II, (MUTP), through LEA International Ltd. Canada and LEA Associates South Asia Pvt. Ltd, India, July.

Realestatemumbai, (2005), Residential and Office Space Prices/Rents in Mumbai, available at http://www.realestatemumbai.com/ (accessed in Mumbai on 14-02-2007).

SRA (2005), Resettlement and Rehabilitation of Slum Dewellers in Mumbai, Griha Nirman Bhavan, Bandra, Mumbai, India, Slum Rehabilitation Authority, Government of Maharashtra (http://www.sra.gov.in/).

5

A MODEL FOR SERVICE LEVEL BASED PRICING OF SHARED RESOURCES AT CONTAINER DEPOTS

Sudhir K. Sinha
N. Rangaraj
N. Hemachandra

ABSTRACT

Till recently, Container Corporation of India (CONCOR), a public sector enterprise, was the sole operator of the inland rail container movement in India. With the opening up of containerised operations by the Government of India to both public and private operators, many new firms are willing to participate in these activities. However, such firms, in their initial period of operations, have to set up the required infrastructure in terms of Inland Container Depots (ICDs), etc. One business model that such firms can follow is to use the infrastructure of existing ICD owners such as CONCOR (Rangaraj et al. 2006). In this paper, we concentrate on the case where an ICD owner can share its ICD. In such a situation, the ICD owner is simultaneously a resource provider as well as a resource manager. We use an aggregate model for the ICD and model it as a single server. We assume that an ICD owner has a steady poisson demand for their ICD facilities. We denote this class of customers as primary class of customers. It is assumed that the primary class has to be ensured a given expected steady state waiting time. Further, it is also assumed that the collective poisson demand rate of firms that want to use ICD owner's facility, called secondary class customers, will be a linear function of unit price charged and expected waiting time that is offered. The ICD owner, as a resource manager, will be using a dynamic priority queue management discipline while managing the ICD. The model developed here is a constrained optimisation problem that selects a suitable pricing policy for the secondary class customers, a pair of price and expected waiting time, which can be used by the ICD owner to maximise its long run revenue rate while ensuring that the expected waiting time to its existing customers is met. An algorithm that selects the optimal pricing policy for secondary class customers as well as the optimal dynamic priority queue discipline to be employed for management of the resulting 2-class queue is developed and illustrated with a numerical example.

1. INTRODUCTION

Inland rail container movement in India till recently was solely managed by Container Corporation of India Ltd (CONCOR), a public sector enterprise, under the Ministry of Railways, Government of India. The Government felt that Concor, while profitable, is not able to grow at the required rate to support the growing market. This sector has become viable to support a certain number of large firms without the requirement of a monopoly service provider. Competition in this sector is seen as highly desirable to increase reach and provide the most effective logistical service to customers. As a consequence, the Ministry of Railways has opened up its containerised operations to other private and public sector players.

Interested companies have to make their own arrangements for a rail-linked inland container depot (ICD) and have to procure flat wagons for transporting containers. An ICD resembles a warehouse facility which offers services for the handling, temporary storage as well as customs clearance of both containers and general cargo that enters or leaves the ICD in containers. Interested companies can build their own ICD, lease it or share it from the existing ICD owners. Due to high infrastructural set up cost, the new firms may be seeking to lease some resources like ICDs from the existing ICD owners (presently only CONCOR possesses a rail-linked ICD) in initial years of operations. Under this scenario, the ICD owner is simultaneously a resource operator and manager (Rangaraj *et. al.* 2006).

ICD operations can be modeled by a network of queues. But on an aggregate level the facility can be thought of as a single server serving a two-class queue. Here, the primary class customers are ICD owner's existing customers and the new firms are called secondary class customers. The price charged and service level offered to customers may vary with their class. A commonly used measure of customers' service level is the steady-state expected waiting time of customers in the system. It is possible that there exists a long term agreement between the ICD owner and the primary class customers which specifies the committed Quality of Service (QOS) level to the primary class customers. We postulate that this prevailing agreement results in a steady demand process of the primary class customers. We now model below, the sharing of an ICD facility by ICD owners such as CONCOR is considered.

The inclusion of secondary class customers into the system increases traffic intensity at the ICD, which in turn, affects not only the system utilisation but also the effective service level offered to the primary class customers. Therefore, there is a need to control the arrival rate of the secondary class customers into the system. We assume that the demand of the secondary class customers depends not only on the price charged but also on the assured service level to them. That is, the pricing scheme is a combination of price charged per customer and the service level offered. As the pricing scheme influences the secondary class customers' demand, it can be viewed as a mechanism to control the traffic intensity at the ICD.

The customer's service level that we consider is a steady-state expected waiting time for its class and it depends on the queuing discipline employed at the facility. A queuing discipline used will therefore, affect the secondary class customers' arrival process whose demand is sensitive to price as well as assured service level. That, in turn, also affects the effective service level offered to the primary class customers. Thus, the queue discipline used can be viewed as another mechanism to control the traffic intensity at the ICD. The simplest queuing discipline is a first come first serve (FCFS) basis where, waiting jobs are selected for service based on their order of arrivals irrespective of their class. The FCFS queuing discipline does not provide differentiated service levels. A differentiated service level between customers can be achieved by using priority queues. The priority scheme can be either static or dynamic. In a static priority scheme, customers are divided into two or more priority classes and the waiting job with highest priority is served first, regardless of the order of arrival. The static priority scheme may cause long delays to the jobs of low priority customers. A dynamic priority scheme aims to eliminate the disadvantages of FCFS and other static priority disciplines by selecting jobs for service using criteria that depend on actual waiting times as well as customers' class.

The details of the operational setting and the revenue maximisation problem are presented in Section 2. We present an algorithm to select these optimal policies and provide a numerical illustration of the same in Section 3. It is clear that the model we consider is valid for any other resource that can be shared over time by 2 different classes of customers that arrive as streams. This aspect, including the details of the optimisation problem that lead to the algorithm, is presented in Sinha *et al.* (2008) and Sinha (2008).

2. REVENUE MAXIMISATION PROBLEM

In this system, we assume that the arrivals of primary and secondary class customers follow independent Poisson processes with means λ_p and λ_s respectively. As the service requirements of the primary and secondary class customers are identical in nature, we assume that the successive service times, i.e., the time taken by the ICD to complete a job irrespective of customer's class, are independent and identically distributed with mean $1/\mu$ and variance σ^2. Further, the queue discipline employed at the resource is head-on-line (non-preemptive) delay dependent priority scheme. A schematic view of the system is shown in Figure 1.

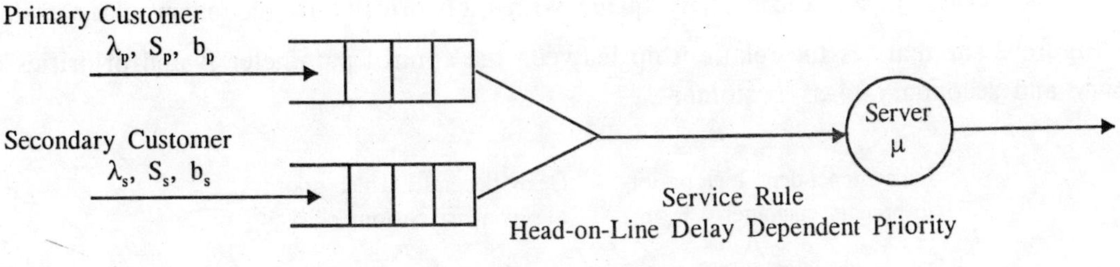

Fig. 1: Schematic view of the System

The delay dependent priority scheme is an example of dynamic priority scheme. A queuing system with delay dependent priority scheme was first studied by Kleinrock (1964). It consists of P priority classes associated with a set of variable parameters $\{b_p\}_1^P$, where $0 \leq b_1 \leq b_2 \leq \ldots \leq b_P$. The instantaneous priority at time t of a class p job that arrived at time T_p is given by $q_p(t) = (t - T_p)b_p$. After a service completion, the server chooses the next job with highest instantaneous priority $q_p(.)$ from all available jobs. If there is a tie for the highest instantaneous priority, then it is broken by using FCFS rule. Here, a higher priority job gains priority at faster rate than lower priority jobs. The steady state expected waiting time in queue for a class p job in M/G/1 head-on-line delay dependent queue is given by the following recursion (Kleinrock 1964, Kanet 1982):

$$W_p = \frac{\dfrac{W_0}{1-\rho} - \sum_{i=1}^{p-1} \rho_i W_i \left(1 - \dfrac{b_i}{b_p}\right)}{1 - \sum_{i=p+1}^{P} \rho_i \left(1 - \dfrac{b_p}{b_i}\right)}, \qquad p \in \{1,2,\ldots,P\} \qquad \ldots (1)$$

where $\rho_i = \dfrac{\lambda_i}{\mu_i}$, $\rho = \sum_{p=1}^{P} \rho_i$, $W_0 = \sum_{p=1}^{P} \dfrac{\lambda_p}{2}\left(\sigma_p^2 + \dfrac{1}{\mu_p^2}\right)$ and $0 \le \rho < 1$. We note that the queue parameters $\{b_p\}_1^P$ only appear as ratios b_p/b_{p+1} in the expression for.

Let b_p and b_s be the parameters associated with the primary and secondary class customers respectively in our system. Alternatively, we define relative priority queue discipline management parameter as a ratio of the associated queue parameters to the primary and the secondary class customers, i.e., $\beta = b_s/b_p$. The selection of the relative priority queue discipline management parameter defines different regimes of the delay dependent priority queue and is as follows:

- $\beta < 1 (b_s < b_p)$. This implies that the primary class customers get higher priority than the secondary class customers. When β approaches zero, the queuing system becomes equivalent to a static priority queue with high priority to primary class customers.
- $\beta = 1 (b_s = b_p)$. This implies that both classes of customers get equal priorities. Thus, the queuing discipline is FCFS.
- $\beta > 1 (b_s > b_p)$. This implies that the secondary class customers get higher priority than the primary class customers When β approaches infinity, the queuing system becomes equivalent to a static priority queue with high priority to secondary class customers.

Figure 2 summarises the relationship between the control parameter β and priorities of the primary and secondary class customers.

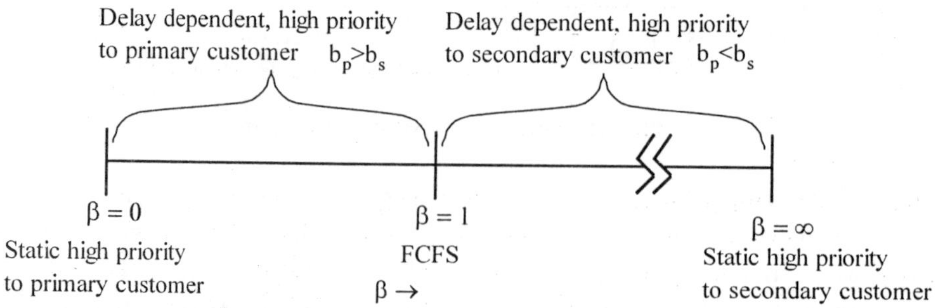

Fig. 2: Effect of Queue Management Parameter on Queue Discipline

Recall that we assume that the service level of a class S is measured in terms of the steady-state expected waiting time of customers in the queue W for that class. Here, an assured service level S for a class of customers implies that the steady-state expected waiting time of customers in queue of its class will be less than or equal to the assured service level, *i.e.*, $W \leq S$. We note that the high value of S corresponds to a low customer service level. In our setting, it is assumed that there exists an agreement between the ICD owner and the primary class customers which assure a given service level S_p to them. This prevailing agreement results in a Poisson stream of primary class customers with mean arrival rate λ_p. In the absence of secondary class customers, it is assumed that the ICD owner is able to fulfill the assured service level to the primary class customers but the facility is still under-utilised. Given the mean arrival rate of primary class customers λ_p where $\lambda_p < \mu$, let $\hat{S}_p$ be the expected waiting time for the primary class customers when the ICD is *dedicated* to primary class customers. The assumption that the resource owner is able to fulfill the assured service level to the primary class customers in the absence of the secondary class customers is only true if and only if $S_p \geq \hat{S}_p$.

The potential mean arrival rate or demand rate of the secondary class customers depends on the unit price charged θ and the assured service level S, to the secondary class customers. Let Λ, (θ, S_s) be the corresponding potential mean arrival rate of the secondary class customers with a charged price of per completed job and assured service level of S_s. We assume that the potential mean arrival rate of secondary class customers is a linear function of unit price and assured service level,

$$\Lambda s, (\theta, S_s) = a - b\theta - cS_s \qquad \text{... (2)}$$

for some given constants $a, b, c > 0$. . The coefficients a, b and c represent the maximum attainable mean arrival rate (market potential), price sensitivity and service level sensitivity respectively. The linear demand function is commonly used to study pricing and lead time decisions of a firm serving customers that are sensitive to quoted price and lead time. Palaka *et al*. (1998) and Pekgun *et al*. (2007) have modeled customer demand as a linear function of price and offered lead time whereas, Ray and Jewkes (2004) have extended the linear customer demand model by assuming that price itself is function of lead time. The customer demand can also be modeled by other functional relationship, for example, log-linear Cobb-Douglas demand function (So and Song 1998).

We have assumed a linear demand function because it is convenient and it exhibits the following desirable properties (Palaka *et al*. 1998):

- The price elasticity of demand, $-b\theta/a - b\theta - cS_s)$, increases with increase in θ and S. This results in higher price elasticity of demand at higher per customer price θ and higher service level S_p. Thus, customers are more sensitive to high prices when they wait for longer periods of time in the queue.
- The service level elasticity of demand, $-cS_s/a - b\theta - cS_s)$, increases with increase in θ and S_s. This results in higher service level elasticity of demand at higher per customer price θ and higher service level S_s. Thus, customers are more sensitive to long waiting times when they pay a high price.

- The demand function is separable of price and assured service level and thus, considers price and service level as substitutes.

The traffic intensity at the ICD is proportional to the sum of mean arrival rates of the primary and secondary class customers. We know that the expected waiting times of the customers in queue depend on the traffic intensity at the resource and the relative queue discipline management parameter. As the mean arrival rate of the primary class customers remains fixed, the expected waiting times of the customers depend only on the mean arrival rate of the secondary class customers λ_s, and relative queue discipline management parameter β. Let $W_p(\lambda_s, \beta)$ and be the steady-state expected waiting times in the queue for the primary and the secondary class customers respectively.

ICD owner aims to select an appropriate arrival rate of the secondary class customers λ_s, a suitable pair of pricing parameters θ and S_s for the secondary class customers and a queue discipline management parameter β that will maximise its expected revenue from the inclusion of secondary class customers while ensuring the service level, S_p, to the primary class customers. The resulting revenue maximisation problem of ICD owner is given as follows:

$$P0: \quad \underset{\lambda_s, \theta, S_s, \beta}{Max} \quad \theta \lambda_s \qquad \text{... (3)}$$

Subjected to

$$W_p(\lambda_s, \beta) \leq S_p \qquad \text{... (4)}$$

$$S_s \geq W_s(\lambda_s, \beta) \qquad \text{... (5)}$$

$$\lambda_s \leq \mu - \lambda_p \qquad \text{... (6)}$$

$$\lambda_s \leq a - b\theta - cS_s \qquad \text{... (7)}$$

$$\lambda_s, \theta, S_s, \beta \geq 0 \qquad \text{... (8)}$$

Here, constraint (4) ensures that the ICD owner does not violate the existing service level commitment to the primary class customers while sharing the resource. The constraint (5) restricts the resource owner to offering a service level commitment to secondary class customers within the system capability. The constraint (6) sets a restriction on maximum permissible mean arrival rate of secondary class customers based on processing capability of the system, i.e., it avoids instability of the multi-class queue. This constraint indeed remains non-binding at the optimum and ensures stability of the multi-class queue (Sinha *et al.* 2008, Sinha 2008). The constraint (7) ensures that the mean arrival rate of secondary class customers should not exceed the demand generated by charged price θ and offered service level S_s. The last constraint captures the non-negativity of the mean arrival rate of secondary class customers λ_s, price θ, assured service level S_s and queue discipline management parameter β. We have assumed that the ICD owner is able to fulfill the assured service level to the primary class customers in the absence of the secondary class customers. Thus, S_p takes values larger than $\hat{S}_p$. Here, $\hat{S}_p$ is the expected waiting time for a typical primary class customer when the resource is *dedicated* to the primary class customers alone.

The constraint (7) will hold as equality in an optimal solution given that the demand is a separable function of both price and assured service level (Palaka *et al*. 1998). Next, we claim that the constraint (5) will also hold as equality in an optimal solution. Now, let us consider that the optimal solution of the revenue maximisation problem is given by mean arrival rate of secondary class customers λ_s^*, price θ^*, assured service level S_s^* and queue discipline management parameter β^* such that $S_s^* > W_s(\lambda_s^*, \beta^*)$. We have already established that the constraint (7) will hold as equality in an optimal solution. Therefore, the objective function can be rewritten as $\frac{1}{b}[a\lambda_s - \lambda_s^2 - c\lambda_s S_s]$. Since the objective function is a decreasing function of S_s, an assured services level S_s' such that $S_s^* > S_s' \geq W_s(\lambda_s^*, \beta^*)$ will increase the earned revenue of the resource owner. Therefore, the constraint (5) must hold as equality in the optimal solution.

The presence of above equality constraints in the optimal solution implies that the revenue maximisation problem of the ICD owner (P0) reduces to

$$P1: \quad \underset{\lambda_s, \beta}{Max} \; \frac{1}{b}[a\lambda_s - \lambda_s^2 - c\lambda_s W_s(\lambda_s, \beta)] \qquad \text{... (9)}$$

Subjected to

$$W_p(\lambda_s, \beta) \leq S_p \qquad \text{... (10)}$$

$$\lambda_s \leq \mu - \lambda_p \qquad \text{... (11)}$$

$$\lambda_s, \beta \geq 0 \qquad \text{... (12)}$$

Once, the optimal mean arrival rate of the secondary class customers λ_s^* and queue discipline management parameter β^* is known, the optimal price θ^* and assured service level S_s^* is obtained using equalities $\lambda_s^* = a - b\theta^* - cS_s^*$ and $S_s^* = W_s(\lambda_s^*, \beta^*)$. The objective function (9) indicates that the optimal choices of λ_s and β remain *insensitive* to price sensitivity coefficient b of the secondary class customers.

Using recursion (1), the expected waiting times in queue for the primary and secondary class customers are given as

$$W_p(\lambda_s, \beta) = \frac{\lambda\psi[\mu - \lambda[1-\beta]]}{\mu[\mu-\lambda][\mu-\lambda_p[1-\beta]]} 1_{\{\beta \leq 1\}} + \frac{\lambda\psi}{[\mu-\lambda][\mu-\lambda_s[1-\frac{1}{\beta}]]} 1_{\{\beta > 1\}} \qquad \text{... (13)}$$

$$W_s(\lambda_s, \beta) = \frac{\lambda\psi}{[\mu-\lambda][\mu-\lambda_p[1-\beta]]} 1_{\{\beta \leq 1\}} + \frac{\lambda\psi\,[\mu - \lambda[1-\frac{1}{\beta}]]}{\mu[\mu-\lambda][\mu-\lambda_s[1-\frac{1}{\beta}]]} 1_{\{\beta > 1\}} \qquad \text{... (14)}$$

where $\lambda = \lambda_p + \lambda_s$, $\psi = [1 + \sigma^2\mu^2]/2$ and $1_{\{.\}}$ denotes the indicator function which is equal to 1 if the statement between braces is true and 0 otherwise. We note that the objective function and the constraint are defined distinctly in the region $\beta \leq 1$ and $\beta > 1$. This aspect distinguishes the optimisation problem P1 from a classical optimisation problem. $W_p(\lambda_s, \beta)$ and $W_s(\lambda_s, \beta)$ have the following properties (The proofs are available in Sinha (2008):

1. $W_p(\lambda_s, \beta)$ and $W_s(\lambda_s, \beta)$ are increasing convex function of λ_s in the interval $[0, \mu - \lambda_p)$.
2. $W_p(\lambda_s, \beta)$ is an increasing concave function of $\beta \geq 0$ whereas, $W_s(\lambda_s, \beta)$ is a decreasing convex function of $\beta \geq 0$.
3. $W_p(\lambda_s, \beta)$ is neither a convex nor a concave function of (λ_s, β) where $\lambda_s \in [0, \mu - \lambda_p)$ and $\beta \geq 0$. Also, $W_p(\lambda_s, \beta)$ is not a quasi-convex function of (λ_s, β).
4. $\lambda_s W_s(\lambda_s, \beta)$ is neither a convex nor a concave function of (λ_s, β) where ls e(0, m - λ_p) and $\beta \geq 0$.

It is to be noted that the revenue maximisation problem P1 is a non-convex constrained optimisation problem.

3. ALGORITHM AND NUMERICAL ILLUSTRATION

The exhaustive search of the Kuhn-Tucker points of constrained optimisation problem P1 results in strict local optimum point if S_p falls within an interval and ratio *a/c* exceeds a critical number. This interval and the critical number are defined by the input parameters of the system. The details are given in Sinha *et al*. (2008) and Sinha (2008). The Kuhn-Tucker first order necessary conditions inherently assume ûnite values of the decision variables. Therefore, the exhaustive search results in the Kuhn-Tucker points where both λ_s and β are finite. But $\beta = \infty$ is a valid decision in our optimisation problem. Therefore, we separately analyse the resulting one-dimensional optimisation problem in λ_s by setting $\beta = \infty$ in the constrained optimisation problem P1. The following algorithm is derived based on the synthesis of the results obtained from the exhaustive search of Kuhn-Tucker points and the analysis of the one-dimensional optimisation problem.

3.1 Algorithm

Given λ_p, μ, σ, a, b, c and S_p, the following algorithm results in the optimum mean arrival rate of secondary class customers $\lambda_s^* > 0$ and the relative queue discipline management parameter β^* that maximises the revenue of the ICD owner. Define $\psi = [1 + \sigma^2 \mu^2]/2$.

1. If either $S_p \leq \hat{S}_p \equiv \dfrac{\lambda_p \psi}{\mu[\mu - \lambda_p]}$ or $\dfrac{a}{c} \leq \dfrac{\lambda_p}{\mu^2}\psi$ then Stop. There is no feasible solution.

2. If $\dfrac{\mu - \lambda_p}{\mu \lambda_p} > \dfrac{a\lambda_p - c\psi}{2\mu\lambda_p^2 + c\psi(\mu + \lambda_p)}$ then find $\lambda_s^{(3)}$ the unique root of the cubic $\tilde{G}(\lambda_s)$ in the interval $(0, \mu - \lambda_p)$.

$$\tilde{G}(\lambda_s) \equiv 2\mu\lambda_s^3 - [a\mu + c\psi + 4\mu^2]\lambda_s^2 + 2\mu[a\mu + c\psi + \mu^2]\lambda_s - \mu[a\mu^2 - c\psi\lambda_p]$$

Calculate $\bar{S}_p = W_p(\lambda_s^{(3)}, \beta = \infty)$. If $S_p > \bar{S}_p$ then assign $\lambda_s^* = \lambda_s^{(3)}$, $\beta^* = \infty$ and Stop. Else go to the next step.

3. If $\frac{a}{c} \le \frac{\lambda_p(2\mu - \lambda_p)}{\mu(\mu - \lambda_p)^2}\psi$ then define an interval $J = (\hat{S}_p, \bar{S}_p]$ if $\bar{S}_p$ exists otherwise $(\hat{S}_p, \infty)$.

   Assign, $\lambda_s^* = \frac{1}{2S_p}\left[S_p[2\mu - \lambda_p] + \psi - \sqrt{[S_p\lambda_p + \psi]^2 + 4\mu\psi S_p}\right]$, $\beta^* = \infty$ for any value of $S_p \in J$ and Stop. Else go to next step.

4. Find $\lambda_s^{(1)}$ the unique root of the cubic $G(\lambda_s)$ in the interval $(0, \mu - \lambda_p)$.

$$G(\lambda_s) \equiv 2\mu\lambda_s^3 - [c\psi + \mu(a + 4\varphi_0)]\lambda_s^2 + 2\varphi_0[c\psi + \mu(a + \varphi_0)]\lambda_s - a\mu\varphi_0^2 + c\psi\lambda_p(\mu + \varphi_0)$$

   where $\varphi_0 = \mu - \lambda_p$. Calculate $I_\ell = \frac{\psi\lambda}{\mu[\mu - \lambda_p]}$ and $I_u = \frac{\psi\lambda}{[\mu - \lambda_s^{(1)}][\mu - \lambda]}$ where $\lambda = \lambda_p + \lambda_s^{(1)}$.

5. Define intervals: $I^- = [\hat{S}_p, I_\ell)$, $I = [I_\ell, I_u)$ and $I^+ = [I_u, \bar{S}_p]$ if $\bar{S}_p$ exists otherwise $[I_u, \infty)$.

   (a) If $S_p \in I^-$, then assign $\lambda_s^* = \frac{\mu[\mu - \lambda_p]S_p}{\psi} - \lambda_p$ and $\beta^* = 0$

   (b) If $S_p \in I$, then assign $\lambda_s^* = \lambda_s^{(1)}$ and

$$\beta^* = \begin{cases} \frac{[\mu - \lambda][\mu S_p[\mu - \lambda_p] - \psi\lambda]}{\psi\lambda^2 - \mu S_p\lambda_p[\mu - \lambda]} & \text{for } \frac{\psi\lambda}{\mu[\mu - \lambda_p]} \le S_p \le \frac{\psi\lambda}{\mu[\mu - \lambda]} \\ \frac{S_p\lambda_s^*[\mu - \lambda]}{\psi\lambda - S_p[\mu - \lambda_s^*][\mu - \lambda]} & \text{for } \frac{\psi\lambda}{\mu[\mu - \lambda]} < S_p < \frac{\psi\lambda}{[\mu - \lambda_s^*][\mu - \lambda]} \end{cases}$$

   (c) If $S_p \in I^+$, then assign

$$\lambda_s^* = \frac{1}{2S_p}\left[S_p[2\mu - \lambda_p] + \psi - \sqrt{[S_p\lambda_p + \psi]^2 + 4\mu\psi S_p}\right] \text{ and } \beta^* = \infty.$$

The optimum assured service level to the secondary class customers is $S_s^* = W_s(\lambda_s^*, \beta^*)$ and the optimal price charged to the secondary class customers is $\theta^* = \frac{1}{b}[a - \lambda_s^* - cS_s^*]$.

The above defined algorithm divides the feasible region of S_p into intervals of S_p. We notice that either λ_s^* or β^* remains constant in those intervals. For example, the optimum queue discipline management parameter $\beta^* = 0$ and ∞ for $S_p \varepsilon I^-$ and I^+ respectively whereas, the optimum mean arrival rate of the secondary class customers λ_s^* remains constant in the interval I.

3.2 Numerical Illustration

Let us assume that the secondary class customers' demand function $\Lambda_s(\theta, S_s)$ is $100 - 0.2\theta - 0.1S_s$. Also, λ_p= 8 customers/hr, μ = 10 customers/hr. and σ = 0.1 hr/customer. We get $\psi=1$, $\hat{S}_p = 0.4$ hr/customers, $\frac{a}{c}$ = 1000 hr/customer, $\frac{\lambda_p}{\mu^2}\psi$ =0.08 hr/customer, $\frac{\lambda_p(2\mu-\lambda_p)}{\mu(\mu-\lambda_p)^2}\psi$ =2.4 hr/customer, $\frac{\mu-\lambda_p}{\mu\lambda_p}$ = 0.025 hr./customer and $\frac{a\lambda_p - c\psi}{2\mu\lambda_p^2 + c\psi(\mu+\lambda_p)}$ = 0.624 hr/customer.

We note that a feasible solution will exist if $S_p > 0.4$ as $\frac{a}{c} > \frac{\lambda_p}{\mu^2}\psi$. As $\frac{\mu-\lambda_p}{\mu\lambda_p} < \frac{a\lambda_p - c\psi}{2\mu\lambda_p^2 + c\psi(\mu+\lambda_p)}$ and $\frac{a}{c} > \frac{\lambda_p(2\mu-\lambda_p)}{\mu(\mu-\lambda_p)^2}\psi$, we directly go to step 4. Calculations at step 4 results in $\lambda_s^{(1)}$ =1.898, I_l = 0.4949 and I_u = 11.97. The intervals I^-, I and I^+ are (0.4, 0.4949), [0.4949, 11.97) and [11.97, ∞) respectively. A few results corresponding to distinct values of S_p are presented in Table 1.

Table 1: Representative Results of the Numerical Example

S_p	*Priority* β^*	*Arrival rate* λ_s^*	*Price* θ^*	*Assured SL* S_s^*	*Revenue* O^*
0.41	0	0.2	497.86	2.28	99.57
0.42	0	0.4	496.69	2.62	198.68
0.45	0	1	492.75	4.5	492.75
0.4949	0	1.898	466.25	48.52	884.94
1	0.01	1.898	467.32	46.39	886.96
3	0.07	1.898	471.53	37.95	894.97
6	0.23	1.898	477.85	25.32	906.96
9.703	1	1.898	485.66	9.70	921.78
10	1.18	1.898	486.27	8.48	922.96
11	2.64	1.898	488.39	4.24	926.96
11.97		1.898	490.46	0.122	930.87
13		1.905	490.41	0.122	934.65
14		1.912	490.37	0.123	937.82
15		1.918	490.35	0.123	940.58

We observe from the algorithm that the optimum decisions depend on the prevailing QOS level to the primary class customers as well as on the ratio a/c of the coefficients of secondary class customers' demand function. If the ratio a/c is low, then the optimum policy assigns static high priority to the secondary class customers and allows maximum possible arrival rate of secondary class customers that does not violate the prevailing QoS level to the primary class customers.

On the other hand, if the ratio a/c is high then the QoS level to the primary class customers is divided into three regions of operation corresponding to low, moderate and high values of S_p. Note that lower the value of S_p, higher the QoS level to the primary class customers. The optimum policy depends on region of operation, *i.e.*, the prevailing QoS level to the primary class customers. When QoS level to primary class customers is high (low S_p), then the optimum policy assigns static high priority to the primary class customers and allows maximum possible arrival rate of the secondary class customers that does not violate the prevailing QoS level to the primary class customers. Similarly, when QoS level to primary class customers is low (high S_p), then the optimum policy assigns static high priority to the secondary class customers and allows maximum possible arrival rate of the secondary class customers that does not violate the prevailing QoS level to the primary class customers. In contrast, when QoS level to primary class customers is moderate (moderate S_p), then the optimum policy chooses a constant arrival rate of the secondary class customers for any value of in that interval and employs a dynamic priority scheme.

REFERENCES

Kanet, J.J. (1982), A Mixed delay Dependent Queue Discipline, *Operations Research*, Vol. 30, pp. 93–96.

Kleinrock, L. (1964), A Delay Dependent Queue Discipline, *Naval Research Logistics Quarterly*, Vol. 11, pp. 329–341.

Palaka, K., Erlebacher, S. and Kropp, D. (1998), Lead-time Setting, Capacity Utilisation, and Pricing Decisions under Lead-time Dependent Demand, *IIE Transactions*, Vol. 30, pp. 151–163.

Pekgun, P., Griûn, P.M. and Keskinocak, P. (2007), Coordination of Marketing and Production for Price and Lead-time Decisions, *IIE Transactions*, Vol. 40, pp. 12-30.

Rangaraj, N., Taneja, D. and Burrus, J. (2006), Logistics Infrastructure for Container Operations in India — Models for Shared Resources, Summit on Indian Manufacturing Competitiveness: Global Manufacturing and Service Networks, Indian School of Business, Hyderabad.

Ray, S. and Jewkes, E. (2004), Customer led Time Management when both Demand and Price are Lead Time Sensitive, *European Journal of Operational Research*, Vol.153, pp.769–781.

Sinha, S.K., Rangaraj, N. and Hemachandra, N. (2008), Pricing Surplus Server Capacity for Mean Waiting Time Sensitive Customers, Technical Report, Industrial Engineering and Operations Research, IIT Bombay, Mumbai.

Sinha, S.K. (2008), Service Level Contracts for Supply Chains, Ph.D. thesis, Industrial Engineering and Operations Research, IIT Bombay, Mumbai.

So, K.C. and Song, J. (1998), Price, Delivery time Guarantees and Capacity Selection, *European Journal of Operational Research*, Vol. 111, pp. 28–49.

6

IMPROVEMENT OF TAXI AND AUTO SERVICES IN THE CITY — AN ECONOMIC PERSPECTIVE

Debabrata Datta

ABSTRACT

The paper looks at a practical problem of excess charges in the market for taxicab services. It is argued that this problem should not be viewed only as inability on the part of the government to enforce government regulation. Rather, it is felt necessary to concentrate on the market inefficiency involved in the market for taxi/auto-rickshaw service as is prevalent in India. Much of the inefficiency and high price arise from the one-shot game and local monopoly character of the taxi/auto-rickshaw service market. Since the game is one-shot, there is no scope for reputation building. The requirement, therefore, is the introduction of reputation factor by policy-induced branding. The economic model constructed in this regard shows how such branding can improve the working of the market and help consumers to get higher consumers' surplus.

1. INTRODUCTION

The quality of taxi/auto service in various cities of India leaves much to be desired. In most of the cities, taxis/auto rickshaws try to charge fares, much higher than the metered rates. It is quite common that in spite of the presence of meters in the vehicle, the drivers demand an arbitrary amount (auto-rickshaws in Chennai are an example). Even if the vehicle driver agrees to charge the metered rate, the meters are found to be defective in many cases (This is often the case with taxicabs in Kolkata). Another common practice to dupe the consumer is to take a longer route to reach a destination. (Auto-rickshaws in Delhi are notorious for this practice). The government machinery is found to be wanting in preventing such extortion practices and saving the travellers, particularly the newcomers, from being cheated.

The important feature of the taxicab segment of the ground passenger transportation industry (hereafter "taxicab industry") particularly in less developed countries like India is that it is a local business with regulated prices. Since taxi markets are highly geographically segmented, the nationwide taxicab industry is actually a collection of hundreds of independent city-level markets, reflecting considerable variations. This traditional taxicab market seldom gives rise to price competition. This is the reason for which Shreiber (1975) argues that the taxicab market should be subjected to price regulation. While in most industries a seller can expect to get more business by cutting price, an individual cab operator acting independently cannot gain more passengers if he reduces the price. Rather he is to gain if he increases the price as the passenger on the road, needing the service urgently has no other option but to hire the taxi. Otherwise, she will have to wait for a period, the duration of which is not known to her. In such cases, the taxi cab driver makes gain by charging extra rent. When the price is regulated, he clandestinely extracts higher price, often by tampering with the meter.

An important question that arises, therefore, is whether price regulation is adequate enough to give respite to the passengers from higher prices. Our observations on the market scenario in different cities of India, derived from casual empiricism, show that the regulation is never full-proof. Then the issue is: what is the mechanism that can ensure the effective implementation of the regulation? Fortunately, the taxi service market can now function better on account of technology-driven changes in the conditions for the market and this can offer a solution, as argued in this paper.

While the early literature on the taxicab industry puts forward the arguments for regulation, the subsequent literature takes into account the changes in the market and presents a case for deregulation as well. Gwilliam (1980) and Coffman (1977) argue that the market situation is no longer characterised by local monopoly only. Taxi fleet and order by telephone are the important features of the taxicab market of the developed countries. In this new situation it is not unlikely that price competition emerges in the market. The results of industrial organisation literature can also be applied to the taxicab industry in this market set up (Rawley 2006).

The issue of regulation in the transport sector has emerged as an important topic of discussion in literature particularly after the shift of paradigm from a situation of hyper regulation of markets to one based on market prices. Some prominent contributions in this area are Teal and Berglund (1987), Gwilliam (1980, 1989). The matter is also discussed in the context of less developed countries in Gwilliam (2001).

In this paper, we are not looking at the deregulation issue but consider the role of changes in market conditions in better implementation of the regulation. The factor that we highlight in this regard is the role of trust and reputation. The literature shows that the reputation factor can play a useful role in improving the quality of the product. Klein and Leffler (1981) show how fear of switching of the customer can ensure performance of the contract. Cabral (2005) shows that there are essentially two mechanisms that lead to working of trust and reputation. One is based on repeated interaction which is called the bootstrap mechanism. The other one is based on Bayesian updating of beliefs and is called the Bayesian mechanism.

The main argument that we put forward in this paper is that the individual taxicab driver-dominated faceless taxicab market generates a local monopoly. It is a monopoly because once the passenger is on the road she can choose only one taxi and she has no respite if that taxi does not provide satisfactory service. The consequence of this local monopoly is play of a one shot game, higher price and an extra mark–up. It is shown that this problem should not be viewed only as inability of the government to enforce government regulation. To put the matter in the right perspective, it is necessary to concentrate on market inefficiency involved in the market for taxi/auto-rickshaw service, as is prevalent in India. The paper argues that much of the inefficiency and high price, as described above, arises from the one-shot game and local monopoly character of the taxi/auto-rickshaw service market. Asymmetric information and one-shot game results in the problem of both adverse selection and moral hazards in this transport service. Since the game is one-shot, there is no scope for reputation building and Bayesian updating. At the same time, the bootstrap mechanism is also not working due to persistence of moral hazard problem. The requirement, therefore, is the introduction of the reputation factor that can lead to the threat of switching in the minds of the services provider and prevention of excess pricing. For this purpose, policies can be adopted to induce branding. The economic model constructed in this regard shows how such branding can improve the working of the market and help consumers to get higher consumers' surplus.

In what follows, Section 2 describes the model of local monopoly. Section 3 analyses the effects of oligopoly formation, brand naming and reputation and finally, Section 4 ends the paper with a concluding note.

2. MODELS

2.1 Local monopoly

In this model we look at the behaviour of an individual taxicab driver who acts as a local monopolist. Once the taxi cab boarder (B) enters a contract with a particular taxi cab driver (D) under a system of individual based faceless taxi cab system, it becomes a one shot game between a local monopolist and the boarder.

The following assumptions are made:

The taxi driver is a profit maximiser. There are two types of passengers (B) – one informed, who can detect the extra charge and the other uninformed and unable to detect or prevent the extra payment. We assume that out of a total N number of passengers, who use the service, λ $\left[0 \leq \lambda \leq 1\right]$ is the percentage of uninformed buyer. The taxi cab driver can extract extra money from the uninformed passenger but not from the informed buyer. The extra payment is μ percentage over the true charge (m). We assume that there is an inverse relation between μ and λ i.e. $\lambda = \lambda(\mu)$ where $\lambda'(\mu) < 0$. this implies that if the taxi cab driver wants to extract more and more extra charges, more and more passengers will get to know that they are being charged extra amount.[1]

Proposition 1: The individual taxicab driver charges a positive extra mark up (μ).

Proof: The revenue function of the monopoly driver is

$$R = m(1+\mu)\lambda N + m(1-\lambda)N$$

The driver chooses that maximises R.

$$R = m(1+\mu)\lambda N + m(1-\lambda)N$$

$$\frac{dR}{d\mu} = m\lambda N + m(1+\mu)\lambda' N - m\lambda' N = 0$$

$$m\lambda N + m\mu\lambda' N = 0$$

$$\mu^* = -\frac{\lambda^*(\mu^*)}{\lambda'(\mu^*)} > 0$$

$$\frac{d^2R}{d\mu^2} = m\lambda' N + m\mu\lambda'' N + m\lambda' N < 0$$

under assumption that $\lambda'' \leq 0$

It should be noted that μ^* is positive implying that D will charge a positive extra mark up (μ).

Let us now examine whether, penalty (K) can take care of the problem. It is obvious that if every case of extra charge can be detected and penalty imposed, the problem is over. But this is impossible on account of prohibitive cost of implementation of such full scale detection. Hence, we assume that there is a probability of detection (q), which is positively related with λ *i.e.*, higher the number of boarders cheated higher is the probability of detection. Hence, $q = q(\lambda)$ where $q'(\lambda) > 0$.

Proposition 2: Even after a penalty the extra mark up is positive. The mark up may even increase after introduction of a penalty system.

Proof: Given $q = q(\lambda)$ where $q'(\lambda) > 0$, the net revenue function is

$$R = m(1+\mu)\lambda N + m(1-\lambda)N - q(\lambda(\mu))K$$

$$\frac{dR}{d\mu} = m\lambda N + m(1+\mu)\lambda' N - m\lambda' N - q'\lambda' K = 0$$

$$\frac{dR}{d\mu} = m\lambda N + m\mu\lambda' N - q'\lambda' K = 0$$

$$\frac{d^2R}{d\mu^2} = m\lambda' N + m\mu\lambda'' N + m\lambda' N < 0$$

under assumption that $\lambda'' \leq 0$

Still we do not get $\frac{dR}{d\mu} < 0$ so that μ can be zero.

$$\mu^{**} = \frac{q'\lambda' K - m\lambda N}{m\lambda' N} = \frac{Kq'}{mN} - \frac{\lambda(\mu^{**})}{\lambda'(\mu^{**})}$$

μ^{**} may exceed, equal or be less than μ^{*}.

2.2 Oligopoly formation, brand naming, reputation

Let us now introduce the formation of firms that provide the taxi services under some brand name. When such brand names are introduced, there arises a role of reputation and trust. Under such arrangements the transaction between the taxi service — firm and the passenger is no longer of the nature of a one-shot game. Since the passenger now has the option to choose among the firms in future as well, the game is a repeated game. In order to capture the scenario, we consider a duopoly market where there are two firms competing between them.

In order to capture the reputation factor, we have to introduce a game played between two infinitely lived seller and infinitely lived buyers. In each period, sellers and buyers play the game. One of the possible equilibrium of this repeated game is simply the repetition of the one-period game. We thus, consider two periods where the first period is the present period but all subsequent periods are covered by the second period.

The analysis is based on a number of simplifying assumptions. Our basic aim is to find out an equilibrium concerning the extra mark up μ. Thus, there are two profit maximising firms 1 and 2 in a market where there is a charge of m, net of the cost, fixed by the authority. N is the demand for service, which is assumed to be given for simplicity. The firms can charge the extra mark up for the uninformed buyers but the firm which charges the higher mark up will earn a bad name and lose all the customers in the second period. This happens on account of Bayesian learning in the second period on the basis of the experiences in the first period. If both firm charges the same extra mark up in the first period the passengers will simply be divided between the two firms. The implication of this assumption is as under. The profit function for firm 1 is as follows:

$$R_1 = \begin{cases} \frac{1}{2}\big(m(1+\mu_1)\lambda N + m(1-\lambda)N\big) + \delta\big(m(1+\mu_1)\lambda N + m(1-\lambda)N\big) & \text{if } \mu_1 < \mu_2 \text{...........(1)} \\ \frac{1}{2}\big(m(1+\mu_1)\lambda N + m(1-\lambda)N\big) + \frac{1}{2}\delta\big(m(1+\mu_1)\lambda N + m(1-\lambda)N\big) & \text{if } \mu_1 = \mu_2 \text{...........(2)} \\ \frac{1}{2}\big(m(1+\mu_1)\lambda N + m(1-\lambda)N\big) & \text{if } \mu_1 > \mu_2 \text{..........................(3)} \end{cases}$$

The profit function for firm 2 is analogous.

This model may be regarded as a two player game with strategy space $\mu = [0, \infty)$ for both players and with pay off functions R_i. The game is symmetric. The pay-off function of the firms in this model is discontinuous.

We are interested in Nash equilibrium of the above game that is, those mark up

(μ_i^*, μ_j^*) for which $R_i(\mu_i^*, \mu_j^*) \geq R_i(\mu_i, \mu_2^*)$

***Proposition* 3:**

$\mu_i^{max}\lambda < \delta$ is necessary and sufficient condition for the mark up $\mu_1^* = \mu_2^* = 0$ to form a symmetric Nash equilibrium.

Proof: $\mu_i^{max}\lambda < \delta$ implies

$$\frac{1}{2}\left(m(1+\mu_i^{max})\lambda N + m(1-\lambda)N\right) < \frac{1}{2}(m\lambda N + m(1-\lambda)N) + \frac{1}{2}\delta\left(m\lambda N + m(1-\lambda)N\right) \text{ for } \mu_j = 0$$

(2) is better even for zero mark up

$$m\mu_i^{max}\lambda N + mN < mN + \delta mN$$

$$\mu_i^{max}\lambda < \delta$$

Then $R_i(0,0) > R_i(\mu_i, 0)$ for $\mu_i > 0$.

So for $\mu_j = 0$, $\mu_i = 0$ is the best response. Similarly

for $\mu_i = 0$, $\mu_j > 0$ is ruled out. This completes the proof.

***Proposition* 4:**

The NE, shown above is unique.

Proof: Suppose there is another NE ($\mu_1 > 0$, $\mu_2 > 0$)

Assume $\mu_1 \leq \mu_2$ without any loss of generality.

Case 1: $\mu_1 < \mu_2$. Then since (2) > (3) deviation by firm 2 to make $\mu_1 = \mu_2$ is gainful.

Case 2: $\mu_1 = \mu_2 > 0$. Since (1) > (2) undercut by firm (1) is gainful

The above results show that under individual taxicab service provision, the extra mark up is positive, implying loss of consumers' welfare. The surprising result is that even a penalty cannot take care of this extra charge problem. However, if the market develops into a service with brand names of taxi fleet operators, competition leads to zero extra mark up. This is on account of the threat of switching over by the dis-satisfied customers in the second period. Since our result is critically dependent on the arguments similar to those used in the Bertrand model, one can argue that a repeated game framework may lead to collusive behaviour and higher pricing. This is however possible only if entry is totally restricted. If there is chance of entry of any new firm, no firm will hazard the loss of reputation. This is particularly true if the game is over an infinite period. It is said that reputation is built over a long period but it takes a single period to lose that reputation. The benefits of reputation are received over all the future periods. Hence, when a firm expects that any new firm may enter in the next period, by the logic of rationality it should not find it worthwhile to collude.

4. CONCLUSIONS

We deal with a practical problem present in the market for an essential transport service. It is observed that instead of large number of faceless taxicab service providers, taxi fleet services by oligopolistic firms under brand names can improve the quality of services, provided, of course, the market has free entry. Policies should, therefore, need the withdrawal of restrictions, if any, on the formation of taxi fleet firms. There is a deep seated belief in many quarters that small is beautiful and therefore there may be policy level restrictions in many areas about the entry of such large firms, which provide taxi services. But as shown in the paper these policies helps in creating market with local monopoly character and therefore, should be reformed. Policy suggestions, based on the existing knowledge of the literature can improve the working of markets, characterised by asymmetric information. In India, this realisation has hardly dawned upon the policy makers that economic analysis of markets can solve many practical problems. Rather, problems of the market are tried to be tackled by more than optimum government intervention. But government intervention is not likely to be successful unless the problem of market imperfection is properly addressed, as shown in our analysis.

Note:

1. A prisoners' dilemma may operate in this case. Each driver finds it profitable to charge extra but as a whole the total demand falls for which the driver may not ultimately gain.

REFERENCES

Gómez-Lobo, A. (2006), Why Competition Does Not Work in Urban Bus Markets: Some New Wheels for Some Old Ideas, Working Paper, Department of Economics, University of Chili.

Cabral, Luýs, M.B. (2005), The Economics of Trust and Reputation: A Primer, Working Paper, New York University and CEPR.

Coffman, R.B. (1977), The Economic Reasons for Price and Entry Regulation of Taxicabs: a Comment, *Journal of Transport Economics and Policy*, Vol. 11, No.3, pp.288-297.

Gwilliam, K.M. (1980), The Economic Reasons for Price and Entry Regulation of Taxicabs: a Comment, *Journal of Transport Economics and Policy*, Vol. 14, No.1, pp.105-112.

Gwilliam, K.M. (1989), Setting the Market Free; Deregulation of the Bus Industry, *Journal of Transport Economics and Policy*, Vol. 23, No.1.

Gwilliam, K.M. (2001), Competition in Urban Passenger Transport in the Developing World, *Journal of Transport Economics and Policy*, Vol. 35, No.1, pp. 99-118.

Klein, B. & Leffler, K.B. (1981), The Role of Switching Cost in Assuring Contractual Performance, *Journal of Political Economy*, Vol. 89 No. 4.

Rawley, E. (2006), Diversification and Adaptation: How Organisation Drives Taxi Firm Performance, Working Paper, University of California, Berkeley.

Shreiber, C. (1975), The Economic Reasons for Price and Entry Regulation of Taxicabs, *Journal of Transport Economics and Policy*, Vol. 21, No.3.

Teal and Berglund (1987), The Impact of Taxicab Regulation in USA, *Journal of Transport Economics and Policy*, Vol. 9, No.1.

7

MAKING THE HOUSING-TRANSPORT LINK: CAN WE DO BETTER?

Christo Venter

ABSTRACT

Cities of the world are facing increasing sustainability challenges, on account of environmental impacts, urbanisation and other related challenges. Housing and transport are the two key areas which need attention from a policy perspective point of view. Housing helps determine transport demand and both are important attributes of the liveability of cities. This paper considers these questions with a view to arriving at an understanding of the need for better integration between housing and transport and the potential direction for action in this field. The paper attempts to locate the housing-transport link within the larger policy debates around sustainability and urban poverty issues, in both developed and developing countries. The emphases are different, as are the specific features of the solutions likely to be applicable in different parts of the world.

1. INTRODUCTION

It is widely acknowledged that cities of the world are facing increasing sustainability challenges. While the dimensions of these challenges differ across regions, they all relate in some way to the environmental (in the broadest sense) impacts of urban living, and questions around the collective ability of our institutions and processes to manage and mitigate these impacts effectively. The very complexity and interrelatedness of the challenges makes this task all the more harder.

Traditionally, our understanding of problems and our means of dealing with them have entailed a "divide and rule" approach, where we attempt to break problems down into infrastructure problems, education problems, and so forth which are then handled by separate departments and officials. The departmentalisation of urban problems has made them more manageable in the short term, given political and technical limitations. But it is increasingly clear that the significant leaps forward that are needed to solve future challenges will have to come from successful integration of thought and action across these disciplinary boundaries. De-departmentalisation is needed not only of planning processes, arenas of institutional action, and resource allocation — the technical particulars of government — but of the very knowledge domains on which a mutual understanding of the problems we face can be constructed. For instance, spatial analysts have been calling for years for better integration of land use and transport development. Yet results have been limited, in no insignificant measure due to the "historically fragmented professional and socio-technical cultures and practices" typical across the urban planning and engineering disciplines (Behrens and Wilkinson, 2003).

Two key areas of Government engagement, in which the benefits of greater integration seem obvious, are housing and transport. Local and State Governments are typically involved in both the development of policy guidance and in the actual provision of services and infrastructure in these two areas. Intuitively the two areas are highly interlinked. Housing (in both location and density) helps determine transport demand, while the quality and cost of transport help determine where people want to live. Together, housing and transport are both important attributes of the liveability of cities (Vuchic, 1999). Both housing and transport shape patterns of spatial inclusion and exclusion, while thus, defining or reinforcing patterns of social equality, marginalisation, and poverty (Church et al., 2000).

Yet, it has been pointed out that, in the developing world at least, "linkages between transport and urban poor housing represents a gap in policy debates in both fields. The idea that urban poor housing issues should be considered when making transport policy choices has rarely been discussed" (Barter, 2002). Experience from developed countries suggests that this is true not only for "poor" housing but more generally for housing of working families and older people. The questions that are raised are: to what extent can housing and transport policy be better integrated; what benefits (if any) could result; and, what could such integration look like?

This paper considers these questions with a view to arriving at an understanding of the need for better integration between housing and transport; and the potential direction for action in this field. The paper starts by examining theoretical and empirical evidence of the links between housing and transport in cities. We then consider the extent to which housing and transport policies have been integrated, both in developing and developed parts of the world, and discuss some of the outcomes. The case of South Africa, as a middle-income country reflecting issues typical of both developed and developing countries, is used as an illustration. Lastly, some thoughts on successful integration initiatives and the way forward are presented.

2. THEORETICAL LINKS BETWEEN HOUSING AND TRANSPORT

Theoretical arguments for the link between housing and transport are rooted in the residential location theories of Alonso and others (for reviews see Giuliano (1986), Deakin (1991) and Cadwallader (1996)). They essentially conceptualised residential location choice as a trade-off between housing and transport cost. In an idealised monocentric city, housing cost increases towards the centre due to the higher land rent demanded by its more accessible location. Transport cost, specifically commute cost for the trip to work, increases for houses further away from the centre due to longer trip distances. A utility maximising (or cost minimising) location exists for each household, but this differs across households depending on their relative preferences for consumption of housing and transport.

The simple model can be extended to account for some complexities of real land markets, but, in essence, it leads to some simple theoretical conclusions:

- The theory predicts a housing density gradient in cities, with higher density housing located near the centre as the higher land rent leads households to reduce dwelling sizes while remaining within overall budget constraints.
- Centrally located residents should consume less transport, to compensate for their higher housing cost.
- Theoretically housing expenditures should decline further away from the city centre. However, there is an income effect. Higher income households are usually assumed to value housing more highly than lower income households, making them willing to consume more housing in lower-density suburban locations (where lower land rates are offset by bigger plot sizes, leading to higher prices per dwelling), even while paying more for the additional commuting involved.
- Cost-reducing transport investments such as freeway improvements or public transport investments impact housing markets by making more income available for consumption (even at constant total incomes). This is used either to consume more housing — thus, raising the value of housing located near improved facilities — or more transport — leading to outward migration of households to more distant locations.
- Any failure of the market to locate a household at their utility maximising location is a market failure and results in lower overall welfare.

3. EMPIRICAL FINDINGS AND POLICY DEBATES IN NORTH AMERICA AND EUROPE

Research in both developed and developing countries has to a large extent validated the main predictions of the theory, but it has also raised some further questions. Both land prices and population densities tend to decline with distance from the city centre (*e.g.*, Mills and Tan, 1980), although, increasing polycentricity of cities makes the relationship harder to verify empirically (Giuliano, 1995). The density gradients of cities in both North America and Europe have also declined over time in response to transport system improvements (Giuliano, 1986; Banister, 2005).

Significant evidence exists of a change in land values in the vicinity of transport investments (Rodríguez and Targa, 2004), although, the relationship is context dependent in both size and direction. For instance, land values in Portland, Oregon, have been shown to increase near light rail stations, but to decrease next to the rail lines themselves due to noise and nuisance factors (Ding et al., cited in Dunphy, 1998). A flurry of recent studies documented how public transport investments significantly raised house prices in Asia (So et. al., 1997), Europe (*e.g.*, Debrezion *et al.*, 2006; Adair *et al.*, 2000), Australia (TRB, 2003) and South America (Rodríguez and Targa, 2004). There is furthermore empirical support for the notion that lower-income households place a high value on accessibility to opportunities in developed (*e.g.*, Adair *et al.*, 2000) as well as developing countries (World Bank, 2002; Turner cited in Gilbert and Gugler, 1992, p.119).

Studies of household expenditures confirm that many consumers are indeed trading off higher transport costs for lower housing (and other) costs. The relative affordability of housing in suburban locations is a major reason for the continued demand for decentralised housing developments, both in the US and elsewhere. However, suburban housing locations are typically associated with higher transport costs resulting from longer travel distances and because living in transit-poor suburbs usually implies the necessity of owning and operating a car at a higher cost (STPP 2001; Sanchez et. al., 2007). Figure 1 reflects this trade-off as calculated by the Center for Housing Policy (Lipman, 2006) for 28 major US cities. The combined cost of housing and transportation (as a percentage of household incomes) typically rises up to a distance of about 15 miles (22 km) from major employment centres, from where it declines very slightly.

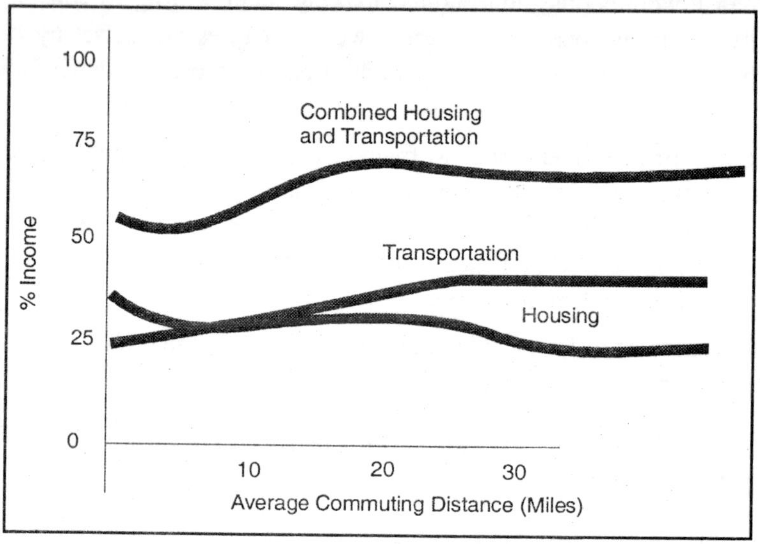

Fig. 1: Relative contribution of housing and transport to household expenditure in 28 metropolitan areas in the United States

Source: Lipman, 2006.

If the market theory works in practice, what then is the need for government intervention in the housing and transport arena? In line with conventional economic thinking, government intervention is warranted when the market fails to produce an efficient allocation of consumption or resources. In the area of housing and transport, market failure has been noted for two primary reasons: the impacts of externalities, and the imperfect supply of housing. These two issues will be discussed, in turn, together with the policy interventions proposed or attempted to correct for them.

It would be useful however, at this stage to bracket the discussion with an acknowledgment that the classical housing-transport cost trade-off does not account for many other factors that shape housing preferences and housing choice. Housing location choice also reflect factors such as school and neighbourhood quality (Molin and Timmermans, 2003; Wachs et al., 1993), the need for two-earner households to access two job locations (Giuliano & Small, 1993), and complex non-work activity needs such as childcare (Jarvis, 2003). It can therefore, be expected that any policy intervention in this complex field will likely not only have limited success, but also cause unintended consequences.

3.1 Market Failure Due To Externalities

Externalities cause the well-known conflict between an equilibrium solution based on private costs and one based on social costs. In short, when selecting a housing location-transport consumption bundle, households do not consider the societal costs of their choice, in particular those relating to transport externalities. The user optimal distribution of housing and activities in a city will therefore, result in more travel — specifically by private car, with its attendant environmental costs — than is optimal from a city sustainability point of view.

There is a rapidly growing literature that seeks to estimate and contrast the higher social costs (in terms of infrastructure supply, traffic fatalities, emissions and the like) of sprawling forms of urban development, with those of denser, more compact cities (*e.g.*, Ewing et al., 2003; Burchell and Galley, 2003). Higher densities — particularly higher residential densities — are often regarded as the single most important land use factor needed to support a more sustainable, less travel-intensive city (Hall, 2007; Newman & Kenworthy, 1989), although, there is no agreement on this (Banister, 2005).

The economist's solution is to "get the prices right" by pricing transport closer to its true marginal social costs. While congestion pricing, fully priced parking, and so on are seeing greater adoption internationally (most recently and significantly in London), the number of schemes that fail due to public and political opposition far outnumbers the few successes. This remains unlikely to change soon. In the absence of true market pricing of transport, some analysts argue that direct public intervention in the housing market deserves consideration as a second-best alternative (Cervero, 1996).

One such planning intervention to correct for market failure is for government to positively influence the balance between housing and jobs in an area. The notion of jobs-housing balance was first put forward by Cervero (1989) as a measure of the amount of housing relative to job opportunities in a region. Imbalances between jobs and housing at the regional or city scale leads to excessive commuting, which government spatial policy (housing, transport, employment) should aim to reduce through better coordination of housing, transportation and land-use (Cervero, 1989; 2002). Jobs-housing balance targets were briefly adopted by some planning authorities in the US during the 1990s, but have since been neglected because they are difficult to enforce (Cervero, 1996).

There is some empirical evidence supporting the notion that the balance of jobs and housing has an important effect on the amount of travel occurring in a geographical area, despite methodological arguments around how big this area should be and how it should be measured. Levinson (1996) presented evidence from Washington DC showing that increasing housing availability in job-rich areas reduces commute times for people working there, even while it increases commutes for people living there by increasing competition for proximate jobs. Cervero (1996) cites evidence from Toronto (see Nowlan and Stewart, 1991) that showed that serious traffic congestion was averted in Toronto's central core despite an office building boom in the 1970s and 1980s, through accelerated downtown housing construction.

Critics of government intervention to balance jobs and housing have argued that many factors prevent people from living near their workplaces, and that over time market forces will take care of reducing imbalances between housing and jobs so as to keep average commute times more or less constant (Giuliano, 1992; Gordon *et al.*, 1991; Peng, 1997). Various empirical studies have supported the notion of the constant average travel time budget (Levinson and Kumar, 1994; Wachs et al., 1993), or argued that, at the least, commute times are not increasing at the same rate as congestion and trip making (Levinson, 1996). This results *inter alia* from the co-location of jobs and housing — which is evidence of a working market. Over time, jobs relocate to follow workers. From an analysis of commuting and urban structure in Los Angeles, Giuliano and Small (1993) furthermore concluded that urban structure explains only a small fraction of commute patterns, and that people elect to travel more than they need to.

More recently, the emphasis has shifted to interventions at the local and neighbourhood level, for instance, through better urban design and provision of higher density housing and mixed-use development in areas around public transport nodes (so-called Transit-Oriented Development (TOD)). Many US cities claim to embrace "Smart Growth" by promoting well-designed, compact communities offering a variety of housing, transport, employment, and recreation opportunities. There is a resurgent appreciation of the importance of good quality public transport — at least as important (if not more) as land use density and design issues, according to Hall (2007) — in moving from sprawling, suburban land use patterns towards less car oriented cities.

What all of this implies is that, while there is a virtually uncontested recognition that externalities in the housing-transport market cause suboptimal development and transport patterns, there is no agreement internationally on the extent to which governments should try to correct it, nor on the form that such intervention should take. With regard to policies for housing and transport, the emphasis has shifted from regional questions around the number of jobs versus houses, towards more micro-scale actions: improving public transport, designing better neighbourhoods around stops and stations, matching housing with other opportunities in the local area. This is not to say that sprawling patterns of suburbanisation are not continuing (Burchell and Galley, 2003); but to the extent that alternatives are purposively being pursued there appears to be a narrowing of the divide between housing policy (in the context of policies for overall spatial development) and transport policy.

3.2 Market Failure Due To Insufficient Housing Supply

In a fully efficient market, any unmet demand for housing in more accessible locations, as expressed by lower income households who favour accessibility over travel, would result in an increase in supply in these locations. This would lower the price of accessible housing until a new equilibrium is established.

However, two factors can prevent this equilibrium from being achieved: restricted supply of housing due to the unavailability of land (which is a finite resource) and restricted supply of housing due to regulatory barriers. Both types of restrictions disbenefit poorer households: housing prices or rents in central places remain out of reach, and households respond either by living elsewhere where they incur higher transport costs, or, in the extreme, by locating in "slums" or on pavements on highly accessible land (World Bank, 2002).

Regulatory barriers can take the form of zoning restrictions, minimum lot sizes, minimum parking requirements, or high rates charges, and usually result from a resistance among existing residents to allow higher density affordable developments for lower income families in their vicinity. Cervero (1996) cites examples from the US where well-to-do, job-surplus communities restricted housing growth for fiscal or parochial reasons, and shows how it prevented lower income workers from locating close to large job pools. Ultimately such exclusionary practices may harm the region, as they raise transport costs and promote marginalisation of certain groups.

The market itself can also fail to adequately deliver housing at affordable price levels in accessible locations. Theoretically, as prices per square meter increase in well-located areas, lower income households will demand smaller and smaller quantities of it in order to remain within their household budgets. However, households need a certain minimum floor area, so that the minimum price or rent of a dwelling may simply be unaffordable to many low-income families. Furthermore, supply of more housing in dense urban centres often takes a long time to materialise, so that, temporarily high prices due to supply-demand disequilibrium may persist for a while.

Several studies have recently examined the impacts of housing affordability on households. There is convincing evidence that many poorer households who can not afford the higher housing costs of accessible locations, are forced to locate in less central areas against their preference. As most US suburbs are typically less well served by public transport, these households face the higher transport costs of owning and operating a car, leading to problems of affordability (Lipman, 2006; Rice, 2004). Sanchez et al. (2007) found that the vast majority of low-income neighbourhoods in major US cities spend more than the national average on housing and transport combined, often not leaving enough income for education, home ownership and other wealth creating assets. Nationally, the combined costs of transportation and housing accounts for 52% of household expenditure; this figure is higher for lower-income households, and likely to climb as transport energy costs rise (Bernstein et al., 2005).

Similar evidence from Paris shows that, between 1978 and 1995, the proportion of low-income households living in the city centre dropped as high housing costs forced such households to locate in the periphery, particularly when they want to purchase their homes (Berri, 2007). This peripheral location involves high car expenditures, which endangers their financial condition and their ability to repay home loans.

Aided by advocacy from non-profit organisations, the market responded to the affordability problem by developing a mechanism to assist households that prefer urban living in affording the higher housing costs of doing so. "Location efficient mortgage" (Center for Transit-Oriented Development, 2006) is an innovative product that allows households to qualify for higher mortgages to buy property in transit-accessible locations, by taking into account the savings in transport costs that such households would realise due to their location. It thus, effectively, treats transport cost savings as additional income to be spent on housing.

Public policies to promote the provision of housing across the whole range of price levels, and particularly in fast-growing employment areas, usually imply strong government intervention. Successful policies to make municipalities "think regionally and act locally" have included tax-base sharing across municipalities, rent control, and regional control of land uses (Cervero, 1996). Huge political and institutional obstacles exist to such interventions. Alternatively, governments often opt to become involved in the provision of affordable housing themselves, either through public housing projects, or through subsidisation mechanisms such as voucher programmes.

While it is not the intention of this paper to review the literature on housing assistance in developed world cities, it is pertinent to note that debates continue on the efficacy of various approaches. In the United Kingdom, research on mobility and social exclusion has highlighted the problems of poor public transport access to urban housing estates (*e.g.*, Grieco cited in Church, 2000: 195). While Church et al. (2000) warned that social exclusion is caused by many factors, only some of which relate to transport. Thus, transport interventions such as reverse commute programmes to help welfare recipients in central cities access suburban jobs have seen some success, but do not eliminate poverty and welfare by itself (Wachs and Taylor, 1998). In fact there is evidence that the use of semi-market mechanisms such as vouchers for housing or transport, are more effective in reducing poverty by giving recipients the spatial and economic flexibility to optimise their housing location and to reduce their commute distance and time (Bania *et al.*, 2003).

4. HOUSING AND TRANSPORT ISSUES IN DEVELOPING COUNTRIES: THE CASE OF SOUTH AFRICA

While the same general principles apply regarding housing and transport trade-offs across the world, both the nature of market failures, and the social and political contexts within which housing and transport policy operates, differ significantly between the developed and developing worlds. This section illustrates the nature of these differences by focussing on the housing and transport problem in South Africa. As a middle income country with a strong market economy, South African housing markets exhibit many signs of efficient, rational functioning, in which many households are presumably able to optimise the housing-transport trade-off. Yet large parts of the market, particularly those related to lower-income and informal housing, are distorted due to past discriminatory policies. South African cities face problems of severe housing deficiencies (leading to what might be termed *slums* elsewhere) similar to other fast-growing, underdeveloped areas in the world. What is ironic, though, is that most of the recent efforts by the current democratic government to address housing backlogs have *exacerbated* problems of coordinating transport and housing in a manner that benefits both residents and society. The evidence, reasons, and impacts of this are briefly examined below.

4.1 Housing Policy and Delivery

The historic role of housing policy in South Africa to spatially marginalise Black people in cities, primarily by housing them in segregated settlements on the urban periphery, is well documented (*e.g.*, Lemon, 1991; Swilling *et al.*, 1991). During the transition from apartheid to democracy in the 1990s, debates on housing were intertwined with debates on desirable urban form, particularly around the need for achieving more compact and integrated (spatially and socially) cities (Todes, 2003). Compact city objectives were emphatically adopted as a means of restructuring cities away from apartheid city form. While also acknowledging the city efficiency and externalities argument more prevalent in developed countries, this was only a secondary consideration in the case of South Africa.

Compact city objectives formed part of the core principles of the 1995 Development Facilitation Act, which was intended to guide all physical planning and development. Transport legislation — notably the National Land Transport Transition Act (2003) — also took up this vision, instructing planning authorities to promote land use/transport integration *inter alia* by curbing sprawl and by directing new development to in-fill and densification sites along key transport corridors. Densification of transport corridors is identified as the "key component of the urban passenger strategy" articulated by the 1999 Moving South Africa Strategy Document (DOT, 1999).

While compact city ideals saturated official vocabulary, the implementation of housing policy on the ground was largely eclipsed by the overwhelming need for formalised housing. In 1994, the newly elected government committed itself to building a million houses in its first 5-year term (Napier, 2007). The National Housing Subsidy Scheme was introduced to finance the delivery of subsidised housing to qualifying low-income households. The state became agent and funder, charging Provincial Housing Development Boards in collaboration with local municipalities with reaching low-income housing delivery targets. Delivery of subsidised housing was primarily achieved through replication of a standard product: a basic, freestanding 30m^2 to 40m^2 one or two-roomed house on a serviced stand, allocated according to waiting lists in each region. The subsidy was initially capped at R15 000 per house, but has since been increased several times to a current level of R39 000 (Department of Housing, 2007:www.housing.gov.za).

4.2 Sprawl led by the market and by the state

The ideals of compaction and integration have so far not been realised. Since 1994, the state has succeeded in building and transferring some two million houses through the government grant system (Department of Housing, 2007: www.housing.gov.za). However, the vast majority of this housing has been located on the peripheries of cities and towns, and in many cases isolated from economic opportunities and social amenities. For example, Figure 2 shows the distribution of housing projects around Gauteng Province by 2003. The projects are in many cases located even further away from traditional job nodes than are existing townships.

Several reasons have been put forward for this continued peripheralisation of low-income housing in post-Apartheid South Africa. The first is the emphasis of national housing policy on achieving targets in terms of the number of houses delivered, rather than on the quality of livelihoods that result (*e.g.*, Todes, 2003; Pieterse, 2004; Napier, 2007). The periphery is where land is most cheaply available and delivery delays due to political opposition least likely. In an attempt to allow for more "well-located" developments, an additional subsidy of up to 15% was made available for houses located close to substantial employment nodes or transport routes. However, the additional subsidy is entirely inadequate to cover the actual price of land in inner city areas (Charlton, 2003; Behrens & Wilkinson, 2003).

Coupled to this is institutional fragmentation between provincial housing departments responsible for disbursing subsidies and overseeing delivery, and local/metropolitan governments given the

Fig. 2: State-subsidised housing projects, 1994-2003, Gauteng Province

Source: Tomlinson, 2003.

task of actual identification and delivery of housing projects. There is little incentive for officials required to achieve housing delivery targets to consider the transport impacts associated with the choice of a particular settlement location — transport provision and subsidisation being the responsibility of a separate department. The Integrated Development Planning process was intended to provide a framework for guiding such contradictory incentives, but it has largely failed to secure actual unity of vision and cooperative action across local government departments (Pieterse, 2004).

Compounding the lack of institutional integration has been the critical disjuncture between the planning and the implementation of public transport in South Africa. Some cities have made good progress towards planning for more integrated, rationally organised and expanded public transport services (DOT, 2006). However, the implementation of these improvements has often been blocked by institutional inertia, lack of government capacity, and vested interests from operators (Cameron, 2007). As a result, the additional funds that might have become available from improved economies of scale and scope in an integrated, rational system, and that might ultimately have been used for expanding public transport services to new settlements, have not materialised. There are some examples of transport planning considerations successfully influencing decision-making around settlement location. For instance, in Durban the metropolitan council has reportedly succeeded in directing housing towards well-located areas that are broadly related to the city's planned High Priority Public Transport Network (Charlton, cited in Todes, 2003: 115). However, by and large, the improved transport services on which such considerations are premised have not materialised, leading in practice to severe housing/transport disjunctures. The impacts of such disjunctures on commuters and the state are discussed below.

Governments in developing countries have often resorted to relocation or slum-clearance as a strategy to deal with overcrowding and unsatisfactory housing conditions. Relocation has been severely criticised as it often results in the poorest being housed in more isolated places where social networks and livelihoods activities are disrupted (Barter, 2003; Anand and Tiwari, 2006). In South Africa, city governments are generally committed to upgrading existing informal settlements where possible, rather than relocating people. The problem is that, at least in South Africa, few informal settlements are located in accessible places, due to the limited availability of land for settlement. Upgrading is thus, likely to reinforce existing patterns of spatial development and transport deprivation (Todes, 2003).

Meanwhile, homeowners in the medium to higher income ranges have continued to express a preference for low-density suburban housing. High housing demand among the emerging middle class is primarily satisfied through greenfield developments on the urban periphery. In this regard, the patterns of suburbanisation, and their travel impacts, are very similar to those found in North American cities. A unique feature of the new South African housing landscape is the emergence of housing in security villages. These estates occur at a variety of densities (sometimes more dense than the traditional suburb) and sizes, but are entirely car-oriented through their disregard for public transport and mixed land use within their walls. It is increasingly being accepted that the amount and type of travel that results contributes to traffic congestion and urban sustainability problems (Landman, 2000).

At the same time, it is also true that the popularity of more central locations closer to high-end jobs seems to be reviving in some segments of the market. This is driven in part by distaste for the high commute cost incurred by living in congested suburbs, and supported by the improved attractiveness of central areas following government's seemingly successful urban renewal efforts in the downtowns of cities like Johannesburg and Cape Town (Fraser, 2007; Cokayne, 2007).

The demand is for more mixed-use "live-work-play" environments — environments that still value easy access by car to major metropolitan nodes (as evidenced by the significant parking structures erected in mixed-use nodes like Melrose Arch in Johannesburg), but cater for an emerging gap in the housing-transport continuum.

In the vast majority of subsidised as well as non-subsidised housing developments, however, practices of neighbourhood design and traffic engineering that prioritise vehicular mobility over walkability and local access persist. Provision of rows of freestanding subsidised houses along low order residential streets, surrounded by higher-order roads designed for mobility rather than access, has been criticised for its failure to accommodate the real needs of low-income people, which is for safe walking and public transport access and opportunities for local economic development (Behrens, 2005; Dewar & Todeschini, 2004). Also, in other developing countries, the mismatch between engineering/town planning standards and community needs has been blamed for raising development costs and contributing to the unaffordability of low-income housing (Barter, 2002; Gannon & Liu, 1997).

4.3 Impacts of Housing-Transport Disjuncture

What are the results, in terms of transport impacts, of the locational and urban design biases characterising subsidised housing provision in South Africa? The experience has been mixed. In some cities, where institutional integration between housing and transport planning is better, housing seems to have been located in *better* locations than in the past, even though, the close relationships between housing, transport and employment envisioned by the traditional notion of urban compaction have not been achieved (Todes, 2003). To the extent that this allows some poorer households to exercise a preference for accessible locations, while being able to afford housing, housing policy has achieved success. As an example, Figure 3 shows the monthly travel costs of residents in Cato Manor, a low-income locality close to the Durban CBD, versus those of more peripheral and rural locations within the metropolitan boundary (Venter *et al.*, 2007). Not only do central households spend less on getting to work (due to a much higher use of

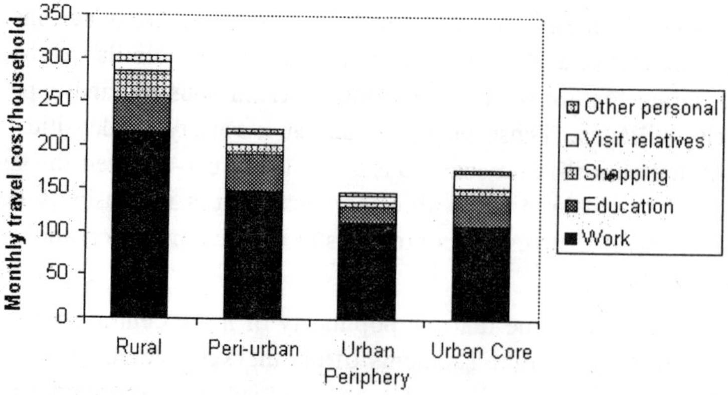

Fig. 3: Travel cost for low-income households, by locality within eThekwini Metropolitan Area, South Africa

Source: Venter *et al.*, 2007.

walking, amongst other reasons), but they also engage more in social visits than similar households elsewhere, indicating perhaps enhanced resources for social interaction.

There is however, significant evidence that the continued peripheralisation of housing imposes excessive transport burdens on individuals and on the state, and that it represents market failure to the extent that it prevents poor households from optimising their resources. Various researchers have documented the long distances and travel times faced by low-income households located far away from employment and other opportunities (*e.g.,* Behrens and Wilkinson, 2003). Work trip lengths of public transport users in South Africa are much longer than in other parts of the world: trip lengths average around 20 km in SA, as compared to 11 km in Europe, and 9 km in developing Asia (DOT, 1999). Long distances combine with use of slower modes to lengthen travel times; in Durban, for instance, low-income people living in peripheral locations spend around 40% more time travelling per month than residents of more central areas (Figure 4). Peripheral location tends to be particularly problematic for women workers or work seekers who face the double burden of long trips and multiple household reproductive tasks. Similar evidence around the role of residential location and the importance of local access as a livelihoods strategy for low-income women has been reported in India (Anand & Tiwari, 2006; Srinivasan, 2005).

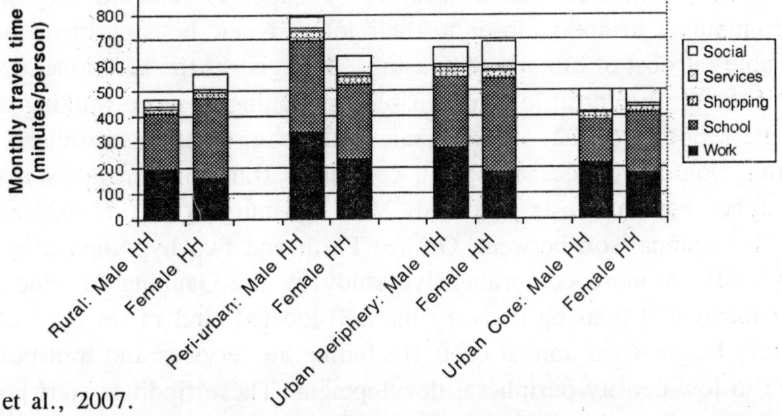

Source: Venter et al., 2007.

Fig. 4: Travel time expenditure for low-income households, by locality within The kwini Metropolitan Area, South Africa

In terms of expenditures, public transport users end up paying a significant portion of their incomes for transport. Figure 3 above demonstrates how peri-urban and rural localities in Durban incur 25% and 75% higher travel expenditures than central localities (Venter *et al.,* 2007). Households in localities labelled *urban periphery* spend somewhat less than in the urban core, due to extensive use of walking to school. High transport costs have been partly blamed for the frequent inability among subsidised housing recipients to consolidate wealth through continued investment in their houses. Instead, houses are often rented out in order to generate consumption income for the owners (Napier, 2007). This undermines the very premise on which state provision of basic housing stock is based, which is that once the poor is given access to the asset, they will further invest in it (Tomlinson, 2003) and use it as "a reliable urban perch with which to build an asset base" (Cross, cited by Napier, 2007:17).

The State carries at least part of the high transport cost, through subsidisation of formal bus and train services. While serving to improve affordability of transport for many low-income users, it causes at least two problems. The first is the massive subsidy burden imposed on the state. Both bus and rail subsidies are essentially distance-based, so that, the long travel distances caused by continued peripheral housing location have caused subsidy payments to balloon to unsustainable levels (Behrens & Wilkinson, 2003). For long distance trips, 60 to 70% of costs are covered by subsidies (DOT, 1999). As a result, the government has been reluctant to expand subsidised services to new areas. This directly causes the second problem, which is that relatively few residents in peripherally located settlements actually have access to subsidised services. Recent evidence in Orange Farm, an isolated settlement 40km from Johannesburg, indicates that 20% of those passengers who are captive to public transport have access to subsidised services (Ntuli, 2007). New settlements are typically located away from traditional bus and rail routes, leaving the privately operated informal minibus-taxi mode to fill the gap. Minibus-taxis provide a crucial transport service to residents, but impose high fares and social costs in terms of accidents and congestion.

Several studies have demonstrated the high overall cost to society of peripheral housing, and the potential savings to be gained from better integrating the state's housing and transport decisions. Naudé (1984) estimated that it would be cheaper to relocate long-distance (longer than 30km) bus commuters to areas closer to their jobs, if new housing could be provided for less than about double the cost of hinterland housing. This ignores the additional transport savings that would result if the more central location enabled switching to more walking or unsubsidised modes. Aucamp and Moodley (2002) showed that, in Durban, locating subsidised housing closer to job opportunities would produce savings in commuter transport subsidies that would more than off-set the higher housing costs involved. Van Rensburg *et al.*, (1992) reported similar findings in a detailed comparison between Orange Farm and two hypothetical settlements near the Johannesburg CBD. A more comprehensive study by the Gauteng Provincial Government (Biermann, 2005) found that housing delivery on well-located land raises once-off capital costs by 34%, but reduces longer-term annual costs (including all services and transport) by 18% per year, as compared to low-density peripheral development. These findings start pointing towards the types of actions that might be needed to rationalise the state's role in transport and housing provision.

5. CURRENT AND POTENTIAL RESPONSES

If it is accepted that housing-transport markets can deliver greater efficiency and greater welfare outcomes to urban residents with a range of needs, and that these markets are presently distorted by both unpriced externalities and suboptimal government interventions, how then can the situation be improved? It is suggested that the answer lies along at least three dimensions: improving prices, locations, and projects.

5.1 Prices

The first relates to improved pricing. Calls for pricing travel closer to its true cost are not new even in South Africa (*e.g.*, DOT, 1997). There are clear theoretical arguments that pricing better for the externalities of travel would help correct market distortions which lead to suboptimal housing-transport outcomes. However, the desirability and feasibility of schemes like congestion pricing need to be tested against local political, social, and economic realities; the debate around them is yet to happen in developing countries, including in South Africa. It might also be useful to consider second-best alternatives, such as charging higher municipal rates or developer contributions for peripheral residential developments to better reflect the cost of sprawl to society.

Linked to the pricing of travel is the need for the correction of distortions in the land market itself. Outright discrimination, exclusionary zoning, and poorly functioning land markets (Napier, 2007) can reduce the ability of low-income households to move house in order to reduce their transport burden (Gannon & Liu, 1997). Land market reform is thus critical, to this debate.

5.2 Locations

An obvious remedy for the problem of the fragmentation of housing and transport decisions is improved integration and rationalisation of spatial planning at the regional level. If location decisions around subsidised housing took account of the overall project cost, including that of land, top structures, services, and transport, which are incurred at a location over the lifetime of the settlement, outcomes that are more beneficial to both the state and poor households can be expected. We would simply see less peripheral, isolated development.

Of course it is neither likely nor necessarily desirable that all subsidised housing be located near city centres. Housing variety should reflect the range of needs and preferences of households (Todes, 2003). The benefits of proximity to central city opportunities are clear. Yet, as formal employment declines, proximity to secondary employment nodes and low-density residential areas offering opportunities for informal trade or domestic service employment may be more valuable to low-income households than proximity to the traditional urban core (Todes, 2003; Venter *et al.*, 2004). Furthermore, a location that may seem "badly located" today, may become better located tomorrow, as the urban area grows and it becomes better integrated into transport routes (Venter *et al.*, 2004). Research since the 1990s suggests that the diversity of poor households' livelihoods strategies is putting new demands on the housing environment. Several authors have argued that the semi-rural locations on the edge of metropolitan areas offer important benefits to residents by allowing them to avoid the high cost of formal urban services, while being able to diversify their income sources through sub-letting, urban agriculture, and informal work (*e.g.*, Cross et al. cited in Todes, 2003).

It follows that rational and integrated housing planning cannot follow a prescription that simply equates "well-located" housing with proximity to the city centre. More nuanced analyses, supported by effective consultation, are needed to identify "better located" sites and forms for housing. Recent government initiatives to provide inclusionary housing for a range of income groups seem to be moving in the right direction. In the US, inclusionary housing policies which locate lower-income families in wealthier suburban areas, closer to suburban job opportunities and amenities, are credited with reducing travel and promoting quality of life (Smit and Purchase, 2006).

Problems of local government capacity, lack of institutional coordination, parochial competition between municipalities, and fragmented planning processes have been identified as significant barriers to the improvement of spatial planning and control (*e.g.*, Pieterse, 2004). Some of these challenges are being addressed, albeit slowly, but it remains clear that unless incentives for coordinated planning are improved, it is hard to see actual progress being made with regard to the above (Behrens & Wilkinson, 2003).

A further reality that limits the state's ability to provide housing in very accessible central locations is affordability. Biermann (2005) recently found that, while housing delivery on well-located land reduces overall long-term recurrent costs, the implications are very different for government and for individuals. While most of the savings accrue to national and provincial governments (in the form of reduced environmental and land costs associated with peripheral development), households bear a significant share of the costs of living on well-located land. While household transport costs reduce slightly, housing costs increase significantly under existing cost recovery mechanisms. Biermann concluded that "even if the entire capital cost of housing [in well-located places] is subsidised by provincial government in the form of a location subsidy, the recurrent housing expenditure requirements are not affordable by households under current conditions of low income levels and unemployment" (Biermann, 2005 p. 20). Unless urban poverty itself decreases significantly, locating large numbers of low-income people in sustainable, affordable housing in highly accessible locations seems infeasible.

5.3 Projects

The third approach relates to actions that are perhaps easier for local government to execute and control, namely the closer integration of housing and transport considerations at the local or project level. There is a growing body of work pointing to the mutually reinforcing links between poverty and transport deprivation (Gannon and Liu, 1997; World Bank, 2002). By increasing the mobility and accessibility of low-income people in general, their choices are widened with regard to finding suitable housing options (Barter, 2002). Pro-poor actions such as improving non-motorised transport access, public transport availability and affordability, and traffic safety should thus, be better integrated into government housing projects.

In most South African cities, significant opportunities are currently arising for purposefully making a closer link between public transport and affordable housing. Many cities are planning for improved road-based public transport in the form of Bus Rapid Transit (BRT) systems, to be implemented over the next twelve years in terms of the Department of Transport's Public Transport Strategy (DOT, 2006). Treasury has allocated billions of Rands for these systems that will consist of fast and attractive bus services running on dedicated lanes, connecting major nodes across each city. Part of the intention is to provide more affordable and integrated mobility to low-income users. Municipalities can link the deployment of BRT lines with the development of affordable housing, which can be designed along Transit-Oriented Development (TOD) principles to improve access to BRT stations. This would have the double benefit of ensuring affordable access to opportunities for residents, and guaranteed ridership for the BRT system, thus, promoting financial sustainability of both public transport and housing. BRT stations should be designed to address uniquely local issues, including the need for local economic development and informal trade (Dewar & Todeschini, 2004). The concept of TOD is already being explored locally, and it shows promise to help make housing/transport costs more affordable, especially for lower-middle income households which do not qualify for housing subsidies, provided the transport cost savings can be used to off-set housing costs through a location efficient mortgage (Wilkinson and Marks, 2007).

Significant investment in improved public transport in congested areas might also bring further opportunities for the state to capitalise on the market value of the accessibility improvements obtained. Some authors have argued for the development of mechanisms for value capture through which "increments in land value attributed to public and community interventions are recouped by the public sector" (Brown-Luthango, cited by Napier, 2007). Given the growing premium being placed by private developers on high accessibility, in the face of growing road traffic congestion, it would seem that it would be worthwhile for government to pursue opportunities for capturing at least part of the increased land rent, which could be redirected into promoting affordable housing and transport.

It is instructive to consider examples from elsewhere in the developing world of successful integration of housing and transport policy at the local level. An excellent example appears to be the Metrovivienda programme in Bogota, Colombia (Cervero, 2005). Bogota is well-known in the transport world for its successful Bus Rapid Transit system, TransMilenio, which since 2000 has been extended to cover a network of 55 kilometer of dedicated busway supported by feeder services and non-motorised transport facilities. Metrovivienda is a programme by which the city acquires open, peripheral land at relatively cheap prices, titles and services it, and then sells it to private developers. Developers are bound contractually to sell the property as affordable housing to lower-income households. What is significant is that the land is mostly sited near TransMilenio's terminuses, thus, providing high accessibility *and* affordable travel to housing beneficiaries. It also benefits TransMilenio by virtually guaranteeing ridership (and perhaps an impetus for further development and densification) from/to the ends of the line. An important feature of the programme is the acquisition of land well in advance of TransMilenio services, as land prices (and rent) have been found to rise once TransMilenio enters an area (Rodriguez and Targa, 2004). This coordination is achieved through the fact that Metrovivienda officials serve on the board of TransMilenio, creating opportunities for mutual cooperation and co-planning.

6. CONCLUSIONS

Can we do better at making the housing-transport link? The answer is clearly yes. Housing and transport problems are closely linked, as they represent two sides of the locational decision that households make when choosing a home. When this decision is constrained by a distorted or inefficient market, sub-optimal housing *and* transport consumption results. Individuals – especially lower-income people with fewer options — as well as society bear the cost. As Cervero (2002) puts it, "transport problems are also housing problems."

The paper attempts to locate the housing-transport link within the larger policy debates around sustainability and urban poverty issues, in both developed and developing countries. The emphases are different, as are the specific features of the solutions likely to be applicable in different parts of the world. Yet, the overall conclusion — that markets can be made less distorted, and that good practice in urban design and multimodal transport planning can go a long way towards solving housing-transport dilemmas — seems to apply everywhere.

REFERENCES

Adair, A., McGreal, S., Smyth, A., Cooper, J., Ryley, T. (2000), 'House Prices and Accessibility: The Testing of Relationships within the Belfast Urban Area', *Housing Studies*, Vol. 15, No. 5, pp. 699-716.

Anand, A., and Tiwari, G. (2006), 'A Gendered Perspective of the Shelter–Transport–Livelihood Link: The Case of Poor Women in Delhi', *Transport Reviews*, Vol. 26, No.1, pp. 63–80.

Aucamp, C.A., and Moodley, G.Y. (2002), 'Making low-cost housing projects more accessible for public transport in Ethekwini: What are the costs?' *Proceedings: 21st Annual Southern African Transport Conference*, Pretoria, South Africa.

Bania, N., Coulton, C., Leete, L. (2003), 'Public Housing Assistance, Public Transportation, and the Welfare-to-Work Transition', Cityscape: *Policy Development and Research*, Vol. 6, No. 2.

Banister, D. (2005), Unsustainable Transport. Routledge , Abingdon (UK).

Barter, P. (2002), 'Transport and Housing security in the Klang Valley, Malaysia', Singapore *Journal of Tropical Geography*, Vol. 23, No. 3, pp. 268-287.

Behrens, R. and Wilkinson, P. (2003), 'Housing and Urban Passenger Transport Policy and Planning in South African Cities: A Problematic Relationship?', Confronting Fragmentation: Housing and Urban Development in a Democratising Society, (P Harrison, M Huchzermeyer and M Mayekiso (eds.)), UCT Press, Cape Town.

Behrens, R. (2005), 'Accommodating Walking as a Travel Mode in South African Cities: Towards Improved Neighbourhood Movement Network Design Practices', *Planning, Practice & Research*, Vol. 20, No. 2, pp. 163-182.

Bernstein, S., Makarewicz, C. and McCarty, K. (2005), Driven to Spend: Pumping Dollars Out of Our Households and Communities, Washington DC: *Center for Neighbourhood Technology and Surface Transportation Policy Project*. (Accessed from www.transact.org).

Berri, A. (2007), 'Residential location and household expenditures on transport and housing: the example of the Greater Paris region', Paper presented at 11th World Conference on Transport Research, 24-28 June 2007, Berkeley, USA.

Biermann, S. (2005), Affording a directional change in housing delivery (Executive Summary). Contract Report, Council for Scientific and Industrial Research, Pretoria.

Burchell, R.W. and Galley, C.C. (2003), 'Projecting Incidence and Costs of Sprawl in the United States', *Transportation Research Record* 1831, pp. 150-157.

Cadwallader, M.T. (1996), Urban Geography: An Analytical Approach, Upper Saddle River, Prentice-Hall, N J.

Cameron, J.W.M. (2007), 'The Time Has Come ...To Talk Of Many Things... Of Empires And Silos... And Study Tour Flings'. Proceedings: 26th Annual Southern African Transport Conference, Pretoria, South Africa.

Center for Transit-Oriented Development and Center for Neighbourhood Technology (2006), The Affordability Index: A New Tool for Measuring the True Affordability of a Housing Choice, Washington DC: The Brookings Institution. (Accessed from www.brookings.edu).

Cervero, R. (1989), 'Jobs-housing balance and regional mobility', *Journal of the American Planning Association,* Vol. 55, No. 2, pp. 136-150.

Cervero, R. (1996), 'Jobs-housing balance revisited', Journal of the American Planning Association, Vol. 62, No. 4, pp. 492-511.

Cervero, R. (2002), Transport and Land Use: Key Issues in Metropolitan Planning and Smart Growth. University of California Transportation Centre, Berkeley (Accessed from www.uctc.net on 6 November 2007).

Cervero, R. (2005), 'Progressive Transport and the Poor: Bogotá's Bold Steps Forward', Access, Fall 2005, University of California Transportation Center, Berkeley, pp. 24-30.

Charlton, S. (2003), 'The Integrated Delivery of Housing: A Local Government Perspective from Durban', Confronting Fragmentation: Housing and Urban Development in a Democratising Society, (P Harrison, M Huchzermeyer and M Mayekiso (eds)), UCT Press, Cape Town.

Church, A., Frost, M, Sullivan, K. (2000) 'Transport and Social Exclusion in London', *Transport Policy*, Vol. 7, No. 2000, pp. 195-205.

Cokayne, R. (2007), 'Land shortage, traffic to drive house prices'. Business Report, 17 August, 2007. Johannesburg.

Deakin, E.A. (1991), 'Jobs, Housing, and Transportation: Theory and Evidence on Interactions between Land Use and Transportation', Transportation, Urban Form, and the Environment. Special Report 231, Transportation Research Board, Washington, DC.

Debrezion, G., Pels, E., Rietveld, P. (2006), 'The impact of rail transport on real estate prices: Empirical study of the Dutch housing market'. Paper presented at 85th Annual Meeting of the Transportation Research Board, Transportation Research Board, Washington DC.

Dewar, D. and Todeschini, F. (2004), Rethinking Urban Transport After Modernism: Lessons from South Africa, Ashgate, United Kingdom.

DOT (1999), Moving South Africa — An Action Agenda, Department of Transport, Pretoria.

DOT (2006), Draft Strategy to Accelerate Public Transport Implementation via a WIN-WIN-WIN partnership between Government, Existing Operators and Labour, Department of Transport, Pretoria.

Dunphy, R.T. (1998), The Cost of Being Close: Land Values and Housing Prices in Portland's High Tech Corridor, ULI Working Paper Series Number 660, Urban Land Institute (accessed from www.uli.org).

Ewing, R., Pendall, R., Chen, D. (2003), 'Measuring Sprawl and Its Transportation Impacts', *Transportation Research Record,* 1831, pp. 175-183.

Fraser, N. (2007), Transportation: the key to unlocking quality urban form. www.eprop.co.za, Johannesburg.

Gannon, C.A. and Liu, Z. (1997), Poverty and Transport, Discussion paper, TWU Papers TWU-30. The World Bank, Washington DC.

Gilbert, A. and Gugler, J. (1992), Cities, poverty and development: Urbanisation in the Thrid World, Second Edition. Oxford: Oxford University Press.

Giuliano, G. (1986), 'Land Use Impacts of Transportation Investments: Highways and Transit', *The geography of urban transportation*, S Hanson (ed.) New York: Guilford Press 247-279.

Giuliano, G. (1992), 'Is Jobs-Housing Balance a Transportation Issue?' *Transportation Research Record* , Vol. 1305, pp. 305-312.

Giuliano, G. and Small, K.A. (1993), 'Is the Journey to Work Explained by Urban Structure?',*Urban Studies*, Vol. 30, No. 9, pp. 1485-1500.

Giuliano, G. (1995), 'The Weakening Transportation-Land Use Connection', Access, Spring 1995, Berkeley: University of California Transportation Center, pp. 6-7.

Gordon, P., Richardson, H. and Jun, M. (1991), 'The Commuting Paradox: Evidence from the Top Twenty', *Journal of the American Planning Association*,Vol. 57, No.4, pp. 416-420.

Hall, P. (2007), 'Beyond the Automobile?' Access, Spring 2007, Berkeley: University of California Transportation Center, pp. 10-15.

Jarvis, H. (2003), 'Dispelling the Myth that Preference makes Practice in Residential Location and Transport Behaviour', *Housing Studies,* Vol. 18, No. 4, pp. 587-606.

Landman, K. (2000), Gated communities and urban sustainability: Taking a closer look at the future. Proceedings: Strategies for a Sustainable Built Environment, Pretoria, 23-25 August 2000 (accessed from www.sustainablesettlement.co.za).

Lemon, A. (ed.). (1991), Homes Apart: South Africa's Segregated Cities, David Philip Publishers, Cape Town.

Levinson, D.M. and Kumar, A. (1994), 'The Rational Locator: Why Travel Times Have Remained Stable', *Journal of the American Planning Association,* Vol. 60, No. 3, pp. 319-331.

Levinson, D.M. (1996), 'Accessibility and the Journey to Work', *Journal of Transport Geography,* Vol.6, No.1, pp. 11-21.

Lipman, B.J.(2006), 'A Heavy Load: The Combined Housing and Transportation Burdens of Working Families'. Centre for Housing Policy (accessed from www.nhc.org), Washington DC.

Mills, E.S. and Tan, J.P. (1980), 'A Comparison of Urban Population Density Functions in Developed and Developing Countries', *Urban Studies,* Vol. 17, No. 3, pp. 313-321.

Molin, E. and Timmermans, H. (2003), 'Accessibility Considerations in Residential Choice Decisions: Accumulated Evidence from the Benelux', Paper presented at 82nd Annual Meeting of the Transportation Research Board, Transportation Research Board, Washington DC.

Napier, M. (2007), 'Making Urban Land Markets Work Better in South African Cities and Towns: Arguing the basis for access by the poor'. Paper presented at Fourth Urban Research Symposium, The World Bank, Washington DC (accessed from http://researchspace.csir.co.za/dspace/handle/10204/1053).

Naudé, A.H. (1984), Public transport regulations and subsidies — a cost-based examination of the issues. Research Report RR590. Council for Scientific and Industrial Research, Pretoria.

Newman, P.W.G. and Kenworthy, J.R. (1989), Cities and Automobile Dependence — An International Sourcebook. Gower, Aldershot.

Nowlan, D.M. and Stewart, G. (1991), 'Downtown population growth and commuting trips: recent experience in Toronto', *Journal of the American Planning Association*, Vol. 57, No. 2, pp. 165-182.

Ntuli, G.S. (2007), Effectiveness of transport subsidy targeting, and the potential for user-side subsidies, Master of Science (Applied Science) thesis, University of Pretoria, Pretoria.

Peng, Z.(1997), 'The Jobs-Housing Balance and Urban Commuting', *Urban Studies,* Vol. 34, No. 8, pp. 1215-1235.

Pieterse, E. (2004), 'Recasting urban integration and fragmentation in post-apartheid South Africa' Development Update, Johannesburg: SANGOCO (accessed from www.isandla.org.za)

Rice, L. (2004), Transportation Spending by Low-Income California Households: Lessons for the San Francisco Bay Area. San Francisco, CA: Public Policy Institute of California (accessed from www.ppic.org).

Rodríguez, D.A. and Targa, F. (2004), 'Value of Accessibility to Bogotá's Bus Rapid Transit System', *Transport Reviews*, Vol. 24, No. 5, pp. 587–610.

Sanchez, T.W., Makarewicz, C., Haas, P.M., Dawkins, C.J. (2007), 'Transportation Costs, Inequities, and Tradeoffs'. Paper presented at 86th Annual Meeting of the Transportation Research Board, Transportation Research Board, Washington DC.

Smit, D., Purchase, J. (2006), A Review of The International Experience With Inclusionary Housing Programmes: Implications For South Africa, Paper prepared for Department of Housing (accessed from www.housing.gov.za on 26 October 2007).

So, H.M., Tse, R.Y.C., Ganesan, S. (1997), 'Estimating the influence of transport on house prices: evidence from Hong Kong', *Journal of Property Valuation and Investment*, Vol. 15, No. 1, pp. 40-47.

Srinivasan, S. (2005), 'Influence of Residential Location on Travel Behavior of Women in Chennai, India', Research on Women's Issues in Transportation: Report of a Conference (Volume 2), November 18–20, 2004. Transportation Research Board. Chicago, Illinois. Washington, D.C.

STPP (2001), Driven to Spend: The Impact of Sprawl on Household Transportation Expenses. Surface Transportation Policy Project, Washington DC.

Swilling, M., Humphries, R., Shubane, K. (eds.) (1991), *Apartheid City in Transition.*, Oxford University Press, Cape Town, South Africa.

Todes, A. (2003), 'Housing, Integrated Urban Development and the Compact City Debate', Confronting Fragmentation: Housing and Urban Development in a Democratising Society, (P Harrison, M Huchzermeyer and M Mayekiso (eds)), UCT Press, Cape Town, South Africa.

Tomlinson, R. (2003), 'HIV/Aids and Urban Disintegration in Johannesburg', Confronting Fragmentation: Housing and Urban Development in a Democratising Society, (P Harrison, M Huchzermeyer and M Mayekiso (eds)), UCT Press., Cape Town, South Africa.

TRB (2003), Bus Rapid Transit, TCRP Report 90, Washington DC: Transportation Research Board.

Van, Rensburg, M., Wepener, D. and Engelbrecht, R. (1992), Improvement of Mobility as a Result of Land Use Planning. Report South African Roads Board, Pretoria.

Venter, C.J., Biermann, S., Van, Ryneveld, M. (2004), 'Low-cost housing location in South African cities: Empirical findings on costs and benefits'. Proceedings: 23th Annual Southern African Transport Conference, Pretoria, South Africa.

Venter, C., Vokolkova, V., Michalek, J. (2007), 'Gender, Residential Location, and Household Travel: Empirical Findings from Low-Income Urban Settlements in Durban, South Africa', *Transport Reviews,* Vol. 27, No. 6, pp 653-677.

Vuchic, V.R. (1999), Transportation for Livable Cities, CUPR Press, New Brunswick.

Wachs, M. and Taylor, B.D. (1998), 'Can Transportation Strategies Help Meet the Welfare Challenge?', *Journal of the American Planning Association*, Vol.64, No.1, pp.15-17.

Wachs, M., Taylor, B.D., Levine, N., Ong, P. (1993) 'The Changing Commute: A Case-study of the Jobs-Housing Relationship over Time', *Urban Studies*, Vol. 30, No.10, pp. 1711-1729.

Wilkinson, P., Marks, A. (2007), 'Promoting Transit Oriented Development In The Atlantis Corridor, Cape Town: Towards An Implementable Model'. Proceedings: 26th Annual Southern African Transport Conference, Pretoria, South Africa.

World Bank (2002), Cities on the move: World Bank Urban Transport Strategy Review. The World Bank, Washington, DC.

8

WEIGHING OUTCOMES OF ACCESSIBILITY CHANGES IN AN ECOLOGICALLY FRAGILE BELT OF THE INDIAN HIMALAYAS

Rinki Sarkar

ABSTRACT

This paper evaluates the outcomes of accessibility changes in the Indian Himalayas. In the post-planning era, the notion of accessibility has been usually linked to 'motorable' roads, in this region. Large fractions of budgets in hill-states continues to be allocated for road construction and maintenance in keeping with the essentials of the 'development paradigm' targeted at bringing more and more remote villages under the influence of 'modernisation' and change. While road mileage has been expanded at a fairly rapid pace, the environmental externalities associated with these mountain roads have received less attention. Research studies conducted across different sectors of the Himalayan region indicate that poorly aligned road linkages which pay less heed to geomorphologic constraints have aggravated the chances of landslides in a region inherently prone to natural hazards. Forests felled to make way for road construction activities, accentuates the possibility of landslides and road closures. The social and economic costs of these road closures can be quite high. While the flow of motorized traffic has increased manifold so has the vulnerability to mishaps as evident from official records on fatalities due to road accidents, in the mountains. The paper highlights these issues by recourse to relevant literature and field insights based on ground studies conducted in an ecologically fragile belt of Himachal Pradesh.

1. INTRODUCTION

In the Indian Himalayas, 'motorable' roads are a feature of the post-planning era. A region where seasonal transhumance was the only form of major human and livestock movement, the undulating landscape is marked by a hierarchy of roads, today. Local inhabitants perceive roads as a sure path for improving their economic well-being and overall progress. These aspirations have been fully exploited by politicians who promise 'road-connectivity' while campaigning for votes in their local constituencies. Some of these promises are delivered and a number of rural link roads in this region have therefore come up, often in haste, due to local political pressure.

Major arteries in the Himalayas, however, have their origins linked to national security requirements. This 'exogenous' strategic measure instituted to ensure territorial claims in the event of insurgencies and invasion from bordering countries, has had other far-reaching socio-economic consequences (Kreutzmann, 1991, 2004). Aligned to ensure steady supplies to military garrisons, these border roads have indirectly benefited the local community all along the route and even further away, integrating the region with the outside world.

The objective of this paper is to empirically evaluate outcomes of these accessibility changes in an ecologically fragile belt of the Middle Himalayas. The exercise is based on a scrutiny of the relevant literature and field studies conducted in 82 villages located between 1800 and 3000 meters in height, within a homogenous ecological belt but across a fairly wide geographical expanse of Himachal Pradesh. Roads have no doubt triggered the process of transformation and change in the Himalayas. This is exemplified by unearthing variations in well-being and development attributable to variations in accessibility in the study area through quantitative trends and ethnographic accounts. An attempt has also been made to reflect upon the negative environmental externalities that have emerged concomitant to these changes.

The paper is essentially divided into six sections. In the second section a brief account of accessibility developments in the region based on documented archival evidence and other sources is presented. As a prelude to the field findings, the evolving debate on the link between transport and development is briefly reviewed in section 3. The core section 4 assesses the impact of accessibility changes in the study area, based on quantitative trends enriched by qualitative accounts and oral histories that were gathered by residing in each village. Environmental externalities associated with mountain roads are scrutinised in the penultimate section 5 The concluding section delves on the implications emerging from this study for developing a framework that evolves more sustainable means of transport in the ecologically sensitive belts of the Himalayas.

2. ACCESSIBILITY DEVELOPMENTS IN THE HIMALAYAS: FROM FOOT-TRACKS TO MOTORABLE ROADS

Villages located in the Himalayas have exhibited a high degree of endurance and resilience for overcoming obstacles to accessibility on account of the difficult nature of the terrain, in the past. They evolved ingenious ways of adapting to these environmental constraints. Evidence of these indigenous systems of transport exists even today. Archival accounts[1] indicate that in the pre-colonial period local movement corridors co-existed with internal as well as trans-montane trade routes. For instance, in Himachal Pradesh, trade with neighboring Tibet was fairly common for procuring necessities such as salt and wool in exchange for barley and wheat obtained from grain surplus regions such as Mandi, Kangra and the Punjab plains. A network of mule tracks and foot-paths facilitated this kind of goods movement, connecting the plains to trans-Himalayan cold desert belts across lofty mountain passes. Very often, these paths could be traversed only by sheep that served as baggage animals for enabling trade. Such goods transport movements were intricately synchronised with the long-distance seasonal transhumance trails necessary for livestock rearing. Besides internal and trans-montane trade routes, there were innumerable foot-paths connecting villages across the region. The construction of these paths appears to have called forth great engineering ingenuity as well as human nerve, given the rugged nature of the terrain. Similar remarks apply for the different kinds of ropeways installed for transporting people across turbulent streams flowing through Himachal. The bridges constructed from local timber, willow and birch twigs are classic examples of indigenous engineering.

British presence in the region, led to further extension and strengthening of existing mule-tracks. A fleet of runners, baggage animals and mules catered to their mobility requirements. The underlying motive was to provide better connectivity to administrative colonial bases in the hills. 'Bridal paths' in remote areas were also carved out for exploring potential timber forest reserves that could cater to their imperial needs of ship-building and railway construction. However, rail-heads ended in the foot-hills of the Himalayas. Despite success in some ventures,[2] a verdict against the construction of rail links in the Himalayan range was unanimously passed due to threats such as recurring occurrences of natural hazards that could completely jeopardize the sustainability of such capital intensive transport systems. Symbolically it signified colonial incapability of bringing modern traffic into the mountains (Kreutzmann, 2004).

Motorable roads are essentially a mark of the post independence planning era, in the Indian Himalayas. In the early phase, major arteries were constructed for strategic reasons following aggression threats from nations bordering the Himalayan arc.[3] It is estimated that nearly 10,000 kilometers of highways were constructed during this period (Ives and Messerli, 1989). Over time, however, the policy perception has essentially been to expand roads for accelerating the overall development process of the region. In keeping with these objectives, 51% of the total plan outlay of the First Five Year Plan, in Himachal, was allocated to the Transport sector.[4] Although, the share of the transport sector has declined over the years, as the energy and social sectors have assumed more significance, a sizeable amount of resources continues to be invested in development of physical infrastructure such as roads.

The road development strategy has focussed on expanding the transport network in to the interior regions gradually, along with the construction of strong cantilever and suspension bridges at intermittent locations. There has been remarkable progress in terms of road length expansion. In 1950-51, Himachal's surface road length of 8.5 kilometers per one lakh population, was the lowest in India (Planning Commission, 2005). Since then, there has been a steady increase in the length of the road network, as reflected in Figure 1. Today, the State has a little over 27,000 kilometers which amounts to 454 kilometers per one lakh population. Nearly 80% of the road network caters to the predominantly rural population in the State[5] and nearly 60% of the villages have been connected by roads so far.[6] The quality of the road network has also improved. In 1948, the State had only 37 miles of metalled roads, 183 miles of unmetalled roads and 500 miles of mule tracks or bridal paths (Govt. of Himachal Pradesh, 2002). At present, 43% of the entire road network is metalled.[7] In the more contemporary context, the emphasis is to develop roads for facilitating the construction of hydro-electric projects, to boost tourism and to enhance better marketability of horticulture produce and other cash crops. Potential cost savings that have resulted due to improvements in the road transport system are phenomenal as depicted in Table 1, which provides a comparative perspective on transport costs of apple boxes by traditional and modern modes of goods transportation.

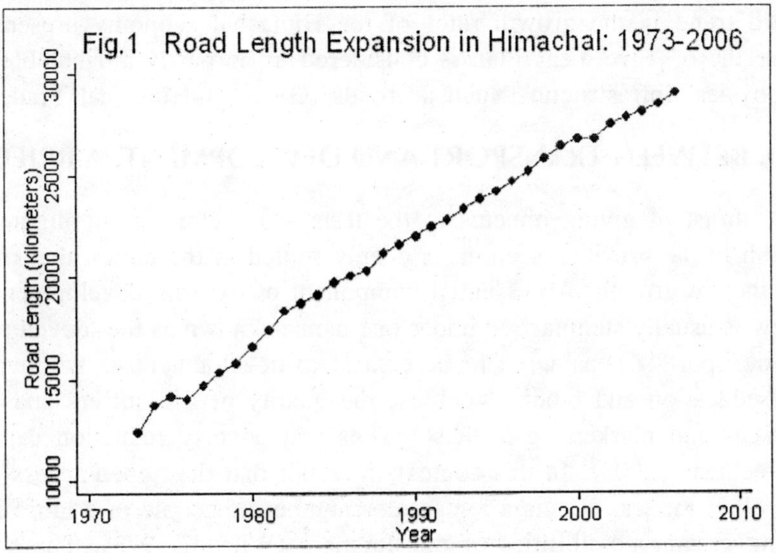

Table 1: Transport Costs across Different Modes of Travel

Modes of Transport	*Cost per kilometer per Apple-box of 20 kgs.(Rs.)*
Human porterage (head-load)	20.00
Mules	4.50
Ropeway	4.50
Motor carrier (unmetalled road)	0.50
Motor carrier (metalled road)	0.25

Source: Interactions in Shimla district, 2007.

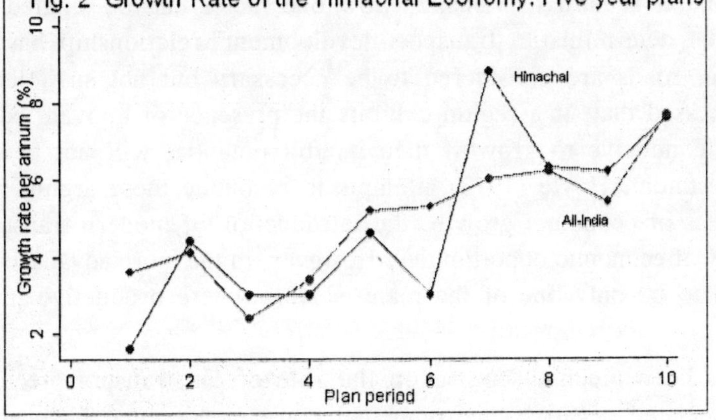

The upward trend in the growth rates of the Himachal economy presented in Figure 2, particularly after the 6th Five Year Plan is considered to be partly attributable to returns from investment in physical infrastructure such as roads (Govt. of Himachal Pradesh, 2002).

3. THE LINK BETWEEN TRANSPORT AND DEVELOPMENT: A BRIEF DIGRESSION

The policy thrust of giving impetus to the transport sector, as highlighted in the case of Himachal Pradesh in the previous section, is deeply rooted in the notion that transport is a pre-requisite for economic growth. An essential component of existing development policy debates, this point of view is usually summarised under one banner known as the 'development argument.' In a nut-shell, transport is considered to be central to development as without physical access to jobs, health, education and other amenities, the quality of life suffers and without physical access to resources and markets, growth stagnates and poverty reduction cannot be sustained (Banister & Berechman, 2000). In this context, it is felt that the "open-access" nature of roads as compared to other modes, affects a far greater number of people in a more intimate fashion, thereby, enabling greater possibilities of development (Wilson, 1973). The policy thrust in a number of developing countries has been largely in consensus with this historic[8] and most common view of the role of transport and particularly roads, in the development process. Creigtney's (1993) comprehensive review of empirical longitudinal studies undertaken in a number of developing countries in Latin America, Africa, South and South-East Asia indicated that good quality transport improved economic performance and human well-being, in general. Besides overall benefits from travel time savings, better accessibility led to enhanced levels of agricultural output in rural belts, increased fertilizer usage, improved access to credit and there was greater scope for technological diffusion. Educational attainment was better and access to health facilities was easier as educational institutions and health centres were found to be located closer to the road network.

Despite widespread belief in the role of accessibility changes, criticues have consistently expressed skepticism about the inevitability of outcomes associated with investment in transport infrastructure (Wilson, 1973, Gauthier, 1973). The argument put forth is that development is a complex process and it is hard to visualize how one factor can be singled out as a causal agent.[9] Thereafter, the deterministic 'transport-development' relationship has been somewhat reformulated wherein, roads are considered to be necessary but not sufficient for economic development. It is stressed that, if a region exhibits the presence of buoyant economic or other particular conditions conducive to growth, then its full potential will not be realised without further transport investment. Hoyle (1973) attempts to reconcile these arguments by indicating that in the initial stages of economic growth, the introduction of modern transport does tend to open up a wide variety of economic opportunities. However, in the more advanced stages, transport should be considered to be only one of the many sectors where productive investment can be channeled.

While there has been much discourse on the role of the transport sector in promoting development, the associated negative environmental consequences that have arisen on account of roads has been less addressed both in academic and policy circles. This is a serious lacuna as much of the analytical endeavors have tended to concentrate on physical, quantifiable aspects rather than the social and environmental qualitative aspects linked to the 'transport-development' debate (Banister & Berechman, 2000). An attempt is made to throw light on the nature of these externalities in Section 5.

4. Impact of Accessibility Changes in the Study Area:

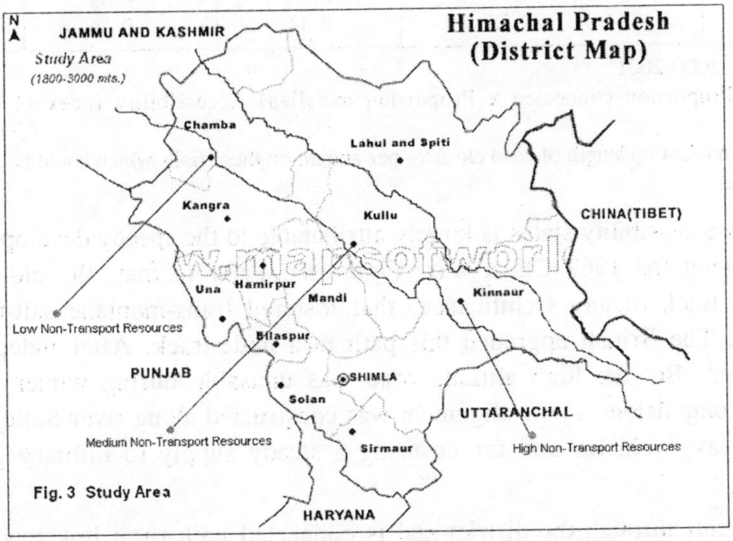

Fig. 3 Study Area

In order to assess the impact of accessibility changes more closely, field studies were initiated in 82 villages across a fairly wide geographical expanse of the Middle Himalyas in Himachal Pradesh, encompassing the three districts of Chamba, Kullu and Kinnaur. The study area, indicated in Figure 3, was selected to represent a fairly homogenous ecological belt between 1800 and 3000 meters above mean sea-level. Field work, conducted between 2000 and 2001, was based on structured household and village level questionnaires. Participatory methods were also used for documentaing oral histories as well as other information that could not be coded or quantified. The intension was to determine variations in accessibility outcomes across the districts in the study area. Attempts were also made to identify other contributory factors that could have affected these outcomes in addition to accessibility changes.

Over the last 25 years, there has been a marked change in accessibility conditions across the study area.[10] While the nearest motorable road was around 8-9 kilometers away from a village, the mean distance to a road is only around 4 kilometers, resulting in travel time savings of nearly 2.5 hours. About 10% more villages have been connected by roads during this period[11] and the road surface has also improved. In 1975, only 12% of the village roads were metalled. However, in 2000, 54% of the rural road links, in the region, have been upgraded from unmetalled to metalled roads. An accessibiliy index was developed for ranking the three districts in terms of village connectivity and the quality of the link-road surface. The results are presented in Table 2 below. In the current context, Kinnaur is 3.4 times more accessible than Chamba and two times more accessible than Kullu.

Table 2: Index of Accessibility across Districts in the Study Area

Districts	*Proportion of villages connected*	*Proportion of metalled links*	*Accessibility Index***	*Rank*
Kinnaur	0.46	0.67	0.31	1
Chamba	0.18	0.5	0.09	3
Kullu	0.36	0.44	0.16	2

Source: Field Survey, 2000-2001.

** Accessibility=(Proportion connected x Proportion metalled) Accessibility Index=1 indicates complete accessibility.

*** *Note:* There was no data on length of road closures per annum on these links which could have been incorporated into the measure.

Kinnaur's high accessibility status is largely attributable to the speedy development of National Highway 22, following the 1962 China war (Figure 4). Prior to that, the old-Hindustan Tibet Road was the only track of any significance, that fostered trans-montane salt-trade with Tibet since ancient times. The British upgraded this path to a mule-track. After independence, a jeep road was constructed. But the high altitude road was unusable during winter months. Due to emerging strategic compulsions a new alignment was constructed along river Sutlej, for facilitating the movement of heavy vehicles and for ensuring a steady supply to military garrisons all the year round.

The Highway cuts through the district and is connected with rural link roads on either side of the mountain façade where most of the villages are located. Interactions with the local community revealed that the highway has been a potent force for boosting horticulture development in the region by facilitating the transporation of the apple produce to major whole sale market centres

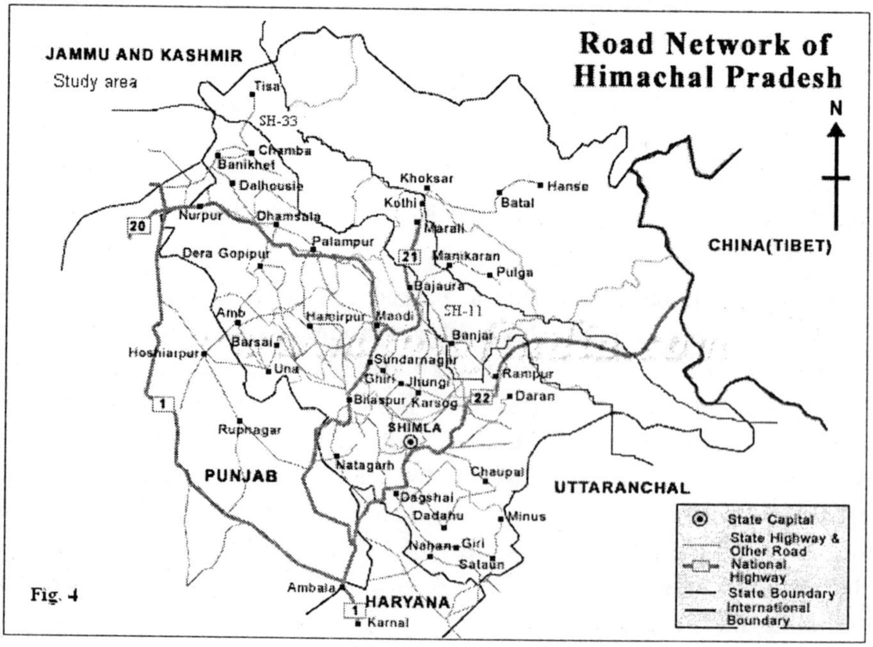

Fig. 4: Himachal Pradesh

all over India. As Kinnaur is a Tribal area, special assistance funds are allocated for catering to infrastructural needs of the region under the 'Integrated Tribal Development Programme'. A large fraction of these funds have been invested for improving and extending the road network. This is another factor responsible for better accessibility conditions in Kinnaur as compared to Kullu and Chamba which are esentially non-tribal areas, except for Bharmour tahsil in Chamba district.[12] Besides, the region has always had a politically favoured status, as representatives from the erstwhile local Bushahr dynasty or influential educated local visioneries such as T.S. Negi, have consistently assumed office at the State government level, influencing infrastructural fund disbursals to the region.

As compared to Kinnaur, assessibility developments have been less of an all-pervasive phenomenon, in Kullu district. National Highway 21 meanders through one part of Kullu district along the right bank of River Beas (Figure 4). The highway was developed and patronised by Nehru who frequented the region as a retreat from Delhi. After the 1962 China agression, the road assumed strategic importance for linking areas such as Ladakh and Lahaul Spiti. A parallel road known as the left bank-road was developed to promote horticulture in the more fertile belts along the river. After State formation in 1971, visioneries such as Lal Chand Prarthi and Pratap Singh Kehro urged the locals to plant apple trees in place of conventional grains. They promised to arrange for supplies from the booming granaries of Punjab, for which roads were essential. The post '85 tourist influx, following insurgency problems in Kashmir, has increased the significance of National Highway 21 as a road of touristic importance as well. All along the highway cash crops such as vegetables are grown in the lower altitude belts while horticulture and tourism flourishes in the high altitude areas. However, accessibility developments in other parts of Kullu district such as interiors of Sainj and Banjar tahsil have received comparatively less impetus.[13] These regions have flourished less in comparison to the belts along National Highway 21. In these more remote areas the local population continues to rely on traditioanl occupations such as livestock rearing supplemented by income from illegal sale of opium and cannabis as well as income from 'high value-low weight' medicinal herbs that have assumed high commercial significance over the last two decades.

There are no major arteries passing through the study area in Chamba district. It is only after the 'Satrundi-massacre' in 1998, suspected to be caused by terrorists, that State Highway 33 has assumed strategic importance for catering to the newly stationed 'Indo-Tibet Border Police' regiments. Except for the tribal belt of Bharmour, rural link roads have mostly come up in response to routine State road expansion programmes, that too wherever the local politicians or panchayat representatives have been able to voice their demands more eloquenty and forecefully. Accessibility developments in Chamba are also more recent as compared to Kinnaur and Kullu and it appeared that the impact of new roads has yet to be fully realised. The local population essentially relies on traditional sources of income supplemented by casual employment in Block Development programmes, private construction sector and in road maintenance ventures of the State Public Works Department. On the whole, the level of commercialisation was found to be weak.

Variations in accessibility and economic well-being, across the three districts, is summarised in Table 3 below. The overall trends do indicate a positive link between accessibility levels and economic status. Roads facilitate acess to markets and higher returns from cash crops.

Table 3: Accessibility and Economic well-being in the Study Area

Districts	*Accessibility Index*	*Mean Consumption expenditure per household per annum (Rs.)*	*Mean Per capita consumption expenditure per household per annum (Rs.)*
Kinnaur	0.31	61,223	10,764
Chamba	0.09	30,302	5,749
Kullu	0.16	38,777	7,114

Source: Field Survey, 2000-2001.

The Mean annual income from cash crops, for a household in Kinnaur is more than 2.5 times of what is earned in Kullu and nearly 30 times that of what is generated in Chamba from the same source. The trends also indicate that roads open up more non-farm sources of income in the region such as casual employment in private sector construction activities, casual employment in government sector roads as well as other decentralised community develop programmes and self-employment in petty retail trade activities.[14] Further, roads tend to attract other forms of physical and social infrastructure such as schools, health centres and banks that further boost the productive potential of the region.[15] A glimpse at the status of education of the current school going age cohort clearly indicates that the proportion of drop-outs and those not attending schools increase with remoteness and weaker accessibility conditions. This is evident from Table 4 below. Most of the respondents indicated that proximity to the school is an important consideration affecting school enrollment and attendance. The mean age of drop-outs was found to be 16 years and their educational attainment was limited to middle school level. This is because, Primary and Middle schools have largely been established in close proximity to the village, while High School, Inter-Mediate Schools and Colleges tend to be located closer to the road.

Table 4: Access and Status of Education

(% of Total in the School going age cohort: 5-19 years)

Districts	*Accessibility Index*	*Studying (%)*	*Drop-outs (%)*	*Illiterate (%)*
Kinnaur	0.31	86.22	8	5.78
Chamba	0.09	65.87	14.55	19.57
Kullu	0.16	84.45	9.08	6.46

On the whole, the trends do depict a connection between the level of accessibility and economic performance and human well-being, as well. These trends reinforce empirical evidence obtained from studies undertaken in other developing countries (Creigtney, 1993).

It may be worthwhile to note that in addition to accessibility changes, a host of other 'non-transport factors' may have influenced these outcomes. For instance, Kinnaur has better natural resource endowments. The average land holding is also higher as compared to Chamba and Kullu.[16] Water from melting glaciers can be seasonally tapped for irrigating the apple orchards which enriches the fertility of the soil. As Kinnaur is located at a relatively higher altitude, the apple produce matures after the crop has reached the market from other areas in the State. As a result the fruit fetches a high off-peak price (Sarkar, 2007). Further, the local population has judiciously exploited access to non-farm avenues of employment because of the special tribal job reservation policy benefits granted to them. Progress on the literacy front has also been somewhat higher as compared to Kullu and Chamba for historical reasons[17] and also because education is perceived to play an intrumental role for having access to reserved jobs in various government departments. Other more qualitative factors include the 'entrepreuneurial' abilities of the local population who have a history of engaging in trans-montane trade with Tibet since tarditional times. In contrast to Kinnaur, the productivity of land, which is entirely rain-fed, is lower in Chamba and so is the average land holding that thwarts attempts to shift to horticulture, a risky venture with gestation periods of as long as 12 years. Chamba is also administratively and politically less favoured as compared to Kinnaur. There are very few State level bureaucrats who hail from the region due to low educational status and therefore, villages are not patronised for special treatment in policy quarters. The region is known to have conistently hosted less motivated political leadership that has further crippled whatever, development potential exists. Kullu lies somewhere in between as regards landholding endowments, soil fertility and the degree of political patronage. The more accessible regions have progressed in predictable ways as compared to the less connected pockets of the district. However, accessibility developments in the more remote pockets of Kullu might play an important role in tapping unexploited potentials for development that already exist but cannot be fully exploited due to weak road-connectivity constraints. This will also prevent excessive extraction of 'non-timber' forest products such as medicinal hebs that threaten the region's biodiversity and other illegal activities that are socially harmful.

To summarise, traditionally, the occupation structure of the region was essentially characterised by dependence on agriculture and livestock rearing supplemented by trade links with Tibet for basic necessities such as salt. In the more contemporary context, occupation-shifts have occurred in most villages in the sample. The broad emerging trend is a progressive shift towards commercialisation of agriculture supplemented by non-farm avenues of employment particularly casual employment in the private or government sector (Sarkar, 1999). Agriculture continues to be the primary occupation, though, it is no longer entire for self-consumption. The intensity of production for the market varies from region to region and is no doubt linked to the nature of road-access.

Fig. 5 Population change (1975-2000)

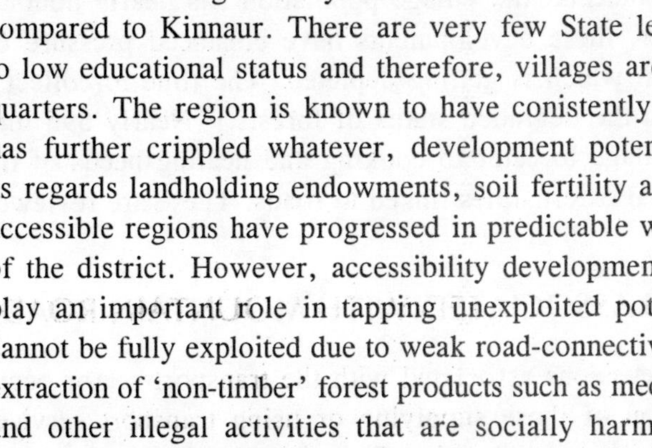

Changes in accessibility have also led to more sedentary patterns of living. As roads generate potentials for generating more cash sources of income both in the farm as well as in the non-farm sectors and as roads attract more infrastructural facilities, the local communities prefer to be based in their villages for catering to their livelihood needs. The survey data indicates that only 4% of the households in a village have migrated out, over the last 25 years.[18] There was not much evidence of male out-migration and nearly 90% of the households in the study area were found to be male-headed. Further, remittances account for a mere 4% of the total consumption expenditure of a household. These are all evidences, supportive of sedentary living patterns in contrast to Kreutzmann's (2004) findings on the impact of the Karakoram Highway in the northern mountainous belts of Pakistan. Though, there has been a gradual transition to cultivation of cash crops with improvements in accessibility conditions, he found that the value of food supplies, imported from the plains, cannot be covered through cash crop receipts. The balance is paid through remittances received from migrants, who are compelled to work in cities such as Karachi. The Karakoram Highway is considered to be the life-line for these food-deficit ridden parts of North Pakistan. However, due to the peculiar circumstance, a kind of 'down-country dependency' has gradually resulted.

Due to sedentary living conditions in Himachal, the village population has nearly doubled during the last 25 years (Figure 5). However, these developments have enhanced pressure on the fragile natural resource base of the region which is getting depleted. The time to collect a bundle of firewood has nearly doubled due to the degraded status of forests.[19] Nearly 595 tons of firewood needs to be extracted by each village to cater to cooking and heating needs of the local community. There are other environmental externalities linked to roads. These are reviewed in the following section.

5. ENVIRONMENTAL EXTERNALITIES ASSOCIATED WITH MOUNTAIN ROADS

Environmental depletion and other repercussions associated with the transport sector occur because these are external to the cost function of those supplying or using transport services Rather than mitigating these distortions, there is evidence that State intervention in transport markets has accentuated the incidence of environmental externalities because governments tend to manipulate transport provision in the hope of achieving regional growth and development as well as other social objectives or simply give vend to political motives, instead of fully taking the environmental costs into account (Button, 1999). In mountain States, implementation of projects such as roads, hydro-electric projects, SEZs and mining ventures are classic cases that have such ramifications. Local, global and inter-temporal environmental effects associated with these projects are hard to quantify and assess. These are either ignored or passed of as 'trade-offs' necessary for giving priority to other local and national development goals and objectives.

There seems to be a consensus that road construction activities in the Himalayas have been pursued disregarding the binding geomorphologic constraints that characterise the region. Development interventions are proposed and undertaken without taking cognizance of hazardous zones through detailed hydro-geophysical analysis and mapping (Gardener, 2000). For instance, the unanticipated shock of the Chinese military presence along the Himalayan frontier led to massive road construction programmes that were put into effect in great haste because military expediencies outweighed sound engineering (Ives and Messerli, 1989). Poorly designed roads constructed across fragile belts of the Himalayas, inherently susceptible to tectonic movements and natural hazards, have aggravated the occurrence of landslides (Owen, 1996). Poor design and faulty alignments have not only threatened the surrounding environment but has also undermined the high capital infusion invested to construct roads in the Himalayas.

In a more contemporary context, roads have been prescribed in all policy documents as an important necessity for promoting administrative, commercial, military or recreational activities. Local public opinion is invariably linked to the more vivid economic benefits associated with roads. As a consequence both local and government perceptions appear to be somewhat myopic to the increasing risks of natural hazards such as landslides which road construction activities may aggravate. In most cases therefore, the policy thrust has been to tackle such disasters after these have occurred rather than to mitigate or anticipate these hazards through research based environmental regulations or engineering works. Pilgrim (1999) in his field studies of a Kinnaur district village in Himachal Pradesh, found that official grants allocated for conservation measures directed at averting the threat of natural calamities were often diverted to more immediate local needs such as irrigation water or road maintenance or just wasted.

In many other cases roads have been constructed in haste because of potential political gains. Politicians have tried to initiate road projects in many areas for gaining political support. But once their purpose is met, many of these projects are not completed and others are not well-maintained. In an intensive all-India study on the politics of infrastructure provision, Wilkinson (2006) empirically showed that electoral volatility is related to both road spending and actual road construction, but much of this construction seems to be of poor quality. An assessment report on roads in Himachal Pradesh (Planning Commission, 2005) indicated that the quality of roads was not up to the mark with poor compaction and drainage design causing disintegration particularly during monsoon months. The same report also found that road design and construction paid little or no heed to environmental considerations concluding that among the man-induced causes, road construction in hilly terrain is more responsible for mounting occurrences of landslides in the region. The use of heavy explosives for road construction, such as dynamite can also aggravate the occurrence of landslides. It has been estimated that in the Indian Himalayas, for each linear kilometer of mountain road, nearly 10 small to medium landslides occur as a result of slope instability caused by road construction (Ives and Messerli, 1989). Such landslides can cause highway blockages and high maintenance costs especially during the monsoons. For instance, in Himachal Pradesh, a whopping amount of Rs. 514 crores had to be spent by the public works department to cater to road infrastructure damage and roads blockages during the monsoons, in 2007. Imputing monetary values to the social and economic losses caused to the local population on account of these road closures will most certainly inflate this figure.

Pilgrim (1999) and Gardener (2000) attribute the increasing occurrence of landslides to anthropogenic disturbances in terms of changing village morphology marked by land use changes propelled by road construction. These perceptible land use changes include the expansion of major settlements that are of administrative, commercial or recreational importance, infilling of cultivated areas by buildings and the ribbon development of buildings along roads. Further, roads have been constructed at lower altitudes along rivers to ensure all-weather conditions and to facilitate the movement of heavy equipment and tonnage. Such developments also enhance the susceptibility to damage due to floods. The same holds good for roads that have come up to cater to the construction of hydro-electric projects. There is a need for greater public awareness both at the local level and in policy circles about disaster protection associated with these new developments.

Road debris generation and disposal is another oft-quoted source of environmental degradation in the hills. A kilometer of road requires the removal of nearly 60,000 -80,000 cubic meter of debris. This causes slope instability and can aggravate the occurrence of landslides. Even after construction, the slope instability continues to produce enormous volumes of debris amounting to nearly 600-700 m^3 per annum, per kilometer of road. The debris is usually dumped down slope causing damage to vegetation, forests, pastures and agricultural lands. Ives and Messerli (1989) quote a number of studies that accredit the enormous annual amounts of debris production to unsatisfactory road alignment and poor design.

Deforestation caused due to road construction is invariably defended on development grounds. Although, 'compensatory afforestation' is a mandatory requirement, the success rate of such plantation programmes is usually very low. Loss of such stabilising vegetation deprives the region of all the tangible and intangible ecosystem services that forests provide in terms of watershed protection, soil conservation and carbon sequestration thereby magnifying environmental problems in the region.

Roads are also known to accentuate illegal smuggling of timber by the so called timber mafia. Official records on the extent of total deforestation caused by road construction, or the level of illegal felling due to road access are rare to come by. Ali et al. (2004) and Kreutzmann (2004)[20] found that the Karakoram Highway, constructed in 1978 for strategic reasons, played an active role in accelerating deforestation in Northern Mountainous belts of Pakistan. The smuggling of timber and firewood is also reported to have flourished with the opening up of the highway (Kreutzmann, 1991).

Fig. 6 Accidents: Himachal Pradesh (1971-2006)

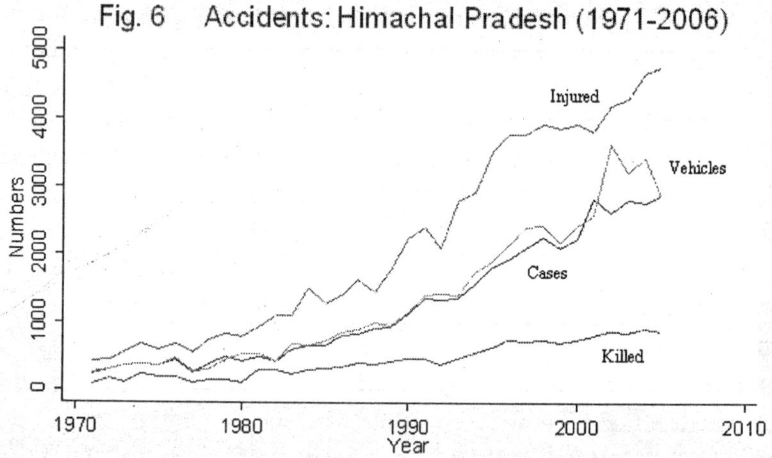

While roads in Himachal Pradesh, have expanded at a steady pace, so have the vulnerability to road accidents (Figure 6) Roads are prone to accidents in the mountainous terrain because of high road curvature, slope and narrow width that causes fatigue and visibility problems. Night driving can also be risky due to poor visibility and undulating nature of roads. Accidents in the mountains have been found to be more fatal due to these geotechnical constraints and also because of delay in access to post accident medical care for the victims (Rautela, et al., 2007). The fatality index,[21] for the high mountain districts of Himachal was found to be 0.31 which is twice the value computed for the lower altitude areas and plains.[22]

6. CONCLUSIONS

Over the last five decades, the expansion of the road network across the Himalayas has been truly phenomenal, particularly in States such as Himachal Pradesh. There is no doubt that roads have been instrumental in promoting economic growth and in opening up a haven of opportunities especially in potentially buoyant areas. This was quite evident from field studies conducted in the region as exemplified in this paper. However, concomitant to these changes, undesirable environmental consequences have arisen. Reckless road construction activities initiated under strategic, political or economic compulsions have adversely affected the fragile environment of the region. There is an ardent need to take account of these environmental externalities for sustaining the pace of accessibility developments. Some measures need to be immediately incorporated into the existing policy framework. Road design has to be integrated with geomorphological information pertaining to the region. There is meager data in this respect. Geomorphological data needs to be mapped and monitored so that, ecologically fragile areas can be avoided while designing road alignments. Recourse to environmentally benign technology for constructing roads is crucial. Some road stretches are particularly prone to accidents. These zones must be tended to through adequate safety measures. Above all, local, global as well as inter-temporal environmental costs need be anticipated and accurately incorporated into road investment appraisal mechanisms. Wherever possible, sustainable means of transport such as ropeways that work on gravity must be installed as an effective alternative to rural link roads. These measures will need to be articulated effectively to the local community by highlighting the environmental benefits. The effectiveness of such public education will of course depend on the pace of social change and the concomitant sensitivity to environmental issues at the local level.

NOTES:

1. See for instance Singh, C (1998) and Kreutzmann, H. (2004) for archival accounts this section, presents
2. Such as the Kalka-Simla 91903), Haridwar-Dehradun (1900) and Siliguri-Darjeeling (1886) rail links.
3. After the 1962 Indo-China war and the extended Kashmir conflict with Pakistan.
4. See Appendix, Table 2A for more details.
5. See Appendix, Table 2A for more details.
6. State Public Works Department, 2007
7. See Appendix, Table 3A for more details.
8. As early as 1892, the colonial administrator, Lord Lugard wrote that the material development of Africa could be summed up in one word-"transport". In similar vein, Munby, in his academic work on the transport sector which was published in the 60s, emphasised that there is no escape from transport (Hoyle, 1973).
9. Wilson (1973) stresses that the existence of other 'non-transport' factors such as appropriate psychological attitudes towards economic activity and change, entrepreneurial and technical abilities and education, the legal, political and social environment and the amount of natural resources are all very crucial for economic growth and development.
10. See Table 4A in the Appendix.
11. See Table 5A in the Appendix.
12. See Table 6A in the Appendix for variation in road access conditions across tribal and non-tribal 'tahsils'
13. The mean distance to the road from a village is 9 kilometers in Sainj and 7 kilometers in Banjar tahsil
14. See Table 7A in the Appendix for trends pertaining to income from cash crops and non-farm avenues.
15. See Table 8A in the Appendix for trends on access to schools and Table 9A for trends on access to other forms of infrastructure in the study area.
16. The average land holding in Kinnaur is 0.96 hectares, in Kullu it is 0.64 hectares and in Chamba it is 0.54 hectares.

17. Ethnographic interviews in many villages in the region indicated the presence of educated elderly villagers who took great pains to secure education by residing away from the village due to accessibility constraints. Kings from the local dynasty were also responsible for encouraging literacy by awarding scholarships to aspiring students.
18. See tables 8A, 9A and 10A in the Appendix.
19. See Table 14A in the Appendix.
20. There studies were based in neighboring 'Basho' and 'Hunza' valleys of North Pakistan.
21. Fatality index is the ratio of fatalities to people injured in accidents.
22. See Table 14A in the Appendix.

REFERENCES

Ali, Jawad and A. Benjaminsen (2004), *'Fuelwood, Timber and Deforestation in the Himalayas. The Case of Basho Valley, Baltistan Region, Pakistan'* Mountain Research and Development, Vol. 24, No. 4, November, pp. 312-318.

Banister, D. and J. Berechman (2000), *Transport Investment and Economic Development'*, Routledge.

Button, K. (1999), *'Environmental Externalities and Transport Policy'* in Hayashi, Y., Button, K. and Nijkamp, P. (eds.) 'The Environment and Transport. Environmental Analysis and Economic Policy, An Elgar Reference Collection, pp. 1-16.

Creightney, C.D. (1993), *'Transport and Economic Performance A Survey of Developing Countries'*, World Bank Technical Paper No. 232, Africa Technical Deptt. Series,The World Bank.

Gauthier, H.L. (1973), *'Geography, Transportation and Regional Development'*, in Hoyle, B.S. ed. 'Transport and Development', Geographic Readings, Macmillan Press Ltd, pp. 19-31.

Government of Himachal Pradesh (2002), *'Himachal Pradesh Human Development Report'*.

Government of Himachal Pradesh (2006), 'Statistical Outline', Department of Economics and Statistics.

Grotzbach, E. and Stadel, C. (1997), 'Mountain People and Cultures', in Messerli, B. and Ives. J.D. (eds.) 'Mountains of the World a Global Priority', pp. 17-38.

Haigh, M.J., Rawat, J.S. and Bartarya, S.K. (1989), 'Environmental Indicators of Landslide Activity along Kilbury Road, Nainital, Kumaon Lesser Himalaya', *Mountain Research and Development*, Vol. 9, No. 1, pp. 25-33.

Hewitt, K. (1997), *'Risks and Disasters in Mountain Lands'* in Messerli, B. and Ives. J.D. (eds.) 'Mountains of the World a Global Priority', pp. 371-406.

Hoyle, B.S. (1973), *'Transport and Development'*, Geographic Readings, Macmillan Press Ltd.

Ives, J.D. and Messerli, B. (1989), *'The Himalayan Dilemma. Reconciling Development and Conservation'*, Routledge, London and New York.

Kreutzmann, H. (1991), 'The Karakoram Highway: The Impact of Road Construction on Mountain Societies', *Modern Asian Studies*, Vol. 25, No. 4, pp. 711-736.

Kreutzmann, H. (2004), 'Accessibility for High Asia: Comparative Perspectives on Northern Pakistan's Traffic Infrastructure and Linkages with its Neighbors in the Hindukush-Karakoram-Himalaya', *Journal of Mountain Science*, Vol. 1, No. 3, pp. 193-210.

Owen, L. (1996), 'High Roads High Risks', *The Geographical Magazine*, January, pp. 12-15.

Planning Commission (2005), *'Himachal Pradesh Development Report'*, Government of India. Chaps 1, 3, 13 and 17.

Petley, D.A., Hearn, G.J., Hart,A., Rosser, N.J., Dunning, S.A., Oven, K., Mitchell, W.A. (2006), 'Trends in Landslide Occurrence in Nepal', *Natural Hazards*, November.

Rautela, P. and S.S. Pant (2007), 'Delineating Road Accident Risk along Mountain Roads', *Disaster Prevention and Management*, Vol. 16, No. 3 pp.334-343.

Rawat, D.S. and Sharma, S. (1997), 'The Development of a Road Network and its Impact on the Growth of infrastructure; A Study of Almora District in the Central Himalayas', *Mountain Research and Development,* Vol. 17, No. 2, pp. 117-126.

Rowe, R., Sharma, N. and Browder, J. (1992), *'Deforestation: Problems, Causes and Concerns'* in Sharma, N.P. (ed.) *'Managing the World's Forests. Looking for a Balance between Conservation and Development',* Chapter 3.

Sanan, D. (2004), 'Delivering basic Public Services in Himachal Pradesh. Is the Success Sustainable?',*Economic and Political Weekly*, February 28, pp. 975-978.

Sarkar, R. (1998), 'Understanding Sustainability. Study of a Hill Settlement', *Economic & Political Weekly,* Vol. XXXIII, No. 34, October 31.

Sarkar, R. (2007), *'Development and Change in Kinnaur',* Interview with R.S. Negi, Seminar, Vol. 577, September, www.cised.org/wp-content/uploads/seminar-kinnaur-2007.pdf

Sarkar, S., Kanumgo, D.P. and Patra, A.K. (2005), 'Landslides in the Alaknanda Valley of Garhwal Himalaya', *Quarterly Journal of Engineering Geology & Hydrogeology,* Vol. 39, pp.79-82.

Singh, C. (1998), *'Natural Premises. Ecology and Peasant Life in the Western Himalaya 1800-1950',* Oxford University Press, Delhi.

Wilson, G. (1973), *'Towards a Theory of Transport and Development',* in Hoyle, B.S. 'Transport and Development', Geographic Readings, Macmillan Press Ltd, pp. 208-230.

Watts, J (2006), 'Protests as Tibet-China Rail Link Opens', *The Gaurdian*, June 30, Friday.

Wilkinson, S.I. (2006), *'The Politics of Infrastructure Spending In India',* July, under publication.

APPENDIX

Table 1A: Plan outlay on Roads: Himachal Pradesh

Five year Plans	*Period*	*% Share*	*Outlay on Roads and Bridges (Rs. Lakhs)*	*% Share (Roads & Bridges)*
First	1951-56	51.4	225.40	93%
Second	1956-61	40.1	533.84	90%
Third	1961-66	35.2	1018.11	85%
Fourth	1969-74	29	2800.00	92%
Fifth	1974-79	24	4700.00	90%
Sixth	1980-85	18	10176.00	85%
Seventh	1985-90	15	15889.13	85%
Eighth	1992-97	13	32122.28	84%
Ninth	1997-2002	14	90892.84	85%
Tenth	2002-2007	16	117291.00	95%

Source: Various Statistical Abstracts, Deptt. of Economics & Statistics, Himachal Pradesh & Public Works Deptt. Himachal Pradesh, 2007.

Table 2A: Hierarchy of Roads in Himachal Pradesh

	Road length (kms)	*Percentage*
National Highways	1241	4%
State Highways	1824	7%
Major District Roads	1770	6%
Border Roads	720	3%
Rural Roads	22,029	80%
TOTAL	27,584	100%

Source: Public Works Dept. Himachal Pradesh, 2007.

Table 3A: Road Quality Over Two Time-Periods in Himachal Pradesh

Year: Districts	*1979-80*		*2006-2007*	
	Road Length	*% Unmetalled*	*Road Length*	*% Unmetalled*
Hilly terrain	6844	67	15,791	48
Less Hillly terrain	5149	66	11,793	29
Total	11,993	67	27,584	57

Source: Statistical Outline, Deptt. of Economics & Statistics, Himachal Pradesh & Public Works Deptt. Himachal Pradesh.

Table 4A: Change in Mean Distance to the Road & Associated Time Savings

Districts Study Area	*Now (kilometers)*	*Std. Dev*	*25 years ago (kilometers)*	*Std. Dev*
Kinnaur	2.65	4.31	2.77	4.36
Kullu	3.38	4.11	7.12	7.02
Chamba	3.6	3.91	11.08	12.26
OVERALL	3.39	4	8.55	10.33
Time to access road	(hours)		(hours)	
OVERALL	1.02		2.3	

Source: Field Survey, 2000-2001.

Table 5A: Villages Connected by Roads in the Study Area

Districts	*Total Villages*	*Now*		*25 years ago*	
		Roads	*of which Metalled Roads*	*Roads*	*of which Metalled Roads*
Kinnaur	13	46%	67%	46%	17%
Chamba	44	18%	50%	5%	0%
Kullu	25	36%	44%	20%	20%
OVERALL		33%	54%	24%	12%

Source: Field Survey, 2000-2001.

Table 6A: Variations in Access across Tribal & Non-Tribal Tahsils.

Variable	*Tahsils*	*Mean*	*Std. Dev.*	*Min*	*Max*
TRIBAL					
Distance to road (kms.)	4	2.79	2.72017	0.125	6
NON TRIBAL					
Distance to road (kms.)	7	4.45	2.83353	1.3	9.33

Source: Field Survey 2000-2001.

Table 7A: Access and Income Sources: Study Area

Districts	*Accessibility*	*Mean Income_cash crops (Rs.)*	*Mean Income Nonfarm avenues (Rs.)*
Kinnaur	0.31	41,069	50,012
Chamba	0.09	1440	20,776
Kullu	0.16	17,810	19,571

Source: Field Survey 2000-2001.

Table 8A: Distance to Schools Across Study Districts

Districts	*Accessibility*	*Distance to primary school (kms.)*	*Distance to middle school (kms.)*	*Distance to high school (kms.)*
Kinnaur	0.31	0	0.23	3.3
Chamba	0.09	0.2	1.86	5.67
Kullu	0.16	0.3	2.45	3.57

Source: Field Survey 2000-2001.

Table 9A: Access to Other Infrastructure Across Districts

Districts	*Accessibility*	*Distance to nearest bus-stop (kms.)*	*Distance to nearest primary health centre(kms.)*	*Distance to nearest Bank(kms)*
Kinnaur	0.31	3.42	2.07	6.88
Chamba	0.09	5.2	12.61	11.98
Kullu	0.16	3.84	9.94	9.76

Source: Field Survey 2000-2001.

Table 10A: Male Headed Households

Gender (Household Head)	*Households*	*Percent*	*Cum.*
(Male)	1,461	89.3	89.3
(Female)	175	10.7	100
Total	1,636	100	

Source: Field Survey 2000-2001.

Table 11A: Proportion of Consumption Expenditure Accounted for by Remittances

	Households	*Mean*	*Std. Dev.*
Proportion remittances	1636	0.0365	0.17494

Source: Field Survey 2000-2001.

Table12A: Out-migrating households per village Over the last 25 years

	Villages	*Mean*	*Std. Dev.*
Out-migrant households	82	4	7.76

Source: Field Survey 2000-2001.

Table 13A: Time to Collect a bundle of firewood

	Variable	*Villages*	*Mean Std. Dev.*
Time to collect (now)	82	2.84	1.935746
Time to collect (25 years ago)	82	1.68	1.368165

Source: Field Survey 2000-2001.

Table 14A: Inter-district Fatality Index: Himachal Pradesh (2005-06)

	Fatality Index
High Mountains Districts	
Chamba	0.29787234
Kinnaur	0.379310345
Kullu	0.203076923
Lahaul & Spiti	0.787878788
Shimla	0.170666667
Sirmaur	0.185595568
Mandi	0.137978142
Mean	0.31
Low hills/plains districts	
Bilaspur	0.261484099
Hamirpur	0.141993958
Kangra	0.1863581
Solan	0.189035917
Una	0.089514066
Mean	0.17

Source: Statistical outline, Deptt. of Economics and Statistics, Himachal Pradesh.

9

ISSUES OF ACCESSIBILITY AND MOBILITY — A CASE STUDY OF SURAT CITY

M. R. Tagore
Mridula Krishna

ABSTRACT

In this paper, a new accessibility measure which takes into account the supply characteristics of transport system (mobility) is used for assessing the accessibility levels in various zones of Surat. The improvement in the accessibility levels with the proposed Integrated Public Transit System is also assessed. As mobility is dependent on socio-economic characteristics and transport supply, an analysis of the socio-economic characteristics of the people of Surat is also presented in this paper. The analysis is based on the household travel surveys conducted in Surat as part of Study on Integrated Public Transit System for the City Of Surat by Gujarat Infrastructure Development Board, Ahmedabad.

1. INTRODUCTION

Over a long period of time, transport planning has been pursued with a bias towards provision of capital intensive infrastructures for private vehicle users. This has now changed to a philosophy where the objective has been demand management, *i.e.*, minimisation of travel demands by manipulation of land uses. Thus, the focus has shifted from *vehicular mobility* to *personal mobility* and accessibility provisions. In addition, increasing emphasis is being laid on providing good accessibility to all the sections of the society to participate in activities like employment, educational needs, and other basic requirements.

Accessibility indicators should constitute an important component of transport planning and modelling, as it is one of the basic determinants of urban form. Since accessibility is a function of the land use patterns and the performance of the transport system, it is an important link between transport and land use. It has a significant influence on the location of industrial, commercial and residential developments. With the changing emphasis of transport planning to provision of equitable accessibility to different sections of society, future transport models are required to consider an effective and sensitive accessibility measure, more directly than their fore-runners.

Transport and land use are highly inter-dependent. Personal modes of transport particularly two wheelers can grow incrementally leading to more dispersed pattern of land use. Public transport, including bus transport, require relatively high levels of investment and therefore, require an integrated land use transport plan. High density development can support public transport and high capacity public transport gives rise to patterns of high accessibility that need to be harnessed by optimum levels of density of land use development that can provide adequate levels of ridership for sustainable operation.

In this paper, a new accessibility measure which takes into account the supply characteristics of transport system (mobility) is used for assessing the accessibility levels in various zones of Surat. The improvement in accessibility levels with the proposed *Integrated Public Transit System* is also assessed. As mobility is dependent on socio-economic characteristics and the transport supply, an analysis of the socio-economic characteristics of the people of Surat is also presented in this paper. The analysis is based on the household travel surveys conducted in Surat as part of *Study on Integrated Public Transit System for the City of Surat undertaken by the Gujarat Infrastructure Development Board, Ahmedabad.*

2. ACCESSIBILITY

The simplest definition of accessibility of a given location is in terms of how easy it is to reach a place. It, therefore, indicates the spatial relationship between one location and others. There are three essential components of an accessibility measure *viz.*, (*i*) the location and characteristics of resident population, (*ii*) geographical distribution and intensity of economic activities and (*iii*) the characteristics of the existing transportation system. Accessibility can also be defined as the ease with which any land-use activity can be reached from a location, using a particular transportation system (*Dalvi, 1979*). Accessibility, thus, indicates the location of a household or a group of households in relation to the distribution of activities and to the transport system connecting them. In this paper, accessibility is defined as the potential of opportunities for interaction. This definition differs from the usual one in that it is a measure of the possible intensity level of the interaction rather than just a measure of the ease of interaction.

2.1 Accessibility Measures

A variety of accessibility measures starting from Hansen's (1959) gravity type to Williams' (1976) consumer surplus approach have been proposed and have been applied to wide ranging problems. But in all the previous studies, mobility characteristics of groups of individuals have not been taken care of in the accessibility measure. In *Tagore and Sikdar, (1995a)* a new accessibility measure has been developed taking account of mobility parameters in addition to transport characteristics and activity spread. The proposed accessibility measure can very well fit in the land use transport models, as it includes the attraction of the zone expressed in terms of transport supply characteristics.

In addition to sensitivity to both transport supply and activity spread, any accessibility measure must also take account of the mobility achievable by population groups. The new accessibility measure developed (*Tagore and Sikdar, 1995a*), is similar to the normalised version of Hansen's gravity type accessibility, except that this includes the variable representing mobility achievable by population groups in addition to a measure of the activity potential and ease of interaction. The functional form of the proposed measure is given in equation (1).

$$A_i = \frac{\sum_j S_j f(C_{ij})}{\sum_j S_j} \qquad \dots (1)$$

A_i = measure of accessibility of zone i to activities located in the remaining zones

S_j = the size of activity in zone j, such as the number of jobs, population, etc.

$f(C_{ij})$ = a travel deterrence function

3. MOBILITY

The term 'mobility' of an individual or a group of individuals represents, in general, a measure of the propensity of movement (Bajpai, 1980). Such a notion of mobility is commonly used in explaining various facets of human behaviour such as social mobility, residential/ employment mobility, migration, etc. In the context of transport, mobility is defined as the ability to travel from one place to another in an urban area, and is associated with a particular group of urban residents (Kirby and McGillivray, 1979).

Clark et. al. (1974) have defined personal mobility as the number of annual kilometers of travel (by all modes, including walking and cycling). Hillman et. al. (1973) defined mobility as the capacity that a person possesses for getting around in his daily life. The Independent Commission on Transport (1974) found that the term mobility refers to the ease with which a person can move about or the amount of movement he performs. A variety of different measures were also used to characterise the mobility of a particular resident or a group of residents.

As summarised by Dalvi (1979), mobility can be defined in two distinct senses; first as a concept and then in terms of some physical measure of that concept. As a concept mobility refers to the degree to which a person is free of ties in the home or elsewhere. In this respect a mother with young children would be considered less mobile than someone without. As a physical measure, however, mobility indicates the ease with which a person can move about, measured in terms of number of trips made by all modes, the availability of different modes and presumably some indication of the resources one can spend on travel.

3.1 Mobility Measures

Mobility is, therefore, mostly measured in terms of number of trips performed by an individual or household, and sometimes in terms of total amount of travel (number of annual kilometres per person, etc.). Unfortunately in all these measures, attention has been focussed on the amount of travel undertaken, rather than potential for travel and this point encourages the planners of transport systems to increase trip rates and to overlook the point that travel is a derived demand. From the literature, it is observed that the number of trips made still remains the indicator of mobility used in most of the transportation planning studies [including the studies done in India by Bajpai (1980) and Central Road Research Institute (CRRI, 1988)]. It was well pointed out by Morris *et. al.* (1979) that the concept of mobility has been used rather indiscriminately to refer to both the supply and demand side of transport services. But mobility is strictly related to the supply side of transport (Dalvi, 1979).

In the present paper, mobility is interpreted to mean the ability of individuals to move from place to place and depends on the performance of the transport system (transport service availability and frequency/waiting time for the service, etc.) and characteristics of individual (income, vehicle ownership and resources that one can be spend on travel, etc.).

To take account of the mobility, the generalised time, which takes into consideration the mobility parameters, is considered as the deterrence function for the public transport. The components of generalised time are In-Vehicle Travel Time (IVTT), Waiting Time (WT), Transfer Time (TR), and fare in time units. Accordingly, the generalised time, GT, is worked out as

$$GT = \text{IVTT} + WTFAC{*}WT + \text{TRFAC*TR} + FARE \,/\, \text{VOT}$$

where,

GT = Generalised time in minutes

WTFAC = Wait time factor worked out as a ratio between value of *WT* and value of *IVTT*

TRFAC = Transfer time factor worked out as a ratio between value of *TR* and value of *IVTT*

VOT = Value of travel time, in Rs per minute

FARE = Fare paid for journey between origin and destination in Rs.

4. CASE STUDY — SURAT CITY

The study area is that under the *Surat Urban Development Authority (SUDA),* which covers an area of 722.0 sq. km. The study area includes areas within Surat Municipal Corporation (SMC) and 130 villages in the peripheral areas. For the purpose of analysis, the study area is divided into three parts:

(*i*) Walled City

(*ii*) SMC area excluding Walled City

(*iii*) SUDA Area (excluding SMC area)

The Surat Municipal Corporation (SMC) area is spread over an area of 112.28 sq. km and had a total population of 14.99 lakhs in 1991. The Walled City covers an area of 8.22 sq km. As per 2001 Census, the SMC population was about 24.34 lakhs with an average gross density of 21676 persons/ sq. km. Recently in the year 2006, Surat Municipal Corporation has increased its area by merging eight SUDA villages (*Nagar Palikas*) into SMC limits. With the extended limits of Surat City, the total population of SMC area (148.67 sq km) was 27,29,482 (2001).

The total population of SUDA area was 9.85 lakhs in 1981, 17.16 lakhs in 1991 and 30.90 lakhs in 2001. The decadal population growth rate of Surat Urban Development Authority area including Surat Municipal Corporation area during 1991-2001 was 80%. The projected population of SUDA area for the year 2011 is about 42 lakhs.

4.1 Growth Profile

During the last decade, Surat has experienced very high growth in economic activities and has earned its name internationally for its textile and diamond business. Alongwith, intensive concentration of trade and commercial activity in the city, the area has been blessed with rich agricultural land. Surat is known for its textile, manufacturing, trade, diamond cutting and polishing industries, intricate zari works, chemical industries and the gas based industries at Hazira. An apparel park has also been planned in the city for production and export facilities to be under one roof and to give a face lift to the textile industry.

4.1.1 Regional Transport System

Surat city is well connected by Road, Rail and Air transport. Surat is well-connected to one of the busiest inter state trunk routes in the country (*National Highway No. 8*) which lies at a distance of about 16 km from eastern boundary of Municipal area and other major regional linkages with State Highways. Being located almost midway on the 500 km long principal rail corridor of Western Railway between Mumbai and Ahmedabad, Surat is provided with 45 pairs of express/ mail/passenger and local trains per day. The state government has also established an air-strip to facilitate smaller aircraft landings, but no domestic air services have started as yet.

4.1.2 Road Network

Surat city has a good road network of the radial and ring grid types. Most of the major roads have divided carriageways. However, the road network in the Walled City is congested due to insufficient road widths. Most of the roads do not have sufficient foot path facilities. All the traffic related problems in the city need detailed studies on assessment of future requirement of transport infrastructure facilities. The annual average growth rate of registered vehicles in Surat during 1994-2005 was 11.89%.

4.2 Socio-Economic Characteristics

An appreciation of the demographic, socio-economic and travel characteristics of the city is essential to understand the travel needs of the people, their propensity to travel, preferences for travel modes, etc. To obtain the required information for the study area, household travel surveys conducted as part of *Study on Integrated Public Transit System for the City of Surat* by *Gujarat Infrastructure Development Board, Ahmedabad* were utilised .

4.2.1 Household Survey Data Analysis

Household travel survey was carried out for 12000 households, spread over 154 Traffic Analysis Zones to gather necessary socio-economic and travel characteristics. In order to appreciate the socio-economic and travel characteristics at a micro level the data has been analysed at four spatial levels within the study area. These are:

1. Walled City
2. SMC area (including Walled City)
3. SUDA Area (excluding SMC area)
4. Study Area

4.2.2 Household Socio-Economic Characteristics

Household Size

Average household size in the study area was observed to be 4.43. The distribution of households by size, at the three spatial levels and the study area is shown graphically in Figure 1. It can be observed that 78.02 percent of households have household size between 3 and 6.

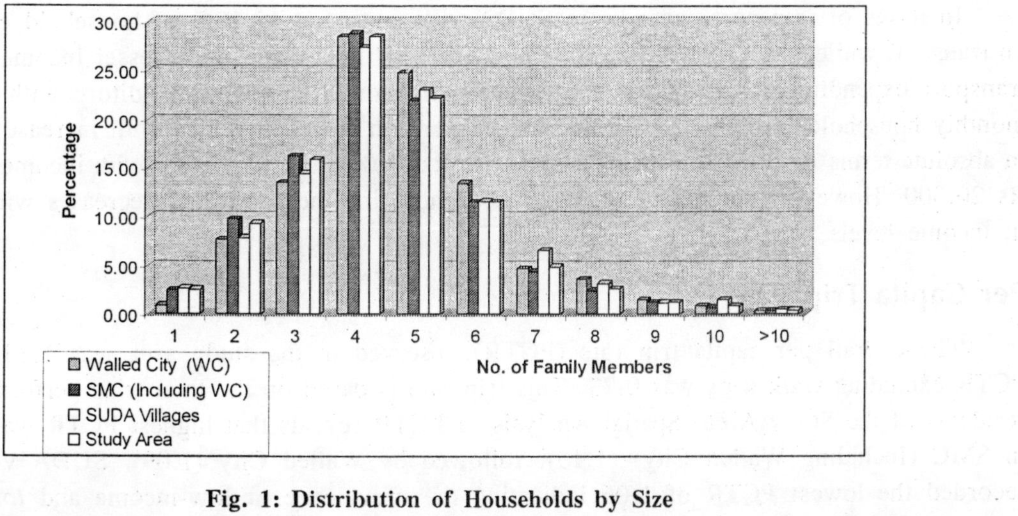

Fig. 1: Distribution of Households by Size

Household Income

Average household income in the study area was found to be Rs. 8,182 per month. The distributions of households under various income groups reveal that majority of the households (43.27%) fall within an income range of Rs. 5001-10000 per month. The distribution of households under different income groups indicate that SMC (including, the Walled City) area exhibit higher incomes compared to SUDA Village area. Average Per Capita Income (PCI) in the Walled City, SMC (Including Walled City), SUDA Village areas were observed to be Rs. 8,487, Rs. 8,342, and Rs.7,649 per month respectively. It is observed that the Walled City has fewer low-income households and more middle-income households, while SUDA villages have more of low-income households than other areas. Further, SUDA villages have fewer middle-income households than other areas.

Vehicle Ownership

Average vehicle ownership rate in the study area was observed to be 0.65 vehicles per household in case of motorized vehicles (two wheelers and car/jeep) and 1.06 vehicles per household when bicycles are also taken into consideration. The Car ownership rates are much lower in comparison to two wheeler and cycle ownership.

Household Monthly Expenditure Pattern

Household expenditure analysis gives an idea on relative priority a household of certain income category attaches to the expenditure on transport vis-à-vis expenditure on other activities. Household expenditure in the study area shows that expenditure on food accounts for the maximum proportion (54.11%) of total household expenditure followed by others (16.31%) and transport (13.22%). It was also observed that on an average a household in the study area spends about Rs. 589 per month on transport, which is nearly 13.2 per cent of total household expenditure. Nearly 37.2 per cent of households spend between Rs. 300 and Rs. 800 on travelling.

In terms of transport expenditure SUDA villages spend 15.10% of household expenditure on transport while SMC spends 12.71% only. Thus SUDA villages have lesser income, but more transport expenditure. As regards the variation in monthly travel expenditure with respect to monthly household income, the average expenditure on travel increases with increase in income in absolute terms *i.e.,* Rs 265 with income upto Rs. 3,000 and Rs. 1,481 with income exceeding Rs 20,000. However, percentage share of household income for travel decreases with increase in income levels.

Per Capita Trip Rate

The overall per capita trip rate (PCTR) observed in the study area was 1.13 while the PCTR excluding walk trips was 0.73. This trip rate is based on the total trips performed by the residents of the Study Area. Spatial Analysis of PCTR reveals that highest PCTR was observed in SMC (Including Walled City) (1.15), followed by Walled City (1.09). SUDA village area recorded the lowest PCTR of 1.06 indicating the prevalence of low-income and *low mobility* level population. The overall PCTR does not vary significantly over spatial entities of the study area.

Mode of Travel

The distribution of trips amongst different modes is presented in Figur 2. Walk trips constitute about 35.28 per cent of total trips in the study area. The share of walk trips in total trips is highest in SMC area (35.66%) followed by SUDA Villages (34.09%). Public transport trips are lowest at 0.48 per cent in SMC area largely due to absence of public transport bus service.

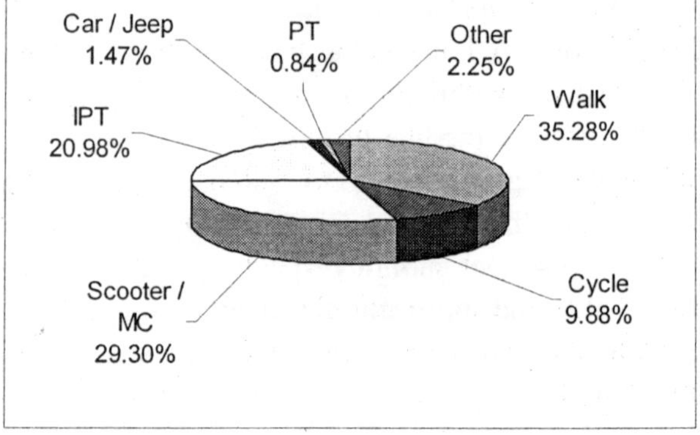

Fig. 2: Mode wise Distribution of Trips

5. ISSUES AND PROBLEMS OF THE CITY TRANSPORT SYSTEM

Some of the major traffic and transportation related problems in Surat city are listed below:

Lack of Functional Hierarchy of Roads: There is a clear lack of functional hierarchy of roads with third order streets and access streets meeting the primary road.

Traffic Congestion: Traffic congestion is acute in some major roads due to increased vehicle ownership with lack of traffic management, which in turn reduce travel speed.

Public Transport and Intermediate Public Transport: Autorickshaw is the major intra-city transport system for people of Surat. A limited intra-city public transport is provided by state transport buses, some mini-buses and contract buses owned by private operators. Inter-city public transport is provided both by GSRTC and private operators. As there is no terminal for private operator they operate from their respective office which turns out to be problematic for both commuters and operator with increase traffic congestion.

Intersections: Surat's road network is characterised by various intersection types- roundabouts, signalized intersections and uncontrolled intersections. Roundabouts at a number of places suffer from insufficient weaving lengths thereby, reducing their capacity, while at a number of signalized intersections the signal phasing is inconsistent with traffic intensity causing delay to traffic. Uncontrolled intersections are major points of conflict and accident-prone locations and impede smooth flow of traffic.

Parking Problem: Parking is a very serious problem in Surat and irregular on street parking is observed on almost all the corridors. There is high conflict between traffic flow and parking manoeuvres affecting capacity and safety.

Transport Infrastructure: Lack of organised terminals for bus transport resulted in indiscriminate parking in open spaces. Lack of organised autorickshaw transport system limit their effectiveness and safety of pedestrians is well hit by almost negligible pedestrian facilities.

Two bus depots are available for StateTransport buses only and private operators use the vacant area near their offices for operation. There is no organised freight movement within Surat. The truck terminal near *Puna Khumbaria* is not organised and trucks coming from outside Surat deliver directly at the point of delivery. This has resulted in an intermingle with local traffic, increasing safety hazards thereby, causing congestion on the city road network.

6. SPECIFIC ISSUES IN SURAT CITY

Based on an initial understanding of the issues in public transportation in Surat City, it was observed that the following issues need to be considered while structuring projects for private sector participation:

1. It must be noted that although there is a supply-side constraint in provision of transportation services through the bus system (as the State Transport Corporation focusses on intra-city interconnectivity, and there is no dedicated intra-city bus provider), the unorganised private sector has not tended to fill this gap through the provision of private services, *chartered services*, etc. This suggests that unlike most other metros of India, there is

no significant existing base of bus traffic that can be channelled into a new systematic organised private sector bus initiative.

2. There is a disproportionately large percentage of commuters using their own vehicles (pre-dominantly two-wheelers). This implies that in order to attract significant usage (and hence, revenue), any new mass transport system that is proposed will need to encourage not only a modal shift but also a shift from personal to public transport. Moreover, the existing transport costs that commuters incur are likely to be relatively low, and hence, there may be a constraint on the range of pricing possibilities on a new mass transport system.

3. It appears that space and Right of Way (ROW) constraints may necessitate implementation of an elevated mass transport system, which implies relatively high capital costs. Taken in conjunction with (possible) limitations on fare pricing and (likely) significant uncertainties in traffic buildup, it seems likely that there will be a requirement for government to facilitate the project by mitigating revenue risks in initial years, or improving returns or a combination of the two.

7. QUANTIFICATION OF ACCESSIBILITY

Zonal accessibility (Hansen) to employment by public transport modes were computed for the year 2006 using employment as the attraction measure. The generalised time by public transport is considered as the deterrence parameter. The generalised time takes into consideration the socio-economic characteristics and the transport supply characteristics. The accessibility was assessed for two cases *viz.*,(*i*) with present transport network and the transport supply and (*ii*) with the proposed transport network including the Bus Mass Transit routes proposed by Surat Municipal Corporation along with BRTS/LRTS along North-South and East-West corridors. Table 1 and Figure 3 show the average accessibility values for different areas in Surat for the two cases :

Table 1: Average Accessibility

Area	*Without IPTS*	*With IPTS*	*% Increase in Accessibility*
Walled City	0.0124	0.0144	17%
SMC	0.0104	0.0123	19%
SUDA	0.0050	0.0057	15%

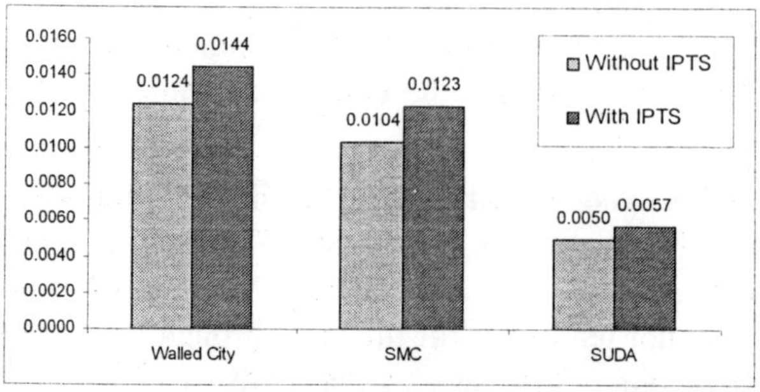

Fig. 3: Average Accessibility

The above accessibility values correspond to accessibility to employment *with* and *without* transport supply improvement for the year 2006. It can be observed that there is a significant increase in accessibility in the Walled City and SMC, which is mainly due to the improved transport supply, *viz.*, proposed bus routes and the LRTS. The new accessibility measure is able to take into consideration the transport supply also in addition to the activity.

REFERENCES

Bajpai, J.N. (1980), Mobility and land-use transportation interaction: Trip generation model revisited. *Traffic Engineering Highway Research Bulletin* 14, IRC Highway Research Board, New Delhi.

Clark, N., Lee J.A. and Ogden K.W. (1974), The use of energy for personal mobility. *Transportation Research,* Vol. 8, No. 4/5.

C.R.R.I. (1988), Mobility levels and transport problems of various population groups. *Report*, Central Road Research Institute, New Delhi.

Dalvi, M.Q. (1979), Behavioural modelling, accessibility, mobility and need: Concepts and measurement. In: *Behavioural Travel Modelling* (Edited by D. A. Hensher and P. R. Stopher), pp. 639-653,Croom Helm, London.

Hansen, W.G. (1959), How accessibility shapes land use. *Journal of American Institute of Planners* Vol. 25, pp.73-76.

Hillman, H., Henderson I. and Wholley A. (1973), *Personal mobility and transport policy.* PEP Broadsheet No. 542.

Independent Commission on Transport (1974), *Changing directions,* Coronet Books, London.

Kirby, R.F. and McGillivray, R.G. (1979), Mobility, accessibility and travel impacts of transport programmes for the elderly and handicapped. In: *Behavioural Travel Modelling* (Edited by D.A. Hensher and P.R. Stopher), pp. 680-691, Croom Helm, London.

Levine, J.C. (1993), Assessing the commute reducing potential of jobs-housing balancing strategies. Paper presented at the *Annual Meeting of the Association of Collegiate Schools of Planning*, Philadelphia.

Morris, J.M., Dumble, P.L. and Wigan, M. R. (1979), Accessibility indicators for transport planning. *Transportation Research,* Vol. 13A, pp. 91-109.

Tagore, M.R. and Sikdar, P.K. (1995), A New Accessibility Measure Accounting Mobility Parameters. Paper presented at the *7th World Conference on Transport Research*, Sydney, Australia (Selected Proceedings Published by *Elsevier Science*).

Tagore, M.R. and Sikdar P.K. (1995b), Accessibility for Guiding Land Use Development. *Proceedings of, ICORT-95*, New Delhi, pp. 1179-1189.

Thibeault, R.W., Kaiser, E.J., Butler, E.W. and McAllister, J. (1973), Accessibility satisfaction, income and residential mobility. *Traffic Quarterly,* Vol. 27, pp. 289-306.

Williams, H.C.W.L. (1976), Travel demand models, duality relations and user benefit analysis. *Journal of Regional Science,* Vol. 16, pp. 147-166.

Wilson, A.G. (1970), Disaggregating elementary residential location models. *Papers of the Regional Science Association*, Vol. XXIV, Ninth European Congress of the Regional Science Association, pp. 103-125.

10

SPACE-DEVELOPMENT MODULE FOR MUMBAI METROPOLITAN REGION (MMR)

M. S. Mir
K. V. K. Rao
J. D. Hunt

ABSTRACT

Metropolitan regions like the Mumbai Metropolitan Region (MMR) in India, are continuously evolving. Populations in this regions are increasing at a tremendous pace, built form is changing fast, and urban sprawl is easily noticeable. To guide the development and transportation needs in these highly dynamic regions and to help the concerned planning/political authorities in taking correct policy decisions, it becomes imperative to develop special land use transport models. The paper describes the methodology for development of a space development module that forms an essential component of the overall land use transport model, being developed for Mumbai Metropolitan Region (MMR). This module represents the actions of developers in the provision of different types of developed space where activities can be located. It includes the demolition and re-development as well as new development that occurs from one point in time to the next. The methodology also gives us flexibility in simulating the space quantities in situations of transition from slum development to non-slum development.

1. INTRODUCTION

With constraints on resources, space, safety and the environment, there are only limited possibilities to extend transport supply to safeguard accessibility. In the long run, the success of most transport policies is dependent on the existence of a supporting urban form (Wegener and Fürst, 1999). Without accompanying land use measures, the effect of many transport policies can become counterproductive. This is true especially in a developing country's context. Regions like the Mumbai Metropolitan Region (MMR) in India are continuously evolving. The populations are increasing at a tremendous pace, built form is changing fast, and urban sprawl is easily noticeable. It is quite clear now that it would call for a holistic approach to policy and investment planning to achieve a diverse and balanced mix of transport modes and a sensible arrangement of land use. To guide the development and transportation needs in these highly dynamic regions and to help the concerned planning/political authorities in taking correct policy decisions, it becomes imperative to develop special land use transport models.

The space development module for the MMR is set-up taking into consideration the existing land categories, existing space types and the various development plans that have been made from time to time. MMR has been divided into 1030 zones for the purpose. Use has been made of the data supplied by Mumbai Metropolitan Regional Development Authority (MMRDA) about the zonal areas under existing land uses, built-up area in each zone and the areas zoned for development under development plans. Space rents have been collected from various real estate sites, ready reckoners like stamp duty ready reckoner and property news material published in various news papers and magazines. Some reconnaissance surveys have also been done to get on the spot information about the characteristics of various space and land categories in the study area. TransCAD has been used to determine the travel time of all the zones from the main CBD and their distances from nearest railway stations.

From the information gained of the study area, the various land categories and space types to be considered in the development of the module is defined. Eight aggregated land categories have been defined for the study area. There are certain space types that are permitted or acknowledged on each type of land category in each zone. The rules applicable to a zone mainly depend on its location in the study area and have been framed mainly based on the information about development controls and regulations given in Regional Plan for MMR, 1996-2011. The maximum Floor Space Index (FSI)/Floor Area Ratio (FAR) value of each space type permitted in a land category in a zone is fixed. The concept of FSI/FAR reduction factor is introduced in the model development. The proportion of existing space quantities, the travel times from the main CBD of the region and the minimum path distances from the nearest railway stations are considered to be the prime factors responsible for encouraging the developers for development and redevelopment of space. The model, first, computes the redevelopment of space types that takes place for a one year time period by allocating the existing space for each space type for land type k among the possible new space types using a logit expression. The total available FAR for each land category is determined to get the potential of development possible in it. The total available FAR for a given land type is the maximum specified FAR less the updated (interim) effective FAR. The share of available FAR on a particular land category that is allocated to a particular space type is determined by allocating the total available FAR for each space type in a land category among the set of possible new types using a logit expression. The quantity of new developed space on a land category is the available FAR allocated to the space type multiplied by the land to space conversion rate (10^6 square metres per square kilometer) and factored (divided) by the FAR reduction factor for space type on that land category. New final quantities of developed space are determined by adding the re-developed and the newly developed quantities.

The utility functions specified need to be calibrated in order to work out the transformation quantities when running the computer programme. The data collected from various sources is compiled and put in the data file that would get used for the estimation. The control/.bin file is coded such that we use a single file for one land category. The computer programme for the

Transformation module of the SD model has been coded in 'C' and once the calibration of the utility equations for both redevelopment and new development is complete the equations is used in the programme to compute the quantities of various space types in the 1030 zones of MMR for various points in time for the future.

2. REVIEW OF THE MODEL

The Production, Exchange and Consumption Allocation System (PECAS) framework (Hunt and Ibrahim, 2003; Hunt and Ibrahim, 2005; Hunt, 2007; Abraham and Hunt, 2005) provides a simulation of the land use component of a land use transport interactive modeling system. PECAS is a recently developed generalised approach for simulating spatial economic systems; a generalisation of the spatial input/output (I/O) modeling approach used in the MEPLAN (Hunt and Simmonds, 1993; Hunt et al., 2005) and TRANUS (de la Barra, 1998; Hunt *et al.*, 2005) land use transport modeling systems. It also includes elements of the land use components of the land use transport modeling systems such as DELTA (Simmonds, 1996). PECAS consists of two basic modules, Activity Allocation (AA) Module and Space Development (SD) Module, as shown in Fig 1. The framework considers flows of exchanges of commodities (goods, labour, capital) from production to exchange zones and from exchange zones to consumption zones allocated by using logit models according to exchange prices and generalised costs. These flows of commodities are converted to transport demands that are loaded to networks in order to determine congested travel utilities. Exchange prices determined for space simulate developer actions and hence, result in changes in space. Thus, the activity allocation module (AA module) in the frame-work results in working out new rents for space quantities for the next time step and the space development module (SD module) uses the rent information to work out the new space quantities for that year. The PECAS space development module is based on a set of logit allocation models. These logit models work out the zonal quantities of land-space and floor-space in each category occurring in the period from one point in time to the next. These logit models take into consideration the zonal and model wide space rents and the influence of existing space quantities.

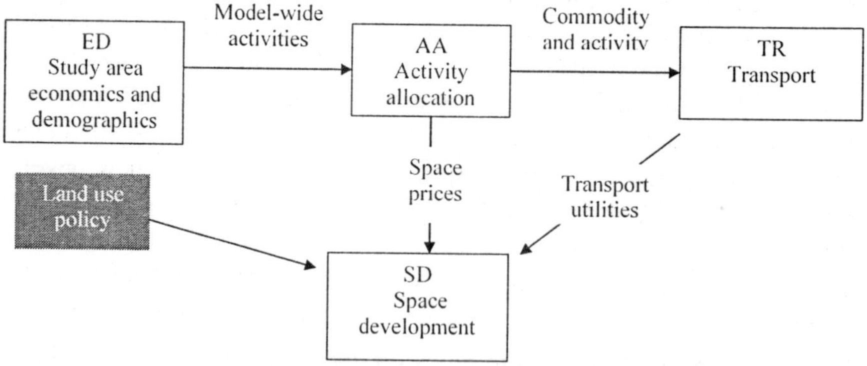

Fig 1: PECAS System of Modules

PECAS or its components are currently being applied in the development of land use transport modeling systems for various North American states and cities like Ohio, Oregon, Sacramento, Calgary and Edmonton and Los Angeles. The methodology has not been applied to any such city of a very dynamic nature like MMR. For applications to such situations of developing countries, special consideration needs to be given to aspects like fast changing economy, heterogeneous setup and speedy floor space and other infrastructure development. The paper describes a methodology adopted to simulate the space development in MMR which would result in the land use change from one point in time to the next (one year). This forms a part of the overall endeavor to develop a running economic spatial model for MMR.

3. THE STUDY REGION AND DATA

The Mumbai Metropolitan Region (MMR) of Maharashtra State, India has been selected as the study region for forming the sub regional land use transport model. A city like Mumbai which is the commercial and financial capital of India, generating about 5% of India's GDP and contributing over one third of the country's tax revenues would be an ideal study region for the development of a regional land use transport model.

MMR covers an area of about 4355 square kilometers, contains 1500 sq km of developable area and supports an overall density of 1300 persons per sq km. It comprises of 1180 villages, 37 census towns, 13 municipal councils and 7 municipal corporations. It has the Arabian Sea coast along its West and South, joins Gujarat in the North and merges with rest of Maharashtra state in the East. The map of MMR showing its sub regions can be seen from MMRDA (2005a). Mumbai, the capital of Maharashtra state and commercial capital of India, is a major constituent of MMR. Greater Mumbai, a major part of MMR as per population, is a well-developed city covering an area of 468 square kilometers. It is the third most populous district in the country (Census, 2001). The rest of MMR, which is in development stage, consists of five municipal corporations, fifteen municipal councils and a number of villages.

With rapid urbanisation and industrialisation during the last three decades in MMR, the population has increased from 9.9 million in 1981 to 18.5 million in 2001. Out of that 17% live on island and 60% in suburbs and New Mumbai. The population of MMR grew at less than 3% per annum during 1991-2001 whereas the vehicles have grown at over 7% per annum contributing to over 50% of cars. The population growth in MMR from 1971 to 2001 based on Mumbai Metropolitan Region Development Authority's (MMRDA) regional plan is shown in Table 1 (MMRDA, 1996a; 2003). The population has led to densities as high as 45,900 persons per sq km in the Island city and above 20,000 per sq. km in suburban Mumbai (Census, 2001). The MMR is well served by major rail and road networks.

3.1 Slum Population and Building Stock

Mumbai Metropolitan Region, in spite of being the commercial hub in India, has 38% of the urban population living in slums in 2001. The same figure for Greater Mumbai part of it is 48.88 %, and Thane is 33%, as per the Mumbai Metropolitan Development Authority (MMRDA) estimates (MMRDA, 2003). Infact, Asia's largest slum, Dharavi is situated in Greater Mumbai sub region of MMR. The concerned authorities like Municipal Corporation of Greater Mumbai (MCGM), Slum Rehabilitation Authority (SRA) and Mumbai Housing and Development Authority (MHADA) are making every possible effort to take the people out of their slum hutments and provide them with affordable accommodation. There is a huge requirement for building stock both in the formal sector as well as that needed for slum resettlements. The data on housing stock in Mumbai is not readily available as most of the housing in Mumbai is managed by private sector, except that for slums. An indicative assessment of housing stock given by MCGM (MCGM, 2005) is reproduced here in Table 2.

The projected increase in total population shown in Table 2 owes partly to the huge in-migration taking place every year in Mumbai due to available job opportunities. As per the data available on existing land use of Greater Mumbai, available land for residential development is only 10 sq km. This suggests that housing sector is severely constrained due to lack of adequate residential land, especially in the city region. To compensate, there is now a sudden change towards rehabilitation of old buildings, and redevelopment of mill land areas. All this has made MMR as one of the most dynamic regions in the world.

3.2 Zoning

MMRDA, with technical assistance from the World Bank under Mumbai Urban Transport Project (MUTP), has undertaken a Comprehensive Transport Study (CTS) for the region titled **"Transportation study for the Region of Mumbai (TransForM)".** The CTS divides MMR into 1030 internal traffic analysis zones (TAZs), out of which 577 zones are in the MCGM area, as shown in Fig 2, and 33 are representing rural areas of MMR. In addition to this 27 external zones are also considered to represent the natural catchment area of the transport links feeding into the study area (MMRDA 2005b). As far as possible the zones have been kept as homogeneous as possible in respect of land use or population composition and trip generation characteristics. The present study considers the same zoning system of CTS for land use zones, since it is the finest available zoning system for MMR and also because the present study uses a part of data that is generated by CTS.

Table 1: Growth of Population in Mumbai Metropolitan Region (MMR)*

Sub-regions of MMR	*Population*			
	1971	*1981*	*1991*	*2001*
Greater Mumbai	5,970,575	8,243,405	9,925,891	11,914,398
North Western Region	30,594	34,940	400,042	989,956
North Eastern Region	625,644	1,441,685	2,549,580	3,828,141
Navi Mumbai Region	—	—	318,447	703,947
Neral Karjat Region	21,549	36,022	69,651	89,340
Panvel Uran Region	39,218	52,241	76,761	217,254
Pen Alibagh Region	23,667	28,823	37,877	49,694
Urban MMR	6,711,247	9,837,116	13,378,249	17,792,730
Rural MMR	1,080,341	1,254,676	1,156,115	1,201,111
Total MMR	7,791,588	11,091,792	14,534,364	18,993,841

* *Source:* MMRDA 2003.

Table 2: Requirement of Slum Housing

Year	*Slum population (Lakh)*	*Total population (Lakh)*	*Formal housing (in lakh)*	*Housing for slums (in lakh)*
2001	69.00	119.14	12.54	12
2010	65.04	129.13	16.03	11
2020	**60.35**	**150.39**	**22.51**	**10**

**Source:* Mumbai City Development Plan 2005-2025, MCGM.

3.3 Data Sets Used for the Study

The data used in the study is mainly secondary data derived mainly from CTS for MMR. The zoning correspondence table and MMR zonal map, quantities of land by category, quantities of floor space by type, and zonal quantities of employment by type are collected from MMRDA. Zonal, current and base, space rents and average space-use rates were got from stamp duty ready reckoners (Kumar et al., 2005), real estate data from internet (Realestatemumbai, 2005), magazines (India Today, 2007), and weekly property news papers. The information about space re-development, for certain areas of MCGM were from MHADA office and Zoning rules (Permitted/acknowledged space types and corresponding max floor area ratios (FARs) by land categories) got from MMRDA

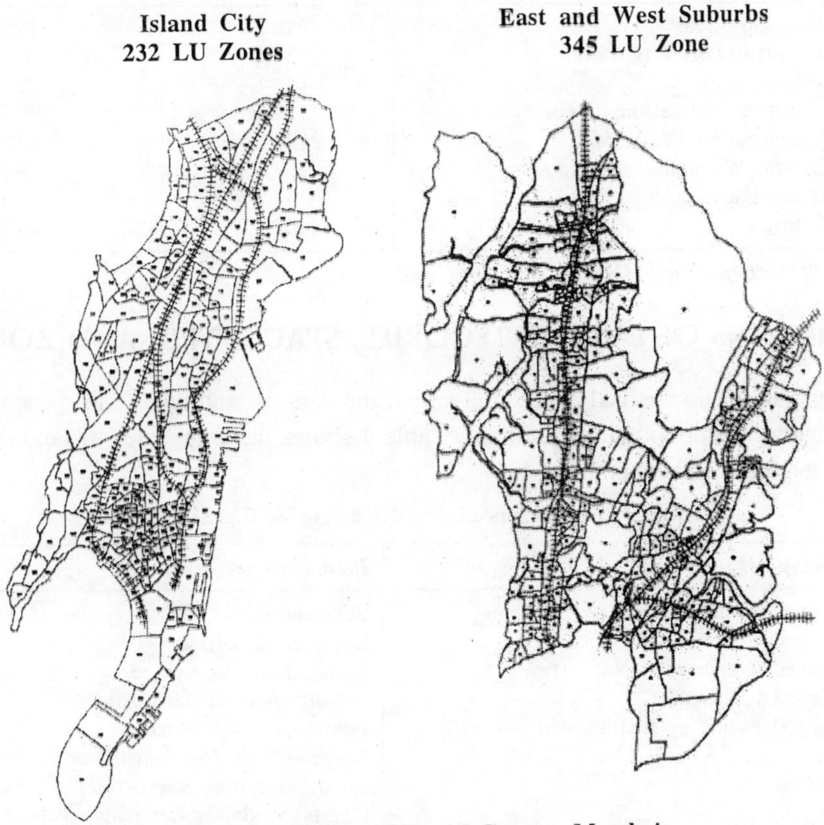

Fig. 1: TA/LU Zoning of Greater Mumbai

regional plan, 1996-2011, (MMRDA 1996b-c), CTS reports (MMRDA, 2005a), and FAR/density calculations on the basis of field observations. Slum details of MMR (slum area and population) have been received from MMRDA's Planning Division/Town and Country Planning, different municipalities of MMR, and SRA for MCGM (SRA, 2005). The transport dis-utilities of various zones like minimum travel times from main CBD and minimum travel distances from nearest railway stations have been determined using TransCad software, knowing the link travel times and travel distances for a layer-based multimodal transport network system.

4. EXISTING LAND USE OF MMR

As per the 2001 land use pattern of MMR, built up land admeasuring 574.76 sqkm was about 13.6% of the total area of the region. This comprised industrial land (2.4%), ports/airport (0.8%) and all other built-up areas (10.4%). The broad existing land use distribution is given in Table 3 (MMRDA, 2005a). More than one-fourth of the land was under forest and plantations (27.9%) while about half of the region has agricultural and open land (50.11%). Coastal wetlands which include mangroves, mud-flats, saltpans account for 6.6% of MMR and water bodies cover about 1.6% of the region.

Table 3: Existing Land Use Distribution for MMR in 2001

S. No.	*Land Use Category*	*Area (Sqkm)*	*Percentage (%)*
1	Built Up Area	438.1	10.41
2	Airport+ Port / Harbour	34.8	0.83
3	Industry	101.8	2.42
4	Forest & Recreational Zone	1177.05	27.98
5	Agriculture+ Waste land	2108.29	50.11
6	Coastal Wetland+ Saltpan	279.87	6.65
7	Water body	67.47	1.6
	Total	**4207.43**	**100.00**

**Source: MMRDA, Report on MMR – Land use, 2005*

5. DEFINITIONS OF LAND CATEGORIES, SPACE TYPES AND ZONING RULES

From the information gained of the study area, the various land types and space types considered in the development of the module is defined. Table 4 shows the categories of land types considered in the development of this module.

Table 4: Definitions of Land Categories for SD Module

S. No.	*Land Type (k)*	*Inclusions*
1.	Developed Residential	Residential
2.	Developed Commercial Office	Commercial office
3.	Developed Commercial Non-office	Commercial non-office
4.	Developed Industrial	Industrial, truck terminal
5.	Developed Public or Institutional	Public or institutional
6.	Green	Recreation, forest, agriculture
7.	Transport	Road, rail, port, airport
8.	Other (etc)	Coastal wetland, salt pans, water bodies

9.	Undeveloped Zoned Residential	New residential
10.	Undeveloped Zoned Commercial office	New commercial office
	Undeveloped Zoned Commercial Non-office	New commercial non-office
11.	Undeveloped Zoned Industrial	New industrial, truck terminal
12.	Undeveloped Zoned Public or Institutional	New public or institutional

The space types for a typical zone is shown in Table 5. The space development/zoning rules are defined for each zone. There are certain space types that are permitted or acknowledged on each type of land category in each zone.

Table 5: Definitions of Space Types for SD Model

S. No.	*Floor Space Type (i)*
1.	Flats/Apartments space
2.	Independent house space
3.	Slums space
4.	Commercial office space
5.	Commercial non-office space (Shops, etc)
6.	Industrial space (Manufacturing industry, warehouse, film industry etc)
7.	Public or institutional space (educational Institutes, entertainment/tourism, public places etc)

The rules applicable to a zone mainly depend on its location in the study area and have been framed mainly based on the information about development controls and regulations given in Regional Plan for MMR, 1996-2011 (MMRDA, 1996b-c). It can be seen that residential land is occupied by three space types, flats/apartments, independent house and slums. Most of the population in MMR lives either in slums or flats/apartments. Overall, more than 37% of the total MMR population lives in slums.

The permitted and acknowledged development actions for a given zone are as shown in Table 6. The space type indicated by 'P' means such space type is actually permitted in the land category in the zone, according to the development rules. The letter 'A' indicates that the space type, although, not permitted in the land category in the zone, as per development plan is 'acknowledged' to get developed.

Table 6: Specification of Zoning, Showing Permitted and Acknowledged Development Actions by Land Type for a Zone

	Space Type (i)	*Flats/ Apart-ments*	*Indepen-dent House*	*Slums*	*Commercial Non-office*	*Commercial Office*	*Indus-trial*	*Public/ Institutional*
		1	2	3	4	5	6	7
Land Type (k)								
Residential	1	P/2	P/1	P/0.9				
Commercial Office	2			A/0.9		P/10		P/ 10
Commercial Non-office	3			A/0.9	P/5			P/10
Industrial	4			A/0.9			P/1	
Public or Institutional	5			A/0.9				P/10
Green	6			A/0.9				
Transport	7			A/0.9				
Other	8		P/1	A/0.9				

Table 6, also shows the maximum FSI/FAR (M_k) values of each space type permitted in a land category in a zone. The concept of FSI/FAR reduction factor is introduced in the model development here which is used especially to reduce the contribution of space of type i to the total actual FAR compared against M_k , the maximum permitted FAR for land of type k in the zone. It can be used, for example, to fit more slums space into a zone already exceeding its maximum FAR. This factor is introduced to have a control on the slum developments in the module.

6. METHODOLOGY AND MODEL SPECIFICATION

Space rents existing in various zones and the proportion of existing space quantities were considered to be the prime factors responsible for instigating the developers for space development and redevelopment. A space type with high zonal and model-wide price in a zone will propel the development of that space type. The existing quantity of a particular space type would also have a positive effect towards its development (Hunt *et al.*, 2003). The transport accessibility available to a zone is bound to have an influence on the development activity taking place in that zone and will have differential effect on the development of various space types. The minimum travel time from the main CBD of the region and the minimum travel distance from the nearest railway station are the transport factors taken into account in the module.

In going from year t to year $t+1$, the module considers each zone z in turn.

If, S_i = quantity of space of type $i(m^2)$, in zone z

then,

$S_i = \sum_k S_{i,k}$ for each i, and

$\sum_k L_k$ = constant for each zone z for all years

where,

$S_{i,k}$ = quantity of space of type i on land of type k (m^2), and

L_K = quantity of land of type k (km^2)

For a zone indexed z in year indexed t the module goes through the following sequential steps:

6.1 Space Transformation/Redevelopment

The quantities of existing space $TS_{i,k,j}$ that are transformed/redeveloped are first determined. Space type i can be transformed into either (*a*) one of the space types that are permitted or acknowledged for land type k according to the zoning for zone z, the space types included in set $I(k)$, or (*b*) its current type i ('transformed' in this case is actually retained). This set of space types that type i in land type k can transform into is designated $J(k)$ and the particular space types included in $J(k)$ are indexed with j

First, the transformation quantities are all initialized to zero:

$TS_{i,k,j} = 0$ for all values of $i \mu I$, $k \mu K$ and $j \mu J$

Then the transformation quantities are determined by allocating the existing space for each type i for land type k among the possible new types j using a logit expression:

$$TS_{i,k,j} = S_{i,k}\left(\frac{e^{UT_{i,k,j}}}{\sum_j \left(e^{UT_{i,k,j}}\right)}\right) \quad \text{... (1)}$$

with

$$UT_{i,k,j} = \alpha^t\left(P_j - PB_j\right) + \theta^t\left(PA_j - PBA_j\right) + \mu^t\left(R_{j,k}\right)^{\pi t} + \phi^t(TTCB_j)$$
$$+ \sigma^t(TDNR_j) + \beta^t{}_{i,j} + \gamma^t{}_{i.j} \quad \text{... (2)}$$

and $$R_{j,k} = \frac{S_{j,k}}{\sum_{j\varepsilon J(k)} S_{j,k}} \quad \text{... (3)}$$

where,

$TS_{i,k,j}$ = quantity of space of type i on land type k that is transformed by redevelopment into space of type j (m2)

i,j = index for space type; I,J = the set of all space types

k = index for land category; K = the set of all land categories

$I(k)$ = set of space types whose development is permitted or acknowledged with land type k according to the zoning rules for the zone z (as shown in Table 6)

$TS_{i,k,j}$ = quantity of space of type i transforming to space of type j in land category k

α^t = zonal price parameter for space transformation allocation

P_j = zonal price (rent) for space type j *(Rs/ m²/year)*

PB_j = zonal base price (rent) for space type j *(Rs/ m²/year)*

θ = modelwide price parameter for space transformation allocation

PA_j = model-wide average price (rent) for space type j *(Rs/ m²/year)*

PBA_j = model-wide average base price (rent) for space type j *(Rs/ m²/year)*

μ^t = inertia multiplicative term for space transformation allocation

$R_{j,k}$ = existing proportion of space type j in land category k

$S_{j,k}$ = quantity of space of type j on land of type k (m^2)

π^t = inertia power term for space transformation allocation

ϕ^t = zonal travel time parameter for space transformation allocation

$TTCB_j$ = Minimum travel time of j zone from main CBD, min

σ^t = zonal travel distace parameter for space transformation allocation

$TDNR_j$ = Minimum travel distance of j zone from nearest railway station, km

$\beta_{i,j}$ = transition constant for permitted transformation from space type i to space type j

$\gamma'_{i,j}$ = transition constant for acknowledged transformation from space type i to space type j

Table 7 shows the various redevelopment/transformation possibilities of space considered for a typical zone in MMR. The utility function shown in Eq 2 is calibrated for all possible space transformations in a zone.

Table 7: Possible Transformation/Redevelopment of Existing Space in MMR

S. No.	*Space Type That is*	*Space Type Transforming to*	*Transforming*
		Residential Land	
1.	Flats/Apartments	Flats/Apartments Independent house Slum	yes no no
2.	Independent House	Flats/Apartments Independent house Slum	yes yes no
3.	Slum	Flats/Apartments Independent house Slum	yes yes yes
		Commercial office Land	
1.	Commercial Office	Commercial office Public/Institutional Slum	yes yes no
2.	Public/Institutional	Commercial office Public/Institutional Slum	yes yes no
3.	Slum	Commercial office Public/Institutional Slum	yes yes yes
		Commercial Non-office Land	
1.	Commercial Non-office	Commercial non-office Public/Institutional Slum	yes yes no
2.	Public/Institutional	Commercial non-office Public/Institutional Slum	yes yes no
3.	Slum	Commercial non-office Public/Institutional Slum	yes yes yes

Industrial Land

1.	Industrial Land	Industrial Slum	yes no
2.	Slum	Industrial Slum	yes yes

Public/Institutional Land

1.	Public/Institutional	Public/Institutional Slum	yes no
2.	Slum	Public/Institutional Slum	yes yes

where,

Q_k = total available FAR for land type k

$M_K = M_K$ = maximum permitted FAR for space of all types combined on land of type k

6.2 Space Updation

The space quantities in a land category are updated after considering the transformation of all existing space types in it.The updated (interim) quantities of space are determined by summing the transformation quantities for the set of all existing space types $i\mu I$ that are transforming into each new space type j for each land type k:

$$XS_{j,k} = \sum_{i\varepsilon I} TS_{i,k,j} \qquad \text{... (4)}$$

where,

$XS_{j,k}$ = updated (interim) quantity of space of type j on land type k (m^2)

6.3 Effective FSI/FAR

The updated (interim) effective FSI/FAR for each land type k for zone based on the updated (interim) quantities of space determined immediately above, is established: The updated (interim) effective FAR for a given land type k is determined by summing the updated (interim) quantities of space for the set of all space types on land type k, each weighted by the FAR reduction factor for the space type on land type k, ($W_{i,k}$) and then dividing that sum by the total quantity of land type k:

$$A_k = \frac{\left(\sum_{i\varepsilon I}\left(W_{i,k} * XS_{i,k}\right)\right)}{L_k} \qquad \text{... (5)}$$

where,

A_k = updated (interim) effective FAR for land type k

$W_{i,k}$ = FAR reduction factor for space of type i on land of type k *(ranges from 0 to 1)*

6.4 Available FSI/FAR in Land Category

To get the potential of development possible in each land category. We determined the total available FAR for each land type *k*.

The total available FAR for a given land type *k* is the maximum specified FAR less the updated (interim) effective FAR:

$$Q_k = [M_k - A_k] \qquad \text{... (6)}$$

6.5 FSI/FAR Allocation

The quantities of available FAR (as undeveloped potential) those are transformed (development) or left untransformed (as a transformation to the same undeveloped type) are now determined. Available FAR can be transformed into either (a) one of the space types that are permitted or acknowledged for land type *k* according to the zoning for zone *z*, the space types included in set *I(k)*, or (b) its current type *i=0* ('transformed' in this case is actually retained as available FAR for the next year and beyond). This set of space types that available FAR can transform into is designated *DI(i)* and the particular space types included in *DI(i)* are indexed with *i*.

The available FAR transformation quantities are determined by allocating the total available FAR for each type *i* for land type *k* among the set of possible new types *iμDI(i)* (including the 'no use' option, which is to be retained as available FAR for subsequent years) using a logit expression.

For each land type *k* in *kμK*:

$$DQ_{i.k} = Q_k \left(\frac{e^{UD_{i.k}}}{\sum_i \left(e^{UD_{i.k}} \right)} \right) \qquad \text{... (7)}$$

with

$$UD_{i,k} = \alpha^d (P_i - PB_i)/W_{i,k} + \theta^d (PA_i - PBA_i)/W_{i,k} + \mu^d (R_{i,k})^{\pi d} + \phi^d (TTCB_i)$$
$$+ \sigma^d (TDNR_i) + \beta^d{}_{i.k} + \gamma^d{}_{i.k} \qquad \text{... (8)}$$

and $$R_{i,k} = \frac{(W_{i,k} * XS_{i,k})}{M_k} \qquad \text{... (9a)}$$

It is for all the permitted and acknowledged space types *i* for land type *k*

$$R_{i,k} = \frac{Q_k}{M_k} \text{ for the 'no use' type (i.e. for } i=0) \qquad \text{... (9b)}$$

Where,

$DQ_{i,k}$ = share of available FAR on land type *k* that is allocated to space type *i*

α^d = zonal price parameter for space development allocation

θ^d = modelwide price parameter for space development allocation

μ^d = inertia multiplicative term for space development allocation

π^d = inertia power term for space development allocation

$\beta^d_{i,k}$ = allocation constant for permitted development of space type *i* for land type *k*

$\gamma^d_{i,k}$ = allocation constant for acknowledged development of space type *i* for land type *k*.

For 'no use' type *(i=0)* the values for P_i, PB_i, PA_i, PBA_i, $TTCB_i$ and $TDNR_i$ are all zero, thereby, removing these terms from the utility function for the 'no use' alternative.

6.6 New Space Development

The quantities of new developed space associated with allocations of available FAR to each space type, are determined now. The quantity of new developed space of type *j* on land type *k* is the available FAR allocated to space type *j* on land type *k* multiplied by the land to space conversion rate (10^6 m² per km²) and factored (divided) by the FAR reduction factor, ($W_{j,k}$) for space of type *j* on that land type *k*.

First, the new developed quantities are all initialised to zero:

$DS_{j,k}$ = 0 for all values of $k\mu K$ and $j\mu J$

Then the new developed quantities are determined by applying the conversion rate and FAR reduction factor to the corresponding $DQ_{i,k}$ value:

$$DS_{j,k} = \frac{\left(DQ_{j,k} * 10^6\right)}{W_{j,k}} \quad \ldots (10)$$

where,

$DS_{j,k}$ = quantity of new developed space of type *j* on land type *k* *(m²)*

6.7 Final Space Quantities

The new final quantities of developed space are determined by adding the redeveloped and the newly developed quantities. These quantities are for the year *t+1*, which becomes the year *t* in the next year.

$$S_{i,k} = \left[XS_{i,k} + DS_{i,k}\right] \quad \ldots (11)$$

where,

$S_{i,k}$ = final quantity of space of type *i* on land type *k* for year *t+1* (m²)

7. CALIBRATION OF SPECIFIED LOGIT MODELS FOR SPACE TRANSFORMATIONS

The utility functions specified in the earlier section need to be calibrated in order to work out the transformation quantities when running the computer programme. These utility functions were specified based on the available data and the theoretical interpretation of the interrelationship between the variables. The parameters need to be determined for each space type transformation (transformation of one into one or more) for each land category in a zone.

The ALOGIT package used for the estimation of parameters. Here in this situation we don't have an absolute discrete choice for estimating the parameters but the proportions of a space type that get transformed into one or more space types. So the normal estimation procedure does not work. Instead an aggregate estimation procedure has to be followed. The data sets prepared for the proportions transforming to different space types for each space type and each land category is prepared and used for the estimation. The current zonal space rents/prices, the current model wide space rents/prices, the base zonal and model wide space rents/prices, the minimum travel time of zones from the main CBD and the minimum travel distance of zones from the nearest railway station were collected from various sources, compiled and put in the data file that would be used for the estimation.

Calibration is basically a process by which the MNL is fitted to the data through the use of maximum-likelihood principles and methodology, and so, the parameters of the utility functions are computed. Moreover, under a trial and retrial procedure the initial functional form of the utility functions can be further adjusted and polished until an optimum fit is achieved. The output evaluation was centred on three pieces of information (Gonzalez-Ayala, 1999):

(*a*) *t-ratio of parameter values*: The t-test simply provides the significance level for rejecting the null hypothesis of having the true parameter value equal zero (rejecting that the parameter has no influence on the utility). A t-test value of ±1.96 means that the parameter is different than zero at a confidence level of about 95%. At a t-test value of ±1.50 the confidence level drops to 85%, which is the lower limit usually recommended to consider a parameter significant.

(*b*) Sign of Parameter Value: The sign of the parameter allows judging if the variable conforms to a priori notions or theory about its overall behaviour with respect to the utility.

(*c*) Rho-squared ($\acute{A}^2$) Index: It provides a value between 0 and 1 as a measure of goodness-of-fit. Values of 0.4 may in fact be excellent fits.

In the present case, the estimations of the utility functions, both for space transformations (for redevelopment) and the FAR allocations (for new development) are in progress.

8. MODEL RUNS AND SPACE FORECASTING

The computer programme for the SD module has been coded in 'C' and once the calibration of the utility equations for both transformation/redevelopment and new development is completed, the equations will be used in the programme to compute the quantities of space types in the 1030 zones of MMR at various points in time for the future. The results of the single/double run will be compared with the space quantity data of 2006/2007 for validation purpose. This may be done separately for redevelopment and new development utility equations. The elasticities of these models will also be checked with respect to price and transport factors.

9. CONCLUSIONS

The paper gives an overview of the PECAS framework. The space development module is taken up thereon. It starts with the information about study area and details of data requirement. The paper then discusses the existing land uses in MMR and goes on to give the specifications about the land categories, space types and zoning rules. The methodology adopted for the SD model development and model specifications are discussed in some detail. The calibration of the logit functions is explained briefly along with the development of module code. Although, the calibrations of utility functions in the logit models of the module are yet to be completed it can still be concluded that PECAS framework provides a very suitable and state-of-the-art methodology for simulating economic spatial systems in highly dynamic regions of developing countries. Given the economic boom in such regions, spatial economic modeling of land use becomes the need of hour. The introduction of FAR/FSI reduction factor gives a good control over the simulation of land use especially in slum infested regions of the world. The developed space development module of MMR will give land use forecasts for every year. By inputting the space prices/rents exogenously it can still work without AA module. This is important because the AA module of PECAS framework may take some time to get developed due to data constrained conditions of developing regions. The proposed methodology can be used to develop space development module that can test various land use transport policy scenarios, in conjunction with a transport model of the region and also on its own.

REFERENCES

Abraham, J.E., Hunt, J.D. (2005), "The Random Utility Theory Foundations of PECAS", *10th International Conference of the Hong Kong Society for Transportation Studies (HKSTS 2005)*, Dec 2005, Hong Kong.

Census of India (2001), Series 28: Maharashtra: Provisional Population Totals. Registrar General, 2A Mansingh Road, New Delhi, India.

de la Barra, T. (1998), "The mathematical and algorithmic structure of TRANUS". Unpublished paper available at http://www.modelistica.com.

Gonzalez-Ayala, S. (1999), "Mode Split Model Application". Tech memo on Development of Travel Demand and Mobile Source Emissions Models for Base Year 1996, Juarez, Instituto Municipal De Investigacion Y Planeacion, Juarez.

Hunt, J.D. (2007), "PECAS Theoretical Formulation", Book in preparatory stage.

Hunt, J.D., Abraham, J. E. (2005), "Design and Implementation of PECAS: A Generalized System for Allocating Economic Production, Exchange and Consumption Quantities," Imprint ELSEVIER, Integrated Land-Use and Transportation Models, Behavioural Foundations, Edited by Martin Lee-Gosselin and Sean Doherty, ISBN 0-08-044669-8, Hardbound, July 2005. www.elsevier.com/locate/ISBN/0080446698 (accessed on 05-06-2006).

Hunt, J.D., Kriger, D. S. and Miller, E.J. (2005), "Current Operational Urban Land-use-Transport Modelling Frameworks: A Review". *Transport Reviews*,Vol.25, No.3, pp.329-376, May 2005.

Hunt, J.D., Abraham, J.E. (2003), "Design And Application Of The PECAS Land Use Modelling System", *8th International Conference on Computers in Urban Planning and Urban Management (CUPUM)*, Sendai, Japan, May 27-29, 2003.

Hunt, J.D. and Simmonds, D.C. (1993), "Theory and application of an integrated land-use and transport modeling framework", *Environment and Planning*, Vol.20B, pp.221-224.

India Today (2007), "Buyer's Guide To Homes in Mumbai," April-Sept 2007.

Kumar, S., and Gupta, S. (2005), Stamp duty ready reckoner and market value of flats in Mumbai. The Architects Publishing Corporation of India, Malad East, Mumbai, India.

MCGM (2005), Mumbai City Development Plan 2005-2025, MCGM, Mumbai, India.

MMRDA (2005a), Report on MMR Land Use. MUTP, through LEA International Ltd. Canada and LEA Associates South Asia Pvt. Ltd, India, December 2005.

MMRDA (2005b), Report on Household Survey Preliminaries: Sampling Framework, Questionnaire Design and Survey Methodology, volume II, July 2005, MUTP, through LEA International Ltd. Canada and LEA Associates South Asia Pvt. Ltd, India.

MMRDA (2003), Population and Employment Profile of Mumbai Metropolitan Region http://www.mmrdamumbai.org/.

MMRDA (1996a), Population Growth, Characteristics and Projections. Chapter-03, Draft Regional Plan of MMR: 1996-2011, Planning Division, MMRDA, http://www.mmrdamumbai.org/

MMRDA (1996b). Development Control. Chapter-14, Draft Regional Plan of MMR: 1996-2011, Planning Division, MMRDA, http://www.mmrdamumbai.org/ .

MMRDA (1996c), Development Control Regulations for MMR. Chapter-15, Draft Regional Plan of MMR: 1996-2011, Planning Division, MMRDA, http://www.mmrdamumbai.org/.

Realestatemumbai (2005), "Residential and Office space prices/Rents in Mumbai", available at http://www.realestatemumbai.com/.

Simmonds, D.C.(1996), "DELTA Model Design", David Simmonds Consultancy, Cambridge UK.

SRA (2005), Resettlement and Rehabilitation of Slum Dewellers in Mumbai, Griha Nirman Bhavan, Bandra, Mumbai, India (http://www.sra.gov.in/).

Wegener, M. and Frurst, F. (1999), "Land-use transport interaction: State of the art". TRANSLAND Integration of Transport and Land Use Planning, Work package 2 Deliverable D2a. Institute of Spatial Planning, University of Dortmund.

11

OMNI-BUSES IN DELHI — CHARACTERISTICS, ISSUES AND POTENTIAL ROLE AS A PUBLIC TRANSPORT MODE

Sanjay Gupta
Amit Bhatt

ABSTRACT

In Delhi, public transportation demand is met by buses provided by the Delhi Transport Corporation (DTC) and private buses. Conventional public transport supply has not kept pace with the demand. As a result, para-transit systems in the form of mini buses, omni buses, auto rickshaws and cycle rickshaws have evolved over time to supplement the public transport supply to bridge the gap. In March 2001, Hindustan Motors introduced its rural transport vehicle on city operations as omni buses. Though, these vehicles are registered as contract carriages, they are operating as stage carriage vehicles. This paper is based on an empirical study carried out on three representative routes in Delhi to fully appreciate the operational characteristics of omni buses and assess their role in the public transport scenario of Delhi.

1. INTRODUCTION

In Delhi, presently about 60% of the total transport demand is met by public transport comprising of DTC & private buses. Conventional public transport supply has not kept pace with the demand. As a result, variants of public transport such as mini buses, auto and other Intermediate Public Transport (IPT) modes are supplementing conventional public transport supply. In March 2001, the Supreme Court banned all non-CNG vehicles from public transport operation in Delhi, creating a severe shortage public transport supply. The problem for the commuter intensified due to slow conversion rate of old diesel buses. Viewing a potential market — Hindustan Motors re-launched its rural transport vehicle (RTV) in March 2001, which became a huge hit in the market. The success of RTV made Mahindra & Mahindra launch its 'Hari Bhari' (a prototype) in October 2001. Presently, omni buses, though, registered as contract carriage, are performing stage carriage operations in Delhi.

2. REVIEW OF GLOBAL EXPERIENCES ON OMNI BUSES AND SUBSCRIPTION BUSES

The Omni bus is a motor vehicle constructed or adapted to carry more than six persons excluding the driver. These buses operate as normal stage carriage buses on a fixed route variable time scenario. While not on fixed time and variable route operation, they run generally as school buses and chartered buses. Omni buses were first started in 1828 in France. They were called 'voiture Omnibus' — meaning 'A Carriage for Every One.' The word 'Omni' is derived from a Latin word 'Omnis' which means "All". The Omni bus was brought to England by George Schllibeer — a coach maker. Early Omni buses were long, narrow coaches pulled by horses and had a seating capacity of 18 passengers. Omni buses in India are running in various parts of the country under private sector operations. The private operations, which essentially started as tourist package services, have evolved over the last two decades into transport services. The change was driven by the business opportunity such a service presented as well as the fact that tour packages were unviable. The omni-bus operation has emerged as a major industry and an avenue for employment in the country besides being a major source of income for the auto-components industry. However, their operation in many parts of the country are not legal as the state governments have not accorded them legal status to operate fearing competition to the State run buses. The operators, who are not licensed to operate transport services, often operate under the garb of package tour operators, with a contract carriage permit.

The International experience

Maunder and Hbara (1996) in their study observed that the privately operated commuter omni buses, which got introduced in Harare in 1993 owing to deregulation of public transport, improved the quality and level of service in Harare. The fleet expansion and the increase in passenger carrying capacity ensured that passenger waiting times decreased and the expansion of routes benefitted the passengers who previously were not provided with a service. Modern omni buses replaced the emergency taxis as a principal travel mode in Harare. On the negative side, it was seen that fares tended to rise especially during the busiest times of the day and congestion at major boarding locations in the city center increased thereby, affecting other road users and the environment, in general.In another study carried out in Cairo on micro bus services, it was observed that in order to meet the transport demand in the city of Cairo small buses in the form of 'Micro Buses', which had seating capacity less then 17 were given the licence to operate. These buses catered to almost 25% of the total demand in cities. It was also observed that only 40% of the drivers had authentic licence to operate the buses. The rapid increase in the microbus market highlighted the poor quality of the public services. Kiran et.al. in a study on subscription bus services in the U.S found that these were basically used for work trips and confirmed to fixed work schedule. It was also noted that very few provided door to door services and seating was of prime importance. In another study of subscription bus services in the US, it was observed that these appealed to every class of the society. These were found to be used for Central Business District (CBD) and non-C.B.D. work trips. It was found that, they were unable to penetrate the short trip category (less than 10 miles).

The Indian Experience

A number of studies have been carried out to assess the role of subscription buses particularly in Delhi. Sachdeva (1982) in his study on subscription buses in Delhi found that they play a vital role in school trips besides offering a high level of service quality. Sarna et.al. (1990) in their study on, chartered buses in Delhi observed that these buses played a significant and supplemental role in public transport and account for four percent of total public transport trips. Nearly 97% of the trips were performed for work purposes. It was found that their average trip length was higher (13.6 km) compared to conventional buses(7.5 km). It was also observed that the people in the higher or the middle income group patronised them. In another study on subscription buses carried out by Venkatesh (1997), it was observed that the high-income group (Rs. 6,001 – Rs. 9,000 per month) patronized them. It was also seen that female patronage was about 40% as compared to 14% in conventional buses. The average trip length by these services was 22km.

3. STUDY AREA CHARACTERISTICS

Delhi, the national capital of India, with an estimated present population of 15 million and an urbanised area of nearly 800 sq. km has emerged as one of the fastest growing metropolitan cities in the country. The city has recorded significant increase in population since independence. The population has increased from 1.74 million in 1951 to 13.78 million by the year 2001 .The share of urban population too has increased from 82% in 1951 to 93% in 2001.The period between 1981 and 2001 has seen a phenomenal increase in the growth of vehicles and traffic in Delhi. The population of vehicles (four wheelers, three wheelers and two wheelers) has increased from 5.13 lakhs in 1981 to 32.38 lakhs in 2001. The bus population increased from 19167 in 1990 to 40692 in the year 2000. The average household income was Rs. 7,737 per month in 2001 while Rs. 1,040 per month was expended on transport by an average household in the city.

There has been a rise in per capita trip rate (excluding walk trips) from 0.72 in 1981 to 0.87 in 2001. Keeping in view the population growth, this translates into an increase from 4.5 million trips to around 11.8 million trips. Based on the rate of increase in the number of trips between 1981 and 2001, it is estimated that the total trips would rise to 28 million by the year 2021, including 25.7 million motorized trips and 2.3 million non-motorised trips. The analyses of model split trend shows that 60% of trips are performed by public transport *i.e.*, bus, 28 % of trips are performed by personalised modes while 12% trips are performed by other modes. The average trip length for buses has increased from 8.6 km to 10.66 km in 1994 while that for cars has gone up from 8.1 km to 11.28 km during the same period. The average trip time in 2001 was 30 minutes.

4. PUBLIC TRANSPORT SYSTEM OF DELHI

In Delhi, public transport is supplied mainly by State owned Delhi Transport Corporation (DTC) and private operators (Blue line). DTC had an average fleet of 3126 buses in 2002-03 and carried 25.16 lakh passengers daily. It is operating interstate services in six states, namely Haryana, Punjab, Uttar Pradesh, Himachal Pradesh, Rajasthan, and Jammu & Kashmir besides Union Territory of Chandigarh.. The Corporation is operating about 133 Interstate Routes with about 727 buses. It has deployed about 2154 CNG buses for the city services. The growth trends of DTC supply are summarised in Table 1 below:

Table 1: Growth Trends in Delhi Transport Corporation Bus Fleet

Items	*1990-91*	*1995-96*	*2001-2002*
Average fleet (nos.)	4403	3206	2921
Fleet Utilisation (%)	84.53	53.71	71.68
Vehicle Utilisation (Kms. per day)	219	269	211
Load Factor (%)	100.79	84.91	82.66
Passengers carried/day(lakhs)	—	15.79	23.4
Passengers carried /bus daily	—	917	1117

Source: DTC Statistical Handbook.

It is observed that while the fleet of DTC has come done over the years, the passengers carried per day have gone up over the years.

The growth of RTV's and 'Hari Bhari' comprising the omni bus system had been negligible prior to March 2001. The major thrust came after March 2001, when the Supreme Court banned all non-CNG vehicles and also after March 2002 when the conversion of diesel buses actually started. Fig 1 shows the growth trend (month-wise) in these vehicles in Delhi between Jan 2001 to July 2002.

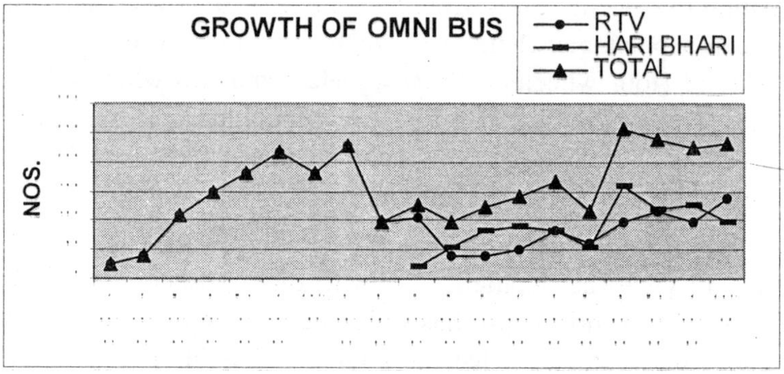

Fig. 1: Growth Trend in Omni Buses in Delhi

The technical details of RTV and Hari Bhari are given in Table 2 below:

Table 2: Technical Details of RTV and Hari Bhari

Technical Details	*RTV*	*Hari Bhari*
Engine type	CNG-4 Cylinder	CNG-4 Cylinder
Fuel	CNG	CNG
Capacity (c.c)	1800	1800
Overall length (mm)	4625	5100
Overall width (mm)	1700	1750
Overall height (mm)	2480	2750
Gross vehicle weight (kg)	3400	3490
Seating (Nos.)	14+1	14+1+10

No. of cylinders	2	2
Cost - ex. Show room (Rs. in lakhs)	5.25 - 5.75	5.45
Availability as per fuel	CNG, Diesel , Petrol	CNG, Diesel , Petrol

5. DATA BASE

Since there was no data available pertaining to Omni bus operations, network (route) and the type of usage of Omni bus, a number of field studies were conducted for which a two-stage survey process was adopted. In the first stage, a reconnaissance survey was conducted on Omni bus routes, while the second stage involved detailed surveys. Eighty routes were identified. Major origin and destination points identified include — Azadpur, AIIMS, Connaught Place, Dilshad garden, ISBT, Janakpuri, New Seemapuri, Shahadra, Lajpat Nagar, Nehru place, Mehrauli, Lal Quila, ITO. For the second stage, field studies, three sections were selected on the following criteria:

- Routing pattern
- Density along the corridors
- Land use along the corridors

The three routes selected were:

- Dilshad Garden to Connaught Place (18 Km)
- Khanpur to Lal Quila (16 Km)
- AIIMS to Azadpur and Azadpur to Sarai kale khan (27 Km)

A number of surveys were conducted which are briefly described below:

On-Board Survey

For On-Board survey, one round trip during peak hour (9-11am) and off peak hour (1-3 p.m.) respectively were conducted both for Omni as well as conventional buses.

User Survey

A samples of 112 users were interviewed for the Omni bus user survey whereas, for conventional bus user survey a sample of 100 was taken up.

Operators Survey

A total of forty Omni bus and thirty conventional bus operators were interviewed for operator's survey.

6. SYSTEM PERFORMANCE CHARACTERISTICS

On-Board Survey

The On- board survey provided information pertaining to system performance across Omni bus and Blue line buses. An attempt has been made to analyse the system performance in terms of:

- two system operating in same environment
- Omni bus across two routes.
- Across two time bands on the same route of Omni buses.

Table 3 gives the salient findings from the survey. While comparing the system performance across two services, namely, omni buses and blue lines on a selected route, it is observed from the Table that compared to Omni buses, the conventional buses (Blue lines) had four times more density of stops/km resulting in better accessibility and consequent higher passenger density per km. The earning per km. which is a function of passenger density, was more in case of Blue lines compared to omni buses. Though, the average dwell time in omni buses was higher compared to blue line buses, the average journey speed was still higher in case of omni buses largely owing to higher running speeds achieved by them.

When comparing the performance of omni buses across routes, it was found that the earning per km was fairly stable at around Rs 11 which dropped by nearly 50% taking into account the off-peak operation.

Table 3: Salient System Performance Characteristics

Parameters (Per Bus)	*Across system (omni buses)*	*Across system (Blue line)*	*Across route (Omni bus)*	*Across time (Omni bus)*
Stops per km	.55	2.05	1.69	1.11
Inter stop spacing (km)	1.8	0.71	1.05	.95
Passenger demand per stop	2.4	5.35	1.3	.8
Passenger per km	1.3	7.5	2.18	.89
Earning per km	11.11	37.5	10.90	6.1
Avg. dwell time at stop (sec)	25	19.28	27	32.5
Avg. journey speed (km/hr)	26.4	21.25	24	24.75
Avg. running speed (km/hr)	37.45	32.12	32.62	34.12

7. USER CHARACTERISTICS

Omni bus user and conventional bus user information were analysed in terms of personal attributes such as gender,age, education, income and trip characteristics (Table 4). It can be seen from the Table that there is a striking similarity in the attributes of both the user sets. There is a marginal difference in the average trip length of omni bus users(11.4 km) compared to 10.7 km in conventional bus users. The average trip time is also lesser in case of omni bus users (32.7 min.) compared to conventional bus users (38.4 min.) which to some extent is a determinant in patronizing omni bus users. It was also found that 21% of Omni bus users have shifted from personalised mechanised mode which exhibits its potential in encouraging modal shifts in favour of public transport.

Table 4: Salient Characteristics of Omni Bus and Conventional Bus Users

Parameters	*Omni bus User*	*Conventional Bus User*
Gender(% males)	77	78
Education level	Graduate and above 70%	Graduate and above 65%
Average age (yr.)	30.50	30.35
Average income (Rs)	9991	9980
Average trip length (km)	11.41	10.73
Average trip cost (Rs)	6.92	5.83
Average travel time (min)	32.77	38.35
Previous mode of travel	Bus 75%, Two wheeler and car 21%	—
Reasons for choosing the system	Comfort 62%, time saving 58%	cheap 74%

8. OPERATIONAL CHARACTERISTICS

The operator survey provided useful information relating to vehicle utilisation, route length, dead kilometrage and staffing pattern across two bus systems. Table 5 gives the results from the survey.

Table 5: Salient Operational Characteristics

Parameters	*Omni Bus*	*Conventional Buses*
Vehicle utilisation(km)	185	225
Average route length(km)	18	21
Average Dead Km	1.5	7.5
Average employees/bus	2.25	3.5

It can be observed that conventional buses have a higher vehicle utilisation (225 km) in excess of 22 % compared to omni buses (185 km). However, conventional buses have a higher average dead kilometrage (7.5 km) compared to Omni bus (1.5 km) indicating the efforts by omni bus operators to keep the non remunerative expenses to the least. Further, the staffing ratio is also in favour of omni buses when compared to conventional buses.

From the analysis, it can be summed up that omni buses are highly un-regulated as seen from the spurt in their growth & concentration of their operations on select routes only.All the Omni buses have contract carriage license but majority of them perform stage carriage operation. Moreover, they don't have any schedule of operation. On the positive side, they offer a high degree of maneuverability with respect to their design, hence, operate effectively in congested areas. They can provide competition to existing public transport thereby, increasing its efficiency.They have the potential to encourage modal shift towards public transport. They have the potential in offering flexibility to operation, *i.e.*, they can be used as public transport mode or school buses or chartered buses or a combination of the above.

9. ASSESSMENT OF THE ROLE OF OMNI BUSES

The role of the Omni bus has been assessed in terms of enhancement in public transport fleet, meeting mobility needs, encouraging modal shifts, alleviating traffic congestion and savings in energy and transport costs. The gross total outputs of omni buses have been estimated based on the application of interpolated values of the sample surveys on the total bus fleets. These aspects are briefly described as under:

(*i*) The estimated share of seat km offered by omni buses increased from 6.6lakh km (0.76%) in April 2001 to 151.2 lakh km (14%) in Dec. 2002 thereby indicating its role in augmenting the public transport supply in the city.

(*ii*) The total estimated trips carried by omni buses in Dec. 2002 was 8.6 lakh/day out of the estimated public transport trips of 78.8 lakh/day thereby, accounting for a share of 11% which attributes its role as a public transport service provider.

(*iii*) Omni buses contributed to a modal shift of 21 % from personalised mechanised modes towards it signifying its potential role in encouraging modal shifts from personalised vehicles in favour of public transport.

(*iv*) Assuming that 21% modal shift is applicable at the city level, it is estimated that the introduction of omni buses have a potential to reduce about 1.12 lakh vehicles and consequently 12.86 lakh vehicle km of private vehicles per day from the city roads indicating the potential role of omni buses in alleviating traffic congestion to some degree besides contributing to savings in energy and reducing pollution costs.

(*v*) Omni buses play largely a supplementary role, with very little of basic role along the case study corridors as shown in Table 6.

Table 6: Role of Omni Buses

	Dilshad Garden to C.P.	*Lal Quila to Khanpur*	*AIIMS to Azadpur*
Peak hour	Supplementary	Supplementary	Supplementary
Off peak hour	Supplementary	Supplementary	Supplementary
After 8 p.m.	Basic	Supplementary	Supplementary
Overall	Supplementary/Basic	Supplementary	Supplementary

10. CONCLUSIONS

Our study of Omni bus performance in Delhi reveals that it is performing the role of conventional public transport system reflected from its high vehicle utilisation (185 km) and long route length (18 km). Their operations are restricted to high-density public transport demand corridors. However, the system suffers from drawback in terms of its unregulated growth, lack of safety concern and profit oriented approach from its operators. Though, the Omni buses have contract carriage license but majority of them perform stage carriage operation. Moreover, they don't have any schedule of operation. On the positive side, they offer high degree of maneuverability with respect to their design, hence, operate effectively in congested areas. A comparative analysis across the systems operating in the same environment reveals that though, conventional buses outscore the Omni buses in terms of passenger serviced per km and earnings per km owing largely due to its capacity. Yet Omni buses are better off in terms of operating speed, comfort and convenience.

The study concludes that Omni buses have a distinct role to play in the public transport scenario of Delhi in terms of enhancing public transport supply, meeting mobility requirements of public transport users, encouraging modal shift towards public transport, alleviating traffic congestion and savings in energy and pollution cost. They also provide flexibility of either being used as a public transport mode for stage carriage operations or on contract service for educational trips or employee trips for institutions. As a thumb rule, these buses have the potential to operate on routes of about 20km length, serving medium to high density residential development and medium to high income zones.

In the light of the potential role of Omni buses the following recommendations are proposed to enhance its role further:

(*i*) Streamlining the unregulated growth of Omni buses and enhancing it in the larger interest of the public transport system of Delhi.

(*ii*) There is big potential role for this system to act as a complementary mode particularly in large residential areas providing feeder services to and from line haul transit systems such as Metro and HCBS.

(*iii*) There is a need to evolve appropriate policies pertaining to planning, development and management of omni buses in Delhi so that these services can co- exist along with conventional buses.

REFERENCES

Maunder, D.A.C. and Mbara, T.C. (1996), Omni Bus Service in Harare, TRRL Report, U.K.

Sarna, A.C.and Agarwal, I.C. (1990), Travel Characteristics of Chartered Buses in Delhi, Indian Highways, April 1990.

Sachdeva, Y.P. (1982), Assessment of the Role of Subscription Bus Services in Delhi, Unpublished Thesis, Department of Transport Planning, School of Planning and Architecture, New Delhi.

Venkatesh, V. (1997), Subscription Bus Service in Delhi: Characteristic, Issues and Potential, Unpublished Thesis, Department of Transport Planning, School of Planning and Architecture, New Delhi.

Bhatt, Amit (2003), Role of Omni Buses in Public Transport: Case Study Delhi, Unpublished Thesis, Department of Transport Planning, School of Planning and Architecture, New Delhi.

12

FINANCIAL CHALLENGES FACING URBAN TRANSPORT UNDERTAKINGS: A STUDY OF KOLHAPUR MUNICIPAL TRANSPORT (KMT)

P. S. Kamble

ABSTRACT

Transport facilities, in general, and road transport means, in particular, play a very vital role in speeding up the process of socio-economic growth of the areas under their jurisdiction. Their role in transporting necessary productive resources, human resources as well as marketing facilities is a vital one. Our analysis reveals that the financial position of the KMT which is significantly weak and unsound has resulted in inefficient, inadequate and inferior quality transport services in Kolhapur city. The study of financial challenges before the city transport undertakings, in general, and the KMT, in particular, is vast with a wide scope and many dimensions. The present study is a small attempt in this direction.

1. INTRODUCTION

The concentration of economic growth and socio-economic overheads in urban areas has been responsible for the rapid urbanisation and growth of cities and metropolitan cities. The centralisation of social services like education, health, as well as employment opportunities is a cause responsible for the migration of population from rural areas to urban areas and thereby, the growth of cities. Transport facilities, in general, and road transport means, in particular, play a very vital role in speeding up the process of socio-economic growth of the areas under jurisdiction. Their role in transporting necessary productive resources, human resources as well as marketing facilities is a vital one.

Urban transport facilities are mainly provided by means of two wheelers, four wheelers, six wheelers such as scooters, motorcycles, auto rickshaws, tempos, trucks, buses and others. City buses play a pivotal role in providing urban transport facilities, when we take into consideration their scope and the number of beneficiaries. Its social value and significance have a special place. Urban road transport facilities are provided mainly through city buses by the urban local bodies or State Transport Corporations.

Transport facilities are a crucial public utility, which provides citizens access to work places, educational institutions and given employers enlarged labour force. They also enable better land use and dispersal of activities and curb spatial concentration.

The efficiency, quality and scope of urban transport facilities are affected by the financial position and financial challenges by city public transport undertakings. It is a fact today, that in Maharashtra out of 13 city public undertaking, no single unit was found to be making profits.

In 2007, the total economic losses of all the city public transport agencies in Maharashtra stood at Rs. 120.81 crore per annum, which run about 5704 city buses on the road. Kolhapur Municipal Corporation (KMC) that runs Kolhapur Municipal Transport (KMT) as its urban transport unit faced a loss of Rs. 2.88 crore in the same year. It was in deficit especially in terms of the revenue deficit. This provides the backdrop to study the financial position, performances and challenges before urban transport units, in general, in India, and particularly, in Maharashtra.

Kolhapur Municipal Transport (KMT) is an important city transport undertaking of the Kolhapur Municipal Corporation (KMC) in Western Maharashtra . Some of the striking features of the finances of the KMT showed an urgent need for a detailed analysis. The income of the KMT from traffic has been declining from 96% of revenue receipts in 2003-04 to 91% in 2007-08. The earnings from other sources were meagre, and showed wide fluctuations. Consequently, the dependence of the KMT on the Kolhapur Corporation has been growing rapidly. Likewise, the KMT has failed to meet its revenue expenditure out of its revenue receipts. It is diverting a part of its capital receipts towards revenue expenditure. Its Revenue deficit was Rs. 353.34 lakh in 2003-04, which significantly rose to Rs. 610.61 lakh in 2007-08.

It is against this overall background, the present research paper tries to examine the finances of the Kolhapur Municipal Transport (KMT), an undertaking of the Kolhapur Municipal Corporation (KMC) for the period 2003-04 to 2007-08. The objective is to examine the financial challenges before the KMT and suggest measures, which will facilitate it to be placed on a sound financial footing that is necessary to provide adequate, efficient, quality city transport facilities for the Kolhapur city.

2. HYPOTHESIS OF THE STUDY

The present study endeavours to test the following hypothesis:

A sound financial position is a pre-requisite for efficient, qualitative, adequate and on time supply of the transport facilities by a city transport undertaking.

3. OBJECTIVES OF THE STUDY

The major objectives of the present study are as follows:

1. To study the overall financial position of Kolhapur Municipal Transport (KMT) during period of 2003-04 to 2007-08.
2. To examine the expenditure of KMT during the same period.
3. To analyse the revenue aspect of the finances of KMT.

4. To identify the financial challenges before the KMT and suggest measures to overcome them.

4. DATA BASE AND RESEARCH METHODOLOGY

The study fully relies on secondary data collected from the budgetary documents of the KMT, its administrative reports, and the publications of the KMC. The secondary data was classified and tabulated in the light of the hypothesis of the study and its major objectives. The tabulated data was processed by employing suitable statistical tools such as compound growth rate (CGR), simple growth rate (SGR), ratio analysis, standard deviation, correlation, regression, so as to draw the interferences, which will enable us to view clearly the financial position of the KMT and also to identify the challenges before it. The study has made use of computer software packages such as Excel, SPSS for the necessary processing of the data.

5. FINANCES OF THE KMT: AN ANALYSIS

The analysis of the finances of KMT enables us to highlight the financial challenges faced by KMT, an urban transport undertaking of the Kolhapur Municipal Corporation (KMC). Urbanisation and industrialisation in India are taking place at a rapid rate. However, this does not seem to be matched with the supply levels of public transport due to financial constraints.

5.1 Overall Financial Position of KMT

A study of the overall financial position of KMT is useful in understanding the extent of its financial strength or weakness. The necessary data is presented in Table 1.

Table 1: Overall Financial Position of KMT

(Rs. in lakh)

Year	*Total Revenue*	*Total Expenditure*	*Surplus (+)/Deficit (-)*
2003-04	2218.22	2572.97	- 354.75
2004-05	2607.76	2969.31	- 361.55
2005-06	2832.14	3008.38	- 176.24
2006-07	3587.30	4415.06	- 827.76
2007-08	2971.85	3582.61	- 610.76
CGR	9.4	11.16	21.10

Source: Budgets of the KMT.
Note: CGR: Annual Compound Growth Rate.

The data in Table 1 clearly reveals that the financial position of KMT worsened during the period from 2003-04 to 2007-08 especially during the latter years. Its total expenditure was always in excess of the total revenue. Likewise, its total expenditure grew more rapidly than its total revenue. This resulted in the problem of deficit in KMT. The growth in its deficit was more rapid than the growth in total expenditure as well as total revenue. The mean as well as standard deviation values were significantly higher of the total expenditure of the KMT than its total revenue and budgetary deficit as well. Rs. 3309.67 lakh, Rs. 2843.45 lakh and Rs. 466.21 lakh were the mean values respectively. Their values of standard deviation stood at Rs. 715.15 lakh, Rs. 504.08 lakh and Rs. 254.50 lakh respectively.

5.2 Financial Position of the KMT on Revenue Account

The overall budgetary deficit of the KMT consisted of the Revenue deficit and Capital deficit. The extent of Revenue deficit of the KMT is shown in Table 2.

Table 2: Financial Position of KMT on Revenue Account

(Rs. in lakh)

Year	*Total Revenue*	*Total Expenditure*	*Surplus (+)/Deficit (–)*
2003-04	1859.98	2213.42	- 353.34
2004-05	2242.57	2603.80	- 361.23
2005-06	2683.52	2869.29	- 185.77
2006-07	2899.80	3727.86	- 828.06
2007-08	2483.50	3094.11	- 610.61
CGR	8.71	10.83	21.21

Source: Same as of Table 1.

It was found that KMT could not incur its Revenue expenditure in accordance with Revenue receipts. Its Revenue expenditure grew more rapidly than increase in its Revenue receipts. As a result, KMT faced the problem of the Revenue deficit, which also grew more rapidly than the growth of Revenue receipts as well as Revenue expenditure. The problem of the Revenue deficit and its growing magnitude indicates the worsening financial position of KMT, as far as current Revenue and Expenditure of KMT is concerned. KMT was mainly depending upon the KMC to meet its revenue deficit. It took financial assistance from the KMC to the tune of Rs. 50 lakh in 2003-04, which rapidly rose to Rs. 300 lakh in 2007-08. Likewise, KMT has also diverted a part of Capital receipts to meet the Revenue deficit. On an average, KMT's Revenue expenditure, Revenue receipts and Revenue deficit stood at Rs. 2,901.69 lakh, Rs. 2,433.87 lakh and Rs. 487.80 lakh respectively during 2003-04 to 2007-08, with significant standard deviation values of Rs. 566.36 lakh, Rs. 402.43 lakh and Rs. 252.08 lakh respectively. A correlation analysis of the problem and of revenue deficit of the KMT with expenditure reveals that revenue deficit was positively and highly correlated with the revenue expenditure (.77) and negatively with the Revenue receipts (.47). The regression analysis showed that rapidly revenue expenditure (Beta 2.24) was an important determinant of the revenue deficit of the KMT.

5.3 Financial Position of KMT on Capital Account

The transactions of the KMT on Capital account are useful in strengthening the ability and quantity as well as quality of transport services. But such transactions should be in the proper direction. The financial situation of the KMT on Capital account is presented in Table 3. It is a good thing that the growth of Capital receipts as well as Capital expenditure was rapid in comparison with the Revenue receipts and expenditure. But it must be noted that the size of both the capital receipts and expenditure was small.

Table 3: Financial Position of KMT on Capital Account

(Rs. in lakh)

Year	*Total Revenue*	*Total Expenditure*	*Surplus (+)/Deficit (–)*
2003-04	358.84	359.55	– 0.71
2004-05	365.19	365.51	– 0.32
2005-06	148.62	139.09	+ 9.53
2006-07	687.50	687.20	+ 0.30
2007-08	488.35	488.50	– 0.15
CGR	13.30	13.25	

Source: Same as of Table 1.

From the data in Table 3, it is observed that the growth in capital receipts as well capital expenditure of the KMT was rapid and significant. But the striking feature of the transactions on Capital account was that KMT had a deficit that was meagre and surplus was somewhat significant. This reveals that transactions of the KMT on capital account have not paid much attention to promote the quantum and quality of the city transport facilities because the size of expenditure was small with considerable fluctuations. The mean value of capital deficit (Rs. 1.73 lakh) was meagre, but of capital expenditure (Rs. 407.97 lakh) and capital receipts (Rs. 409.70 lakh) it was considerable. The capital expenditure of the KMT deviated more than the (Rs. 200.56 lakh) capital receipts (Rs. 197.54 lakh) and capital deficit (Rs. 4.37 lakh) as shown by the standard deviation. The correlation analysis revealed that capital deficit was positively correlated with capital expenditure and positively with the capital receipts with more or less the same degree of (.69, 68) association.

5.4 Composition of Total Revenue of KMT

The study of the composition of Total revenue of the KMT is useful in revealing its dependence on revenue receipts and capital receipts so as to mobilise the revenue necessary for providing transport facilities in Kolhapur. This composition highlights the efforts of the KMT to provide transport services at present or in future. The necessary information is presented in Table 4.

Table 4: Composition of Total Revenue of KMT

(Rs. in lakh)

Year	*Revenue Receipts*	*Capital Receipts*	*Total Revenue*
2003-04	1859.98 (84)	358.84 (16)	2218.22 (100)
2004-05	2242.57 (86)	365.19 (14)	2607.76 (100)
2005-06	2683.52 (95)	148.62 (5)	2832.14 (100)
2006-07	2899.80 (81)	687.50 (19)	3587.30 (100)
2007-08	2483.50 (84)	488.35 (16)	2971.85 (100)
CGR	8.71	13.30	9.4

Source: Same as of Table 1.

Note: Figures into brackets show percentages to Total Revenue.

The data in Table 4 reveals that KMT has focussed more on the present than the future, as a resultof which its share of Revenue receipts was significantly higher (86% average) than the Capital receipts (14%).This indicates that for the growth of city transport facilities potentialities and abilities, KMT has not paid much attention, which is not an indicator of sound financial operations.

5.5 Composition of Revenue Receipts of KMT

Revenue receipts have importance in the context of city transport services, at present. Hence, the analysis of the composition of Revenue receipts highlights before us their sources and reliance of the KMT on different sources in their mobilisation. Table 5 shows the data about revenue receipts.

Table 5: Composition of Revenue Receipts of KMT

(Rs. in lakh)

Source	*2003-04*	*2004-05*	*2005-06*	*2006-07*	*2007-08*	*SGR*
Traffic Income	1776.69 (96)	2095.46 (93)	2382.66 (89)	2585.25 (89)	2272.00 (91)	5.57
Non-traffic Income	34.63 (2)	49.14 (2)	26.87 (1)	38.55 (1)	104.00 (1)	40.06
Income from Diesel & Tyres	—	54.11 (3)	226.69 (8)	220.00 (8)	60.00 (3)	2.72
Nutrition Surcharge	48.65 (2)	53.83 (2)	47.28 (2)	56.00 (2)	47.50 (2)	- 0.47
Revenue Receipts	1859.98 (100)	2242.57 (100)	2683.52 (100)	2899.80 (100)	2483.50 (100)	6.70

Source: Same as of Table 1.

Note: (1) SGR: Annual Average Simple Growth Rate.

(2) Figures into brackets indicate percentages to Revenue Receipts.

The study of the Revenue receipts of KMT reveals that income from traffic and non-traffic sources like advertisements, sale of dead stock, compensation from the insurance companies are the sources of income. The KMT heavily relies on the traffic income to collect the Revenue receipts. Economic fare may be defined as the transport price, which is affordable to the passenger and brings in traffic revenue, which ensures financial viability for transport operators. But the growth in the traffic income was mild and meagre. On the contrary, the share of non-traffic income was insignificant, but the growth rate was considerable one. On an average (mean) KMT has collected traffic and non-traffic income worth of Rs. 2222.41 lakh and Rs. 50.63 lakh respectively during 2003-04 and 2007-08. Its income from the sale of diesel, tyres was also considerable (Rs. 112.16 lakh). Correlation analysis reveals a high degree positive correlation between traffic income and Revenue receipts. Likewise, regression analysis shows the traffic income as a major determinant of revenue receipts of KMT.

5.6 Composition of Capital Receipts of KMT

Capital receipts have a special importance in the context of increasing potentialities of providing city transport services. Increase in Capital receipts availability promotes availability of the capital assets, especially buses, which facilitates increase in the supply of quantity as well as quality of transport services. The study of the composition of capital receipts highlights the nature of capital receipts, sources, variations, growth and their quantum. Table 6 presents the data about the composition of capital receipts of KMT. Correlation analysis indicates that depreciation and capital receipts are highly and positively correlated.

Table 6: Composition of Capital Receipts of KMT

(Rs. in lakh)

Source	*2003-04*	*2004-05*	*2005-06*	*2006-07*	*2007-08*	*SGR*
Depreciation	143.84 (40)	156.08 (43)	148.67 (99)	237.00 (34)	293.35 (60)	20.78
Deposits	—	—	1.95 (1)	0.50 (1)	145.00 (30)	2445.29
Loans	215.00 (60)	209.11 (57)	—	—	—	- 1.36
Revenue Receipts	—	—	—	450.00 (65)	50.00 (10)	- 44.44
Capital Receipts	358.94 (100)	365.19 (100)	148.62 (100)	687.50 (100)	488.35 (100)	7.21

Source: Same as of Table 1.

Note: Figures into brackets show percentages to Capital Receipts.

The data in Table 6 reveals that only depreciation on capital goods were a regular source of capital receipts to the KMT. All the other sources of Capital receipts show wide fluctuations. Loans were normally a significant source of capital receipts. But it requires creditworthiness and ability to repay, which seems lacking in the case of KMT. More recently KMT has been exploiting transfer from revenue receipts as a source of capital receipts.

5.7 Total Expenditure Pattern of KMT

It is not only receipts or revenue, but also their spending that is important, as far as the supply of city transport facilities is concerned. Total expenditure is divided into revenue expenditure and capital expenditure. Revenue expenditure is the expenditure of current and recurrent in nature, and Capital expenditure is concerned with the capital goods. The necessary data about the composition of total expenditure of the KMT is presented in Table 7.

Table 7: Total Expenditure Pattern of KMT

(Rs. In lakh)

Year	*Revenue Expenditure*	*Capital Expenditure*	*Total Expenditure*
2003-04	2213.42 (86)	359.55 (14)	2572.97 (100)
2004-05	2603.80 (88)	365.51 (12)	2969.31 (100)
2005-06	2869.29 (95)	139.09 (5)	3008.38 (100)
2006-07	3727.86 (84)	687.20 (16)	4415.06 (100)

2007-08	3094.11 (86)	4881.50 (14)	3582.61 (100)
CGR	10.83	13.25	11.16

Source: Same as of Table 1.

Note: Figures into brackets show percentages to total expenditure

KMT assigned a major share of total expenditure towards the revenue expenditure (88%), which indicates its efforts to provide city transport services effectively and efficiently at present. The growth in its revenue expenditure was considerable, but not significant. The KMT has assigned about one-fifth share to capital expenditure, which is a good thing. But an analysis of the composition of capital expenditure highlights the direction of capital expenditure. It is noteworthy, that the growth in capital expenditure was significant.

5.8 Revenue Expenditure Pattern of KMT

Revenue expenditure is of vital importance for the supply of transport services at present. The study of revenue expenditure pattern shows the activities undertaken by the KMT to provide city transport facilities at present. Table 8 gives the data about the changing revenue expenditure pattern of the KMT during the period under study.

Table 8: Revenue Expenditure Pattern of KMT

(Rs. In lakh)

Items of Revenue Expenditure	*2003-04*	*2004-05*	*2005-06*	*2006-07*	*2007-08*	*SGR*
Administration	808.70 (37)	954.20 (37)	1005.70 (35)	1085.36 (29)	1273.31 (41)	11.49
Bus Fare	272.84 (12)	318.04 (12)	301.79 (11)	305.00 (8)	85.00 (3)	- 13.76
Repairs & Maintenance	712.19 (32)	9025.50 (35)	1274.33 (44)	1319.75 (35)	1046.50 (35)	9.39
Government Taxes & Other Charges	27.66 (1)	28.27 (1)	31.90 (1)	64.15 (2)	129.10 (4)	73.34
Interest, Provisions, Deposits	252.66 (11)	270.60 (10)	124.70 (4)	753.60 (20)	271.85 (9)	1.51
Depreciation	139.37 (7)	127.19 (5)	130.87 (7)	200.00 (6)	288.35 (9)	21.37
Revenue Expenditure	2213.42 (100)	2603.80 (100)	2869.29 (100)	3727.86 (100)	3094.11	7.95

Source: Same as of Table 1.

Note: Figures into parenthesis indicate percentages to Revenue Expenditure.

The study of revenue expenditure pattern of KMT reveals that Administration (37%) was a major item of expenditure on Revenue account, of which, Traffic section consumed a lion share (50%). It is necessary for providing transport services, which is a major source of Revenue receipts. The thing of serious concern about the revenue expenditure of KMT is its expenditure on Repairs and Maintenance. It indicates the bad conditions of the buses as well as efficiency in providing transport services. It is good to note that KMT has been regularly providing for interest, deposits, depreciation. Regression analysis shows that Administration and Repairs and Maintenance are two determinants of increase in revenue expenditure of the KMT.

5.9 CAPITAL EXPENDITURE PATTERN OF KMT

Capital expenditure has a special importance in strengthening potentialities and abilities of providing city transport services. It can increase the quantum and quality of road transport facilities, but its direction should be proper.

Table 9: Capital Expenditure Pattern of KMT

(Rs. In lakh)

Items of Capital Expenditure	*2003-04*	*2004-05*	*2005-06*	*2006-07*	*2007-08*
Repayment of Loans	324.40 (90)	88.51 (24)	94.13 (68)	2104.75 (15)	242.00 (50)
Purchase of Buses	1.05 (0.29)	218.89 (60)	—	508.50 (74)	195.00 (40)
Purchase of Vehicles & Machines	2.31 (0.64)	—	—	0.35 (0.05)	7.00 (1)
Purchase of Dead Stock	0.05 (0.01)	0.10 (0.02)	—	0.25 (0.03)	0.50 (0.10)
Improvements in & Around Office	5.45 (2)	4.40 (1)	6.04 (4)	7.35 (1)	17.00 (3)
Construction of Terminus	7.34 (2)	16.08 (4)	9.35 (7)	13.00 (2)	17.00 (3)
Transfer to Revenue Account	18.95 (5)	36.45 (10)	29.55 (21)	32.00 (5)	5.00 (2)
Purchase of Computers	— (1)	1.08	0.02 (0.01)	3.00 (1)	5.00 (1)
Capital Expenditure	359.55 (100)	365.51 (100)	139.09 (100)	687.20 (100)	488.50 (100)

Source: Same as of Table 1.
Note: Figures into brackets show percentages to Capital Expenditure.

It is observed that KMT has paid due attention towards the repayment of taken loans and advances. Therefore, it has spent about 49% share of Capital expenditure on the repayment of loans. To purchase buses is an important item of Capital expenditure so as to strengthen potentialities and abilities of providing transport facilities. On an average, KMT has diverted 35% share of Total Capital expenditure towards the purchase of buses, which is a good thing. But there is a need for assigning major share for it, because it is expected that purchase of buses should be a major and important item of capital expenditure for any city transport undertaking.

6. FINANCIAL CHALLENGES BEFORE THE KMT

Our detailed study of the various aspects of the finances of the KMT during the period 2003-04 to 2007-08 reveals the following financial challenges before the KMT.

1. The overall/budgetary deficit is a major financial challenge before the KMT as a city transport undertaking of the KMC. It indicates the financial loss of the KMT in providing the city transport facilities in Kolhapur. It was Rs. 354.75 lakh in 2003-04, which rapidly rose to Rs. 610.76 lakh in 2007-08.
2. The KMT has not succeeded in mobilising the Capital receipts necessary for strengthening the potentialities and abilities of providing city transport services. It could collect only 14% share of Capital receipts in the Total Revenue. Likewise, its depedance upon revenue receipts and assistance from the KMC is serious concern.
3. KMT as a city transport unit of the KMC has totally failed in collecting the income necessary for meeting its current expenditure. It indicates the economic losses of the KMT. Hence, its revenue deficit rapidly grew at 21% p. a. from Rs. 353.34 lakh in 2003-04 to Rs. 610.61 lakh in 2007-08. To correct the revenue deficit is a big financial challenge before the KMT.
4. Even though, the KMT did not face the problem of Capital deficit, the surplus on the Capital account is not a good practice of the KMT. But it is a challenge that KMT must spend all the Capital receipts, which are so much important for improving potentialities and abilities of providing city transport facilities in quantity as well as quality terms.
5. Even though, traffic income is an important and major source of revenue receipts for KMT, it is a financial challenge before the KMT is to increase it rapidly and significantly.
6. Likewise, the non-traffic income collected by the KMT from advertisements, rent, sale of dead stock and others is meagre. It could contribute to revenue receipts by only 2% on an average. There is an urgent need to find out new avenues of the non-traffic income to strengthen the financial position, especially the revenue receipts position of the KMT.
7. To improve and strengthen the creditworthiness of the KMT is an important challenge before it, which will decide the loans and advances that can be raised for the purchase and liquidity of Capital assets. During the period of five years under study, the KMT could take loans only for two years.
8. Dependence of KMT on revenue receipts for mobilising the capital receipts is a bad practice and challenge before the KMT. Because the KMT is in huge revenue deficit, and in this situation its dependence on Revenue receipts for collecting the Capital receipts seems irrational.
9. The small share of capital receipts collected by the KMT in its total revenue has resulted in smaller and inadequate capital expenditure to be incurred by it, which is bad for improving quantity and quality of city transport services being provided. The KMT has spent just 11% share of Total expenditure as a Capital expenditure on an average during 2003-04 to 2007-08. Its a thing of welcome that the Capital expenditure has shown a considerable growth.
10. The lion share in revenue expenditure of Repairs and Maintenance with considerable growth is a financial challenge before KMT. It indicates the bad conditions of buses

and thereby, inadequate quantity and quality of the city transport services provided. Control of expenditure on Repairs and Maintenance, which stood at 35%, is urgently needed.

11. The growing taxes and other charges liabilities of the government by KMT works as an indicator of financial weak position of KMT. And hence, it is a financial challenge before the KMT. The government liabilities of the KMT rapidly rose from Rs. 28 lakh in 2003-04 to Rs. 129 lakh in 2007-08 by showing about seven-fold growth.
12. As a result, of inadequate mobilisation of total revenue, revenue receipts and capital receipts KMT has been increasing its dependence on the KMC for financial assistance as well as posing additional financial burden on the KMC, which is basically weak in financial position. To reduce unnecessary financial burden posed on the KMC is a financial challenge before the KMT. The financial assistance from the KMC rapidly and significantly rose from Rs.50 lakh in 2003-04 to Rs. 3 crore in 2007-08.
13. The present state of city transport services provided by the KMT is inadequate, inferior and inefficient. This can be improved by spending on purchase of buses. The present spending of the KMT on purchase of buses is inadequate, which stood at only 34% of Capital expenditure on an average. To increase spending on buses is a financial challenge before the KMT.
14. It is obligatory to maintain reserves by the KMT as per Bombay (Mumbai)

Provisional Municipal Corporations Act 1949,Article 359 and 360. But it is becoming difficult to maintain such reserves. On the contrary, such reserves are being used by the KMT to meet its deficit. Hence, it is also a financial challenge before the KMT.

7. CONCLUSIONS

The foregoing analysis reveals that the financial position of the KMT is significantly weak, this has posed a number of financial challenges before it. The study adequately proves that the unsound financial position of the KMT has resulted in inefficient, inadequate and inferior quality transport services in the Kolhapur city. The study of financial challenges before the city transport undertakings in general, and the KMT in particular is vast with a wide scope and many dimensions. The present study is a small attempt in this direction. There is plenty of scope to go further in undertaking research on this topic.

REFERENCES

Goel, Tripta (2000), Urban Bus Transit System in Delhi : An Assessment of the Quality of Service, *Indian Journal of Transport Management*, CIRT, Pune, May 2000, July 2005.

Kadam, V.A. and Bagade, M.V. (2000), Transport Pricing in Competitive Environment, *Indian Journal of Transport Management*, CIRT, Pune, July 2000.

Kolhapur Municipal Transport (KMT) (2007-08), The KMT Budget: 2007-08, Kolhapur.

Pathak, M.G. (1992), *Transport and Economic Development*, Edited by Mathur, J.S., Chugh Publications, Allahabad.

13

THE ROLE OF GIS IN MANAGING URBAN TRANSPORT PROBLEMS IN DEVELOPING COUNTRIES WITH REFERENCE TO KHARTOUM CITY

Arif Elhag Aydrous

ABSTRACT

Developing countries all over the world have experienced rapid urbanisation during the past few decades. The failure to provide adequate transport services to match the growing demand in these urban areas has been a major cause of economic inefficiency, which is well manifested in the present chronic shortage of urban transport services in all developing countries. Despite huge investments, adequacy of services had remained a problem. This is partly because of poor utilisation resulting from poor management of transport systems which, in turn, could be attributed to lack of information required for effective decision making. The use of Geographical Information Systems (GIS) has served as an effective way of better utilisation of existing facilities. This paper attempts to examine the role of such systems in the context of managing road passenger traffic in a city like Khartoum, Sudan using Arc GIS programme.

1. INTRODUCTION

During the last few decades, developing countries have experienced rapid urbanisation in the form of a growing number of mega cities and a high percentage of population living in urban areas. As cities in these countries continued to grow and expand, more and more migrants have been encouraged to flow in, as a result of which the percentage of people living in urban areas has grown much faster than the availability of services including transport.

The failure to provide adequate transport services to match the growing demand has been a major cause of economic inefficiency, which is well manifested in the present chronic shortage of urban transport services in all developing countries.

In most major cities in developing countries, public road passenger transport is the primary means of meeting basic transport needs. In many cases, public transport is managed in a traditional way. Services are poor and deteriorating with the city area within vehicle speeds less than

10 kph, often accentuated by long average waiting times resulting in a deficiency of supply. Transport expenditures for work journeys can be as high as 30 per cent of the income earned.

Today, mobility plays an important role in the urban structure of activities. Urban transport has always been viewed as a major dynamic force in influencing quality of life and shaping cities all over the globe. The attractiveness of a particular location depends in part on the relative accessibility to various services and amenities to promote economic development, social and cultural activities, and these in turn, depend on the quality and quantity of the transport system and its related infrastructure. Therefore, the prime objective of any transport system can be defined as one of moving people and goods quickly, efficiently and safely within any area or between areas.

In developing countries, motorized public transport meets a substantial part of the demand but, of late, private cars are being preferred, as a result of which the use of public transport is stagnating or decreasing. However, urban public transport services have a specific role, they have a great influence on urban planning since they allow everyone to move.

Many research studies concerned with urban transport problems in developing countries have confirmed that public transport especially road transport, are unreliable which has turned the attention of many commuters particularly in the middle income class to consider private cars as an alternative mode to the overcrowded mass transport. This has made the urban transport problem a more complex issue particularly in larger cities where the growth of private cars is very high. Paratransit services such as two wheelers, three wheelers, cycling, walking, etc. are widely used in many cities with a varying role as basic, complementary, supplementary or a mix of all, depending on the city and its public transport system.

The growth of private means of transport has had serious implications on the existing road infrastructure, as these modes compete with public road transport and other non-motorised modes, not only affecting the movement of traffic especially during the peak hours but has made the operations of mass transport especially buses unviable. Heavy overcrowding in public transport, congestion on roads, noise and air pollution created by vehicles has serious impact in urban environment and health of urban population. As a result of poor performance, many public transport companies have been incurring huge financial losses as revenue generated from the services often fall short of the required level to improve their performance as well as expanding their network coverage to peripheral areas.

In order to manage urban transport problems to ensure reliable services and reduce congestion on roads, many planning authorities in developing countries have moved from a conventional approach to an integrated technological-based approach in planning and managing their activities. Information technology systems like Geographic Information Systems (GIS) have become the most promising technology for the integrated approach. In spite of the availability of this technology, urban transport problems such as delays, congestion, accidents, etc. have become very common and are of concern to policy makers and planners. This is mainly because of the unavailability or lack of reliable information flow on a real time basis to aid decision-making processes to come up with solutions. This paper attempts to examine the usefulness of these systems in aiding practitioners to solve urban transport problems.

2. INFORMATION SYSTEMS: AN OVERVIEW

Information technology is technically known as a set of interrelated components working together, mainly based on computer networking and communications with prime objectives to process, classify, arrange, calculate, tabulate, encrypt, store, retrieve, present, and disseminate information to support decision-making process to solve problems and control the activities of the organisation. Therefore, information technology besides containing information describes the organisation activities within its boundary and beyond, by processing and tabulating data into a meaningful and useful form also helps managers and decision makers to analyse problems, visualize complex issues and create and/or improves services.

During the past century, almost all public organisations around the globe have started to use information technologies, Public transport authorities have also been utilizing technological development as a tool for managing their services. In the past, information technologies was not considered as an essential asset for many organisations specially the transport sector wherein management processes and decision-making were widely taken on experiences and a personal basis. Today, it is globally recognised that building and understanding information technology via a Geographical Information System (GIS) is essential for many organisations specially urban transport managers and policy makers who need reliable information on time to tackle serious and complex problems, to ensure suitable urban transport services to meet increasingly urban demand for mobility which is vital to developing urban areas and managing growing cities.

What is GIS

Over the years, Geographic Information Systems have been defined by many authors. For example, according to a recently developed website of the U.S. Federal Highway Administration (2004) a GIS "is a collection of computer software, hardware, data and personnel used to store, manipulate, analyse and present geographically referenced information."

Another definition of GIS by Blin et. al. (1993) says that a GIS "is a system of computer hardware, software, and procedures designed to support the compiling, storing, retrieving, analysing, and display of spatially referenced data for addressing planning and management problems. In addition to these technical components, a complete GIS must also include a focus on people, organisations, and standards."

The component of a GIS system intended for application in urban transportation planning and management is commonly known as Geographic Information Systems for Transport GIS-T, including hardware and software, data capture like cameras and video, integration, users and their requirement and finally organisation. These components of a GIS can be illustrated as follows (Figure 1).

In order to make full use and advantages of GIS for solving complex urban issues including urban transportation problems through planning and management process, there are some basic factors that affect the application and use of GIS technology in urban transportation that have to be identified very clearly. According to United Nation (1995), the main factors that would pave the way for wide application and use of GIS by many organisation authorities especially in urban transport planning and management are as follows:

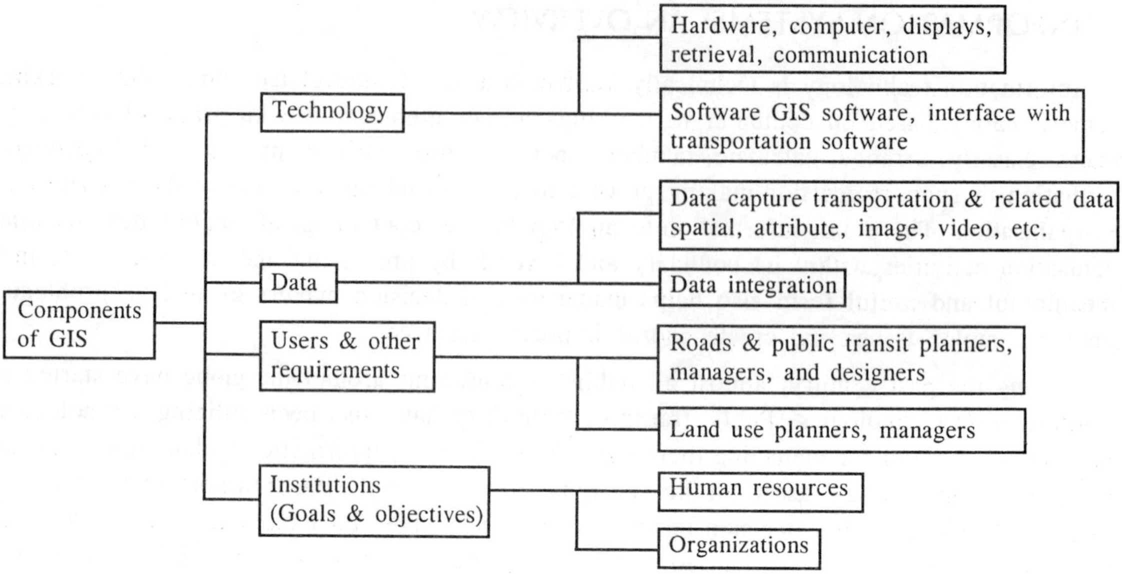

Fig. 1: Components of GIS

1. The knowledge base of users and employees regarding the capabilities of GIS technology.
2. Technological development including both hardware and software.
3. The cost of hardware, software, and operation of the GIS.
4. The organisational factors.

The above mentioned factors and their relationship along with the requirement for the use of GIS in urban transportation are illustrated in (Figure 2).

3. MANAGING TRAFFIC CONGESTION USING GIS: THE KHARTOUM EXPERIENCE

Khartoum is the capital of Sudan and the Khartoum state. It is located at the point where the White Nile, flowing north from Uganda, meets the Blue Nile, flowing west from Ethiopia. The place of merger of the two Niles (where Khartoum is located) is known as "The Mogran". The merged Nile flows north towards Egypt and the Mediterranean sea. The capital Khartoum contains three metropolitan cities i.e., Khartoum, Khartoum North, and Omdurman linked by bridges, and they all together form Khartoum State.

Khartoum is very poor in land use planning compared with other cities in developing countries, with few exclusive areas. Few streets are paved, but the centre is well planned, with tree-lined streets. However, Khartoum has the highest concentration of economic activities in the country. This is slowly changing as major developmental activities are taking place in other parts of the country, like oil exploration in the South, and the Giad Industrial complex and White Nile Sugar project in Central Sudan, and the Merowe Dam in the North. Khartoum city is the main location for most educational institutions and other socio-economic services and facilities. According to

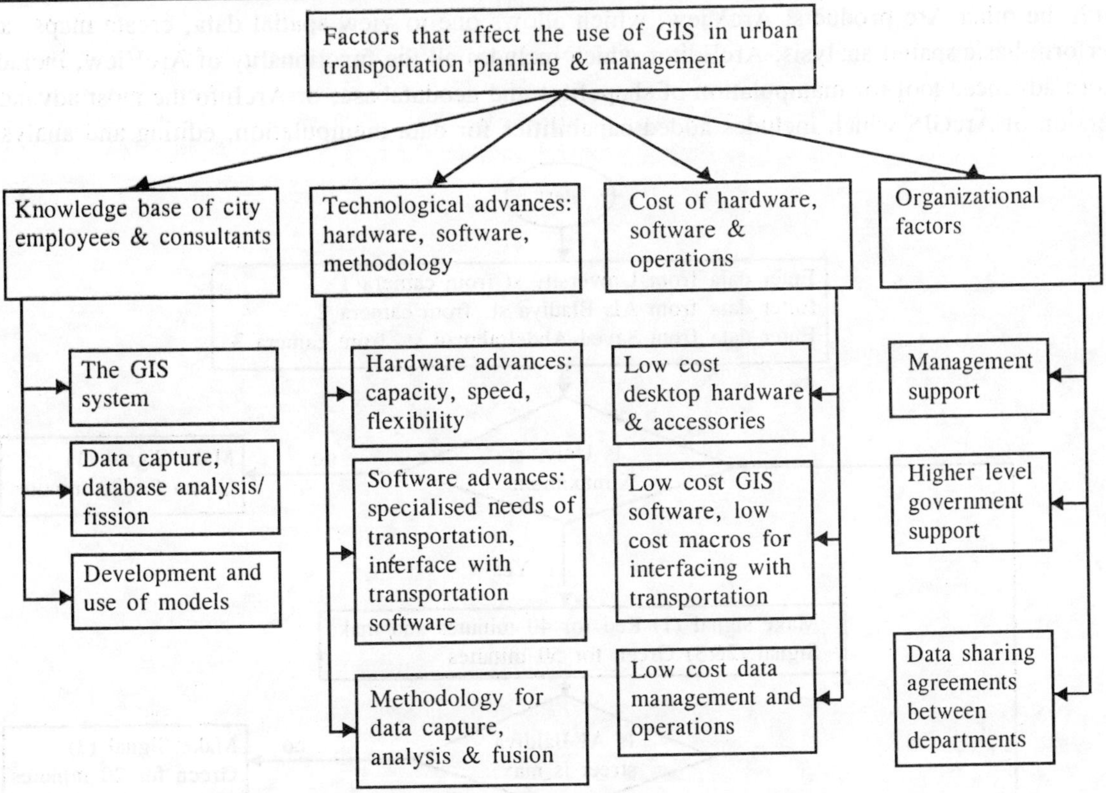

Fig. 2: Factors Affecting the Use of GIS in Urban Transport

the Government of Sudan (2007), the city is inhabited by nearly 20 per cent of the total population of the country.

The urban transport scene in Khartoum city is mainly dominated by private operators regulated by the government, The fleet owned by private operators consist of medium buses (25 passengers), mini buses (14 passengers), taxi etc. Private cars are widely used in the city as an alternative mode.Their number has continuously increased.

Khartoum city like any other city in developing countries faces acute transport problems and bottlenecks reflecting poor quality of services, accidents, delays, overcrowding, poor quality of roads, unreliability, etc. But the most serious problem is the heavy congestion on roads specially those leading to the centre of the city — the CBD — not only during the peak hours but almost throughout the day. This is mainly due to the increasing number of private cars and the competition between them and other modes on the road including three wheelers and non-motorised modes. In addition to this, there are no spaces for parking. Private users usually in many cases use the road sides for parking, reducing roads capacity to only 50 percent of its full capacity.

To ensure better services and reduce the level of congestion on roads, a GIS-method based on computer can be suggested to be applied using ArcGIS programme.

ArcGIS is the name of a group of geographic information system software. At the desktop GIS level, ArcGIS can include, ArcReader, which allows one to view and query maps created with the other Arc products; ArcView, which allows one to view spatial data, create maps, and perform basic spatial analysis; ArcEditor which includes all the functionality of ArcView, includes more advanced tool for manipulation of shapefiles and geodatabase; or ArcInfo the most advanced version of ArcGIS which includes added capabilities for data manipulation, editing and analysis.

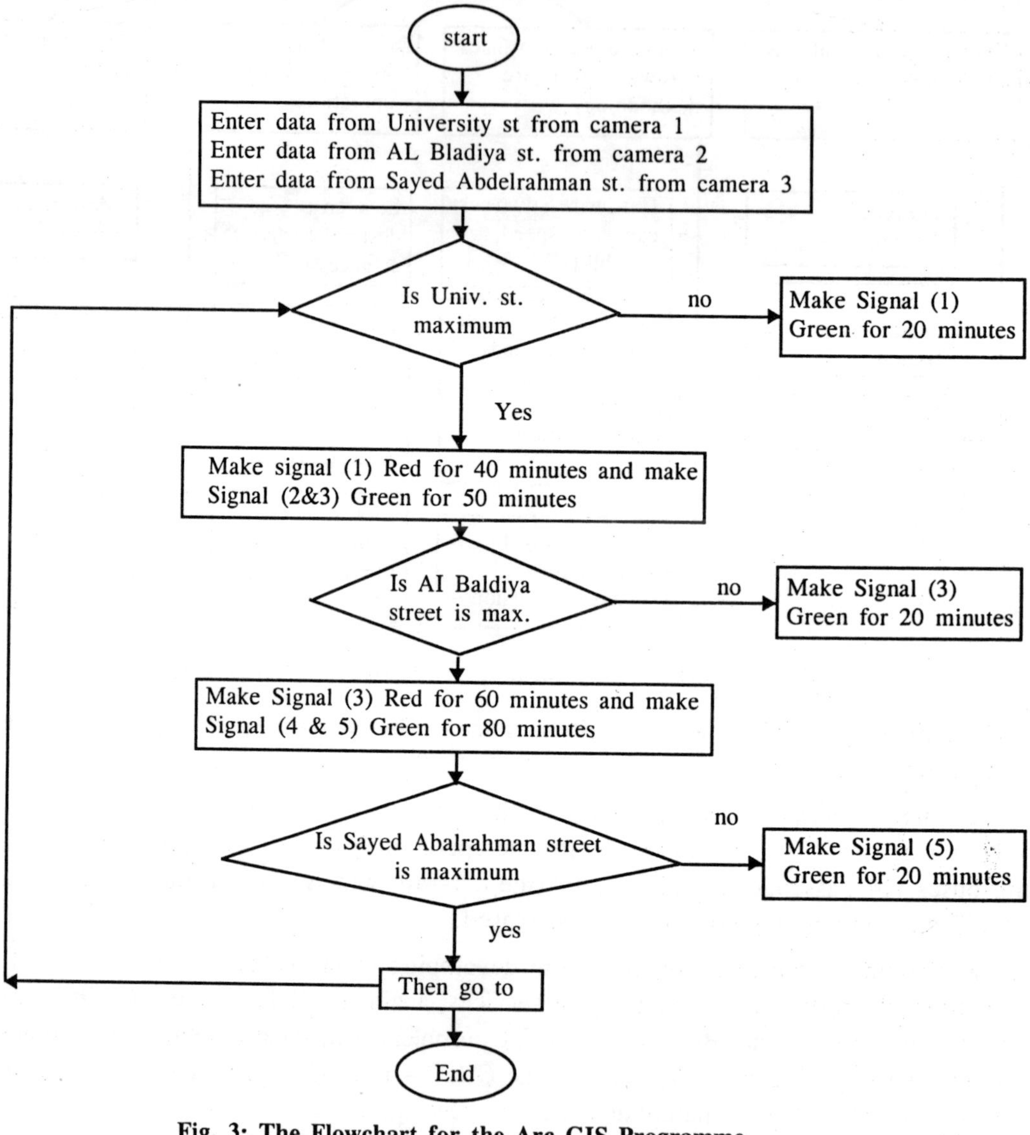

Fig. 3: The Flowchart for the Arc GIS Programme

To develop a programme for managing the traffic movement an ArcGIS software can be used which is illustrated in Figure 3. The full programme code is also shown at the end of the paper (Appendix 1). The main objective of this programme is to monitor and regulate the traffic movement depending on computer. The same system can be applied to some other roads in different zones and then connected together for form a network for traffic monitoring and control. The system can be useful once it is applied specially in Khartoum, because traditional traffic monitoring by traffic police has created a lot of problems. They give priority to private and government cars rather than passenger buses who have to wait for hours to reach the city centre. Secondly, the data collected by cameras and stored in the database can form good information regarding the volume of traffic on specific roads that can help in future planning. It can also help to form a policy to improve passenger transport, at the same time formulate policies and restriction on use of private cars ownership. Furthermore, reducing congestion on roads can reduce fatal accidents. In addition to this, the same programme can be updated to help the government authority to impose electronic pricing policy on private cars entering the city centre. In a nut shell, given the situation of passenger transport in Khartoum city, the system can be useful to regulate traffic and form a good ground to visualize future policies to improve passenger transport and reduce the level of private car ownership which is the main cause of traffic congestion on roads.

REFERENCES

A.E. Aydrous, (1999), Financing Urban Infrastructure with special references to the Transport Sector in Developing Countries, An Unpublished Ph.D. Thesis, submitted to the University of Mumbai, Sept, 1999.

Blin, C.R., et. al. (1993), Geographic Information Systems: A Glossary, Minnesota Extension Service,University of Minnesota, Natural Resources, NR-FO-6097-S, NR-PC-6136-S.

Caliper Corporation 2004, TransCAD, Transportation GIS Software, Overview, Newton, Massachusetts

http://www.caliper.com/tcovu.htm.

Federal High Way Administration (FHWA) 2004, GIS In Transportation.

http://www.gis-fhwa.dot.gov/

Fletcher, D.R., (2000), Geographic Information Systems for Transportation: A Look Forward. Transportation in the New Millennium, Committee on Spatial Data and Information Science, Transportation Research Board, Washington D.C.

GIS Lounge (2004), Components of GIS.

http://www.gislouge.com/libaray/introgis.shtml

Government of Sudan, Sudan in Figures, (2007), Ministry of Council of Ministries, Central Bureau of Statistics, Khartoum, Sudan.

Khan, A.M. (1995), Application of Geographic Information System to Urban Transportation Planning and Managements. Paper Presented at the UN_s Seminar on Urban Geographic Information Systems, City Sustainability and Environment, Dec 1995, Cairo, Egypt.

United Nations, (1995), International Seminar on GIS, City Sustainability and Environment Resolution, Cairo, Egypt.

Appendix-1

Code Of The Programme

```
' Get the view and the line theme
'
aView = av.GetProject.FindDoc("View1")
aStreetFTab = aView.FindTheme("Streets").GetFTab
' Make sure you can perform network analysis on this theme
'
if (not (NetDef.CanMakeFromFTab(aStreetFTab))) then
 msgBox.Error("Can't make a network from this FTab","")
 Exit
end
' Make the NetDef and Network objects
'
aNetDef = NetDef.Make(aStreetFTab)
aNetwork = Network.Make(aNetDef)
' Check for error creating network
'
if (aNetDef.HasError) then
 msgBox.Error("The network has an error","")
 Exit
end
' Show a message box for a user to select a cost field
'
aSelectedCostField = msgBox.Choice(aNetDef.GetCostFields,
 "Select a cost:",
 "Network cost selection")
' Set the cost field for the network problem.
'
aNetwork.SetCostField(aSelectedCostField)
' Get the customer point feature table
'
aCustomerFTab = aView.FindTheme("Customers").GetFtab
aPointField = aCustomerFTab.FindField("Shape")
' Make a list validated points from the customer theme
'
aPointList = {}
for each rec in aCustomerFTab
 p = aCustomerFTab.ReturnValue(aPointField, rec)
 if (aNetwork.IsPointOnNetwork(p)) then
 aPointList.Add(p)
```

```
 end
end
' Find the best way to visit all the customers
'
travelDistance = aNetwork.FindPath(aPointList, True, False)
' Create a graphic representing the route and add it to the view
'
aView.GetGraphics.Add(GraphicShape.Make(aNetwork.ReturnPathShape.
```

14

GEOGRAPHICAL INFORMATION SYSTEM (GIS) FOR URBAN ROAD SAFETY — A CASE OF PUNE CITY

N. Ramasaamy

ABSTRACT

The nature of urban road traffic safety and the ways in which problems created by road traffic conflicts need to be reviewed to promote Urban Road Safety. Of particular interest is the impact of road safety issues on the well-being of the vulnerable urban road users. Urban road users may be particularly disadvantaged, as compared to others, since there is a disproportionately higher risk to involvement in an accident because of the nature of their travel and locational characteristics (e.g., greater dependence on walking and low cost forms of informal public transport). Geographical Information System usage provides spatial analysis, improved display capacities and data integration capabilities. From this perspective, this study attempts to identify and investigate particular problems facing urban road users as a result of road accidents. The study reviews existing material that describes the nature of urban road accidents and safety improvements in Pune. Material to be included would cover (i) Scale and characteristics of traffic accidents in urban areas, identifying common patterns, trends and causes; (ii) Developing a GIS based information system which integrates land use information, traffic and travel characteristics, road accident data to assess urban safety; (iii) Analysis of the impacts of road accidents on the community, covering the physical damage, health care facilities, enforcement agencies, etc particularly in relation to the vulnerable road users; (iv) Analysis of the effectiveness of interventions which have been applied to redress either specific urban road accident problems or the more general nature of road safety (e.g. introduction of traffic calming measures; safety audits; stricter enforcement; publicity campaigns, etc); and (v) Examination of the institutional requirements and capability for planning and implementing urban road safety improvements.

1. INTRODUCTION

A sustainable transport system must provide mobility and accessibility to all urban residents in a safe and environment friendly mode of transport. This is a complex and difficult task when the needs and demands of people are not only different but also often conflicting. If a large proportion of the population cannot afford to use motorized transport modes — public/private — then they have to either walk or ride bicycles for their mobility.

The nature of urban road traffic safety and the ways in which problems created by road traffic conflicts need to be reviewed to promote Urban Road Safety. A particular interest needs to be taken on the impact of road safety issues on the well being of the urban vulnerable road users. From this perspective, our study will identify and investigate particular problems facing the urban vulnerable road users as a result of road accidents. The urban vulnerable road users may be particularly disadvantaged, as compared to others. The urban vulnerable road users may also be at a disproportionately higher risk to involvement in accidents because of the nature of their travel and locational characteristics (e.g. greater dependence on walking and low cost forms of informal public transport).

Geographic Information System (GIS) usage provides spatial analysis, improved display capacities and data integration capabilities. In this study, an attempt is made to identify and to highlight these issues by using GIS information system to aid policy makers and other stakeholders in their endeavour to promote Urban Road Safety.

2. OBJECTIVES AND SCOPE

The main objective of this paper is to present a status report on the nature and impact of road safety in Pune city. The article highlights GIS capabilities such as special analysis tools, graphics and data integration capabilities, etc. to provide enhanced capacity for addressing urban road safety issues relating to vulnerable road users. While attempting to identify priority areas for remedial actions, the study also looks at enforcement issues, traffic control and traffic calming measures. The study is restricted in scope to the urban settlement areas of Pune city under Pune Municipal Corporation area. The GIS will provide a platform to maintain up to date road accident database and use it for further analysis and planning. The scope can also be extended to identify characteristics of traffic accidents. Developing GIS based information system will help to integrate land use information, traffic and travel characteristics, and road accident data to assess urban safety particularly for vulnerable road users.

3. DESIGN CONSIDERATIONS OF GIS

Analysing traffic accident data is an important step in improving road safety in any transportation network. The ability to do this quickly and efficiently requires a suitable information system backed by GIS to focus on identifying and prioritizing safety improvements that are most beneficial to users of the transportation network. To identify a suitable GIS, the following objectives need to be defined:

The selected GIS should be capable of providing:

- Electronic access to accident data; maps and plots of accidents;
- Accident summary reports;
- Data and charts for accident reports;

- Accident rates using traffic volumes;
- User-friendly, data-entry interface; and
- Import functions for accident data in a pre-defined electronic format.

Additionally, the GIS should be capable of supporting multiple users, be cost-effective and be relatively user friendly. After researching and reviewing available products, we selected the ARCVIEW3.1 as the GIS-based software that allows users flexibility in displaying and generating an unlimited number of accident reports.

The approach is to define diversified GIS software in terms of capabilities, availability to a wide range of users, computing power, usability, and budget considerations. Having this diverse background and the magnitude of potential users in mind, there is need to adopt a simple PC based system. Another factor in choosing the basic GIS software is the defined need to integrate images and other data with the vector and tabular data that are the backbone of any geo-referenced data management system that is being considered. This factor was triggered by the desire to enable the use and incorporation of photo-logging data as well as incorporating images from other data sources. The ability to incorporate images of features adds a new dimension to the information system in terms of analysis, decision-making and display.

Several methodologies and approaches can be adopted for integrating GIS into transport planning applications. In order to integrate GIS and transport planning for accident evaluation purposes, there are two main methods in use: the complete integration method and the add-on approach. The complete integrated approach involves development of new forecasting packages or modifying existing ones to run entirely within the GIS to produce outputs useful for accident evaluation as well as transport planning. The main disadvantages of this method relate to the time and efforts required in re-development or modification of the existing model. The add-on approach aims to augment existing transport models. It merely provides an extension to the models already being used, and hence the users would only need to learn how to use the add-on programme. Its main disadvantage involves the issue of compatibility and how to design a single programme one to fit on each of the many different models in use. Finally, going through the merits and demerits of both the approaches, the complete integration method was adopted so as to enable its use by as many users as possible.

Last, but not the least, is the user interface design. The idea is to design the system to be open, user friendly and simple. The term open is used here in the sense that it allows the addition of more applications as required and as data becomes available. To facilitate ease of usage, the interface needs to be simple and user friendly.

4. COMPONENTS OF THE SYSTEM

The system is designed as a practical programme for the analysis of road accident impacts. It is ideal for use by the stakeholders of road safety in evaluating road accidents. It provides capabilities for testing different hypothesis on road safety management. The results of the system enable both a global analysis as well as a local analysis. Computations are done on a link-by-link basis and aggregated to obtain the overall network level impacts. It is developed using the ARCVIEW3.1 GIS based software. It contains four main modules (namely Data manager, Models,

Output and Scenarios) each of which contains a group of functions and tools used to perform specific purposes. These are described below. The modules are embedded in the form of a toolbox like structure and operate in the form of pop-up and pull-down menus. It is easy to use, completely mouse driven and uses the standard Arc view tables. The user is presented with a step-by-step guide to all operations. All input data and output are saved in Arc view format keeping everything simple and uniform.

4.1 Data Manager Module

This module serves as a data capture and input facility system. It presents options that enable the user to create and manage the input data required in the analysis. It has three sub-modules namely "raster image capture", "network", and "workspace", each of which performs a separate and unique function. Through these, the system organises and manages the input data files into a single unified data sharing facility for use by all the separate accident models.

The "raster image capture" module enables the user to create input files containing land use information by heads-on digitizing (that is, digitizing based on screen image). It uses aerial photographs (raster images) of the area, road network layer, and a comprehensive database containing detailed information on each property in the area. When activated, the program overlays the street network layer onto the raster image, which include the location x and y coordinates, and distance from the start node of the link are saved to a (Pune_map) data file in feature image format. The accuracy of the values obtained depends on the accuracy of the coordinates of the street network being used. The street network must therefore be digitally accurate in order to obtain accurate location of each property. Geo-referencing of the map is done using arcview9 software.

The "network" module assists the user in generating a map layer from the data files imputed. These are the theme files (usually defined by the point, polygon and line) and the link description files i.e., the table, which contains the type of the accident, time and date etc. The user may add additional attributes interactively.

The "workspace" module is used to build a new workspace or open an existing workspace to be used in the analysis. A workspace or view in ARCVIEW3.1 is a term used to represent a saved configuration of a working session. It details ARCVIEW Tables and windows opened and used in any particular session. This module organises various used files and tables into a unified data set and also helps to keep track of all processes and outputs during any modelling session.

4.2 Models Module

This module presents options for the estimation and evaluation of a range of planned effects viz., identifying high crash zones, providing detail information about the accidents in a particular area, selection of streets by the user and finding the shortest route, database querying and visual effects.

Each of the above activity is carried out using a separate layer but shares a common data structure and makes use of the graphics display of the GIS in displaying the output.

The visual effects module is designed to provide no computational functions but serves more as a planning and administrative tool. It is added to provide the user a tool for viewing photographs of specific links, intersections and special roadway features of interest. It allows the user to click on a link or intersection or a feature of interest after which an associated plan image of the feature will be displayed. The process is achieved by linking the individual road features in the network layer to scan or to take aerial photographs of the network. The ARCVIEW hot link functions are then used to display the images. It should be noted that several images might be acquired for a particular geographic feature. In such situations, the system offers a variety of images to the user who may choose to view some or all.

4.3 Output Module

Normally, the results for each model for any transport scenario are displayed immediately after processing on the screen for viewing and subsequent printing. At a later stage during the modeling process, the output module enables the user to review on the screen and to generate hard copies and output results of previous runs. The output results are shown in the form of map displays, graphical charts and are tabular text files. The output provides users immediate information about the impact of alternate proposals and policies in the very early design stage. The output may be used to provide an overall transport network plan for the region. These results may be used to provide an up-to-date report on the state of the road safety system. The information gained from such reporting will encourage a move from mere reporting to a proactive means of planning for better urban road safety.

5. CASE OF PUNE CITY

Pune city is an important urban centre in Maharashtra and a rapidly growing metropolis of the country. The metropolitan area of Pune extends over 809 sq km. The Pune Metropolitan Area (PMA) consists of Pune Municipal Corporation (PMC), the Pimpri-Chinchwad Municipal Corporation (PCMC), Cantonment Boards of Pune and Kirkee and some villages. The total length of road network in the PMC area is about 1800 kms.

The importance of Pune as an industrial centre has grown rapidly since the 1960's when industrial expansion in Mumbai region was curtailed. Consequently, Pune has become a major centre in the State, having attracted engineering industry such as the automobile industry, etc. In addition to this, a number of multi-national companies have manufacturing bases within the city. Much of the local industry is concentrated along the main Pune-Bombay highway, enabling manufactured goods to be dispatched.

As per 2001 Census population, Pune is home to 26 lakhs people and 1.5 lakh vehicles. The city has experienced a steady population growth due to inward migration of both skilled and unskilled labour for the rising industrial base and service sector. It still remains a favourite destination for students as well as the retired community. For the last two decades, Pune has registered a steep growth in number of public-private vehicles. But the road infrastructure and the utilities have not expanded in commensurate with the increase in the number of vehicles.

The city reflects all the problems of a metropolis like increase in traffic congestion, speed reduction, environmental pollution, high incidence of road accidents and degradation of quality of life. The problem of road accidents has been brought out by an unprecedented growth in motorized vehicles which is further aggravated by interstate truck movement that flows through the city.

The growth of vehicles in Pune has assumed extraordinary proportions, especially in the case of two wheelers. Currently, there are about 15.6 lakh vehicles registered in PMC and PCMC areas out of which more than 12 lakh vehicles are two wheelers.

Public transport has always been a hallmark of any good transportation system. Commuters in Pune are heavily dependent on the personalised mode of transport like two wheelers and public transport has always taken a back seat. The maximum number of accidents occurs from 0900 to 1300 hrs in the morning and 1800 to 2200 hrs in the evening. Two wheelers, three wheelers and cars are involved in most of these accidents. Two wheeler riders alone are involved in more than 45% of fatal accidents while 39% of the fatal accident victims are pedestrians. Thus, pedestrians and two wheeler riders in Pune city are the most vulnerable road users exposed to high risk of road accidents on Pune city roads.

6. DATA COLLECTION

The data on fatal accidents and serious injury accidents for one year from January to December 2007 was taken up in this current study. The accident data are the secondary data obtained from the Traffic Police branch, Pune. The data was in local language and it was translated into English. The map showing all the corridors of PUNE was obtained from the Ground Water Survey and Analysis Department (GWSAD), Shivajinagar, Pune.

7. GIS SOFTWARE (ARCVIEW 3.1)

The different layers created using GIS software (ARCVIEW 3.1) are shown in the ARCVIEW screen in Figure 1 below:

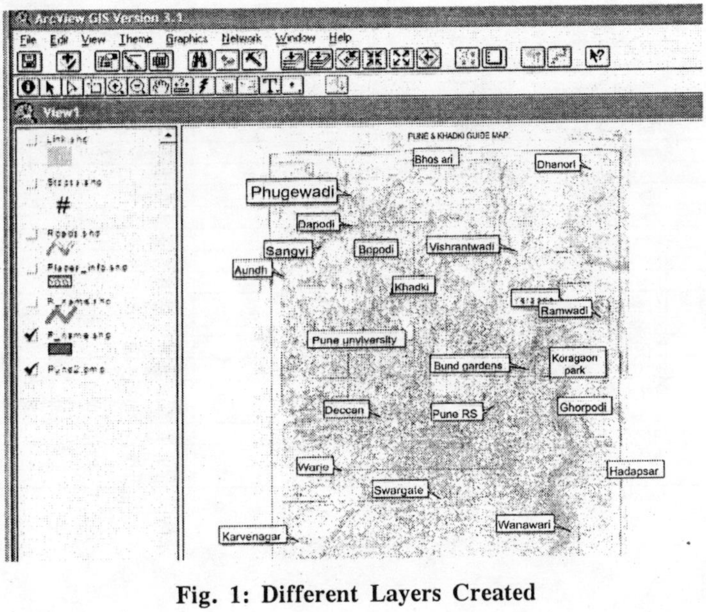

Fig. 1: Different Layers Created

Geo-referencing and digitizing are the primary steps to be carried out for developing the GIS. Geo-referencing is a process to establish a relationship between an image (row, column) co-ordinate system and a map (x, y) co-ordinate system.

Digitizing is the process of encoding geographic features in digital form as X, Y co-ordinates. It is carried out in order to create spatial data from existing documents and hardcopy maps. After completion of the above mentioned processes, the next step was creation of different layers namely, place information, road name, stop, link, label etc. These layers would be stored in the memory with .shp extension. Using ARCVIEW9 software, which is the latest version available and highly effective and accurate, the geo-referencing of Pune city map was carried out. The remaining modules of project I have been worked using the ARCVIEW3.1.

8. DATABASE

By using the accident database on fatal and serious accidents, the following fields were created in ARCVIEW3.1 viz., road name, place name, accident details, number of persons injured/died, type of vehicles involved and date & time, as shown in Figure 2 below:

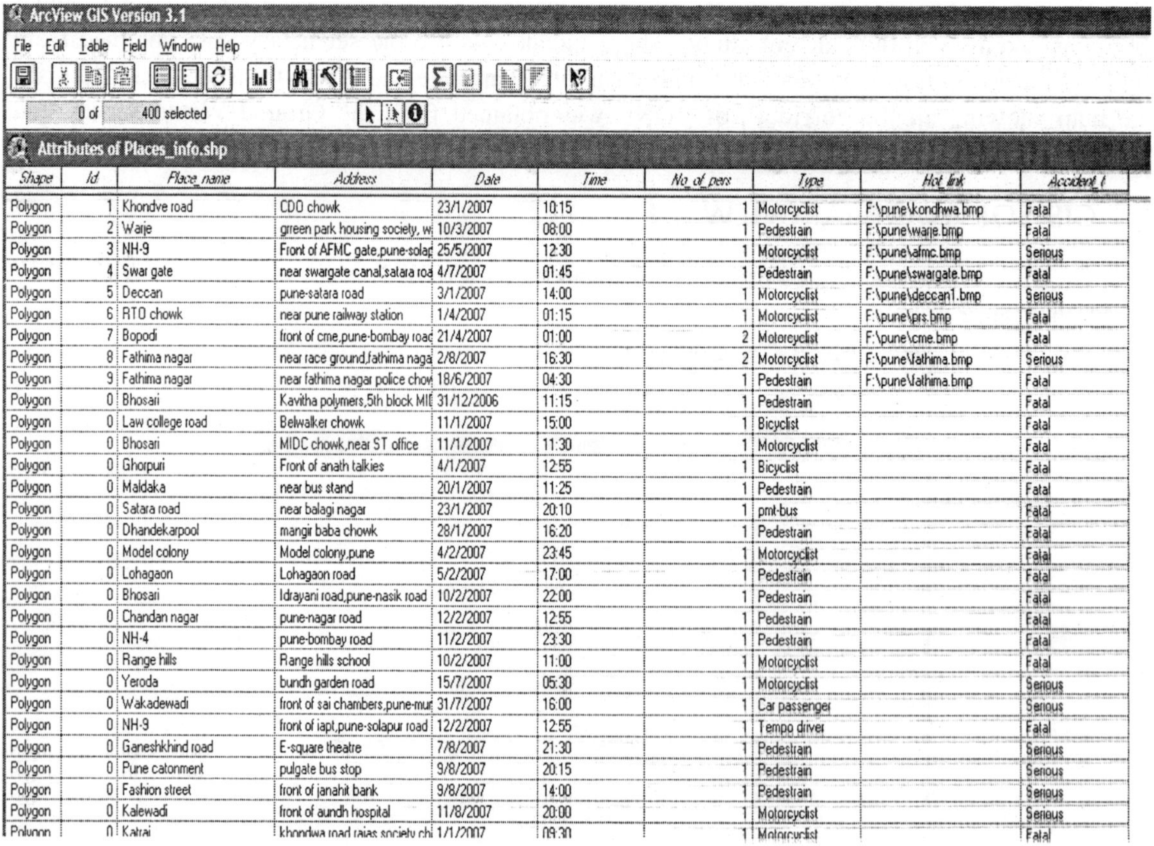

Shape	Id	Place_name	Address	Date	Time	No_of_pers	Type	Hot_link	Accident_t
Polygon	1	Khondve road	CDO chowk	23/1/2007	10:15	1	Motorcyclist	F:\pune\kondhwa.bmp	Fatal
Polygon	2	Warje	grreen park housing society, w	10/3/2007	08:00	1	Pedestrain	F:\pune\warje.bmp	Fatal
Polygon	3	NH-9	Front of AFMC gate,pune-solap	25/5/2007	12:30	1	Motorcyclist	F:\pune\afmc.bmp	Serious
Polygon	4	Swar gate	near swargate canal,satara roa	4/7/2007	01:45	1	Pedestrain	F:\pune\swargate.bmp	Fatal
Polygon	5	Deccan	pune-satara road	3/1/2007	14:00	1	Motorcyclist	F:\pune\deccan1.bmp	Serious
Polygon	6	RTO chowk	near pune railway station	1/4/2007	01:15	1	Motorcyclist	F:\pune\prs.bmp	Fatal
Polygon	7	Bopodi	front of cme,pune-bombay road	21/4/2007	01:00	2	Motorcyclist	F:\pune\cme.bmp	Fatal
Polygon	8	Fathima nagar	near race ground,fathima naga	2/8/2007	16:30	2	Motorcyclist	F:\pune\fathima.bmp	Serious
Polygon	9	Fathima nagar	near fathima nagar police chov	18/6/2007	04:30	1	Pedestrain	F:\pune\fathima.bmp	Fatal
Polygon	0	Bhosari	Kavitha polymers,5th block MID	31/12/2006	11:15	1	Pedestrain		Fatal
Polygon	0	Law college road	Belwalker chowk	11/1/2007	15:00	1	Bicyclist		Fatal
Polygon	0	Bhosari	MIDC chowk,near ST office	11/1/2007	11:30	1	Motorcyclist		Fatal
Polygon	0	Ghorpuri	Front of anath talkies	4/1/2007	12:55	1	Bicyclist		Fatal
Polygon	0	Maldaka	near bus stand	20/1/2007	11:25	1	Pedestrain		Fatal
Polygon	0	Satara road	near balagi nagar	23/1/2007	20:10	1	pmt-bus		Fatal
Polygon	0	Dhandekarpool	mangir baba chowk	28/1/2007	16:20	1	Pedestrain		Fatal
Polygon	0	Model colony	Model colony,pune	4/2/2007	23:45	1	Motorcyclist		Fatal
Polygon	0	Lohagaon	Lohagaon road	5/2/2007	17:00	1	Pedestrain		Fatal
Polygon	0	Bhosari	Idrayani road,pune-nasik road	10/2/2007	22:00	1	Pedestrain		Fatal
Polygon	0	Chandan nagar	pune-nagar road	12/2/2007	12:55	1	Pedestrain		Fatal
Polygon	0	NH-4	pune-bombay road	11/2/2007	23:30	1	Pedestrain		Fatal
Polygon	0	Range hills	Range hills school	10/2/2007	11:00	1	Motorcyclist		Fatal
Polygon	0	Yeroda	bundh garden road	15/7/2007	05:30	1	Motorcyclist		Serious
Polygon	0	Wakadewadi	front of sai chambers,pune-mur	31/7/2007	16:00	1	Car passenger		Serious
Polygon	0	NH-9	front of iapt,pune-solapur road	12/2/2007	12:55	1	Tempo driver		Fatal
Polygon	0	Ganeshkhind road	E-square theatre	7/8/2007	21:30	1	Pedestrain		Serious
Polygon	0	Pune catonment	pulgate bus stop	9/8/2007	20:15	1	Pedestrain		Serious
Polygon	0	Fashion street	front of janahit bank	9/8/2007	14:00	1	Pedestrain		Serious
Polygon	0	Kalewadi	front of aundh hospital	11/8/2007	20:00	1	Motorcyclist		Serious
Polygon	0	Katraj	khondwa road rajas society chi	1/1/2007	09:30	1	Motorcyclist		Fatal

Fig. 2: Database

A major advantage in creating a GIS database as shown in Fig: 3 is that it includes data on the spatial location and the shape of the geographic features recorded as points, polygons, lines, grids cells, areas or tins as well as their attributes. Using an Excel sheet, the fatal and serious accidents were sorted separately into different categories viz., place of accident, time, date, victim type etc.

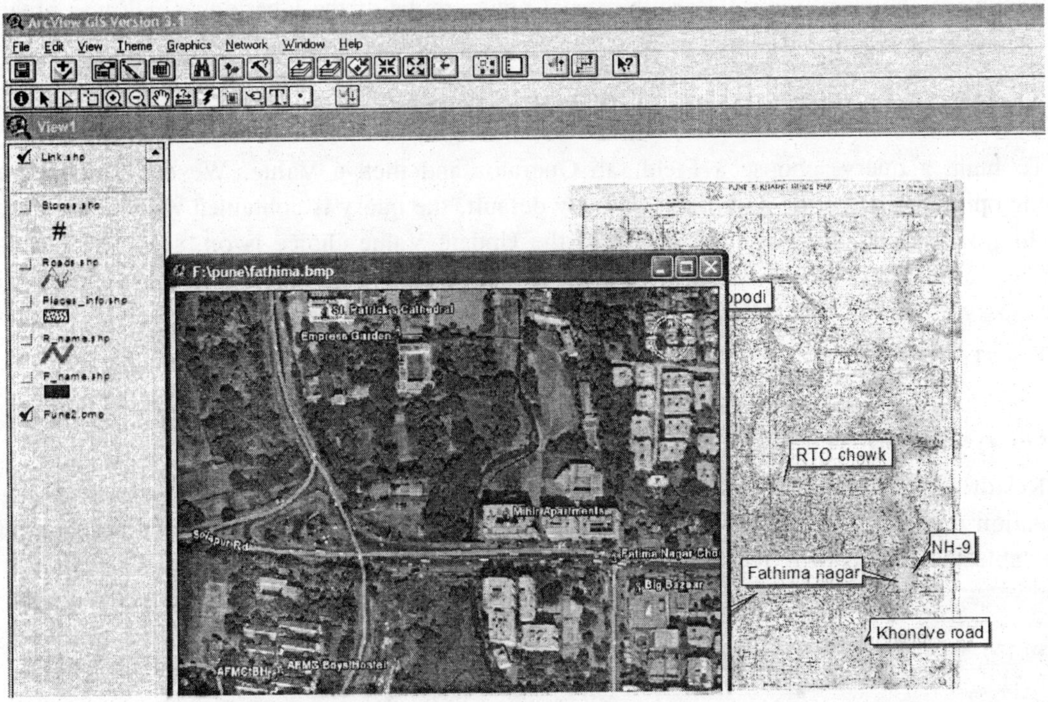

Fig. 3: Hyperlinks

9. HYPERLINK (HOT LINK)

Hot links help us to access virtually any data or application directly from a view. A hot link is followed by clicking on a feature in a theme with the Hot Link tool, Arc View performs

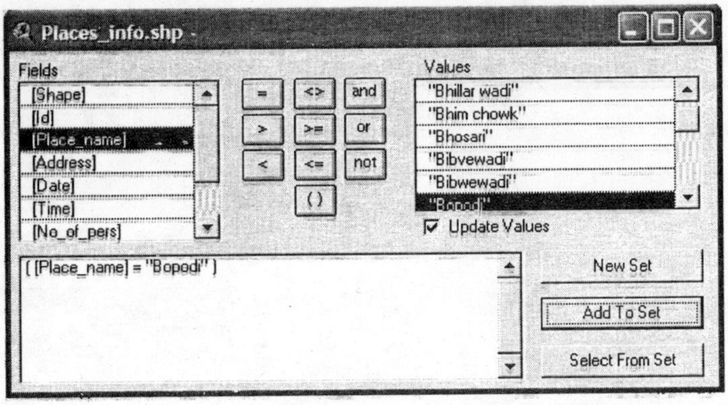

Fig. 4: Query-1

an action using an input value that feature has for a specified field in the theme's attribute table. The action and the field are specified in the Hot Links panel of the Theme Properties dialog. Each theme in a view can have its own hot link definition. There is no default hot link definition. Hot links have to be defined before they can be used. Snaps of the main road & chowk, snaps of important landmarks are shown in Figure 4.

The snaps shown in Figure 4 are the aerial photographs of the location, which was obtained using the Google Earth software.

10. ANALYSIS USING QUERY BUILDER

To build a query, choose a Field, an Operator and then a Value. We can build a query selecting options through the query text box. By default, the query is contained within parentheses, depending on the complexity of the query. If the Update Value choice is on, select a field name to list its value. Field names are always enclosed in square brackets ([]). If the required value in the query is not in the Values list, enter the same into the query text box.

E.g. 1: To select all the information about the place *'Bopodi'*, the following query can be used :

Query: ([Place_name] = "Bopodi")

Result: In the identify Results box, we can the get the output of the query and all the information related to the query will be displayed as shown in Figure 5 and in the corresponding theme table the results will be highlighted as shown in Figure 6.

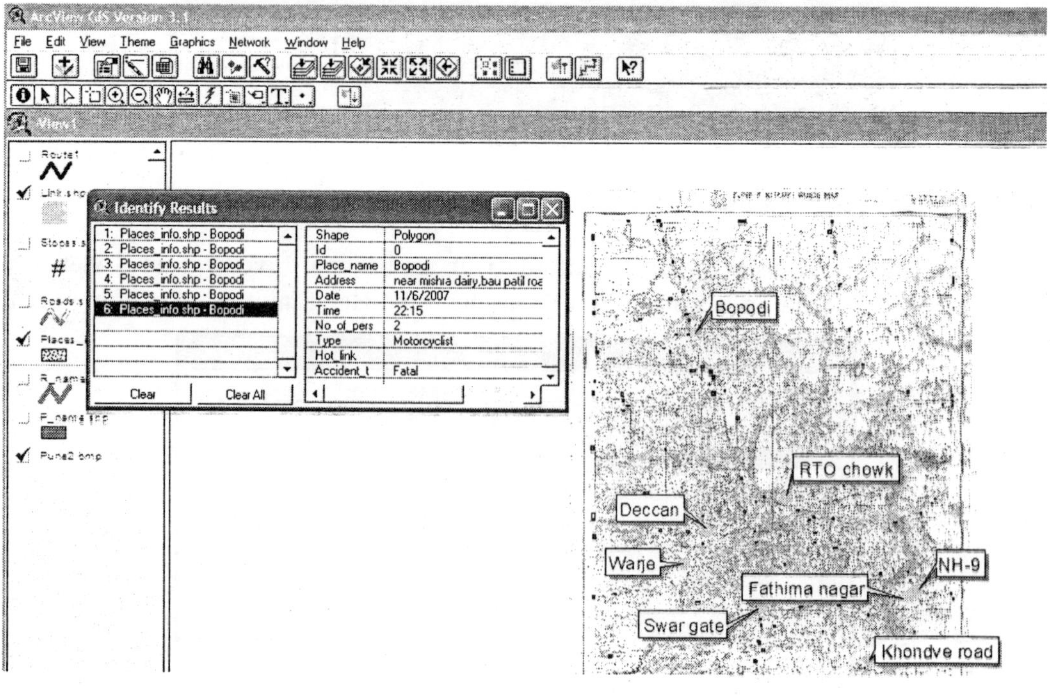

Fig. 5: Result-1 Display

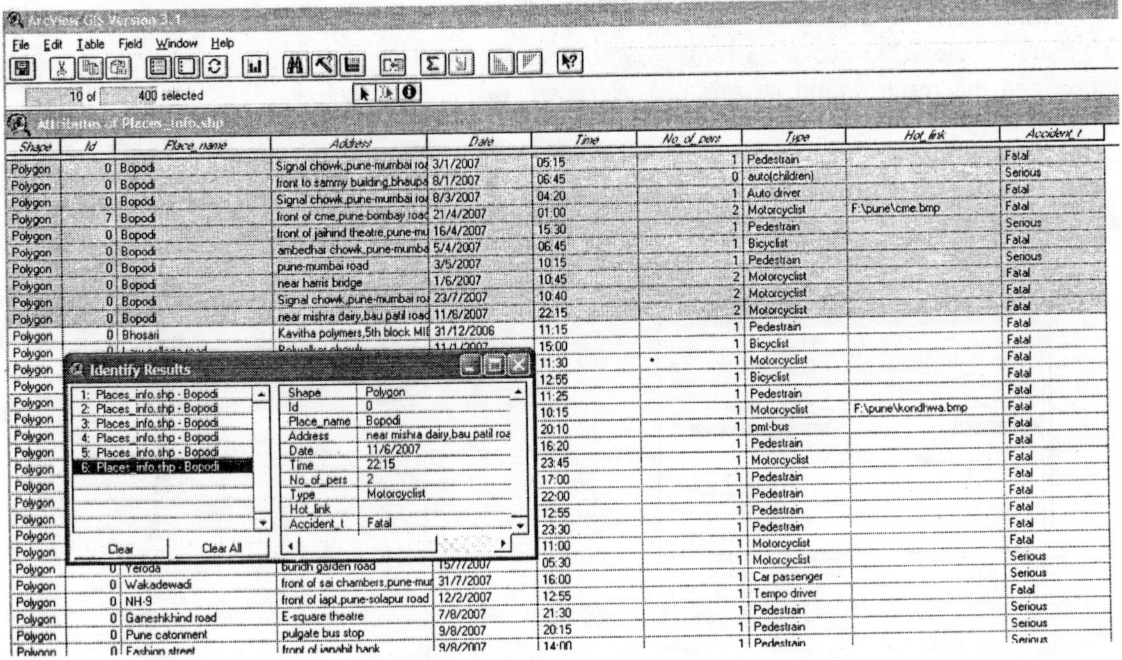

Fig. 6: Result-1 Database

E.g. 2: To select all the accidents, which has happened before a specific time, we could use:

Query: ([Time] < "02.13")

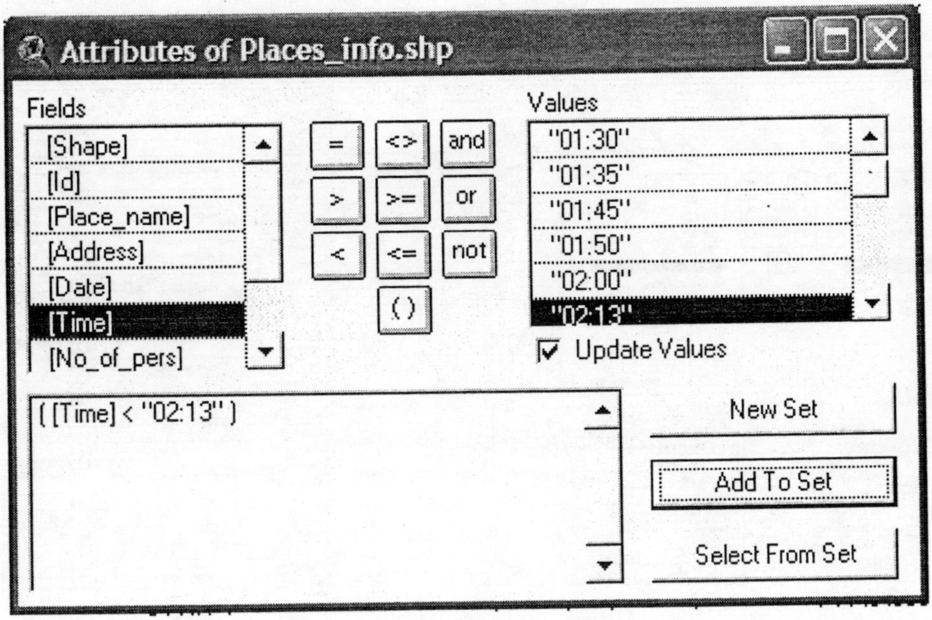

Fig. 7: Query-2

Result: All the accidents, which have happened before 02:13 will be highlighted as shown in Figure 8 below. 32 accidents took place before 02:13. To group them together, use promote button and the result would be grouped as shown in Figure 9 below.

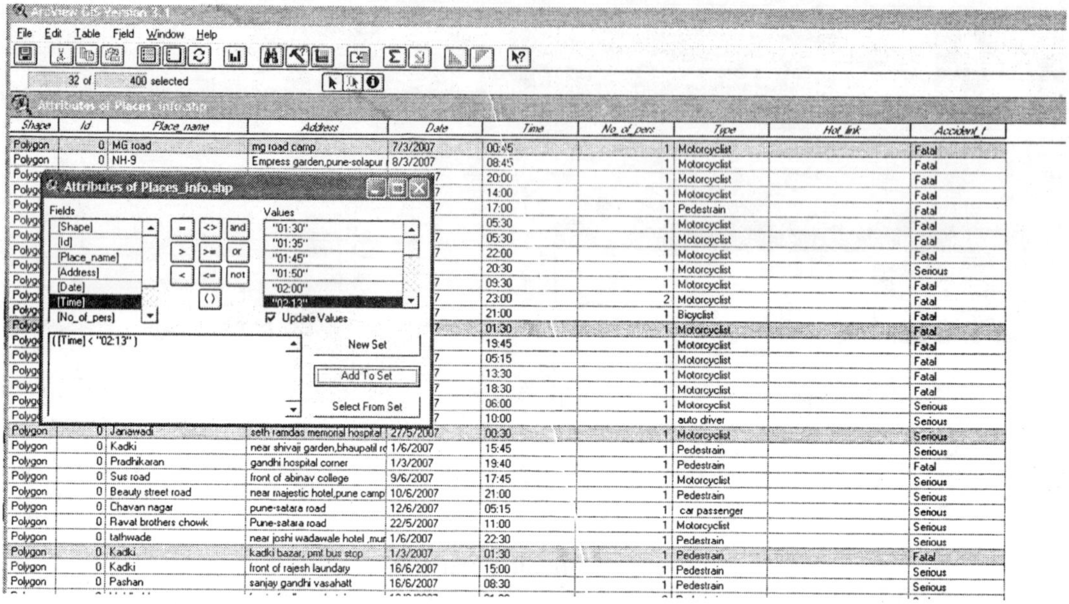

Fig. 8: Result-2

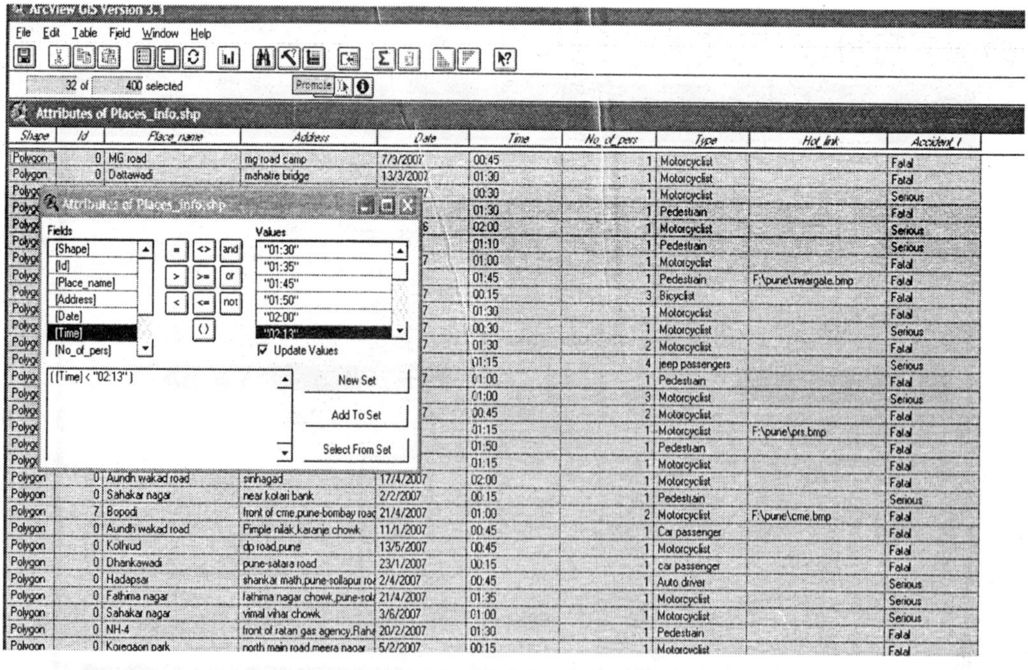

Fig. 9: Promoted Result

By using the query builder, we can get the result for any question, which is helpful for on the spot analysis of the accident.

The percentage share of vulnerable road users among the total victims can be found out by firing a single query. Similarly, the percentage share of two wheelers involved in total number of accidents can also be found out from the accident database using the query facility instantly.

11. NETWORK ANALYST

The Arc View Network Analyst is an extension product designed to help use road networks more efficiently. It can solve common network problems on any theme containing lines that connect. This theme can be a shape file, ARC/INFO coverage, or a CAD drawing. Before solving a problem, we can model networks precisely, including setting up average travel times, one-way streets, prohibited turns, overpasses and underpasses, and closed streets. It also helps to find out efficient travel routes, determine which facility or vehicle is closest, generate travel directions and also to find a service area around a site, etc. Figures 10, 11 and 12 below show how to find the best route between stop1 and stop 2 by using network analyst, loading stops in the route box and querying as to find the best route will give the desired result as highlighted in colour alongwith the information of the directions displayed in the direction dialogue box.

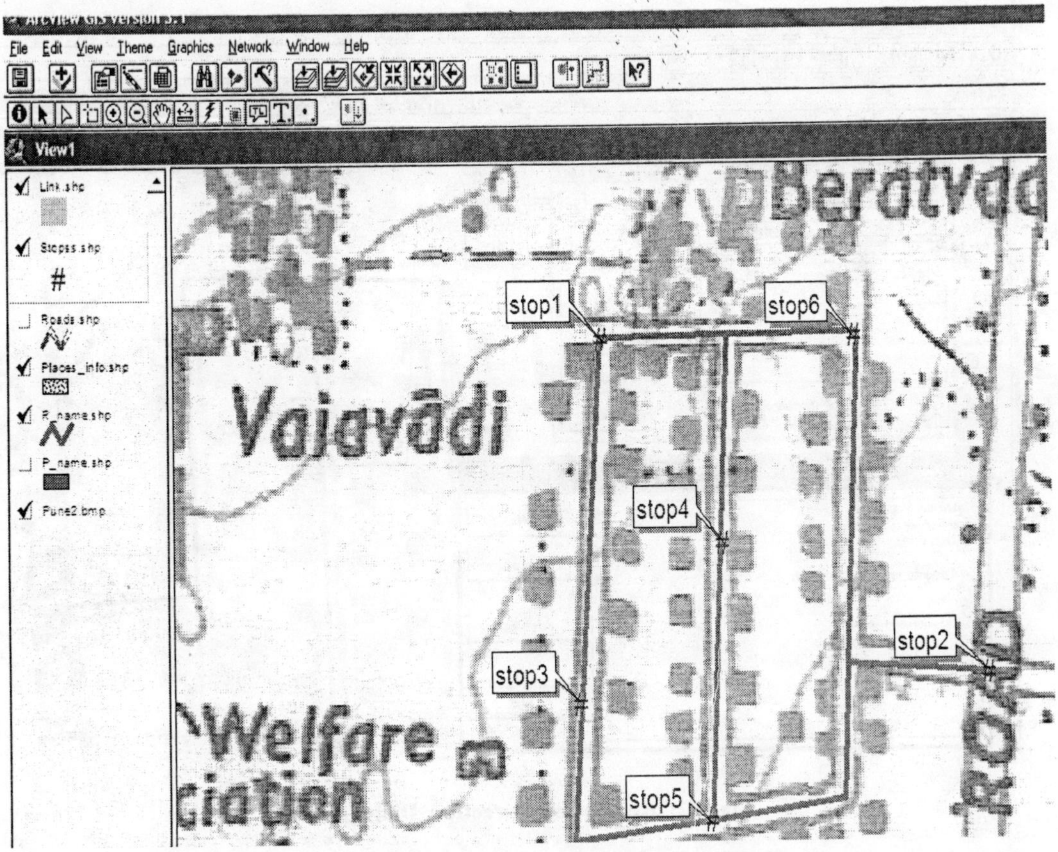

Fig. 10: Network Analyst

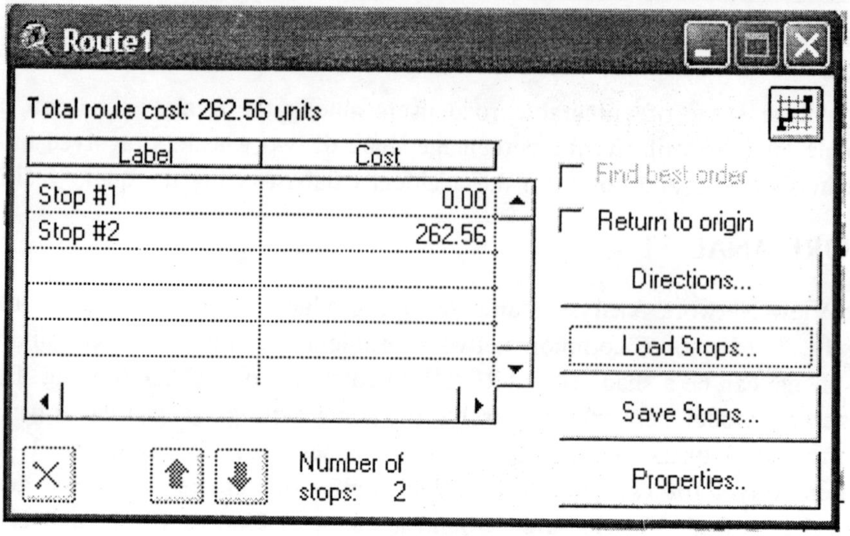

Fig. 11: Route Dialogue Box

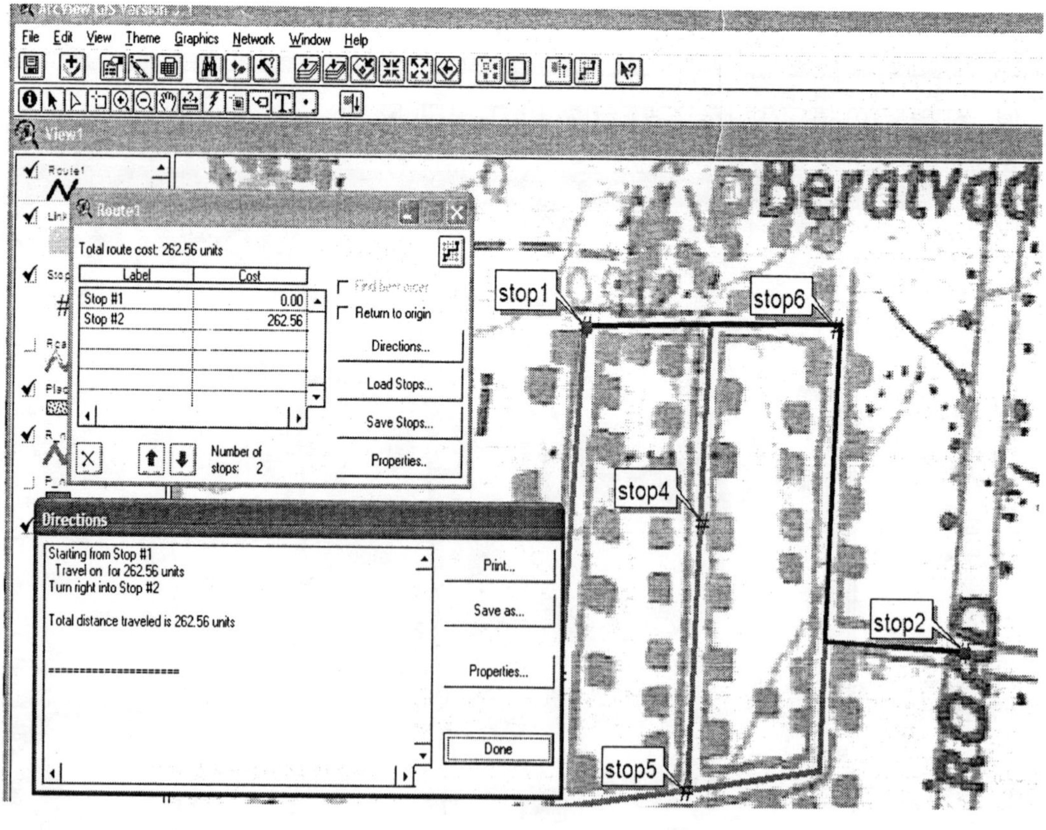

Fig. 12: Result and Direction Dialogue Box

12. CONCLUSIONS

This paper focusses on the management of accident data and performing tasks such as accident analysis and safety studies. To start with, these studies can be taken up on a priority basis along the Mumbai road, Solapur road, Nashik road and Ahmednagar road, which have been found to be the major accident-prone roads in the city as a result of this entire exercise. GIS-based technology is useful especially while conducting corridor analysis, pedestrian safety studies and accident analysis. It provides the tools required to review area-wide safety and prioritize safety improvements that will give maximum impact. It also allows us to update the GIS components, such as street network and other layers, with updated data. The Arc View version allows overlaying the accident data with several other layers such as two wheeler routes and transit centers, etc. Additionally, it permits a view of the actual roadway geometry in collision diagrams and enables the urban planners on the spot analysis.

REFERENCES

Affum, J.K. (1997) *'A GIS-based Method for Estimating the Accidents Impacts of Road Traffi'.*

Downing, A. et.al. (1997) *'Review of Road Safety in Urban Areas'*, Project report PR/INT/200/00, Transport Research Laboratory, U.K.

Mohan, D. (2002) *'Traffic Safety and Health in Indian Cities'. The Asian Journal of Transport and Infrastructure, Vol. 9, No. 1 pp. 79-94.*

Rao, V.T. et.al., 'Intelligent *Transportation System (ITS): A Technology Solution for 21st Century, Public Transport System Management.'*

15

USE OF TELECOMMUNICATION SERVICES AND PASSENGER TRANSPORT: AN URBAN VIEWPOINT

Smruti Bulsari

ABSTRACT

The present study tries to examine the effect of a well-developed telecommunication system on passenger transport. This study is based on a survey of 150 households of Surat city out of which 125 households owned a telephone — a fixed-line phone or a mobile phone or both, whereas 21 households did not own either a fixed-line phone or a mobile phone. The results indicate that the users of telephone were of the opinion that they are able to reduce their expenses on transportation whereas those households not having a telephone opined that they have to incur avoidable expenditure on transportation. The majority of owners of telephones prefer to place orders for day-to-day consumables like vegetables, milk, grocery etc. on phone rather than going to the market. They also use their phones extensively to build and maintain their social network. The respondents owning a telephone also said that they even prefer to book tickets — railway, bus or air — on telephones or the Internet. The households not owning a telephone — fixed-line or mobile, or having access to public telephone found themselves spending a lot of their time for maintaining social contacts. The households not owning or having access to telephones were found to be low-income earners with a large family size and therefore, they could not afford to use phones for any purpose other than emergency calls. Data on macro indicators of transport and telecommunications also reveal similar patterns.

1. INTRODUCTION

Transport and telecommunications are intricately woven in our day-to-day activities. A good quality and well-knit transport as well as a telecommunication network can contribute towards development of an economy in general, and industries in particular.

From the Second Five Year Plan, infrastructure has been accorded high priority in India. Roads are considered to be the back bone of a transport system (CMIE, 1986). According to this report, a well developed road network is important for the development of industries in backward areas, thus, establishing a link between industries and agriculture as well as between producers and consumers. All these linkages give rise to positive externalities in the form of development of nearby geographical areas, especially the backward and rural areas, thereby, contributing to economic development. A telecommunication network, on the other hand, acts as a complement to a well-developed road transport system. This is because a well-developed, good quality telecommunication system can effectively transmit information without any delay. Applications of telecommunication technologies like facsimile (Fax), e-mails, text messaging, etc. can help in saving time and expenses on information dissemination. Information is vital for any business and therefore, information is a requirement for industrial development too. The importance of communication is also explained in a study by Nanavati (2001). According to this study, a good communication network can lead to efficient allocation of resources to the telecommunication and transport sectors. It also reduces traffic intensity, road accidents, pollution and all these lead to overall improvement in work culture. Policymakers of the country have started according high priority to the telecommunication sector in recent years. In the Five Year Plans, the allocation towards developing the telecommunication sector has been continuously rising. The Policy makers have also been quite liberal in setting the limits of Foreign Direct Investments (FDI) in the telecommunication sector. Entry of private players, especially foreign players, have helped in developing telecommunication services at cheaper rates and of world-class quality. The present study tries to examine the effect of a well-developed telecommunication system on passenger transport in urban areas.

An objective of this study is to examine the impact of increasing use of telecommunication services on urban passenger transport. The paper is organised into four sections. Section – 2 discusses the rationale and methodology for this study. The usage pattern of telephones and perceptions of people about using telephones are discussed in Section – 3. Section – 4 summarises the findings of this study.

2. RATIONALE AND METHODOLOGY OF STUDY

There is a dearth of literature examining the relationship between increasing use of telecommunication services in urban areas and urban passenger transport. However, some studies state that people have become more conscious about use and waste of time. Therefore, people have started rating various means of transport in terms of the amount of time that is saved by resorting to that means of transport. Somuyiwa (2007) categorises transport into two parts – one involving physical movement and the second involving non-physical movement. She quotes Oyesiku (2002) that the means of non-physical transport is attained through telecommunication services.

The present study tries to examine the pattern of and perceptions of people towards increasing use of telecommunication services. This study is based on a survey of 150 households of Surat city of Gujarat State. The State of Gujarat, situated on the western coast of India, is one of the major states occupying a leading position in industrial development. Many medium and small-scale industries are located in the South Gujarat region, including Surat. Handloom and handicraft industries are located in Kuchh district as well as other northern and western parts of the State. The long coastline of Gujarat and its proximity to Mumbai have always attracted industrialists and traders to Gujarat. Moreover, Gujarat is the only State in India to have passed the Gujarat Infrastructure Development Act, 1999, in order to provide a legal framework for private sector participation in infrastructure development of the State (Saxena, 2001). Surat is the hub of textile, jari and diamond industries. Moreover, large-scale industries like Reliance, Essar, Kribhco, NTPC etc. are located on the coastal belt of Hazira in Surat district. Today, Surat is one of the fastest growing cities of the world.

The data on 150 households of Surat city was collected using a structured questionnaire. Five clusters were identified on the basis of income groups[1] and samples were drawn from each cluster. Thirty respondents were surveyed from each cluster and snowball sampling was done in each cluster. The respondents were asked to rate on a five point scale the usage pattern of telephones and their perception whether, use of telephones has reduced their expenses and time on transportation. The households not owning a telephone were asked to rate on the same scale whether, they feel disadvantaged and whether they have to spend a lot of money on transportation.

Out of total responses from 150 households, 146 responses were retained after data cleaning. As shown in Table-1, 17 households did not either possess either a fixed-line phone or a mobile phone, where as 91 respondents possessed both fixed-line and mobile phone. 17 respondents possessed only mobile phones only, where as 21 respondents had only fixed-line phone. Micro-level analysis revealed that the households not owning or not having access to telephones were found to be low-income earners with large family size and therefore, they could not afford to use phones for any purpose other than emergency calls.

Table 1: Respondents' Status on Possessing a Telephone

Status of Possessing a Telephone	*Frequency*	*Per cent*	*Valid Per cent*	*Cumulative a Telephone*
None	17	11.6	11.6	11.6
Both	91	62.3	62.3	74.0
Mobile Only	17	11.6	11.6	85.6
Fixed-line Only	21	14.4	14.4	100.0
Total	146	100.0	100.0	

The uses of telephones by respondents are summarised in ensuing paragraphs.

3. NATURE OF USAGE OF TELEPHONES AND RESPONDENTS' PERCEPTIONS

The responses were collected on a five point scale — never, rarely, sometimes, often and always. The users of the telephones were asked about different purposes for which they use telephones. In order to identify the usage patterns, factor analysis[2] was undertaken. Three factors are extracted from 9 variables. Factor-1 explains 24% of variance, factor-2 explains 21% and factor-3 explains 18% of total variance in the model. The total variance explained by these three factors together is 64%.

Table 2: Rotated Component Matrix (a)

Variables	*Component*		
	1	2	3
FL Telebanking	.749		
FL Calling Workplace	.672		
FL Booking Complaints	.658		
FL Booking Local Conveyance	.629		
FL Ticket Booking		.865	
FL Grocery		.744	
FL Social Calls			.847
FL Contact family members			.718
FL Casual Calls		.513	.574

Note:

(*a*) Extraction Method: Principal Component Analysis.

(*b*) Rotation Method: Varimax with Kaiser Normalisation.

(*c*) Rotation converged in 5 iterations.

Table 2 shows that highest loadings are found to be on variables like telebanking, calling workplace to convey change in time schedules, booking complaints for household gadgets and booking local conveyance (like calling an autorickshaw). It can be said that had not a telephone been used for any of these purposes people would have been spending time and money on commuting to do all these chores.The second highest factor loading is found on using telephone for ticket booking for bus/rail/air and placing order for grocery. The variables with third highest factor loading are using fixed-line phone for making social calls, for contacting family members about change in schedule and for making casual calls.

Barring the use of fixed-line phone for contacting family members for conveying change/ delay in schedule, all the other uses of fixed-line phones tend to reduce the need for local conveyance. For example, in the absence of telebanking, one might have to go personally to bank in order to do any transactions. Similarly, for booking complaints on household appliances/gadgets, telephonic talk obviates the need to personally go to the service provider. Booking bus/rail/air tickets through telephone eliminate the need to personally go to railway station/booking office. Thus, use of telephones seems to have significantly reduced the need for local conveyance.[3]

On being specifically asked whether, it results in saving on expenses by doing all these activities through fixed-line phone, 81% respondents said that it reduces their expenses on socialisation. 91% respondents said that they also save on time on social visits, 70% respondents said that they save time on booking complaints for household appliances/gadgets where as 42% respondents said that they save time on shopping.

A similar study of mobile phone users barring the first factor, shows the use of mobile phone to get more for information seeking and for entertainment purpose. The second factor shows that even mobile phone is used for booking complaints of household appliances/gadgets, booking for local conveyance, booking bus/rail/air tickets, telebanking, placing order for milk, vegetables, grocery etc. and calling at work place to convey change in schedules, (see Table 3).

Table 3: Rotated Component Matrix (a)

Variables	*Component*			
	1	**2**	**3**	**4**
CL Photo for evidence	.888			
CL E-mails	.843			
CL MMS for Information	.841			
CL Photo for entertainment	.827			
CL Data Transfer	.825			
CL Internet	.816			
CL Recording Conversation	.778			
CL Task Scheduler	.632			
CL MMS for entertainment	.586		.540	
CL Alarm	.534			
CL Booking Complaints		.818		
CL Booking Local Conveyance		805		
CL Ticket Booking		.757		
CL Telebanking		.752		
CL Grocery		.604		
CL Calling Workplace		.547		
CL Social SMS			.849	
CL Casual SMS			.830	
CL Casual Calls			.789	
CL Social Calls			.674	
CL Contact family members				
CL News Updates				.740

Note:

(*a*) *Extraction Method:* Principal Component Analysis.

(*b*) *Rotation Method:* Varimax with Kaiser Normalisation.

(*c*) Rotation converged in 6 iterations.

Table 3 shows that the third factor includes variables like use of mobile phone for making social and casual calls as well as writing text messages (SMS) for socialisation / casual purpose. The fourth factor shows the use of mobile phones for news updates.

The total variance explained by the first factor is 29%, by second factor is 19.5%, by factor-3 is 15.6% and that by factor-4 is 7%. The total variance explained by all four factors is 69%.

The influence of factor-4 is very less but barring the first factor, factor-2 and factor-3 are indicative of substituting phone calls/text messages for local conveyance. 68% respondents said that they save their time on complaint booking for household appliances/gadgets and 47% said that they save their time on shopping.

When the respondents using mobile phones were asked about whether, they save on conveyance expenses by using mobile phone instead of personally visiting places, 69% said that the use text messages saves expenses on conveyance, 89% said that they make social calls from their mobile phones rather than making social visits.

There were, however, 17 respondents who neither possessed a fixed-line phone nor a mobile phone. When these respondents were asked whether, they feel disadvantaged because of not having a telephone, 9 respondents said that they felt so. When these 9 respondents were asked whether, they have to spend more expense on transportation/local conveyance, they all replied in the positive.

Though, the extent of impact of the use of telecommunication services on urban passenger transport is not measured, but results show that the extent of local conveyance has reduced with the use of fixed-line and mobile phones. At the macro level, the chart shown in Figure 1 gives the rate at which — average distance travelled per passenger and number of telephone connections grew from 1991 to 2003. Average distance traveled per passenger is plotted on Y-axis and telephone connections are on secondary Y-axis. Figure 3 shows that the growth rate of telephone connections is much higher than that of average distance travelled per passengers. The trend of average distance travelled by passengers is more or less linear and steady. The years 1994, 1996, 1999 and 2001 show a decline in the average distance travelled.

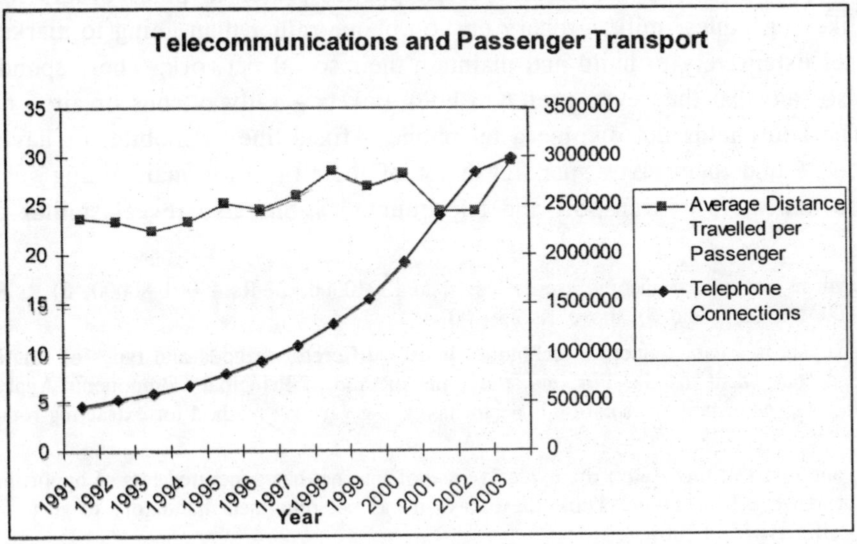

Fig. 1: Telecommunications and Passenger Transport at a Macro Level

Source: Basic Transport Statistics Gujarat (2004) and Socioeconomic Review of Gujarat State (2003-04). Govt. of Gujarat.

It has been mentioned in Section-1 that telecommunications and transport sector are major contributors to economic development. On probing deeper, it was found that though there is decline in average distance traveled by passengers, the revenue per passenger is increasing every year. Moreover, the amount of goods transport is also continuously rising. This shows that use of telephones has made businesses simple and more efficient. Moreover, substituting phone call for local conveyance/transportation can have following benefits:

1. It can decrease traffic density,
2. It can help in saving petrol, a scare energy resource, and thereby save precious foreign exchange that is otherwise used in purchasing the stock of petrol, and
3. Reduced traffic can lead to reduction in pollution level, thereby, conserving our environment.

4. CONCLUSIONS

This study is based on data collected from 150 households of Surat city of Gujarat state for understanding the nature of usage of telecommunication services vis-à-vis local conveyance / transport. Out of 146 responses retained after data cleaning, 17 households did not possess either a fixed-line or a mobile phone. The households not owning or having access to telephones were found to be low-income earners with large family size and therefore, they could not afford to use phones for any purpose other than emergency calls. The results indicate that most of the time, respondents use telephones as substitute to local conveyance. Moreover, the users of telephone were of the opinion that they are able to reduce their expenses and time on local conveyance/transportation whereas those households not having a telephone opined that they have to incur avoidable expenditure on transportation. The majority of owners of telephones prefer to place orders for day-to-day consumables like vegetables, milk, grocery etc. on phone rather than going to market. They also use their phones extensively to build and maintain their social network. The respondents owning a telephone also said that they even prefer to book tickets – railway, bus or air – on telephones or Internet. The households not owning a telephone – fixed-line or mobile, or having access to public telephone found themselves spending a lot of their time for maintaining social contacts. Data on macro indicators of transport and telecommunications also reveal similar patterns.

Notes:

1. The categories for annual income are 1) less than Rs.40000, 2) Rs.40001-80000, 3) Rs.80001-160000, 4) Rs.160001-250000 and 5) above Rs.250000.
2. Factor analysis is a data reduction technique. It uses different methods and types of rotations to extract the rotated component matrix. For this study, the method of Principal Components Analysis is used to extract factors and orthogonal rotation is performed using varimax method for extracting rotated component matrix.
3. Though, not a part of this study, the extensive use of internet has generated lots of opportunities for those who want to work from home. Thus, these days it has not remained mandatory to go to work place for some specific types of jobs.

REFERENCES

Centre for Monitoring Gujarat Economy, Government of Gujarat. (1986), *A Profile on Infrastructure in Gujarat*.

Government of Gujarat, Department of Economics and Statistics, (2007), *Basic Transport Statistics Gujarat*.

Government of Gujarat, Directorate of Economics and Statistics, (2005), Socio-Economic Review.

Indian Journal of Transport Mangement, October-December 2005, pp. 521-524.

Nanavati, A. (2001), Infrastructural Facilities in Gujarat (Gujarat 2010 — Challenges and Opportunites), Seminar Volume, Government of Gujarat, pp. 472-477.

Saxena, R. (2001), Infrastructure Development in Gujarat (Gujarat 2010 — Challenges and Opportunites), Seminar Volume, Government of Gujarat, pp. 472-477.

Somuyiwa, A. (2007), Transport Demand Management: A Conceptual Appraisal, *Indian Journal of Transport Management,* January-March 2007, pp. 4-20.

16

ENVIRONMENTAL IMPACT OF ROAD TRANSPORT ON KOLHAPUR

P.S. Kamble

ABSTRACT

Increased use of urban transport services has significantly increased various environmental problems in cities such as traffic congestion, accidents, air pollution and noise pollution. The environmental degradation has severe effects on the flora, fauna, materials and building and human resources. Of these, human resources are a very important component of the environment, in general, and biosphere, in particular.

It is against this background that this paper attempts to study the environmental effects of urban transport on the human resources in Kolhapur city.

1. INTRODUCTION

Infrastructure facilities have a special importance in the economic development process of an economy since they play a very vital role in the socio-economic development of an economy as a whole. In absence of infrastructure, development is merely a dream rather than a reality. Noteworthy infrastructural facilities are electricity, irrigation, transport, water supply, roads, harbours, airports and so on. Transport, in general, and road transport, in particular, is necessary for the development of an economy, in general, and urban areas, in particular.

Urban road transport facilities create a conducive environment for the development of urban areas through facilitation of movement of productive resources along with the human resources necessary for the production of goods and services through the development of a variety of productive activities as well as marketing of the produced goods and services. Their role in time management and other conveniences is considerable. Important means of urban road transport are the different categories of vehicles like two wheelers, three wheelers, four wheelers and others. But it is a fact that the environmental dimension of urban transport is a neglected one. Not much attention has been paid towards the environmental impacts of road transport.

Increase in the use of urban road transport means has significantly contributed to the environmental impacts such as traffic jams and congestion, accidents, air pollution, noise pollution, etc. The primary air pollutants found in most urban areas are carbon monoxide (Co), nitrogen oxides (No_x), sulphur oxides (So_2), hydrocarbons (Hc) and suspended particulate matter (PM). Urban transport means very badly affect flora, fauna, materials and buildings, human resources. Of these, human resources are a very important component of the environment, and biosphere, in particular. The major consequences of air pollution from urban road transport means are slowing of ciliary beat and mucus flow in the bronchial tree, absorption of toxic gases such as So_2 and production of synergic effects, intrinsically toxic because of physical or chemical characteristics (SPM), bronchoconstriction, throat irritation, eye irritation, coughing (So_2), headache, nausea, vomiting, dizziness, slurring of speech, tendency of collapse, pulmonary edema (No_x), etc. It is against this overall background, that the present study, endeavours to assess the environmental impacts of urban road transport in Kolhapur city, with a focus on impact on human resources.

2. HYPOTHESIS OF THE STUDY

The present study will test the following hypothesis, namely,

Urban transport system (means and facilities) results in very bad environmental impacts on cities, especially on human resources. In the absence of due precautions that need to be taken, this could result in heavy economic losses to a locality.

3. OBJECTIVES OF THE STUDY

The following are the important objectives of the present study:

1. To study the road transport profile of Kolhapur City.
2. To review environmental problems arising from the road transport in Kolhapur.
3. To assess environmental impacts of road transport on Kolhapur city.
4. To suggest policy measures so as to restrict bad environmental impacts on the city.

4. DATA BASE AND RESEARCH METHODOLOGY

The present study relies on both, secondary as well as primary data. The study takes into consideration the period from 2000 to 2004, especially for the secondary data and its interpretation. The necessary secondary data was collected through the sources like Regional Transport Office (RTO) Publications, Environmental Status Report of Kolhapur City and other publications of Kolhapur Municipal Corporation (KMC).

This study has undertaken to collect the necessary primary data by administering a well prepared questionnaire and holding discussions and interviews. The present study conducted a field survey of 50 households selected randomly in Kolhapur city. While conducting the survey, the study took due care of different strata based on socio-economic criteria so as to arrive at a well stratified sample.

Both secondary as well as primary data were classified and tabulated in the light of hypothesis and objectives of the present study. The data was processed by employing simple statistical tools such as growth rate, ratio analysis and others as per needs and requirements. The processed data was studied and interpreted so as to arrive at some conclusions.

5. KOLHAPUR CITY: A PROFILE OF ROAD TRANSPORT

Infrastructural facilities play a very vital role in speeding up the process of socio-economic development of the economy, in general, and a locality, in particular. It is a fact that infrastructure facilities have been concentrated in the urban areas and cities. Likewise, there is a concentration of urban road transport means and facilities in Kolhapur city also. A profile of the road transport in Kolhapur city is presented in Table 1.

Table 1: Road Transport Profile of Kolhapur City

Type of Vehicle	*2000*	*2003*	*2004*	*SGR*
Two wheelers	87145 (79%)	120809 (80.7%)	106323 (16%)	22%
Three wheelers	6272 (6%)	6998 (5%)	7189 (4%)	15%
Four wheelers	16817 (14%)	22624 (14%)	58895 (34%)	250%
Others	32 (1%)	37 (1%)	55 (1%)	72%
Total	110266 (100%)	150468 (100%)	172462 (100%)	56%

Source: RTO, Kolhapur.

Note: SGR: Simple Growth Rate.

Kolhapur is a famous industrialised, religious, historical, educational, cultural city in western Maharashtra. It is also known as "Dakshin Kashi". Therefore, urban road transport means and facilities have been concentrated in the city of Kolhapur. Consequently, the total number as well as different categories of vehicles show a rapid growth in the city during the period from 2000 to 2004.

The data in Table 1 reveals that two wheelers have a prominent share in the total number of vehicles in Kolhapur city. Four wheelers stood at second position, as far as their relative share in city road transport. On the basis of growth, four wheelers (250%) and others (72%) category of vehicles have registered a significant growth. Likewise, total number of road transport means also has indicated (56%) a significant growth during the period under study. To be precise, the growth in road transport means and facilities along with different category of vehicles is significant, which could affect the socio-economic development of the city.

6. ENVIRONMENTAL PROBLEMS DUE TO ROAD TRANSPORT IN KOLHAPUR CITY

It is a fact that growing urban road transport means and facilities in Kolhapur have been significantly contributing to the socio-economic development of the Kolhapur city. But it has also resulted in environmental pollution and environmental problems in Kolhapur city. These environmental problems have been affecting badly human resources and thereby, causing economic losses. In other words, the development of road transport system has produced both economic and social benefits to a large number of people but not without a social cost.

The study of ambient air quality in Kolhapur city shows an increase in air pollution and deterioration in the quality of air in terms of principle pollutants SPM, RPM, So_2, No_x, Co, Hc. Air pollution is observed to have increased in commercial areas such as Dabholkar Chowk, Venus Corner, Bindu Chowk and areas near Kolhapur Municipal Corporation.

Likewise, the levels of noise have crossed their quality standards in many places in the city. Places where there is high of noise as compared to prescribed standards are commercial areas arising due to road transport means and facilities. The noteworthy areas are Tararani Chowk, Dabholkar Corner, Venus Corner, Malkar Corner, Gangavesh, Rankala Bus Stand.

The total number of accidents in Kolhapur city rose from 105 in 2000 to 275 in 2004, which consisted of 6 & 18 fatal. 26 & 28 serious, 56 & 126 slight, 17 & 53 minor.

7. ENVIRONMENTAL IMPACTS OF ROAD TRANSPORT ON KOLHAPUR CITY

The present study has attempted to assess the environmental impacts of road transport on Kolhapur city by using the Contingent Valuation Method (CVM) based on primary data generated by approaching respondents and sufferers. The data in Table 2 gives the number of respondents from the traffic crowded areas in Kolhapur city.

Table 2: Traffic Crowded Area in Kolhapur City

Name of Area	*No. of Respondents*	*Percentage Share*
Rajarampuri	11	22%
ST Stand	04	08%
Dabholkar Corner	06	12%
Venus Corner	09	18%
Shivaji Chowk	10	20%
Rankala ST Stand	10	20%
Total	50	100%

Source: Primary Survey, November 2007.

This study has used stratified random sampling method while selecting the respondents. Table 3 reflects the relevant data in terms of the socio-economic profile.

Table 3: A Profile of Respondents

Sr. No.	*Features*	*No. of Respondents*	*Percentage Share*
1	Age Group		
	(*a*) 0 to 15 years	01	02%
	(*b*) 16 to 60 years	44	88%
	(*c*) Above 60 years	05	10%
2.	Religion		
	(*a*) Hindu	35	70%
	(*b*) Islam	10	20%
	(*c*) Others	05	10%
3.	Occupation		
	(*a*) Service	13	26%
	(*b*) Business	30	60%
	(*c*) Others	07	14%
4.	Level of Income		
	(*a*) Rs. 1000 to Rs. 10000	28	58%
	(*b*) Rs. 11000 to Rs. 25000	19	38%
	(*c*) Above Rs. 26000	03	04%

Source: Same as of Table 2.

The data in Table 3 shows that the present survey has more people in the working population (Age 16 to 60 years, 88%). At the same time businessmen then form (60%) an important group.

Our field survey also reflects the nature and characteristic of road transport and traffic in Kolhapur with reference to the selected respondents. Table 4 gives the necessary information.

Table 4: Nature and Extent of Road Traffic in Kolhapur

Sr. No.	*Details*	*No. of Respondents*	*Percentage Share*
1.	Type of Vehicles		
	(*a*) Two wheelers	30	60%
	(*b*) Three wheelers	08	16%
	(*c*) Four wheelers	12	24%
2.	State of Transport System		
	(*a*) Best	01	02%
	(*b*) Better	08	16%
	(*c*) Good	41	82%
3.	Dominance in City Transport		
	(*a*) Auto Rickshaws	34	68%
	(*b*) Buses	02	04%
	(*c*) Others	14	32%

Source: Same as of Table 2.

Our survey revealed that two wheelers are an important means of transport in the city (60%), which is followed by four wheelers (24%). According to respondents, the road transport system in Kolhapur is good and that auto rickshaws dominated city traffic.

The growth and extent of bad environmental impacts of the road transport depends upon the traffic control and management, and the measures used for the effective traffic management.

Table 5: Role in Traffic Control

Sr. No.	*Description*	*No. of Respondents*	*Percentage Share*
1.	Traffic Jam Area		
	(*a*) ST Stand	21	42%
	(*b*) Rankala Stand	18	36%
	(*c*) Laxmipuri	16	22%
2.	Important Role in Traffic Control		
	(*a*) Municipal Corporation	06	12%
	(*b*) Traffic Police	44	88%
	(*c*) State Government	00	00
3.	Measures on Traffic Control		
	(*a*) Traffic Rules	28	58%
	(*b*) Use of PUC	09	1.8%
	(*c*) Awareness	03	06%
	(*d*) Good Roads	10	18%

Source: Same as of Table 2.

It is observed that the Central ST Stand area (42%) and Rankala ST Stand area (36%) are the crowded areas in Kolhapur city. And it is the traffic police mechanism, which is playing an important role in the control and management of traffic in the city. Our survey reveals that the strict implementation of traffic rules can be effective in the control and proper management of the traffic, and thereby, imposing adverse impacts of the road transport in the city.

Human resources are an important component of the environment in general and biosphere in particular. Table 6 shows the impact of road transport on human beings in Kolhapur city.

Table 6: Impact of Road Transport on Human Beings

Sr. No.	*Description*	*No. of Respondents*	*Percentage Share*
1.	Pains/Troubles		
	(*a*) Body Pains	28	56%
	(*b*) Headache	16	56%
	(*c*) Diseases	06	12%
2.	Effects on Work		
	(*a*) Boring	31	62%
	(*b*) Less Work	17	34%
	(*c*) No Work	02	16%

Source: Same as of Table 2.

It is observed that body pains and headache (58%), are acute due to adverse environmental impacts. Such impacts also result in low level of efforts on the part of people in their jobs. The answers are tabulated in Table 7.

Table 7: Road Transport and Environmental Pollution

Sr. No.	*Description*	*No. of Respondents*	*Percentage Share*
1.	Environmental Pollution		
	(*a*) Air Pollution	49	98%
	(*b*) Noise Pollution	34	68%
	(*c*) Water Pollution	00	00
2.	Causes of Environmental Pollution		
	(*a*) Poisonous Gases	47	94%
	(*b*) Improper Roads	12	24%
	(*c*) Violation of Laws	09	18%
	(*d*) Noise	15	30%
	(*e*) Others	27	54%

Source: Same as of Table 2.

The data analysis in Table 7 reveals that air pollution and noise pollution are the major environmental problems of road transport in Kolhapur city. And poisonous gases emitted, intensive noise, and some other reasons are also responsible for the environmental pollution arising out of road transport means and facilities in Kolhapur.

Road transport facilities in Kolhapur city have been contributing to a significant environmental damage in terms of sickness among people, loss of working man days and other types of loss. The data in Table 8 reveals this.

Table 8 : Road Transport and Environmental Damage

Sr. No.	*Description*	*No. of Respondents*	*Percentage Share*
1	Sickness		
	(*a*) Headache	44	88%
	(*b*) Vomiting	44	88%
	(*c*) Eye & Throat Irritation	48	96%
	(*d*) Others	09	18%
2.	Loss of Man Days		
	(*a*) One day	13	26%
	(*b*) One Week	32	64%
	(*c*) One Month & above	05	10%
3.	Other Damage		
	(*a*) House	13	26%
	(*b*) Public Places	31	62%
	(*c*) Trees	31	62%

Source: Same as of Table 2.

It is observed that a majority of people (96%) are suffering from the sickness like eye & throat irritation, which is followed by headache and vomiting. Besides this, road transport in Kolhapur city is responsible for loss of their working days even to the extent of one week; Likewise, damage to the public places and trees, due to road transport in the city is also significant.

The loss of man days taken into account in physical terms does not adequately reflect the impact of road transport on Kolhapur city.

It is essential to take into consideration the loss in money terms. Some attempts have been made to quantify these losses. This is given in Table 9.

Table 9: Economic Loss due to Road Transport

Sr. No.	*Description*	*Loss*
1.	Loss of Man Days	
	(*a*) Servicemen	10 weeks
	(*b*) Businessmen	28 weeks
	(*c*) Others	12 weeks
2.	Earnings per month	
	(*a*) Servicemen	Rs. 5,000 per month
	(*b*) Businessmen	Rs. 13,000 per month
	(*c*) Others	Rs. 3,000 per month
3.	Loss of Earnings	
	(*a*) Servicemen	Rs. 15,000 per month
	(*b*) Businessmen	Rs. 91,000 per month
	(*c*) Others	Rs. 9,000 per month
	(*d*) Total Loss of Earnings	Rs. 1,15,000 per month
	Total Loss of Earnings	Rs. 13,80,000 per year
4.	Loss due to Other Damage	
	(*a*) House	Rs. 65,000 for a year
	(*b*) Public Places	Rs. 1,55,000 for a year
	(*c*) Trees	Rs. 91,000 for a year
	(*d*) Total Loss of Other Damage	Rs. 2,11,000 for a year
5.	Gross Economic Loss of Road Transport	
	(*a*) Total Loss of Earnings	Rs. 13,80,000 per annum
	(*b*) Total Loss of Other Damage	Rs. 2,11,000 per annum
	(*c*) Gross Economic Loss	Rs. 15,91,000 per annum

Source: Calculated on the basis of primary data collected

The data in Table 9 adequately reveals that businessmen are the major losers of working hours due to sickness because of environmental pollution arising due to road transport services in Kolhapur, which is followed by other categories of working people. Economic loss due to loss of working days was also higher for the businessmen, followed by the servicemen. It stood at Rs. 91,000 per month and Rs. 15,000 per month respectively with the total of Rs. 1,15,000 per month. Economic losses because of damage to public places (Rs. 1,55,000) and trees (Rs. 91,000) were also significant. Thus, total economic loss due to road transport in Kolhapur city consisting of loss of earnings and loss of other damage was significant, and was around Rs 16 lakhs.

8. SOME USEFUL SUGGESTIONS

The following are some suggestions which will be useful in controlling economic loss or cost as well as proper control and management of the road transport system in Kolhapur city.

1. The strict implementation of traffic rules will be useful in the proper management and control of Kolhapur city road transport system.

2. Public awareness of the bad environmental impacts of road transport is required to be spread through education and training programmes.
3. The development of business activities in the suburban areas and peripheries, along with increased use of one way traffic can be of greater use in proper traffic management and thereby loss of human as well as other resources.
4. The Municipal Corporation as well as the state government should look into the matters relating to environmental bad impacts, costs or economic loss with their due interference and necessary action for their reduction and avoidance.
5. The RTO (Regional Transport Officer) can play a very important role in the proper control and management of road transport traffic by effective monitoring of the condition of vehicles on the road.

9. CONCLUSIONS

The foregoing analysis about the environmental impacts of road transport on Kolhapur city adequately tests the hypothesis formulated in the beginning of the present study. The lack of due care of the environmental bad impacts with the growing city road transport means and facilities have been putting a significant economic loss on the people of Kolhapur city, especially the working population. The present study provided various dimensions and insights into the environmental impacts of road transport facilities in cities like Kolhapur. This study is anyway the first of its kind of road transport in cities, with emphasis on environmental impacts, especially economic losses of earnings as well as resources and properties. There is plenty of scope to consider a number of dimensions that have been left untouched in the study.

REFERENCES

Bhattacharya, R. N. (2006), Environmental Economics, Oxford University Press, New Delhi.

Kolhapur Municipal Corporation (2003-04), Environmental Status Report: 2003-04, KMC, Kolhapur.

Kolhapur Municipal Corporation (2006-07), Budgetary Documents, Kolhapur, pp. 18-19.

Rajlaxmi, N. (2002), Environmental Cost and Economic Evaluation, Manak Publications Pvt. Ltd., New Delhi.

17

SPATIAL DECENTRALISATION AND INNOVATIVE APPROACH TO REDUCE THE TRAFFIC CONGESTION – A CASE OF BHOPAL (INDIA)

Kshama Puntambekar
Ashutosh Sharma

ABSTRACT

Transport and built form constitute major components of an urban area. The growth in transport demand is exponential world-wide. The trip generation varies from city to city but certain basic underlying factors are common. These factors may be increase in urban population, size of the city, household income, level of motorization, and industrial and commercial activities. People reside away from the city centres in the suburban areas for want of more space and better amenities. Peri-urban areas require separate vehicles to commute to workplace in the city adding to the traffic. Transport policy and planning need to be put in the context of wider land use-transport planning consideration. Land use decisions affects transport decisions, which means whatever purpose the land is put to, such as market, factories, malls, educational institutes etc. its activities generate trips. These trips, in turn, point up the need of certain type of transport facilities use. Today, the Indian urban population is concentrating only in selected metro cities aggravating the problems. All metros in the developing countries are facing the same problem. The paper will deal with spatial decentralisation specifically locating/ relocating the market places as a selected parameter to reduce the traffic.

1. INTRODUCTION

The automobile population in the country is growing to double in a decade. India is a developing country. The problems related to congestion, overcrowding in cities and pollution are evident. There are the signs of growth in the country but the need is to properly channelize efforts so as to improve the quality of life. The changes can be experienced in social, economic and spatial parameters.

There have been several major trends during the last few decades that changed the way in which Indian cities are socially, economically, and spatially organised; Compact cities have been replaced by outward growth resulting in lower densities. This change was initiated in most cases due to land availability at low prices and was made possible primarily by the automobile. This frequently led to additional traffic from the periphery and necessitated the construction of arterials to the city centers. The buying capacity of the Indian consumer is increasing with the financial growth. This is also reflected in the choice of location for residential purpose. People are residing away from the city centers in the suburban areas for want of more space and better amenities. These areas demand for separate vehicles to commute to workplace in the city. The public transport is not sufficient and comfortable in low density areas, people tend to use private mode of transport generating huge traffic. Earlier any urban area could be approached by foot or other non motorized mode. Today rickshaw, tonga, carts etc are obsolete and they have been replaced by other faster means of motorized vehicles to reach the destination with more comfort and speed. As a result the congestion in the cities is increasing every day. These congested areas are the inner cities, CBD area, and narrow lanes etc. Congestion is outcome of the improved land values and mismanaged traffic. There are means to reduce the inflow of traffic to certain areas. In this paper we emphasise the role of traffic regulation (transport system) and regulated spatial development (land use regulation) in achieving this objective. This paper tries to substantiate the theory of decentralisation with the help of an example.

2. TRANSPORT AND THE EXTENT OF THE MARKET AREA

Major trips are generated between the work place, place of residence and the market. The frequency of the market trip is decided on the basis of the hierarchy level of the market. Figure 1 below shows the relation between the market size and the frequency of the visit. Its distance also affects the frequency.

The Hierarchy of the Market Area

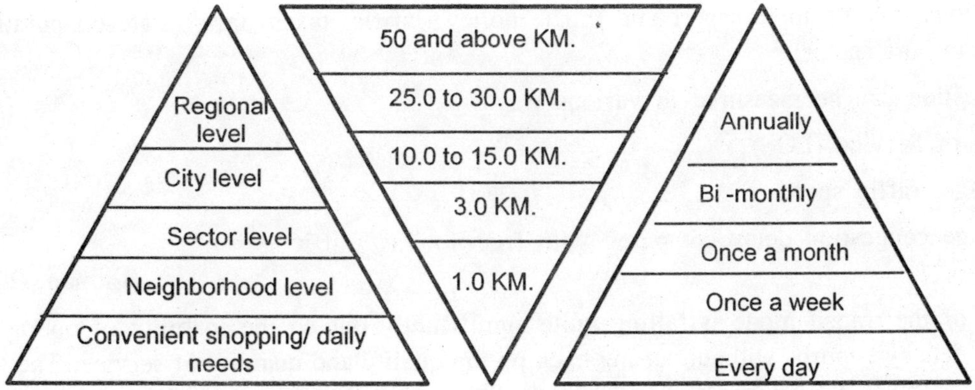

Fig. 1: Hierarchy of Market Places/Regions of Influence

Factors shaping the extent of market areas are as follows:

- Land use: industrial areas can provide little in the way of a consuming population.
- Poor accessibility: this can limit the extent of a centre's market area.
- Competition: this limits the extent of market areas in all directions.
- Technology: high mobility afforded by the automobile allows overlapping of market areas

and factors that stimulate changes in travel behaviour are:

- Increase in the level of automobile ownership.
- Increase in the annual mileage driven stemming not just from longer trips.
- Taking more trips and more trips alone.

Transport and traffic serve the purpose of relocation of people and goods, as well as the conveying of information. The demands imposed on transport and traffic result from the interaction of those areas where people live and where commerce and industry are located, which are interlinked at many different levels and which are:

- Influenced by the number of inhabitants, the structure of human settlement, the general economic standard, the economic-geographical circumstances (such as natural land-use potential, the location of raw materials and production facilities), the production strategies (*e.g.*, just-in-time), and by natural peripheral conditions (the topography),
- A consequence of economic policy (*e.g.*, industrial settlement, the demands of the agricultural sector) and development planning (national development and regional planning), which can be used to control the transport and traffic demand through centralisation and decentralisation.

The type and intensity of transport and traffic depend on

- Existing transport facilities
- Operational measures (transport control systems)
- Decisions relating to transport and traffic policy (tariffs, taxes, laws, state cooperation in the transport sector).

Congestion can be measured in various ways:

- Level of Service (LOS)
- Average traffic speed
- Average congestion delay compared with free-flowing traffic

(Litman, 2004a).

Use of the transit mode is falling quite significantly due to the inability of operators to serve low density suburbs without cutting back on the quality and quantity of service. The transit share of the travel market has continued to decline nationally. Travel has also been impacted by the suburbanisation of jobs and changes in the patterns of the journey to work because of this. Increases in activity spaces have necessitated more travel as well as the creation of edge cities which are perceived to be more accessible even though, they may result in more miles driven.

3. PRIORITIES FOR URBAN TRANSPORT IN INDIA

Indian cities cannot afford to cater only to private cars and two-wheelers and there has to be a general recognition that policy should be designed in such a way that it reduces the need to travel by personalised modes and boosts public transport system. This requires both an increase in quantity as well as quality of public transport and effective use of demand as well as supply-side management measures. At the same time, people should be encouraged to walk and cycle and government should support investments that make cycling and walking safer. Traffic composition in India is of a mixed nature. A wide variety of about a dozen types of both slow- and fast-moving vehicles exists. Two-wheelers and cars (including jeeps) account for more than 80 per cent of the vehicle population in most large cities. Table 1 shows the existing modal split. Table 2 represents a desirable modal split.

Table 1: Existing Modal Split in Indian Cities (as a % of Total Trips)

City Population (in millions)	*Walk*	*Mass Transport*	*IPT*		*Car*	*Two wheeler*	*Bicycle*	*Total*
			Fast	*Slow*				
0.10 - 0.25	37.1	16.4	10.4	20.1	3.3	24.1	25.7	100.0
0.25 - 0.50	37.8	20.6	8.9	17.2	2.6	29.8	20.9	100.0
0.50 - 1.0	30.7	25.4	8.2	12.0	9.5	29.1	15.9	100.0
1.0 - 2.0	29.6	30.6	6.4	8.1	3.3	39.6	12.1	100.0
2.0 - 5.0	28.7	43.3	4.9	3.0	28.9	15.9	100.0	
5.0+	28.4	62.8	3.3	3.7	6.1	14.8	9.4	100.0

Source: Ministry of Urban Development, Government of India, New Delhi. 1998. Traffic and Transportation Policies and Strategies in Urban Areas in India. Final Report.

Table 2: Desirable Modal Split for Indian Cities (as a % of Total Trips)

City Population (in millions)	*Mass Transport*	*Bicycle*	*Other Modes*
0.1 - 0.5	30-40	30-40	25-35
0.5 - 1.0	40-50	25-35	20-30
1.0 - 2.0	50-60	20-30	15-25
2.0 - 5.0	60-70	15-25	10-20
5.0+	70-85	15-20	10-15

Source: Ministry of Urban Development, Government of India, New Delhi. 1998. Traffic and Transportation Policies and Strategies in Urban Areas in India. Final Report.

There are many solutions that can be adopted by different authorities at local and regional level to mitigate the problem of increasing traffic. Some of them are listed below. Each of them can be applied as per local conditions.

- **Creating no traffic zone**: in very busy and happening area where inflow and outflow of population is very large a No Traffic zone is declared. This eases the pedestrian movement and avoids pollution due to slow moving traffic. When a commuter uses private vehicle he/she has to walk a long distance with loads of purchase.
- **Provision of parking lots**: management will have to provide parking lots consuming major portion of the precious land near the happening places. 30% of the land is required for

maneuvering the vehicle. Parking requirement will increase the spread of the sprawl further demanding more parking spaces, again forming a cycle.

- **Congestion pricing**: in many metros one can find that you have to pay extra charges to enter the congestion-pricing zone. Only the privileged can enter the area after paying an extra amount. In London County this method of traffic control is used in the CBD. This forces people to use the public transport and move on foot.
- **Limited hour's entry**: the entry of heavy or all vehicles is restricted to non-peak hrs. for loading and unloading purpose. In government and corporate office zone the heavy vehicles used for goods transport can be restricted in peak hrs.
- **Provision of MRTS**: Is one of the good solutions to reduce the load of private vehicle traffic on the roads. MRTS is possible if the density is high and the system is easily approachable by people at large. Present trend of sprawl shows that people buy land at outskirts because
  - Large parcel of land is available.
  - Pollution is less.
  - They have private means of communication.

  This makes the provision of MRTS difficult and has to rely on inter-modal services.
- **Road Widening:** means increasing road width to accommodate the increasing traffic. This is one of the solutions applied as a measure to reduce congestion on the existing roads. But increase in road widths will invite traffic on the road leading to further congestion. Widening of roads require surgery of the area. This includes displacement of people living and earning daily bread, acquisition of land, dismantling the standing structures etc. may cost a lot of money, time and public non-cooperation. The brought in vehicles will also need the parking space. Road widening is not possible to be applied every where and is a site specific solution where the land permits.
- **One way Traffic:** Eases the traffic moving with fewer accidents and head on collisions. This system increases the total travelled distance by the vehicle to reach the desired destination.
- **Traffic Diversion:** can be done by fly-over and by-passes to divert the through traffic. The fly-over can avoid the congestion at level crossing, and major junctions where the traffic signal timings are more than 180 seconds/side. Many such examples can be seen in the Indian cities which are newly made million plus. By-passes work effectively at regional level where they help to by-pass the city traffic for commuters to the further urban areas.

All the above solutions are condition based and cannot be applied in general. A new concept can which can act as a model solution for reducing the traffic generation through change in land use and termed as ***'Spatial Decentralisation'*** is perhaps required to understand and applied. This paper makes an attempt to do so.

4. SPATIAL DECENTRALISATION

Decentralisation is considered to be, for instance, the transfer of political decision-making authority and institutions from central governments to intermediate or lower administrative levels.

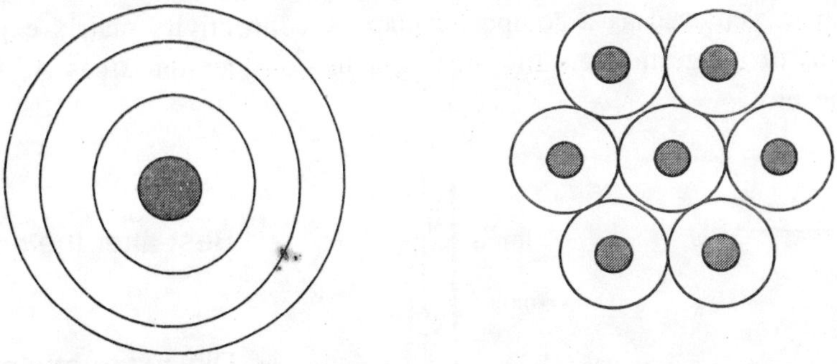

Centralised with one nucleur **Decentralised with many nucleur**

Fig. 2: Decentralisation as multi-nucleus development

In discussing types of decentralisation, there are two important issues that come to mind. Firstly, one must distinguish between the natures of power that is being transferred and therefore, classify the functions that the 'decentralised unit' can effectively perform. Secondly, it is important to consider the institutional nature of the decentralised unit, in order to differentiate between the extent of control that the central Government, continues to exercise over the decentralised unit, post the transfer of powers.

There are four popular typologies of decentralisation:

- Deconcentration
- Delegation
- Devolution
- Privatisation

Decentralisation is in general talked for devolution or distribution of power and money. In this context we are talking about distributing the traffic load on roads by changing or altering the land use. This will change the origin and destination of the trips and thus the generation of the traffic is monitored. This can control the traffic to an extent. Decentralisation in the transport sector can be expected to bring the decision making centres closer to the actual point of delivery of transport services. While the parallel political process is to bring elected officials closer to their constituencies and make them accountable for the decisions they have taken to the public.

The building of more and more roads in cities has left congestion at much the same level as before. A dynamic statistical model is necessary. Policy makers need to be persuaded to take a systems view of all modes, improving one mode may not improve the system as a whole.

To attain a decentralised system of spatial development multicriteria decision-making is required. The constraints for the decision making are:

Physical .... **Land matters**
Environmental .... **Health matters**
Economic .... **Money matters**
Political .... **Influence matters**

The result can be achieved as a composite map. A connectivity matrix explains the traffic flow and the reasons of congestion on any area. Let us consider the areas A, B, C, D, and E are locations in the city.

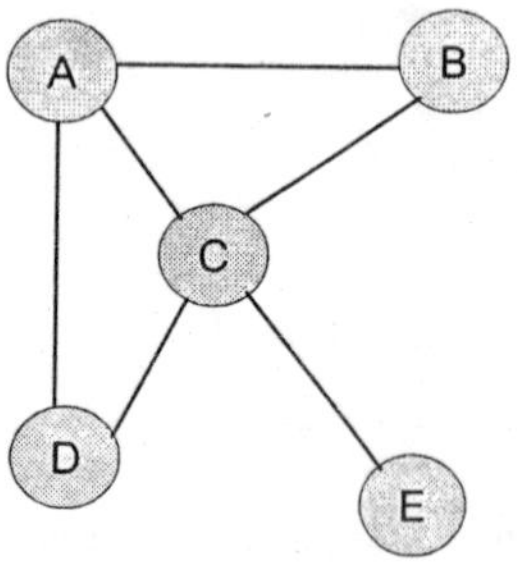

Fig. 3(a): Linkages

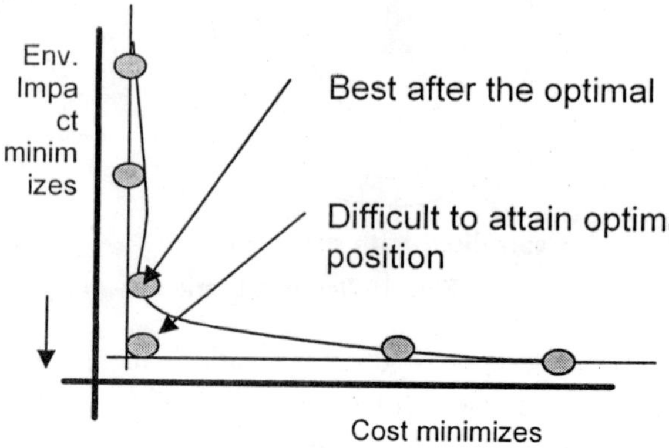

Fig. 3(b): Graph

	A	B	C	D	E
A	0	1	1	1	0
B	1	0	1	0	0
C	1	1	0	1	1
D	1	0	1	0	0
E	0	0	1	0	0

Fig. 3(c):Connectivity Matrix

Fig. 3: Cost-impact relationship

The given figure shows the connectivity between the areas A, B, C, D, and E. The matrix is developed on the basis of the figure. Area "E" is connected to other areas through "C". Hence, all the traffic from "E" causes congestion in "C" and later radiate to the respective areas. Traffic in the area "C" is not necessarily generated in the area but most of it is passing through.

The solution to the congestion in "C" lies in the other areas. The solutions can be

- Connecting the areas directly.
- Building the fly-over for through traffic.
- Decentralise the activities i.e., make it available at both ends.

The first 2 solutions will be short lived but if the third one is possible and made by multicriteria decision method it will have a longer life and reduce the environmental pollution.

4.1 Possible Benefits

Land use and Travel Behaviour: Decentralised land use has a major impact on the travel behaviour. Human behaviour is a complex system. Output of the behavioural pattern is the traffic that is generated. Controlling the spatial development and land utilisation will assist the other stakeholders to reduce the vehicular movement on the roads. With mixed land use most of the facilities are available and approachable to people of all age groups and reduces the pick and drop trips which are evident if the distances are more. Decentralisation generates frequent short trips using non-motorised mode or two-wheeler at times. Decentralisation can thus, help in saving the time, money and environment. In the present urban life in metro cities saving time and money will improve the work efficiency and social life of individual. Less use of motorized transport will give healthy environment.

Urban Scenario: The transport activities are affected by the daily routine of the person. Hence, if the distance between the work place and place of residence is reduced the movement of the traffic will be reduced drastically. The city of Mumbai faces the same problem. There are a lot of commuters towards the south of the city during the morning hours when people rush to the workplace and same scenario is towards the opposite direction in the evening hours.

One more land use which attracts the major traffic is commercial. The market forces act on the development of the market and the traffic is generated between the residences, workplace and the market area.

It is found that if the commercial areas are developed at regular intervals with a certain hierarchy the traffic generated due to this activity is reduced.

One of the examples quoted below is the city of Bhopal which is a capital city and has used the decentralisation of the markets to keep a control of the traffic generation. The mixed land use in the city also contributes to the same.

5. BHOPAL: A CASE STUDY

Bhopal city is the capital of Madhya Pradesh. It was designated as capital city in the year 1956. Since then new Bhopal was accordingly developed.

The physical growth of city started thereafter, due to upcoming government offices and houses for the employees. In 1959-60 first development plan was prepared for the proper development of city. Bharat Heavy Electricals (BHEL) a public sector unit was established in this period only. For factory and township land was allocated 3Km away from the than municipal boundary. In the development plan prepared by Town & Country Planning in 1974 total planning area was 24087 hectares, it includes urban area as Old City, T T Nagar, Bairagarh, and BHEL (Dhote and Sharma 2006).

Thus city can be divided into 4 major sectors namely:

- Old City — Walled City
- New Bhopal — Capitol Complex
- BHEL Township — Industrial Area
- Bairagarh — Predominantly Commercial

Bhopal as the Capital City: In 1956 Bhopal was made the capital city of Madhya Pradesh **(M.P.) A state, which was the result of divulgation of the then central province pushing the** existing capital from Nagpur to Bhopal. This event had a far-reaching significance in the development of Bhopal. Once the capital was formed the large number of administrative and support staff had to be housed in the city. (Bhopal Development Plan (BDP), 1974) However, the compact dimensions of the inner city restricted the possibilities of the same. Hence, the development of the city took a tacit turn and the administrative buildings mounted the unexplored verging hilltops and the government housing populated the slopes below.

Bhopal as an Industrial Town: Bhopal also witnessed the industrialisation wave of India. However, one should not confuse it with the industrialisation era of the west. The Bharat Heavy Electrical Ltd. (BHEL) was one of the major public sector industries, which came up during the socialist political regime of the post independence era. The industrial developments of the time were developed as a composite settlement, which included an extensive township and related services that were erected along with the industry. This type of development led to emergence of a unique typology of the modernist India and was usually rooted in the sanitized conceptions of modernist architects and planners (so called promulgators of the international style), in complete contrast with the culture and organic-ness typical to the Indian cities. Bhopal is unique in containing such a typology concurrently with its ethnic urban form.

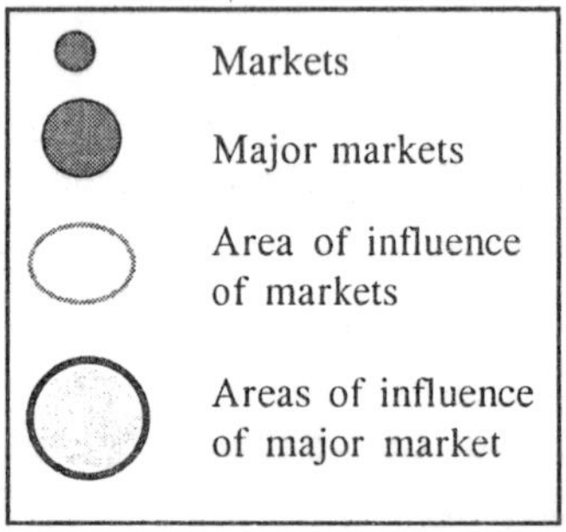

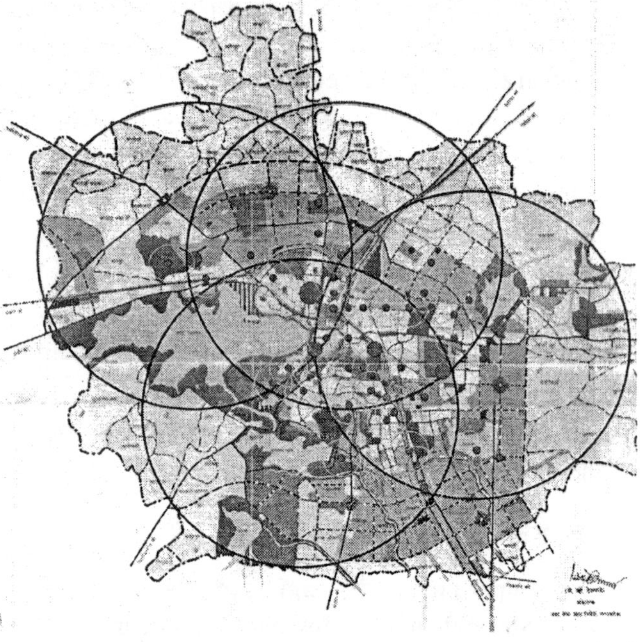

Fig. 4: Spread of market and there influence zone

Bhopal as a refugee Town: The bairagarh area is dominated by the sindhi community who had taken refuge in the refugee camps after partition of August 1947. Presently it has turned to a predominantly commercial area.

The four sectors have been planned and developed in a manner such that they are self sufficient and occasionally have to commute larger distances for there needs. The markets are properly distributed making them more approachable. The map (Figure 4) shows the shopping area hierarchy with there hinterland. Each sector has a major market area with many other smaller ones to cater to the needs of the public.

For study purpose, while considering the market hinterland or influence zone a radius of 1.0km was assumed to generate traffic to the nearest market. This is said to be a comfortable distance for a person to walk down thus, reducing the vehicular traffic generation for the purpose of approaching the market. Major markets marked have influence zone at sector level, city level and also some markets in Bhopal are of district and regional level. These markets were not considered for the study purpose as they are approached on account of any whole sale (quantity) purchase on special occasions or annually. Only major markets at sector level are considered.

6. CONCLUSIONS

The spread of the commercial area in the city is mostly at an interval of distances that are walkable distance. The circles of influence zone show they cover all the residential area. The sector level markets are also evenly distributed covering the entire city. On interviewing the people in the market, we found they belonged to the near-by-areas. The % of population coming from other sectors was negligible. The study thus, support the concept of decentralisation of land uses which will act as a model solution for reducing the traffic generation through change in land use termed as ***'Spatial Decentralisation'***.

REFERENCES

BDP (2005), Bhopal Development Plan 2005.

Briand, Taylor *"Rethinking Traffic Congestion"*.

United States Congress, Senate. Committee on Public Works, Subcommittee on Environmental Pollution, "Implementation of Transportation Controls".

Lee Associates, *(2001), Comprehensive Traffic and transportation Study for Bhopal Urban Area . CRRI New Delhi.*

Puntambekar K (2006), *"Relation Between Land-use and Transportation in Million Plus Cities"*. VI Eco-city Conference, Bangalore.

Sanjay K. S. (2005), "Review of Urban Transportation in India" Indian Institute of Technology Kanpur, *Journal of Public Transportation*, Vol. 8, No. 1, 2005.

Todd Litman *(2006)*, "Smart Transportation Investments II Reevaluating The Role Of Public Transit For Improving Urban Transportation" ,Victoria Transport Policy Institute.

William R. Black (2000), "Social Change and Sustainable Transport" A Summary of Workshop and Conference Activities, Research Needs and Future Directions Indiana University, January.

www.planning-aid-scotland.org.uk/glossary.html

www.bridgefieldgroup.com/glos9.htm

www.southampton.gov.uk/environment/development-control/planning-terms.asp

18

CONTAINERIZATION IN INDIA — BUILDING GLOBAL TRADE COMPETITIVENESS

G. Raghuram
Rachna Gangwar

ABSTRACT

India has 12 major and 187 non major ports along its 7517 km coastline. Cargo traffic handled by Indian ports in 2005-06 was 569 mt, of which 60 mt (5.1 mTEUs) was the container traffic. The compounded annual growth rate (CAGR) of container traffic for the past 6 years (1999-00 to 2005-06) was 11.5%. This was higher than the world's average for the same period. This paper focusses on the future of the container traffic growth, scope of transhipment, potential of the hub operations in India and the connectivity issues. Looking at the container traffic growth in the past few years, there seems to be scope for hub operations in India, possibly one each on the east and west coast. Ports would also need the infrastructural facilities like wide berthing, high crane handling capacity, quicker and safe loading and unloading capabilities and direct shift of containers to the feeder vessels. Further, hinterland connectivity is a critical area to ensure a seamless flow of containers and improved port productivity. There are also issues with respect to evacuation of containers from Internal Container Depots. There is a lot of road based congestion due to insufficient infrastructure. Interfacing with customs is another issue. Thus, a lot of future potential is seen in this sector provided that (i) the ports are equipped to take the challenges emerging from large shipping vessels and (ii) higher throughput is ensured through adequate hinterland connectivity.

1. INTRODUCTION

India has 12 major and 187 non major ports along its 7517 km coastline. The compounded annual growth rate (CAGR) of container traffic in Twenty-foot Equivalent Units (TEUs) for the period 2001-08 was 17.3%, which is higher than the world's average for this period. Given the growing economy and international trade, a lot of future potential is seen in this sector. This however, would be contingent on the maritime sector being equipped to take the challenges emerging from (i) large shipping vessels and deeper draft at ports (ii) hub and feeder operations at ports and along the coast respectively (iii) hinterland connectivity between port and Inland Container Depot (ICD)/Container Freight Station (CFS) and (iv) terminal development on ports and in the hinterland. Other issues relate to use of Information Technology (IT) and better systems to coordinate with bodies like customs and industrial location policy (especially with respect to Special Economic Zones (SEZs). This paper makes an attempt to examine these issues within the framework of maritime operations in the Indian context.

2. POTENTIAL OF CONTAINER TRAFFIC

India handled 723 million tons (mt) (649 mt) of cargo traffic in 2007-08 (2006-07). The total container traffic in 2007-08 (2006-07) was 98 mt (80 mt). In terms of TEUs, it was 7.5 mTEUs (6.1 mTEUs) in 2007-08 (2006-07). Growth rate of container traffic has outstripped the national Gross Domestic Product (GDP) growth rate. Table 1 gives the growth trends of national GDP, total port and container traffic. *Considering the current trends, it appears that 21 mTEUs of originating and terminating traffic is likely to occur by 2015-16 and it is necessary to get prepared for that.*

3. DRIVERS OF CONTAINER TRAFFIC

3.1 International Trade Growth

India's export earnings in 2007-08 topped US $155 billion, recording a 23% growth over the previous year. India's import value in 2007-08 reached US $236 billion, recording a growth of 27% over the previous year. The export to GDP ratio reached 17%, while the import to GDP ratio reached 26% in 2007-08. Table 2 gives the growth of India's import export with respect to national GDP. While trade was growing at over 20% per annum, its impact on container traffic growth could be higher, since, a greater share of trade has been in terms of finished goods requiring containerization.

3.2 Penetration of Containerization

Presently, containerized cargo represents about 30% by value of India's external trade, and this proportion is likely to grow as containerization increasingly penetrates the general cargo trades and increases its share from the current 68% to nearer international levels of around 75-80% [World Bank, 2007]. Of the principal commodities that India trades in, commodities that are containerized include engineering goods, agricultural commodities, textiles and readymade garments, pharmaceutical products (bulk formulations) and machinery (auto and electronic). With increased penetration, and growth in India's trade, container traffic is projected to grow from 4.5 mTEUs per annum. (in 2005) to around 21 mTEUs by 2015 [World Bank, 2007].

3.3 Hub and Feeder

Given the container traffic growth in the past few years, there seems to a scope for hub ports in India, possibly one each on the east and west coast. The absence of a hub port means that a significant share of containers leaving an Indian port goes through feeder, transshipment and then mainline movements. This has implied additional delays due to the feeder voyage from India to the hub port and then at the hub port while it waits for the mainline ship to call. This has resulted in delays of anything between 40 hours to 50 hours at an extra cost of at least US $70 per TEU (Business Line, 2004).

In the absence of a hub port in India, a majority of the country's containers are currently transshipped through other ports ie Colombo (just south of India), Singapore (east), Dubai and Salalah (west). Handling these through the Indian transshipment terminal would result in savings of around (US$ 120 and US$ 320) TEU for the Indian exporter.

Table 1: India's GDP and Port Traffic

Year	*National GDP*		*Total*		*Major Ports*		*Non-Major Ports*		*Container*				
									Major Ports			*Total*	
	US $b[1]	*Growth*[2] *(%)*	*mt*	*Growth (%)*	*mt*	*Growth (%)*	*mt*	*Growth (%)*	*mt*	*000' TEUs*	*Share*** *(%)*	*000' TEUs*	*Growth (%)*
2000-01	409	4.4	368	10.2	281	3.3	87	39.3	32	2468	11.5	2468	13.0
2001-02	441	4.8	384	4.3	288	2.5	96	10.3	37	2886	12.9	2886	16.9
2002-03	467	3.8	419	9.1	314	9.0	105	9.4	44	3366	13.9	3366	16.6
2003-04	554	8.5	466	11.2	345	9.9	121	15.2	51	3900	14.8	3900	15.9
2004-05	633	7.5	522	12.0	384	11.3	138	14.1	55	4233	14.3	4502 *	15.4
2005-06	725	9.0	569	9.0	423	10.2	151	9.4	62	4613	14.6	4998 *	11.0
2006-07	827	9.3	649	14.1	464	9.7	186	22.5	73	5541	15.8	6069 *	19.3
2007-08	899	8.7	723	11.4	519	11.9	204#	9.7	92	6710	17.7	7512 *	23.8

Source: CMIE; IPA, Various Years.
1. At current market prices
2. At factor cost (constant prices)

\# 148 mt from GMB ports

* Includes traffic from Mundra and Pipavav

** Share of container traffic wrt total port traffic

Table 2: International Trade Growth

Year	*National GDP*		*Exports*		*Imports*	
	US $b[1]	*Growth*[2] *(%)*	*US $b*	*Growth (%)*	*US $b*	*Growth (%)*
2000-01	409	4.4	44.1	20.1	50.1	0.5
2001-02	441	4.8	44.0	-0.4	51.6	3.0
2002-03	467	3.8	53.0	20.6	61.7	19.7
2003-04	554	8.5	63.9	20.5	78.2	26.7
2004-05	633	7.5	83.5	30.7	108.0	38.1
2005-06	725	9.0	102.7	23.0	133.4	23.5
2006-07	827	9.3	126.2	22.5	185.6	24.5
2007-08	899	8.7	155.4	23.1	235.9	27.1

Source: CMIE.
1. At current market prices
2. At factor cost (constant prices).

Table 3 gives the container traffic and transshipment at Indian ports. As can be seen, the percentage of transshipment is a very small share of the total traffic, implying that Indian ports are really not providing hub services.

Table 3: Container Traffic and Transshipment at Major Ports

Year	*Total Container Traffic*		*Transshipment*	
	000' TEUs	*Growth (%)*	*000' TEUs*	*%*
2000-01	2468	13.0	25	1.0
2001-02	2886	16.9	169	5.9
2002-03	3366	16.6	187	5.6
2003-04	3900	15.9	208	5.3
2004-05	4233	8.5	162	3.8
2005-06	4613	9.0	181	3.9
2006-07	5541	17.9	284	5.1
2007-08	6710	19.0	423	6.3

Source: IPA, Various Years.

In terms of port traffic, for every transshipment container handled at a hub port, two more handlings would be required at ports, one at the same hub and another at the feeder port. Developing India's container ports to enable direct calls by mainline vessels would provide Indian shippers better access to global markets.

As per the projection above, 9 mTEUs (43%) of the Indian traffic of 21 mTEUs will be hubbed in 2015-16. Of the hubbed traffic, 0.95 mTEUs (11%) will be hubbed in India, implying a transhipment of 1.9 mTEUs. This is conservative. Hubbing in India can and should develop. If 50% hubbing were to take place in India, then 4.5 mTEUs will be hubbed in India, implying transhipment handling of 9 mTEUs. About 7 more mTEUs will need to be handled at hub ports. This requires port handling capacity of 30 mTEUs, with 9 mTEUs as transhipment at hub ports. Moreover, it is observed 35% of the containers handled in the west coast ports are bound for destinations closer to the east coast. This is the optimal route due to cargo aggregation.

Given the above three drivers of container growth, we can get an insight into the break-up of the traffic across various port clusters, as per a World Bank study. The ports in the western region (Mumbai and Gujarat) would handle at least 66% container throughputs in the country, followed by the ports in the southern region at 27% and the balance at the eastern region ports. As per this projection, the eastern ports are underleveraged. With specific interventions in terms of terminal related services and connectivity, the regional balance can move in favour of the eastern ports.

4. SHIPPING TRENDS

Looking at the current as well as future shipping trends that are likely to emerge, it would be the era of large mother vessels, with a minimum of 6000-8000 TEU, and a few as big as 12,000-14,000 TEU. These ships would make only a few calls at mega hub ports to/from where cargo movement would be by transshipment and feedering through the present age ships of 4000 TEU and below. These future generation vessels would require drafts between 13-15.5 mtrs. These ports would also need the infrastructural facilities like wide berthing, high crane handling capacity, quicker and safe loading and unloading capabilities, and direct shift of containers to the feeder vessels.

Emma Maersk (DWT 156,907, overall length 397m, beam 56m, hull height 30m, draft 15.5m) owned by the AP Moller-Maersk Group, when launched in August 2006 became the world's largest container ship ever built, and as of today, the largest ship in use. (The largest ship ever built was the supertanker Knock Nevis, now retired). Officially, as stated by Maersk, Emma Maersk is able to carry around 11,000 TEUs. However, as per standard shipping calculations, it can carry between 13,500 to 14,500 TEUs [http://en.wikipedia.org]. The next generation will be the Malaccamax ship, with 18,000 TEUs of 200,000 DWT, 470 meter long, 60 meter wide, 16 meter of draft, with more than 100 MW power for 25.5 knots. This is expected to be the limit before a major restructuring of world container trade routes [http://en.wikipedia.org].

Hence, it would be useful if hub ports in India should aim for at least 16 meter draft and feeder ports upto 12 meter draft.

5. POTENTIAL HUB PORTS IN INDIA

Given the reality of transshipment and feedering, it is important to focus on few ports on both the coasts with deep draft. The key requirements of a transshipment terminal are its strategic location, potential to reduce total transport cost using 'hub and spoke' arrangement, financial savings in terms of lower land values, less need for dredging and the facility to receive higher-capacity vessels to reduce overall fleet costs. Table 4 shows the container traffic handled at ports (including the non-major ports of Mundra and Pipavav) in 2006-07 and 2005-06. Table 5 provides a comparative analysis of various ports in terms of their physical and efficiency parameters for hub operations.

Table 4: Port-wise Container Traffic

Sl. No.	*Port*	*Operating Company*	*2007-08*		*2006-07*		*2005-06*	
			Total (000' TEUs)	*%*	*Total (000' TEUs)*	*%*	*Total (000' TEUs)*	*%*
1.	JNPT	1. Port 2. DP World 3. AP Moller/Concor	4060	53.3	3298	55.3	2667	53.4
2.	Chennai	1. DP World	1128	14.8	798	13.4	735	14.7
3.	Mundra* (MPSEZ)	1. DP World 2. Adani	712	9.3	393	6.6	299	6.0
4.	Tuticorin	PSA International/SICAL	450	5.9	377	6.3	321	6.4
5.	Kolkata	Port	297	3.9	240	4.0	203	4.1
6.	Cochin	DP World/Concor	254	3.3	227	3.8	203	4.1
7.	Pipavav*	AP Moller	195	2.6	135	2.3	86	1.7
8.	Kandla	ABG	165	2.2	177	3.0	148	3.0
9.	Haldia	Port	128	1.7	110	1.8	110	2.2
10.	Mumbai	Port	118	1.5	128	2.1	156	3.1
11.	Visakhapatnam	DP World	71	0.9	50	0.8	47	0.9
12.	New Mangalore	Port	21	0.3	17	0.3	10	0.2
13.	Mormugao	Port	14	0.2	12	0.2	9	0.2
14.	Paradip	Port	4	0.1	2	0.0	4	0.1
	Total		**7617**	**100.0**	**5964**	**100.0**	**4998**	**100.0**

Source: CI Magazine, 2007; Indian Infrastructure, 2007; IPA, Various Years.
* Non-major and private ports, both under GMB.

In addition,

(*i*) A second container terminal at MPSEZ is nearing completion for operations.

(*ii*) Hazira port in Gujarat, owned by Shell Gas BV is being developed and will be operated by PSA for 1 mTEU per annum,

(*iii*) Dholera Port, owned by JK Group and Adani Group will develop a container terminal,

(*iv*) Maroli port in Gujarat has tendered for bidding for a container terminal,

(*v*) An off-shore container terminal (700 meter) at MPT for 0.8 mTEUs, to be developed by Gammon and Dragoddar

(*vi*) Rewas container terminal in Maharashtra is being developed by Reliance Logistics Investment

(*vii*) Dighi container terminal in Maharashtra is being developed by Balaji Infrastructure Project Ltd

(*viii*) Vizhinjam in Kerala is being tendered for an international container transshipment terminal (in competition to Vallarpadam in Cochin), and

(*ix*) A 0.5 mTEU per annum container terminal at Kulpi in West Bengal is being developed by DP World.

Table 5: Hub Operation Readiness

Readiness Level	*West*	*South*	*East*
High	JNPT, Mundra, Pipavav	Cochin, Chennai	Visakhapatnam
Medium	Kandla, Mumbai	Tuticorin	
Low		New Mangalore, Mormugao	Kolkata, Haldia, Paradip

Source: CRISIL, 2006.

The readiness level is based on the maximum vessel size at berth, high speed equipment, average turnaround time, average pre-berthing time and average parcel size. As per the CRISIL Infrastructure Advisory study, hub ports could be Mundra, Pipavav, JNPT, Cochin, Chennai and Visakhapatnam.

About 50% of the containers exported through Indian ports are transshipped at some point prior to reaching their overseas destination. Approximately 30% of containers are transshipped in either Colombo or Singapore/Klang and another 5% in Dubai or Salalah. About 50% of the container traffic is not transshipped and moves on the same vessel to the final destination port. In the case of JNPT, this proportion is above 80%. Of Indian containers transshipped in Singapore/Klang, Chennai and Kolkata account for 68%, while for Colombo the eastern and southern ports account for 87% (World Bank, 2007). Table 6 gives the share of direct and hub shipments for JNPT and the other ports in the country.

Table 6: Direct and Hub Shipments (2007-08)

(Per cent)

	JNPT	*Other Ports*	*Total*
Share of Container Traffic	54	46	100
Direct	93	27	63
Through Hub	7	73	37

Source: IPA, 2008.

It is useful to note that while 93% of JNPT traffic is direct, 73% of all the other ports is through a hub. Overall, water depths are low in Indian ports compared to those of neighbouring regional hubs. Table 7 gives the draft available in the various ports.

Table 7: Maximum Draft

S. No.	*Terminals*	*Draft (meter)*	*S. No.*	*Terminals*	*Draft (meter)*
1.	JNPT	12.5	8	Kandla	11.7
2.	Chennai	13.4	9	Haldia	10.0
3.	Tuticorin	10.8*	10	Pipavav	12.5*
4.	Mundra	17.5*	11	Visakhapatnam	15.0
5.	Kolkata	7.5*	12	New Mangalore	10.5
6.	Cochin	12.5	13	Mormugao	12.5
7.	Mumbai	10.7	14	Paradip	11.5

*Source:*World Bank, 2007; *Port Website, 2006.

In contrast, Colombo, for example, one of the main hubs for transshipping Indian container cargo, has a draft of 15 metres. This is proposed to be increased further to 17 metres and eventually 20 metres. JNPT, the largest container port in the country has a draft of only 12 metres. JNPT currently handles vessels of upto 4000 TEUs compared to 8500 TEUs at Colombo. Despite handling a higher volume of traffic than Colombo, JNPT is constrained by its deficient draft from offering cheaper and higher quality services, i.e. higher frequency and lower transit times. Other ports in the region like Singapore, Dubai, Port Klang etc have drafts of at least 15 meter and can accommodate vessels upto 11,000 TEUs.

Exhibit 1 (Exhibits are given in Appendix) gives the traffic handled at the top 20 container ports of the world. It is interesting to note that the share of the global throughput of the top 20 ports was 75.9% in 1970. It dropped to 49.6% in 1980, obviously due to a proliferation of container ports. However, since then the share of the top 20 ports has been increasing in a marginally steady manner to reach 56.3% in 2006, showing the trend of concentration due to transshipment and scale economies in the bigger ports.

The market for hub services is highly dependent on patterns of ocean container trade and a specific port's location. Perhaps even more important is the economics of the transshipment business. Rates for transshipping containers are relatively low, typically US $35 per lift. In addition, there is little if any loyalty among customers and a carrier can easily exit the terminal at short notice, giving the carrier a high degree of bargaining power. Ideally the line-haul carrier should have a long-term stake in the facility to ensure its viability [World Bank, 2007].

Based on commercial criteria, JNPT would be the logical choice for a hub port on the west coast. However, from an infrastructure perspective, neither does the JNPT have the draft for the current (and future) generation vessels nor the evacuation capability. Mundra is better placed as far as draft is concerned. As far as evacuation is concerned, while JNPT is congested, significant investments for evacuation capacity are on the anvil. Visakhapatnam is the most viable port for hub operations on the eastern coast. It is in the centre of the India's eastern coast, and can even service Bangladesh and Myanmar. It has a natural water depth of 20 metres within a nautical mile from the coast due to which there is minimal capital dredging requirement. The sea drift there is such that maintenance dredging requirements are also less.

6. HINTERLAND CONNECTIVITY

Hinterland connectivity is probably the most critical area to ensure a seamless flow of containers and improved port productivity. It is an essential part of a world class logistics system that India needs to develop with a strategic focus.

Exhibit 2 provides a comparative insight of the productivity at JNPT. The terminal operated by DP World (developed and operated until 2005 by P&O Australia) has a high level of performance, both in terms of TEUs per crane/year and TEUs/meter quay/year. This terminal has set new benchmarks in terms of efficiency.

JNPT is the most efficient container port in the country and is the preferred port for a majority of the country's container traffic, presently accounting for about 55% of the total. Table 8 presents the distance, travel time and cost of moving a container from the Delhi area to JNPT and to alternate ports. As shown in the table, even though, the Gujarat ports are located a little closer, they take almost twice as long to reach. The east coast ports not only take much longer, but also cost more than twice as much in inland haulage charges. These differences restrict competition, and JNPT therefore, enjoys a dominant position on account of both its better overall shipping service offerings and its superior hinterland connectivity. The Gujarat ports on the other hand, continue to lose out to JNPT due to their relatively poor connectivity, despite enjoying a closer proximity to the north-western hinterland which generates a majority of the container traffic. Even cargo destined for China or other south east Asian countries prefers to be routed through JNPT, rather than ports like Chennai on the east coast which though, closer to the destination offer poor connectivity to the northern hinterland (World Bank, 2007).

Table 8: Inland Haulage Costs for Delhi Container Traffic to JNPT vs Other Ports

Port	*Distance from Delhi (Km)*	*Rail Transit Time (Hrs)*	*Haulage Costs (Rs/TEUs)*	
			*Rail**	*Road*
JNPT	1388	48	18750	32000
Mundra	1295	80	16650	20000
Pipavav	1333	70	17000	24000
Visakhapatnam	1700	67	22450	66000
Chennai	2100	90	30000	70000

Source: World Bank, 2007.

* Excludes terminal charges of roughly 30%.

6.1 Rail Evacuation

Currently, 30% of the JNPT traffic is expected to move hinterland by rail and the remaining moves entirely by road, mostly to nearby CFSs, and some to interior ICDs. Rail capacity is barely sufficient for current demand. As per discussions in CENTRUM 2006, CONCOR monopoly has been a deterrent to quality service. Competition has now been permitted and 16 licenses have been issued, as listed in Table 9. However, many of the licensees have signed up with CONCOR to have access to their wagons and ICDs, as required by the license conditions. This has distorted the competition to an extent.

Table 9: List of Players for Rail Container Operation

Name of Company	*Associated with*
Category I: Rs 50 Crore (can operate on all routes)	
1. Adani Logistics	Adani Group
2. CWC (own ICD)*	
3. CONCOR (own ICD)*	
4. Dinesh/ETA	
5. Gateway Rail Freight (own ICD)*	Gateway Distriparks
6. Hind Terminals and MSC Agency*	Hind Terminals (subsidiary of Sharaf Group, UAE), Mediterranean Shipping Company (Geneva)
7. India Infrastructure and Logistics*	APL India (subsidiary of NOL, Singapore), Hindustan Infrastructure Project and Engineering
8. Container Rail Road Services**	DP World
9. Reliance Infrastructure Leasing	Reliance (ADAG)
10. SICAL Logistics (own ICD)	
11. KRIBHCO	
12. Arshiya Rail Infrastructure	Arshiya International
Category II: Rs 10 Crore (can operate on all routes except JNPT/Mumbai – NCR)	
1. Delhi Assam Roadways	
2. Innovative B2B Logistics Solutions*	Bagadiya Shipping and Bothra Brothers
3. Boxtrans (India) Logistics Services*	JM Baxi & Co
4. Pipavav Rail Corporation	

* Out of the 15 licensed operators, seven have started operations.
** Expected to start in September, 2007.

Presently, for instance, it is estimated that the transport cost of a container from Delhi to Mumbai Port is almost half the total logistics costs of delivering it to a destination in Europe. Inadequate capacities in the hinterland transport modes often lead to higher costs and delays on account of sub-optimal mode choices, circuitous routing and congestion in the hinterland transport links. The Tughlakabad-JNPT (Delhi-Mumbai) line, one of the most highly trafficked corridors in the country is a case in point (Figure 1). With an average line capacity of 50 trains per day, it has been handling over 67 trains per day, operating at a capacity utilisation of 135%t, and several sections are being operated at 160% utilisation levels. Roughly 40 trains on this corridor are passenger trains, leaving a limited capacity for freight trains, which have a lower priority. Congestion at the railways' Tughlakabad ICD near Delhi and on the line itself has resulted in a poor reliability of service, and high value cargo such as containers, which form the majority of the traffic on this corridor, is increasingly shifting to road transport. Presently, less than one-third of the containerized cargo in this corridor is being carried by the Railways. On average, 9,000 loaded trucks move over this corridor everyday, aggregating around 30 mt annually of road freight traffic (World Bank, 2007).

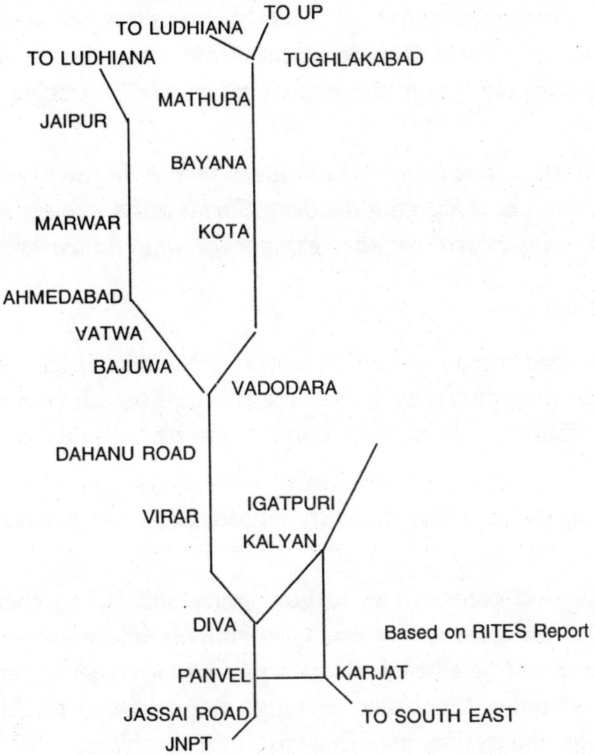

Source: World Bank, 2007.

Fig. 1: Rail Connectivity Mumbai to North-Western Hinterland

The overall data related to hinterland flows at JNPT in Table 10. JNPT faced an acute congestion in 2004. Since then, a third container terminal has been commissioned, bringing the total throughput capacity to 4 mTEUs. A fourth terminal being considered is likely to double the capacity. This will impose serious constraints on the facilities around the port, unless they are addressed concurrently [Raghuram, 2006].

Table 10: Hinterland Flows at JNPT Per cent

Import		Export	
ICD by Rail	33.3	ICD by Rail	22.6
ICD by Road	4.0	ICD by Road	7.5
En Bloc CFS	59.7	CFS by Road + Buffer Yard	26.5 + 7.7
Green Channel	3.0	Factory Stuffed under Excise Seal – RTS	35.7

Source: Chaudhuri, A, 2006.

To provide for the rail based evacuation, the Dedicated Freight Corridor Corporation of India Ltd (DFCCIL) has been set up in 2006, with its first phase being the JNPT to Tughlakabad/

Dadri and Ludhiana to Son Nagar via Dadri corridors. The western corridor will have container trains as its driving traffic.

For 21 mTEU, at 30% movement by rail, and 90 TEU per train, over 190 trains would need to run per day. (Currently, about 40 trains are running per day, over 25 of which are on the JNPT Tughlakabad corridor). Double stack would ease this to about 120 trains per day. About 35-45% of these would be on the stretch near JNPT, picking up an additional 25-30% from the Gujarat ports.

PPP model with ports and related stake holders should be used for rail capacity development. Kutch Railway Corporation and Pipavav Railway Corporation are examples. The DFCCIL should evolve appropriate models, based on past experience and future requirements.

6.2 Road Evacuation

To provide for the road based evacuation, while the National Highways Development Programme is providing inter-regional connectivity with some success, not all port based connectivity projects have been successful. Three such project contracts were recently annulled.

Beyond just the four laning of highways, expressway connectivity to the ports to service major flows would be essential. The currently envisaged future phases of NHDP do not provide for this.

In terms of local road connectivity around ports and ICDs, there is no explicit planning for consequential trailer movements for empty containers and empty trailer movements. Recent studies show that these could be as high as six to seven movements per TEU [Raghuram, 2006]. Similarly, there is no planning for trailer parking, maintenance, facilities for drivers etc. These could lead to avoidable congestion and first/last mile problems.

PPP model for roads around ports can be used with ports and ICD/CFS operators as the stake holders. A need for immediate attention would be the ICD at Tughlakabad.

6.3 Coastal Shipping and Inland Waterways

The potential of coastal shipping and inland waterways is untapped and needs to be developed to lessen the load on the railways and road networks and bring down the costs since cost of cargo movement by sea is significantly less than the cost by road and rail. Feedering from an Indian transshipment port would naturally be a coastal movement.

The possibility of a dedicated sea corridor with inter-port connectivity needs to be explored. Integration with coastal and inland water transport for evacuation needs proactive consideration.

6.4 ICD/CFS Infrastructure

Given that ICD/CFS business is open to anybody, there would not be a concern regarding the supply. The concepts of SEZs and Free Trade Warehousing Zones would only further facilitate such infrastructure. The conditions imposed on the private rail container reinforce this concept.

However, the following aspects would need intervention.

- Location and access, giving consideration to distance to manufacturing units, local connectivity with minimum traffic interference.
- Customs and bonded warehouse
- Rail connection to gateway ports
- Parking spaces and maintenance facility

7. OTHER ISSUES

7.1 Information Technology (IT)

While IT use for container logistics would be commercially driven, policy and industry level interventions would be necessary to develop standards, networking and information sharing, and even knowledge products. Technologies such as Radio Frequency Identification Device (RFID) and Global Positioning System (GPS) should be leveraged to achieve effectiveness and efficiency.

7.2 Domestic Traffic

While container movement has been primarily viewed in the context of international trade, domestic container movement is slowly picking up and needs focus for development. Most of the domestic container movement is expected to be by rail (Concor). During 2006-07, out of over 2 mTEUs moved by Concor, nearly 0.4 mTEUs were for the domestic market (Table 11).

Table 11: CONCOR Traffic

TEU

Year	*International*	*Domestic*	*Total*	*Annual Growth (%)*
2002-03	1,031,925	351,238	1,383,163	12.3
2003-04	1,251,618	350,501	1,602,119	15.8
2004-05	1,376,516	351,460	1,727,976	7.9
2005-06	1,556,714	373,848	1,930,562	11.7
2006-07	1,715,661	389,605	2,105,266	9.0

Source: CONCOR.

This would also create an opportunity for customised containerization. For example, while the standard container does not permit double stacking under electric traction wires, specially designed lower height containers for automobiles have permitted double stacking under wire. Opportunities in customised containerization should be leveraged, as specific segment volumes increase.

7.3 Leasing and Manufacture

Availability of containers, wagons, tractor/trailers and cranes as support equipment is critical. India does not have enough manufacturing base for such equipment. China is currently the world leader in this domain. There is big opportunity for India to develop a manufacturing base, not only to cater to our requirement, but also for the export market.

In the context of containers, leasing by non-shipping line owners has been leveraged internationally for efficient use of containers. However, the share of the leased fleet has dropped from 50% in 1981 to 40% in 2006. With better IT for container tracking, the leased fleet has utilisations over 90%, with the cost of leasing showing a decreasing trend.

Exhibit 3 gives the annual global manufacture of containers, which stands at over three million in 2006. Exhibit 4 brings out the profile of container manufacturers, showing Japanese dominance in 1978, Korean dominance in 1992 and Chinese dominance in 2006. At even US $1500 per TEU, India should be able to compete by manufacturing containers at less than Rs 60,000 per TEU. The manufacturing base in India is small and could do with a focus on incentivized growth.

7.4 Location Policy of Industries Including SEZs

As part of evolving world class export and import logistics, the government has embarked on the policy of developing SEZs. As on August 11, 2008, 250 SEZs had been notified under the SEZ Act apart from the 19 that were operational prior to the SEZ Act of 2005. Of the 250 SEZs (Table 12), 83 are manufacturing driven while the rest are IT and IT enabled services based. Of the 83, 31 are coastal and the rest 52 are away from the coast and would hence require focus on connectivity.

Table 12: Location of SEZs (as on August 11, 2008)

	Coastal	*Non-Coastal*	*Total*
Manufacturing	31	52	83
IT/ITES	47	120	167
Total	78	172	250

Source: Ministry of Commerce and Industry.

As far as possible, it would be a good idea to locate SEZs near ports. The same would apply for industries, where a focus on appropriate zoning of industrial development to minimise connectivity requirements with planned linkages including by Inland Water Transport would be essential. Gujarat has been proactive in this through a policy of port led industrial development.

7.5 Regulation

It is important to ensure appropriate regulation for the following:

Licensing

Issues of ensuring sufficient competition, along with capability to deliver with appropriate national security would be key criteria in licensing. There have been debates on private sector monopoly, when P&O Australia won the bids and operated many terminals in the South Asian region. P&O Australia has now been taken over by DP World and the same issue continues.

There are guidelines on there being at least two operators in a port and no more than two terminals per operator. These guidelines need to be reviewed and linked with TEU capacity and not number of terminals.

Security

Security was a matter of concern in the context of Hutchison bidding for Chennai Even DP World had to give up some of its US acquisitions due to perceived security concerns. Operational security at ports including screening of containers has gained significance after 9/11.

Port Tariffs

While India has a Tariff Authority for Major Ports (TAMP), the question has often been raised as to whether, we need the TAMP, and even if so, whether, the regulation should be cost based. Recently the PSA International operated container terminal at Tuticorin port resisted the reduction in tariffs imposed by TAMP and consequently reduced their throughput.

It would appear that with the number of terminals that India has and is developing, competition is increasing and the market itself can regulate the tariffs.

Shipping Line Conferences

In the container shipping business (which is a hangover of liner business), cartel like conferences of shipping lines operated in route based markets to control schedules and tariffs. While these were frowned upon, they were never regulated. Recently, the Competition Commission of India raised the issue that such conferences were anti competitive and that shipping lines should set tariffs and compete independently.

Independent of conferences, there is an increasing market concentration in the container shipping business. Exhibit 5 gives a perspective on the concentration of container shipping among the top 20 carriers, which has increased from 38.8% in 1990 to 72.7% in 2006. This is reflective of the mergers and acquisitions, which seem to be a rather continuous activity of this business.

Customs

Customs need to become more process friendly with increased usage of green channel. The data gathered by customs, especially with Electronic Data Interchange, can be used to create much required Origin Destination (OD) data for traffic profiling.

Cabotage

The cabotage rules of not allowing foreign flag vessels for coastal shipping need to be reviewed. The main trade of is between protection for Indian flags versus more competition and supply. In today's world of liberalisation led growth, it would appear that cabotage must be lifted as a matter of long term policy. An attendant measure would be to provide the same concessions to coastal shipping as international shipping. As was voiced in CENTRUM 2006, cabotage should not become a sabotage!

Other Areas of Regulation (which are not being elaborated)

- Environment and conservation
- Safety

- Quality of service
- Dispute resolution

8. CONCLUSIONS

Based on the above analysis, the following issues need consideration:

- Landlord port with privately operated terminals would be the way forward. Existing ports should be empowered for this
- There should be clear delineation of roles between landlord and operator. This does not exist at JNPT presently (JNPT vs JNPCT)
- The public port authority will focus more on
    - **landlord function** such as long-term planning, infrastructure development, asset management
    - **regulatory function** such as maritime safety, environment protection and fair competition, and
    - **co-ordination function** such as coordination among governmental agencies, maritime organisations, decision-making authorities and planners of the city, under the commonly shared long-range policy and planning
    - **facilitation/promotion function** such as provision of port EDI, inter-port cooperation and strategic marketing
- There is not enough focus on scale of container terminals. This is necessary to drive down costs.
- Tendering and bidding should be done in a time definite manner. There should be a flexible framework in place for terminal development by private parties under a landlord port. There are significant beauracratic delays (eg second terminals in Tuticorin and Chennai). Labor is not always in favour and needs to be dealt with.
- Global tendering would be essential to get the most competitive supply. Dredging is an example.
- Acts governing ports and related activities need to be reviewed and liberalised (MS Act, IP Act, Maritime Trade Practices Act, etc).
- Training to bring in a supply chain and marketing mind set among executives of all stakeholders in this sector is critical. OD data on port traffic should be systematically gathered and published. IPA should drive this with support from Customs and Concor. EDI based data would help.
- Top management stake holding, especially through the civil service, is not compatible with strategizing port development. Technocrats, with appropriate incentives and accountability should be brought in.

The largest increases in container traffic are expected to occur in the western region, with the Mumbai and Gujarat port clusters together requiring capacity additions on the order of 10 mTEUs, from about 4 mTEUs now to over 14 mTEUs by 2015. Of this about 6 mTEUs of capacity is expected to be needed in the Mumbai cluster, and another 4 mTEUs in the Gujarat cluster. The other cluster where a large increase in container traffic is expected is in the Cochin/Tuticorin cluster where an additional 4 mTEUs of capacity will be needed. These three port clusters would then account for 14 mTEUs of the 16 mTEUs of additional capacity needed for container traffic through the year 2015. Achieving this level of capacity increases in the Mumbai, Gujarat and Cochin/Tuticorin clusters would largely address the container traffic requirements through the year 2015.

The 191 mt or 15 mTEUs capacity shortfall for container traffic projected for 2015 would only partially be filled by capacity expansions planned under the NMDP. The NMDP envisages the creation of an additional 11 mTEUs of container handling capacity in the near term. The remainder would need to be developed in the State ports sector primarily through private investments, and some of these are already being planned or under implementation such as at Mundra and Rewas. The investments proposed under the NMDP include large expansions of container handling capacity at Tuticorin, Cochin, JNPT and Mumbai port. This appears to fit well with the strategy of developing container facilities where the demand is greatest (the western and southern ports) and in the southern cluster which has proximity to international shipping routes [World Bank, 2007].

For 30 mTEUs per annum, as per normal international standards of 1000 TEUs per annum per mt of berth length, we need 30 km of berth length. By JNPT standards where demand is continuously available and productivity is high, this could be as low as 15 km. However, providing for a reasonable 70% occupancy, we need 21 km. At 300mts per berth, this translates to 70 berths. Currently we have 27 berths. An additional nine berths have been signed up as stated earlier in this paper: So there is a need for atleast 30 more berths. While this is a target, market forces will drive the actual berth development.

The additional investment required could be of the order of US $7.5 billion based on a 300 mts berth cost of US $250 million (Rs 1000 crore). With JNPT standards, and focusing on Suezmax vessels at hub ports, berth productivity can be doubled and the investment requirements brought down. A detailed cost benefit analysis, keeping in view the costs of accommodating large vessels and benefits of increased productivity including due to hubbing in India needs to be carried out.

Indian infrastructure for logistics is poor compared to world class and at best reactive to demand. There is need for continued focus on quality infrastructure development with speed. Commercialisation and private involvement through PPP contracts is the key for building global trade competitiveness through containerization.

REFERENCES

1. Chaudhuri, A (2006), 'De-regulation within the Rail Market,' Presentation.
2. CI Magazine (2007), Containerization International, 40th Anniversary Issue, 2007.
3. CMIE (2008), Data from 'Centre for Monitoring Indian Economy.'
4. CRISIL (2006), CRISIL Infrastructure Advisory Study.
5. IPA (2008), 'Major Ports of India,' Indian Ports Association, New Delhi.

6. Raghuram, G (2006), 'A Diagnostic Study of Jawaharlal Nehru Port Trust,' Working Paper No 2006-04-09, Indian Institute of Management, Ahmedabad, April 2006
7. World Bank (2007), 'India: Port Sector Development – Possibilities for Accelerating Growth,' June 26, 2007.
8. http://en.wikipedia.org

APPENDIX

Exhibit 1

Top 20 Container Ports

Port	Traffic (TEU)	Port	Traffic (TEU)	Port	Traffic (TEU)	
1970		**1980**		**2006**		
1.	New York/New Jersey	930,000	New York/New Jersey	1,947,000	Singapore	24,792,400
2.	Oakland	336,364	Rotterdam	1,900,707	Hong Kong	23,230,000
3.	Rotterdam	242,328	Hong Kong	1,464,961	Shanghai	21,710,000
4.	Seattle	223,740	Kaohsiung	979,015	Shenzhen	18,468,900
5.	Antwerp	215,256	Singapore(PSA)	916,989	Busan	12,030,000
6.	Belfast	210,000	Hamburg	783,323	Kaohsiung	9,774,670
7.	Bremen/Bremerhaven	194,812	Oakland	782,175	Rotterdam	9,690,052
8.	Los Angeles	165,000	Seattle	781,563	Dubai	8,923,465
9.	Melbourne	158,127	Kobe	727,313	Hamburg	8,861,545
10.	Tilbury	155,082	Antwerp	724,247	Los Angeles	8,469,853
11.	Larne	147,309	Yokohama	722,025	Qingdao	7,702,000
12.	Virginia	143,231	Bremen/Bremerhaven	702,764	Long Beach	7,290,365
13.	Liverpool	140,419	Baltimore	663,000	Ningbo	7,068,000
14.	Harwich	139,627	Keelung	659,645	Antwerp	7,018,799
15.	Gothenburg	128,270	Busan	632,866	Guangzhou	6,600,000
16.	Philadelphia	120,000	Tokyo	631,505	Port Klang	6,320,000
17.	Sydney	117,985	Los Angeles	620,988	Tianjin	5,900,000
18.	Le Havre	107,995	Jeddah	562,792	New York/New Jersey	5,092,806
19.	Anchorage	100,731	Long Beach	553,709	Port Tanjung Pelepas	4,770,000
20.	Felixstowe	93,099	Melbourne	512,864	Bremen/Bremerhaven	4,450,000
	Total	**4,069,375**	**Total**	**17,269,451**	**Total**	**208,162,855**
	Share of global throughput	75.9%	Share of global throughput	49.6%	Share of global throughput	56.3%
	Global Total	**5,363,235**	**Global Total**	**34,805944**	**Global Total**	**369,719,521***

[CI Magazine, 2007]

* Provisional.

In 1970, the total container traffic was 4.0 mTEUs. In 2006, Singapore alone handled 24.8 mTEUs. There has been a tremendous shift in the throughput. Scale economy, more players (ports), consolidation and bigger ships were some of the factors that accounted for huge throughputs. Asia gained market share in the past 40 years and currently dominate the 2006 container throughput league. In 1970, there was only one Asian port in top 20 lists, the port of Yokohama in Japan. In 2006, 12 out of 20 top ports were from Asian countries. China alone handled more about 50% of traffic in 2006.

Exhibit 2

Container Berth and Crane Productivity Across Ports

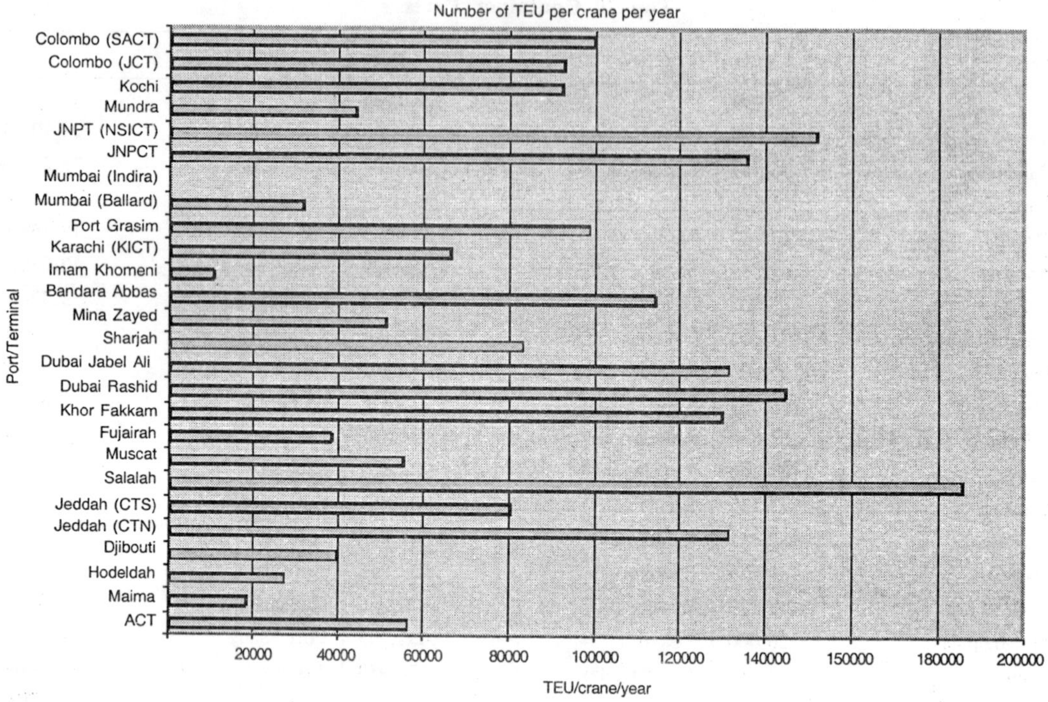

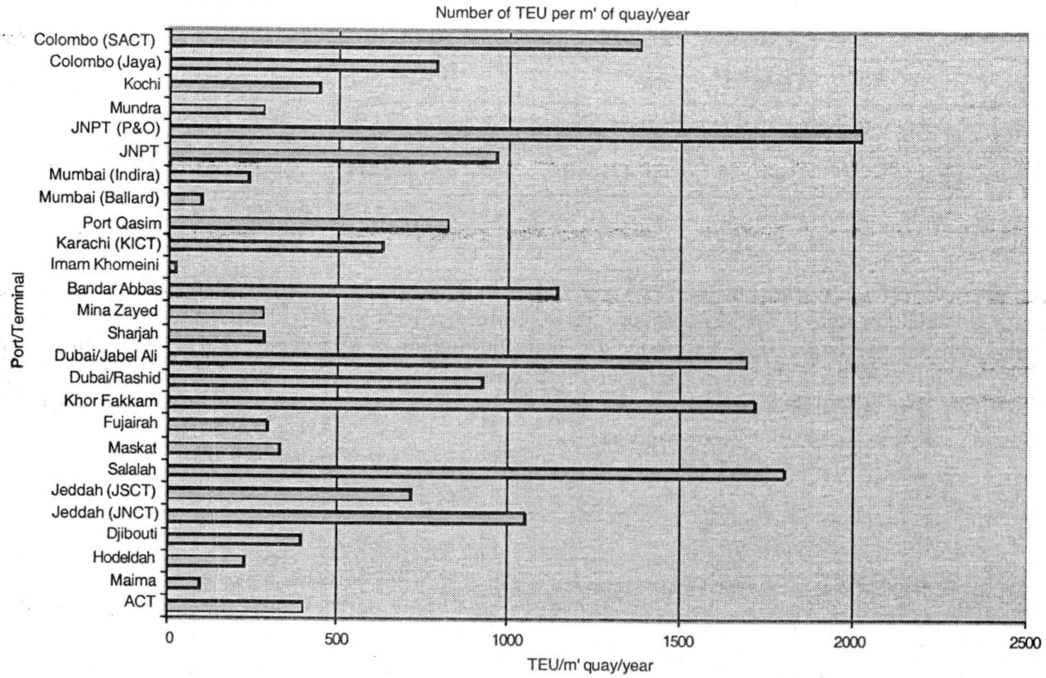

Exhibit 3

Global Production

Year	*Annual Output (TEU)*	*Annualized 20ft Price (US $)*
1966	40,000	1,500
1970	130,000	2,000
1974	185,000	1,800
1978	475,000	2,500
1982	460,000	2,000
1986	430,000	1,700
1990	805,000	2,700
1994	1,150,000	2,300
1998	1,480,000	1,700
2002	1,740,000	1,350
2006	3,050,000	1,850

[CI Magazine, 2007].

Exhibit 4

Top 20 Ocean Carriers

Carrier	*Traffic (TEU)*	*Carrier*	*Traffic (TEU)*
1990		*2006*	
1. Evergreen	130,916	AP Mÿller-Maersk [1]	1,600,012
2. Sea-Land Service	115,367	Mediterranean Shipping Co	937,145
3. Maersk	94,703	CMA CGM [2]	597,677
4. NYK	78,148	Evergreen [3]	539,801
5. Mitsui OSK Lines	70,338	Hapag-Lloyd	448,840
6. APL	66,380	Cosco	385,368
7. OOCL	58,117	China Shipping Container Lines	339,545
8. K Line	55,462	Hanjin Shipping [4]	328,307
9. Cosco Shanghai	54,505	APL	323,319
10. Hapag-Lloyd	53,178	NYK [5]	313,049
11. Hanjin Shipping	49,621	Mitsui OSK Lines	284,848
12. P & O Containers	49,368	OOCL	268,502
13. Yangming	46,817	CSAV [6]	249,885
14. Zim Israel Navigation	44,916	K Line	241,772
15. Nedlloyd Lines	40,335	Yangming	223,192
16. Baltic Shipping Co	36,760	Hamburg Sud [7]	217,018
17. Neptune Orient Lines	35,294	Zim Integrated Shipping Services	213,795
18. ScanDutch	32,948	Hyundai Merchant Marine	153,850
19. CGM	29,040	Pacific International Lines [8]	141,391
20. Delmas Vieljeus	31,204	Wan Hai Lines	117,767
Total	**1,173,413**	**Total**	**7,925,083**
Top 20 Share	**38.8%**	**Top 20 Share**	**72.7%**

[CI Magazine, 2007].

(1) includes Portlink and Safmarine; (2) includes ANL, Delmas, FAS, MacAndrews, OT Africa Line; (3) includes Hatsu, Italia Marittima; (4) includes Senator Lines; (5) includes TSK; (6) includes CSAV Norasia, Libra, Montemar; (7) includes Alianca, Ybarra; (8) includes Advance Container Line

The top 20 carriers accounted for 38.9% of the total fleet capacity in 1990, which increased to 72.7% in 2006. Several mergers and acquisitions took place during this period. Out of the 20 top carriers, 13 were from Asia in 2006, holding a fleet capacity share of 46.6%.

Exhibit 5

The Box Building Hierarchy

Company	*Country*	*Output (TEU)*	*Company*	*Country*	*Output (TEU)*	*Company*	*Country*	*Output (TEU)*
1978 (Japanese Dominance)			***1992 (Korean Dominance)***			***2006 (Chinese Dominance)***		
Tokyu Car	Japan	115,000	Hyundai Precision	South Korea*	230,000	CIMC Group	China	1,565,000
Hyundai Precision	South Korea	25,000	Jindo Corp	South Korea*	90,000	Singamas Group	China*	585,000
Officine Franchin	Italy	18,000	EHIC Group	Taiwan*	70,500	CXIC Group	China	280,000
Nippon Fruehauf	Japan	17,500	Hyosung Metal	South Korea*	50,500	Jindo Corp	China (S Korea)	165,000
Nippon Strick	Japan	17,000	Signgamas Group	China	45,000	Hyundai Mobis	China (S Korea)	90,000
Ste Trailor	France	16,500	Union Container	Taiwan*	45,000	Maersk	China (Denmark)	65,000
Morteo Soprefin	Italy	16,000	Bangkok Cont Ind	Thailand	40,500	China Shipping	China	55,000
Nippon Trailmobile	Japan	15,000	Hung Myung Ind	South Korea	40,000	EHIC (Malaysia)	Malaysia	50,000
Alna Koki Co	Japan	13,500	AIC Group	Taiwan*	36,500	PT Aspex Kumbong	Indonesia	40,000
Fruehauf France	France	11,500	CIMC Group	China	35,000	Hung Dao Container	Vietnam	15,000
Other		210,000	Other		452,000	Other		140,000
Total		**475,000**	**Total**		**1,135,000**	**Total**		**3,050,000**

[CI Magazine, 2007] *Also includes overseas production.

Notes:

1. This paper is a result of deliberations held in CENTRUM (Containerization for Trade Momentum) 2006 (July 12-13, 2006) and 2007 (August 28-29, 2007), New Delhi and further data collection and analysis by the authors.

19

IMPACT OF MORMUGAO PORT ON THE DEVELOPMENTAL PARAMETERS OF GOA: A HISTORICAL AND ECONOMIC PERSPECTIVE

Jeronimo G. R. Monteiro

ABSTRACT

Mormugao port is one of the oldest ports on the west coast of India, with a fine natural harbour. It has been relentlessly serving the nation in its economic development for over a century. Portuguese navigators founded the sea route to India to expand their commerce and trade. Historians say the pre-Portuguese trade of Goa was mostly horses, artifacts among others and during Portuguese rule of 451 years it was spices and a wide variety of other items of economic and historical importance. Down the ages it has been the busiest port catering to a vast hinterland which is very productive and resourceful. Post 1961 (Goa's Liberation) era the port handled "iron ore" as bulk of the cargo for export. Government of India declared it a "Major Port" in 1963. Port literature reveals a positive relationship between existence of a port and overall development of the region. Economic hinterland of this port is very vast and full of resources, which makes this port a centre of activity. The paper examines both historical and economic review of Mormugao Port as well as its contemporary significance.

1. INTRODUCTION

Ports are the drivers of entire economies they serve. Ports are gateways to a country's international trade. Ports play an important role in maritime nation by facilitating foreign trade. They are thus, vital catalyst for social and economic development in any maritime nation.[1] A port is essentially an economic concept, which, through its economic infrastructure, serves the coastal and overseas traffic to a region. Port is a sub-system of the total transport system and a meeting place of other modes of transport.[2]

The development of a modern port is the result of a variety of factors, which the ports face in a competitive and globalised world. This paper focusses on some of the factors which have contributed to the success and development of Mormugao port, the "golden gateway"[3] of

Goa. Some of the factors behind the growth of Mormugao port are clear from the point of view of putting Goa on the path of development and bestowing fine socio-economic indicators. First, Goa is bestowed with a fine natural, all weather port to the west coast of India. It is strategically located on the western seaboard of India, catering to the traffic not only of Goa but also of the neighbouring states as well as of the world. Second, Goa is endowed with many mineral resources, especially iron ore and manganese in the hinterland, which was discovered by private initiatives in 1950s. The port caters to the exports of mainly these minerals from Goa. Third, the port is one of the oldest port (completed 122 years of its existence) of India, achieved greater success after the establishment of the Port Trust in 1963, which is quite obvious that such organisation enables the port to move ahead on the developmental path of its region. And, finally the connectivity to the port was a prime factor for the greater success of Mormugao port. The economic hinterland of Mormugao port is beyond Goa borders.

Historically, ports have played a major and crucial role in the economic development of a region. The origin of Mormugao Port owed to the "Treaty of Lisbon" signed in 1878 between British and Portuguese Governments. The treaty was also known as "Luso-British Treaty". Mormugao port, which has made iron ore mining and its export since 1950s, was primarily instrumental in bestowing on Goa and its people better socio-economic indicators, and a "gateway" to a growing industrial complex in the hinterland of Goa.

Goa, the twenty-fifth state of the Union of India, is a tiny, scenic place which has been variously known as the "Tropical Paradise of Tourists," "Golden Gateway of Commerce and Trade," "Pearl of the Orient," "Rome of the East," and "Kashi of the Konkan." It is situated along Konkan coast of India (western India), has a coastline of 131 kms. It has a partly hilly terrain with Western Ghats to the east and the Arabian Sea in the west. It has an area of 3701 sq. km. and stretches for 60 km. in an east-west direction and about 105 km. from north to south.

Having discussed the histories of Goa and Mormugao Port, the paper now looks at the developmental parameters from the historical and economic perspectives. The remainder of the paper is organised as follows section 2 looks at the historical perspective of development of trade, commerce up to 1961, when Goa became part of India. The building of a rail line to Goa's hinterland and Mormugao Port by a British company marked the turning point for the expansion and growth of this region. Section 3 looks at the economic perspective of Mormugao Port, after Goa became part of India in 1961. We intend to present here the economic aspects briefly of pre 1961 era of the port and an analytical discussion of the post 1961 era. The developmental parameters here to be highlighted and discussed are cargo traded, population growth in Goa, and some others, on account of a Port. Today, the port stands tall among the major ports of India, because of its contribution to iron ore exports of the country. It exports around forty percent of iron ore of India. Besides, the port survives the era of global competition and is trying to expand its base in areas such container handling, catering to international passenger ships, cruise ships and tourism related development.[4] Section 4 provides the concluding remarks.

2. MORMUGAO PORT: A HISTORICAL PERSPECTIVE

Goa has a long historical attachment to maritime trade. It had quite a few ports in its territory which were of historical importance till the advent of the Portuguese 1510. Among the earliest port was Chandrapur followed by port of Old Goa and then New Goa (Panaji). The maritime history of coastal Goa can be traced back to the period of the Indian Emperor Ashoka. Indian trade and commerce traveled to distant lands farther from India during Ashoka's rule.[5] Commerce with foreign countries like Arabia, Persia and Turkey continued by land as well as by sea. Sea-borne trade, however, played an increasingly important role in medieval India. The port of Goa was visited by merchants of all nationalities and was best suited for maritime trade.[6] Goa was one of the principal emporia of trade on the west coast of India and a great centre, which attracted people of various races, cultures and creeds from different parts of Asia.[7] The presence of rich merchants of all nationalities added to its greatness. Magnificent edifices, residences, mansions, buildings adorned the city of Old Goa. As Tome Pires (1886) observed in 1511, Goans were well known for their skills in ship-building which was possible due to availability of timber and other raw materials and of course their craftsman, gave it a fine reputation for quality vessels. Besides, sea-men hailing from this area were known for the skills and bravery in navigation.

The port city of Goa grew in importance because of the trade in horses imported from Persia, Arabia, Hormuz and from the Kingdom of Cambay (Gujarat). Besides horses; Goa also traded betel, areca, calico, fine muslin, rice velvets, satin, damask and chinaware. Later on historians, says that Goa traded pepper, ginger and other spices which were brought from other parts of India. The port city of Goa from fifteenth century (1510) came under foreign rule led by Afonso de Albuquerque. During the Portuguese rule, the city of Goa got a further boost and trade continued to expand beyond Indian boundaries. Goa in those years was in the international mainstream due to Portuguese's influence. However, soon the Portuguese territory of Goa entered a period of decline and stagnation in the seventeenth century,[8] due to Portuguese neglect of Goa on account of failure to link Goa with vast rail network of British India. Another reason was the flourishing trade in Bombay (now Mumbai) which acted as a convenient corridor and exit point for all purpose. Historians also attributed the decline of Portuguese India due to the treaty signed by the Portuguese in 1661[9] in Lisbon to cede the rights over Bombay.

Goa's earliest port was shifted from interior Chandrapur to Old Goa and again to 'New Goa' (Panaji) in 1818.[10] All these three earlier ports of Goa were not sufficient to serve international trade and also could not cater to big size vessels. Besides, they had navigational problems. It was later on found that the mouth of Zuari River was an easy point to construct a full-fledged Port for Goa. British initiative was called upon by the Portuguese to build a Port for Goa suiting to changing needs of the time. This port later came to be known as 'Mormugao Port'.[11] This port would have tremendous potential to cater to the demands of trade and industry and to contribute to the economic development of not only of the region but also of the nation.

Mormugao Port owed its origin to the Treaty of Lisbon of 1878 between the British and Portuguese Governments. An agreement was signed between the Western India Portuguese Guaranteed Railway Company (WIPGR) and Portuguese Government for the construction, operation and maintenance of the port and the connected Railway line in 1881. The Mormugao port was virtually gifted by the Portuguese administration to a British Company "Western India Portuguese Guaranteed Railway" (WIPGR). The implication of this gift was that the British Company would link the hinterland of the Deccan to a new port (Mormugao) on the west coast of India through a railway line.[12] This treaty *inter alia,* was meant for the purpose of having a union of commercial interests between India and Goa. The Port was to provide adequate accommodation for all the hinterland trade of the Southern Maratha and other districts of India which were in close proximity to Goa and for all such commercial purposes, it was to function in exactly the same manner as a port of transit.[13] This was the turning point in the expansion of business, industrial capacities of hinterland and the overall growth of the port of Mormugao. The actual work of construction of the Harbour and the Railway line started in 1882. As the construction of these gigantic projects was underway in April 1885, *S.S. Westbourne*, with a draft of 25 feet, sailed into Mormugao for the first time.[14] According to Lopes Mendes (1886) the steamer *S.S. Westbourne*[15] was carrying a cargo of 2700 tonnes consisting of heavy machinery for the railway line then under construction. It was a "new era", wrote Lopes Mendes.[16] The Port and its connected railway line up to Castle Rock commenced functioning in 1888, the year when Bombay's prestigious Victoria dock was constructed. Mormugao port is described as a good and safe port and one of the best all-weather natural harbours in the world formed by the promontories of the two peninsulas namely Salcette and Bardez. Mormugoa port provides anchorage to vessels of all sizes in all seasons.

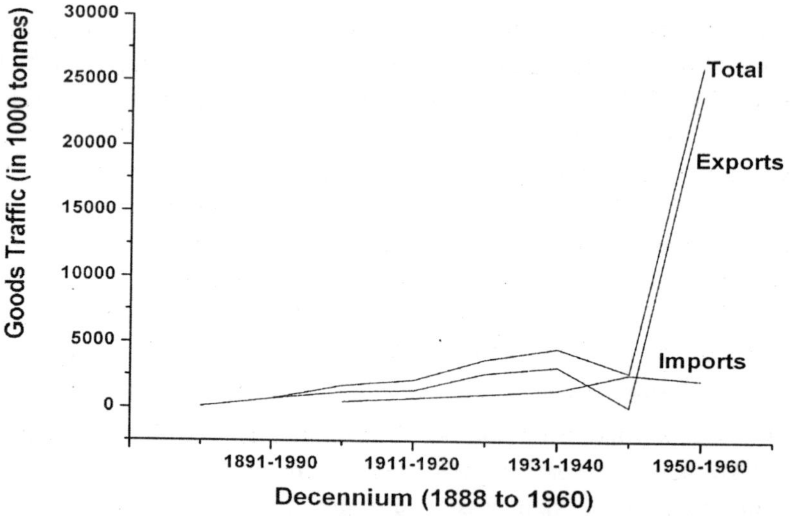

Fig. 1: Imports and Exports through Mormugao Port, 1888-1960

Figure 1 presents the goods traffic handled by Mormugao port from 1888 to 1960. It shows the trends in exports and imports for the last seventy years or so of the Portuguese occupation of Goa. Mormugao Port was at that time, providing easy accessibility for its local and international trade. The figure shows a substantial increase in goods handled over this period. This may be attributed to the fact that the variety of exports increased to include areca, betel, spices, cotton and minerals. The prosperity of the hinterland contributed to the supply of these goods to the port. On the other hand, imports were mostly petroleum, oil and lubricants; food grains; and iron and steel machinery. Overall exports in each decade between 1901 and 1960 were, on average, about two and one-half times greater than imports. It may be noted that exports drastically decreased from 1940 due to the advent of World War II. But exports, especially of iron ore, increased sharply in the 1950s as private investors developed the mining industry to take advantage of incentives provided by the Portuguese administration.

3. MORMUGAO PORT: ECONOMIC PERSPECTIVE

The port of Mormugao entered a new phase in early 1961. Many developments took place with regard to the port and the railway line. The Indian economic blockade of the 1950s, likely designed to induce the Portuguese to leave Goa, had a severe impact in the early 1960s. Due to the closure of the India-Goa border there was a sudden change in the administration of Mormugao port and the railway. Indeed, the Southern Railway, which was operating and managing the port railway, ceased all its operations in Goa. In April 1961, an autonomous body called the Junta Autonoma dos Portos e Caminhos de Ferro (Autonomous Commission for Ports and Railways) was created to replace the WIPGR Company and took over the Port and the Railway Administration.[17] This occurred before 19 December 1961 when Goa became part of India. With this, the Administration of the Port and its Railway link were taken over by the Indian Government through the appointment of an Administrative Officer on 8 January 1962.

Like other major ports, the port of Mormugao came under the direct control of the Ministry of Transport in November 1962. The railway section too from Vasco da Gama to the border of Goa was transferred to the Southern Railway in May 1963. The Indian Ports Act, 1908 was extended to Mormugao Port, and on 2 December 1963 the Ministry of Transport declared Mormugao Port the country's seventh major port. Thereafter, the Major Port Trust Act, 1963 became applicable and a Board of Trustees was appointed on 1 July 1964. When Goa became part of India the port had seven berths with a breakwater of 2500 feet. Since then, the facilities at Mormugao have been increased to comprise twelve berths, a traffic management system, a twenty-four hour signal station, tractor tugs, a mechanical ore-handling plant and a variety of other equipment to handle containers, oil and general cargo.

India at present is ranked as the world's seventeenth most important maritime nation[18] based upon the volume of tonnage entering and clearing its ports. Situated at the confluence of the Arabian Sea, Indian Ocean and Bay of Bengal, India also has locational advantage[19] and Mormugao Port is part of this. The port is the country's premier iron ore exporter with an annual throughput of around thirty million tonnes, which accounts for about forty percent of India's iron ore exports. This increase in rapid growth of traffic is due to excellent inland waterway system based upon the Zuari and Mandovi rivers and the Cumbarjua Canal. This system has been used to bring ore economically from the mines to the harbour.

Figure 2 shows that most of the cargo handled in the post-Portuguese era was exports, except in 1999-2000 when exports decreased by 3.43 per cent while imports increased by twenty-nine percent over the previous year. The fall in export traffic was attributable to a drop in iron ore exports due to a lack of overseas demand. A noteworthy feature in Figure 2 is that after the 1990s imports increased while transhipment cargoes decreased to zero after 2002-2003. The new development at Mormugao Port is that vessels of 70,000 dwt and above could now be berthed. This is the result of a continuous increase in the quality of port services in recent years.

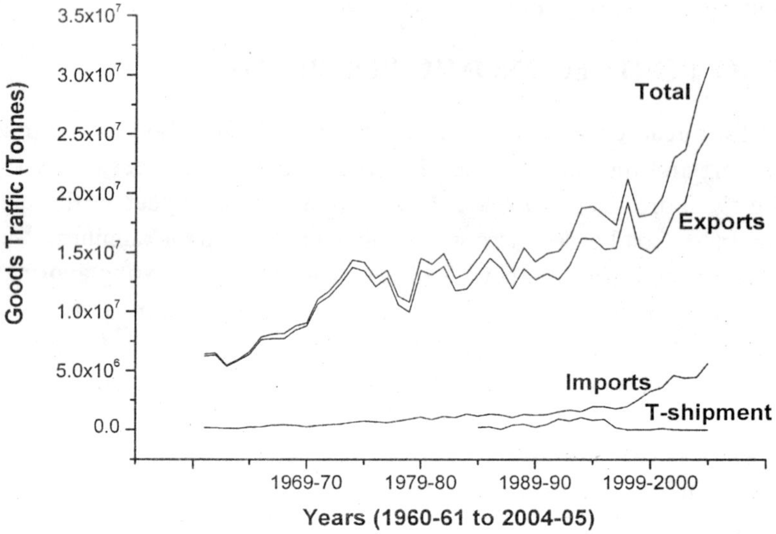

Fig. 2: Variations in Imports, Exports and Transhipment Cargoes after 1960

The major ports of India have accounted for the bulk of cargo traffic. In the 1960s the major ports handled about eighty-five percent of the traffic; this figure has risen to about ninety-five percent in the 1990s. Figure 3 shows the absolute growth of cargo handled by all the major ports in India and Mormugao's share of total cargo handled. The overall cargo handled by the major

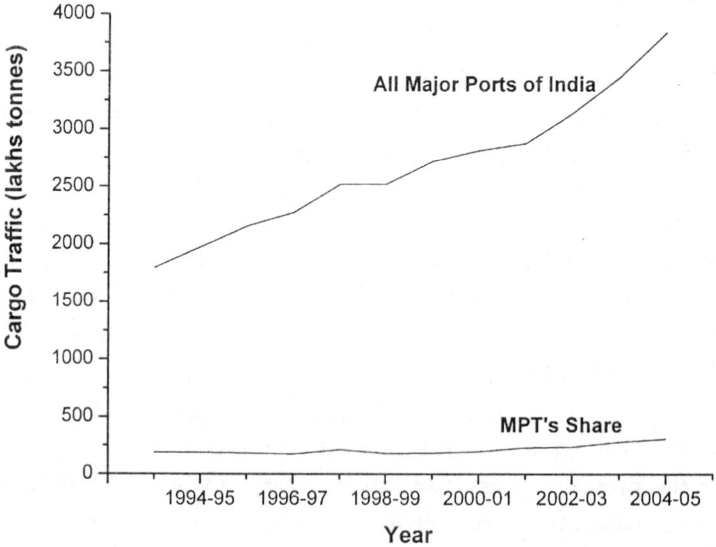

Fig. 3: Cargo Handled at the Major Ports of India and at Mormugao, 1901-2005

major ports in 1993-1994 was on the order of 1792.60 *lakh* tonnes.[20] This has increased to 1972.62 *lakh* tonnes in 1994-1995, a growth of 10.04 percent. When tonnage handled touching an all-time high of 3836.25 *lakh* tonnes in 2004-2005, growth increased to 11.26 per cent. Mormugao's share over the years increased from nearly 187.17 lakh tonnes to 306.59 lakh tonnes during the same period. A noteworthy development for the MPT is that almost forty percent of the exports were iron ore.

The commodities that comprised imports and exports in Mormugao were different than that during the Portuguese era. Imports used to comprise lubricants, food grains, cement, mineral oils and fertilizers, while exports consisted of iron ore, manganese, oil cakes, bauxite and general cargo. The composition of trade after 1961 has changed significantly due to Goa's increased exploitation of mineral resources.[21] The Port also started to serve other regions outside of Goa. In terms of export tonnage, Mormugao assumed second place among all the major ports, wresting this position from Calcutta in 1968-1969.

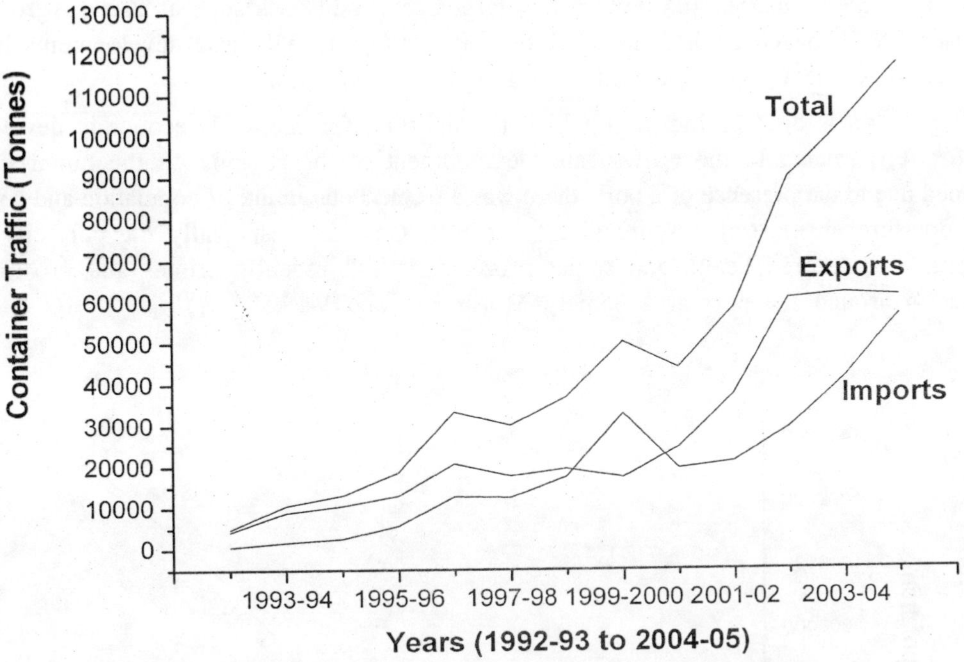

Fig. 4: Container Traffic Handled at Mormugao, 1992/1993-2004/2005

The rise in container traffic has been particularly noticeable in recent years. Since 1992, there has been a regular container feeder service from the port. Figure 4 shows the rise in container traffic. In the container sector, exports have exceeded imports except in 1999-2000.

As far as performance of MPT is concerned, the average pre-berthing and average turn around time has declined quite significantly. It was 2.98 and 6.61 days for average pre-berthing and average turn around time in 1994-95 declined to 1.92 and 2.79 days in 2002-03, for both the performance indicators respectively. (See Table 5) A study in the growth of the port's other increased considerably. The growth was especially notable among the largest ships visiting the port. The total number of ore vessels has increased from 421 in 1962-63 to 501 in 1970-71. In 2006 MPT has installed a new generation modern technology transshipped ship with a storage capacity of 123,000 tonnes, thereby, giving a competitive edge to MPT.[22]

From this foregoing discussion, two interesting and healthy trends can be seen with regard to traffic patterns of the Port during the post-Portuguese period: (*i*) a tendency towards diversification of the Port's traffic, with a growing volume of non-ore traffic (from mono-commodity to multi-commodity), and (*ii*) the expansion of Mormugao's service-area to areas beyond Goa. Mormugao Port today, caters to a vast hinterland beyond the Goa borders. This is indeed a healthy trend, since it encourages the growth of diversified port-services and also reduces the Port's undue dependence on a single-commodity-traffic. The economic hinterland of the port comprises 57,400 sq. miles of total area.[23] Goa was on a path to industrial development after 1961 and many entrepreneurs showed interest in investing in Goa, though, there were no specific incentives like those they have today. As of now, Goa has eighteen Industrial Estates comprising little over 4000 small scale industries and quite a few large scale industries such as Zuari Agro Chemicals Industries Ltd, Ciba Geigy Ltd, MRF Rubber Pvt. Ltd, etc All these developments in Goa can be the result of heavy goods transit by sea and a railway link.

Population is another indicator which is important for the socio-economic development of Goa, for it is related to the growth and development of the region. As the hinterland of Goa developed due to the presence of a port, there was a tremendous influx of population and consequently heavy pressure on existing resources. As a result, Goa, and especially the port city of Vasco da Gama, encountered health and social problems.[24] Till recently crimes and prostitution was rampant in around the port area namely Mormugao and Vasco.

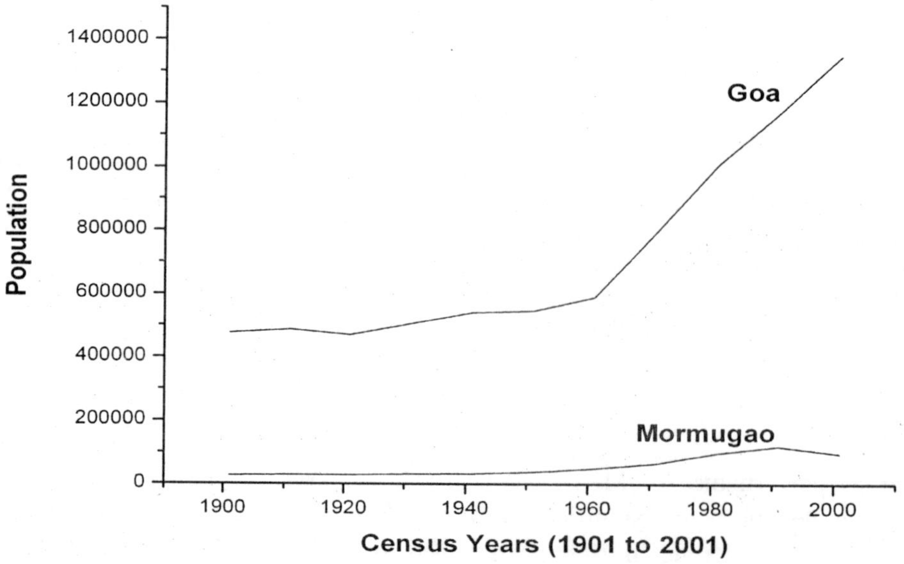

Fig. 5: Population of Goa and Mormugao, 1901-2001

It was earlier noted in this paper that skin, tuberculosis and other ailments related to the dust of the iron ore is most common in mining areas of Goa.[25] Figure 5 shows the trends of population growth in Goa and Mormugao. Today, Mormugao is a fastest growing *taluka* (zone) of Goa. About seventy percent of all workers in the port are migrants. The cargo-handling department alone of the port as of 2005 comprised of eighty percent of migrant workers. The growth of population in both Goa and Mormugao show substantial increases in the post-Portuguese era due to the much freer influx of people from neighbouring States on account of increased employment opportunities in the unskilled, semi-skilled and technical sectors. Goa has had an influx of around seven *lakhs* of population from the other states of India as recent study shows. This may be due to the fact that manual physical jobs are more lucrative and easily available in Goa. Goans are *sussegado*,[26] and do not wish to do the hard physical work which is often required in the port. As a result this void is filled in by the migrants of neighbouring states of Goa. All mining areas and also fisheries attract migrant labours. The development of the port and its hinterland has had important roles to play in this economic development.

4. CONCLUSIONS

Mormugao Port has indeed been a "golden gateway" to Goa. The Luso-British Treaty of 1881 brought about sweeping changes in the Portuguese territory, and Mormugao has played a large role in many of these.

The port rose to prominence and became even more international after 1510. It was the first foothold of the Europeans on the lucrative spice routes. By the end of the tumultuous sixteenth century, Goa was one of the most dynamic cities in the world, larger than contemporary Paris or London and at the heart of the fabulously wealthy maritime empire that stretched from Japan to the southern coast of Africa. The Portuguese promoted Mormugao port across the globe. The port has been well placed historically on important trade routes between East and West. It continues to be important in modern India as a facilitator of global trade. Almost forty percent of the iron ore of India is exported from Mormugao, largely due to improvements in infrastructure and an exceptionally good network of inland waterways, road and rail links. And the success of this modern port is also due to the private mine owners who discovered and exploited important natural resources from the 1950s.

REFERENCES

A India Portuguese, (1907), *'The Port of Mormugao'*, Nova Goa Imprensa Nacional, 1907.

Amonçar, Gundu Sitaram, (1945), *'A Fast Geography of Goa'*, Tipografia Rangel, Bastora, 1945.

Angle, Prabhakar, S. (2001), *'Goa: An Economic Update'*, Goa Hindu Association, Mumbai, India.

Batra, Satkartar (1967), *'Port of Bombay'*, Published by The Kandla Commercial, Kandla Adipur, India 1967.

Bennathan, Esra and A. A. Walters (1979), *'Port Pricing and Investment Policy for Developing Countries'*, Oxford University Press, New York.

Bhatt, S.C. and Gopal K. Bhargava, (ed.) (2005), *'Land and People'*, Vol.7, Kalpaz Publications, Delhi.

Bird, James (1971), *'Seaports and Seaport Terminals'*, Hutchinson University Library, London.

Bose, Santu. Kumar (2001), 'Cargo Handling of Major Ports in India: A Case Study', *Economic and Political Weekly*, Vol XXXV, No. 34, pp 3284-88.

Button, Kenneth J. (1982),*'Transport Economics'*, 2nd Edition, Edward Elgar Publishing Company, USA.

Cabral e Sa, Mario (1985), *'Song of the Golden Gateway'*, Vikas Publishing House Pvt. Ltd., New Delhi.

Cabral e Sa, Mario (1997), *'Destination Goa: The Investor – Friendly Paradise'*, Vikas Publishing House Pvt. Ltd., New Delhi.

De Mendonca-Noronha, Silvia M. (1990), 'The Economic Scene in Goa (1926- 1961)', in De Souza, Teotonio R.(ed) (1990): *'Goa Through the Ages: An Economic History'*, Vol. II, Concept Publishing Company, New Delhi, India.

De Souza, Teotonio R.(ed) (1990), *'Goa Through the Ages: An Economic History'*, Vol. II, Concept Publishing Company, New Delhi, India.

Ghosh, Buddhadeb., Prabir, De., (1998), 'Role of Infrastructure in Regional Development: A Study over the Plan Period', *Economic and Politcal Weekly*, Vol XXV, No 18-19, pp 3039-48.

Ghosh, Buddhadeb., Prabir, De., (2001), 'Indian Ports and Globalisation: Grounding Economics in Geography', *Economic and Political Weekly*, Vol XXXVI, No 34 pp 3271-83.

Government of Goa, Daman & Diu, Directorate of Planning, Statistics and Evaluation, *Statistical Yearbook*, various years, Panaji Goa.

Government of India, Third Lok Sabha, Estimates Committee (1964-65), 67th Report, New Delhi.

Government of India, Seventh Lok Sabha, Estimates Committee (1981-82), 32nd Report, New Delhi.

Government of India, Ministry of Finance, (2006), *'Economic Survey 2006'*, Government of India, New Delhi.

Gune, V. T. (1990), 'Goa's Coastal and Overseas Trade: From the earliest times till 1510 A.D.', in De Souza, Teotonio R.(ed) (1990): *'Goa Through the Ages: An Economic History'*, Vol. II, Concept Publishing Company, New Delhi, India.

Jansson, Jan Owen and Dan Shneerson, (1982), *'Port Economics'*, The MIT Press, New York.

Kamat, Pratima P. (1990), 'Historical Geography and Natural Resources', in De Souza, Teotonio R.(ed) (1990), *'Goa Through the Ages: An Economic History'*, Vol. II, Concept Publishing Company, New Delhi, India.

Kamat, Varsha. (2000), 'Trade and Commerce under Yusuf Adil Shah (1489-1510)', in Mhamai, S. H. K. (ed) (2000): *Goa: Trade and Commerce Through the Ages,* (Seminar Papers) Directorate of Archives and Archaeology, Government of Goa, Panaji Goa.

Lopes Mendes, Antonio, (1886), *'A India Portuguesa'*, 2 Vols. Lisboa, Portugal.

Mascarenhas, Nascimento J. (2006), *'Mormugao's Rich Heritage'*, Published by Nascimento J.Mascarenhas, Vasco-da-Gama.

Mathew, K.S. (1990), 'Trade and Commerce in Sixteenth Century Goa', in De Souza, Teotonio R.(ed) (1990), *'Goa Through the Ages: An Economic History'*, Vol. II, Concept Publishing Company, New Delhi, India.

Mhamai, S. H. K. (ed) (2000), *Goa: Trade and Commerce Through the Ages,* (Seminar Papers) Directorate of Archives and Archaeology, Government of Goa, Panaji Goa.

Mormugao Port Trust (1997), *'Anchoring in the Future'*, Presented and Published by MPT, Mormugao Goa.

Munby, Denys (ed) (1969), *'Transport', (selected Readings),* Penguin Books, London.

Pearson, M. N. (1990), 'Goa-based Seaborne Trade (17th-18th Centuries)', in De Souza, Teotonio R.(ed) (1990), *'Goa Through the Ages: An Economic History'*, Vol. II, Concept Publishing Company, New Delhi, India.

Pereira, Amaro A. (1981), *'History of Mormugao Port'*, Issued by Mormugao Port Trust, Vasco-da-Gama, Goa.

Pinto, Celsa (1990), 'Goa-based Overseas and Coastal Trade (18th-19th Centuries)', in De Souza, Teotonio R.(ed) (1990), *'Goa Through the Ages: An Economic History'*, Vol. II, Concept Publishing Company, New Delhi, India.

Pinto, Celsa (1994), *'Trade and Finance in Portuguese India'*, Concept Publishing Company, New Delhi.

Sau, S. N. (1990), 'Economics of Calcutta-Haldia Port Complex', *Economic and Political Weekly*, May 5-12, 1990 pp 1015-26.

Sen, Arun Prasad (1993), '*Some Aspects of Calcutta Port*', Centre for Urban Economic Studies, Department of Economics, University of Calcutta, Discussion Paper No. 12, Calcutta, April 1993.

Sriraman, S. (1998), 'The Two Gateways: Mumbai and Jawaharlal Nehru Ports', *Asian Transport Journal,* Annual Number, December 1998.

UNCTAD (1969), '*Development of Ports*', United Nations, New York, 1969.

APPENDIX

Data used in the paper is presented below:

Table 1 (Figure 1)

Imports and Exports through Mormugao Port 1888-1960 *(in 1000 tonnes)*

Decennium	*Imports*	*Exports*	*Total*
1888-1890	—	111.249	111.249
1891-1990	—	713.942	713.942
1901-1910	498.655	1226.715	1725.37
1911-1920	779.000	1376.000	2155.00
1921-1930	1074.599	2665.333	3739.932
1931-1940	1398.754	3174.38	4573.134
1941-1950	2607.269	137.667	2744.936
1951-1960	2175.356	23936.74	26112.1

Table 2 (Figure 2)

Variations in Imports, Exports and Transhipment Cargoes after 1960 at MPT

(in 1000 metric tonnes)

Year	*Exports*	*Imports*	*Transhipped*	*Total*
1960-61	6227801	183991		6411792
1961-62	6342953	162473		6505426
1962-63	5353906	112077		5465983
1963-64	5840958	115405		5956363
1964-65	6403356	216352		6619708
1965-66	7620975	239127		7860102
1966-67	7688932	396764		8085696
1967-68	7714105	417682		8131787
1968-69	8409416	369468		8778884
1969-70	8787984	241255		9029239
1970-71	10651838	353134		11004972
1971-72	11264812	435395		11700207
1972-73	12360380	486110		12846490
1973-74	13705780	629244		14335024
1974-75	13408455	723875		14132330
1975-76	12092836	675057		12767893
1976-77	12835832	617888		13453720
1977-78	10556062	725594		11281656
1978-79	9931434	866638		10798072
1979-80	13450459	1054778		14505237
1980-81	13096000	858000		13954000
1981-82	13773000	1115000		14888000
1982-83	11760000	1028000		12788000
1983-84	11903000	1311000		13214000
1984-85	13149637	1149980	211060	14510677
1985-86	14494298	1324483	235835	16054616
1986-87	13626670	1260812	31953	14919435
1987-88	11922249	1013603	395883	13331735
1988-89	13605615	1293087	489945	15388647
1989-90	12685293	1251549	231088	14167930
1990-91	13189950	1277716	443768	14911434
1991-92	12702755	1505264	890493	15098512

1992-93	13920195	1644405	749053	16313653
1993-94	16182458	1513588	1021280	18717326
1994-95	16149000	1940000	792000	18881000
1995-96	15276000	1948000	871000	18095000
1996-97	15361000	1761000	190000	17312000
1997-98	19204000	1958000	20000	21182000
1998-99	15460000	2536000	24000	18020000
1999-2000	14929000	3285000	12000	18226000
2000-01	15938000	3574000	116000	19628000
2001-02	18308838	4599655	18995	22927488
2002-03	19269535	4379780	0	23649315
2003-04	23406131	4467779	0	27873910
2004-05	25027988	5631475	0	30659463

Table 3 (Figure 3)

Cargo Handled at the Major Ports of India and at Mormgugao 1993-94 to 2004-05 (in Lakhs tonnes)

Year	*All Major Port's Cargo*	*MPT's Share*
1993-94	1792.6	187.17
1994-95	1972.62	188.81
1995-96	2153.38	180.95
1996-97	2272.57	173.12
1997-98	2516.59	211.82
1998-99	2517.2	180.2
1999-2000	2719.23	182.26
2000-01	2811.05	196.28
2001-02	2875.79	229.27
2002-03	3135.29	236.49
2003-04	3447.99	278.73
2004-05	3836.25	306.59

Table4 (Figure 4)

Container Traffic Handled at MPT 1992-2005 (*in tonnes*)

Year	*Exports*	*Imports*	*Total*
1992-93	4270	579	4849
1993-94	8899	1645	10544
1994-95	10455	2553	13008
1995-96	12882	5663	18545
1996-97	20621	12602	33223
1997-98	17608	12390	29998
1998-99	19378	17418	36796
1999-2000	17312	32841	50153
2000-01	24402	19381	43783
2001-02	37474	20937	58411
2002-03	60562	29230	89792
2003-04	61745	41269	103014
2004-05	60978	56361	117339

Table 5

Average pre-berthing and Turnaround time at MPT, 1994-95 to 2002-03(in days)

Year	*Average pre-berthing time*	*Average Turnaround time*
1994-95	2.98	6.61
1995-96	2.78	6.29
1996-97	2.17	6.28
1997-98	1.87	5.60
1998-99	1.40	4.81
1999-2000	1.09	3.21
2000-01	1.32	2.93
2001-02	1.74	2.90
2002-03	1.92	2.79

Table 6 (Figure 5)

Population Growth in Goa 1881, and from 1901 to 2001 (in Lakhs)

Year	*Total Population*	*Population of Mormugao*
1881	420868	24767
1901	475513	26439
1911	48752	27838
1921	469494	28320
1931	505281	32061
1941	540925	32875
1951	547448	38076
1961	589997	49068
1971	795120	65511
1981	1007749	98541
1991	1169793	120503
2001	1347668	97154

Notes:

1. United Nations Conference on Trade and Development, Development of Ports (New York, 1969), 4-9.
2. Buddhadeb Ghosh and Prabhir De, "Indian Ports and Globalisation: Grounding Economics in Geography," Economic and Political Weekly, XXXVI, No. 34 (25 August 2001), 3271-3283.
3. In Portuguese India, Goa was known as "Goa Dourado" (Golden Goa) hence the name came for Mormugao port as "Golden Gateway' of Goa.
4. Ministry of Shipping and Ministry of Tourism, Government of India, have identified Mormugao Port Trust as one of the port for cruise tourism. Hence MPT has already a work on building a new berth only for cruise tourism. One must not forget that Goa has a brand name in tourism.
5. V. T. Gune, "Goa's Coastal and Overseas Trade: From the earliest times till 1510 A.D.," in Teotonio R de Souza (ed), Goa Through the Ages, Vol. II. (Concept Publishing House, New Delhi, 1990), 117-136.
6. K.S. Mathew, "Trade and Commerce in Sixteenth Century Goa," in Teotonio R de Souza (ed), Goa Through the Ages, Vol. II. (Concept Publishing House, New Delhi, 1990), 137-145.
7. Varsha Kamat, "Trade and Commerce under Yusuf Adil Shah," in S.K Mhamai (ed), *Goa:Trade and Commerce through the Ages.*(Panaji,2000), 43-55.
8. Celsa Pinto, Trade and Finance in Portuguese India: A Study of the Portuguese Country Trade 1770-1840, (Concept Publishing Company, New Delhi, 1994), 29-60.
9. This treaty was signed by the Portuguese to gift Bombay (now Mumbai) as dowry to Charles II of Great Britain, who married Infanta Catherine of Portugal. Decline of Portuguese India was also attributed to this treaty.

10. A note is to be made here, that Chandrapur and Old Goa were also rated as important cities of Goa some centuries ago because of a good surrounding and environment they possessed.
11. Port City of Goa was shifted in three different historical periods from Chandrapur to Old Goa and to Panaji. Portuguese shifted this to Mormugao, as new port was to be built here by the British Company (WIPGR). Hence there was a time when Mormugao was known as "the pearl necklace" and also "the village of pearls", because it was surrounded by many islands and string of volcanic rocks which looked like necklace around the neck of 'Goa Dourado' (Golden Goa),[Cabral e Sa 1985].
12. Mario Cabral e Sa, *op.cit.*, p. 8.
13. V. T. Gune, *op. cit.*, p. 669.
14. Mario Cabral e Sa, *op.cit.*, p. 8.
15. The first ship "S.S. Westbourne" to visit the port on an unspecified day of April 1885. Hence Mormugao port completed its centenary in 1985. Today the port is in 121st year of its operation.
16. Lopes Mendes, Antonio, A Portuguesa, (2 Vols.), (Lisboa, 1886); Mario Cabral e Sa, *op.cit.*, p. 8-15.
17. Gune (ed.) *Gazetteer,* 670.
18. Government of India, Ministry of Shipping, *Maritime Draft Policy,* 1-60.
19. Government of India, Seventh Lok Sabha, Estimates Committee (1981-1982), 32nd Report, 1-2; and Arun Prasad Sen, "Some Aspects of Calcutta Port" (Discussion Paper No. 12, Centre for Urban Economic Studies, Department of Economics, University of Calcutta, 1993), 6-7.
20. A *lahk* tonne is equal to 100,000 tonnes.
21. Goa's mineral resources were exploited over the years by entrepreneurs like V.M. Salgaocar, V.D. Chowgule and V.S. Dempo. Goa's mineral resources are privately owned by these three individuals among others.
22. Herald (Panjim Goa), 11 April 2006.
23. The economic hinterland of Mormugao Port covers the entire territory of Goa and extends to the hinterland regions of three neighbouring states: south-west Maharashtra, north Karnataka and west Andhra Pradesh.
24. Goa today is experiencing a tremendous influx of population from the neighbouring states. This is helpful to Mormugao, which requires a good deal of physical labour. Goa has more than a *lakh* of its educated youth unemployed. This figure for a small state like Goa is very high compared to other states in India.
25. This study do not go deeper into the health and social aspects of the port, however, studies are conducted by others on these areas of concern to Goa.
26. The Portuguese word for 'easy going', tranquil people.

20

PORT AND HINTERLAND CONNECTIVITY

P. Anbalagan

ABSTRACT

Linkages of ports with the hinterland are one of the important determinants of performance of ports. This is especially true of land locked regions for their socio-economic development. The port of Tuticorin is one of the youngest of the major ports in India with high growth potential. The traffic handled in the port has witnessed significant increase over a period of time; particularly container traffic. The port hinterland has enormous future for its industrial, agricultural, trade and commerce. Availability of vast land, geographical location, favourable investment climate, cheap manpower, dry climate, acceptable basic amenities, and reasonable transport infrastructure are great advantages for the Tuticorin port to become a hub port in Asia. This paper examines the effectiveness of the current modal linkages with the port from the point of view of examining its potential to handle emerging requirements.

1. INTRODUCTION

The efficiency of a port in operational terms depends on the availability of infrastructure and superstructure and the utility of the port to trade depends on its hinterland connectivity. Hinterland has been defined as organised and developed land space which is connected with a port by means of transport lines and which receives goods laden ships through that port (Weigend,1958). In short, the hinterland is the place where a port receives and dispatches cargo and passengers. The actual size and shape of the hinterland are determined by the facts of physical geography, the pattern of trade, location of industrial establishments, transport facilities for movement of raw materials and distribution of agricultural produce and finished goods. The objective of a port is often to maximise economic impact on the hinterland by port planning, investment and operation. This may be interpreted as maximising: (a) competitiveness of hinterland economy, by introducing effective port capacity and throughput changes; (b) direct and indirect employment at the port including ripple or spin-off effects and, (c) development of the port related to dependent industry by provision of land, facilities, access and port capacity (Ernst, 1987). Any port has generally two hinterlands viz. primary and secondary hinterland. Primary hinterland has very high proximity with the ports, whereas secondary hinterland is away from the ports.

The objective of this paper is to analyse port connectivity with road and rail transport network and also to examine the hinterland development of the port. The scope of the study is limited to an analysis of Turicorin port connectivity during the period 1990-91 to 2005-06. This study is confined to cargo movement alone. Various regional, national and international level secondary data have been used for the purpose of study.

The structure of the paper is as follows. Section 2 provides brief review of the literature. Section 3 discusses the road and rail network links with Tuticorin port. Section 4 discusses the socio-economic development of hinterland district of Tutcorin port. In Section 5, investment patterns, industrial and agricultural development and employment generation of different sectors of the hinterland are examined. The next Section contains a discussion on transport sector contribution to the GDP and per capita income of the hinterland districts. Empirical relationship between the variables is also dealt in this Section. Section 7 gives the concluding remarks.

2. REVIEW OF LITERATURE

There are several studies and reports on the various aspects of port infrastructural development. These studies have mainly focused on historical background, performance, financial position, relationship with trade, private and public sector participation. The Report of the United Nations Conference on Trade and Development (2003) on 50 African Ports aimed to assess the consequences of public-private sector partnership. In Africa, 90 per cent of its international trade is maritime trade. The average freight rate is 47 per cent higher than in other developing countries and twice the rate of developed countries. The study showed that only 40 per cent of the investments involved private sector participation in port infrastructure development, as most of African ports found it difficult to attract private investment. This study suggests that regional transport policies that can link port reforms to other modes of transport like rail and road related modernisation and privatisation are required. The report also suggested that the African states must adopt comprehensive strategies and embrace the full apparatus of government, which will strengthen the port infrastructure of the states.

In the past history of the USA, ports played a remarkable role in foreign trade and economic development. Pisani (1989) stated that 64 per cent of the USA ports is under the private sector, which mainly handle dry and liquid cargos. Other ports come under the public sector and these ports mainly handle general cargos. The study concludes that the overall growth of the ports infrastructure in the USA had experienced a number of setbacks. Therefore the study suggests building industrial parks around the ports to strengthen the multimodal transport system and to improve efficiency of port management.

Lakshmanan (2001) highlighted the factors that underlie Rotterdam's port's (Europe) success as a major port in the world. It had a superior delivery system of cargo as a result of which cargo reached European markets within 48 hours and is also well connected by rail, road, pipelines and storage systems. This study found a hinterland connectivity shift from road to rail and inland shipping which occurred over the period of 1994-98. The share of road transport declined 64 per cent to 52 per cent and the share of rail and inland waterways transport increased. The study found that the Rotterdam port has a well-emerged system of transport points and has remained at the forefront of transportation activities for the past four decades. The main point observed from this study is that the cause for success of Rotterdam port is sound connectivity which promoted effective forward and backward linkages of transport.

Inter-mode transport connectivity has a critical value for economic development of the country. Blauwens and Van De Voorde (1988) have examined the impact of port choice on inland transport in the Antwerp port of Belgium. In the flow model that was estimated, transport flows between regions for 15 commodities groups were indicated. The study concluded that port investment is directly associated with the inland transport traffic volume.

Takeuchi (1983) examined port sector development and economic growth in Japan during 1952-1980. The empirical results showed that GNP and total cargo volume through the port have a positive relationship. Further, the paper states that port development has increased employment by 20 per cent and increased economic activity by 44 per cent in the region. This paper concluded that Japan's ports had contributed significantly to its economic development of various regions.

The history of port development in India is often an epitome of changing economic, political and technological circumstances on various scales and over varying periods of time. There are many studies on the development and performance of the Indian ports. Prabir De (1999) attempted to measure the performance of all major ports in India by developing a composite index called Port Performance Index (PPI), comprising three major indicators namely operational, assets and financial performance. The study identified the best three ports as Kandala, Mumbai and Chennai and the worst three ports as Mormugao, New Mangalore and Cochin. It suggests that favourable and effective policies are necessary for further development of Indian ports.

Ghosh and De (2001) have examined the role of ports in India's regional economic development and the relationship between port performance and overseas traffic. This empirical study found that port performance depends on many variables like share of overseas port traffic, port traffic and Per Capita Net State Domestic Product (PCNSDP). The finding showed that port performance is highly contingent upon overseas traffic, while port traffic and PCNSDP are significant. There is also the lack of an integrated policy aimed at developing the transport network. It was also pointed out that over the plan periods the share of fund allocations came down.

Bose (2001) in his study attempted to analyse the performance of major ports in India taking into account the absolute cargo handled by them during 1951-52 to 1992-93. This study primarily focused on the Culcutta-Haldia port. It found that Culcutta port traffic increased 68 per cent over the period of 1928-29 to 1992-93, while the Bombay recorded 3,507 per cent, Chennai 1,122 per cent and Visakhapatnam 1,788 per cent. However, this study does not produce any empirical evidence to show the relation between the traffic and other economic variables.

Ramakrishnan (1998) examined the development of Indian Ports between 1960-61 and 1996-97. This study observed that traffic of the ports in India has increased tremendously in the post-liberalisation era. The study identified problems faced by ports and also gave remedial measures to solve them. It suggested that the Indian government should give more attention to modernisation and privatisation of ports.

Iyer and Balaji (2001) empirically examined the relationship between development and Indian east coast ports. This study kept container traffic as dependent variable and export, import and transhipment as independent variables of the time series data from 1992-93 to 1998-99. As per the result of the regression model, in the case of Tuticorin and Chennai ports, movement was related to 95% of export and import. In the case of other three ports namely Visakhapatnam, Haldia and Calcutta, these are also positively related. Traffic projections of Tuticorin port was estimated at 221 TEU '000' in 2009-10. This study restricted its analysis only tc container traffic, which though significant was dominated by other cargo movement.

Sasikumar and Bhasi (2004) have studied the performance of eleven major ports of India in 2001. Ports are ranked, based on four important performance indicators viz. operation performance, financial performance, facilities available and manpower and its utilisation. The study found that the port of Jawaharlal Nehru stood first in overall performance followed by Mangalore and Visakhapatnam and poor performance by Mumbai port. The study showed that the Cochin and Tuticorin ports are very close to each other in performance. The analysis concludes that the overall progress of new ports of India is comparatively better than the old ports with the exception of Visakhapatnam port.

Our review of literature has brought out many current issues relating to port infrastructure at the international and national levels. It is observed that the developing countries ports are facing many more hurdles than the developed countries. The main cause for the backwardness of the developing countries ports is the lack of connectivity or ports with the surface transport, in particular road and rail. Hence, there is a need to analyse the port connectivity with different modes of transport especially land transport.

3. HINTERLAND CONNECTIVITY

India does not have well-established riverine-based hinterland connectivity. The surface connectivity through rail and road network has some advantages. The advantages of road are speed and flexibility, whereas the advantages of rail are bulk throughput. Therefore, hinterland connectivity to port should ideally comprise both rail and road. Due to improvement of connectivity, the cost of marine freight has come down 6.6 per cent in 1980 to 4.17 per cent in 1999 in the advanced countries, while in developing countries it dropped from 10.4 per cent to 8.04 per cent in the corresponding period. In India, it is still at the 10 per cent level (Anantharaman, 2005).

One important aspect of any port analysis is the determination of the actual and potential port hinterland or the area served by the port. The port of Tuticorin commands the southern most part of the state of Tamil Nadu, enveloping an area of 44,086 sq.km (Indian Port Association, 1985) spread over 11 districts. The Indian Port Association (IPA) has divided the hinterland into primary, secondary and tertiary as indicated below.

Primary hinterland	—	Tuticorin, Tirunelveli, Kanyakumari and Virudhunagar districts
Secondary hinterland	—	Ramanathapuram, Pudukottai, Dindigul, Madurai, Theni and Sivagangai districts
Tertiary hinterland	—	Part of Tiruchirappalli district

Our study adopts this classification for the analysis. In the case of tertiary hinterland of Tuticorin port, i.e., part of Tiruchirappalli district, the part of the district is very small and it was also difficult to get the data. Therefore, this study restricts its analysis to primary and secondary hinterland alone. The development of trade and commerce through Tuticorin port greatly depends on the generation of industrial capacity in the hinterland of the port. The port of Tuticorin is connected with various parts business centres directly and indirectly by means of rail, road, waterways and airways, in which rail and road are most the important.

3.1 Road Connectivity with Tuticorin Port Hinterland

For accessing the markets of industrial and agriculture products, transport plays a unique role in the economy. The road network is the major artery of communication for the country. Since road movement of goods plays a significant role in the traffic to or from Tuticorin port, a detailed discussion is taken up below.

The main roads available at present were formed in the early sixties and service roads and approach arm roads were laid during the year 1975-76. The link roads of Tuticorin port with other major cities are:

NH7A linking Tuticorin with Palyankottai via. Tirunelveli (2 lane) — Total length 51 km

NH45B linking Tuticorin with Trichirappalli via. Madurai, Ettayapuram, Aruppukottai (2 lane) — Total length 257 km (known as Ettayapuram road)

Major District Roads (MDR) linking Tuticorin with Kanyakumari via Tiruchandur (2 lane) along the east coast.

Many other important NH, SH and MDR which serve the hinterland districts of Tuticorin port are Tiruvananthapuram — Kanyakumari — NH47, Kanyakumari - Madurai NH7, Ramanathapuram — Madurai — NH49 that passes through Sivagangai. The East Coast Road (ECR) that connects Nagapattinam, Ramanathapuram, Tuticorin and Kanyakumari (to be upgraded) are notable roads in the hinterland districts. The National Highway Authority of India (NHAI) has come up with a project for improvement of road connectivity to Tuticorin port by widening the two lane highway NH7A (connecting Tuticorin and Tirunelveli) into 4 lanes at an approximate cost of Rs.180 crore and Tuticorin port has agreed to contribute in the form of equity in the Special Purpose Vehicle (SPV) to 11 per cent of the project cost or Rs. 25 crore. Four laning of NH45B is between Tuticorin — *Ettayapuram* — *Kovilpatti* - NH7 will be taken up in Phase II. Improvement of NH45B between *Ettayapuram* and Madurai via *Aruppukottai* will be taken up in Phase III under NHDP. The work would be taken up at a cost of Rs. 650 crore. Government of India also plans to convert the MDR to Kanyakumari into a NH, which will be a great boon to limenite sand exporters, DCW and TATA's Titanium Oxide Project. The East Coast Road (ECR) from Chennai to *Cuddalore*, 166 km via Pondicherry, was improved to two-lane facility with Asian Development Bank loan of US $ 24.47 million in 1993-98. This project is a part of ECR from Chennai to Kanyakumari a distance of 737 km. Hence, the coastal road from *Nagapattinam* to Tuticorin has been selected in phase I, and the other corridors have been selected in phase II-A to give equal importance to roads in different regions. Apart from the NH, efforts are underway to upgrade the State Highway (SH) network as well. For this purpose, the Tamil

Nadu Road Sector Project has been launched with an outlay of Rs.2160 crore in 2004. This will enable the construction of 330 km road linking *Nagapattinam* to Tuticorin.

The Tuticorin port hinterland road networks giving the different categories are presented in Table 1. The total hinterland of Tuticorin port road network was 40,552.11 km in 2003-04, accounting for 22.7 per cent of the total state's area. The length of NH in the district of Ramanathapuram and Tirunelveli is the highest among the hinterland districts, while the SH length is highest in the districts of Dindigul and Tuticorin. The overall hinterland of Tuticorin port road density was (943.18 per thousand sq.km) less than the state level density in 2002-03. When compared to road infrastructure available in the hinterland districts, apart from Kanyakumari (2983.54 per thousand sq.km), the road length per thousand sq. km. in hinterland districts is less than average of the state (1372.81 per thousand sq.km). Though the overall length of the road network in this region is inadequate, the NH is a prime category for carrying cargo from and to the port. It has a 3 per cent share of the total network of the hinterland. At the State level, 31.7 per cent of the total NH and 13.44 per cent of SH runs are in this region. Tuticorin port cargo mainly passes through two NHs, namely NH7A and NH45B. Traffic on these highways has increased continually. The average number heavy vehicles that passed through these two highways point near Tuticorin port were 2265 and 2517 respectively in the year 2002.

Table 1: Road Infrastructure Facilities in Hinterland of Tuticorin Port (2003-04)

Hinterland Districts	*Road length (in km.)*				*Distance from Tuticorin Port*
	National Highways	*State Highways*	*Total**	*Density***	
Primary Hinterland Districts					
Tuticorin	112.40	1994.23	4705.06	1018.41	—
Tirunelveli	178.00	435.20	3648.10	535.70	51
Kanyakumari	63.20	1209.46	5027.26	2983.54	130
Virudhunagar	147.60	163.76	2724.01	635.26	106
Secondary Hinterland Districts					
Ramanathapuram	187.8	201.24	4992.50	1179.70	112
Sivagangai	54.50	62.02	4404.20	1077.88	163
Pudukottai	86.82	291.78	3596.28	773.23	221
Madurai	145.00	114.00	1972.00	494.73	139
Theni	131.45	725.67	2170.43	841.58	202
Dindigul	113.70	2295.74	7312.27	1207.04	210
Hinterland total	1220.47	7493.10	40552.11	943.18	—
Tamil Nadu	3851.00	55755.00	178545.00	1372.81	—
% of Primary to total hinterland	41.07	50.75	39.71	925.38	—
% of Secondary to total hinterland	58.93	49.25	60.29	955.29	—

Note: * Including Corporation, Municipalities, Town Panchayats and other roads.
** Per thousand sq.km.

Source: Various District Statistical Handbook 2003-04, Assistant Director of Statistics, Govt. of Tamil Nadu and Tamil Nadu Survey and Land Record Department, Govt. of Tamil Nadu

The distances from the Tuticorin port to the district headquarters of hinterland districts are given in the Table 1. The district of Tirunelveli is very close to and Pudukottai which is far from Tuticorin port, which are connected with various types of road network. Many district headquarters and the trading centres of hinterland are connected with ports through the road network, which lack upkeep. Many of the highways are single and double lanes. Another important bottleneck found was that some of the hinterland district headquarters (Ramanathapuram, Sivagangai, Pudukottai and Theni) and commercial cities are not directly connected with the Tuticorin port. Consequently, the processes of economic development of such districts are slow.

The State of Tamil Nadu is poised to benefit immensely from the Golden Quadrilateral project that connects the four metropolitan cities. In Tamil Nadu, 314 km of NH are being covered under this programme. Another important road connectivity programme is North-South and East-West corridor connecting Kanyakumari with Kashmir for which 851 km of NH are being developed in Tamil Nadu, while NH covering other areas in the state is also being upgraded (FICCI, 2004). NHAI have now taken up the work of upgrading the road sections in NH4, NH5, NH7, NH46 and NH47, which form part of the 'Golden Quadrilateral' and North-South Corridor projects (GOI, 2005). The object of these projects is mainly converting the NH into four lanes, which will render huge benefits to the hinterland of the Tuticorin port.

3.2 Rail Connectivity with Tuticorin Port Hinterland

Railways are important links in the supply chain for global trade. Port – Rail connectivity is a very important aspect, to ensure a better performance by both the ports and railways. The port was linked to the broad-gauge system in 1993 and a daily express train service between Tuticorin and Chennai, known as Pearl City Express and Mysore Express runs between Tuticorin and Mysore. The Southern Railway is operating its services up to the harbour. The harbour site is connected by a broad gauge siding to *Milavittan*, a station on Tuticorin - *Maniyachi* line.

The coverage by railways in Tamil Nadu was 4166.80 km in 2003-04 and 51 per cent of it is broad gauge and the rest is metre gauge. About 30 per cent of the total rail route length is in the Tuticorin port hinterland districts in the state. The share of metre gauge in the hinterland is higher at 63 per cent, which is greater than the state's average as shown in Table 2. 71 per cent of the primary hinterland district rail route mainly consists of broad-gauge system that is close to Tuticorin port. All the primary hinterland districts are directly connected with the port through the Maniyachi junction. Majority of the secondary hinterland districts are not directly connected by rail and except from Madurai and Dindigul, there is no train service to the port. As a result these districts mainly depend on road service to reach the port.

The density of the rail route in the hinterland districts is lower with 27.84 km per thousand sq. km, compared to 32.04 km in Tamil Nadu as a whole during 2003-04. The average density in the primary hinterland districts is higher than the secondary hinterland districts. The Southern Railway took up conversion of 324.42 km metre gauge into broad gauge line connectivity to Karur, Dindigul, Tuticorin and Tirunelveli at a cost of Rs 42.82 crore in 1985. In the year 2003, the Southern Railways has undertaken 13 projects, including laying new lines and gauge conversions of existing lines, covering about 2000 km at a cost of Rs. 3422.15 crore. The project

Table 2: Rail Infrastructure Facilities in Hinterland of Tuticorin Port (2003-04)

Hinterland Districts	*Railways route length (in km.)*				
	Broad Gauge	*Metre Gauge*	*Total*	*Density per hundred sq. km.*	*Distance from Tuticorin Port*
Primary Hinterland Districts					
Tuticorin	73.45	40.00	113.45	24.56	—
Tirunelveli	77.00	125.00	202.00	29.66	60
Kanyakumari	78.00	—	78.00	46.29	150
Virudhunagar	95.78	72.06	127.84	29.81	116
Secondary Hinterland Districts					
Ramanathapuram	—	98.37	98.37	23.24	267
Sivagangai	—	142.50	142.50	34.88	199
Pudukottai	—	63.50	63.50	13.65	373
Madurai	62.95	81.95	144.90	36.35	159
Theni	—	41.09	41.09	15.93	234
Dindigul	69.15	116.12	185.27	30.58	225
Hinterland total	456.33	780.59	1196.92	27.84	—
Tamil Nadu	2061.19	2105.61	4166.80	32.04	—
% of Primary to total hinterland	71.05	30.37	43.55	29.95	—
% of Secondary to total hinterland	28.95	69.63	56.45	26.40	—

Source: District Statistical Handbook 2003-04, Assistant Director of Statistics, Govt. of Tamil Nadu (various issues) and www.southernrailway.org

includes (*a*) New line from Madurai to Tuticorin via. *Parambupatti, Aruppukkottai, Vilattikulam* with an alternative route via Virudhunagar, *Aruppukkottai* and *Vilattikulam*; (*b*) gauge conversion between Madurai and *Coimbtore*; and (*c*) new BG line between Madurai and *Kottayam*. If these projects are implemented, this would greatly benefit the Tuticorin port hinterland in achieving faster economic growth.

Several measures have been taken by the Indian Government to improve the port connectivity. However, completion of *Villupurum-Kumbakonam-Tanjavur* and Tirunelveli-*Quilon* broad gauge conversion projects, double laning of Madurai-Dindigul and improving connectivity to *Coimbatore* will be of interest to Tuticorin port. When compared to the distance between Tuticorin port and hinterland district road and rail, the former one is the best choice because of flexibility, less time consumption, easy approach, and transport frequency. The primary hinterland has better transport infrastructure, both road and rail. Therefore, these regions receive immense benefits than the secondary hinterland.

4. SOCIO-ECONOMIC DEVELOPMENT OF TUTICORIN PORT HINTERLAND

Port hinterland study consists of the evaluation of the developments in socio-economic activities that are likely to affect or be affected by the demand for port commerce. Some comparison data of hinterland districts of Tuticorin port are presented in Table 3. The hinterland districts have one-third of the total geographical area of the state. There have accounted for 27.43 per cent of the population as per 2001 census. The percentage of urban population is higher in primary hinterland than in the secondary hinterland. The rate of literacy is higher in Kanyakumari and Tuticorin compared to state's average, while other hinterland districts almost equal the state's average. The percentage of population increase from 1991 to 2001 was lower than the state's growth rate in all hinterland districts except Virudhunagar and Tirunelveli. Half of the hinterland districts are above the state level average in terms of working population, in which Dindigul was the highest, followed by Virudhunagar and the least was Kanyakumari in 2001. The percentage of Below Poverty Line (BPL) families is higher in the hinterland districts, in which Kanyakumari registered the lowest with 17.7 per cent. An interesting finding is that the port district of Tuticorin witnessed the maximum percentage of families below the poverty line. The district of Virudhunagar accounted for the highest per capita income in the hinterland districts followed by Tuticorin, while the majority of seven district's per capita income accounted for less than the state's average.

Table 3: Tuticorin Port Hinterland Districts Development Comparison (2001)

Socio-economic indicators	*Primary Hinterland Districts*				*Secondary Hinterland Districts*						
	Tuticorin	*Tirunel-veli*	*Kanya-kumari*	*Virudhu-nagar*	*Ramanatha-puram*	*Siva-gangai*	*Pudu-kottai*	*Madurai*	*Theni*	*Dindigul*	*Tamil Nadu*
Area (Sq. km)	4620	6810	1685	4288	4232	4086	4651	3986	2579	6058	130058
Population(in lakh)	15.72	27.24	16.76	17.51	11.87	11.55	14.59	25.78	10.94	19.23	624.06
% of Urban population	42.28	48.03	65.27	44.39	25.46	28.22	17.02	56.01	54.10	35.01	44.04
Density per Sq.km.	339	411	992	409	287	275	312	733	357	317	480
% of Literacy	81.52	76.09	87.55	73.70	72.96	72.18	71.12	77.82	71.58	69.35	73.45
% of increase population (1991-2001)	7.54	11.97	4.34	11.92	5.73	4.32	9.43	6.75	4.33	8.99	11.19
% of workers	43.03	46.79	32.68	50.27	44.00	44.27	46.64	42.22	47.45	50.69	44.78
% of BPL* families (2000)	37.81	28.85	17.67	30.94	29.35	29.35	28.75	31.79	27.81	23.24	29.16
Per capita Income(Rs.) (2001-02) @	16150	13566	12260	21271	10851	10384	10435	16028	12437	13937	14700
HDI# (1999)	0.703	0.658	0.711	0.651	0.629	0.640	0.618	0.661	0.628	0.640	0.657

*Note:** BPL - Below Poverty Line, @ Per capita income to the Gross Domestic Product at constant 1993-94 price, # HDI – Human Development Index

Source: Annual Statistical Abstract of Tamil Nadu 2002-03; Directorate of Rural Development Department and Various District Statistical Handbook, Government of Tamil Nadu.

Another important measure of development of the district is Human Development Index (HDI). The primary hinterland district's HDI value is greater than the state's average except Virudhunagar. Conversely, other than Madurai district, in the secondary hinterland districts, values are less than the state values. This study found that the higher percapita income districts are Tuticorin, Virudhunagar and Madurai and also percentage of the BPL families are higher. The general observation from the Table 3 is that, districts like Madurai, Tirunelveli and Tuticorin are in the forefront in many aspects. The former one is naturally urban-based economy and various types of infrastructure facilities are also sufficiently available, which is a greater advantage for the district's development. But the subsequent two districts are dominant in trade and commerce, because of their proximity to the port of Tuticorin.

5. INVESTMENT IN THE TUTICORIN PORT HINTERLAND

Investments in various projects in the hinterland is shown in Table 4. Notable investors in the hinterland districts are NHAI, Southern Railways, Government of Tamil Nadu and Tuticorin Port Trust. NHAI has mainly invested in NH7, NH7A, NH45B and in some bypasses projects.

Southern Railways concentrated on route conversions and the Government of Tamil Nadu concentrated on SH development. It is clear that the port district of Tuticorin and its adjoining district, Tirunelveli, received huge amount of investment among the hinterland districts. These two districts share 94 to 98 per cent of the total hinterland investment between 1999 and 2005. Since Theni is an agricultural district, it received less investment and in general, industrially developed districts attracted more investments. In addition, Table 4 shows that the primary hinterland received more than 95 per cent of investment from the total hinterland investment between 1999 and 2005.

In case of small scale industries (SSIs), the secondary hinterland received around 52 per cent of investment, while even the primary hinterland consisting of four districts, received considerable level of investment. It is clearly observed that primary hinterland districts received massive investment. However, the secondary hinterland districts except Madurai received comparatively less investment in this period.

Table 4: Investments in Tuticorin Port Hinterland (Rs. in crore)

Hinterland Districts	*Project Investment*							*SSIs* (2002-2003)*
	1999	*2000*	*2001*	*2002*	*2003*	*2004*	*2005*	
Primary Hinterland Districts								
Tuticorin	12933.1	10699.5	14333.0	16114.0	10472.0	10561.0	11090.0	410.4
Tirunelveli	11963.3	12238.3	15196.5	17363.0	17043.0	16257.0	16387.0	391.8
Kanyakumari	450.0	18.0	18.0	39.2	139.1	157.7	250.2	354.0
Virudhunagar	200.0	237.0	237.0	205.0	231.0	333.0	247.0	555.5
Secondary Hinterland Districts								
Ramanathapuram	112.5	118.5	356.0	356.0	317.0	87.4	481.4	178.8
Sivagangai	30.0	30.0	30.0	30.0	30.0	30.0	30.0	230.3
Pudukottai	9.0	40.0	—	—		7.0	188.0	319.7
Madurai	857.0	849.8	894.3	40.1	98.4	273.4	333.5	671.5
Theni	—	—	—	—	8.7	10.0	1.3	123.9
Dindigul	15.0	21.0	-	30.50	131.90	84.5	244.0	351.4
Hinterland total	26569.9	24252.1	31064.8	34177.8	28471.1	27801	29252.4	3587.3
Tamil Nadu	137364	155723	156785	164566	129160	132723	158974	12569
% of primary to total hinterland investment	96.15	95.63	95.88	98.66	97.94	98.23	95.63	47.72
% of secondary to total hinterland investment	3.85	4.37	4.12	1.34	2.06	1.77	4.37	52.28

Note: * SSIs — Small Scale Industries.

Source: CMIE, Monthly Review of Tamil Nadu Economy (Various Issues of 2004 & 2005) and Director of Industries and Commerce, Government of Tamil Nadu.

5.1 Industrial and Agricultural Development in Tuticorin Port Hinterland

The industrial development of the Tuticorin port hinterland is centered in and around a few selected urban centres like Madurai, Dindigul, Virudhunagar, Rajapalayam, Sattur, Thirumangalam, Sivakasi, Theni and Tuticorin. Traditional industries like salt manufacturing, sea foods, wood and other small and medium scale industries are located in the hinterland of Tuticorin Port. State Industries Promotion Corporation of Tamil Nadu (SIPCOT), a fully state government owned premier institution, established in the year 1972, has been a catalyst in development of industries in Tamil Nadu. There are 16 SIPCOTs functioning in Tamil Nadu, in which Tuticorin SIPCOT is a notable one. It is located 13 km away from Tuticorin Port on the highways of NH45B on a 1083 acre complex. Sterilite Industry (India) Limited, Kilburn Chemicals, Amalya seafoods, other export oriented and textile industries are notable industries that are located in the SIPCOT. These industries mainly depend on the Tuticorin port for their trade activities.

The development of trade and commerce greatly depends on the generation of industrial capacity in the hinterland of the port. Many of the industries are identified as port based. There are 1,26,737 SSI units which were located in the Tuticorin port hinterland in 2002-03, accounting for more than one-fourth of the total industries in Tamil Nadu as shown in Annexure I. Notable small-scale industries like readymade garments units (1,16,093), food-processing units (39,805), paper and paper products units (26,124) and cotton textile units (24,752) were functioning in this hinterland in 2002-03. Number of SSIs is the highest in the district of Madurai followed by Virudhunagar, Tuticorin and Tirunelveli districts in 2002-03. The hinterland districts SSIs CAGR was higher than the state's average (12.21 per cent), in which Virudhunagar witnessed highest CAGR of 19.34 per cent and lowest in Kanyakumari district between 1990-91 and 2002-03. Tamil Nadu Industrial Investment Corporation (TIIC) sanctioned 550 projects out of 1630 total projects in Tamil Nadu, with Rs. 47.17 crore in Tuticorin port's hinterland i.e. 23.55 per cent of investment inflow in this region during 2003-04. The share of total SSI units in the hinterland increased to 28.2 per cent from 25.0 per cent in the corresponding period at the state level.

Salt production in Tuticorin region has been in vogue for over 200 years. It is one of the major industries providing employment potential to a large number of people, providing employment to more than 50,000 persons directly and 1,00,000 persons indirectly, in-and-around Tuticorin region. Due to natural disasters in 2005, in many countries, Tuticorin salt was imported, particularly by China, Israel, Germany, Japan, America and the Arab countries, resulted in a boom and acted as a fillip to find new international markets for the salt produced in Tuticorin.

Factories are larger units than the SSIs. The hinterland district's factories have sizably increased, from 4285 units in 1990-91 to 10,359 units in 2002-03, with 7.63 per cent of CAGR against 6.70 per cent at the state level as given in Annexure I . Due to adequate infrastructure facilities and potential for export opportunities, large-scale industries are concentrated in the primary hinterland. Among the hinterland districts, Virudhunagar recorded the highest growth rate with 11.02 per cent followed by Tuticorin and the lowest growth was witnessed in Pudukottai between 1990-91 and 2002-03. It is clear that the primary hinterland districts are progressing more in industrial development than the distant districts of hinterland.

The vast vacant hinterland, rapidly growing infrastructure facilities, easily accessible foreign market through the Tuticorin port, cheaply available manpower, abundant power supply could be the big boosters to industrialisation in this region in future. Some of the old industries are being expanded and some new ones are being established on a large scale. The coastline length of the hinterland is 593 km (about 55 per cent to the state's coastal length) and it consists of five districts namely Tuticorin, Tirunelveli, Kanyakumari, Ramanathapuram and Pudukottai, in which Ramanathapuram has the longest coastal line followed by Tuticorin. The 'wedge bank' off this coast is claimed to be the world's richest fishing ground. The availability of adequate marine infrastructure facilities is a great boon to the marine fish production in this region. The hinterland districts account for 60 per cent of the state's total marine fish production, amounting to 2.26 lakh tonne in 2002-03 against about 70 per cent and 1.92 lakh tonne respectively in 1990-91. The CAGR of marine fish production in Ramanathapuram district was the highest with 5.02 per cent and a negative growth was recorded in Kanyakumari district. Marine fish production in the secondary hinterland district was larger, because length of coastal line of these districts, 313 km, is longer than the primary hinterland districts. It also has the richest fishing sources in this region. Even though there is higher potential for marine fish in this region, the available infrastructures like transport; storage facilities, boats are insufficient, which are bottlenecks for its development. India earns a huge amount of foreign exchange through export of marine products.

Mineral is an important cargo handled in the port. Mineral production in the hinterland districts has drastically come down between 1990-91 and 2002-03 due to increase in cost of production. Though inputs like power and fertilizer for agriculture are available in plenty, its foodgrains production has come down from 2055 thousand tonnes in 1990-91 to 1481 thousand tonnes in 2002-03 in the hinterland of Tuticorin port. The major reasons for the negative growth of foodgrain production are high cost of production, spreading of industrialisation, frequent failure of monsoon, and low market price.

5.2 Employment Generation in Tuticorin Port Hinterland

Transport sector plays an important role for creating employment opportunity. Due to transit of commodities and passengers through various transport modes, the primary, secondary and tertiary sectors can expand and generate more employment. Annexure II reveals the comparison of employment in various sectors of economy in the hinterland districts of Tuticorin port. The SSIs created directly and indirectly more employment opportunities. They have created 8.8 lakh employment opportunities directly during 2002-03 in the hinterland. It was about 28 per cent to the state's total. Estimation of indirect employment generation is very difficult, though it is definitely large. The districts of Madurai, Virudhunagar and Tuticorin are generating more employment through SSI units. Even though the share of employment of the primary hinterland is little less, it plays a significant role in generating employment in this region.

Factories have also been playing a substantial role in generating employment in the hinterland region. Total share of employment from factories was about 27 per cent in 2002-03, which was 30 per cent during 1990-91 to the state's total. Number of employees was the highest in the primary hinterland, in which district of Virudhunagar accounted for 121.8 thousands in the factories, followed by Kanyakumari, and then by Tuticorin, where robust growth rates were recorded between 1990-91 and 2002-03. The CAGR of employment in the factories is positive in the primary hinterland except Tuticorin in the corresponding year. Even though many large-scale units are located in the Tuticorin district, the growth rate of employment is negative since they are adopting sophisticated modern technology in the production process. This may be the cause of many BPL families in the district.

Marine fishing has potential for generating employment opportunities in the coastal region. Tuticorin port hinterland has more than half of the total coastal length in Tamil Nadu, accounted one-third of state's total employment through marine fishing during 2002-03. The primary hinterland benefited much from higher employment rate than the secondary hinterland, in which the districts of Kanyakumari and Tuticorin have the highest number of fishermen engaged in this activity. Though India as well as Tamil Nadu depends on agriculture to a marked extent, the hinterland region of Tuticorin port's dependency was smaller with 26 per cent when compared to the state's total as per 2001 census. The number of agricultural workers was the highest in Tirunelveli district in 1991. An interesting observation is that all the primary hinterland districts have registered negative growth rate of agriculture workers between 1991 and 2001, particularly, in the district of Kanyakumari, where the rate had drastically come down. Faster industrialisation and commercialisation in the primary hinterland are the main causes for bringing down agricultural employment.

An analysis of the employment data relating to the service sector clearly shows that the primary hinterland districts have a greater advantage than the secondary hinterland districts in terms of employment growth rate. The study observes that the primary hinterland has significantly benefited by employment generation, except in the agriculture sector. The hinterland of the port has potential employment opportunity, for which infrastructure facilities must be strengthened, specifically port connectivity in this region requires improvement.

5. ECONOMIC DEVELOPMENT IN TUTICORIN PORT HINTERLAND

The economic development in the hinterland of Tuticorin port has been increasing rapidly over the period. The overall economic development of the hinterland districts is measured in terms of the District Gross Domestic Product (DGDP). The DGDP of the hinterland increased

Table 5: District Gross Domestic Product (DGDP) of the Tuticorin Port Hinterland

Districts	*Rail transport contributed to the GDP (in %)*		*Other means OF transport contributed to the GDP(in%)*		*Per capita income (in Rs.)*			*GDP (Rs. in crore)*		
	1993-1994	*2002-2003*	*1993-1994*	*2002-2003*	*1993-1994*	*2002-2003*	*CAGR (in %)*	*1993-1994*	*2002-2003*	*CAGR (in %)*
Primary Hinterland Districts										
Tuticorin	0.27	0.23	7.94	6.26	11865	16974	4.06	1783.39	2679.82	4.63
Tirunelveli	0.40	0.34	2.78	3.54	9823	14618	4.52	1783.39	4005.08	9.41
Kanyakumari	0.34	0.35	3.58	4.63	9083	12555	3.66	1500.71	2100.25	3.81
Virudhunagar	0.17	0.12	2.20	2.51	14090	20264	4.12	2276.61	3588.85	5.19
Secondary Hinterland Districts										
Ramanathapuram	0.23	0.22	3.64	3.78	7539	12332	5.62	890.43	1459.12	5.64
Sivagangai	0.37	0.35	3.35	4.05	7597	11305	4.52	845.63	1309.57	4.98
Pudukottai							0.25	0.25	2.79	3.90
7061	10406	4.40	967.45	1530.66	5.23					
Madurai	0.53	0.53	5.62	5.50	10239	14984	4.32	2268.84	3875.09	6.13
Theni	0.49	0.46	4.52	4.36	8555	17249	8.10	1151.05	1801.60	5.10
Dindigul	0.29	0.29	3.06	3.16	9358	14260	5.36	1700.94	2759.82	5.53
Hinterland total	0.32	0.32	3.99	4.16	9521	14495	4.78	15168.44	23784.6	5.56
Tamil Nadu	0.63	0.64	4.91	4.71	9979	14532	4.26	57549.02	91703.24	5.19
% of primary to total hinterland	39.13	39.12	49.74	47.60	11215#	16103#	4.10	48.42	49.28	4.82
% of secondary to total hinterland	60.87	60.88	50.26	52.40	8392 #	13423#	5.36	51.58	50.72	5.86

Note: GDP-Gross Domestic Product at constant (1993-94) price, # per capita of primary and secondary hinterland in rupees.

Source: District Income Estimates 1993-94 to 2002-03, Directorate of Economic and Statistics, Government of Tamil Nadu.

to Rs. 23,784.60 crore in 2002-03 from Rs. 15,168.44 crore in 1993-94, with the average annual growth rate of 5.6 per cent as against 5.19 per cent of the state level (Table 5). The hinterland was maintaining about 26 per cent of the share to the total DGDP of the state of Tamil Nadu during both the periods. An interesting observation is that half of the hinterland districts' CAGR of DGDP is lower than the state average between 1993-94 and 2002-03.

Even though rail transport has a significant role in development of this region, its contribution to the DGDP is too negligible. The share of rail transport contribution to the DGDP of the hinterland is just about half of the state level. Lack of interconnectivity of transport network, lack of train services and cumbersome procedure for loading and unloading are the major bottlenecks for low contribution to the DGDP in many of the hinterland districts. The other means of transport viz. road, water, air and port, contributed to the DGDP significantly increase in the hinterland. In general, the other means of transport contributed to the DGDP in a positive manner in most of the hinterland districts, in which Tuticorin district contributed the maximum of 6.26 per cent to the DGDP in 2002-03, against 7.94 per cent in 1993-94. The DGDP in the primary hinterland witnessed a higher growth in both the points because of the transport sector development.

The per capita income in the over all hinterland was lower both in 1993-94 and 2002-03, when compared with state average. Virudhunagar ranked first in the per capita income among the hinterland districts followed by Theni and Tuticorin and the last was Sivagangai. In general, the primary hinterland districts show better performance in per capita income except Kanyakumari district. Figure 1 shows the comparison of per capita income trends of Tuticorin port hinterland between 1993-94 and 2002-03 with GDP at constant price. The general trend of the per capita income is on the rise in both the primary and secondary hinterland districts. However, the primary hinterland per capita income trend is greater than the secondary hinterland and state of Tamil Nadu.

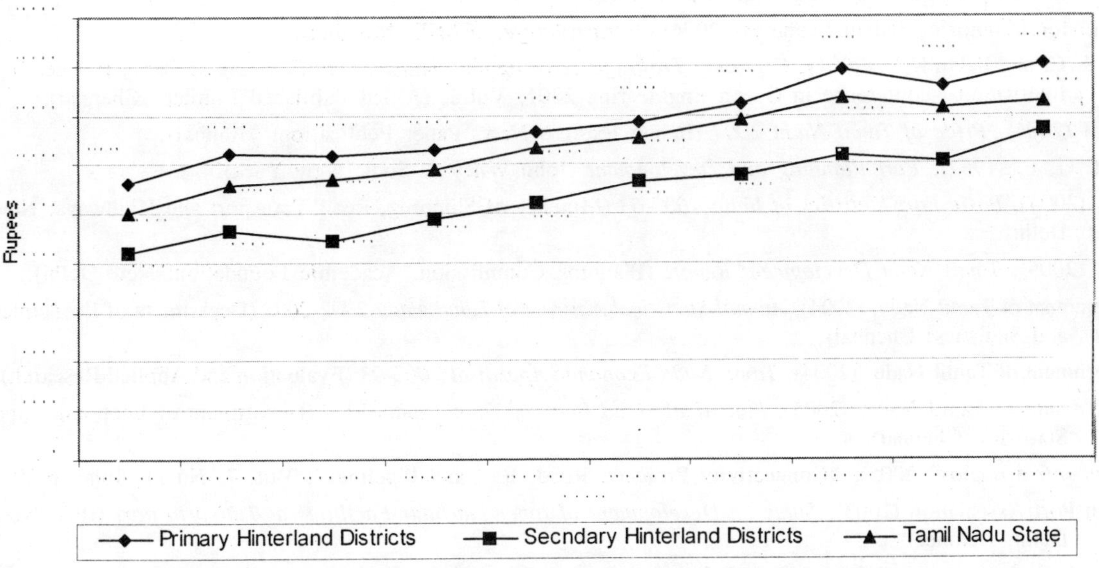

Fig. 1: Per capita income of the Tuticorin Port Hinterland

The port connectivity and the industrial development of the hinterland receive benefits directly and indirectly. The direct benefits are saving in vehicle operation cost due to reduction in distance and in congestion; saving in travel time; improved levels of comfort and accessibility between the port of Tuticorin and its hinterland; and accelerated growth in the region. Indirect benefits are increase in demand and land prices due to improved accessibility in the influence zone; accelerated economic development of Tuticorin and nearby regions; economic integration with neighbouring states; environment improvement and reduced population levels; improved safety due to reduction in accidents; improvement in trade and trade competitiveness through faster and improved logistics.

6. CONCLUSIONS

Logistic linkage of port connectivity is one of the important determinants of performance of ports. Road and port connectivity are very much useful to land locked regions for their socio-economic development. The port of Tuticorin is one of the youngest major ports in India with high growth potential. The traffic handled in the port has witnessed significant increase over the period; particularly container traffic.The port hinterland has enormous future for its industrial, agricultural, trade and commerce. Availability of vast land, geographical location, favourable investment climate, cheap manpower, dry climate, acceptable basic amenities, and reasonable transport infrastructure are great advantages for the Tuticorin port to become a hub port in Asia.

REFERENCES

Anantharaman, S. (2005), *History and Organisation of Railways in India* (Railway Staff College: Vadodara).

Blauwens, G. and Voorde, E.V. (1988),"The impact of Port Choice on inland Transportation", *Maritime Policy and Management*, Vol. 15, No.2, pp. 127-148.

Ghosh, B. and De, P. (2001), "Indian Ports and Globalisation grounding Economic in Geography", *Economic and Political Weekly*, August 25, pp.3271-3283.

Centre for Monitoring Indian Economy (2004), *Infrastructure*, (CMIE: Mumbai).

Iyer, K C. and Balaji K.B. (2001), *Container Traffic forecasting and the impact in Planning of Ports*, Proceedings International conference in Ocean Engineering 2001, Vol.2, (Allied Published Limited: Chennai).

FICCI (2004), *Pride of Tamil Nadu 2004* (Indian Express News Paper Publication: Mumbai).

Ernst, G, F. (1987), *Port Planning and Development* (John Wiley & Sons: New York).

GOI, (2004), *Basic Port Statistics of India 2002-03* (Ministry of Shipping, Road Transport and Highways: New Delhi).

GOI, (2005), *Tamil Nadu Development Report* (Planning Commission, Academic Foundation: New Delhi).

Government of Tamil Nadu, (2004), *Annual Statistical Abstract of Tamil Nadu 2002-2003* (Department of Economics and Statistics: Chennai).

Government of Tamil Nadu, (2004), *Tamil Nadu Economic Appraisal 2002-03* (Evaluation and Applied Research).

Government of Tamil Nadu, (2005), *Statistical Hand Book of Tamil Nadu 2004* (Department of Economics and Statistics: Chennai).

Indian Infrastructure (2005), "Connectivity Projects: Road, Rail and Pipelines", Vol. 7, No.11, June, p.30.

Indian Port Association (2003), *Study on Development of Inner Harbour Facilities at Tuticorin port* (IPA: New Delhi, October).

Indian Port Association (2004), *Major Ports of India — A Profile 2003-04* (IPA: New Delhi).

Indian Ports Association (1985), *Tuticorin Port: Master Plan Study Volume-I — Traffic Analysis and Forecast* (IPA: New Delhi, April).

Pisani, J.M. (1989), *Port Development in United States*, Report presented in 16th World Conference, Miami Beach, Florida, April, 22-29 (The IAPH foundation: Tokyo, Japan).

Lakshmanan, T.R. (2001), *Rotterdam: A strategic Hub in Global trade — Transport Chain, in Integration of Transport and Trade Facilitation — Selected Regional Case Studies* (The World Bank: Washington D.C.).

National Council of Applied Economic Research (1959), *Traffic Survey of the Port of Tuticorin* (Asia Publishing House: New Delhi).

Rietveld, P. (1977), Policy aspects of Interconnectivity in networks, in Cristina Capineri and Piet Rietveld (Eds), *Networks in Transport and Communications - A Policy Approach* (Ashgate Publishing Company: Vermont, USA).

De. P. (1999), "Performance of Indian Ports", *Indian Ports*, Vol. 31No.2, October, pp.5-12.

Ramakrishnan, R. (2003), "Scenario of Port Handling & Vision", *Indian Ports*, Vol. 35 No.2, October, pp.5-17.

Bose, S.K. (2001), "Cargo Handling of Major Ports in India - A case study", *Economic and Political Weekly*, August 25, pp.3284-3288.

Sasikumar, R. and Bhasi, M. (2004), "A comparative study of performance of India major Seaports", *Indian Ports,* Vol. 36, No2, pp.9-18.

Tuticorin Port (2005), *Shipping Routes Connecting Sethusamudram Channel* (Tuticorin Port Trust: Tuticorin).

Tuticorin Port (1985a), *Master Plan Study, Vol. I, Traffic Analysis and Forecast, Indian* (Ports Association: New Delhi).

Tuticorin Port (1985b), *Master Plan Study Volume-II - Planning of port Facilities* (Indian Port Association: New Delhi).

Tuticorin Port (2004), 25th Administration Report of the Tuticorin Port Trust 2003-04 (Tuticorin Port Trust, Tuticorin).

United Nations Conference of Trade and Development, (2003), *African Ports Reforms and the Role of Private Sector* (Report by the Secretariat, UNCTAD, 31, March).

Weigend, G. (1958), Some Elements in the Study of Port Geography, *Geographical Review*, Vol. 48, pp. 185-200.

Takeuchi, Y. (1988), *The Economic Impact of Ports in Japan — in Port Development Policy* (Proceeding of a Seminar held at Bangkok in January 1983: Thailand).

Annexure I

Comparative Development of Selected Sectors in Tuticorin Port Hinterland Districts

Hinterland Districts	*Small Scale Industries (in Nos.)*			*Factories (in Nos.)*			*Marine Products (in '000' Tonne)*			*Minerals Production (in '000' Tonne)*			*Agricultural total Food grains production (in '000' Tonne)*		
	1990-1991	*2002-2003*	*CAGR (in %)*	*1990-1991*	*2002-2003*	*CAGR (in %)*	*1990-1991*	*2002-2003*	*CAGR (in %)*	*1990-1991*	*2002-2003*	*CAGR (in %)*	*1990-1991*	*2002-2003*	*CAGR (in %)*
Primary Hinterland Districts															
Tuticorin	3377	14153	12.68	679	2276	10.61	39.57	31.59	1.84	87.00	2.10	-26.68	158	107	-3.20
Tirunelveli	3650	13511	11.52	553	1036	5.37	5.29	5.93	0.95	1129.40	178.00	-14.27	301	284	-0.48
Kanyakumari	7213	12205	4.48	358	658	5.20	37.28	19.64	-5.15	1.60	9.10	15.59	117	100	-1.30
Virudhunagar	2618	21845	19.34	1029	3606	11.02	—	—	—	784.00	206.40	-10.53	148	128	-1.20
Secondary Hinterland Districts															
Ramanathapuram	964	6166	16.72	65	96	3.30	60.30	108.28	5.02	2.00	—	—	185	163	-1.05
Sivagangai	1385	7942	15.67	169	206	1.66	—	—	—	—	17.9	—	176	140	-1.89
Pudukottai	3168	11025	10.95	195	232	1.46	49.89	60.54	1.60	—	—	—	254	161	-3.73
Madurai		23155			1325		—	—	—	5.40	3.30	-4.02		135	-5.66
Theni	7166	4272	11.83	832	297	5.72	—	—	—	—	—	—	463	95	
Dindigul	2273	12463	15.24	405	627	3.71	—	—	—	760.00	2.60	-3.77	253	168	-3.35
Hinterland total	31814	126737	12.21	4285	10359	7.63	192.33	225.98	1.32	2769.40	419.40	-14.55	2055	1481	-2.69
Tamil Nadu	127202	448905	11.08	15652	34071	6.70	287.40	379.21	2.34	18543.5	10192.0	-4.87	7481	4460	-4.22
% of primary to total hinterland	52.99	48.69	11.42	69.38	73.13	9.26	42.71	25.29	-2.93	72.29	94.33	-12.64	35.23	41.80	-1.30
% of secondary to total hinterland	47.01	51.31	13.03	30.62	26.87	4.37	57.29	74.71	3.44	27.71	5.67	-25.13	64.77	58.20	-3.56

Note: CAGR – Compound Average Growth Rate.

Source: Various issues of Annual Statistical Abstract of Tamil Nadu, Department of Economic and Statistics, Government of Tamil Nadu.

Annexure II

Employment growth in Tuticorin Port Hinterland Districts

(in '000' Nos)

Hinterland Districts	*Small Scale Industries*	*Factories*			*Agricultural Workers*			*Service Sectors*		
	2002-2003	*1990-1991*	*2002-2003*	*CAGR (in %)*	*1991*	*2001*	*CAGR (in %)*	*1991*	*2001*	*CAGR (in %)*
Primary Hinterland Districts										
Tuticorin	99.73	87.6	39.2	-6.48	301.66	238.73	-2.31	253.90	389.95	4.38
Tirunelveli	94.98	27.2	29.2	0.59	600.33	508.26	-1.65	337.97	505.26	4.10
Kanyakumari	85.32	31.7	54.6	4.64	238.98	98.07	-8.52	211.73	413.60	6.92
Virudhunagar	151.65	79.8	121.8	3.59	390.25	282.2	-3.19	331.51	548.76	5.17
Secondary Hinterland Districts										
Ramanathapuram	40.63	3.9	3.0	-2.16	317.14	304.04	-0.42	124.18	189.93	4.34
Sivagangai	53.77	8.3	8.2	-0.1	308.72	331.17	0.70	110.87	168.66	4.28
Pudukottai	76.59	8.8	7.7	-1.11	384.77	477.91	2.19	124.74	184.95	4.02
Madurai	161.35	41.8	38.8	1.23	886.07	458.14	-1.10	548.96	589.13	3.40
Theni	26.61		9.6			335.06			177.59	
Dindigul	87.23	19.5	22.7	1.27	582.90	606.95	0.41	230.94	345.41	4.11
Hinterland total	877.85	308.6	334.8	0.68	4010.82	3640.53	-0.96	2274.80	3513.24	4.44
Tamil Nadu	3142.34	1024.7	1256.1	1.71	13560.39	13779.40	0.16	8435.73	12624.80	4.11
% of primary to total hinterland	49.17	73.33	73.12	0.66	38.18	30.96	-3.02	49.99	52.88	5.05
% of secondary to total hinterland	50.83	26.67	26.88	0.75	61.82	69.04	0.13	50.01	47.12	3.81

Source: Same as in Annexure I.

21

IMPROVING INDIA'S PUBLIC TRANSPORT SYSTEMS: COMPARING GOVERNANCE IN INDIAN RAILWAYS AND IN AIR INDIA

Ashima Goyal

ABSTRACT

The paper examines the basic reasons and feasible remedies for organisational weakness, and the possible contribution of ownership, industry and management structure, leadership, social norms, and institutional incentives to alleviating the weaknesses in the Indian context. The arguments are illustrated with reference to the public rail and air services and help to understand why some public sector transport undertakings performed better than others. The most effective changes are those that create incentives, broadly defined, for individuals to improve productivity.

1. INTRODUCTION

Among factors impacting organisational weakness in public service provision are ownership, industry and management structure, leadership, social norms, and institutional incentives We will illustrate each with the experience of public rail and air services in India to draw implications for improved governance.

Williamson (1999) suggests the "remediableness criterion" — what is a feasible replacement for or modification of an inefficient organisation? He further defines "governance as the means by which *order* is accomplished in a relation in which potential *conflict* threatens to undo or upset opportunities to realise *mutual* gains (pp.312)" thus lowering transaction costs. We search for this order in the context of the Indian transport sector, examining design elements that improve incentives for the delivery of public services. Incentives are not just monetary but include mechanisms that motivate players to cooperate and compete at those margins that raise productivity.[1] Rise in quality and decrease in the cost of public services has great potential for improving the quality of life for the average citizen.

Air India (AI)

Both the public air and rail networks were created by nationalisation of private lines. The State owned Indian Airlines (IA) (largely domestic) and Air India (AI) (the International carrier), under the Ministry of Civil Aviation, have now (2007) been merged with the brand name Air India. But with the repeal of the Air Corporations Act in 1993, Government monopoly was abolished. A number of private players entered, and the number of aircraft increased rapidly, although remaining below international standards. Competition reduced fares, innovation improved facilities and conveniences offered and no frills airlines make it possible for the common man to fly, a task government airlines could not achieve (Srinivasa Raghavan, 2007, Wikipedia, 2007). Other restrictions continue—foreign airlines cannot invest more than 49 percent in any private India-based airline, the Airports Authority of India still largely controls airports, and taxation and other charges are high by international standards. Since severe congestion had developed at airports, expansion is on going under private participation. Fifty percent of the revenue collected in air travel goes to the government. Although all airlines suffered under the oil shocks of 2008, the market share of the new Air India has shrunk and it has gone deep into the red, despite advantages such as better airport space.

Indian Railways (IR)

The Indian railway (IR) is a department of the Government of India, managed by the Railway Board, under the Ministry of Railways. After nationalisation of private and princely lines in 1951 Indian railways has a monopoly on rail transport. The network already largely covered the country at the time of independence, but carrying capacity has increased substantially in the period since. Both passenger and freight traffic increased about 8 times, and train density doubled. But while the growth in freight traffic has been less than that of GDP, increase in passenger traffic has far exceeded population growth, as mobility increased. For many years railways barely covered operating expenses, and depended on government transfers for expenditures on maintenance, capacity expansion and upgradation for safety. Shortfall in capital expenditure is met by borrowings through the Railway Finance Corporation and budgetary transfers from the Central Government. Indian railways also pays dividend to the Central Government on capital-at-charge.[2] Inefficiency, wage costs, populist cross-subsidisation (without attention to elasticity of demand) and inability to raise fares, contributed to this state of affairs. Remunerative freight traffic was over-priced compared to passenger fares and lost to competitors. Even so, it contributed 70 % of rail revenues and made profits compared to losses on passenger traffic. The highest-to-lowest passenger fare ratio was 14.4 in the late 1990s. Second class ordinary passengers were 71 percent of the total passenger traffic but contributed only 16 per cent of the revenue in 2003-04. Employment in the railways peaked at 1.6 million[3] in the late 90s, and provisions for pensions were about 20% of operating costs in 2005-06 (Gokarn, 2007, Wikipedia, 2007). There has been some rationalisation of freight and premium passenger fares. IR has 16 zones further divided into divisions (67 in all) reporting to the board. Functional specialists report to their division heads.

Under the United Progressive Alliance (UPA) Government rail minister Lallu Yadav (2004-2009), rail finances have seen a turnaround with passenger and freight traffic and revenue rising. The operating ratio was 80 per cent and fund balance of Rs. 20,000 crores expected in 2007.

The primary contribution has been from management innovations and better use of resources and new technology. Load limits for freight wagons were raised by 11percent, and turnaround times improved. There are attempts to structure like a corporation, even while fulfilling social responsibilities. Liberalisers generally push for privatisation and raising user charges. But partial privatisation, better utilisation of assets, and corporatisation or restructuring of management are delivering. The ideas were there, but someone to push and implement, seems to have made a difference. Among partial privatisation initiatives are outsourcing stations management, rail hospitals, allowing companies to run their own container trains, letting suburban trains run as separate companies, raise funds through and accept the discipline of markets. The management structure has been largely unchanged since independence. Restructuring of departments and reorganisation along corporate lines would be helpful.

Comparing AI and IR

Both IR and AI are planning massive modernisation expenditures with a thrust on infrastructure—modern freight corridor for IR, aircraft acquisition for IA, largesse coming from the higher growth of the economy, improved demand and government finances.

IA also made a profit in 2003 after a loss the previous year. But profits as a percentage of revenues were only 2.7 compared to 20.7 for IR in 2005-06, and its revenues were only 8.5 percent of the IR revenues.[4] The costs of the merger is ecpected to be about Rs 1000 crores. Productivity has plummeted with hectic lobbying at the ministry for reduced posts. AI was operating in a more competitive environment compared to IR yet IR has done better. IA had the opportunity to learn and adopt the best practices of its rivals, but did not. It has gone in the space of a few years from being a monopoly player to not even being the dominant player.[5] Neither ownership nor industry structure is able to explain these outcomes. Ownership was the same and IA was operating in a better market structure. It is true that AI did not have full commercial freedom. There was no acquisition over 1999-2003 when private airlines were expanding, passenger service was poor, there was a shortage of pilots, fuel prices shot up but, other airlines and the railways did well in similar circumstances. Below we explore the other factors that matter.

The structure of the paper is as follows. Section 2 asks what are fundamental organisational weaknesses and feasible responses. The subsequent sections take up these responses one by one and analyse their performance as actual or suitability as potential reform of Indian railways and airlines. Section 3 examines the contribution of varying degrees of ownership, the extent to which an activity should be in the public or in the private sector. While Section 4 turns to the industry structure. Section 5 looks at the role of leaders and organisation norms. Further Section 6 points out the need for the management reforms and individual incentives while Section 7 emphasises institutional incentives. Section 8 makes a concluding assessment.

2. Organisation structures as a response to transaction costs and contracting failures

Transaction cost economics (Williamson, 1999) says that alternative modes of governance differ with respect to incentive intensity, administrative controls and the contract law regime. Markets emphasise autonomy by the combination of high-powered incentives, few controls, and legalistic dispute settlement; hierarchy seeks to achieve cooperation through low-powered incentives, extensive controls, and internal dispute resolution.

A variety of institutional features have evolved to enforce commitments.[6] Renegotiations, laws, regulations, sanctions, private conflict resolution mechanisms, organisational forms, and norms, all have a role in providing the required mix of commitment and flexibility. The ex-post bargaining position is important. Residual rights of control, in uncontracted for circumstances, determine agents' incentives. For example, either residual control rights must be given to the party who makes a relationship specific investment or that party will underinvest. When such allocation of control is not possible, internalising the transaction within a firm can improve welfare.

If control rights are conferred on a single group it may result in self-serving actions. Therefore control rights have to be carefully divided and civic society and other democratic pressures used. Supervisory or coercive mechanisms may be required to ensure that parties respect their commitments, but these should not restrict the flexibility required to ensure ex-post optimal coordination. Different transaction structures solve the coordination problem to different degrees. If complete contracts could be written public or private provision of public services would be equivalent.

3. OWNERSHIP: PUBLIC OR PRIVATE SECTOR OR A COMBINATION?

A number of factors affect the decision on whether an activity should be in the public or the private sector. A division between public and private based on first principles can improve outcomes. Since modern technology facilitates unbundling this is no longer an either or decision—various degrees of privatisation are possible.

The prime motive for public ownership and control comes from externalities that the private sector would neglect in its decisions. In rail transport in a poor country these include universal service obligations (USO). Public ownership or at least regulation is essential to prevent potential exploitation of consumers since network economies of scale give rail transport some features of a natural monopoly. But an ineffective public sector can fail to meet these obligations.[7]

The more specific assets are to the particular service, the more ownership and control should stay with the public sector. The private sector would have an incentive to under invest, since it is liable to "holdup" once it has invested in assets, which have no use elsewhere.

Incentives

Wherever multiple objectives have to be satisfied the public sector is more likely to provide them. Incentives have to be low for bureaucrats to satisfy multiple objectives, some of which are not measurable. Consider a regulated public service firm. Two extremes in pricing rules have opposite effects on incentives. With a price cap, incentives are high-powered since the residual profit share lies with the producer. The latter is motivated to decrease costs. Since rate of return regulation reimburses the cost of the service, incentives are low-powered. Profits from improvements do not stay with the producer. Thus there is a trade-off between rent extraction and providing incentives for additional effort. With a low enough price cap the regulator extracts all rent, but incentives to invest and improve quality may fall. Since costs rise with quality low-powered incentives are required for the provision of quality. Better accounting and more transparency makes price caps possible. Laffont (2005) argues that poor monitoring in developing countries limits the power of incentives that regulators can give public service providers. But technology is changing this. He advocates cost plus pricing initially in developing countries and a shift to price caps later as accounting improves.

Quality

Public sector provision should dominate, the greater the uncertainty affecting the quality, and the more difficult it is to enforce quality standards. Quality is expected to be higher in the public sector because incentives to reduce costs and quality are too high for the private sector. Public goods and services are often experience rather than search goods—only consuming reveals their quality. All dimensions of quality of service cannot be fully specified and enforced in market provision.

In the public sector, the bureaucrat-manager has poor incentives or control rights since he is transferable, but mission, reputation or career concerns, or political pressure may enforce quality service. Hart et. al. (1997) point out that while private provision will always have lower costs than public, quality in private provision may be lower if quality requires higher costs but higher if quality increases with innovation. The latter is normally higher under private provision and is likely to be more important in some kinds of services. Private provision would be superior in cases where quality can be contracted for, or is insensitive to cost reduction, or opportunities for cost reduction are small. Private provision will also dominate if incentives for quality improvement are poor for public managers, or low quality is used as a means of rationing.

The latter may explain the poor quality associated with provision of public sector services in India? Competitive populism in an era of political fragmentation did not allow user charges to rise after the 1970s oil price shocks. This effectively meant price caps were low. Even costs were not covered. This over-extraction of rent created a disincentive to invest and expand capacity. Even the sunk costs made for investment were expropriated. Low quality, delays and overcrowding, served as a rationing device helping target the poor, but made things worse as revenue sources found alternatives leaving only the subsidy burden. In railways, the revenue to cost ratio fell steadily from the early 70s. The ratio of the public sector deflator to GDP deflator was below 100 since 1961, there was a sharp fall in 1973, some recovery, but in 2001 it was still 83 % of its level in 1961 (Nagaraj, 2006). The Indian railways were eating reserves: "all along the provision for depreciation was tampered with for presenting an unreal rosy picture (Sriraman 1998, p. 282)." The large numbers of engineers in the Indian railway service were meant to enhance safety, but accidents became more frequent as funds for spending on safety were compromised.

Maintaining quality and servicing the poor in the context of a natural monopoly are strong arguments for a public railway service, but neither objective has been achieved very satisfactorily. Other changes we examine below can improve outcomes even with public ownership.

4. INDUSTRY STRUCTURE

It is frequently argued that the change in industry structure with more competition due to entry of the private sector and the opening of the economy has led to improvements in the public sector also. It did lead to more freedom from political interference and more managerial autonomy. High debt made it difficult for the government to continue to fund losses through taxpayers' money, forcing attempts at commercial viability. More information about and examples of best practices were available. But as we saw, competition has not helped Indian Airlines. The railways did better with milder competition from other modes of transport such as roads.

Competition is not dependent on industry structure. Despite many public services being local monopolies, a regulator can introduce elements of yardstick competition. For example, one railway zone or division can be benchmarked with another similarly placed section, and thus forced to reduce costs. There can be competitive bidding for the award of service utility contracts. Unbundling makes competitive supply possible for parts of the public good or service. If the latter is a search good, where consumers can assess quality for themselves, and suppliers are perfectly competitive at each level of quality, private supply would face socially optimal incentives (Hart et. al. 1999). Citizen or user groups are another useful source of information for the regulator, to discipline public monopolies. Such countervailing pressures make it feasible for incentives to be high powered even in the provision of public goods. Divesting and trading shares is another way to achieve market discipline. The necessity of publishing quarterly annual reports increases transparency.

That railways have performed better than public airlines despite limited changes in industry structure, suggests other changes have greater impact. Market pressures can be created even without formal changes in industry structure.

5. SOCIAL, CULTURAL AND PSYCHOLOGICAL FACTORS

Other important factors affecting performance are the culture of an organisation, and psychological and social ways of coping. Since social norms become sticky, leaders have a major role as change agents.

Cultural attributes come from national characteristics interacting with an organisations own culture and history. Thus AI focused on Indian hospitality and is known for its good food. A strong sense of hierarchy meant that VIPs were very well cared for.[8] But, in the Indian way, other relationships are taken for granted and communication is poor. If the culture is healthy, a large public sector organisation can do better than a small one. History, pride, belonging and participation can all contribute. Peer pressure can be more effective in a large organisation.[9] On this count IR is doing better than AI currently.

Psychological and cultural traits interact with economic conditions. Public transport systems are known for frequent breakdowns and delays, with minimal information given to and arrangements made for passengers affected. The strategy routinely used is similar to the "kheechna" textile exporters in Gujarat use to draw in the buyer. Knowing that once he has sunk costs he will adjust to delays, they assure a buyer that they will deliver by a certain date, knowing that if it rains the dyes will not dry and the consignment will not be ready. Similarly, in IA technical snags and expected delays are never clearly communicated. If any communication is made a blanket optimistic tone is adopted to make people accept delays longer than their initial tolerance levels. Systems that are prone to shocks lead to stratagems such as "kheechna". But they become habitual, being used even when they are not necessary. A clear well communicated contingency plan would lower costs and raise welfare. Habit and culture perhaps explains why IA has not emulated private competitors who are doing much better in these respects.[10]

"Passing the buck" is another frequent coping strategy. The remedy for this is decentralisation with clear individual rather than collective responsibility. Sometimes delays are consciously created as a way of rationing limited resources.

Corruption

A major problem, often spoken of sotto voice, is the pervasive corruption that hemorrhages revenues, diverts subsidies, and leads to sub-standard procurement. Shocks that made corruption the norm probably occurred in India around the seventies. First, political fragmentation weakened the government, multiple power centers developed. Second, user charges were not raised in the face of large cost shocks, as populism increased. The transport undertakings found it difficult to meet costs, salaries were also squeezed, encouraging extra-legal means of making money.

Jalan (2005, pp. 112) quotes from a former cabinet secretary's memoirs, "Politics having become the most lucrative business in the country, with few checks and controls, there is a compulsion for the minister or political leader to attempt to coerce civil servants to collude with him for mutual benefit. The service rules and procedures have been progressively adapted to facilitate this process."

Corruption has decreased to the extent discretionary controls have been dismantled, but it continues, especially with State governments, where arbitrary decisions are taken and there is a lack of accountability, or special favors and sanctions are required. Reforms that have reduced corruption at the Centre need to be carried out also in the States.

In procurement etc. operations, sub-standard materials allowed suppliers to make money while officials siphoned off payments. This is what Shleifer and Vishny (1993) call corruption with theft. The redistribution motive in the presence of shortages necessitated a discretionary allocation structure and monitoring for consumers more than for officers. Populist employment creation created multiple points where consumers were subjected to the discretionary powers. Relatively free entry into bribe collection and weak or collusive governments that were unable to punish, meant that officials functioned as independent monopolists. In such conditions, the bribe prices rise while revenue and sale of government goods fall as people seek alternatives.

In a multiple hierarchy between politicians and the people, middle layers can have an information advantage, which facilitates theft. It is human nature as well as feudal practice to give something for getting something. This reciprocity benefits middle-rung officials charged with re-distribution or rationing allocation. The Right to Information (RTI) Act and the realisation that officials are there to implement a citizen right, not for doing a favour, can help change this.

More accountability to the public with penalty for non-delivery is required. But too strict punishment does not work also, since that can paralyze individual effort and risk-taking. Established norms are difficult to change. But better accounting systems with random checks facilitated by the use of ICT can check corruption with theft. Competitive supply of the government good, as occurs for example through Internet enabled non-discretionary sale of tickets, can reduce monopolistic bribe collection. Better systems together with RTI reduce discretionary powers in general. One department should be clearly responsible for one objective, with competition in delivery. There should be multiple provision, but not multiple responsibility. Better finances with more market-linked discipline can also help.

If equating marginal returns to the marginal cost of corruption determines equilibrium extraction, then any measure that reduces the return and raises costs of corruption would lower extraction. Higher probability of getting caught, with online accounting systems, increases the cost of corruption. Changes in management routines are necessary to break out of habitual coping modes. Better systems would also reduce the necessity for such modes.

6. MANAGEMENT REFORM

In much of the public sector, management systems reflect the old structure of government, which was oriented towards command and control. In terms of Williamson's classification, the Indian public sector is characterised by low-powered incentives, hierarchical administrative controls, and legalistic dispute settlement across departments even though the latter is normally found in market-based non-hierarchical structures. A large percentage of cases pending in the courts originate in the public sector.

Jalan (2005, pp. 105), records the decay in Indian public services: "the system is dominated by internal conflicts of interest (for example, powerful but separate trade unions for different classes of government employees), political interference, statutory provisions, complicated seniority bound procedures, fiscal stringency and the proliferation of agencies which operate at cross purposes without any clear division of work".But he (2005, pp. 197) also notes that real successes were achieved where "old and cumbersome administrative procedures" based on multiple discretionary approvals were "replaced by a rule-based system largely based on self-certification" as in release of foreign exchange.

Incentives and Innovation

More competition and hardening of the budget constraint enforce some discipline, but losses will truly affect performance only when they affect individual salaries and jobs. Technology allows breakup of jobs so that there are no longer multiple people for same function and there is clear individual responsibility. Improved accounting of actual costs and outputs possible may also make it possible to give high-powered incentives to staff, so that they are able to retain gains from efficiency and are motivated to accept more accountability. Whether incentives are high or low powered is tied to information availability (Tirole, 1994). Technology and transparency allow less rigid rules. Reduction in theft from the government, and unbundling and restructuring that improves efficiency, may allow better services without large price increases.

Incentive compatibility is the key; he who gains from something should be given responsibility for it. Management changes that give space for individual creativity and initiative are required to support these changes. The gain can be recognition, reputation, and interaction, leading to a better work culture, encouraging innovations such as APEX pricing to differentiate between and suit the requirements of different market segments that have contributed to the growth of Indian aviation. Non-discretionary outcome related assessment and high-powered incentives would encourage similar innovation in public airlines. At present, the officers are only concerned to please their superiors who write their performance reports. This is also a source of corruption as political, bureaucratic bosses, assessment committees and their families are lavishly hosted at the taxpayer's expense.

Accounting reform should make possible a shift to modern management information systems, which clearly allocate responsibility for outcomes, measured as variance from budgeted amounts, right down the hierarchy, together with continuous feedback. Mid-term correction becomes feasible ensuring delivery. Daily expenditure control is possible.

Since bureaucrats have multiple objectives it is normally difficult to give high-powered incentives. But public sector transport undertakings provide a paid service. Although money does follow the service the providers continue to have fixed salaries. This can change. Even where the job is not so clearly linked to one measurable output, new technology makes better measurement of work possible. Hammer et. al.(2007) point out that worldwide money follows the delivery of public services, fixed salaries do not work.

It is possible to design management systems with variable pay linked to performance. Regular appraisals with clear performance targets get taken seriously. These have been newly introduced even in Indian private corporate organisations and the government is also exploring performance-linked pay.[11] Performance can include that of the individual and organisation as a whole.

Overcoming conflicts

Mr. Sreedharan, who set up the Konkan railway line and the Delhi Metro demonstrated that good management is possible in public sector transport projects. The projects were completed in record time, without delays and cost overruns, and were of high quality. Planning, conceptualization and implementation were all good. Delhi Metro was also given the critical freedom from political interference, for example there was no pressure to provide employment. The Delhi government made the land available for the metro, and ensured that nothing concerning the Metro was negotiable in a court of law (Sankhe, 2007).

Arbitration and support across government departments are required. A special agency should be set up for inter-sectoral coordination and public hearings.[12] Most of the massive infrastructure projects the Government has taken up are delayed. Mumbai flyovers are an example. One department blames the other for delays, since one is responsible for construction, the other for clearances and the third for facilities. Anyone affected by a project can lobby against it. Bureaucrats do not want to be blamed, so the matter goes to the courts, resulting in years of delay.

Turning again to Williamson's three categories, to the extent technology is making it possible to shift to more high powered incentives, administrative controls can be reduced. Encouraging arbitration is one way of reducing the excessive dependence on the legal system. To the extent a public sector organisation continues to consist of multiple hierarchies with differential information in the different layers the reliance on legalistic modes of conflict resolution can be reduced. Arbitration based on this information advantage would work well in conjunction with the formal legal system (Dixit, 2004). Private modes of conflict resolution have the informational advantage of more industry specific knowledge and better verifiability. Arbitration tribunals could be set up with the law promising to enforce the judgements of the tribunals subject to appeals. More reliance on other private informal enforcement such as handshakes and oral agreements will reduce the cost of using the legal system, and improve the work atmosphere. Apart from costs arising from problems of verifiability, lack of industry specific knowledge, requirements of disclosure in any formal legal system, the huge delays in the backlogged Indian legal system are a major cost. Reducing the public sector's reliance on this system will also reduce the pressures on and delays in the system.

Public Private Partnership (PPP)

PPP is another type of restructuring to overcome specific weaknesses of public ownership and of markets. A choice of PPP in a particular public service delivery normally offers a menu of contract choices, ranging from outright privatisation or divestiture, to long-term concessions or management contracts where asset ownership remains in the public sector, to outsourcing of specific jobs. Control, asset ownership and risk shared by the private sector falls in moving from the first to the last. The general principle is that risk should stay with the agency most able to bear and best able to alleviate it. Service contracts normally vary over a period of 6 months to 2 years. Private sector expertise is used or it may be developed and competition increased. The responsibility for coordination and for investment rests with the public sector. Management contracts transfer responsibility for operation and maintenance (O & M) also to the private sector. These run typically for 3 to 5 years. They may have a fixed fee and include a performance target. In a lease contract the private party buys rights to the income stream so it assumes the commercial risk. Incentives for reducing costs and quality standards can be written in. Concessions last for 25 to 30 years. Responsibility for operation and management (O&M) as well as investment is transferred while asset ownership remains with the Government. The contracts set out performance targets, standards, investment amounts, mechanisms for adjusting tariffs, and arrangements for arbitrating disputes. Assets are to be returned in good condition and consumers are to be protected from monopoly pricing. Under divestiture, asset ownership also passes into private hands and the Government is only left with the task of regulation. Given the existing large management establishments in the public transport sector political willingness at present seems only to consider service contracts. Outsourcing hygiene, security, dining etc can be a way to improve these services and also earn revenue Goyal (2004). These contracts should give preference to developing local entrepreneurship over large foreign firms pushed by aid agencies. The latter may have more management experience but lack local knowledge and tend to generate political resistance.

The private sector may be able to provide funds that highly indebted governments lack. But the former will be motivated to provide the funds only if it is possible to recover the investments through user charges. Therefore pricing becomes a key reform. Reasonable user charges can make either a public or a private project viable, and a larger customer base will increase profitability. A financially constrained public sector entity has a greater incentive to outsource, and a larger population or consumer density will make outsourcing more feasible without large price increases.

Theoretical arguments of maintaining quality support public ownership of assets, but the command and control management structure has strained finances and reduced quality. Therefore, reform of management is the essential precondition that may allow assets to remain in the public sector while improved quality of services are provided at reasonable prices.

7. Institutional Incentives

In so far as public sector enterprises will continue to have unique features, and remain a forum for resolving the competing claims of different stakeholders, checks and balances will continue to be required. These reduce efficiency, but institutional structures with better incentives can be designed to motivate bureaucrats, reduce corruption and delay.

Optimal cross-subsidisation is derived if social welfare is maximised subject to a budget constraint. This gives the Ramsey-Boiteux rule that the price marginal cost gap should be inversely proportional to elasticities of demand. Thus the poor should be charged higher prices if they have a lower elasticity of demand, but they can be cross-subsidised as long as the budget is balanced. The rule has been generalised into the theory of optimal non-linear tariffs. These pricing principles are violated if, in the aggregate, charges do not even cover costs. Cross subsidisation is then excessive and generates inefficiencies that raise cost further. Moreover, competitive entry occurs if, with cross subsidisation, the price in any sub-market exceeds cost, or if new technology lowers cost or breaks a natural monopoly. Then government revenues from these sub-sectors fall further. This happened as Indian Airlines lost its natural monopoly; railways lost freight traffic to the roadways due to higher freight prices. It is necessary to pay attention to changes in to the elasticity of demand and the development of competing transport modes. Beyond a point, subsidies for USO should come from the general budget not from other traffic. One-way of achieving this is to switch controls to managers or bureaucrats and away from politicians during waves of competitive populism, for example, by empowering regulators. In the Indian democracy, other checks and balances are in place but politicians have gained too much power over bureaucrats.

In budgetary processes, separation of powers can reduce expenditure if it removes conflict of interest, for example, the agent who has proposal rights over expenditure should not be the one who stands to directly gain from it. Whoever cuts a cake should not be responsible for distribution of the slices. The countervailing pressures generated induce, although they may not ensure, a more fair and efficient allocation. Tirole (1994) suggests multiple control rights with control switching to a more conservative agency when finances are under strain.

Budgetary implementation through control and monitoring make incentives low powered. The use of self-motivation is minimal; agents are supposed to just obey instructions. This works better for simple processes where effective and low-cost monitoring is feasible. In more complex processes monitoring needs to be complemented by delegation to residual claimants. The latter have high-powered incentives, since the returns from greater efficiency stay with them. Following the control philosophy, budgetary implementation in India, although quite detailed, tends to focus on monitoring inputs. This makes participants strategic and forward-looking. They try to maximise their allocations, but have little incentives for delivery. Modern management information systems, in contrast, build in strong incentives for delivery.

Rules

To the extent bureaucrats or politicians are self-interested, or there is the possibility of regulatory capture, processes that restrict efficiency have to be designed. Since public sector organisations have a multi-hierarchical structure, parts may have more information compared to others. If they have sufficient discretion they could use the informational advantage to benefit interest groups they favour. In general interest groups that benefit from withholding of information stand to gain. They have an incentive to persuade the official not to release information that harms them. If the officials have to follow a rulebook, then interest groups have less of a stake in the decision and therefore less incentive for regulatory capture. This is one reason officials are made to follow rules. Thus low-powered cost plus rules are less subject to regulatory capture, since they leave low rents with the firm, and the regulator has little discretion. If high-powered incentive schemes such as price caps are to be retained then alternative pressure groups such as user groups are required to guard against regulatory capture by the supplier. Control rights need to be divided among countervailing groups.

In government auctions, discretion in judging quality gives scope for favouritism. Therefore tangible variables such as price are given precedence (Tirole, 1994). Large discretion in the award of contracts can lead to allegations of payoffs received from the firms selected. Transparent rules that minimise discretion may be necessary even at the cost of some flexibility.

Other ways of getting around the above problem are (i) short-term public service contracts that are subject to re-bidding, and (ii) checks and balances designed to prevent corrupt politicians making money from privatisation or using public utilities for patronage.

In many situations social welfare is enhanced if a benevolent government can make an intertemporal commitment — this would remove fears of expropriation and encourage utilities to achieve optimal efficiency and investment. But short-term commitments provide a check against decisions taken to favour interest groups. Thus re-bidding rail or air service contracts may not only keep a check on costs but also allow removal of a corrupt or inefficient firm (Tirole, 1994). Since governments can loose elections they cannot commit not to 'hold-up' sector specific investment, so private investment would not be optimal.

In addition to the division of control rights among the judiciary, executive, and the legislature, the media, user and other independent groups must be given a formal role. Often advocacy by each group reveals valuable information for a decision-maker (Tirole, 1994).

To the extent corruption is widespread in public life, more independent private sector management or sale of public utilities would be beneficial. The latter would prevent the non public-spirited politician from obliging special interest groups such as trade union vote banks of sources of illicit funding (Hart et al. 1997).

8. CONCLUSIONS

Our survey of relevant theoretical insights is motivated by the differential performance of Indian public rail and air rail, and helps to explain it. It suggests that there may be grounds for public sector control of assets and delivery of public services. Just changes in ownership, industry structure and competition will not necessarily improve delivery and quality. Better individual motivation, through changes in management structure and institutional design holds the key. All types of organisations are imperfect, but context-specific feasible modifications exist that can improve outcomes. We identify such that could apply to Indian rail and air services.

Market structure alone was not enough to improve the performance of Air India. Indian Railways have done better as leadership implemented managerial changes, which created better incentives.

Leaders are important to push change when dysfunctional social and organisational norms set in. Their main contribution is in implementing better systems against resistance or inertia. A few good people can make a difference; but good systems can induce better behavior from most people.

Notes:

1. Goyal 1999, 2003, 2004 and 2007 has explored such incentives in the context of public deficits, budgets, provision of water and design of welfare schemes. This paper draws on and extends the earlier analysis and applies it to public transport undertakings. An expanded earlier version of this paper was published as Goyal (2008).
2. This was 6 percent in the early nineties. At this time an accounting reform made the railways depreciation reserve fund (DRF) count as part of capital-at-charge creating perpetual dividend liability owed to the Government.
3. Indian railways are the second largest employer in the world after the Chinese army.
4. AI had been making profits since 2002-03 after a string of losses, but made a loss of over 500 crores in 2006-07 (it is probably even higher since doubtful accounting practices adopted led to dissent notes from the board) the biggest in its 70 year history. Indian made a small profit of 57 crores (Economic Times, November 24, 2007).
5. India Aviation's profiles the fall in IA's market share from 100% in 1994, 40% in 2004 and just 20% by 2007. See http://indiaaviation.aero/news/airlineCarrier/view/77/107/Indian+Airlines
6. The discussion in this section draws upon Tirole (1994), Hart. et.al. (1997), Williamson (1999) Brousseau and Glachant (2002), papers collected in the latter, and Goyal (2004).
7. A participant at ICOTSS remarked that Indian municipal departments are often only interested in collecting revenue not in providing services.
8. Thus a media celebrity (Vir Sanghvi) complained in his Hindustan Times column that Air India's record of hospitality was being spoilt by outsourcing to foreign workers. A German girl was rude to him—presumably she did not recognise him, as an Indian would have. VIPs do not experience and therefore do not understand the shabby treatment given to the average traveler.
9. Hammer et. al. (2007) suggest that large public sector hospitals deliver better services than other public health care partly for these reasons.
10. A managing director of Indian Airlines had written in their flight magazine that Indian Airlines does not consider ten minutes to be a delay!

11. The GVR group introduced such a system recently. The Mumbai administration has in 2007 introduced 5 key parameters on which bureaucrats will be given a ranking of 1 to 10 on their annual Performance Appraisal Report. These are time-bound disposal of files, utilisation of state and central funds, implementation of the relevant minister's assurances in the state legislature, satisfying auditor's queries, and filling up departmental vacancies and promotions. The 6th Pay Commission has asked IIMA to study the feasibility of measuring performance in government employment through five parameters of skill, effort, output, productivity and quality.
12. Professor Agarwal pointed out at ICOTSS that interdepartmental conflict makes change difficult. For example, in IR electronic and mechanical engineers were fighting since one wanted digitalisation and the other did not.

REFERENCES

Brousseau, E., and J.-M. Glachant (2002), 'The Economics of Contracts and the Renewal of Economics' in Brousseau, E., and J.-M. Glachant (eds.) *The Economics of Contracts: Theories and Applications*, Cambridge University Press, UK.

Dixit, A. K. (2004), *Lawlessness and Economics: Alternative Modes of Governance*. Princeton, NJ and Oxford, Princeton University Press, UK.

Gokarn, S. (2007), 'Railways', entry in the *Oxford Companion to Economics in India*, K. Basu (ed.), OUP, New Delhi.

Goyal, A.(2008), 'Governance in India's Public Transport Systems: Comparing Indian Railways and Airlines', *Economic and Political Weekly*, July12-18, Vol. XLIII No.28, pp. 119-127.

Goyal, A. (2007), "NREGS, Local Infrastructure and Governance," Box 1.6, Chapter 1 in *IIR 2007 – Rural Infrastructure*, (Eds.) P. Kalra and A. Rastogi, New Delhi: 3iNetwork and Oxford University Press, pp. 22-24.

Goyal, A. (2004),'Getting Water from Public Private Partnerships', chapter 12.1 in *India Infrastructure Report 2004, Bringing about value for money in infrastructure*, Morris S. (ed.), New Delhi: 3iNetwork and Oxford University Press.

Goyal, A. (2003),'Budgetary Processes: A Political Economy Perspective', chapter 2.2 in *India Infrastructure Report 2003, Public Expenditure Allocation and Accountability*, Morris S. (ed.), 3iNetwork and Oxford University Press, New Delhi.

Goyal, A. (1999),'The Political Economy of the Revenue Deficit', in *India Development Report 1999-2000*, K. S. Parikh (ed.), IGIDR and Oxford University Press, New Delhi.

Hammer, J., Y. Aiyar, S.Samji, (20070, "Understanding Government Failure in Public Health Services," *Economic and Political Weekly*, October 6, pp. 4049-4057.

Hart, Oliver, Andrei Shleifer, Robert Vishny (1997), 'The Proper Scope of Government: Theory and an Application to Prisons', *Quarterly Journal of Economics*, 112, pp. 1127-61.

Jalan, B. (2005), "The Future of India: Politics, Economics and Governance",Viking, Penguin Books India Ltd., New Delhi.

Laffont, J-J. (2005), *Regulation and Development*, Frederico Caffe Lectures, New York, USA and Cambridge,Cambridge University Press, UK.

Nagaraj, R. (2006), "Public Sector Performance since 1950: A fresh look," *Economic and Political Weekly*, Vol. XLI, No. 25, June, pp. 2551-2557.

Sankhe, S. (2007), "Creating a **modern Indian city:** An interview with Delhi's chief minister", McKinsey Quarterly, November, accessed on November 15, 2007, from http://www.mckinseyquarterly.com/Economic_Studies/Productivity_Performance.

Sheifer, A. and R.W. Vishny (1993), "Corruption", *Quarterly Journal of Economics*, pp. 599-617.

Srinivasa Raghavan, T.C.A. (2007), "Aviation", entry in the *Oxford Companion to Economics in India*, K. Basu (ed.), OUP, New Delhi.

Sriraman, S. (1997), "Financing Transport Infrastructure and Services", in D.M. Nachane and M.J.M. Rao (eds.) *Macroeconomic Challenges and Development Issues*, pp.276-293, Himalaya Publishing House, Mumbai.

Tirole, J. (1994), 'The Internal Organisation of Government', *Oxford Economic Papers*, 46, pp. 1-29.

Williamson, O. (1999), "Public and Private Bureaucracies: A Transaction Cost Economics Perspective", *Journal of Law Economics and Organisation,* Vol.15, No. 1, pp. 306-342.

Wikipedia, 2007, http://en.wikipedia.org/wiki/Indian_Railways, and

http://en.wikipedia.org/wiki/Indian_Airlines, accessed on 19th November.

22

REVITALIZATION OF THE PASSENGER TRANSPORT SECTOR IN INDIA

T. V. Ramanayya
G. Ramesh

ABSTRACT

Passenger Road Transport Sector in India is passing through a critical period. The required assistance from both Central and State Governments is not forthcoming. On the advise of Planning Commission during the Seventh Plan review period, some of the States have opened up this sector in a big way to private operators. However, the private sector involvement has not been up to the expectations. Their operations are mostly limited to the profitable segments. There is a need to revitalize this sector in the interest of 60 million passengers daily using this system, energy conservation and to optimize the investments in road construction. This paper outlines a systematic review and demand estimation for public transport system in India; relative roles of public and private operators. This paper also emphasizes the need for policy intervention along with a financial package to keep this sector on a sustainable track in the years to come.

1. INTRODUCTION

State Road Transport Undertakings (SRTUs) were promoted in each State in sequel to the Road Transport Corporations Act, 1950 of Government of India. Both the Central and the State Governments financially supported the State Road Transport Undertakings. Subsequently amendments made to the Motor Vehicles Tax and the RTC Act between 1956 and 1969, enabled nationalization of passenger transport services leading towards State monopoly in many areas. Thus, the State Road Transport Undertakings were formed to shoulder the responsibility of providing affordable transport services throughout the country. At present there are 53 Undertakings functioning in different parts of the country with a total fleet strength of over 1,13,000 buses and with an investment of over Rs. 8,100 crores.

As a change of strategy, in the Seventh Five Year Plan, it was decided to encourage private sector participation as it was thought that SRTUs alone may not be in a position to cater to the growing demand for passenger transport services. This was however, not followed up with a comprehensive Road Transport Policy and Regulatory Framework. Consequently, many private operators are involved in providing service to the public but have not been able to provide them up to the desired level. A comparative analysis of private bus operators with STUs in terms of efficiency parameters is difficult to undertake due to lack of data relating to private operators. The absence of a comprehensive passenger transport policy and regulatory framework has resulted in the proliferation of personalized transport vehicles and also some unsafe methods of transport.

The number of buses registered in the country has gone up from about 34,000 in 1951 to about 600,000 by the end of 2005. Enquiries with private operators reveal that bulk of the registered private vehicles are contract vehicles. Only about 45,000 to 50,000 buses are being regularly used for passenger operations across the country. The performance of SRTUs today is a reflection of the policy environment in which these operate. Even though these are operationally efficient, they are financially weak. Public transport services whether provided by the State or private operators are subsidized in most countries. For example, in European countries like the U.K., France, Sweden, and Switzerland, the States subsidizes about 40% to 75% of the cost of operation of public transport buses. The global trend is also to encourage public transport and discourage private owned vehicles. The taxation policy of public transport in India has been hampering its growth. The private operators are equally in a quandary about their role and future prospects.

It may be noted that from Table 1 fleet strength of SRTUs has been more or less stagnant during the last 10 years. In 2007, the SRTUs fleet strength is about 18% of total bus fleet registered in India.

Table 1: Fleet strength of SRTUs between the period 1976-77 and 2006-07

Year	*Public sector buses*	*Private buses (Contract + Stage + Public Sector Co. buses)*	*Total*	*Percentage of Public Sector Buses*
1976	52200	62800	115000	45.39
1981	69600	923000	161900	42.99
1986	84000	143300	227300	36.96
1991	104106	225000	331100	31.44
1996	111100	338700	449800	24.70
2001	115000	411980	525680	21.88
2003	114900	435980	546380	21.03
2004	111400	450980	564280	19.74
2005	113300	465000	567790	19.95
2006	112380	465000	577380	19.46
2007	98809	465000	563809	17.53

Source: Central Institute of Road Transport, Pune.

However, there is a need to encourage public transport from the point of view of energy conservation, providing mobility to different sections of society and to optimize the use of road infrastructure. A comprehensive development of business plans for the passenger road transport sector is an immediate necessity. For this purpose, Passenger Transport operations can be divided into four categories, viz.,

- Urban operation
- Intra-District and Rural services
- Inter District services
- Inter-State operations

The characteristics of each of these segments (see. Table 2) vary and each segment may need a different policy and support. This paper deals with demand for passenger transport under these four categories and strategy to be followed in Revitalization of the Passenger Transport Sector in India.

Table 2: Characteristics of Different Segments

Category	*VU (Kms/day)*	*Service Types*	*Players*	*Profitability*	*Competitors to SRTUs*
Urban	*200-250*	Ordinary, limited halt	Public, private, autos	Mostly loss making	Illegal contract buses, maxi cabs, autos
Intra- District and Rural	250-350	Express, ordinary, limited halt	Public, private, maxi cabs	Low and loss making	Illegal contract buses, maxi cabs
Inter District	300-450	Luxury, express, Volvo	Public & private	Moderate and high	Private
Inter State	>600	Volvo, luxury, deluxe	Public & private	Very high	Private

2. URBAN OPERATIONS

Urban areas contribute to nearly 60% of GDP of India. Provision of public transport is crucial in cities with more than one million population. As per 2001 census, there are 35 cities with more than one million population and an attempt has been made to forecast the need for public transport of these cities.

Table 3: Norms for Bus Fleet Size

	Buses Required/Lakh	
Pop. Range	*Desirable*	*Minimum*
> 80 Lakhs	100	80
60-80 Lakhs	80	60
40-60 Lakhs	60	50
20-40 lakhs	50	40
10-20 Lakhs	40	30

We consider below four scenarios. Scenario–1 considers the growth of urban sprawl, the resultant increase in trip lengths and the number of trips a bus could make in a day between two places on the given network. Scenario-2 visualizes less urban sprawl and consequently reduced trip lengths. These assumptions have been discussed with the officials of Bangalore Metropolitan Transport Corporation (BMTC), Andhra Pradesh State Road Transport Corporation (APSRTC) and other experts and the norms suggested in the above table are in line with their perceptions. The requirement of fleet strength for the urban areas is computed on the basis of norms suggested above. The population growth of these areas for the next 10 years has computed and the bus fleet for the years 2011 and 2016 also computed (Ref. Table 4). These norms are modified in cities where sub-urban train services were in operation (a maximum of 50% in Mumbai and a minimum of 10% in Delhi).

Table 4: Bus Fleet Requirements of Urban Areas

Sl. No.	*Name of cities*	*As per 2001 Census*		*2006*		*2011*		*2016*	
		Scen. 1	**Scen. 2**	**Scen. 1**	**Scen. 2**	**Scen. 1**	**Scen. 2**	**Scen. 1**	**Scen. 2**
		Buses	**Buses**	**Buses**	**Buses**	**Buses**	**Buses**	**Buses**	**Buses**
01	G Mumbai	8184	6547	10203	8184	12788	10230	15984	12788
02	Kolkata	9257	10573	11564	9252	14456	11564	18069	14456
03	Delhi	10223	8186	12791	10233	15989	12791	19987	15989
04	Chennai	5140	3855	5622	4497	7027	5622	8784	7027
05	Bangalore	3412	2843	5687	4265	8886	7109	11107	8886
06	Hyderabad	3320	2767	5534	4150	8646	6917	10808	8646
07	Ahmedabad	2712	2260	3389	2825	5649	4237	8827	7061
08	Pune	1878	1502	2817	2347	3521	2934	5868	4401
09	Surat	1406	1125	1757	1406	2636	2196	3295	2746
10	Kanpur	1345	1076	1682	1345	2522	2102	3153	2627
11	Jaipur	1162	930	1453	1162	1816	1453	2724	2270
12	Lucknow	1133	907	1417	1133	1771	1417	2657	2214
13	Nagpur	1061	849	1327	1061	1659	1327	2488	2073
14	Patna	512	341	1067	854	1334	1067	1667	1334
15	Indore	492	328	1024	820	1281	1024	1601	1281
16	Vadodara	448	298	560	373	1166	933	1457	1166
17	Bhopal	436	291	546	364	1137	909	14211	1137
18	Coimbatore	434	289	542	362	1130	904	1412	1130
19	Ludhiana	419	279	523	349	1090	872	1362	1090
20	Kochi	407	271	508	339	1059	847	1324	1059
21	Visakhapatnam	399	266	499	332	1039	831	1298	1039
22	Agra	396	264	496	330	1032	826	1290	1032
23	Varanasi	364	232	454	303	757	568	1183	947
24	Madurai	358	239	448	299	747	560	1167	933
25	Meerut	350	233	438	292	730	547	1140	912
26	Nasik	346	230	432	288	720	540	1125	900
27	Jabalpur	335	223	419	279	698	524	1091	873
28	Jamshedpur	331	220	413	275	689	516	1076	861
29	Anansol	327	218	409	273	681	511	1065	852
30	Dhanbad	319	213	399	266	665	499	1039	832
31	Faridabad	316	211	396	264	659	495	1030	824
32	Allahabad	315	210	394	262	656	492	1025	820
33	Amritsar	303	202	379	253	632	474	790	593
34	Vijayawada	303	202	379	253	632	474	790	592
35	Rajkot	301	200	376	251	626	470	783	587
	Total	**58444**	**45708**	**76344**	**59541**	**106526**	**84728**	**152677**	**111978**

The bus required for million plus urban areas by 2011 varies from a minimum of 84,700 to a desirable number of 106500. By 2016, the demand for buses range from 1,00,000 to 1,52,000. Moreover, some more cities might reach the million plus mark by the year 2016 and the bus fleet requirement could go up. Data is not available about the number of buses in operation exclusively in different cities of India. The requirement of buses for metropolitan cities of India for 2006, 2011 & 2016 are separately tabulated in Tables 5a to 5c respectively. By 2016, the deficit increases between 58,000 to 76,500 based on the relevant scenario.

Table 5a: Requirement of Buses for Metropolitan cities in India 2006

Name of City	*Buses as on 2006*	*Requirement*		*Correction for Rail Network*	*Net Requirement*		*Deficit*	
		Scenario1	*Scenario2*		*Scenario1*	*Scenario2*	*Scenario1*	*Scenario2*
Ahmedabad	540	3389	2825	0	3389	2825	2849	2285
Bangalore	3925	5687	4265	0	5687	4265	1762	340
Chennai	2737	8031	6425	30	5622	4497	2885	1760
Delhi 2434	15989	12791	20	12791	10233	10357	7799	
Bombay	3391	20460	16368	50	10230	8184	6839	4793
Hyderabad	2838	5534	4150	0	5534	4150	2696	1312
Kolkatta	1144	16521	13217	30	11564	9252	10420	8108
Total	17009	75611	60041		54817	43406	37808	26397

Table 5b: Requirement of Buses for Metropolitan Cities in India 2011

Name of City	*Buses as on 2006*	*Requirement*		*Correction for Rail Network*	*Net Requirement*		*Deficit*	
		Scenario1	*Scenario2*		*Scenario1*	*Scenario2*	*Scenario1*	*Scenario2*
Ahmedabad	540	5649	4237	0	5649	4237	5109	3697
Bangalore	3925	8886	7109	0	8886	7109	4961	3184
Chennai	2737	10038	8031	30	7027	5622	4290	2885
Delhi	2434	19987	15989	20	15989	12791	13555	10357
Bombay	3391	25575	20460	50	12788	10230	9397	6839
Hyderabad	2838	8646	6917	0	8646	6917	5808	4079
Kolkatta	1144	20651	16521	30	14456	11564	13312	10420
Total	17009	99432	79263		73441	58470	56432	41461

Table 5c: Requirement of Buses for Metropolitan Cities in India 2016

Name of City	*Buses as on 2006*	*Requirement*		*Correction for Rail Network*	*Net Requirement*		*Deficit*	
		Scenario1	*Scenario2*		*Scenario1*	*Scenario2*	*Scenario1*	*Scenario2*
Ahmedabad	540	8827	7061	0	8827	7061	8287	6521
Bangalore	3925	11107	8886	0	11107	8886	7182	4961
Chennai	2737	12548	10038	30	8784	7027	6047	4290
Delhi	2434	24983	19987	20	19987	15989	17553	13555
Bombay	3391	31969	25575	50	15984	12788	12593	9397
Hyderabad	2838	10808	8646	0	10808	8646	7970	5808
Kolkatta	1144	25814	20651	30	18069	14456	16925	13312
Total	17009	126056	100844		93566	74853	76557	57844

The information presented in Tables 5a to 5c indicate that current scenario in metropolitan cities is very dismal and thus needs urgent remedial action which partly explains the formidable problems of commuters in metropolitan cities.

3. INTRA DISTRICT AND RURAL OPERATIONS

The demand for these services is linked to:

- Number of settlements in the State
- Number of economic activity centers in the taluk or mandal

One bus on an average will be able to cater to four rural settlements. In addition, it is felt that six buses may be required per lakh of population to link various economic activity centers in the vicinity of these villages. This criterion is validated by applying these norms in the State of Andhra Pradesh through stakeholders survey and discussions with the employees of APSRTC. At the all India level, the requirement to cater to this segment will be around 198000 during 2006 and 20700 by 2016 (Table 6).

Table 6: Bus fleet for Intra and Rural Operations in India

Item	*2006*	*2011*	*2016*
Number of Settlements	600000	600000	600000
Buses@ 1 for 4 settlements	150000	150000	150000
Rural Population(Lakhs)	8055	8747	9500
Buses @ 6 per lakh	48327	52484	56998
Total Bus Fleet Needed	**198327**	**202484**	**206998**

4. INTER-DISTRICT OPERATIONS

The demand for inter district services depends upon major economic and administrative places of importance in a State, the intensity of economic activity and linkages provided by railways. The total population of a State also contributes to the demand for these services. The demand for this category of services comprises of:

- Number of economic activity centers in a State (Number of towns)
- The total population of a State

At the macro level, the number of buses required per town will be about 5. The number of buses required per lakh of total population will be about 8. This empirical model is validated in the State of Andhra Pradesh. The requirements of buses at all India level to cater to this demand at different time periods are presented in Table 7.

Table 7: Buses needed at Different Time Periods in India

Item	*2001*	*2006*	*2011*	*2016*
Population in lakh	10270	11313	12462	13727
Buses @ 8 Per Lakh	82161	90505	99695	109819
Number of Census Towns	400	420	440	475
Buses @ 5 Per census town	2000	2100	2200	2375
Total Fleet needed	**84161**	**92605**	**101895**	**112194**

5. INTER-STATE OPERATIONS

Inter State Services will be mostly buses plying to the neighboring states for business, religious and tourist locations. At the macro level, the demand for the number of buses will be about 3 buses per lakh of population. This assumption was tested with the data of Andhra Pradesh and found appropriate. The demand for inter-state services in India for different time periods is tabulated in Table 8.

Table 8: Buses Required in India at different time periods

Item	*2001*	*2006*	*2011*	*2016*
Total Population in lakhs	10270	11762	13471	15428
Bus fleet @ 3 per lakh	30810	35287	40413	46284

6. TOTAL DEMAND FOR PASSENGER BUS FLEET AT THE NATIONAL LEVEL

The previous sections provided bus fleet requirements for different segments at different time periods. The total requirement bus fleet is provided in Table 9.

Table 9: Total Requirement of Bus Fleet in India

Type of Service	*Scenario 1*			*Scenario 2*		
	2006	*2011*	*2016*	*2006*	*2011*	*2016*
Urban Operations	76344	106526	152677	59541	84728	111978
Intra District and Rural Services	198327	202484	206998	198327	202484	206998
Inter District Services	92605	101895	112194	92605	101895	112194
Inter State Operations	35287	40413	46284	35287	40413	46284
Total Requirements	402563	451318	518153	385760	429520	477454

7. CONTRIBUTION OF PRIVATE OPERATORS TO PASSENGER BUS OPERATIONS

Private operators are involved in all the segments of passenger bus operations. However, their participation is dependant on the profitability of the segment. Interviews were conducted with a number of private operators and the maximum percentage of contribution in each segment is tabulated below (Table 10).

Table 10: Share of Private Operators by Service

Type of Service	*Percentage*
Urban Operations	25%
Intra District and Rural Services	30%
Inter District Services	50%
Inter State Operations	50%

Based on the information presented above, the possible business opportunities for private operators in India for different types of operations are presented in Table 11.

Table 11: Business opportunities for Private Operators

Type of Service/Year	*Scenario 1*			*Scenario 2*		
	2006	***2011***	***2016***	***2006***	***2011***	***2016***
Urban Operations	19086	26632	38169	14885	21182	27995
Intra District and Rural Services	59498	60745	62099	59498	60745	62099
Inter District Services	46303	50948	56097	46303	50948	56097
Inter State Operations	17644	20207	23142	17644	20207	23142
Total Requirements	142530	158531	179508	138329	153081	169333
Estimated fleet in operation in 2006	50000					
Augmentation needed	92500	108531	129508	88329	103081	119333

Thus, there is enough scope for private operators to consider this as a business activity. However, the government needs to develop appropriate strategies and policies to encourage private sector participation.

8. REQUIREMENTS TO BE MET BY PUBLIC OPERATORS (SRTUs)

The requirement of fleet that need to be operated by SRTUs, after adjusting for private sector involvement, is presented in Table 12. Thus the number of additional buses to be procured in different years for both the desirable and minimum scenarios is also included in Table 12.

Table 12: Business Opportunities for SRTUs Operators and Additional Fleet required

Type of Service/Year	*Scenario 1 (desirable)*			*Scenario 2 (minimum)*		
	2006	*2011*	*2016*	*2006*	*2011*	*2016*
Urban Operations	57258	79895	114508	44656	63546	83984
Intra District and Rural Services	138829	141739	144899	138829	141739	144899
Inter District Services	46303	50948	56097	46303	50948	56097
Inter State Operations	17644	20207	23142	17644	20207	23142
Total Requirements	260033	292787	338645	247431	276439	308121
Fleet as on March 2006	112380	112380	112380	112380	112380	112380
Fleet to be Procured	147653	180407	226265	135051	164059	195741
Fleet as on March 2006	112380	112380	112380	112380	112380	112380
Additional Fleet to be procured	147653	180407	226265	135051	164059	195741

9. COMPETITIVE ADVANTAGES OF SRTUs

Currently SRTUs are playing a key role and they have built huge organizational capital in terms of:

- Huge Fleet Strength
- Vast network of services
- Significant infrastructure in terms of depots, workshops, and bus terminals
- Management capabilities in terms of traffic management, fleet management, transport engineering capabilities, and human relations.

These capabilities of SRTUs need to be further strengthened in the national interest. Experience suggests that the private operators will not be able to replicate these facilities in the near future and they will not be able to scale up their services to the desired level. Experiences of Madhya

Pradesh and Orissa shows that even closing SRTUs can be a costly proposition. This money is better spent on strengthening these Public corporations. Thus a positive policy framework and a strong regulatory institution are essential to create a favorable environment for both SRTUs and private operators, to ensure quality service to the stakeholders.

10. POLICY PRESCRIPTIONS TO REVITALIZE THE PASSENGER TRANSPORT SECTOR IN INDIA

SRTUs are providing concessions to many sections of commuters. The revenue losses from student concessions are currently estimated at Rs.2,000 crores and increasing at 10% every year. This burden needs to be shared by the States, SRTUs and students in the ratio of 50 : 25 : 25.

The States should stop viewing public transport services as a source of revenue. Global experience shows that public transport services on the contrary are subsidized by governments. There is a wide variation in Motor Vehicle tax among States. The States should move towards a common tax structure preferably close to a nominal life time tax situation on public transport services. The rate can be 5.5% Motor Vehicles Tax as a benchmark rate during the XI Plan period.

SRTUs will continue to operate rural services and certain urban services which are loss making. About 20% of the losses incurred by the SRTUs can be attributed to this factor alone. The SRTUs need to be compensated for these operations. The resources for compensating the SRTUs for these operations may be raised by way of a cess levied on luxury and express buses, and as Deficit Charges from private operators who are unlikely to operate on loss making routes in the interior rural areas and urban agglomerations. The cess needed could be just 50 paise per ticket on Inter-state and Inter-district operations.

Use of Information Technology by STUs should be encouraged for improving operational efficiency and passenger convenience. Use of alternative fuels like compressed natural gas and bio-fuels should be encouraged through specific plan schemes during the XI Five Year Plan. The expenditure should be borne by the Governments initially for a period of 3 years.

The accumulated debt burden of the SRTUs is estimated to be around Rs. 8000 crores. It is felt that at least 50% of the outstanding debts should be taken over and discharged by the Centre and the States.

In addition, a financial package of about Rs.50,000 crores during the XI Plan period by both central and state governments for improving the public transport system is an urgent necessity. This could be justified in view of the benefits that would accrue to over 20 million passengers using SRTU services on any given day. This is much more cost effective investment compared to the investment of about Rs.12,000 crores to Rs.15,000 crores required for building a Metro rail system in one State capital in the country which would probably cater to only about one million passenger trips per day. Jawaharlal Nehru National Urban Renewal Mission (JNNURM) funds could take care of part of this financial package.

The financial implications of all the measures proposed above do not add up to more than Rs.25,000 crores for the entire period of the XI Five Year Plan for the Central Government.

Similarly the support required from all the State Governments put together will come to about Rs.30,000 Crores for the entire Plan period. Thus the annual support needed from the Central Government would be only Rs.5,000 crores and that from all the State Governments about Rs.6,000 crores annually. The information on financial implications (Centre and States) is presented in Table 13.

Table13: Financial Implications of Various Policies for Center, States and SRTUs

Items	*Suggestion*	*Financial Implication*	*Contribution from Centre*	*Contribution from States*	*STUs*
MV tax	Benchmark MV tax Rate above this governments has to bear	Rs.800 crores per year	Losses to be compensated by Center for Three years	States to Bear the Loss after three years	
Students Concessions	Policy for revision of fares No indiscriminate issue of passes	Rs.1500 crores annually	No obligation	States to bear 50% of the costs	SRTUs to bear 25% of the costs Students 25%
Univeral Service Obligation	Service goals to be specified	30% of the losses of all corporations can be attributed to this	To prescribe national benchmarks To support urban services	States to compensate SRTUs for losses incurred on this. State Government can collect cess on luxury and express services buses for this	SRTUs will be compensated only based on achieving some benchmark performance standards
Fleet Augmentation	Fleet Augmentation plan to be made	Rs.10,000 crores total for five years	Centre to bear 25% of this through capital contribution. Also to reduce duties and excise on bus chassis	States to bear 25% through capital contribution. Also to reduce Sales Tax on bus body building and spare partsStates to guarantee loan	SRTUs to raise this through borrowings from Financial Institutions
Capital Support	To create clean balance sheet	Aggregate cumulative borrowings of all statesRs.8000 crores (estd)	Centre to share 25% of the accumulated borrowings	States to share 25% of the accumulated borrowings	SRTUs to service 50% balance borrowings

11. ROLE OF PRIVATE OPERATORS

At present, most of the private operators are operating less than two buses. Fleet operators owning more than 50 buses are very few and they perceive there is no level playing ground between SRTUs and large fleet operators. Due to innumerable number of private operators and the absence of any regulatory mechanism, they have not created any large scale passenger amenity centers like bus shelters, bus stands etc. Most of them do not maintain proper records. The private operators were mostly for policy and tax concessions than financial concessions. They are keen that whatever concessions that are extended to SRTUs should be made available to them also. As a corollary, they should also be willing to bear some of the social responsibilities or pay though universal service obligations (USO). They would like to have a stable policy regime on licensing, privatization, fare structure, students' concessions, uneconomic routes, etc. The policy should be framed such that this sector can attract larger and corporate operators. They can be given license for a cluster of routes to make it viable for larger operators. They will have no problems in sourcing funds from banks if the policy prescriptions are clear. Any support should be contingent upon private operators being obliged to maintain all service records and proper documentation on the lines of SRTUs.

12. CONCLUSIONS

This paper outlines an analysis of both public and private sector bus operations, analyzes the demand for public transport system, provide policy inputs for revitalizing public transport system and suggests a revival package for sustainable development.

In the VII Five Year Plan review it was decided to encourage private sector participation as it was thought that SRTUs alone may not be in a position to cater to the growing demand for passenger transport services. The absence of a comprehensive passenger transport policy and regulatory framework has resulted in the retarded growth of the bus transport sector and proliferation of personalized transport vehicles and some unsafe modes of transport.

The SRTUs physical and financial performance is commendable. The fleet strength of SRTUs as a share of the total number of buses in the country declined from 45.4 per cent in 1976 to about 20 per cent today *i.e.*, in 2006. The capital contribution to SRTUs from Governments is estimated to be around Rs.8,000 crores but the value of the assets owned by all the SRTUs far exceeds this and is around Rs.15,000 crores taking into account the rolling stock, the lands, buildings, and other items of infrastructure owned by them. In operational parameters SRTUs show considerable variation among states. Some States show consistently good physical performance. Overall fuel efficiency in STUs has improved from 4.41 km per liter (kmpl) to 4.78 kmpl during 1995-96 to 2004-05. However, the share of the fuel costs for the STUs at the all India level has increased from 25.20 % in 2000-01 to 35.66% in 2005-06 mainly due to phenomenal increase in fuel prices.

SRTUs are among the biggest employers in the country with nearly 700,000 people employed by them directly with substantial indirect employment also being generated by them. The Staff per bus ratio of SRTUs has been steadily declining and is presently at 6.90 persons in 2004-05. In spite of the reduced staff per bus ratio the personnel costs of SRTU operations has steadily increased over the years from 395 ps/km in 1995-96 to 687 ps/km in 2004-05 at an annual compounded average increase of 5.69% mainly due to wage revisions. The 'No Growth Policy' also affects SRTUs in achieving efficiencies as on the one hand their growth opportunities are sealed and, on other hand, they cannot go in for a rationalization of the work force.

The annual revenues of all the SRTUs is in the order of Rs.20,000 crores; but, most of them are incurring losses mainly due to students concession, excessive MV (passenger) Tax, rise in fuel prices and obligation to maintain uneconomical routes. Public perception as per Indian Institute of Management, Bangalore study reveal that most people prefer a state monopoly or coexistence of state owned and private operators. Public are against the monopoly of private operators. The private operators are equally in a quandary about their role and future prospects. The majority of the operators are small fleet operators who operate with less than 2 buses and their sustainability and viability are always a problem.

SRTUs have a strong role to play as they have built a huge organizational capital in terms of the huge fleet strength, vast network of services, significant infrastructure in terms of depots, workshops, and bus terminals, management capabilities in terms of traffic management, fleet management, transport engineering capabilities, and human relations.

In order to revitalize this sector, there is an urgent necessity to rationalize MV (passenger) Tax to about 5.5% of the earnings. The undertakings need to be reimbursed the revenue losses incurred with respect to students concessions and uneconomical routes. The Central and State Governments should help SRTUs to reduce their accumulated debt burden of Rs.8,000 crores at least by 50 percent. In addition, financial support of Rs.50,000 crore for the entire Eleventh Plan period is essential to put this sector in sustainable mode. This works out to an annual commitment of Rs.4,000 crores by Central Government and Rs.6,000 crores by all the State Governments put together. JNURM funds could be utilized for this purpose.

There is a need to encourage big private operators, capable of operating more than 100 buses, providing a long-term sustainable policy for their effective participation. However, this support may be provided only if they maintain all the records regularly similar to that of SRTUs.

REFERENCES

Ramanayya, T.V., Nagadevara, V, and Shyamal Roy. (2003), Comparative Study of Nationalised and Non- Nationalized Transport Services and Facilities in Karnataka, Sponsored by KSRTC, Government of Karnataka.

Ramanayya, T.V. Ramesh, G. and Ravi Kumar, R. (2005), Holistic Organizational Transformation Strategies (HOTS) for APSRTC, report submitted to Government of Andhra Pradesh.

Ramanayya, T.V. and Ramesh, G. (2007), Revitalization of Passenger Transport Sector in India, report submitted to the Association State Road Transport Undertakings.

Nagadevara, V. and Ramanayya, T.V. (2007), Factors affecting passenger satisfaction levels – a case study of Andhra Pradesh State Road Transport Corporation (India), 10th International conference on competition and ownership in land passenger road transport, Hamilton, Australia.

Ramesh, G. and Ramanayya, T.V. (2007), Economic Contribution of Public Passenger Transport Organisations — An application of EVA^{R} methodology, *VISION — The Journal of Business Perspective*, Vol. 11, No.3, July-Sept.

23

"PUBLIC OR PRIVATE?" PASSENGER PERCEPTION OF BUS TRANSPORTATION IN GOA[1]

Anand Venkatesh
Tuba Modassir
Aditya Bhagat
Sampada Dev
Pratik Nowlakhe
Shashikant Ganti

ABSTRACT

It is a commonly held view that state transport undertakings need to be privatised. It is also perceived that the service levels provided by private operators is far superior to that of state transport undertakings. The present study examines this view by comparing the service levels of Kadamba Transport Corporation (KTC), a Government of Goa Undertaking and the private bus operators in Goa. The main objective of the study was to analyse the relative efficacy of KTC vis-à-vis private operators. The study attempts to do this by means of observation techniques, indepth interviews and primary surveys. The performance indicators for KTC and Private Operators were compared by soliciting the perception of passengers on these performance indicators. Data was collected through a questionnaire returned by 218 passengers which was subjected to regression analysis. Based on our findings, we challenge the view that state transport undertakings, particularly government corporations, need to be privatised. We also conclude that the current service levels of KTC need to be improved and an effective regulatory mechanism for Private Bus Operators should be initiated.

1. INTRODUCTION

Kadamba Transport Corporation Limited (henceforth referred to as KTC) is a Government of Goa Undertaking, registered under the Companies Act 1956. It was established in October 1980 to provide regular, reliable, comfortable and safe transport service to the people of Goa.

Prior to the establishment of KTC, passenger road transport was in the hands of the private operators. Private bus operators were unwilling to operate along low earning routes in the interior villages of Goa. KTC was set up with the objective of connecting these interior villages to urban areas in order to assist in the socio-economic development of the rural areas.

The corporation runs its services parallel to private operators and has to compete with them on almost all routes. Only three major trunk routes, namely Panjim-Vasco, Panjim-Margao and Margao-Vasco routes have been nationalised by the government and are serviced only by KTC buses.

The capital city Panjim and its surrounding areas are serviced primarily by buses run by private operators. These private operators resort to unfair practices such as not issuing tickets and heavy undercutting of fairs. KTC faces a stiff competition from these private operators mainly due to two reasons. First, unfair practices followed by the private operators and secondly fewer KTC buses operating on the route.Generally, private operators provide a poor level of service to passengers in terms of staff behaviour, crowding of buses, cleanliness and punctuality. But given the lack of alternatives on these routes, passengers are compelled to travel by private buses.

To eliminate these problems, KTC has striven to introduce more buses and offer high quality passenger service. In order to do so, it is essential to understand the passenger's perception of the current situation as well as their needs. This paper attempts to find the indicators of passenger satisfaction and measure the same for KTC as well as private operators. By drawing out comparisons between the two, this paper attempts to understand the service perception and highlight issues from a passenger perspective. The outline of this paper is as follows: In the following Section the objectives of the study are stated. This is followed by an overview of bus transportation scenario in goa in Section 3, which puts the study in proper perspective. The methodology adopted for the study is elaborated in Section 4. Section 5 presents a comparative analysis between KTC and private bus services in terms of passenger perception of various service attributes. In Section 6 the results of the empirical analysis have been presented. In Sections 7 and 8 the conclusions and key findings respectively have been stated.

2. OBJECTIVES OF THE STUDY

- To understand the bus transportation scenario in Goa state.
- To bring to light **specific performance and passenger satisfaction indicators** for KTC and private bus services and identify characteristics of service delivery associated with 'high quality' service.
- To evaluate **comparative performance indicators** for KTC bus service vis-à-vis private bus services.
- To **highlight issues** from a **passenger perspective**, which would assist in identifying appropriate corrective actions that need to be taken.

3. THE BUS TRANSPORTATION SCENARIO IN GOA: AN OVERVIEW

Bus Transportation in Goa has two major players, viz., KTC, the state owned transport corporation and private operators. KTC is the single largest bus operating body with around 432 vehicles in 2004-05. However when viewed against the total number of passenger buses in Goa, this is just about 10-15% of the total vehicles. Thus private operators, as a unit own and operate anywhere between 3000 to 4000 buses. The limited number of buses, coupled with the requirement of KTC to service uneconomic routes, reduces its ability to compete with private operators. Though the state transport department does talk about encouraging "healthy competition" in bus transportation, the same is conspicuous by its absence. On one hand, while KTC is highly regulated in virtually every aspect, particularly pricing, as well as provision of socially obligatory services, the private operators, by default run only on profit making routes. Moreover, private bus transportation in Goa is run by a powerful lobby of businessmen flout the existing regulations. From our discussions and interviews with KTC officials, it was evident that KTC does not have an appropriate investment policy. They have to operate with a relatively older fleet. Private operators too operate buses that have crossed the permissible age limit. These buses are highly polluting as well as unsafe. Also, private operators do not follow the mandatory practice of issuing tickets to passengers and hence data regarding revenue is extremely unreliable and obviously passenger taxes paid by private operators has been observed to be less than KTC. Some of the physical performance indicators as well as financial performance for KTC are provided in Annexures I and II respectively. It can be seen therein, financial profitability of KTC has been declining over the years. Though there has been an increase in some physical productivity indicators, the same has not translated for into better financial performance. Also, a major cause for concern has been declining load factors in KTC. Perhaps one may have to exercise a bit of caution in interpreting the same as a pure decline in demand as load factor has a supply side element as well. It could corroborate our earlier mentioned point that KTC has to deploy its fleet in rural areas where demand is sparse unlike private operators who ensure that they operate along the financially lucrative routes in Goa and also do not provide buses during late evenings and night time. Thus one observes that despite being one of India's prime tourist destinations, public bus transport in Goa leaves a lot to be desired.

4. METHODOLOGY

4.1 Research Design

As mentioned earlier, the main objective of the study was to analyse the relative efficacy of KTC vis-à-vis private operators. The study attempted this by means of observation techniques, in depth interviews as well as primary surveys. The area of study was Panjim city and adjoining areas. Panjim was chosen firstly because it is the capital city of Goa and secondly, it was observed that despite being a key commercial center, the level of bus services was not up to the mark, both qualitatively and quantitatively.

In order to understand the market for bus services in Panjim city, the observation technique was employed. This involved traveling in both KTC and private operators' buses and observing the behaviour of passengers and bus staff. Apart from this, factors such as frequency of operation, punctuality, condition and cleanliness of the bus, driving habits, passenger comfort, availability of alternative modes of transport, etc. were also observed. These observations enabled us to formulate and test certain hypotheses pertaining to passenger perceptions.

Apart from observation techniques, in depth interviews with drivers, conductors and passengers of both KTC as well as private buses were conducted. Interviews with officials of KTC were also conducted. It proved very difficult to obtain any co-operation from private operators both for data as well as for qualitative information. These helped us to obtain valuable qualitative information regarding various features of bus services in Goa and customer perception of KTC as well as private bus services. The observation studies and interviews were conducted during different times of the day so as to clearly understand differences between peak and off peak bus travel characteristics.

The qualitative techniques mentioned above helped to gather useful inputs for formulating the structured questionnaire. This questionnaire aimed at eliciting responses from passengers on various dimensions of bus travel and service. Responses were obtained using a five point Likert scale, which were then used for statistical analysis. For each attribute, the respondent was asked to rate KTC as well as private bus services. Prior to administering the questionnaire to the actual sample, it was pre tested through a pilot survey. Based on the pilot survey, the necessary modifications were made and the final version of the questionnaire was prepared.

4.2 Data Collection

The study was mainly based on primary data collected through surveys. The units for the primary surveys were passengers and staff of KTC and private buses. Data from statistical statements of KTC, RTO records as well as and other KTC publications were used for background research. As mentioned before, the study was conducted in Panjim city and the surrounding areas. The objective was to collect as representative a sample as possible. This was done by ensuring that the passenger profile covered all age groups, gender and occupations. The total number of passengers sampled was 218. Convenience sampling was used to collect data from passengers in different categories. Passengers were surveyed at several locations such as bus stops, workplaces, schools and colleges and on the bus during transit.[2]

4.3 Data Analysis

In order to analyse the passenger perception for KTC and private operators, both descriptive and inferential statistical techniques were used. Descriptive techniques essentially involved graphical depiction of preferences and contingency tables. The inferential statistical techniques used were multiple regression and testing the independence of attributes by means of chi square test for independence.

Two regressions, one each for KTC and Private Bus Services were run. For each regression, the specification of dependent and independent variables were identical. The dependent variable in the regression function was overall satisfaction from the bus service. Symbolically the relationship hypothesized was;

Overall satisfaction = a + b(beh) + c(safety) + d(wilstop) + e(buscond) + f(seatavail) + g(punc) + h(freq)

Where:

a = Intercept

Beh = Behaviour of the bus staff

Safety = perceived safety of the bus service

Wilstop = willingness of the driver to pickup passengers between stops

Buscond = Condition of the bus

Seatavail = availability of seat in bus

Punc = punctuality of service

Freq = frequency of bus

4.4 Sampling Plan

A sample of 218 people was taken which included passengers across ages, gender, occupation and various localities in Goa. We selected our sample through convenient sampling by randomly surveying the passengers. The Table 1 below shows the sample profile.

Table 1: Sample profile

BASE: All respondents	**218**
SEX	%
Male	35
Female	65
TOTAL	**100**
AGE	%
Below 18	34
18 - 23	35
24 - 30	18
31 - 40	6
41 - 50	3
50 and above	4
TOTAL	**100**
OCCUPATIONAL DISTRIBUTION	%
Student	66
Service/Job	28
Housewife	3
Business	1
Others	2
TOTAL	**100**

5. KEY FINDINGS FROM THE OBSERVATION STUDY

As mentioned earlier observation studies were carried out aboard private and KTC buses and on the bus stands. Few of the typical passenger comments have been recorded as shown in Box 1.

Box 1

COMMENTS BY PASSENGERS

"Stop private buses and introduce KTC buses on all routes. Behaviour of staff in private buses towards women and school children is absolutely bad and sometimes abusive"
"If KTC does not stop now and then at every minor stop I am willing to wait extra time for a KTC bus."
"More KTC buses"
"Conductors should not be harsh and very fast driving should be prohibited"
"Employees should be properly trained to cooperate with passengers"
"One way pass system should be introduced in all KTC buses"

5.1 KTC buses

KTC buses run between 7 A.M. to 6 P.M. in the evening making a total of 7 trips a day. The buses stop for approximately 30-40 seconds at each stop. Also, the number of stops for a KTC bus was much less in comparison to the private buses. Printed tickets are issued to passengers of KTC buses, a system which is not followed in private buses. Moreover, KTC buses were better maintained than the private buses. KTC buses were also less crowded with not more than eight people standing at any time in the bus. They also showcased a lot of promotional schemes and messages of public interest inside the buses.

5.2 Bus stands

At any point of time about four private buses were usually parked in line, very close to one another. On certain occasions, this led to freak mishaps. The conductors of private buses constantly engaged in verbal arguments amongst each other and fought for customers making the atmosphere uncongenial.

5.3 Private Buses

Private buses operated along fixed routes and made a definite number of trips each day. Overcrowding in private buses was rampant and passengers were filled in the bus indiscriminately, without any regard to passenger comfort or convenience. Private buses were usually dirty and badly maintained. Some of the seats were damaged and spit marks on the walls were a common sight. While smoking was strictly banned in KTC buses and the rule was strictly adhered to, it was sometimes flouted in private buses. They stopped at many places and took more time to reach the destination as compared to the KTC buses. The price structure of private bus services is similar to that of KTC. This raveled an often overlooked fact that private bus operators invariably follow public sector pricing practices. But private bus operators sometimes resort to undercutting of prices for regular passengers. As far as the behaviour of staff was concerned school going children and other passengers complained that the bus staff was sometimes rude to them. The poor service quality was clearly evident from the fact that there were no seats reserved for women or disabled people.

Table 2: Respondent Profile

Mode of Transport	*Users (%)*
Personal Vehicle	26
Rented Vehicle	2
Auto Rickshaw	5
Pilot Carrier	6
No Alternate Mode	58
Others	3

Table 2 above shows us the alternate modes of transport used by bus travelers. While 26% of the respondents sometimes used their personal vehicles, a mere 10%of the respondents used other modes of transport. It shows us that majority i.e. 58% respondents were totally dependant upon bus services.

Table 3: Vehicle Ownership Pattern

Vehicle Ownership Pattern	*Respondents (%)*
Four Wheeler	9
Two Wheeler	39
No Vehicle	51
Others	1

Table 3 gives an idea of the ownership pattern of vehicles among the respondents and the modes of transport they use. Out of the sample surveyed, 58% have said that they use only Bus as medium of transport which when extrapolated means a huge potential to be serviced by KTC. 26% have said that they use their personal vehicles apart from KTC buses for travel. Also 51% have said that they do not own a vehicle of their own which makes them completely dependant on buses for their travel needs.

5.4 Comparison between passenger perception of KTC and Private Bus Services

5.4.1 Overall Satisfaction Level

4.78% of the respondents have rated KTC service as very good compared to only 0.46% for Private. The proportion of respondents rating KTC services as Good is almost three times

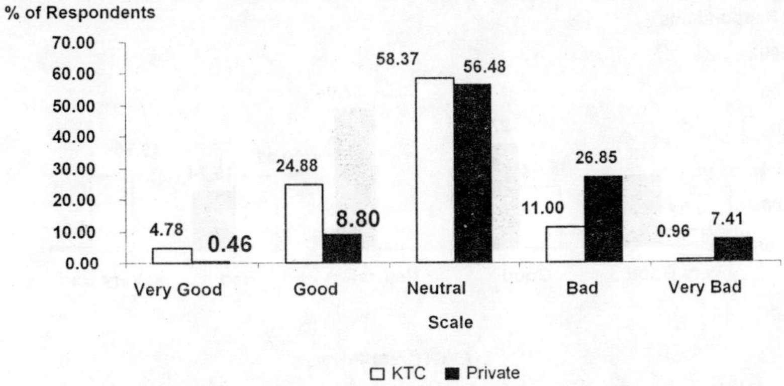

Fig. 1: Overall Satisfaction Level of Bus Services

that of private bus services. While the proportion of respondents rating private bus services as Bad or Very Bad is quiet high than that of KTC services. It is clearly seen that the satisfaction levels are much higher for KTC (see Fig.1.)

5.4.2 Specific Service Characteristics

Punctuality

It is seen here that almost 86% of respondents rate KTC services in Very Good - Neutral range while its only 45% for Private. 54% of the respondents feel that the Private operators are Bad or Very Bad with regard to punctuality. As a result KTC services are viewed as a lot more punctual than private operators (see Fig.2)

Willingness to stop buses

45% people say that the willingness to stop according to their requirements was good or very good in Private buses while only 20% said the same for KTC. 37% of the people were not happy with KTC in this aspect. Passengers consider Private operators more flexible when it comes to meeting their requirement of halting between stops (Fig. 3).

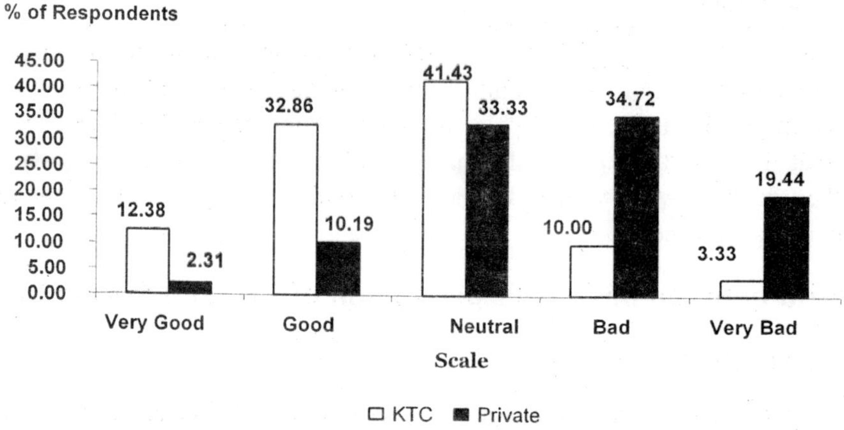

Fig. 2: Punctuality of Bus Services

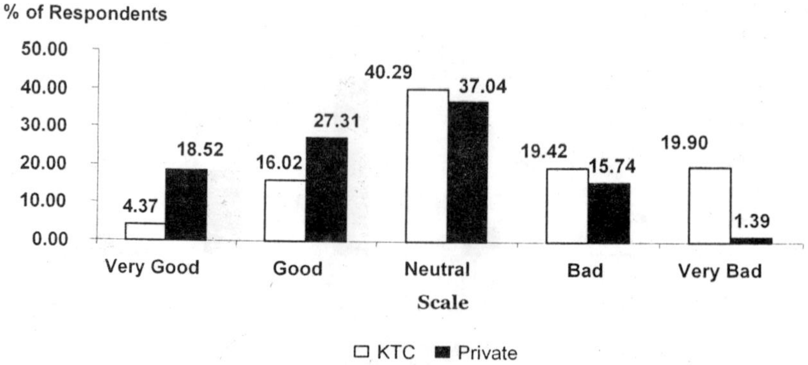

Fig. 3: Willingness for stopping the bus according to Passenger Requirements

Length of Trip

From the graph above, we can see that more people strongly agree that the time taken for a trip by a private bus service is appropriate while a majority gave a neutral rating on the same parameter for KTC bus service. (Fig. 4)

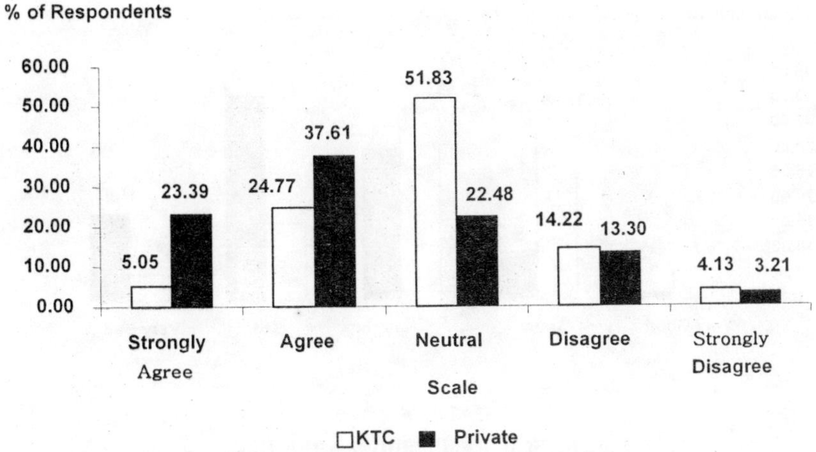

Fig. 4: Length of the Trip is Appropriate

5.4.3.On-Board Attributes

Bus Condition

29% people rate KTC buses as Good or Very Good as compared to 18% for Private operators. The number of people, who rated this factor as Neutral, stands almost equal for KTC and Private buses. On the whole KTC may be seen as slightly better than Private Buses but there is not a very large difference in the overall sentiment regarding cleanliness, maintenance and condition of the bus (Fig. 5).

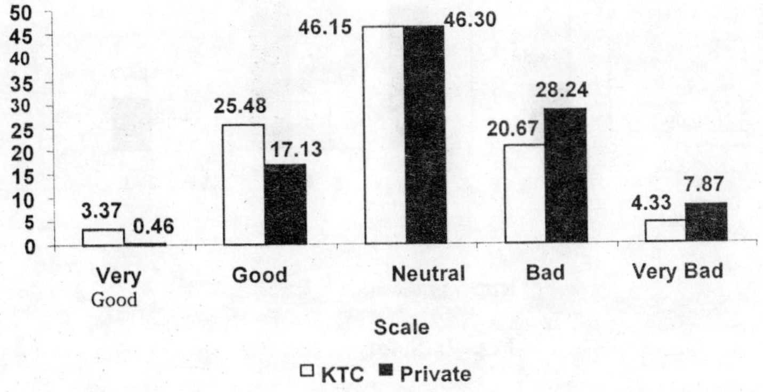

Fig. 5: Condition of the Bus

Seat Availability

58% feel that the availability of seats in the Private Buses is Bad, while 21% feel similarly for KTC. 41% have rated the seat availability in KTC as Good or Very Good. It indicates that there is over crowding in Private buses due to which there is low seat availability. (Fig. 6)

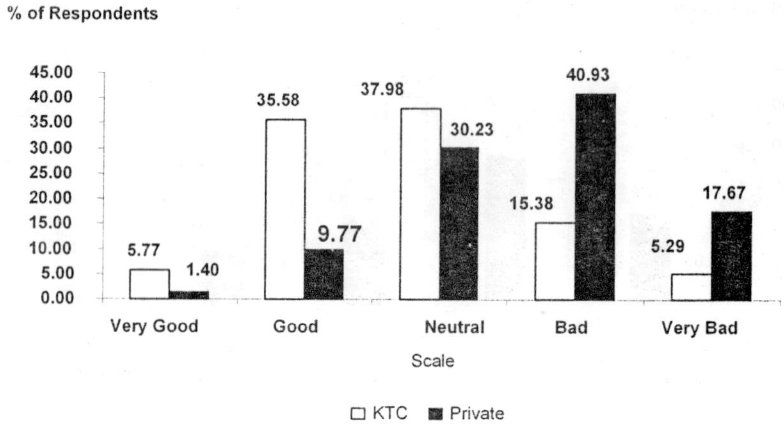

Fig. 6: Seat Availability on the Bus

Perceptions Regarding Safety

82% people rate KTC in the range of very good to Neutral. Approximately 86% people rated Private buses as Neutral, Bad or Very Bad. This clearly indicates that most people consider KTC much safer and Private Operators may be seen as rather rash due to overtaking and speeding. (Fig. 7).

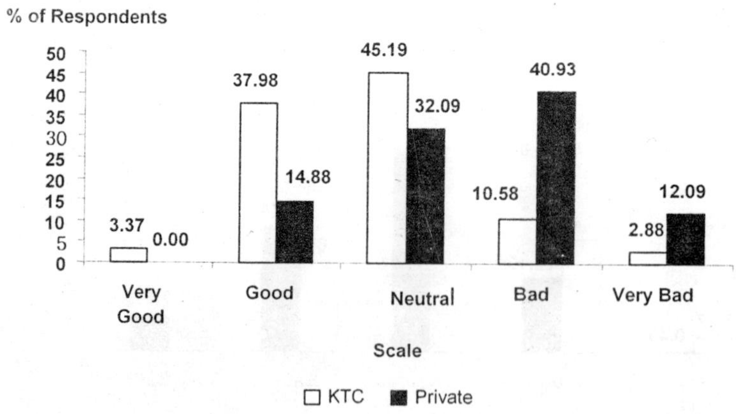

Fig. 7: Safety

Service Frequency

32% people rate frequency of KTC buses as Bad or Very Bad as compared to 26% for private buses. Thus, private buses have an edge over KTC buses with regard to frequency (Fig. 8).

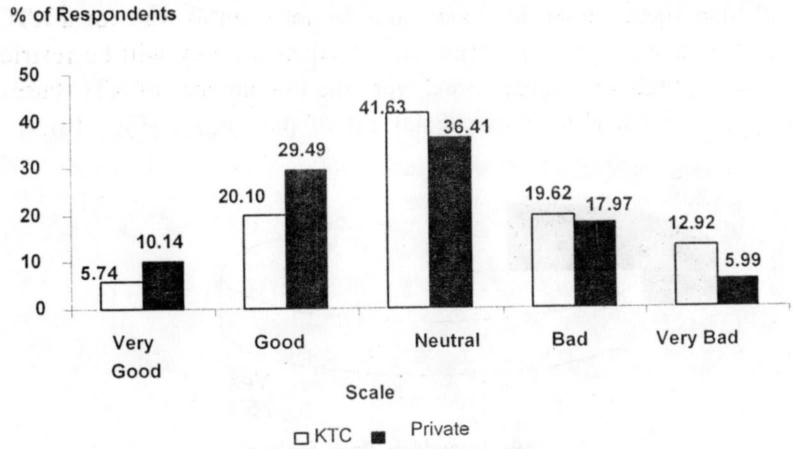

Fig. 8: Frequency of Buses

5.4.4. Staff-Related Service Aspects

Staff Behaviour

Around 43% of the people rated the behaviour of KTC conductors as Very Good or Good as compared to less than 11% for Private Operators. 8% people rated the behaviour of KTC bus staff as Bad or Very Bad as compared to 47% for private operators. There is a clear difference of opinion regarding politeness and cooperation shown by the driver and conductor for the two services. A very large number of people view private bus conductors as impolite and harsh (Fig. 9).

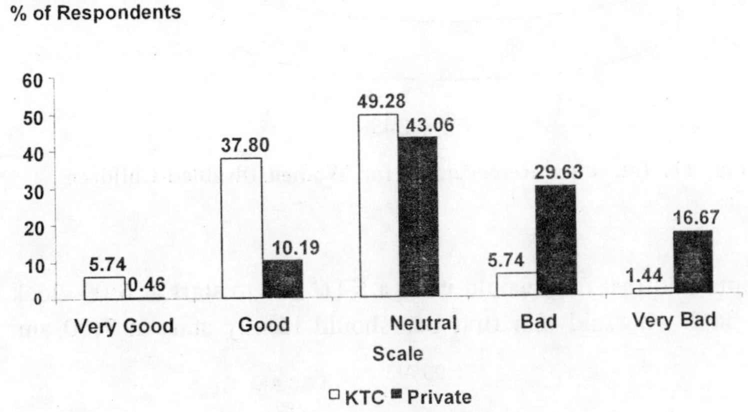

Fig. 9: Staff Behaviour

5.4.5. Passenger Perception on Special Services

Special Service

75% of the people are willing to travel only by KTC if they get discounts on fares in the form of a pass system. A majority of the remaining 25% would still prefer a KTC bus but they prioritise low travel time ahead of service levels and do not want to wait for a KTC bus for extra time. Thus, a Pass System would act as a hindrance to them as they will be restricted to a fewer number of buses. Other apprehensions expressed were the low number of KTC buses and inflexible timings which may be a problem for a particular set of passengers (Fig. 10).

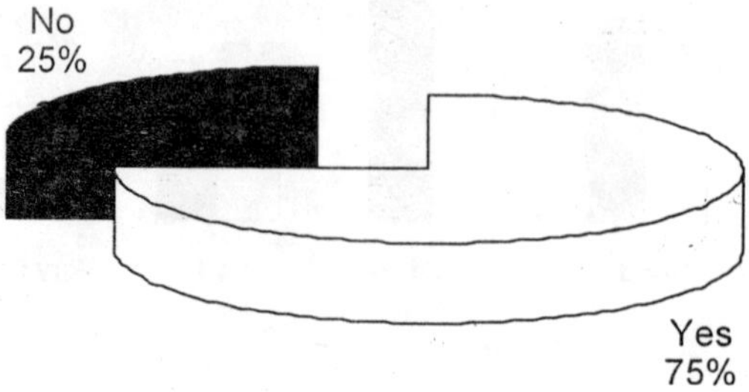

Fig. 10: Introduce Pass System

Reservation for Women/Children/Disabled

According to the research findings, 94% of the sample size finds it useful to have seats reserved for women, children, elderly or disabled. However people insist that the reservation would be beneficial only if it is implemented (Fig. 11).

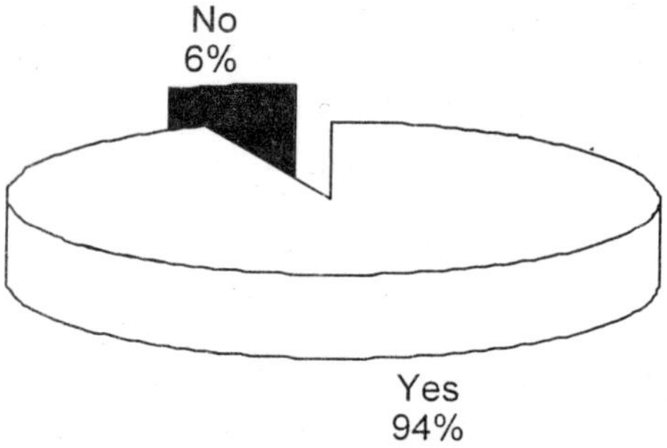

Fig. 11: Introduce Reservations for Women/Disabled/Children

Service Hours

38% of the people said that they would want a KTC bus to start at 6:00 clock in the morning closely followed by 36% who said that first bus should ideally start at 7:00 am. A majority of

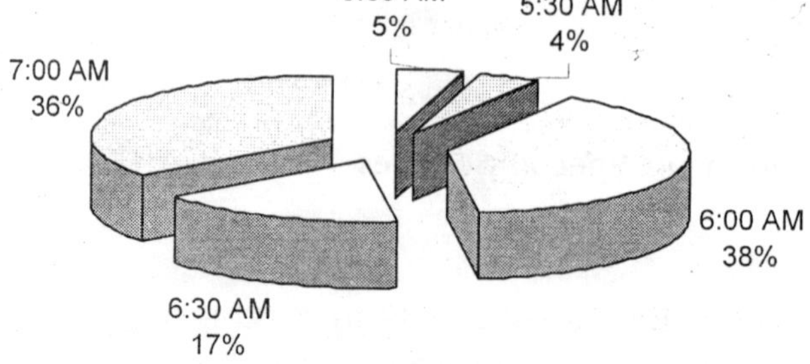

Fig. 12: Expected Starting Time

people also said that they would like the timings of the last bus to be extended to 9'O clock in the night followed by 26% who said the last bus should start at 10'O clock (Fig. 12).

5.4.6. Passenger Attitude towards Kadamba Bus Service

Trade off between service hours and willingness to pay extra

Amongst the total of 62 people who perceived the overall service levels to be Very Good or Good, 35% of the respondents were not ready to pay extra for the desired service, whereas the remaining 65% of the respondents were willing to pay extra for the desired service The breakup for the amount to pay extra is shown in the chart below (Fig. 13).

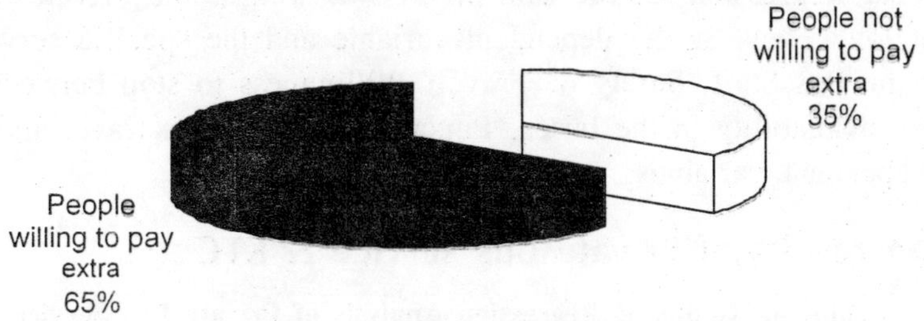

Fig. 13: Overall Service Level v/s Willingness to Pay Extra

Willingness to Pay extra

46% of the people would not be willing to pay extra even if service quality was improved. 36% of the passengers say that they would pay Rs 1 to 2 extra while 15% would pay Rs 3 to 4 extra for the improved service levels (Fig. 14).

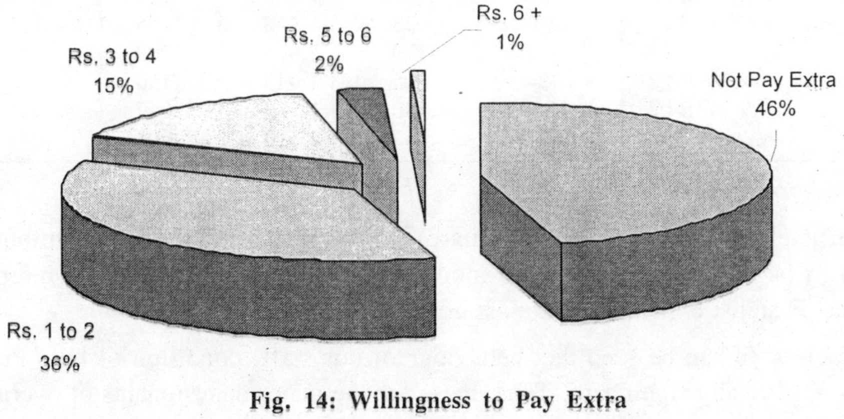

Fig. 14: Willingness to Pay Extra

Overall service time v/s willingness to wait for a KTC bus

In the chart above, out of the total number of people who found the overall service levels to be Very Good or Good (62 people), 39% of them Strongly Agreed or Agreed to wait for a KTC Bus, whereas the remaining 61% were Neutral, Disagreed or Strongly Disagreed to wait for the KTC Bus (Fig. 15).

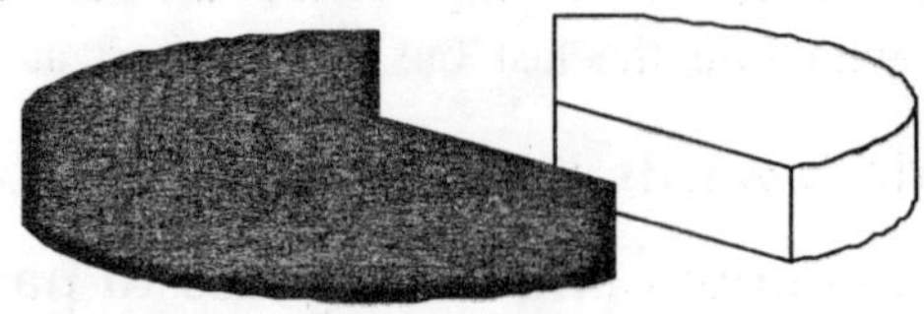

Fig. 15: Overall Service Levels v/s Willingness to Wait for a KTC Bus

6. RESULTS OF REGRESSION ANALYSIS

We ran Linear Regression for the data of KTC as well as the Private Bus Operators with "Overall Satisfaction Level" as the dependent variable and the specific service attributes such as Behaviour of the Bus Staff, Safety of Travel, Willingness to stop between stops, Condition of the buses, Seat availability in the buses, Punctuality of the bus travel and Frequency of the buses as the independent variables.

6.1 Regression results of Private bus service & KTC

Table 4: Results of Regression Analysis of Private Bus Service

Model		*Unstandardised Coefficients*		*Standardised Coefficients*	*t*	*Sig*	*95% Confidence interval for B*	
		B	*Std. Error*	*Beta*			*Lower Bound*	*Upper Bound*
1	(Constant)	.887	.302		2.937	.004	292	1.483
	Behaviour	.181	.058	.217	3.152	.002	.068	.295
	Safety	8.798E-02	.057	.103	1.545	.124	–.024	.200
	Wilingne	–.021	.047	–.028	–.448	.655	–.113	.071
	Condon	.161	.060	.179	2.663	.008	.042	.280
	Seat_Avl	7.736E-02	.054	.095	1.445	.150	–.028	.183
	Punct	9.913E-02	.050	.130	1.982	.049	.001	.198
	Freq	.136	.047	.187	2.890	.004	.043	.228

a. Dependent Variable: OVERALL

The coefficient of determination (R square) for the model is 29.4%. Even though R square doesn't seem to be particularly high, the model as a whole is significant as inferred from the p value of the F statistic, which is almost zero.

From Table 4, it can be seen that behaviour of bus staff, condition of bus, Punctuality and Frequency are statistically significant. Thus, these are the major determinants of overall satisfaction for the services of private operators.

A similar regression was run for KTC as well. The results of this regression are as reported in Table 5. R square for this model is 0.5. It can also be seen that behaviour of bus staff, condition of bus, Punctuality and Frequency are statistically significant. As opposed to private operators, variables like bus staff behaviour and safety are statistically significant for KTC. The coefficient of the "willingness" variable is 0.12 i.e., positive. This means that the overall satisfaction from KTC services increases with lower willingness to stop in between scheduled stops. This finding at first seems contrary to intuitive perception that passengers prefer to board and alight from buses as per their convenience. However, a closer look reveals that passengers attach a greater weight to travel time rather than boarding and alighting conveniences.

Table 5: Results of Regression Analysis of KTC Bus Service

Model		*Unstandardised Coefficients*		*Standardised Coefficients*			*95% Confidence interval for B*	
		B	*Std. Error*	*Beta*	*1*	*Sig*	*Lower Bound*	*Upper Bound*
1	(CONSTANT)	231	.198		1.168	.244	-.159	.621
	BEHAVIOUR	178	.058	.182	3.083	.002	.064	.292
	SAFETY	9.941E-02	.054	.111	1.848	.066	-.007	.205
	WILLING	.102	.038	.154	2.707	.007	.028	.176
	CONDTN	113	.047	.133	2.404	.017	.020	.205
	SEAT_AVL	5.934E-02	.044	.076	1.339	182	-.028	.147
	PUNCT	.291	.044	.372	6.569	.000	.204	.378
	FREQ	7.325E-02	.040	.107	1.843	.067	-.005	.152

a. Dependent Variable OVERALL

7. CONCLUSIONS

Based on our qualitative as well as quantitative analysis, the following are the conclusions of the study:

- The overall satisfaction levels of KTC's services were relatively higher than those for private operators' services. It is seen that virtually on every count of passenger satisfaction, KTC outscored the private operators.
- The common determinants of passenger satisfaction for both KTC and private operators were bus staff behaviour, bus condition, punctuality and frequency. However, aspects such as safety and timely travel were significant determinants of passenger satisfaction for KTC's services.
- KTC should retain its present policy of halting only at scheduled bus stops, as passengers seem to attach a premium to travel time. Thus, any attempt to replicate the private operators' "halt and ride" policy should be resisted by KTC.
- Another important distinguishing feature was behaviour of bus staff on which count KTC significantly outscored the private operators. However when viewed at an absolute level, we realise that there is still a lot of scope of improvement. The staff of KTC needs to be sensitized to the importance of cordial behaviour towards passengers.
- KTC should ensure optimal scheduling of its buses. Services should be available to passengers early in the morning as well as during later hours of the night.
- KTC should increase its fleet size, which would enable it to improve its service levels, both quantitatively as well as qualitatively. For this it requires financial support from the state government.
- Socially obligatory services of KTC need to be explicitly subsidised.
- Private operators should be strictly regulated and should not be allowed to flout rules.

8. KEY FINDING

This study challenges the commonly held view that state transport undertakings, particularly government corporations, need to be privatised. This is substantiated by the findings that overall service levels provided by KTC are far superior to that of private operators. An optimal solution would be to improve the current service levels of KTC and to initiate an effective regulatory mechanism for the Private Bus Operators.

ANNEXURE I

Fleet Utilisation and Load Factor for KTC

Year	*Fleet Utilisation (FU)(%)*	*Load Factor (%)*
1999-00	74	49.99
2000-01	76.6	52.73
2001-02	78	54.62
2002-03	79	57.09
2003-04	79.6	53.50
2004-05	82	51.07

ANNEXURE II

Financial Performance of KTC from 1999-00 to 2004-05

Year	*Total Revenue (Rs. Lakhs)*	*Total Cost (Rs. lakhs)*	*Loss (Rs. lakhs)*
1999-00	3030.41	3374.33	- 343.92
2000-01	3542.62	3921.81	- 379.19
2001-02	3872.23	4295.6	- 423.37
2002-03	4171.9	4548.72	- 376.82
2003-04	4614.17	5033.49	- 419.32
2004-05	4907.03	5811.95	- 904.92

Notes:

1. This was a project done by students of Goa Institute of Management (GIM) under the guidance of Prof. Anand Venkatesh
2. We could survey only a few passengers inside the bus as the heavy peak hour crowd prevented us from having any meaningful interaction.

REFERENCES

Button, K.J., (1995), Bus Deregulation: Ten Years on Policy Preview, *Tranport Reviews*, No.3.

Button, K.J., (1993), *Transport Economics*, Third Edition, Edward Elgar, England.

Cole, S., (2005), *Applied Transport Economics— Policy, Management and Decision Making,* Third Edition, Kogan Page Limited, England.

Dalvi, M.Q., (1997), *Transport Planning and Policy in India*, Himalaya Publishing House, Mumbai.

24

COMPETITION ISSUES IN THE ROAD GOODS TRANSPORT INDUSTRY (RGTI) IN INDIA WITH SPECIAL REFERENCE TO THE MUMBAI METROPOLITAN REGION

S. Sriraman
Anand Venkatesh
Manisha Karne
Vidya Mohite

ABSTRACT

Given the dominance of small operators in the industry, it is natural to expect a competitive regime to prevail. However, given that the industry is segmented in terms of market players and market makers, it has been an emerging feeling that this is a sector, which is prone to be dominated by some of the players and makers. It is against this background that this study was undertaken. The study reveals that the role of the middlemen is crucial in price fixation as well as in allocation of quantum of movement. But, given the large number of players, both operators and intermediaries, it is being ensured that the structure is driven by market forces. Though, there could be situations wherein these intermediaries seem to be colluding with each other in fixing freight rate as well as the conditions and terms of freight movement, the existence of a large number of these intermediaries especially in the significant sections of the overall movement reveals an overwhelming tendency towards a market determined revenue sharing arrangement. The Mumbai market reflects this scenario to a very large extent.

1. INTRODUCTION

Though emerging as a dominant mode the road goods transport sector in India has, it is observed, hardly been able to emerge out of the traditional unorganised framework over a period of time. It has been a widespread feeling that the market structure of the industry in terms of the supply of services is very highly competitive. Given the dominance of small operators, it is natural to expect a competitive regime to prevail. However, given the segmentation of the industry in terms of market players and market makers, it has been an emerging feeling that this is a sector, which is prone to be dominated by some of the players and makers. In the case of specialised traffic like movement of petroleum products, routine contractual traffic (big ones), it is most likely that there is absence of competition - in a market - where single buyers are faced with number of sellers of services. This argument can perhaps be extended to manufactured items like chemicals, pharmaceuticals, which are supplied in bulk all over the country. Even in the case of general freight where the small operators dominate (in terms of numbers), it is recognised that the role of the middlemen is crucial in price fixation as well as in allocation of quantum of movement as far as the small operators are concerned. In other words, it has been an evolving feeling that a significant part of the sector may not be really operating within a competitive market structure as is normally thought out to be. It is against this background that we felt the need for a detailed study on possible anticompetitive practices in the RGTI in India. This study was taken up at the instance of the Competition Commission of India.

Insights from Literature

Deregulation in the transport sector has taken place in many countries in the past two decades or so. It has been observed that the effects of deregulation have depended on the extent to which the industry was regulated earlier. However, broadly the effects have been as follows:

- The capacity available for common use has increased significantly with increasing dominance by highly competitive small operators.
- Rates have fallen considerably as a result of more capacity and introduction better technological features.
- Falling rates have benefited customers but with costs not reducing to such an extent, profit levels have fallen though operators offering higher levels of service have achieved higher profit levels.

The roads goods transport industry in India has never been regulated the way it has been in many other countries. But as mentioned earlier, a regulatory framework in the form of the MV Act has been in place since 1939. This did provide for restrictions on permits but over a period of time these have been relaxed to a very large extent permitting easy entry into the industry and for movement all over the country. This is perhaps the only deregulatory move that has taken place in India as far as the trucking sector goes. And the credit for this development goes to the Indian railways, which had no capacity to offer on a regular basis even with regard to bulk items. But as observed by the various Committees and pointed out by the different studies, the Motor Vehicle departments of the States have mainly focused on the collection of revenue (tax and otherwise) rather than on effective enforcement of the provisions of the Motor Vehicles Act (MV Act). As a result, an effective regulatory framework has, in our opinion, never been attempted to be put in place. This has emerged over the years as a major external impediment (in terms of a number of dimensions) to the effective growth of the trucking industry in India. This is a matter of concern especially when viewed in the context of an emerging globalised competitive economy. In this context, it becomes imperative to point out the major internal impediment that the industry faces in the form of its internal organisational structure, which has implications for efficient operations. It was observed earlier that the industry offered low rates in India. Basically, the industry is characterised by skews- large number of operators and users and sufficiently large number of intermediaries between these two players. The question - what are the agreements between the various players? Some are formal while most seem to be informal. These informal agreements appeared to be often highly iniquitous as a direct consequence of the intermediaries' access to information. The power the intermediaries exert over the industry is not, however, matched by the capital employed by them. This suggests that there is an imbalance here in the way the revenue is being shared by the various players in the industry. Clearly, there is a need to bring the intermediaries under the purview of regulation. However, effective interaction between the various elements of the industry needs to be encouraged by government policies, which are necessary for the healthy growth of the industry.

A survey of the literature related to the trucking sector put our study in the proper perspective. The study team believed that it needed to fill certain gaps. First of all, it was pertinent to take a critical look at the supply chain related to trucking, in the sense of who actually determined the price of trucking services and more specifically, the role of the operators and other intermediaries in determination of the price. The basic objective was to examine the possibility of price fixation at levels not really reflecting competitive benchmark rates. Thus, a related objective was to take a look at various costs related to operations and the returns derived thereby. Given the state of the market and knowledge of the cost structure, it was possible to make conjectures related to breaking even, earning of positive or negative economic profit, the rationale for overloading, and so forth. However, this required some understanding of policy and regulatory elements, which would ultimately have an impact on fixation of tariffs.

2. FREIGHT RATES, OPERATOR COSTS AND INDUSTRY PROFITABILITY

Despite the provision in the MV Act regarding fixing of fare and freight, no definite mechanism has been evolved for their determination and enforcement. Consequently, at present, there is no State, which has fixed the freight rates for the industry. We now turn to an examination of freight rates and operator costs in the Indian context with a view to assessing the profitability of operations. The objective behind this examination is to look at the trend in movement — in terms of increase or decrease in freight rates and then examine profitability of operators. Figure 1 below shows the interrelationships between various factors driving operator profitability.

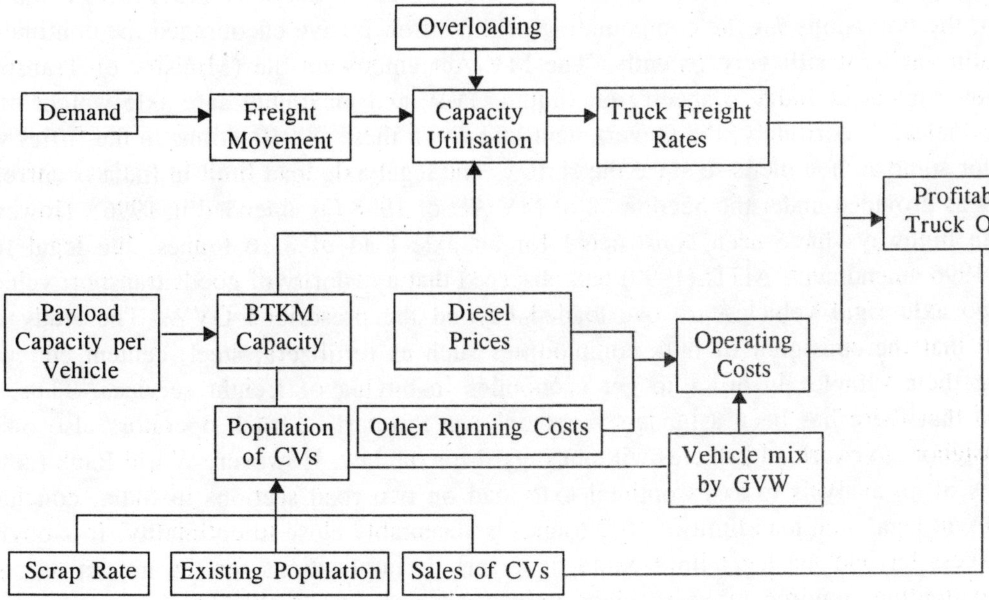

Fig. 1: Profitability of Truck Operators

Source: Deloitte Study (2003).

One point of view that has emerged over a period of time is that there has been only a gradual (though some what consistent) increase in freight rates in India due to the entry of a large number of operators. With increasing fuel costs, it is claimed that profitability has decreased considerably with many operators just able to break-even. It may be mentioned that the rate of inflation during the past few years has been hovering around 4.5 per cent on an annual basis.

Given a basic analytical model, an attempt was made to understand the profitability of operations for average freight rates on the **different routes.** Further, some simulation exercises, which take into account varying payloads, different distances in terms of total annual operations along with some deviations in the interest charged on truck loans were conducted to examine the potential profitability.

It was found that only for an aggregate distance of 90,000Kms. (around 300kms. per day) and loading to the extent of 15 tonnes, there was a reasonable return on almost all the routes. Our surveys of truck operators indicated that, on an average, a truck moves around 250-300 Kms. per day especially when they are involved in inter-regional movements. Given the lower limit of moving around 250Kms. (or even slightly less) there was a financial loss. Even with a possibility of covering a slightly greater distance, say, 275 kms., there could only be a very modest profit level if not a break-even situation for the industry. This has also pointed out by World Bank (2005). On a comparison of freight rates and estimated costs, it was then suggested that only in a competitive market, one could expect freight rates to vary little from costs.

The question arose how does an operator survive? To do so, the operator was required to overload - a common feature on Indian Highways. Though the MV Act is against overloading (the statutory provisions dealing with overloading are set out in Sections 113,114,194 and 200 of the Act), the provisions for the compounding of this offence have encouraged the continuance of overloading at least still very recently. The MV Act empowers the (Ministry of Transport) (MOT), Government of India to specify maximum GVW and maximum safe axle weight of all transport vehicles. Accordingly, the Government laid down these specifications in the fifties with provision for some ad hoc increase since the sixties. The legal axle load limit in India is currently 10.2 tonnes as provided under the Section 58 of MV Act of 1988 (as amended in 1996). However, most Indian highways have been constructed for an axle load of 8.16 tonnes, the legal limit before the 1996 amendment. AITD (1999) had observed that a majority of goods transport vehicles that are two axle rigid vehicles are overloaded beyond the prescribed GVW. The study also pointed out that the consignor of bulk commodities such as fertilizers, steel, cement etc. were overloading their vehicles in order to get economies in buying of freight services. Thus, the study noted that there has been a tendency not only on the part of truck operators also on the part of consignors to overload vehicles without regard for the law. However, World Bank (2005), on the basis of an analysis to asses optimal axle load on two road sections in India, concluded that the present legal axle load limit of 10.2 tonnes is acceptably close to optimality. It is obvious that any excess beyond the legal limit could have serious implications for the impact on roads and for the funding required to keep roads maintained at an acceptable level.

Given the pressures on margins, it was very clear that it is only with a certain level of overloading that operations turn out to be viable. This is a wide spread practice with axle loads well in excess of the legal limit — a practice aided significantly by laxity of enforcement of axle load controls by the concerned regulatory authorities in different States. Though it must be noted that a higher level of movement to the extent of 108000 or even 120000 Kms. could enable operations to be viable with the registered payload (simulation exercises relating to these figures revealed the trend towards viability of operations). Given a situation where overloading is no longer expected to be a possibility (as a result of Judicial intervention — judgment of Supreme Court on overloading, November 9, 2005 and strict implementation), it is more likely that the overall demand for trucking services (in terms of vehicles) at any point of time would increase these by shifting the demand curve for such services. This can no doubt result in a higher freight rate in the market. But the issue is: whether this higher realisation would eventually reach the operators? It is also a moot question whether a higher level of movement by trucks on a daily basis is possible given the existing barriers to free trade flows on an inter-State basis. In order to understand these issues, we examined the structure of the industry in terms of the market, its players, the relationships and the implications for the different players. Our entire analysis is based on surveys mainly conducted in the Mumbai Region and to a small extent in Goa and Satara.

3. THE INDUSTRY – ITS STRUCTURE, MARKET SURVEYS AND ANALYSIS

3.1 The Industry Structure: the Market Players

The structure of the road goods transport industry in India is very complex as it has always been identified (and continues to be so) as a system comprising of many players in the field which include among many but mainly the transport operators (who could be small or fleet operators providing the real haulage services), the user/consignor (constituting the ultimate demand for services), the intermediaries — booking agents/transport companies (who could be operators also) and brokers (who could be placed on either side of the booking agents and normally work for a commission). Figure 2 gives the most general picturisation of the structure of the industry in terms of the market players and their functions.

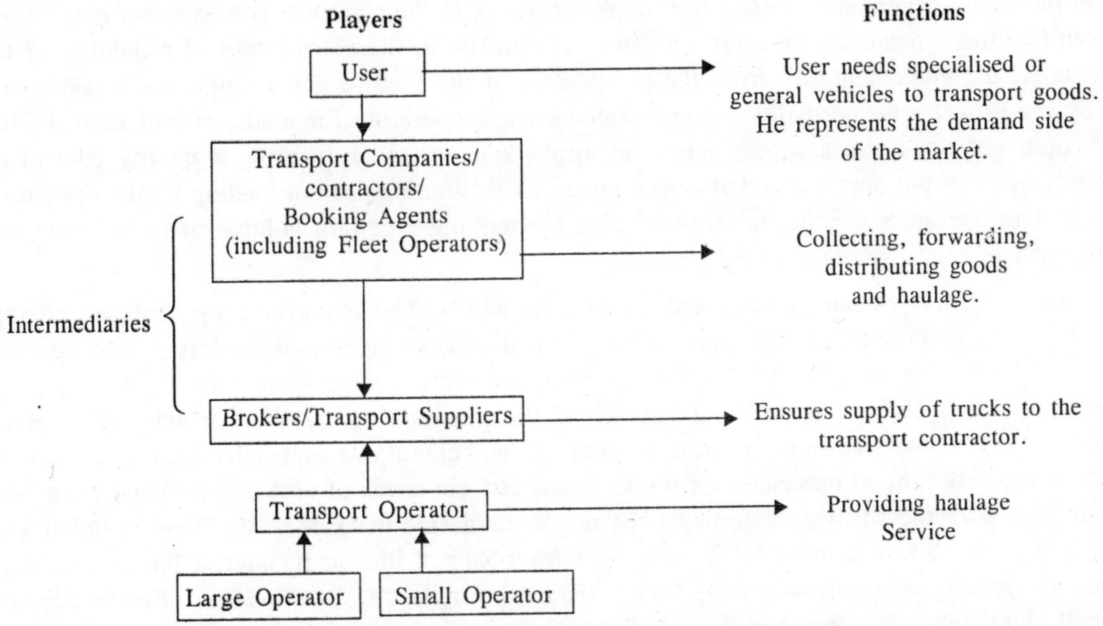

Fig. 2: Market Players and their Functions

Users: The users of road goods transport are the manufacturers, distributors, retailers of goods and the general public who are typically expected to represent the demand side of the market. Their choice of road transport, it appears, is influenced by a number of considerations including the inability of its main competitor, namely, the railways to provide wagons for loading on time. Above all, a relatively better customer orientation also provides the cutting edge. This gets reflected by lower transit time, reliability, etc. though freight rates may be marginally or even much higher.

Intermediaries: The intermediaries seem to play a significant role in the provision of road goods transport services. These can be normally of two categories, namely,

(a) Booking agents/Transport companies/transport contractors: Booking agents are firms or persons who accept and store goods, both parcels and bulk and arrange for their movement through operators. This agent is really the person who represents the demand i.e. he negotiates with and on behalf of the users. He is responsible for collecting, forwarding or distributing goods carried by goods carriages and also for cargo loss and damage claims while performing other customer service functions. In some cases, the agents own trucks and also function as operators. In addition to these services, the agents also advance money to operators (especially small ones) to help meet their working capital requirements and by discounting bills on unloading. As regards the volume of business handled by this category of intermediaries, it is generally accepted that they have a virtual monopoly of most inter-State and long-distance movement.

(b) Brokers/Commission agents/Suppliers of Vehicles: A Broker is normally expected to represent the supply side i.e., the truck operators, though in the past there have been booking brokers who have represented user interests for a commission. The broker takes a commission from the truck owners and ensures the supply of trucks to the transport company/booking agent. Given that the dependence on small operators is significant, there are issues of reliability of the operators, the movement etc. from the perspective of the User which is supposedly taken care of by the broker who normally is sought out by truck operators for loads. World Bank (2005) also observed the necessary role played by brokers in terms of ensuring a quality control on the reliability of the operator and also as a means of facilitating prompt loading by the operators. Large fleet operators depend on these brokers for moving a certain volume of traffic over and above what their own fleet would permit.

In the course of our surveys and discussions with different players, we made an attempt to find out the number of intermediaries — brokers and transport agents/contractors — who operated in the Mumbai Region. Broadly speaking, there are three areas from which most of these intermediaries operate. A significant location is the Masjid Bunder/ Wadi Bunder/ P.D'Mello (city) area. This has traditionally been the area of their operations especially till the last decade since when only limited movement of trucks in the city (in terms of area and timings) have been permitted. With the shifting of some of the major wholesale markets to the New Mumbai area and emergence of warehousing facilities in New Mumbai and Bhiwandi, intermediaries have been operating from these two areas as well. Though the market in the city area (in terms of intermediaries) is still significant, their number in the other two areas is increasing fast. Though a provision for a major truck terminal has been made by the MMRDA at Wadala, the lack of facilities here has been a major factor inhibiting truckers from using this facility. As a result, the intermediaries have also not moved into this area from the city. MMRDA sources say that work on readying the terminal for use is in full swing and is expected to be over by end 2006.

As for booking agents/transport companies, it estimated that there are around 5000 of them operating in the Mumbai region. About 1200 of these are formally associated with the Bombay Goods Transport Association (BGTA) as members. On further queries, we understand that most of these members were partnership or proprietary concerns with the remaining being private limited companies. Most of them are involved as booking agents only while a good number are operators with limited fleet capacity. Some of them are also custom agents and multimodal operators in addition to being booking agents. Custom agents are all registered with the Bombay Customs House and are all members (totaling 1162 presently) of the Bombay Custom House Agents Association.

Operators: Operators are expected to provide the services in terms of movement. The truck ownership profile in India as brought out in the CIRT study (1998) is given in Figure 3.

The current ownership profile is somewhat different from what existed in1971 (as given by NCAER, 1979) when the number of operators owning up to 5 vehicles constituted nearly 98 per cent of the fleet. The situation was only slightly different in the early 1990s when it was estimated that the 95 per cent of the vehicles belong to those operators who had less that 5

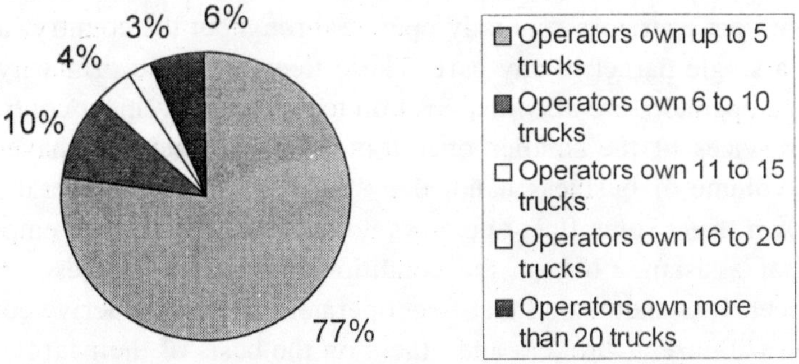

Fig. 3: Truck Ownership Profile in India

Source: Deloitte (2003).

vehicles. This reflects a definite change in the pattern of ownership though it is still true that small owner operators dominate the same. We have not been able to get any idea regarding the relevant ownership profile in the context of vehicles registered in the Mumbai region. The number of goods vehicles in the region totaled nearly 200,000 in 2001. Given that there are a number of operators from other States plying their vehicles in the region, it was considered neither feasible nor necessary to examine this profile. However, some figures are available in terms of the regular operators who ply their vehicles between JNPT and different locations. There are nearly 100 operators who own around 25 vehicles while there are 50 of them who own around 50 vehicles and 10 to 15 operators own around 100 vehicles. There are very few of them owning much more than 100 vehicles. These figures are based on discussion with some of the port based container truck operators.

Broadly, the operators can be categorised as follows:

1. Small Truck Operators: This category includes the single (or small truck operators owning 1-5 trucks) truck operator, who are very large in number. Entry barriers are low in the sense that: (*a*) there are low capital requirements, (*b*) Ease of availability of capital though at high cost, (*c*) very little expertise required in terms of educational skills, and (*d*) ease of obtaining driving licenses and permits. The presence of a large number of operators has led to a fragmented industry structure. Moreover, though the entry into this market is supposedly easy, information regarding availability of freight is a formidable problem. There is dependence on the brokers who give them business. The small operators, as can be seen from the above Figure, just provide the haulage service. The small operators are involved mainly in the physical movement of goods and depend on brokers and other fleet operators who, in turn, depend on booking agents for obtaining business. The small operators are not in a position to perform functions of aggregating, handling, delivering of cargo and marketing. These operators do not have the geographical reach and necessary infrastructure to tap business on a continuous basis and hence are forced to rely on brokers. They do not come into direct business contact with the users. This was the feedback from all most all the small operators interviewed so far. Though the exit option also seems likely in regard to these operators, it is observed it is a very difficult one since there is no alternative to this work. Therefore, there is hardly any scope for easy exit.

2. Fleet operators: The Large fleet operators are small in number even in a region like Mumbai. The large fleet operators generally operate throughout the country, and have the capacity to even transport a single parcel in any part. These fleet operators primarily work on a hub and spoke model. Large operators are also in a position to bid for movement contracts with companies. They utilise the services of the smaller operators when they need to have additional vehicles. Accordingly, the volume of business handled by them is normally several times more than the capacity of their own fleet. Some fleet operators do encourage their own employees to own trucks with some financial assistance but on the condition that these vehicles should be permanently attached to their fleet. It is understood that fleet operators attempt to derive considerable advantage in their interaction with users, brokers and others on the basis of their larger size and bargaining strength derived from size. But an emerging feature is the move from an asset-based model of operations to a non-asset based model.

3.2 The Industry Structure: The Market Makers?

The unique ownership profile has created middlemen who act as liaison agents. Our review of the sector in the Indian context revealed the sustained role of the middlemen. GOI (1966) pointed out the growing role of booking agencies which act as intermediaries and accept consignments for transport. GOI (1967) observed "the bulk of the trucks engaged in inter-city transport, which carry commodities which are comparatively and in smalls, have necessarily to depend on booking agencies" (p.48). GOI (1980) also observed the dependence of a majority of operators on goods booking agencies for their operations. Though the NCAER study (1979) found that more than 80 per cent of the small operators depended on booking agents, subsequent studies by CIRT (1994) and AITD (1999) revealed that about 70 per cent and 65 per cent of the operators depended fully on middlemen for their business. This is only one part of the story. Almost all the Reports/ Studies emphasise a significant role especially for the booking agents and a somewhat limited role for the broker (except for the CIRT study (1994) which reported a role for the broker in price fixation). In the context of booking agents, GOI (1980) specified three main types of their operations. The first relates to an agreement between the agent and the operator for a stipulated period during which the former arranges guaranteed freight at rates fixed in advance. Secondly, booking agents have day-to-day arrangements and offer goods to operators at prevailing market rates. Thirdly, the agent acts an intermediary between the consignor and the operator charging commission from both. Having received representations that booking agents have been exploiting the smaller operators by retaining high margins of commission on freight and charging exorbitant interest rates wherever they act as financiers, the Committee (GOI, 1980) looked into the issue but concluded that "we have not come across any concrete evidence to show that booking agents exploit operators as they seem to be operating in a competitive market" (p.197). This was quite contrary to the opinion of an earlier Committee (GOI, 1967) which admitted the existence of high margins though these may not have been as much as suggested by the operators.

The evidence that has emerged over quite some period of time is that the middlemen/ intermediaries, which include the booking agents and the brokers, are the dominant players in the market and they in fact are the real "makers" of the market. Given this feature, the issue is: who and/or what determines the freight rates? NCAER (1979) indicated that the booking agents, besides other functions, also had a role in fixing freight rates i.e., the rate charged to the user and the rate given to operators. AITD (1999) was more emphatic in observing that these two categories acted as the real power centers ('powerful agents') in the industry and therefore had a major role to play in determining freight rates. One emerging view is that as a result of significant increase in the number of operators in the industry, the competitive nature of the market has been strengthened as a result of which competitive rates prevail. However, it must be recognised that since the early nineties, freight movement in general has not been in tune with the growth in capacity in the trucking sector as a result of which average capacity utilisation over the period 1990-91 to 2001-02 has been only in the range of 57 per cent to 63 per cent which along with a manifold increase in diesel prices has seriously affected profitability of operators (Deloitte, 2003). This situation has reflected an excess supply, which has depressed freight rates. For instance, over the period 1995-96- 2001-02, freight rates have increased only marginally by 10 per cent on the Mumbai- Delhi route. But equally significant if not more important was the observation "that the freight charges paid to the truck owners have no relationship with the rate settled between the consignor and the booking agent" (AITD, 1999 p.45). It is widely believed that the rate paid by the consignor is a competitive one based on market forces of demand and supply. Even the most recent study of the World Bank (2005) brought out this feature clearly while admitting at the same time that the low cost to the user was at the expense of quality. This really brings us to the question: if the consignor is being offered a competitive rate, which is low, how much lower is the final rate offered to the operator given that the final rate has no relationship to the consignor rate? Would the rate to the consignor be lower given only reasonable margins to the booking agents? These are some of the questions that we examined among the many others on the basis of surveys conducted mainly in Mumbai but to a smaller extent in Goa and Satara.

3.3 Market Surveys and Analysis

Any attempt to understand a market for a product/service and its characteristics would necessarily have to begin with the relevant definitions, which can be primarily in terms of the product/service that is offered, the geographic area which it serves, the nature of substitution possibilities within and outside and the ease of entry and/or exit into the sector in terms of policy/regulatory elements and factors within the sector. All these features can ultimately affect the quantity and quality of services offered as also the price that is charged to the consumer and the revenue realisation of the producer. We attempt below some relevant definitions in the context of the RGTI in India.

Service Differentiation

In the context of trucking operations in India, there is a reasonable variety of services that is offered by the industry. One service relates to the parcel or smalls business. These mainly refer to small packages booked by different customers, which are consolidated into a truckload for dispatch (this is possibly most equivalent to the LTL segment in the context of countries like the United States and those of the European Union). Another relates to larger consignments, which could constitute a FTL or a number of FTL. The emergence of containers has only sought to provide some consolidation in these two product categories. Given that the parcels are smaller units and there is need to consolidate these, their charges are invariably higher per unit of weight. A third category may take the form of specialised traffic moving in specialised vehicles such as tankers etc. According to CIRT (1994), specialised movement accounted for less than 10 per cent with parcels traffic accounting for about 20 per cent. According to market sources, currently the parcels traffic might account for about 25 per cent of the movement.

Areas of Operation

Trucking operations can also be classified into Local, Regional and National on the basis of the spread and the extent of operations. We now examine these in some detail.

There are some operators who operate at the local level only. Many more seem to be operating on specific routes on an inter-regional basis. Some others operate on a national basis. Figure 4 gives this delineation.

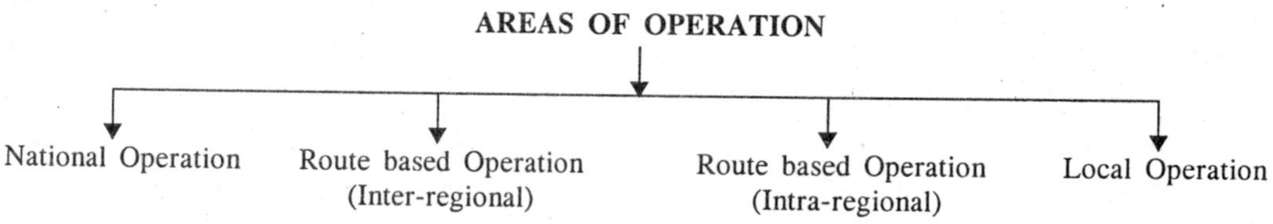

Fig. 4: Areas of Operation

Substitution Possibilities

In almost all the categories of services offered and distances moved (exceptions being local movements), choice of railways as a mode has always been a possibility. This is especially true in the case of long-distance movements in which case the railways have inherent advantages, which get reflected in lower tariffs. However, the railway system in India has been consistently

Table 1: Road-Rail Rate Differential

Particulars		*2001-02*		
		Road	*Railway*	*Difference*[1] *(per cent)*
Distance (Mumbai-Delhi)	Km	1,407	1,389	—
Average freight rate	Rs. per tonne	1,395	805	73.2
Loadings/unloadings in truck	Nos.	2	4	—
Loadings/unloadings in railway	Nos.	0	2	—
Loading/unloading charges for truck	Rs. per tonne	90	90	—
Loading/unloading charges for railway	Rs. per tonne	0	50	—
Handeling loss per loading/unloading	Per cent	2	2	—
Effective freight cost	Rs. per tonne	1,631	1,362	19.7
Effective freight cost	Rs. per t-km	1.16	0.98	18.2

1. Percentage differential between road and rail freight rates over rail freight rates.

Note: (1) Road freight rate is the average freight rate on the Mumbai-Delhi route.

(2) Railway freight rate is for the distance slab of 1,400 Km.

Source: Deloitte (2003).

under performing in terms of its potential as reflected by the inefficiency on the system (Rao and Sriraman (1985), Sriraman (2000)). As a result, significant movement of bulk items over long distances has been a common feature especially since the late 1960s. With the trucking industry offering the advantages of customer-tailored schedules, easy availability of equipment, easier maneuverability, smaller cargo acceptance, flexibility in operation and organisation, door-to-door service, etc., there has been a continuous shift to road movement despite the higher explicit costs of movement by road (See Table 1).

With the development of high quality roads in different parts of the country including the up gradation of important sections of the National Highway network, it is expected that the share of road movement would go up further. However, the emergence of a different railway approach in the past year or so in meeting the demands of the market in terms of different strategies involving tariffs, insistence on higher utilisation of assets, development of exclusive freight corridors can be expected to restrict shifts to some extent. The Indian Railways have begun offering highly competitive services in regard to parcel movement by going in for lease of space for parcel movement on scheduled trains running from different cities on the network. More recently, the space being offered has been increased in terms of provision for higher loads (4 tonnes), which still comes within the category of 'smalls' or 'parcels'. Though dedicated freight corridors may take quite some time to emerge, their emergence (which is expected to be fast) will definitely slacken the move towards roads if not divert back movement to the railways.

Ease of Entry and Exit

The absence of barriers to entry and exit reflect a fairly competitive market. There could arise private barriers in the form of structural barriers (product differentiation, extent of sunk costs, etc.) and strategic barriers in the form of particular behavioral strategies of incumbents (in the form of threats, pre-emptive behavior, etc.) while public barriers arise in the form of licensing and other regulations imposed by the Government.

"There are no entry barriers to this industry; almost anyone who can manage to own a rickety truck gets into it" (CIRT, 1994, p.8). This observation is perhaps true to a large extent. Low entry barriers can be attributed to some of the following factors:

- Low capital requirement as compared to other self-employment options (particularly for buying not so new trucks).
- Easy availability of capital (through unorganised financiers although at a significantly higher cost for the small operator).
- No expertise required in terms of business or educational skills. A basic driving skill is the only prerequisite coupled with the fact that driving licenses and clearances are simple to obtain.
- Liberal issue of permits — at State and National levels- has enabled emergence of the perception that the market for these services is huge.

Given the low entry barriers in the Indian context (in terms of both private and public ones), the normal consideration for entry into any economic activity, at least on *a priori* basis would be the existence of good (or more than good) returns. Our surveys did reveal such a consideration on the part of operators especially the smaller ones. This was based on the observation (rather cursory) that other operators were fairly successful in terms of the financial performance. At the same time, there was only little awareness of their own limitations in terms of their ability to identify demand for their services. This fear was to some extent removed on the possibilities of attachment to the larger ones or other intermediaries. In other words, the new entrants would not normally know where the demand for their services lay except through the players they are attached to. Thus even basic information requirements are not available to new entrants. Though this is not perceived to be a barrier to entry, the problem is formidable and gets resolved only by an almost complete surrender to intermediaries by which time exit is also ruled out an option.. Thus, there are information asymmetries to contend with. Given the lack of alternative employment opportunities, exit was not considered. Many of the smaller operators confessed that they held on to the business and given that their families were all located at their native villages, as single individuals, they managed to continue their operations especially in urban areas.

As for competition within the industry, we examine these issues below in some detail taking into account the areas of operations and the extent of involvement of the different players in terms of different relationships in different operations.

3.4 Interrelationships

The surveys focused on different supply linkages with a view to examine the inter-relationships between various players in this market. The following patterns have emerged from this examination. This has been explained in terms of different models in the form of flowcharts below.

1st Model

The above model is applicable only in case of local (within a particular city or peripheral areas of the city) movements. Given that the geographical spread of operations is very limited and the informational requirements are minimal, **there is almost no role for intermediaries in these operations**.

In the Mumbai context, our surveys reveal the possibilities of such control on freight rates mostly in case of light commercial vehicles (mostly tempos) in and around the ports (Dock Local Unions), in and around Industrial Estates like Andheri Industrial Estate (MIDC) in Mumbai, Wagle Industrial Estate in Thane and industrial area in Bhiwandi.

2nd Model

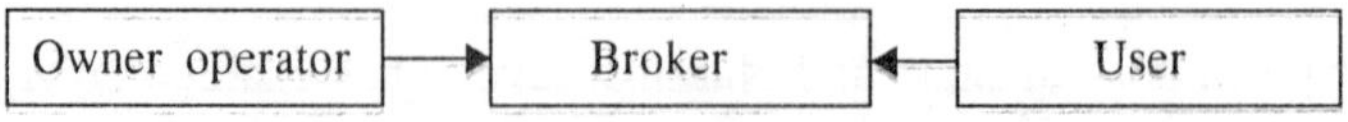

The market for this service is seen to be a perfectly competitive one with existence of a large number of users and a large number of operators. But it can be seen that in the above structure there is an intermediary who is a broker here and who gets paid a certain fixed commission for his service. This type of model is prevails mainly where the area of operation is limited i.e. **area of operations is mainly within the state**. In this case, the informational and other requirements are limited and hence provided by the broker.

3rd Model

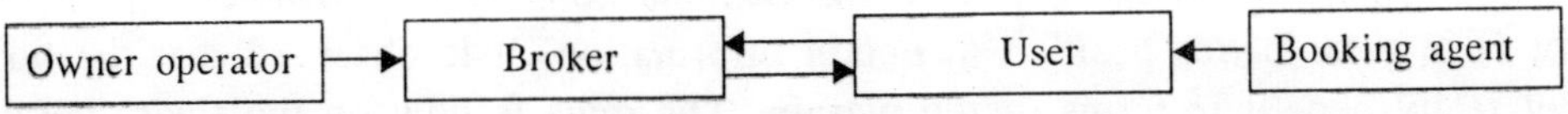

This structure is very much evident in the case of players on certain specified routes. Some of the important routes are Mumbai- Panipat, Mumbai- Jodhpur, Mumbai_ Cochin, Mumbai-Lothian, Mumbai-Agra, Mumbai-Calcutta, Mumbai-Bangalore, and Mumbai- Hubble. In addition to the presence of a broker on whom the operator depends, there is also a booking agent with whom the user is in contact. Thus there is no direct business contact of the operator with the user. It is thus expected that the brokers and booking agents negotiate on behalf of the operators and users respectively and hence supposed to play a dominant role in determining the freight rate. **In a sense, we could say that the brokers represent the supply side of the market while the booking agents constitute really the demand side of the market.**

4th Model

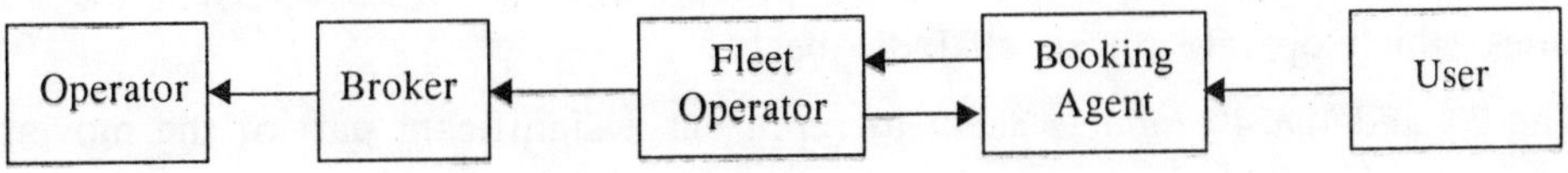

This is a variant of the third model in that there is demand for a fleet of vehicles for handling movements perhaps on a continuous basis. This model is also evident in case of specific routes. The large fleet operators get the freight through the booking agents but outsource it through the brokers to the small operators. Thus, the fleet operators in a way also play the role of intermediaries here for which they either take commission or just pay lower freight to the small operators. Here again the booking agent does seem to have a significant role. The issue is: whether the intermediaries dominate the scene?

One observation (made by many Committees in the past) that is pertinent here is that the freight charges paid to the truck owners have no relationship to the rate settled between the user/ consignor and the booking agent. With the broker being a more passive player relative to the booking agent, we suspected a fairly high margin for the booking agent. GOI (1967) observed 'It has been alleged that at times the margin of profits realised by booking agencies from truck operations is as much as 50 per cent of the freight they charge from clients' (p.49). In our surveys, the operators quoted margins of booking agents to be 25 to 35 per cent on the freight realised. More specifically, a figure of Rs. 4,000/- on freight realisation of Rs.10,000/- was quoted by a number of operators especially the smaller operators. The booking agents themselves admitted only to a margin of 10 to 15 per cent of the revenue realised. Some of them even revealed specific figures of Rs. 1,000 on revenue of Rs. 10,000/-. World Bank (2005) observed that the transporters/ booking agents admit that the amount they have to pay to the truck operators on any given day can vary from half of their revenue to more than 100 per cent of the revenue. In the context of the peak season, it was revealed by some booking agents that the higher realisation is not necessarily passed on to the operator. Once again it is to be noted that it is lack of information flows which gives rise to this problem for the operator. Whereas it is the information flow that gives the intermediaries some advantage in the market.

In the 4th model again the booking agent plays the same role vis-a-vis the user as in the third model depending on the nature of the demand conditions. However, given that the fleet operator is in a far better position to obtain information, it is observed that the booking agent does not really benefit in terms of the margin. The onus is now on the fleet operator since he is in an advantageous position vis-a-vis the smaller operators. Our surveys revealed that the smaller operators were victims in this regard though not on a regular basis.

In Goa, some of the small operators who are involved in long distance movements have a tie up with a fleet operator, say, Transport Corporation of India (TCI) a major player on an all India basis. TCI provides the framework under which the small operator act as a franchise in a formal way for which they charge a price in addition to the margin available to the fleet operator in the case of an attached vehicle. The survey revealed that there are few companies operating on all India bases. These companies need to have warehousing facilities, branches all over the country, network of hubs and sub-centers. Accordingly their costs also differ. It was revealed to us that the user prefers specific route operators when there is full truckload, as they are faster and less costly. But when small parcels have to be transported, the users approach companies which operate on an all-India basis.

The 3rd and the 4th models seem to represent a significant part of the movement in terms of the tonnage handled, in short, the output produced. Even though there is segmentation of markets in terms of region wise movements, given the large number of players in terms of various categories constituting the markets, structure of the market thus seem to be market driven and appears to be serving it reasonably well.

5th Model

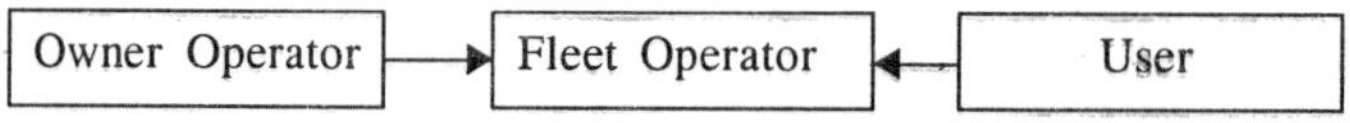

In the above model there are three players but no middlemen. The fleet operators generally bid for contracts and have formal contracts. This is the case where there is 'competition for the market' which though not a substitute for 'competition in the market' is a good surrogate. The basis for this is auction theory, which traditionally promised to deliver many of the gains that competition in the market would have delivered. The implicit assumption was that the number of potential providers in the sector would be large enough to allow competition for the market to be effective. This has not happened in many of the infrastructure related sectors.

This model is observed in case of the market for highly specialised vehicles where large fleet operators have access to the market for bidding but small operators do not e enter because of various entry barriers. It is observed that the large fleet operators actually bid for the contract with users. They utilise the services of the small operators. That is, in case additional vehicles are required then they outsource them from the small truck operators. So the fleet operator here is playing a multiple role — that of a booking agent, a broker as well as an operator.

From a detailed analysis of the above-mentioned supply chain models one could say that the market appears to be segmented on various basis, say as per area of operation, as per routes, i.e., operators as well as booking and commission agents seem to have certain preferred routes. The preference for the area of operation is in general based on familiarity with the route, contacts on that route, infrastructure required, which in turn reduces associated risks. Historically, this kind of market segmentation seems to have led to more powers in the hands of intermediaries as the information flow was normally accessible to the intermediaries only. Therefore, in the past, these intermediaries have enjoyed higher margins and have been in such a position so as to exploit the market situation in their favour. However, over a period of time, the entry of a large number of players, both operators and intermediaries, is ensuring that the structure is driven by market forces. Given the dominance of small operators and the user requirements in terms of reliable haulage, loss protection, the role of the intermediaries is substantial and proving to be useful to both from demand and supply perspectives. Though, there could be situations wherein these intermediaries seem to be colluding with each other in fixing freight rate as well as the conditions and terms of freight movement, the existence of a large number of these intermediaries especially in the significant sections of the overall movement reveals an overwhelming tendency towards a market determined revenue sharing arrangement. The Mumbai market reflects this scenario to a very large extent. However, concerns have been raised regarding cartelisation practices in local movements and bid rigging practices in the context of attempts to compete for the market by way of tenders and open bid procedures. These concerns need to be looked into and such practices removed/curbed.

4. EFFECTS OF POLICY AND REGULATORY REGIMES ON COMPETITIVENESS OF THE INDUSTRY

Several studies have, in the past, pointed out the implications of policy and regulatory regimes on the efficiency and viability of operations of the trucking sector and thereby its competitiveness in the Indian context. We examine some of these aspects now. We begin with issues related to policies and then take up the regulatory aspects.

4.1 Some Policy Effects

Taxation Regime

Taxes of various kinds and in varying rates are often imposed without consideration to their distorting aspects. States have often attempted to reduce taxes in a competitive spirit to attract trade and industry to the State concerned[J]. Such competition in sales tax leads to legitimate concerns and there has also been an attempt to unify and harmonise sales tax rates so as to move towards a value added tax (VAT). However, there is also the issue that in an attempt to absorb the resultant revenue loss from lowering of sales tax rates, States have sought to identify new sources for levying taxes. There has, thus, been a growing tendency to transfer tax liability to the transportation sector for quite some time.

The tax regime is both transport-specific and commodity-specific. Vehicles are detained for checking payment of commodity-specific taxes such as sales tax, octroi and other local taxes.

These checks are generally done by the respective agencies at separate points, resulting in more than one detention for this purpose. At the same time, there are specific taxes levied on the transportation sector, for instance, road tax, national and state permits, etc. Taxation of motor vehicles is a widely used instrument for raising resources. Usually, the transport carrier is detained at five different locations for collection of tax or checking the papers at the State and District level.

According to Debroy and Kaushik (2001) what differentiates the existing system in India with that of taxation systems practiced outside India is the delay and harassment in the tax recovery system. Domestic trade taxes in India are in need of reform. The tax regime that is in place today is archaic, irrational and complex. It interferes with the free play of market forces and competition, causes economic distortions and entails high costs of compliance and administration. Under the Constitution, the basis of excise duties and sales tax, the two principal components of the domestic trade taxes, are distinctly defined – excise duty as a tax on production of goods and sales tax on consumption (sale or purchase). In practice, the two have come to overlap because of problems in administering taxes at the retail level.

Vehicle and Operation related Taxes

In the context of assessing tax burden on a unit of operation, say, a truck operating at a certain utilisation level and moving over a certain distance, GOI (1950) observed "these taxes alone amounted in the case of lorries to 100 per cent more than the average earning per ton-mile for carrying traffic by rail" (p.25). The general conclusion was that the prevalent taxation policies of the Central and State governments do not conform with their overall policy of developing road transport as a national enterprise. GOI (1967) was more specific when it pointed out "that the burden of taxation on the road transport industry has been increasing. The margin left with the transport operators after the payment of taxes is not sufficient to enable them to plough earnings in an adequate measure for replacement let alone expansion" (p.63). The general conclusion was that the tax element in the cost of operation had become a definite disincentive to the healthy development of transport. NCAER (1979), on the basis of a detailed exercise, found that the situation had not improved and pointed out the need to rationalise the tax structure so as to ensure that taxation would be growth oriented rather than a hindrance, as it had been in the past. According to World Bank (1989), the position in regard to the incidence on vehicles was most unsatisfactory in India. Since vehicle taxation in India was road damage related but levied on the basis of gross vehicle weight rather than on potential axle loads resulting in under taxation of 2 axle trucks compared to those with more axles. Since the former is a major source of revenue to the States (accounting for one-fifth of the revenue from road users), it has been felt that there is need for rationalisation/restructuring to ensure that the tax burden is distributed fairly among different types of vehicles according to PCU (passenger car unit) dimensions as well as the road damage caused by each type of vehicle according to the equivalent standard axle.

As for the taxation element in the operating cost, GOI (1967) had come up with a figure of 35.2 per cent. NCAER's (1979) figure was at higher at 42 per cent. The corresponding figures for the US and the UK were 5 per cent and 17 per cent respectively for the early seventies. More recent estimates (Sriraman, et.al., 1998) of the tax burden in the price of the vehicle were

31 per cent and in the operating cost 57 per cent. A high tax burden would naturally affect competitiveness of services especially viewed from the perspective of growing liberalisation and globalisation of markets. While it was reasonable to expect this burden to come down to levels obtaining in advanced countries, rationalisation should necessarily lead to a lowering of the tax burden to about 15 to 20 percent (of the operating cost) - which are close to figures emerging out of optimal tax exercises conducted in the context of developing countries (Newbery and Stern, 1987, Ray, 1993). A detailed enquiry is called for in this regard.

Commodity-related Taxes

An important feature of the prevailing tax system is the existence of a large number of barriers for passenger and goods. Documents received by check-posts help the transport department to monitor flow of goods into the State and also make an assessment of tax. These check-posts, however, interfere with the free flow of traffic within a State and cause harassment to a large body of dealers, the majority of whom are not liable to pay tax. Studies undertaken on the efficiency of check-posts in different States reveal that the existence of check-posts does not contribute significantly to checking tax evasion. On the contrary, the more the number of check-posts, the higher is the wastage resulting from stoppage of traffic.

4.2 Regulatory Effects

The MV Act of 1988 (1939 as amended over a period of time) prescribes conditions for regulation of all types of road transport, viz, passenger transport in public and private sectors, tourist transport, contract carriages and goods transport. The regulatory aspects (in terms of different dimensions) relate to quality of vehicles, safety, labour, environment, loading, policing, etc. The Motor Vehicles Departments of the various States are concerned with the enforcement of the provisions of the Act. Almost every high -powered Committee that has gone into an examination of the issues of road transport in the Indian context has observed that the focus of these departments has been on collection of tax revenue from motor vehicles and not on effective enforcement of the various provisions of the Act. As a result, other important functions related to aspects such as mobility, safety, fuel conservation, environmental protection, etc. have hardly been attended to. In fact, AITD (1999) observed, "the regulatory mechanism has fallen far short of expectations" (p. 24). However, even this limited focus has, it appears, given rise to a number of problems especially smooth flows of movements thereby affecting efficiency of operations.

One important index for measuring the efficiency of a transport system is its adequacy. Adequacy is not merely influenced by the size of the fleet in operation but much more importantly by whether a given fleet moves frees without restraints so that its effective capacity is utilised and hence productivity enhanced during a given period of time. The smooth flow of road goods traffic is hampered by frequent detentions of vehicles for one reason or the other at various check points and mid way. Vehicles are detained for checking essential documents such as registration book, driving license, permits, etc. (RTO checking). They are also detained for checking payment of commercial taxes such as sales tax, octroi, other local levies, etc. In addition, detentions take place for booking traffic rule violations (Police checking) and also at State borders (Border Post checking).

The consequences of detention of vehicles are loss of time leading to underutilisation of truck capacity, avoidable consumption of fuel (due to deceleration and acceleration, stopping and restart of engines) and lastly, corruption and graft. GOI (1950), while pointing out to the delays due to octroi levies observed, "the delays that occur while goods are being examined and weighed at octroi posts are as harmful or even more harmful to the economy of the country than the levy made on the goods themselves especially when these levies are relatively light" (p.23). GOI (1967) pointed out, "Octroi and similar check posts which detain vehicles frequently are impediments to the growth of the economy and the time they consume is a serious obstacle in the way of quick turn round" (p. 83). The Committee also observed that octroi was a fertile source of corrupt practices and concluded that octroi is one of the greatest hindrances in the way of commerce and economic development of the country. NCAER (1979) noted that considering the total time wasted at the various detention points which were of the order of 20 to 35 per cent of the running time, carrying capacity equivalent to nearly 80000 trucks or capital investment equal. to Rs.650 crores is locked up due to check posts. Further, there was a huge wastage of fuel as a result of idling. In terms of gratification and other social costs, the study revealed that the incidence of gratification on different routes was almost as much as the total fees levied on those routes. CIRT (1994) surveys revealed that detentions on the different routes ranged between an average of 2 hours and "more than 24 hours." In the course of our surveys, most operators emphatically pointed out that problems arising out of exploitation by an intermediary in the trade were of no consequence to them when viewed in relation to those they faced on the road on a day-to-day basis. "The broker is a much lesser evil than the police or the RTO official," it was observed every time we raised the issue of exploitation by the intermediary. The implications are many. One of them, as pointed out earlier, relates to low utilisation that results from less movement in a day. Our exercises relating to freight rates and operators reveal that at a higher lever of operations in terms of more movements per day, say, 350 to 400 kilometers, operators' returns turn out to be positive even with legal loads. With less to be paid by way of wayside expenses, the returns could be higher. Debroy and Kaushik (2001) conclude that on the basis of personal interviews with transporters, if all the additional costs were eliminated, the delays could be reduced by approximately 3 days and transportation costs halved. World Bank (2005) pointed out the low cost of movement by trucks while at the same time it was inefficient. If inefficiencies could be reduced, the cost to the user could go down further which means rates would be more competitive. Given that there could be very little provision for overloading in future, the demand for truck services can go up significantly thereby pushing up freight rates and restore some respectability to the viability of operators especially the smaller ones.

Several Committees and Study reports have, in the past, pointed out the implications of several policy and regulatory regimes on the efficiency and viability of operations of the trucking sector and thereby its competitiveness in the Indian context. The present study also points out the deleterious effects of the taxation regime (vehicle and operation related as also commodity related) on costs of operations. Further, it also points out to a number of problems resulting from the regulatory regime especially smooth flow of movements due to barriers there by affecting efficiency of operations and competitiveness.

5. COMPETITION ADVOCACY MEASURES AND INITIATIVES

A key function of competition authorities in many countries has been advocacy of the application of competition principles in the design of governmental policies and measures including the elimination of unnecessary regulation and the adoption of least anti-competitive means of achieving various policy and regulatory objectives (UNCTAD, 1998). One outstanding example of competition advocacy has been the clarion call given by the former Chairman of the United States Federal Trade Commission in the early seventies, Lewis Engman, for deregulation of the transport sector, which has often been cited as being among the first contemporary evidence of useful competition advocacy. Accordingly, competition laws in several countries have sought to intervene in legislation or administrative processes, while others may intervene only if the competition authority is requested to do so. In Canada and the United States, competition authorities participate in proceedings before regulatory authorities relating to competition policy and also undertake general advocacy efforts. In the United States, the Department of Justice participates in executive branch deliberations and has played an important role in deregulation. In the Republic of Korea, competition law requires other governmental authorities to consult with the competition authority when they wish to introduce, amend or enact any legislation that might restrain competition. In short, active competition advocacy efforts are a necessary part of any competition authority's work profile though it is not quite sure as to how such efforts (thereby recommendations) have actually been implemented. Competition advocacy is an essential part of the work of the Competition Commission of India. Having examined issues relating to competition in the RGTI in India, we now attempt to provide some guidelines, which can be part of advocacy measures to be put forward to the Government in regard to RGTI in India. We provide these in two parts — some structural — relating to measures to promote efficiency within the industry and the others — policy and regulatory oriented-relating to measures aimed at removing barriers to movement with a view to increasing the industry's efficiencies and thereby its competitiveness.

5.1 Structural and Behaviourial

(*i*) In the context of local operations, the Regional Transport Authority (RTA) can be requested to provide parking spaces where operators could be located and also to notify (based on discussions with the operators and users) a price band within which the operators could compete until such time that the market has effective competition. Thus, the State Governments through the RTA could eliminate price fixation practices in local movements.

(*ii*) It is necessary that the Central and State Governments and other public sector bodies enhance the efficiency and competitiveness of competitive tendering through more careful attention to the tendering process. Given that there is provision for action against bid rigging or collusive rigging in the Competition Act, 2002, the Commission's advocacy role would be to impress upon Governments for an active oversight of the competitive tendering process to ensure sustainability of competition failing which active competition enforcement would be resorted to by the agency.

(*iii*) An effective public sector role (Central and State) can be in facilitating applications and adaptability of information technology and Intelligent Transport Systems (ITS) to all aspects of trucking operations so that information asymmetries which continue to plague profitable operations can be minimised if not eliminated.

(*iv*) State legislation providing for cooperative efforts already exists. What are required are some efforts on the part of the respective State Governments to encourage operators based in the State to get down to formation of such cooperative units of operators. The Commission can actively promote this idea with the State Governments as an advocacy measure.

(*v*) The Commission, in its advocacy initiative, must lay particular emphasis on the emergence of a mechanism for a competitive price regime in the market for container movement by rail and also point out the need for a fair allocation of services in terms of access between the players (the multimodal operators) in the market.

(*vi*) As an advocacy measure, the Commission needs to point out the anomalies resulting from Customs' bonding requirements in the context of truck container movement from the ports which need to be removed to provide a level playing field to the trucking sector.

5.2 Policy and Regulation related

(*vii*) Service quality of trucking services is poor - which does not augur well for our domestic as well as our international expansion efforts in terms of competitiveness of the economy. Advocacy should cover the quality aspect of the trucking service (industry) also in terms of requiring proper enforcement of standards provided by the MV Act.

(*viii*) The relevant provisions relating to fixation of minimum and maximum rates contained in Section 67(1) and Section 79(2)(iv) are redundant and should be dropped from the Act. This is to ensure that there is no more clamor for minimum rates under the existing regulatory framework.

(*ix*) As an advocacy measure, Governments need to be advised on the issue of the current perverse system of financial incentives such as high tax rates and tolls on multi axle vehicles so as to ensure a tax regime that results in more efficient use of trucking and road capacity. This is especially important in the context of our competitiveness in international markets.

(*x*) The Commission, as an advocacy measure, should advise the Central Government to initiate a review into the requirements for an efficient and sustainable nation freight transport system (encompassing all freight transport modes). Taking into account reforms to date and also the various detailed studies undertaken in this regard, the review should map out what is required to:

- Achieve competitive neutrality across all transport modes;
- Address barriers to competition and efficiency in individual modes; and
- Enhance interfaces between modes.

This is an important advocacy measure which could ultimately result in policies which can help ensure that the mix of transport modes reflects the intrinsic efficiency of the different modes compared to current Government policies and regulations that favored one mode to other.

(*xi*) With an economy dominated by roads and road transport, it is increasingly important that truckers have much the same right as the railways to travel interstate with a minimum of delays. Legal and administrative reforms are needed in this area are needed for India to function effectively as a single market. As a measure of competition advocacy, the Commission needs to emphasise the importance of elimination of regulatory and physical barriers which can pave the way for a seamless national (single) market to begin with. The State Governments should be encouraged to carry out competition audit of existing regulations especially those providing for the present system of checkpoints administered by the States and involve a number of agencies (which involve restrictions on flow of commodities, the fiscal regime, etc) to determine the need for their continuation.

ACKNOWLEDGEMENT

This paper is based on a study titled "Competition Issues in the Road Goods Transport Industry in India with special reference to the Mumbai Metropolitan Region" undertaken by the Department of Economics, University of Mumbai and commissioned by the Competition Commission of India (CCI) as part of the advocacy programme of CCI. The copy right of the study rests with the CCI. This is being published with the explicit consent of CCI. However, the views expressed herein should, in no way, be treated as official views of the Competition Commission of India or of its officials.

REFERENCES

AITD (1999), 'Trucking Operations in India', Asian Institute of Transport Development, New Delhi.

CIRT (1994), 'Road Goods Transport in India — A Study of its Structure and Organisation', Central Institute of Road Transport, Pune.

Debroy,B. and Kaushik, P.D. (2001), Barriers to Inter- State Trade: the Case of Road Transport, Paper submitted to the Ministry of Law, Justice and Company Affairs, Government of India.

Deloitte (2003), 'Modernisation of the Trucking Industry', Report submitted to the Advisory Group on Trucking Industry in India, All India Motor Transport Congress and All India Confederation of Goods Vehicles Owners' Association.

Dugar, S. M., (1997), *'Law of Monopolistic, Restrictive and Unfair Trade Practices'*,3rd edition, Wadhwa & Company, Nagpur.

Dutz, M. (2002), Competition Policy Issues in Developing and Transition Markets, Paper presented at the OECD Global Forum on Competition, March.

GOI (1932), 'Report of Mitchell- Kirkness Committee', Government of India.

GOI (1932): 'Report of Wedgewood Committee', Government of India.

GOI (1950), 'Report of the Motor Vehicle Taxation Enquiry Committee', Ministry of Transport, Government of India, Delhi.

GOI (1953), 'Report of the Taxation Enquiry Committee', Government of India, Delhi.

GOI (1958), 'Report of the Road Transport Reorganisation Committee', Government of India, Delhi.

GOI (1966), 'Report of the Committee on Transport Policy and Coordination', Planning Commission, Government of India, New Delhi.

GOI (1967), 'Final Report of the Road Transport Taxation Enquiry Committee', Ministry of Transport, Government of India, New Delhi.

GOI (1980), 'Report of the National Transport Policy Committee', Planning Commission, Government of India, New Delhi.

GOI (1987), 'Report of the Planning Group on Road Transport for the Twentieth Century', Planning Commission, Government of India, New Delhi.

Kessides, C. (1993), Institutional Options for Provision of Infrastructure, Discussion Paper No. 212, World Bank, Washington D.C.

Kessides, I.N. (2004), *Reforming Infrastructure: Privatisation, Regulation and Competition,* A World Bank Policy Research Report, Oxford University Press and World Bank, Washington D.C.

Lakshmanan, T.R. and Anderson, W.P. (2000), Case Studies in Trade and Transport Integration, Centre for Transport Studies, Boston University, Report prepared for the World Bank Group on Infrastructure, March.

Lata,. M. (2005), 'Infrastructural Impediments and Rising Costs of International Trade: A Case Study of India's Export Competitiveness in the Global Market', Ph. D. Thesis submitted to the University of Mumbai.

NCAER (1979), *'Road Transport Industry',* National Council of Applied Economic Research, New Delhi.

Newbery, D.M. and Stern, N., (1987), *The Theory of Taxation for Developing Countries*, Oxford University Press.

OECD (2001), 'Competition Issues in Road Transport'.

Rao, T.V.S.R. and Sriraman S., (1985), *'Disequilibrium in Rail Freight Services'*, Ajanta Publication, New Delhi.

Savage, I., (1995), 'Panzar and Rosse Style Tests of Market Structure in the U.S. Motor Carrier Industry', Logistics and Transportation Review Volume 31, No.2.

Smith, H. L. (1995), *'Deregulation and Privatisation in the UK Freight, Bus and Coach Industries,* Volume III, Regulatory Policy Research Centre, Oxford.

Sriraman, S. (1998), 'Road Transport Development in India', *Current Science*, October.

Sriraman, S., (1997), 'Road and Road Transport Development in India', Asian Transport *Journal, Asian Institute of Transport Development*, New Delhi.

Sriraman, et al. (1998), Report of the Sub-Committee on Financing, Taxation, Fares and Freight and Insurance submitted to the Steering Committee on "Trucking Operations in India", Asian Institute of Transport Development, New Delhi.

Sriraman, S., (2000), 'Indian Railway Finances — Critical Issues and Emerging Options', *Economic and Political Weekly*, Vol.XXXV, No.12, March 18.

Sriraman, S., (2006), 'The Transport Sector in India: Has it been technology driven or demand induced?', Directions, Vol.7, No.4, Indian Institute of Technology, Kanpur.

Taylor, J.C., (1995), *Regulation of Trucking by the States, Regulation: CATO Review of Business and Government,* CATO Institute, Washington D.C.

Thukral, K. L., (2002), 'Enhancing the Quality of Trucking Services', Report prepared by Asian Institute of Transport Development, New Delhi for Asian Development Bank, Manila.

UNCTAD (1998), Empirical Evidence of the Benefits from Applying Competition Law and Policy Principles to Economic Development in order to Achieving Greater Efficiency in International Trade and Development, Report of the United Nations Conference on Trade and Development, July.

Winston, C. et.al. (1990), *'The Economic Effects of Surface Freight Deregulation'*, The Brookings Institution, Washington D.C.

World Bank (1989), *'Vehicle Fleet Modernisation Road User Cost Study'*, World Bank, Washington D.C.

World Bank (1997), '*Economic Development in India: Achievements and Challenges, A World Bank Country Study*', World Bank, Washington D.C.

World Bank (2002), *'India's Transport Sector: The Challenges Ahead'*, Volume 1, World Bank, Washington, DC.

World Bank (2005), 'Road Transport Service Efficiency Study', Mimeograph, World Bank, Washington D.C.

25

COMPETITIVENESS OF FIRMS IN THE INDIAN AUTOMOBILE INDUSTRY

L. G. Burange
Shruti Yamini

ABSTRACT

Although the opening up of the economy in the early 1990s gave the much-awaited impetus to the Indian automobile industry, it is recognised that the industry has grown in the last five years as never before. Well supported by the changing economic conditions particularly in the financial sector and in foreign direct investment, increasing number of global players are entering the Indian economy by way of joint ventures, collaborations with the domestic firms or wholly owned subsidiaries, which have led to increased competition among firms in the industry. In this paper, this trend in competitiveness among the firms in the Indian automobile industry has been assessed by understanding the factors that determine its competitive advantage. An attempt has been made to construct a competitiveness index for a sample of fourteen firms for the year 2005-06, which represents around 85% of each segment of the industry namely passenger vehicles, commercial vehicles, three-wheelers and two-wheelers. Separate indices have been constructed for the financial and non-financial indicators as well as for the various segments of the industry. About 50% of the sample firms have recorded above industry average performance from all the segments of the automobile industry. The marginal difference between the competitiveness of different firms reveals tough competition among the firms in the automobile industry in India.

1. INTRODUCTION

The automotive industry, globally, as well in India, is a key sector of any economy. Due to its deep forward and backward linkages with several major segments of the economy, the industry has a strong multiplier effect on industrial growth. The rise in efficiency and productivity helps directly and indirectly to accelerate the efficiency of other sectors through movements of goods and people in the economy. Therefore, the industry is recognised as one of the drivers of economic growth as it contributes significantly to the overall GDP of a nation. It has been identified at different forums as a sector with a high potential to increase exports and employment. It also helps in attaining two critical goals of the Common Minimum Programme that of increasing manufacturing output and of providing employment. Though indirectly, it also facilitates the third objective of increasing agricultural productivity through farm mechanisation and the needs of agro-produce transportation (Ministry of Heavy Industries and Public Enterprises, 2006b).

The Indian automotive industry has flourished after economic liberalisation in 1990s like never before. This extra-ordinary growth of the industry has been mainly due to the higher disposable incomes of the middle class and the resultant increase in their living standards. This has been well supported by the economic conditions particularly in the financial sector, which has played a big role in boosting the demand and sustaining the long-term growth in the industry.

The Indian automobile sector has several competitive advantages. The competitive landscape of the industry has been developed using the Porter (1990) Diamond Framework by India Brand Equity Foundation (2006) which is depicted in Figure 1.

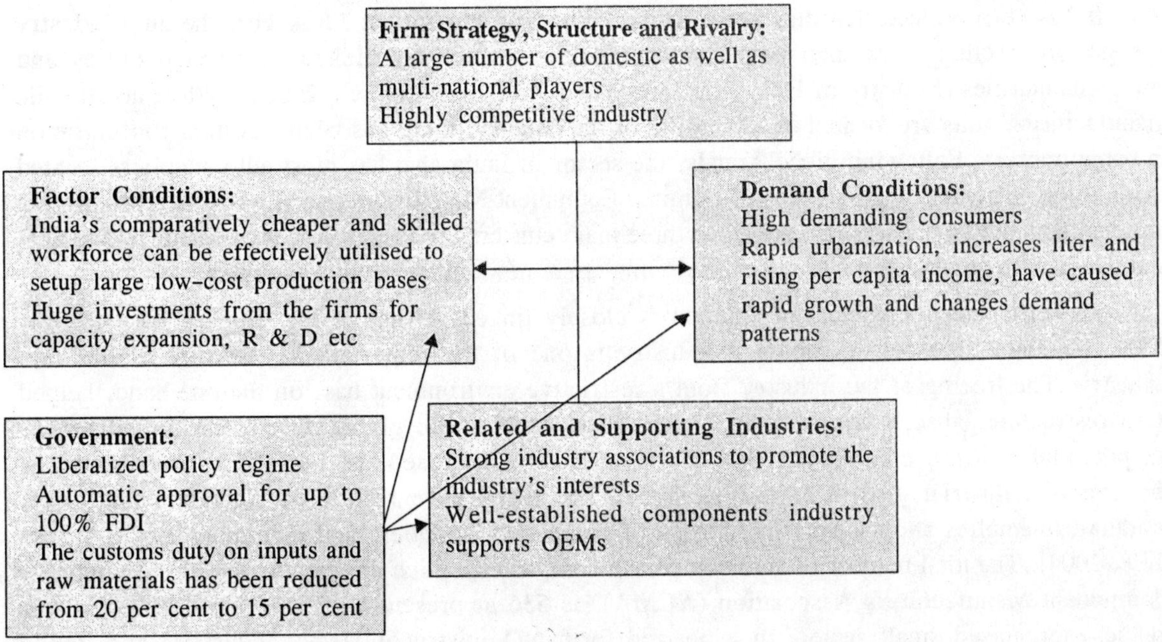

Fig. 1: Competitive Landscape of the Indian Automobile Industry

The present paper has tried to bring out the competitive flavour of the Indian automobile industry. Intense competition has gripped the industry in recent years with major world players entering the market bringing better technology and long experience. Therefore, the study on competitiveness of firms in the industry in the domestic market, in its present state is interesting to examine. With this objective, an effort has been made to construct an index, which benchmarks the firms according to their competitive position in the industry.

The paper is organised in five sections. In the second Section, the structure and evolution of the Indian automobile industry is discussed in the light of its current status. The third Section deals with the methodology used for constructing the competitiveness index. Section four addresses the results and analysis, followed by conclusions of the study.

2. AN OVERVIEW OF THE INDIAN AUTOMOBILE INDUSTRY

2.1 Structure of the Automobile Industry in India

The Indian automotive sector has a presence across all vehicle segments and comprises of key component manufactures which are in concentrated in regional clusters.

The Indian automobile market is still in its evolutionary stage. Therefore, no fixed or widely accepted method of segmenting the market has evolved as yet. Segmentation has mostly been done on the basis of product types, its weight/size or product uses. It is broadly categorised into the following four segments; commercial vehicles, passenger vehicles, two wheelers and three wheelers, which cover 5%, 14%, 77% and 4% of the total market share of the industry respectively (Society of Indian Automobile Manufacturers, 2007).

It has been noticed that due to its strong backward and forward linkages, the auto industry has grown in clusters of inter-connected companies, which are linked by commonalities and complementarities (Ministry of Heavy Industries and Public Enterprises, 2006a). While automobile manufacturing units are located in all regions of the country, there has been a certain concentration in some pockets. Following global trends, the sector in India also has most auto suppliers located close to the manufacturing locations of Original Equipment Manufacturers (OEMs), thereby forming regional automotive clusters. Broadly, the three main clusters are centered around Chennai, Mumbai and Delhi. However, Pune is also developing as a new cluster in the country.

The efficiency of vehicle production is closely linked to that of the supplier base (Singh, 2004). In India, the auto component industry is one of the important key sectors of the auto industry. The freeing of the industry from a restrictive environment has, on the one hand, helped it to restructure, absorb newer technologies, align itself to the global developments and realise its potential. On the other hand, this has significantly increased the industry's contribution to the overall industrial growth of the economy. The firms have resorted to common platforms, modular assemblies and systems integration of component suppliers and e-commerce (CII-DSIR-IIFT, 2004). The total number of auto component companies, which are members of the Automotive Component Manufacturers Association (ACMA), is 536 at present with more than 10,000 firms in the unorganised small sector, in a tierized format (Ministry of Heavy Industries and Public Enterprises, 2006b). The industry is however dominated by a few industrial business houses. The industry in the country has made rapid strides and is growing at a fast pace, which can be seen from the following Figure 2. The industry has grown at an annual compound growth rate of 17% from 2000-01 to reach a size (in value terms) of around US $10 billion in 2005-06, while component exports have grown at around 25% per annum (IBEF, 2006).

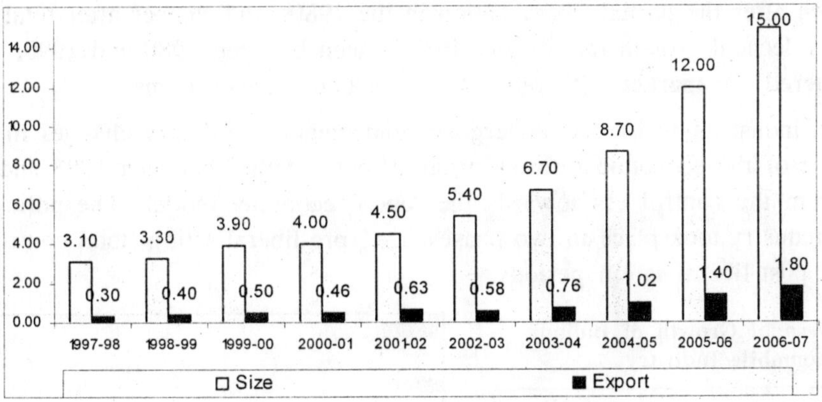

Source: ACMA 2007.

Fig. 2: Size and Export of Indian Auto Component Industry (In US $ billion)

The auto component industry has the potential of becoming the export driver of the auto industry due to increasing globalisation of the supply chain processes and the cost advantage in many component groups supported by relatively (compared to other developing markets) well-developed labour skills and engineering base (Khisty, 2000). This will help the industry mark its global presence.

2.2 Evolution of the Indian Automobile Industry

It was in 1898 that the first motorcar rode down India's roads in Mumbai (then Bombay) which had its first taxicabs in the early 1900. Then, for many years, cars were imported to satisfy domestic demand. Till the First World War, about 4,000 cars were directly imported to India from foreign manufacturers (Auto India Mart, 2007). The growing demand for these cars established the underlying requirements of the Indian auto market that these merchants were quick to pounce upon. Between 1910 and 1920, the automobile industry made a humble beginning by setting up assembly plants in Mumbai, Calcutta and Chennai. The import/assembly of vehicles grew consistently after the 1920s, crossing the 30,000 mark in 1930 (India Infoline, 2007).

The Hindustan Motors (HM) and Premier Autobackmobile (PAL) were established in 1942 and 1944 respectively to manufacture automobiles in India. However, it was PAL who produced the first car in India in 1946 by assembling 'Dodge De Soto' and 'Plymouth' cars at its Kurla plant in Mumbai, as HM concentrated on auto components and could produce their first car only in 1949. After a short period of time, it was another company, Mahindra and Mahindra (M&M), which manufactured sturdier utility vehicles, namely, the American Jeep.

In the 1950s, the Government of India granted approval to only 7 car dealers to operate in India. The1960s witnessed the establishment of the two and three wheeler industry in India, and for some time things remained much the same. Since the 1980s, the Indian car industry has seen a major resurgence with the opening up of Indian industry to foreign manufacturers and collaborators. The 1990s became the melting point for the car industry when large number of foreign players came into the country through collaborations and partnerships. Table 1 below shows the trend of growth of production in the industry. It can be seen from Figure 3 that the growth was steep after the partial liberalisation in the 1980s and steeper after total decontrol in 1991. Maximum decadal growth rate of 347.46% is seen between 1980 and 1990, when Maruti Udyog Ltd. entered the market with other Japanese two-wheeler firms.

The Indian industrial sector has undergone fundamental regulatory changes in recent times as a consequence of the economic reforms program put together between 1988 and 1991. India moved away from the control era towards the 'open' economy model. The policy changes in the automobile industry took place in two phases, *i.e.*, pre-liberalisation (total control and partial de-control) and post-liberalisation periods.

Table 1: Decadal Growth of Indian Automobile Industry

Years	*Production*	
	Number	*Growth (%)*
1960-61	41535	—
1970-71	181752	337.59
1980-81	625143	243.95
1990-91	2797241	347.46
2000-01	5497416	96.53
2006-07	11065142	101.28

Source: SIAM, 2007

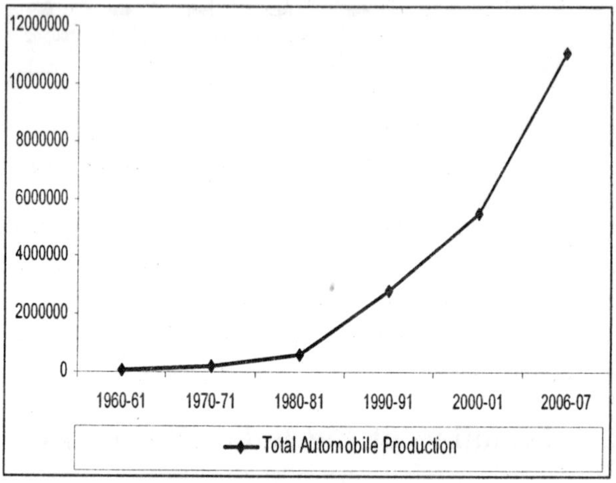

Fig. 3: Trend of Production in Indian Automobile Industry

The automobile industry in India grew under a highly regulated and protected economic environment over the period 1950 to 1985. There were quantitative restrictions on imports of raw materials, components, and equipments through licensing and a tariff structure designed to restrict the market. Also, there were restrictions on foreign direct investment and imposition of the condition of indigenisation of components production which protected the domestic market. The initial changes, introduced in 1985, eased the licensing requirements, broad-based the classification of vehicles for issue of licenses, allowed selective expansion of capacity and partially relaxed controls with regard to foreign collaborations, imports of capital goods, raw materials and spares. Though these measures represented 'domestic liberalisation', the policy environment continued to be geared towards imposing trade and investment regulations, constraining the growth of big business houses and regulating exchange rates (Narayanan, 2001).

Liberalisation of economic policies and the outward orientation introduced since 1991 brought about a dramatic change in this industry. These new measures effectively dismantled the license raj which had made it difficult for Indian firms to import machinery and know-how, and had disallowed equity ownerships by foreign firms (Krishnan, 2002). Since July 1991, approvals have been given to foreign technology agreements and up to 51% foreign equity investment was allowed in the automotive sector. Further, in 1997, some more reforms were introduced wherein in the case of new foreign entrants which sought to establish actual production facilities, the minimum foreign equity was raised to $50 million, and the minimum indigenisation allowed was to the extent of the 50%. The auto policy announced by the government in 2002 (Ministry of Heavy Industries and Public Enterprises, 2002) permitted 100% foreign equity on an automatic basis. The Automotive Mission Plan 2006-2016 was released in 2007, which visualizes India emerging as a destination of choice in the world for design and manufacture of automobiles and auto components with output reaching a level of $ 145 billion accounting for more than 10% of the GDP and providing additional employment to 25 million people by 2016.

2.3 Current Status of the Indian Automobile Industry

The growth trends of key industry indicators are improving every year as seen from Table 2. Industry volumes, export performance as well as domestic sales are increasing at a steady rate even given that there is a potential for much higher growth in the domestic market due to the fact that the current car penetration level in India is just 7 cars per thousand persons compared to 12 in Sri Lanka/Pakistan and over 100 in Europe/US.

Domestic manufacturers acting as a global hub for exports are also gaining acceptance. Though exports are not necessarily lucrative, it will enable domestic players to increase exposure and maintain capacity utilisation at a healthy level. Expansion of auto component industry is also evident today.

Table 2: Growth Trends of Key Variables of the Industry

Years	*Production*		*Domestic Sales*		*Export*	
	Number	*Growth (%)*	*Number*	*Growth (%)*	*Number*	*Growth (%)*
2001-02	5316302	—	5225788	—	184680	—
2002-03	6279967	18.13	5941535	13.70	307308	66.40
2003-04	7243564	15.34	6810537	14.63	479919	56.17
2004-05	8467853	16.90	7897629	15.96	629544	31.18
2005-06	9743503	15.06	8906428	12.77	806222	28.06
2006-07	11065142	13.56	10109037	13.50	1011278	25.43

Source: SIAM 2007.

The following observations are in order:

1. Consolidation of the industry has gained momentum. Foreign automotive firms have arrived and are in queue. There is a long list of foreign companies that are forging alliances with their Indian counterparts. Corporate participation in these alliances varies from 10 to 100 percent of equities (i.e. wholly owned foreign subsidiaries) (Nath, 2006).
2. India is becoming an important destination for automobile research and development as it is fully equipped to take up design, engineering and components manufacture.
3. Armed with higher purchasing power and an ever-increasing expectation from products and services, the customer is undoubtedly the king and has propelled fierce competition among the major players in the market.
4. In the case of commercial vehicles, the significance of large-tonnage multi-axle vehicles and light commercial vehicles is on the rise and is likely to increase further on account of superior economies in transportation they offer.

5. The dominant basis of competition in the Indian passenger car industry has changed from price to price-value, especially in the passenger car segment. The market for multi-utility vehicles has also been redefined.
6. Recent years have witnessed a robust growth in motorcycle sales and a decline in the share of scooters in the overall Indian two-wheelers market and hence a demand shift.

3. THE METHODOLOGY

There are numerous methodological choices encountered in the problem of construction of composite indices, which can measure competitiveness at any level of aggregation. The technique used for construction of competitiveness index for the Indian automobile industry at the firm level is discussed below.

3.1 Competitiveness Index

An immediate problem in analysing competitiveness is that despite widespread acceptance of its importance for economic performance and growth, no consensus exists on its definition and measurement. The Oxford Dictionary of Economics defines the term competitiveness as 'the ability to compete in markets for goods or services' and The Free Dictionary explains it as 'an aggressive willingness to compete'. These are the most fundamental definitions of competitiveness, although are deceptive ignoring the ambiguity of the concept.

There are several interpretations of the concept of competitiveness in which some distinctions have been made. The most fundamental being the difference between microeconomic and macroeconomic concepts. Competitiveness can be observed from different perspectives, through products, firms, industry and branches of the economy or national economies. At each level of aggregation, there are different measures or indicators of competitiveness. The second issue relating to competitiveness is the distinction between one-dimensional and multi-dimensional concepts, in terms of the number of the dimensions it integrates and measures. The number of dimensions included in its measurement can be seen as a mark of complexity of the concept (Siggel, 2003). We are mainly concerned with the firm-level multidimensional concept of competitiveness in the domestic market.

One of the interesting attempts to capture more than one dimension of a firm's competitiveness was made by Buckley et. al.. (1988). According to him, "a firm is competitive if it can produce products and services of superior quality and at lower costs than its domestic and international competitors. Competitiveness is synonymous with a firm's long-run profit performance and its ability to compensate its employees and provide superior returns to its owners". Of the micro indicators assessing the multi-dimensionality of the concept of competitiveness, the best known attempt was made by Porter (1990) in his 'Diamond Framework'. He identified four main determinants of competitiveness of enterprises as their strategy; structure and rivalry, the demand conditions they face, the factor supply conditions they encounter, and the conditions of related industries. Although there are a multitude of factors that influence the competitiveness of firms, Porter classified those under four above mentioned facets only.

Gelei (2003) has used the definition of firm competitiveness as 'the basic capability of perceiving changes in both the external and internal environments and the capability of adapting to these changes in a way that the profit flow generated guarantees the long term operation of the firm'. According to him, firm competitiveness is basically a function of two factors. First, it is determined by the extent a company can identify those value dimensions that are important for their customers. These are the main features of the firm's complex product and service package a customer expects. The second factor of firm competitiveness is the sum of resources and capabilities that make a firm capable to create and deliver the identified important value dimensions for the customer. Prahalad and Hamel (1990) call these core competences.

A *White Paper* on competitiveness by the UK Government (Department of Trade and Industry, 1994) offers a multi-notion definition at the company level, which says, 'for a firm, competitiveness is the ability to produce the right goods and services of the right quality, at the right price, at the right time. It means meeting customers' needs more efficiently and more effectively than other firms'.

Defining competitiveness is not easy as it is linked to a large number of variables. Equally problematic is the measurement of competitiveness, it being a broad, relative concept without bearing any direct relationship with economic performance indicators. The multi-dimensionality in the definition of competitiveness has made the construction of a composite index, which can measure it in some mathematical fashion, very important. Keeping this in mind, an effort has been made to build up a competitiveness composite index that can measure a firm's competitive position in the industry which it can sustain in medium to long run.

A composite indicator is the mathematical combination of individual indicators that represent different dimensions of a concept whose description is the objective of the analysis (Saisana, 2002). Composite index represents aggregate measures of a combination of complex phenomena (Booysen, 2002). Composite indicators can be used to summarise complex or multidimensional issues, in view of supporting decision-makers (Saisana, 2005). In the context of policy analysis, indicators are useful in identifying trends and drawing attention to particular issues. They can also be helpful in benchmarking or monitoring performance.

3.2 Data-Coverage and Adjustments

Variables are included in an index if they are relevant to the concept that is being measured (Salzman, 2003). The variables that compose the competitiveness composite index for Indian auto industry have been identified on the basis of factors related to competitiveness at the firm level, considering specific issues peculiar to the Indian automobile industry.

Total number of sub-indicators used for the competitiveness index are 62 out of which 38 (61%) are taken from PROWESS database of Centre for Monitoring Indian Economy (CMIE) and 24 (39%) from other data sources. Other data sources include a questionnaire survey, which was carried out for all sample firms. Some of the other sources used for preparing the database are company websites, SIAM and ACMA websites and other publications.

For consumer satisfaction index, J.D. Power scores of Consumer Satisfaction Index (J.D. Power Asia Pacific, 2007) have been used because of non-availability of data. The two sub-indicators for which this substitute has been used are number of customer complaints in a year and customer complaint response time. Industry averages are used for those firms not included in the J. D. Power study. One of the sub-indicators used for the technological index is the environmental indicator, which includes total emissions from plants, product disposal expenditure and environmental management expenditure. Due to lack of response from the sample firms, we used Centre for Science and Environment (CSE) scores of Green Rating Project (CSE, 2001), which include similar indicators. The sub-indicators, which are used to construct the competitiveness index of the firm, are listed in Table 3. All of these sub-indicators are grouped into ten main indicators that clearly describe its components.

Table 3: Description of the Sub-indicators in the Competitiveness Index for Indian Automobile Industry

	Indicators	*Sub-indicators*
1.	Productive Performance	• Capacity Utilisation • Labour Productivity
2.	Financial Performance	Liquidity Ratio: • Current Ratio • Quick Ratio Leverage Ratio: • Debt-Equity Ratio • Interest Coverage Ratio Efficiency Ratio: • Inventory Management • Debtors Turnover Ratio Profitability Ratio: • Net Margin Ratio • Return on Assets Ratio • Return on Net Worth (ROE) • Return on Capital Employed (ROCE) Other Ratios: • Net Working Capital Cycle • Solvency Ratio • Asset Turnover Ratio
3.	Cost Effectiveness	• Cost as % of Gross Sales Other Cost Indicators: • Raw Materials, Stores etc. • Financial Charges
4.	Sales and Marketing Strategy	• Market Share • Department for Brand Management • Number of Dealers • Expenditure on Marketing • Expenditure on Advertising • Expenditure on Distribution
5.	Stock Market Performance	• Earnings Per Share • Price-Earning Ratio • Book Value Per Share

6.	Consumer Satisfaction	• Number of Years of Warranty • Number of Authorised Service Stations or Workshops • Average Number of Free Servicing to the Vehicle • Customer Complaint Response Time • Number of Customer Complaints
7.	Technology and Environmental Indicators	Technology Acquisition: • Technology Strategy: Import or In-House Development • Foreign Exchange Spending on Capital Goods • Royalty know how expenses • R & D Expenditure • Technology Management: • Expansion of Production Base to other Segments • Number of Production Plants • Product Differentiation • Power and Fuel Expenses • Alternative Fuel Models Environmental Indicators: • Total Emissions • Product Disposal Expenditure • Environmental Management Expenditure
8.	Human Resource Development and Social Indicators	• Employment Generation • Expenditure on Salaries and Wages as % of Total Cost • Performance Incentives to Employees • Skill Enhancing Training • Certification to Plants (Health And Safety) • Safety Awareness Training • Loss Due to Labour Unrest
9.	Foreign Trade Measure	• Net Foreign Exchange Earned • Exports as % of Gross Sales
10.	Growth Variables and Potential	Growth Variables (over previous year): • Total Assets • PAT (NNRT) • Net Sales • Total Exports Future Plans: • Firm's Investment Plans over the Next 2 Years • Plans to Launch any New Models in Next 2 Years Contingency Planning: • Insurance Premium Expenses • Any Department for Disaster Management • Maintenance — Plant and Machinery Repairs Expenditure

3.3 Sample Selection

The sample of firms has been chosen on the basis of market share data given by SIAM (2007) for the year 2005-06. Efforts have been made to include a representative sample, which covers at least 85% of the market share in each of the segment of the industry.

Other important consideration was availability of data. As about 61% of the data has been taken from Prowess Database, listing of companies on the portal become very important. This forced the exclusion of some firms not listed on National Stock Exchange (NSE) and hence on the database, even with greater market share than others. The companies of this sort in the passenger car segment are Toyota Kirloskar Motor Pvt. Ltd. (4.05%), General Motors India Ltd. (2.70%) and Ford India Pvt. Ltd. (2.53%). However, Honda Seil Motors and Hyundai Motors are two companies, which are also not listed on NSE, but they are on PROWESS and hence included in the study. Piaggio Vehicles with 30.26% of market share in three-wheeler segment had to be excluded from sample because of non-availability of data. In the two-wheeler segment, Honda Motorcycle & Scooter (7.97%) and Yamaha Motor India Pvt. Ltd. (2.91%) are also excluded from the study. The details of the sample and their respective market shares are given in Table 4.

Table 4: Market Share of Sample Firms in Automobile Industry in 2005-06

Firm	*Market Share (%)*
Passenger Vehicle Segment	
1. Maruti Udyog Ltd	46.11
2. Tata Motors Ltd	16.52
3. Hyundai Motor India Ltd	13.91
4. Mahindra & Mahindra	7.35
5. Honda Siel Cars India Ltd	3.74
Total Market Share	87.63
Commercial Vehicle Segment	
Tata Motors Ltd	62.04
6. Ashok Leyland Ltd	27.00
7. Eicher Motors Ltd	7.44
8. Swaraj Mazda Ltd	3.03
Total Market Share	99.51
Three Wheeler Segment	
9. Bajaj Auto Ltd	49.11
Mahindra & Mahindra	6.23
10. Force Motors Ltd	5.72
11. Scooters India	4.22
Total Market Share	65.28
Two Wheeler Segment	
12. Hero Honda Motors Ltd	41.24
Bajaj Auto Ltd	26.29
13. TVS Motor Company Ltd	17.90
14. Kinetic Motor Co Ltd	1.08
Total Market Share	86.51

Source: SIAM, 2007.

3.4 Normalising Technique, Weighting and Aggregation of Indicators

Normalisation is required prior to any data aggregation to render them comparable as the indicators in a raw form often have different characteristics. Therefore this has to be transformed into pure, dimensionless numbers. For this, a number of normalisation methods can be used (Freudenberg, 2003; Jacobs, 2004).

The normalisation method used should take into account the data properties, as well as the objectives of the study (Giovannini, 2005). Considering this we used the range equalisation method where variables are re-scaled between 0 to 100 with the help of equation 1 given below. This requires points of reference relative to which indicators can be scaled. A minimum and a maximum value are identified for each of the variables. Subtracting the minimum value of the particular variable from its actual value and dividing it by the difference between the selected maximum and minimum values determines the values of the indicators. This value of the indicators is multiplied by 100, so that it ranges between 0 (worst performer) and 100 (best performer). This method of re-scaling the data widens the range of indicators, which makes the differences more distinct.

$$\text{Normalisation} = \frac{\text{Actual Value} - \text{Minimum Value}}{\text{Maximum Value} - \text{Minimum Value}} \times 100 \qquad \text{... (1)}$$

Different factors of competitiveness have different impact on the competitiveness index, both negative and positive. For this reverse of the value i.e., '100- value' of the index is taken, which solves the issue of directionality.

For benchmarking, weights can have a significant effect on the overall composite index and the rankings. Different weights may be assigned to indicators to reflect their economic significance, statistical adequacy, cyclical conformity, speed of available of data, etc. A number of weighting techniques are available of which some are derived from statistical models, such as factor analysis, data envelopment analysis and unobserved components models or from participatory methods like budget allocation, analytic hierarchy processes and conjoint analysis.

Statistical methods could not be used for the purpose as most of them are based on the correlations between the indicators. Correlations do not necessarily represent the *real influence* of the sub-indicators on the phenomenon being measured (Nardo et al., 2005). Also there must be a sufficiently large size of the sample to use most popular methods such as factor analysis and principal component analysis.

Considering the nature of the problem the budget allocation method for weighting has been used. Budget allocation is a participatory method in which experts are given a 'budget' of *N* points, to be distributed over a number of sub-indicators, 'paying' more for those indicators whose importance they want to stress. In this, experts' opinions are likely to increase the legitimacy of the composite and create a forum of discussion around which to form a consensus for policy action (Nardo et al., 2005).

In the present study, ten broad categories of indicators (given in Table 5) were listed in the questionnaires itself so that experts in the field could assign weights to them out of 100 depending on their relative importance in the competitiveness of the firm. This reduced the subjectivity in the index as officials already working in the industry have clear insights into the problem of competitiveness. The weights were then averaged across the sample firms. However, for sub-indicators, equal weights have been used as asking relative importance of 62 sub-indicators to the officials of the firm was not possible due to their unwillingness as it involved too much time.

Table 5: Weights of the Indicators

Indicators	*Average Weight*
1. Productive Performance	14
2. Financial Performance	12
3. Cost Effectiveness	7
4. Sales and Marketing Strategy	12
5. Stock Market Performance	4
6. Consumer Satisfaction	14
7. Technological and Environmental Factors	11
8. Human Resource Development and Social Indicators	10
9. Foreign trade: Export and Import	8
10. Growth Performance and Potential	8
Total	100

After weight allocation to each component index, these scores are aggregated into a composite score. The aggregation of indices tends to be of either of an additive or a functional nature (Booysen, 2002). The most widespread method of linear aggregation is used in the index construction where the mere summation of weighted and normalised indicators is done.

The aggregate index for each of the ten indicators is derived first using relevant variables (sub-indicators). The formula used for this is given below:

$$V_i = \frac{1}{n}\sum_{i=1}^{n} x_i \qquad \text{... (2)}$$

where, V_i is i^{th} indicator, x_i is the ith sub-indicator , n is the number of sub-indicators within the indicators.

The next step is that of aggregating these ten indicator indices into one competitiveness index for a firm in the automobile industry. This is done in the same manner as in equation 2.

$$C_j = \frac{\sum_{i=1}^{n} W_i V_i}{\sum_{i=1}^{n} W_{ii}} \qquad \text{... (3)}$$

where, C_j is the competitiveness index of *j*th firm, W_i is weight of the *i*th indicator, V_i is *i*th indicator (i = 1 to 10) and n is the number of indicators.

The ten indicators are then grouped in two groups namely Financial and Non-Financial Indicators. We constructed both the indices for the purpose of analysis and have also averaged the scores of the sample firms to benchmark the average competitiveness in the industry.

4. RESULTS AND ANALYSIS

The results are presented in Table 6 and Figure 4. The industry average score of competitiveness index has been calculated at 40.98, which is used to analyse the competitive performance of firms above and below it. It is hence used to benchmark the firms' competitive standings in the industry. Seven firms from the sample of fourteen firms i.e. 50% of the total sample size, show performance above industry average and remaining seven are below this average. The firms that showed better performance comprise of all the segments of the industry. Out of these seven, 4 of them namely Maruti Udyog Ltd., Tata Motors Ltd., Hyundai Motor India Ltd. and Mahindra & Mahindra Ltd. manufactured passenger vehicles in 2005-06. Firms like Bajaj Auto Ltd., Hero Honda Motors Ltd. and TVS Motors Ltd. produces two-wheeler vehicles, whereas Bajaj Auto Ltd. and Mahindra & Mahindra Ltd. also manufacture three-wheeler vehicles. Of course Tata Motors Ltd. is the only firm, which manufactures commercial vehicles also. This indicates the competition in passenger vehicle segment and in two-wheeler segment is relatively more intense.

The firms, which recorded performance below industry average, are mainly from commercial vehicles such as Ashok Leyland Ltd., Eicher Motors Ltd. and Swaraj Mazda Ltd. Honda Siel Cars India Ltd. is the only passenger vehicle producer that is below industry average during 2005-06. Force Motors Ltd. and Scooters India Ltd. are three-wheeler manufacturers below industry average and Kinetic Motors Co. Ltd. is the only two-wheeler producer below industry average in the ranking of competitiveness index during 2005-06.

Table 6: Overall Rankings and Scores of Automobile Firms

Company	*Rank*	*Score*
Maruti Udyog Ltd.	1	64.06
Bajaj Auto Ltd.	2	57.52
Hero Honda Motors Ltd.	3	54.89
Tata Motors Ltd.	4	48.80
Hyundai Motor India Ltd.	5	47.77
Mahindra & Mahindra Ltd.	6	46.44
TVS Motor Co. Ltd.	7	43.67
Industry Average		**40.98**
Ashok Leyland Ltd.	8	39.21
Honda Siel Cars India Ltd.	9	33.55
Eicher Motors Ltd.	10	31.03
Force Motors Ltd.	11	29.32
Scooters India Ltd.	12	28.42
Swaraj Mazda Ltd.	13	28.14
Kinetic Motors Co. Ltd.	14	20.97

4.1 Competitiveness of Firms

In the overall competitiveness rankings, Maruti Udyog Limited comes first with 64.06 score. From Table 7 it is observed that this is largely due to its position in the productive performance and consumer satisfaction indicator. The good competitive position it enjoys in productive performance is because of its highest capacity utilisation and labour productivity in the automobile industry. In case of consumer satisfaction, it holds the highest position in the industry. However, the company's performance in foreign trade is scored very low and is on 12th position in the list of sample firms. This is mainly because of its negative net foreign exchange earnings due to high imports (mainly of components). The percentage of exports in total sales basket is also very low at only 3.85% where the highest is 27.32%. In all the other indicators, it has performed above average of the industry.

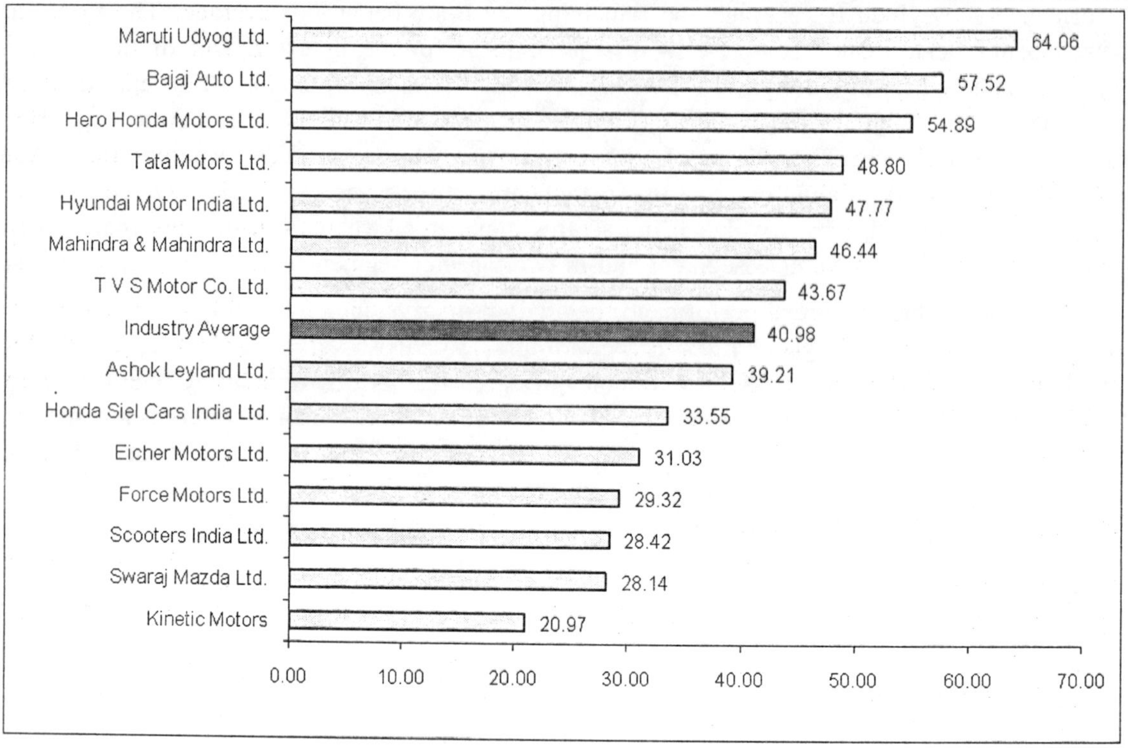

Fig. 4: Scores of Automobile Firms in Competitiveness Index

Bajaj Auto Limited is at the second position in the competitiveness index and 1st in the financial index as it gets 8.93 score there. It can be noted here that this company has 1st ranks in five indicators. It has got a second ranking in the overall index mainly because of poor performance in productivity where it stands 13th. The difference in the total productivity score is very wide where Maruti Udyog has got 14 and Bajaj Auto gets only 1.61 score due to its low capacity utilisation of 56% and low labour productivity, which is only 0.74 as compared to 3.61 in case of Maruti Udyog. Low foreign exchange spending on technology acquisition, R & D expenditure and royalty know-how expenses has led the company to 7th ranking in technological indicators too, further pulling down the total score.

The difference in total score between Hero Honda and Bajaj Auto is only 2 points (both two-wheelers). Hence, performance wise, the company is doing well as it stands at number 3 position. The company holds 1st position in cost effectiveness as it has lowest cost component in its gross sales. Also raw materials etc and financial charges are the lowest. Human resource, growth variables and foreign trade measures have pulled it down to this position although it is 2nd in regard to other 4 sub-indicators such as productive and financial performance, sales and marketing strategy and customer satisfaction.

The overall score of Tata Motors is 48.80 on the basis of technology. The company tops the list mainly because of highest R&D expenditure and good product differentiation, as it caters to two segments in the industry namely passenger vehicles and commercial vehicles. In terms of growth, the company performs well, as sales and profits both showed good growth and also

Table 7

Scores and Ranks of the Firms for Indicators

Firm	Productive Performance		Financial Performance		Cost Effectiveness		Sales and Marketing Strategy		Stock Market Performance		Consumer Satisfaction		Technology and Environmental Indicators		Human Resource Development		Foreign Trade Measure		Growth Variable and Potential	
	Score	Rank	Score	Rank	Score	Rank	Score	Rank	Score	Rank	Score	Rank	Score	Rank	Score	Rank	Score	Rank	Score	Rank
Maruti Udyog Ltd.	14.00	1	7.97	3	6.44	3	5.41	6	2.17	2	11.38	1	4.28	3	6.88	5	0.55	12	4.97	4
Bajaj Auto Ltd.	1.61	13	8.93	1	6.38	4	7.52	1	3.38	1	6.82	3	3.20	7	7.55	3	6.34	1	5.78	1
Hero Honda Motors Ltd.	6.59	2	8.63	2	6.90	1	6.93	2	1.81	6	8.85	2	4.05	4	5.42	9	1.75	11	3.96	7
Tata Motors Ltd.	3.01	6	5.32	11	5.74	6	6.03	4	1.98	3	3.92	6	5.25	1	7.33	4	4.91	3	5.30	2
Hyundai Motor India Ltd.	3.96	5	7.04	4	5.76	5	4.54	8	0.85	10	3.87	7	3.64	6	7.72	2	5.89	2	4.51	5
Mahindra & Mahindra Ltd.	4.01	4	5.73	10	6.54	2	6.23	3	1.86	5	3.41	8	3.85	5	6.32	6	3.35	5	5.14	3
TVS Motor Co. Ltd.	2.17	12	5.72	11	5.27	8	5.76	5	1.94	4	5.07	5	2.91	8	8.56	1	2.88	7	3.38	10
Ashok Leyland Ltd.	2.72	8	6.54	7	5.04	9	3.68	10	1.17	9	1.52	13	4.80	2	6.30	7	3.55	4	3.89	8
Honda Siel Cars India Ltd.	2.44	8	6.88	5	5.71	7	0.72	14	0.85	10	5.18	4	2.25	10	5.53	8	0.42	13	3.56	9
Eicher Motors Ltd.	2.35	11	5.79	9	4.22	12	5.13	7	1.73	7	3.04	11	1.17	12	2.10	13	3.19	6	2.31	11
Force Motors Ltd.	0.04	14	5.09	12	4.55	11	4.20	9	0.57	11	3.05	10	2.33	9	3.05	11	2.14	10	4.30	6
Scooters India Ltd.	2.73	7	6.56	6	5.29	8	1.97	13	0.57	11	3.05	10	0.46	14	3.40	10	2.34	9	2.06	12
Swaraj Mazda Ltd.	4.62	3	6.21	8	3.87	13	2.07	12	1.47	8	2.13	12	1.57	11	1.80	14	2.68	8	1.72	13
Kinetic Motors Co. Ltd.	2.40	10	2.96	13	0.80	14	3.05	11	0.51	12	3.35	9	1.01	13	2.49	12	2.68	8	1.72	13
Industry Average	3.76	—	6.38	—	5.18	—	4.52	—	1.49	—	4.62	—	2.91	—	5.20	—	3.05	—	3.76	-

Note: Shaded scores of firms indicate above industry average performance in that particular indicator.

their plans to launch new models in future. However, the company's performance in other indicators is average and exceptionally poor in financial indicators such as liquidity ratios and interest coverage ratio.

In the list of competitive performance, 5th, 6th and 7th positions are held by Hyundai, Mahindra & Mahindra and TVS Motors, with very little difference in their total scores. Nevertheless, the strength of Hyundai lies in getting the second highest rank in human resource and foreign trade indicator with 27.32% of export in total sales. But it lags behind in stock market performance as is not listed on NSE and hence its score is zero for the indicator. Mahindra & Mahindra is doing well in cost effectiveness and sales and marketing strategy whereas financial performance is relatively very poor. Human resource performance is strongest for TVS Motor Co. Limited where it is ranked first, which is offset by poor productive and financial performance.

All the firms discussed above in terms of their competitive performance in various indicators are above the industry average and hence showing good competitive behavior. The remaining other firms, which are below the industry average, are discussed below.

Ashok Leyland, Honda Siel Cars India and Eicher Motors are 8th, 9th and 10th in the list of competitive rankings getting 39.21, 33.55 and 31.03 scores respectively. All are very close with each other although Ashok Leyland is exceptionally good in technological indicators and average in other indicators. Honda Siel's strength seems to be consumer satisfaction where it has 3rd position but because of poor performance in sales and foreign trade the overall score is very low. Whereas, Eicher Motors has below average performance in all the indicators of competitiveness.

Firms such as Force Motors, Scooter India and Swaraj Mazda have the 11th, 12th, and 13th rankings respectively in the list of index of competitiveness being very close in scores except for Kinetic Motors, which is 14th with avery low score. Scooters India at 11th has done above average performance in financial and productive variables. Swaraj Mazda is ranked 3rd in productive performance because of 99% capacity utilisation. Kinetic Motors has consistently been in the last two in four indicators, only doing better in foreign trade measure as net foreign exchange earnings has positive value. In case of other indicators, all these four firms show below industry average performance.

If we divide the industry in segments then it can be seen that the two-wheeler segment and three-wheeler segments is dominated by Bajaj Auto as it is the most competitive as reflected by its high scores. The passenger vehicle segment is obviously ruled by Maruti Udyog whereas the commercial vehicles segment is dominated by Tata Motors.

The pattern of difference of scores can be observed from the overall index of all the sample firms. It is seen that the maximum difference is between the 13th and 14th positions i.e. Swaraj Mazda and Kinetic Motors (7.17) which shows exceptional relatively poor performance of the later in terms of competitiveness. Next is the difference between Maruti Udyog and Bajaj Auto (6.54) showing the dominance of the former on the automobile industry. The gap between Hero Honda and Tata motors (6.09) is also large, which is followed by Ashok Leyland and Honda Seil (5.65). All the other firms are very close in competitive scores, which show close competition among them.

4.2 FINANCIAL AND NON-FINANCIAL INDICES

Competitiveness is concerned with the ability of firms to perform better than rivals, where performance is dependent on both financial and non-financial conditions of the firm. For the purpose of analysis, competitiveness index has been divided into financial index and non-financial index. The objective is to ascertain which of the two indices has more effect on the overall competitiveness index of a firm.

For this purpose financial indicators such as different financial ratios, cost effectiveness, stock market performance and foreign trade indicators are grouped under financial index and other indicators such as productive performance, sales and marketing strategy, consumer satisfaction, technological issues, human resource and growth variables are grouped under non-financial indicators. The former has 31% of the total weights whereas the later gets remaining 69%. Importance to non-financial factors is given visibly more by the industry experts in the survey of sample firms (Table 5). Using the weighted average of the sub-indicator indices, financial and non-financial indices are constructed.

It can be seen from Table 8 that although Maruti Udyog stands first in non- financial index, it is on sixth position in financial index reflecting its weakness in four of the financial indicators such as foreign trade and financial ratios. It is way ahead of all other firms in non-financial indicators as reflected by the score of the index. The company can dominate the industry completely if it tries to improve its financial performance. This is the only firm from the sample firms whose non-financial performance is superior to financial performance (Figure 5).

However, opposite is the case with Bajaj Auto as it has highest score in financial and is third highest in non- financial index. It has ranked 1st in all of the financial indicators except in cost effectiveness where it stands 4th. But the company has got the 3rd rank in terms of non-financial performance because of its relatively poor performance in productivity and technological indicators.

The performance of Hero Honda is marginally better in non-financial than in financial index. However, Tata Motors and Mahindra & Mahindra are the two firms, which have same ranks in both the indices. But the performance of Tata Motors is much superior to Mahindra & Mahindra because Tata Motors could maintain the same rank in the overall index but Mahindra & Mahindra went down by one rank i.e., from 5th to 6th (Table 8). Hyundai despite being very strong in financial performance has lagged behind due to weakness in non-financial index. There is only a marginal unevenness in the comparative position of other firms, which has altered their overall rankings in the competitive index. However, exceptions to this are Honda Seil and Eicher Motors where ranks have interchanged in the two indices. Although Kinetic Motors has poor performance in terms of both the indices, its relative weakness is much higher in financial than in non-financial index.

Table 8: Comparison of Rankings in Financial and Non-financial Indicators

Firm	*Overall Index*		*Financial Index*		*Non-financial Index*	
	Score	*Rank*	*Score*	*Rank*	*Score*	*Rank*
Maruti Udyog Ltd.	64.06	1	55.27	6	68.00	1
Bajaj Auto Ltd.	57.52	2	80.75	1	47.08	3
Hero Honda Motors Ltd.	54.89	3	61.59	3	51.88	2
Tata Motors Ltd.	48.80	4	57.92	4	44.70	4
Hyundai Motor India Ltd.	47.77	5	63.02	2	40.92	6
Mahindra & Mahindra Ltd.	46.44	6	56.38	5	41.97	5
TVS Motor Co. Ltd.	43.71	7	51.03	8	40.36	7
Ashok Leyland Ltd.	39.21	8	52.59	7	33.20	8
Honda Siel Cars India Ltd.	33.55	9	44.70	12	28.55	9
Eicher Motors Ltd.	31.03	10	48.16	9	23.34	11
Force Motors Ltd.	29.32	11	39.80	13	24.61	10
Scooters India Ltd.	28.42	12	47.61	10	19.80	14
Swaraj Mazda Ltd.	28.14	13	45.90	11	20.16	13
Kinetic Motors Co. Ltd.	20.97	14	22.41	14	20.32	12

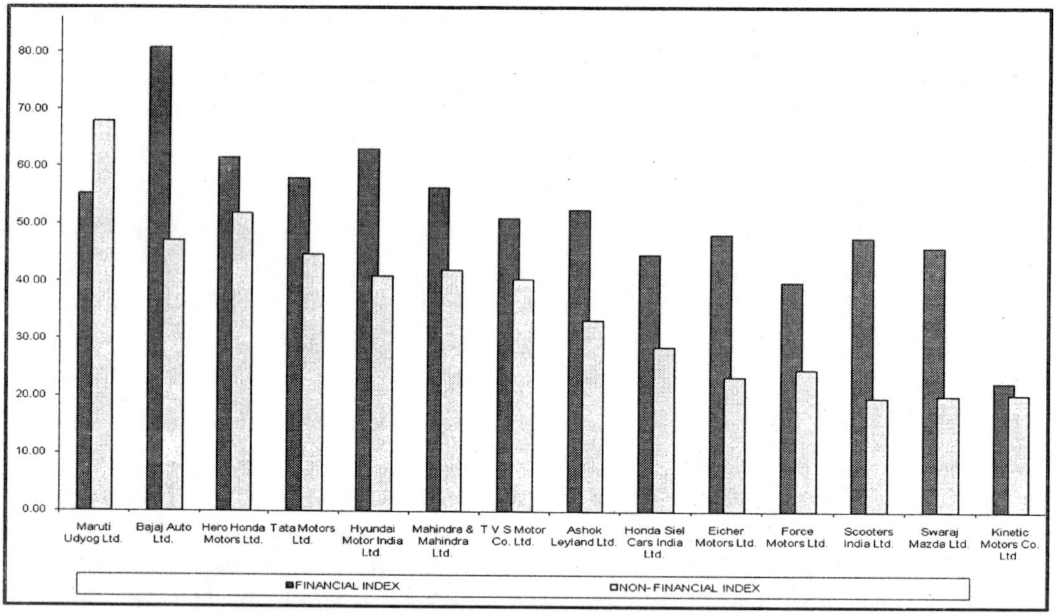

Fig. 5: Comparison of Financial and Non-financial Indices

5. CONCLUSIONS

Efforts have been made in the paper to build up an index that reflects the competitiveness of firms in the Indian automobile industry. An attempt has also been made to study the current status and evolution of the industry. A composite competitiveness index is defined as the mathematical combination of individual indicators that represent different dimensions of the concept whose description is the objective of the analysis.

The finding of the study reflects the relative competitive position of the sample firms and also the overall picture of the industry. Out of fourteen sample firms, performance of seven firms was above the industry average. Maruti Udyog Limited scored highest in the group getting top most ranking mainly because of non-financial indicators such as productive performance, customer satisfaction etc. This is followed by Bajaj Auto, which has scored second rank due to better financial performance in terms of stock market performance, financial ratios and foreign trade. Looking at the financial and non-financial index separately, it is seen that the rankings differ slightly as some firms perform better in one than the other.

It is also observed that out of first seven firms, only two are from three-wheeler segment. This shows that competition is more intense in the passenger vehicle and two-wheeler segments. The commercial vehicle segment seems to be dominated by Tata Motors.

It can be hoped that the overall index, sub-indicator index and financial/non-financial index prove to be helpful in framing competitive policies by the firms. It will also be useful to consumers to judge the competitive performance of these firms from the product quality and investment point of view.

REFERENCES

1. Automotive Component Manufacturers Association (2007), *Engine of Growth Driving the Indian Manufacturing Sector*, Status Report of Indian Automotive Component Industry.
2. Booysen, Frederik (2002), An Overview and Evaluation of Composite Indices of Development, *Social Indicators Research* 59, pp. 115–151.
3. Buckley, Peter J., Christopher L. Pass, and Kate Prescott (1988), Measures of International Competitiveness: A Critical Survey, *Journal of Marketing Management* 4 (2).
4. Centre for Science and Environment (2001), Mileage: Environmental Rating of Indian Automobile Sector, *Green Rating Project*, New Delhi.
5. CII-DSIR-IIFT (2004), *Technology Financing for SMEs,* A Survey Report on Auto Component SMEs, CII, DSIR and IIFT, New Delhi.
6. Department of Trade and Industry (1994), *Competitiveness*, White Paper, Cm 2563, London, HMSO.
7. Freudenberg, M. (2003), *Composite Indicators of Country Performance: A Critical Assessment*, Directorate for Science, Technology and Industry, Working Paper 2003/16, Organisation for Economic Cooperation and Development (OECD), Paris.
8. Gelei, Andrea (2003), *Competitiveness: A Match between Value Drivers and Competencies In The Hungarian Automotive Supply Chain*, Budapest University of Economic Sciences and Public Administration, Hungary.
9. Giovannini, E. *et al.* (2005), *Handbook on Constructing Composite Indicators: Methodology and User Guide*, OECD Statistics Working Paper, STD/DOC (2005)3, OECD Publishing. Paris, France.
10. Gooroochurn, Nishaal and Guntur Sugiyarto (2004), *Measuring Competitiveness in the Travel and Tourism Industry,* Discussion Paper 7, Tourism and Travel Research Institute, Nottingham University, U. K.
11. India Brand Equity Foundation (2006), *Automotive*, Report by KPMG for IBEF, Gurgaon.
12. Jacobs, Rowena, Peter Smith and Maria Goddard (2004), *Measuring Performance: An Examination of Composite Performance Indicators,* Technical Paper Series 29, Centre for Health Economics, University of York, United Kingdom.
13. J.D. Power Asia Pacific (2007), *India Customer Satisfaction Index (CSI) Study*, Press Release, J.D. Power and Associates, McGraw-Hill Companies, Singapore.
14. Khisty, Vasant (2000), *Globalisation and Competitiveness of Indian Auto Component Industry*, Associated with RAHA - World Independent Writers' Home in Exile, World News, Kabul Press.
15. Krishnan, Viswanathan (2002), *Indian Automotive Industry: Opportunities and Challenges Posed by Recent Developments*, IMV Publication No. 0104a, International Motor Vehicle Program at the Massachusetts Institute of Technology, Cambridge.

16. Ministry of Heavy Industries and Public Enterprises (2006a), *Automotive Mission Plan 2006-2016*, Government of India, New Delhi.

17. Ministry of Heavy Industries and Public Enterprises (2006b), *Automotive Industry, Eleventh Five Year Plan (2007-2012)*, Report of Working Group, Department of Heavy Industry, Government of India, New Delhi.

18. Ministry of Heavy Industries and Public Enterprises (2002), *Auto Policy 2002,* Department of Heavy Industry, Government of India, New Delhi.

19. Narayanan, K. (2001), *Liberalisation and the Differential Conduct and Performance of Firms: A Study of the Indian Automobile Sector*, Discussion Paper Series- A No. 414, The Institute of Economic Research, Hitotsubashi University and United Nations University Institute of Advanced Studies, Japan.

20. Nardo, Michela, Michaela Saisana, Andrea Saltelli & Stefano Tarantola (2005), *Tools for Composite Indicators Building,* EUR 21682 EN, Institute for the Protection and Security of the Citizen, JRC, Ispra, Italy.

21. Nath, Aditya (2006), *India: The Next Automobile Giant*, Business Performance Consulting, CGN & Associates Inc.

22. Porter, M. E. (1990), *The Competitive Advantage of Nations*. New York: Free Press.

23. Prahalad, C. K. and G. Hamel (1990), The Core Competence of the Corporation, *Harvard Business Review*, Vol. 68, No.3, pp.79-81.

24. Saisana, Michaela (2005), *State-of-the-Art Report on Composite Indicators for the Knowledge-based Economy,* Work-package 5, KEI-project, European Commission: Joint Research Centre, Ispra, Italy.

25. Saisana, M. and S. Tarantola, (2002), *State-of-the-art Report on Current Methodologies and Practices for Composite Indicator Development*, EUR 20408 EN, Institute for the Protection and Security of the Citizen, JRC Ispra, Italy.

26. Salzman, J. (2003), *Methodological Choices Encountered in the Construction of Composite Indices of Economic and Social Well-Being*, mimeo, Center for the Study of Living Standards, Ontario.

27. Siggel, Eckhard (2003), *Concepts and Measurements of Competitiveness and Comparative Advantage: Towards an Integrated Approach*, paper prepared for the International Industrial Organisation Conference at Northeastern University, Boston, Massachusetts.

28. Singh, Neelam (2004), *Strategic Approach to Strengthening the International Competitiveness in Knowledge Based Industries: The Case of Indian Automotive Industry*, RIS Discussion Paper Series No. 82, Research and Information System for the Non-Aligned and Other Developing Countries, New Delhi.

29. Society of Indian Automobile Manufacturers (2007), *Market Share Analysis Report*, Report VII, SOP 11-F-09/01, New Delhi.

30. Society of Indian Automobile Manufacturers (2004), *Automobile Industry: Advantage India Indian Automobile Industry – An Agenda for Global Leadership*, Speech by Mukesh D. Ambani, Annual Convention, New Delhi.

WEBSITES

ACMA (2007), Retrieved on 08-09-2007 from

http://acmainfo.com/docmgr/Status of Auto Industry/Status Indian Auto Industry.pdf

Auto India Mart (2007), Retrieved on 21-09-2007 from

http://auto.indiamart.com/index.html

India Infoline (2003), Automobile- Cars, Sector Report, retrieved on 01-09-2007 from

http://www.indiainfoline.com/sect/atca/ch01.html

SIAM (2007), Industry Statistics, Market Share, retrieved on 01-10-2007 from

http://www.siamindia.com/scripts/market-share.aspx

The Great Idea Finder (2005), Wheel, Retrieved on 22-09-2007 from http://www.ideafinder.com/history/inventions/wheel

26

COMPARISON OF TRANSPORTATION PROJECT EVALUATION METHODOLOGIES IN DEVELOPED AND DEVELOPING COUNTRIES

Kayitha Ravinder
S. Velmurugan
S. Gangopadhyay

ABSTRACT

Cost-Benefit Analysis (CBA) as a tool is basically the most commonly used technique to measure the direct impacts in monetary values and to evaluate the economic efficiency of a transportation project. Some countries follow Multi-Criteria Analysis (MCA) in addition to Cost -Benefit Analysis depending on the importance and objectives of the transportation project. In this regard it is necessary for researchers and investment/decision makers to understand what are the methodologies followed all over the world to take appropriate investment decisions and further which are the grey areas in this field. The present paper examines what are practices followed all over world in evaluating the transportation project appraisals in developed as well as developing countries and also emphasises the grey areas in which research is yet to be carried out. For this purpose developed countries like Japan, United Kingdom (UK), Germany, France, USA and India as a developing country have been compared. In this paper the methodology and parameters adopted by the above mentioned appraisals have been examined critically.

1. INTRODUCTION

Cost-Benefit Analysis (CBA) as a tool is basically the most commonly used technique to measure the direct impacts in monetary values and to evaluate the economic efficiency of a transportation project. Some countries follow the Multi-Criteria Analysis (MCA) in addition to Cost -Benefit Analysis depending on the importance and objectives of the transportation project. In this regard, it has been found necessary for researchers and investment/decision makers to understand the different methodologies followed all over the world to take appropriate investment decisions and also examine the grey areas in this field. The present paper looks at practices followed all over world in evaluating transportation project appraisals in developed as well as developing countries and also emphasising the grey areas in which research is yet to be carried out.

In this paper, it is proposed to compare transportation project evaluation considering the following parameters for different countries:

- Institutional setup
- System of transportation project evaluation
- Manuals for project evaluation
- Traffic forecasting demand
- Value of time
- Traffic safety
- Environmental impact Assessments
- Regional economic impacts
- Efficiency criteria
- Post evaluation

The paper has been structured as follows. Section 2 describes the Institutional setup in the transportation sector. Section 3 describes the comparison of transportation project evaluation methodologies and parameters in developed and developing countries and finally conclusions drawn from this paper are presented in Section 4.

2. INSTITUTIONAL SETUP IN TRANSPORTATION SECTOR

From Table 1, it is observed that institutional set up for developed and developing counties looks more or less similar. In developed countries regarding the road network hierarchy except in the case of Germany (Rothengatter,2000) the national transport master plan was prepared and being decided by the federal government and all other state and local governments would be integrated with the federal government where decisions in their state and local government spatial integration are concerned. France (Quinet, 2000) has decentralised all decision making, financing, tariff system except in Paris. US and the UK partly decentralised decision making expect in case of the national/truck road network. The national government would fund the projects, but most of the construction work would be carried out by the states only.

Regarding the funding in the US (Lee, 2000), all the user tax instruments would be routed to the federal government, and then revenue would be given to the states and local government projects. Further, the state and local governments would contribute the rest of the funding. The UK (Vickerman, 2000) adopted the centralised funding based on the plans prepared by local governments. Japan (Morisugi, 1995, 2000) has been funding national/expressways through earmarked road taxes.

In India, national highways planning and funding is being undertaken totally by the Central Government through an agency (NHAI). Further, BOT/BLT/PPP toll fee tariff has been fixed

Table 1: Comparison of Institutional aspects of the Transportation Sector

Point of Comparison	*USA*	*UK*	*France*	*Germany*	*Japan*	*India*
Road Network Management	Highways are owned and maintained by either State or Local Government authorities	National Highways are owned by DETR through Highway agency: regional and local roads and the responsibility of local authorities	Highways are owned and maintained by either National or Local Government authorities	Federal government is responsible for national roads. Regional, local roads and public transport are the responsibility of State governments.	National toll/non tolled roads are responsibility of central government. Ordinary roads are managed and funded by central and local government.	National highways are funded and maintained by central Government trough NHAI.State highways, local roads are responsibility of state governments. Rural roads are partly funded by NRRDA and state governments
Planning, Policy ,decision making and funding	States and local governments propose the projects and do most of the construction. Federal government pays about 70% depending up on the importance of the projects, rest the state/local governments would manage.	National Government is in charge of overall policy of making and funding the road projects. Local governments prepare the annual plans for regional and local roads for the approval of state governments. National government funds national roads through the National Highway agency. State and local roads are funded by local governments, However sometimes National governments will also fund depending upon the importance of the projects.	Public agency *Sindicat des Transports Parisiens (STP)* decides on new investments and tariffs.Except for Paris, decision making financing on urban roads are decentralized. For non urban roads national highways are the state in consultations with local authorities.National highways are funded by the national government or local authority with cross subsidyLocal roads are funded by local authorities.	Federal Government prepares national transport master plans as decided by the federal parliament. States governments can suggest the projects. State governments have to integrate their spatial structure in the state government plans. National transportation infrastructure projects was directly funded by national government. Regional and local infrastructure developmental plans will be funded by states and local governments partly funded by Federal government.	Funding for roads is from earmarked road tax and general tax revenues. Funding for toll roads are based on debts later recovered through tax revenues.	National highways planning and expansion works are manly by central government in funding as well as construction. State highways and local roads are by state governments and local authorities. Rural roads maintenance was with state governments and partly by NRRDA.

Table 1 (Contd.)

Point of Comparison	*USA*	*UK*	*France*	*Germany*	*Japan*	*India*
Mass Transport/ Transit operations	LRT/Subway systems, public transportation etc, are operated by public corporations subsided by national/ state/local governments	Rail transportation was privatized and subsidized by the national government.	Metros and tramways given subsidy by state governments	National railways are owned by federal government, managed and coordinated by the four operating companies.	Railways operated by private companies, Subway systems, public transport by state governments	Railways are owned by the National government. Metro systems are run by the central from the cross subsidies from national government. Public corporation looks after its construction, maintenance and operations.
Toll way operations	Toll roads for highway pricing picking up recently. Bridge toll pricing existing over a good number of bridges. Toll authorities are having full independence to set the toll fee. Toll tariffs are set to repay the bonds.	BOT concept for the bridges and tunnels either in the form of PPP/public private partnerships exists. Provision for the public private partner ship for all highway operations.	Toll fee will be decided by the Government. Concept of toll roads was just started.	As of now, no toll roads in operation. However, there are some demonstrative toll roads projects based on weight and emissions standards.	Japan Highway Public Corporation as self sustaining corporation by use of toll revenues collected from toll charges.	Concept of toll bridges was in operation. Toll roads are exclusively on BOT basis. However National highways toll and toll rates for the BOT projects are decided by the National government.

by the National Government. The state and local road network were planned and funded by the state/local governments. Recently, a central government level NRRDA (National Rural Road Development Agency) was established to take up rural road development. Funding for these projects would be given to the state governments and construction activity and maintenance would the state government responsibility. For the mass transport/LRT in India there are separate agencies which were formed for construction and maintenance.

3. COMPARISON OF TRANSPORTATION PROJECT EVALUATION METHODOLOGIES AND PARAMETERS IN DEVELOPED AND DEVELOPING COUNTRIES

3.1 Transportation project evaluation

From Table 2, it is seen that developed countries and a developing country like India would be using the Cost Benefit Analysis (CBA) by giving preferential weightage to some parameters as in the case of France and Germany which use the Multi-Criteria Analysis (MCA). In the UK the weightage would be time savings and accident reduction, while in France more importance is given to impact on local development of urban and intercity investments. Japan considers the global and environmental impacts while Germany gives importance to other alternative options.

3.2 Manuals for project evaluation

Each country has project evaluation packages and manuals. The US uses packages and manuals prepared by the Association of States Highway Transport Organisation (ASHTO) further revised by the federal administration. In addition to this for big projects it is mandatory that environmental impact assessment statements are also produced. In the UK, the National Association of Traffic Authorities (NATA) guidelines are followed for roads and bridges. In Germany, in addition to manual laid procedures, ecological impact assessment is also mandatory for major projects. Similarly, in Japan, the environmental impact assessment of road investment projects are mandatory. In India the Indian Road Congress (IRC) manual is used. In developing countries for World Bank funded projects, it is mandatory to use the Highway Design and Maintenance (HDM) analysis (see Table 3).

3.3 Traffic forecasting demand

It is observed from Table 4; all the developed and developing countries use a step wise procedure for traffic forecasting. In addition to the above, some countries like the US, the UK and France consider induced traffic in addition to India. The US uses implicitly diverted traffic. Further, in developing countries for the World Bank funded projects it is mandatory to work based on economic growth based on GDP growth elasticities. In Germany, only fixed matrix table is used.

3.4 Value of time

From the Table 5, it is seen that most developed countries use the wage rate approach in addition to stated preference and revealed approaches in case of non-working time. In India,

Table 2: Comparison of System of Transportation Project Evaluation

Point of Comparison	*USA*	*UK*	*France*	*Germany*	*Japan*	*India*
Criteria	Cost-Benefit Analysis (CBA) considering equity. Multi Criteria Analysis (MCA) will be used for regional projects	CBA	MCA aggregating the results after the each criteria.	CBA	MCA	CBA
Parameters and scope of impact	Following Travel impacts were consideredTravel time, cost savings, safety, induced traffic, environmental effects.	Travel time savings. accidents reduction, environmental effects	Weight assignments were given to decision makers. Impacts on local regional level are least considered.	Reduction in travel time, cost savings, spatial connectivity, reduction in accidents and environmental pollution, improved safety.	Main benefits are travel time savings, cost reduction, environmental benefits, accident benefits, safety and induced travel demand, improvement in life styles and living standards.	Reduction in travel time, cost savings, induced safety. accidents reduction.
Implementation of Policy Evaluation	Economic development impacts are considered in addition to CBA ratio.	CBA ratio helps in determining the ranking of the project	PDU process helps in determine the set goals of the project	Guide to prepare the comparative statement of priority of the projects. Considering the impacts of regional developments.	Uses the BIT (Benefit Incidence Table) by considering all the sectoral benefits in arriving the Social Net Benefits	CBA forms the basis for decision making of the project.

Table 3: Comparison of Manuals for Project Evaluation

Point of Comparison	*USA*	*UK*	*France*	*Germany*	*Japan*	*India*
Evaluation packages	Uses the packages developed by AASHTO (1977)and further revised guidelines by the Federal Aviation Administration (1998)	Design Manual for Roads and Bridges and NATA guidelines procedures.	Uses various techniques as specified in a number of manuals and procedures.	Federal Transport Infrastructure Plan main guide line.	There are manuals for road railways, airports and sea ports and navigation systems projects.	IRC mauls (Road Investment Decision Software), However developing countries mostly used package as per World Bank guidelines and HDM analysis.
Manuals	Depending upon the importance of the project specified guidance on selected topic would be prepared. However, it is mandatory for the big projects to get Environmental Impact Assessment Statement.	NATA has formal guidance produces on producing AST.Guidance on Methodology for the multi-modal studies are under preparation	Manual for intercity road Investment appraisal. Manuals on rail Infrastructure and urban Infrastructure.	Ecological Risk assessment for large projects is mandatory.	Environmental Impact Assessment Statement is mandatory for all major projects	IRC SP-30, and the Environmental Impact Assessment Statement is mandatory for the major projects.

Table 4: Comparison of Traffic Forecasting Demand

Point of Comparison	*USA*	*UK*	*France*	*Germany*	*Japan*	*India*
Method of forecasting	Conventional step wise forecasting	Conventional step wise method, the growth rate set by NRTF to reflect the localized conditions	Conventional step wise method	Conventional step wise method integrated with the rail, road and waterways.	Conventional step wise method for road, railways. For Seaways and air ports no specific methods are applied.	Conventional step wise method. Further growth rates for World Bank projects based on GDP growth elasticities. No specific method for railways, seaway and airways.
Induced demand	Induced demand was considered however taken as implicitly.	Uses both fixed and variable trip matrix.	Sometimes induced demand considered.	No project relates to induced demand. Only fixed matrix table considered.	Fixed OD tables. Only some specific projects consider induced demand.	Induced demand considered explicitly.
Other parameters	Forecasting includes diverted traffic that will be treated implicitly.	Traffic growth on each link would be same on the whole network.	Minimum sacrifice method would be adopted to estimate the traffic volume of TGV diverted from air traffic.	Forecast is integrated based on multi modal base.	Minimum sacrifice method is used estimate the traffic on air planes.	In some conventional projects, diversion curves are used to get diverted traffic.

stated preference is used (Reddy et all, 2003). In Japan some times, a mode choice model is used to calculate the disutility of congestion on roads in comparison with train. The Value of Travel (VOT) for working and non-working is different for US, UK and Germany. The same values are considered for the weekday and holidays in France and Japan. Values of VOT for each country that has been given in Table 5 shows that the values reflects more or less the same range for developed countries. For Indian conditions, the highest value on VOT adopted is around $1.5/hour.

3.5 Traffic Safety

All the countries presented use the traffic safety from estimated as the summation of the product of cost per accident, multiplied by traffic accident occurrence. Estimated methods on physical damage are different among the countries. Presently two methods are employed, namely willingness to pay and other is based on gross production method. Monetary value for physical damage would be based on market values commonly adopted. While Japan uses insurance statistics for the valuation of the physical damage, most other countries estimate the probability of the accident based on accident statistics. The accident cost for the different country has been given in the Table 6 indicates that the highest value is around $ 2.6 million with the least value being around $0.27 million for Japan. In India (Reddy et all,2003, IRC SP-30) it would be around 0.02 million (fatal accident cost) excluding the physical costs. However, the accident compensation is worked out on a case to case basis in India.

3.6 Environmental Impact Assessment

In developed countries like France, Japan and Germany attempts are being made to take into account the monetary terms of environmental impacts into the analysis. In the UK, these impacts are included in physical terms. In the USA environmental impacts are considered separately occasionally. In India, though the environmental impacts are assessed for major projects, (for the projects exceeding above Rs 50 cores) monetary values of environmental impacts in the cost benefit analysis has not been considered. France and Japan estimate the damage due to noise based on the hedonic approach while Germany adopts the criteria in terms of the amount of investment for noise reduction. Only France and Japan take into account global warming as an item for evaluation. All this is reflected in Table 7.

3.7 Regional economic impacts

Most of the developed countries do not consider this impact so as to avoid double counting. In case of Germany as shown in Table 8, employment effects due to transportation construction and operation are estimated. In India, these effects are not considered and not included in the cost benefit analysis of the projects.

3.8 Efficiency criteria

From Table 9 it is observed that only Japan and Germany consider the cost benefit ratio, net present values being the main criteria used. France adopts the modified net present value method. As far as ranking is concerned the UK, France and Germany explicitly state some criteria.

Table 5: Comparison of Value of Time

Point of Comparison	*USA*	*UK*	*France*	*Germany*	*Japan*	*India*
Method of estimation of VOT followed	Wage rate approach	Working hours based on wage rate approach. Non working time based on SP and RP studies	Wage rate approach	Mainly wage rate approach.	Mainly wage rate approach. Mode choice model sometimes used to calculate the disutility of congestion in comparison with the train.	Stated preference For types of routes,
Types of modes considered and by purposes	Working travel based on wage rate by trip purpose	By vehicle types mode wise VOT. Working and Non working purposes are also considered.	Working and non working rates are the same.	2 categories purpose wise.Four categories mode wise.(Car, bus , LCV, HCV)	Four types of modes wise. (car , bus, LCV HCVs) one category for rail mode.	Secondary and trunk routes (modes new cars, old brand cars, Mini bus, standard bus)
Approximate VOT ($/hour)	$ 40	$ 35~40	$ 21	$ 20	$ 20	$1.5

Table 6: Comparison of Traffic Safety Evaluation Methods

Point of Comparison	*USA*	*UK*	*France*	*Germany*	*Japan*	*India*
Items considered for evaluation	Material damage, Physical damage (injury and fatalities)	Value of life, injury physical damage, police costs, other cost dealing with accidents.	Material damage, Physical damage (injury and fatalities)	Material damage, Slight injury, Severe injury. Fatalities of road and rail based on statistics and forecasts. Value of life and insurance	Material damage physical damage, police costs, other cost dealing with accidents. Damage of ships	Material damage, Physical damage (injury and fatalities)
Methods employed	Based on market price of the material damage. Injuries and fatalities based on willingness to pay to avoid accidents and gross production. Accident occurrence is probability based.	Based on willingness to pay to avoid the accidents. Past accidents data on road types. Resources cost of accident differentiated by road.	Based on market price of the material damage. Injuries and fatalities based on willingness to pay to avoid the accidents. Accident occurrence is probability based.	Gross loss of production for physical damage. No subjective measure of human value.	Based on market price of the material damage. Injuries and fatalities based insurance statistics. Accident occurrence probability based.	Based on market price of material damage.
Value of human life ($ millions)	2.6	1.0	0.56	0.79	0.27	0.02 (excluding the physical damage cost)

Table 7: Comparison of Environmental Impact Assessments

Point of Comparison	*USA*	*UK*	*France*	*Germany*	*Japan*	*India*
Evaluation criteria	Not evaluated in monetary terms.	Not evaluated in monetary terms.	Not evaluated in monetary terms.	Included in monetary terms in CBA and additional risk indicator.	Not evaluated in monetary terms.	Not evaluated in monetary terms.
Items considered for the Evaluation	—	—	Global environmental impact carbon emissions), local air pollution, noise pollution.	Air pollution, all types ecological risk indicators.	Global warning, air pollution (NO_2), Noise.	Air pollution and ecological impact.
Methods employed	—	—	CO_2 tax,Hedonic Approach	Material damage cost, health damage costs. Willingness to pay	Hedonic approach, PCC report,	Procedure laid by IRC & Ministry of environment and Forests.

Table 8: Comparison of Regional Economic Impacts

Point of Comparison	*USA*	*UK*	*France*	*Germany*	*Japan*	*India*
Evaluation criteria	Not Evaluated	Not Evaluated, however generation impacts are included in NATA	Not Evaluated	Evaluated in monetary terms. For major projects impacts in terms of additional equity indicators.	Not Evaluated	Not Evaluated
Items considered for the Evaluation	—	Direct generation impacts.	—	Employment on construction phase and operation phase. Effects on development of low developed regions.	—	—
Methods to be considered	—	Employment directly due to project.	—	Time cost savings for region concerned are taken as base indicator and weighted by regional preference factors.	—	—

Table 9: Comparison of Efficiency Criteria and Post Evaluation

Point of Comparison	*USA*	*UK*	*France*	*Germany*	*Japan*	*India*
Project life	20 years for road20-30 years for air port 50 years for port	30 years	20 years	40 years	40 years	30 years
Discount rate	7%	6 ~ 8%	8%	3%	4%	10 ~ 12%
Criteria indices	Net present Value	Net present value and cost benefit ratio	Modified net present value	Cost-benefit ratio	Net present value	Cost-benefit ratio
Criteria employed	Cost benefit ratio to rank the project, in addition the equity also considered.	Cost benefit ratio to rank the project but not for decision making.	Cost benefit ratio to rank the project, in addition equity also considered.	Project with higher cost befit ratio > 3 would be included in the high priority projects. Cost benefit ratio 1-3 included in low priority, other are eliminated.	Cost-benefit ratios are used for efficiency. Further equity is also considered in decision making.	Cost benefit ratio would be used in addition to other parameters which the project would be influencing.
Financial Evaluation	Conducted for all the projects	Conducted for private financed projects	Conducted for all the projects	Conducted for major projects financed through PPP.	Conducted for all commercialized projects	Conducted for all projects.
Post-Evaluation	No explicit study	None	No explicit study	—	Ex-post evaluation is formal	None

In India in addition to the Cost benefit criteria, other considerations including the budget constraint influence the ranking of the project.

3.9 Post evaluation

According to Table 9, financial evaluation is to be carried out for all projects in developed and developing countries depending upon the type of project and especially when funded through PPP. Further post-evaluation though stated as a necessity by some developed countries, it is normally observed that explicit treatment has yet to be done.

4. CONCLUSIONS

In this paper, we try to bring some of the salient features of the transportation project evaluation methodologies and parameters that are taken in developed countries and in India. Further, in discussing the each of the mythology and parameters, we have also highlighted the some importance of the VOT (value of time), considering the monetary values of environmental impact assessments, and SDR (Social Discount Rates) based on observable economic data rather than on assumed value which reflects the actual economic conditions

Acknowledgements

Authors are thankful to Dr.Vikram Kumar Director, CRRI for his kind permission to publish the paper. The usual disclaimers nevertheless apply.

REFERENCES

Bristow, A. L.and Nellthorp, J., (2000) 'Transport project appraisal in the European Union', *Transport Policy*, Vol.7, pp.51-60.

IRC SP-30, 1993 'Indian Roads Congress Special Publication-30'.

Lee, Jr., D.B., (2000) 'Methods for evaluation of transportation projects in the USA'. *Transport Policy*, Vol.7, pp.41-50.

Morisugi, H. and Ohno, E., (1995) 'Proposal of a benefit incidence matrix for urban development projects', *Regional Science and Urban Economics* , Vol.25, pp.461-481.

Morisugi, H., (2000) 'Evaluation methodologies of transportation projects in Japan'. *Transport Policy*, Vol.7, pp.35-40.

Quinet, E., (2000),'Evaluation methodologies of transportation projects in France'. *Transport Policy*,Vol.7, pp.27-34.

Reddy, T.S., Velmurugan S., Madhu. E., Ramalingaiah A (2003) " Updation of Road User Cost and Revised Software for Evaluation of Highway Projects", Paper No.493, *Journal of the Indian Roads Congress*, Vol. 64, No.2, pp 207-267.

Rothengatter, W., (2000), 'Evaluation of infrastructure investments in Germany'. *Transport Policy, Vol.* 7, pp.17- 25.

Standing Advisory Committee on Trunk Road Assessment (SACTRA), (1999), Transport and the Economy, HMSO, London.

Vickerman, R., (2000), 'Evaluation methodologies transportation projects in the United Kingdom,. *Transport Policy, Vol.* 7, pp.7-16.

27

DEMAND SIDE FACTORS IN INFRASTRUCTURE SECTOR: A CASE STUDY OF ROAD PROJECTS

M. K. Datar
G. A. Tadas

ABSTRACT

Inadequacy of appropriate infrastructure facilities often becoming a constraint on development is a widely accepted position. Perhaps as a result, the supply side perspective is generally dominantly displayed among discussions regarding infrastructure "problems ". However, demand side factors which too would influence viability of infrastructure services are not explicitly accounted in any such an assessment. Inadequate demand would inevitably affect efficiency & profitability of such projects. Potential investors would certainly consider these aspects and would therefore influence investment flows in such projects. Inadequacy of demand may result from either price related or other activity related factors. This paper situates analysis of demand side factors in the context of infrastructure projects. Though it would seek to establish relevance of these factors for infrastructure projects in general, its focus would be on road projects wherein demand side factors are likely to be more important. The paper would also gauge the actual experience of a few road projects in relation to demand experienced over time. Finally, it would also suggest measures to deal with demand uncertainty in designing road projects in order to render private investment in these projects more attractive.

1. INTRODUCTION

That inadequacy of appropriate infrastructure facilities is becoming, a constraint on development is a widely accepted proposition. Perhaps, as a result, the supply side perspective is given more prominence in discussions regarding infrastructure "problems". In the context of an emerging market, a lack of infrastructure services is perceived as the main, if not the only, constraint. The real challenge, therefore, appears to be to create additional capacities to enhance the supply of a wide range of infrastructure services that is required. If public investment fails to expand due to budgetary constraints, private investment needs to be encouraged to meet investment shortfalls. In 1996, the Rakesh Mohan Committee (1996) prepared estimates of required investments in Indian infrastructure sectors. These estimates have been updated regularly since then, and different measures are suggested for augmenting investment flows from different sources-public and private - be it domestic or foreign. Surprisingly, demand side factors are rarely mentioned though demand side factors would also be equally important. Inadequate demand would inevitably affect efficiency & profitability of such infrastructure projects. Potential investors, particularly those from the private sector, would certainly consider this aspect though public sector investors, mainly government, may not be so particular as they could wait for a longer period for adequate return on investments. In the context of augmenting private investment flows, it would be necessary to analyse explicitly demand side factors for successful design and implementation of infrastructure projects. Inadequacy of demand may result from either price related or activity related factors.

This paper attempts to analyse demand side factors in the context of infrastructure projects. Though the paper seeks to establish the relevance of such factors for infrastructure projects in general, its focus would primarily be on road projects wherein demand side factors are likely to be far more important. As demand side factors are likely to be different in rural & urban areas, the analysis in this paper may prove to be useful to assess problems in the development of road infrastructure in semi-urban/rural areas where demand side factors may be more relevant.

The paper is divided into four sections. Section 2 analyses impact of demand side factors on infrastructure projects including road projects. The analysis would draw implications for project viability, pricing and returns to private investors. Section 3 extends the analysis to road projects where private operators/investors have limited degrees of freedom given the dimensions of a concessionaire agreement. The paper suggests ways to address potential risk concerns due to demand uncertainty. Section 4 describes the road sector in India while Section 5 explains the mechanism for private involvement in development of this sector. Finally, Section 6 presents an empirical analysis on the basis of private investment projects followed by concluding observations.

2. IMPACT OF DEMAND FACTORS

The world over, infrastructure projects are beset with time and cost overruns. Flyvbjerg (2005) and Flyvberg et. al. (2005a) find sustained increase in estimated cost and time required to complete large infrastructure projects in several countries over long stretches of time. They identified technical, psychological and politico- economic factors that led to systemic & sustained underestimation of costs and overestimation of benefits. More importantly, is that, as the deviation between estimates & actuals are not uniform (reflected in large standard deviations), this phenomenon could affect the choice of projects where by sub-optimal projects may get selected. Psychological factors — delusional optimism — as also politico economic factors would lead to overestimation of project benefits. This could happen mainly through overestimation of traffic volumes in road and port segments. Such phenomena, also discernible in electricity or telecom sectors, could lead to projects appearing more attractive with lesser pay back periods.

Infrastructure services are being expanded by encouraging participation of private investment in many countries in the world. The method of privatisation chosen (direct sale, divestment etc.,), to a large extent determines the outcome of such efforts. Hence the choice of the right mode is most crucial. In the case of infrastructure segments, generally national monopolies, concession agreements are found to be most suitable to achieve a proper risk distribution which does not leave room for opportunistic behavior and renegotiations (Calva and Felipe 1998). Experiences in Korea, which has a long record of private participation in Infrastructure (PPI), indicates that bidding out projects is a very complex and also politically sensitive process that needs to be certain, predictable and transparent so as to enhance competition. It was often found that cartelisation in the construction industry and a lack of expertise in regulatory authorities were the other constraints in achievement a higher level of success in privatisation. The Latin American experience highlights the importance of improving the balance of risk and expected return on projects to enhance private sector participation. Unless governments take effective measures to reduce regulatory risk, to improve framework for PPI and to strengthen risk mitigation mechanisms, private participation may remain limited (Fay and Morrison, 2007). It is, therefore, necessary for public authorities to address the concerns of private investors with regard to project related risks and the overall business risk.

The overall demand for various infrastructure services is generally linked with macro economic factors (growth in GDP, exports etc), which may get overestimated under optimistic growth scenarios. While prices are in general expected to have a negative impact on demand, such direct price effects may not be very significant in the case of infrastructure services. As service providers operate in monopoly or monopolistic market, prices would not change to balance the demand and supply gap in infrastructure segments. However, in some segments demand could be price sensitive, as for instance, in electricity where demand was found to be price sensitive when retail customers were given access to spot and forward markets in electricity in California.

However, it would be far from correct to conclude that prices have no economic role in infrastructure projects. Price of infrastructure services are set at levels which would help recoup the investments over a reasonable period (Gans, 2004). However, low levels of realised demand may lead to projects operating at sub-optimal capacity (low Plant Load Factor, low usage of telecom network or cargo handled in ports) and would result in longer payback periods. This can have adverse effects on generating resources for planned investments, particularly private investment. If current prices fail to generate sufficient surpluses, it may warrant provision for higher prices in order to maintain pay back periods within acceptable limits. But the resulting higher costs (prices) of infrastructure services may lead to a high cost structure in a wide range of sectors, which cannot but have an impact on overall costs & competitiveness of the national economy. After all, benefits from removal of infrastructure bottlenecks would flow through reduced effective cost, which themselves would arise from higher availability and/or better quality infrastructure. Prices would also perform a demand allocation role whereby demand would be channeled to a particular mode. For example, prices may not impact demand for transport services as such but these could shift demand between road & railways or railways and airlines.

The role of prices would be different across different infrastructure segments. In the case of electricity, lack of demand in a particular region can be made good by transmission of electricity to other regions (or even to other countries). Such flexibility would be virtually non-existent in space specific infrastructure services like roads & ports.

In view of the special characteristics of the infrastructure sectors, concession agreements are the preferred mode of encouraging private sector participation. Under this arrangement project developers are entitled to operate the project for a specific period at the end of which the project would be transferred to government. Under such arrangements, price variables are important parameters in design of such concession agreements. Concession rights are offered on the basis of (lowest) price of services to the final consumer. However, concession agreements are infamous for frequent renegotiations and initial conditions being subsequently changed, more often than not, at the cost of exchequer and to the benefit of private operator/ investor. A Concession agreement is an important tool for risk sharing between governments and private investors. It also has an important bearing on "competition for markets" which is characteristic of infrastructure segment unlike commodities signified by "competition in the markets." The price and demand for infrastructure services are, therefore, prima facie, important as these signify the nature and extent of competition. The manner in which these factors would operate depends on sector specific characteristics. Excess demand for power may lead to rationing of electricity but heavy demand for road services would result in air & sound pollution, traffic congestion and consequent delays. Similarly, low demand for electricity could be made good by transporting it to other regions/ sectors but low traffic volume would impair the operations of a road/ port projects. It may, therefore, be useful to study in greater detail the potential impact of demand side factors specifically for road sector.

3. ANALYSIS OF ROAD PROJECTS

A basic requirement for a successful road project is that "it should attract sufficient traffic so that the project benefits would exceed project costs" (Duncan & Lumain , 2006). The benefits would be in terms of reduced journey time and lowered vehicle operating costs. Moreover, improved roads would augment availability of privately operated passenger and goods transport services leading to higher competition resulting in lower cost and/or better quality of services for customers. An Asian Development Bank sector review also found that rapid and sustained economic growth was found to be instrumental in success of ADB funded highway projects. This was largely because economic growth was a leading factor in determination of volume & pace of road sector investment. Positive impact of road percolate through demand for transport services, vehicle ownership and government revenues, which in turn may add to the fresh capacities. It appears that while lack of proper roads & bridges may be a bottleneck in the growth process of all areas, road projects in fast growing areas would be utilised fully and hence more successful.

With a view to augment investment flows, private sector participation is sought through different mechanisms of business risk sharing as this would encourage private investors to assume risks they have been so far unfamiliar. This could be done by two alternative ways.

First, it can be done through an annuity route wherein government or government-sponsored entity would assure certain payments to the road developer on a regular basis. The annuity amount is derived so that project developer gets a reasonable return on capital cost of road construction and recurring cost of road maintenance. This scheme of arrangement provides an assured fair return to the developer provided he can implement the project without overruns and maintenance costs are controlled within estimated levels. The developer assumes project construction & maintenance risk. The business risk is assumed by government through annuity payments. However, annuity mechanism can only be of limited use as government's inability to find enough resource for infrastructure investments is the main reason to encourage private investment.

Secondly, under a concession arrangement, the developer gets a right to collect toll from road users over the period of concession agreement. The users of road services are required to pay a toll per use. While toll rates may not have a direct impact on road usage, the level of tolls is a potentially sensitive matter. Therefore, the government usually fixes the level of toll. Hence, the period of concession over which the road developer has a right to collect toll (at government specified rate) remains the principal factor, on the basis of which different bidders would compete while bidding for the project. The toll rates are fixed by the government based on toll levels on similar roads elsewhere and these are set to increase periodically at a fixed, pre-determined rate. The bidder, who asks for a low concession period (subject to fixed level of toll and standards of road construction & maintenance) would succeed in getting a road contract. In such an arrangement, the price factor has a limited direct role. However, demand for roads, which is a principal business risk factor, is largely borne by the concessionaire i.e., the private road developer. In such a situation, if demand rises more briskly than anticipated, the private operators would get all the benefits as the concession period is pre-fixed. If, on the other hand, demand rises at a lower than anticipated pace, the private operator would bear the full brunt of low demand. As compared to the annuity note, private developers assume large risks, i.e. project construction and maintenance risk in addition to business risk. It is likely that under these circumstances, private sector participation would be limited to only such roads that connect economically booming cities.

Though concession agreements require private developers to assume higher risks, in practice, private parties generally avoid significant risk sharing. They would abandon the projects in extreme cases forcing the government to re-award the contracts. But more often they would lobby for renegotiation of concession agreement or extending the period thereof. Renegotiation of concession agreement results in private sector successfully shifting the burden of risk sharing back to government. Renegotiations of concession agreements are quite widespread. Such phenomenon could be checked if there is provision for balanced risk sharing between private and public entities since inception of the project.

The process of bidding could be designed in such a manner that risks arising from uncertain traffic volumes are properly recognised with a view to facilitate wider participation of private players. This may be achieved by linking concession period to a fixed volume of traffic. If the pace of demand is brisk, the concession period is shortened; while in case the pace of demand is slack, the road developer and operator would get a higher concession period. This is achieved by a system of least Present Value of Revenue (PVR) auctions (Engel, Fischer & Galetovic, 2002). Under the system, bidders are chosen on the basis of PVR, given the toll rate fixed by the government quoted by the bidder. The bidder quoting the lowest value would win the bid. Thus, the amount of traffic volume is recognised while choosing among different bidders. The mechanism of discounting (even discount rate need to be specified by government) would accommodate different time profile of traffic growth. If the time profiles were altered, the operator would neither get the benefit nor bear the burden alone. Such a system would allow better risk sharing and therefore evoke wider participation of private investors.

Given the significant impact of economic growth in generating requisite volume of traffic, rural areas would in general be at a disadvantage as the risk of generating requisite traffic volume would be higher for rural road projects. Mechanism of PVR auctions provides a better framework for risk sharing. Risk of slow increase in traffic volumes would be adequately compensated by correspondingly larger concession period. In addition, as an added incentive, the specified discount rate could be different for urban (i.e. areas with high/certain traffic volumes) and rural (uncertain/ low traffic volumes). It is most likely that debt investors in rural projects would demand a higher interest rate as compared to investors in, say, road projects in metropolitan areas. This can be reflected in a higher discount rate that may be allowed for PVR auctions of rural road projects.

4. THE ROAD NETWORK IN INDIA

Between 1950-51 and 2005-06, freight traffic on Indian roads increased by 154 times - from 6 billion tonne kilometre (btkm) to 921.5 btkm - while passenger traffic increased by 178 times, from 23 bilion per kilometer (bpkm) to 4,089 bpkm. India's road sector needs massive investment restructuring to cope with the rising demand for road transport services. Road transport services account for about 85 percent of passenger movement and 70 percent of surface freight movement. The balance of the services is met by Indian Railways. It is estimated that 80-90 per cent of the roads (NH and SH) are not even suitable for the permissible axle loads of 10.2 tonnes. This situation is further aggravated by the fact that most vehicles are overloaded.

A well-developed network of highways can result in savings in vehicle operating costs due to lower fuel consumption and reduced maintenance costs, safer and faster journeys, benefits to trade, especially in the movement of perishables, and all-round economic development. Currently, though India's road network is the world's second largest, it is severely deficient in many ways. There is congestion on nearly 25 per cent of the national and state highways. It is widely reported that, commercial vehicles in India can traverse only 250-300 km (average speed of 30 kmph) in a single day, as against 600 km (average speed of 60-70 kmph) in developed countries.

During the Eleventh Five Year Plan (2007-12), total investment in the road sector is envisaged at Rs. 2,21,758 crore, of which Rs.1,19,735 crore (54%) is expected to be contributed by private sector. This shows the importance private sector investment would get in meeting the plan targets. To facilitate private sector participation government has taken various initiatives by way of extending tax benefits and schemes of viability gap funding.

5. THE MECHANISM FOR PRIVATE SECTOR PARTICIPATION IN ROAD PROJECTS

The Government, recognising the fact that infrastructure projects may not always be financially viable because of long gestation periods and limited financial returns, has acknowledged the need for extending financial support to Public Private Partnerships (PPPs) in Infrastructure. A PPP project, as is generally understood, means a project based on a contract or concession agreement, between a Government or statutory entity on the one side and a private sector company on the other side, for delivering an infrastructure service on payment of user charges. The sectors eligible for Viability Gap Funding under this Scheme are:

(*i*) Roads and bridges, railways, seaports, airports, inland waterways;
(*ii*) Power;
(*iii*) Urban transport, water supply, sewerage, solid waste management and other physical infrastructure in urban areas;
(*iv*) Infrastructure projects in Special Economic Zones; and
(*v*) International convention centres and other tourism infrastructure projects.

5.1 Model Concession Agreement

The concession agreement between the government/government agency and the concessionaire (promoter/developer) defines the framework within which road projects operate. In January 2006, government put in place a new Model Concession Agreement (MCA) for road contracts. This has standardised the documentation to a great extent for National Highway projects. However, it is observed that there are substantial differences in the State highway project contract terms vis-à-vis MCA. It is desirable that a unified MCA is adopted across the states to eliminate uncertainties in approaches being followed by different States.

We restrict our analysis to certain clauses which have a direct bearing on our analysis, i.e. those affecting time and cost over-runs, and traffic risks, with consequent effects on the earning capacity of the project. The penalty clauses in the MCA try to address the delays in project completion in some ways. For instance, in build own operate (BOT) Annuity based projects, the concessionaire will either receive a bonus for the early completion of the project or face a reduction in the annuity for delayed completion. While this might discourage delays, attributable to concessionaire, it may prove to be ineffective in preventing the delays which are beyond the control of concessionaire. As regards project cost escalation, The National Highways Authority of India (NHAI) mainly considers cost increases due to design/scope changes approved by it and not the cost escalations due to other factors. There is no specific provision in the MCA which states that traffic risk may be shared between the NHAI and the concessionaire, and hence, it is assumed that the same is to be borne by the concessionaire.

The projects are offered to private agencies by way of either BOT-toll based projects, or BOT-Annuity based projects, or Special Purpose Vehichle (SPV) projects. Under BOT-toll based projects, the concessionaire is responsible for the construction and maintenance of the project highway, and generates revenues through toll collection during the period of concession (which varies from 20 years to 30 years). After the completion of the concession period, the project highway is transferred back to NHAI. Under this approach, the concessionaire assumes the traffic risk. Under the BOT-annuity-based projects, the concessionaire is responsible for the construction and maintenance of the project highway, and NHAI would pay the concessionaire a semi-annual payment (annuity). The concession contract is awarded to the bidder quoting the lowest annuity amount. Under this approach, there is no direct reference to the number of vehicles using the highway, and hence the traffic risk is borne by NHAI. However, the NHAI, retains the right to charge toll at any stage of the project. In addition, it also retains all rights relating to property development, advertising along the project site and other revenue-generating sources. SPV projects are projects implemented by special purpose vehicles (SPVs) with NHAI participation. Projects with typical returns (IRR) of 5-10 per cent have been identified for development through the SPV route. Initially, NHAI planned to implement projects, especially port connectivity stretches, through the SPV route. All the projects identified under the SPV route are to be tolled.

From the point of view of our analysis, BOT-toll and BOT-Annuity based projects may be more relevant and hence, some discussion on the risk sharing (arising out of traffic uncertainty) between various parties is desirable. As mentioned above, in respect of Annuity projects, NHAI awards the projects to the bidder quoting the lowest annuity amount. NHAI pays the concessionaire a semi-annual payment, and hence the traffic risk is borne by NHAI. However, as the award is based on lowest annuity amount quoted, it is critical that the cost escalation, if any, is within acceptable limits so as to take care of debt servicing. It is pertinent to note that cost escalation not considered/accepted by NHAI for making revisions in annuity payment, will have to be absorbed by the concessionaire, and if not would directly affect the debt servicing ability of the project. It is observed that debt-equity ratio is generally much higher (some times 9:1) in respect of annuity based projects. Debt service coverage ratio is seen around 1.05-1.10, with hardly any margin to accommodate variations in costs, either project cost escalation or operation & maintenance cost increases. Coming to the BOT-toll based projects, it is evident that the traffic risk is borne by the concessionaire. As the projects are awarded on the basis of lowest concession period, in case of non-realisation of projected traffic in the initial years, the promoter suffers reduced revenue and associated debt service difficulties, and consequential lower than expected returns on the project. In such situation, there is a tendency to seek elongation of concession period, which may be deserving, but not necessarily or only partially conceded to by the government.

The choice between BOT-annuity based and BOT-toll based methods depends upon the level of optimism about expected traffic. Considering that annuity is a fixed guaranteed payment by the government/government agency, it has implication for the government budget in case the traffic is inadequate to cover the annuities. This may put limits on the number of such projects that government can take on. Moreover, if the objective is to promote greater private sector participation based on risk sharing basis, annuity projects may not be the preferred mode. On the other hand, BOT-toll based projects throw open many opportunities for private sector participation, and also reduce the need for budgetary support as required in the case of annuity projects. The solution lies in designing appropriate method of risk sharing (arising out of traffic uncertainty) between the government, concessionaire and the lenders.

6. PERFORMANCE OF PPP ROAD PROJECTS

Over 200 National highway projects have been awarded by the NHAI to private players till date under BOT/SPV and Annuity route. Majority of these are still under implementation. Even for completed projects, little information is available. Hence, our empirical analysis is necessarily based on a tiny number of projects for which information is available in the public domain.

Under Phase I of the National Highway Development Programme (NHDP)out of a total of seven BOT toll stretches awarded, five have been completed. Stretches like Jaipur-Kishangarh,

Tumkur-Nelamangla have witnessed higher traffic numbers than anticipated. The recently completed Satara-Kagal stretch, is recording lower than the anticipated traffic volumes.

As mentioned earlier, there is a tendency on the part of PPP players to under-estimate costs and over-estimate traffic in a bid to win the project contracts. An analysis of financial performance of PPP road projects in the past few years would provide useful insights in this regard. Unfortunately, data on financials for most road project companies are generally not available. In what follows, an attempt is made to piece together available data based on various sources to enable some reasonable understanding of these issues. We present three sets of experiences – two BOT-toll based projects, for which financials could not be obtained, but certain basic information is available; two BOT-annuity based projects and one BOT-toll based project for which some financial data are available.

6.1 BOT Annuity based projects

The two annuity based road projects selected for the analysis are those undertaken by the GMR group companies, Hyderabad viz. Ankapalli-Tuni (60 km between Tuni and Tindivanam in Andhra Pradesh and Tambaram-Tindivanam Annuity projects (90 km between between Tambaram and Tindivanam in Tamil Nadu). Both these stretches were considered having a high traffic density (a daily traffic of 16,000-20,000 PCUs on the Ankapalli-Tuni stretch, and 32,750 PCUs on the Tambaram-Tindivanam stretch as in 1999). The EPC cost of the Ankapalli-Tuni (NH-5 for stretch of 60 kms) and Tambaram-Tindivanam (NH-45 for a stretch of 93 kms) projects were estimated to cost around Rs.315 crore and Rs.430 crore respectively. The projects achieved financial closure in June 2002, and had a debt-equity ratio of 4:1. The concession period is 17.5 years, of which construction period is 2.5 years. The Ankapalli-Tuni project commenced operations in December 2004 as per schedule, while Tambaram-Tindivanam did in October 2004 (one month ahead of schedule). Being Annuity projects, there is no traffic risk, and the company is expected to get annuities as per the Concession Agreement. However, based on the summary results presented in Table 1, some interesting patterns emerge. The total income, being an annuity project, would more or less be fixed. Net profit may vary depending upon variations in operating costs and interest payment. In the instant cases, net profit marginally declined during 2006-07 compared to 2005-06. Interest coverage is around 1.05-1.10, which is lower than the desired levels. The return on capital employed is about 9-10%, which may consider reasonable for Annuity projects. As data relate only to two years, we desist from making any generalised conclusions. However, it may be noted that interest coverage being just over one, there would be difficulties in debt repayment unless supported by additional resources.

Table 1: Select Financials for BOT Annuity based projects

Sr.	*Company Name*	*PAT*		*Interest coverage employed (%)*		*Return on capital*	
No.		*Mar-05*	*Mar-06*	*Mar-05*	*Mar-06*	*Mar-05*	*Mar-06*
1.	G M R Tambaram-Tindivanam Expressways Pvt. Ltd.	7.86	4.84	1.62	1.12	na	10.01
2.	G M R Tuni-Anakapalli Expressways Pvt. Ltd.	8.8	1.37	2.46	1.04	na	9.47

Further, if the projects face time and cost over-run (which may be possible in many road projects), given the fixed annuity payments and high debt-equity ratio, debt servicing will be adversely affected. It is desirable that the debt-equity ratio is kept at a reasonable level in respect of annuity projects as a cushion against such eventualities.

6.2 BOT Toll based road projects

The Tumkur-Nelamangla project involved four-laning of the 32-km stretch between Tumkur and Nelamangala (on NH-4, near Bangalore in Karnataka). The project was awarded to Jayaswals-Neco (of the Neco group, formerly known as the Nagpur Engineering Company Ltd) that quoted the lowest grant of Rs.24.8 crore (including a capital grant of Rs.20.8 crore and an O&M grant of Rs.4.1 crore). The project was implemented through an SPV, Jas Toll Road Company (JTRC). The concession is for a period of 19 years (including 2 years for construction). The overall project cost was estimated at around Rs.155 crore. A consortium of banks and financial institutions funded the project and the financial closure was attained in the last quarter of 2002. The traffic on this stretch was estimated at 24,000 PCUs (as of 1999). The current traffic level is around 34,617 PCUs per day. The company has registered net profits and taking advantage of good financials, it has in the past securitised the toll receivables to pre-pay high cost debt. The Jaipur-Kishangarh 90.38-km project (lying on NH-8 in Rajasthan) involved six-laning of the existing two lanes on the section. This is a high-density corridor on NH-8, linking Delhi with Mumbai and the important coastal centres of Gujarat. The bidding for this project occurred three times due to various issues. It was finally awarded to the consortium of GVK International NV and B Seenaiah & Company (Projects) Ltd., as it sought the lowest capital grant of Rs.211 crore from NHAI. (The consortium of Larsen & Toubro and Joannou & Paraskevaides of Cyprus, the only other bidder to submit price bids, had sought a capital grant of Rs.225 crore). The project was implemented through an SPV, namely GVK Jaipur-Kishangarh Expressway Pvt Ltd. The concession period is for 20 years, including the construction period of 30 months, from the date of financial closure. The project cost was estimated at Rs. 615 crore and was proposed to be financed on a debt equity ratio of 3:1. The project achieved financial closure in May 2003. It is understood that the concessionaire company's traffic projections were different from that prepared by NHAI. NHAI has accepted the traffic projections prepared by L&T, with the clause that if there is higher traffic and consequently higher revenue, 20 per cent of the additional revenue will be ploughed back for road maintenance, 40 per cent will go to the concessionaires, and the balance 40 per cent to NHAI. It is understood that the project company has been able to achieve satisfactory financials.

Although, the above success stories of toll based road projects are not directly aiding our analysis, they have been identified as cases in study for award of toll based projects in similar road projects. However, it may be interesting to further analyse traffic turnover with a view to reflect on the possibility of cutting short the concession period in such successful projects.

6.3 NOIDA Toll Bridge Co. Ltd.

The only road project which is in operation for quite some time now and for which reasonable amount of data are available is the NOIDA Toll Bridge Co. Ltd. It is recognised that it generally takes 4-5 years for the traffic to pick up as the users need time to evaluate the full benefits of the tolled roads. Some detailed account of NOIDA Toll Bridge Co. Ltd. would be helpful in gaining a better understanding of the dynamics of performance of road project companies. The concession for the Delhi Noida Toll bridge project (NTB) was awarded in 1997. The NTB project comprises a main bridge (spanning 552 metres), three minor bridges, and an 8-lane expressway (length of 7 km). The project was developed by Noida Toll Bridge Company Ltd (NTBCL), an SPV promoted by NOIDA and IL&FS. Strategic investors, like AIG Indian Sectoral Equity Fund, Asian Infrastructure Mezzanine Capital Fund and the World Bank also have a stake in the SPV. The bridge, which opened to traffic in February 2001, was among the first few projects to have been developed as a Public Private Partnership (PPP) in India. The contract typically, had not given the Public Authority NOIDA a role in assessing the reasonableness of capital and operational costs reported by the concessionaire. Shortfalls in returns for previous years would, thus, result in a corresponding increase in project cost, on which further returns are payable. As a result, the initial capital cost of Rs.408 crore had risen to Rs.953 crore as at March-end 2006. A review of the contract has shown that the concession agreement for the Delhi Noida bridge project has several features that appear to weigh the contract in favour of the private partner and that, from a public policy viewpoint, depart from best practice contract design (Sheoli Pargal, 2007). However, it may noted that contract documents and procedure followed since then have undergone considerable changes and there is now a feeling that system has been made more transparent over the years.

Table 2: Performance of NOIDA Toll Bride Co. Ltd

Year (March)	*Total Income (Rs. crore)*	*PAT (Rs. crore)*	*Interest Coverage*	*Cash profits (Rs. crore)*	*Long Term Bank Borrowing*	*Return on Capital Employed*
2000-01	1.29	-4.73	0.05	-4.28	95.5	na
2001-02	11.27	-45.62	-0.08	-37.27	133	-1.02
2002-03	18.22	-28.6	0.07	-20.75	141.84	0.59
2003-04	25.29	-21.11	0.42	-19.43	148.36	3.67
2004-05	30.97	-16.5	0.5	-11.79	128.39	3.65
2005-06	40.27	2.61	1.09	8.75	103.94	4.21
2006-07	47.76	11.06	1.68	23.73	39.25	4.41

In the initial years of its operations, the traffic fell short of expectations/projections. The low traffic coupled with the high cost of debt (at 16 per cent), resulted in the company suffering cash losses till 2004-05, requiring granting of restructuring package by the banks and institutions in February 2003 (Table 2). However, the traffic growth has been substantial in the past 3 years, which can be seen from the turn-around in financials. The company realised profit (PAT) for the first time in 2005-06, which has been on the rise in the subsequent year. There has also been a decrease in total costs, which may be interpreted to mean consolidation in costs and scope for controlling costs with the passage of time as the operations stabilise. The return on capital employed has improved, although lower than general expectations from toll-based projects.

Thus, it might be said that initial years generally pose difficulties for the Road project companies. Even the Mumbai-Pune Expressway, on which there were high expectations, faced similar problems in the beginning. The Mumbai-Pune Expressway is a 6-lane, 95 km long, access controlled concrete expressway, implemented by the Maharashtra State Road Development Corporation

(MSRDC). The project (except the Panvel Bypass) was completed in May 2001; however, it was partially opened to traffic from July 2000. However, the corridor traffic was estimated at 50 per cent of the initial projections. Further, the overall traffic diversion from the existing NH-4 to the expressway was lower than expected. Though the traffic diversion for cars was estimated at more than 80 per cent, it was just around 30 per cent in the case of high toll paying traffic, such as trucks and multi-axle vehicles. This could be partly attributed to the perception of high toll rates on the expressway and the availability of an alternate toll free route (NH-4). As a significant portion of the debt had to be repaid in the initial 3-4 years of operation, and the fact that project cash flows in the initial years were not sufficient to meet even the interest payment, MSRDC needed significant infusion of funds for the project.

7. CONCLUSIONS

It is no wonder that National highways or state highways that are not part of heavy traffic corridors would need proper scrutiny in terms of traffic projections and reasonableness of cost to avoid any potential debt service defaults and consequent threats to viability. The debt structuring for such road projects should also factor in conservativism, if one may so use the term, while evaluating these projects. Further, sufficient cushion should be provided in the initial years by considering longer moratorium and lower repayment installments.

Our analysis reveals risk prone financials of completed projects. In the case of annuity based projects, interest coverage ratio barely exceeds one which implies capacity to repay principal dues is uncertain. In the case of only one toll based project analysed above the project faced difficulties in initial years mainly due to low traffic volumes. During the initial years low traffic the company had to face financial problems necessitating financial restructuring as also extension of concession period. Despite the empirical finding are from a small sample, these clearly support the importance proper risk sharing mechanism. This aspect also comes out very clearly from international experience.

It is felt that PVR auctions would provide a flexible risk sharing mechanism to tackle the main business risk for road project viz. uncertain traffic volumes. This would encourage wider participation by private sector over a whole range of road projects both in urban and rural areas.

One encouraging sign is government is trying innovative ways to fund road projects. It is worth noting that a new financial structure has been tried for certain road projects (Vadapa-Gonde and Pimpalgaon-Dhule) in the recent past. Under this, the concessionaire would get a positive grant during the early years of the concession period, to be compensated by a negative grant towards the end of the concession period. This type of financial restructuring can create a positive environment for the BOT projects in the days to come.

REFERENCES

Andres, et. al. (2007), *Do Regulation and Institutional design matter for Infrastructure Sector Performance?* Policy Research Working Paper 4378, World Bank.

CMIE Data Base.

Cris-Infac Study on Road Sector, Centre for Railway Information System, New Delhi.

Duncan, and Lumain, (2006), *Learning from Successful Road Projects; A Case Study from the 2006 Annual Evaluation Review*, Asian Development Bank.

Engel, Fischer, and Galetovic, (2002), *A New Approach to Private Roads*, Regulation.

Estache, and Serebrisky, (2004), *Where do we stand on Transport Infrastructure Deregulation and Public– Private Partnership?*, Policy Research Working Paper 3356 World Bank.

Fay, M. and Morrison, M. (2007), *Infrastructure in Latin America and the Caribbean: Recent Developments and Key Challenges*, World Bank.

Flyvbjerg, (2005), *Policy & Planning for Large Infrastructure Projects: Problems, Causes & Cure,* Policy Research Working Paper 3781, World Bank.

Flyvbjerg Bent et al (2005a), *How (In)accurate are demand forecasts in public works projects?*, Journal of American Planning Association, 71(2) Spring pp. 131-46.

Gans, S. (2004), *Access Pricing and Infrastructure Investment*, Melbourne Business School , University of Melbourne.

Graham.D. and Glaister, S. (2002), *Review of Income & Price Elasticity of Demand for Road Traffic,* Centre for Transport Studies, Imperial College of Science, Technologies & Medicine.

India Infrastructure Report, 3i Network Oxfor University Press, various Issues.

Lopez, and Felipe (1998), *On Privatisation Methods*, Development Discussion Paper No. 665, Harvard Institute for International Development, Harvard University.

NHAI Website.

Paul, and Dinghem, (2005), *Private Participation in Infrastructure Projects in the Republic of Korea*, World Bank Policy Research Working Paper.

Rakesh Mohan Committee Report (1996), *The India Infrastructure Report,* Ministry of Finance, Govt. of India.

Sheoli,(2007), *Concession for the Delhi Noida Bridge*, August, Planning Commission.

Virmani, A.(2004), *Infrastructure Development and Financing*, ICRIER.

28

FUTURE MOBILITY IN INDIA: IMPLICATIONS FOR ENERGY DEMAND AND CO_2 EMISSIONS

Sanjay Kumar Singh

ABSTRACT

The aim of this study is threefold. First, it aims to provide a reliable data set of land-based passenger traffic volumes in India from 1950-51 to 2000-01 for the five major motorized modes of transport — two-wheelers, cars, auto-rickshaws, buses, and railways. Second, based on this data set, it aims to estimate the long-term trends in motorized traffic volume and modal split up to the year 2020-21. Third, based on the projected values of aggregate traffic volume and modal split, this study aims to estimate the level and growth of energy demand and CO_2 emission from the passenger transport sector in India. It is found that the motorized traffic volume in India will be of the order of around 13000 billion passenger-kilometers in 2020-21, out of which 91.7% will be on the roads and the rest on railways. If there is no reduction in modal energy and CO_2 intensities, energy demand is projected to increase from 1060.8 peta joules in 2000-01 to 5584.4 peta joules in 2020-21 and CO_2 emission will increase from 19.80 to 93.25 million metric tons of carbon equivalent during the same period.

1. INTRODUCTION

Passenger mobility in India relies heavily on rail and road. Passenger travel by air and water is negligible in comparison to rail and road. On an average, an Indian traveled 285 Kms in a year during 1950-51, out of which 185 Kms was by rail and 100 Kms by road. In a span of five decades their annual travel figure jumped to 3470 Kms - 449 Kms by rail and 3021 Kms by road. From 1950-51 to 2000-01, passenger travel per capita (measured in terms of passenger-kilometers per capita; PKm/cap) by road and rail taken together increased at the rate of 5.13% per annum against the per capita Gross Domestic Product (GDP) growth of around 2.23% per annum.[1] It is perhaps surprising to know that between 1970-71 and 2000-01, in light of an 88% population growth, absolute motorized mobility (measured in terms of passenger-kilometers; PKm) has risen by 888% in India. The growth of road-based passenger mobility (PKm) during the last 50 years has been around 9.17% per year against the corresponding compound annual growth rate of 3.93% by rail. Consequently, the road share in passenger mobility increased from 35% in 1950-51 to 87% in 2000-01.

Rapid increase in travel demand and increasing reliance on road transport has serious implications for various issues related to energy and environment. Already, the transport sector is a major cause of air pollution in urban areas. It contributes significantly to major environmental challenges both at local as well as global levels. The transport sector is a major consumer of energy particularly petroleum fuels. Designing and implementation of effective strategies to reduce transport sector's impact on environment and energy demand require a reliable projection of motorized mobility for the forthcoming years. This paper lays the foundation for the same.

The main aim of this study is to forecast the level of traffic mobility, energy demand, and CO_2 (carbon dioxide) emission from the land-based passenger transportation in India up to the year 2020-21. There are typically two ways to estimate future traffic mobility. The first approach is generally based on independent projections of traffic volume per mode of transport over time. Typically, each modal projection is built on a different method, and the total traffic volume becomes simply an aggregate of the independent estimates for the various modes. The second approach is based on a projection of motorized mobility (the aggregate traffic volume of two-wheelers, cars,[2] auto-rickshaws, buses, and trains) in a first step and the related modal split is computed afterwards. The second approach is a better one for developing long-term scenarios since it takes into account the competition between modes (Schafer, 1998). Projections based on the first approach offer some glimpses into the future, often in the form of multiple scenarios that bound a large range of possibilities, but offer little guidance about the most likely ones (Schafer and Victor, 2000). This paper follows the second approach to allow formulation of aggregate and long-term scenarios. The aim is to project total mobility and the share of each mode far away in the future. This aggregate approach will be useful when we analyse the transport systems' impact on the environment and energy demand. The forecasting model used in this paper is mainly built on only two explanatory variables: GDP and population. Annual data from 1950-51 to 2000-01 are used to forecast the future mobility in India. The statistical program LIMDEP Version 8.0 is used for the required regression analysis.

The paper is organised as follows. Section 2 presents the aggregate as well as mode-wise traffic volume data from 1950-51 to 2000-01. Section 3 deals with the model, model estimation, projection of per capita as well as absolute mobility, and estimation of modal split changes from 2000-01 to 2020-21. Section 4 describes the energy demand and CO_2 emission scenarios. The paper's findings are summarised in Section 5.

2. PASSENGER MOBILITY IN INDIA DURING THE PAST FIVE DECADES

The paper presents for the first time, annual time series data of land-based traffic volume in terms of passenger-kilometer from 1950-51 to 2000-01.[3] These data account for the five major modes of transport, namely cars, two-wheelers, auto-rickshaws, buses and railways. The data sources and estimation methods are summarised in the Appendix.

Passenger traffic volume in India increased from 102 billion passenger-kilometers (BPKm) in 1950-51 to 3536 BPKm in 2000-01 due to a 12.18-fold increase in annual distance traveled by the people (from 285 Kms in 1950-51 to 3470 Kms in 2000-01), and a 2.84-fold rise in population (from 359 million in 1950-51 to 1019 million in 2000-01). Analysis of per capita mobility data shows that the average annual distance traveled by the people tripled every two decades (Figure 1). Although a large proportion of the mobility need is still catered to by the buses, there is increasing reliance on automobiles in recent years. For example, during 1990s per capita mobility by two-wheelers, auto-rickshaws and cars increased by 124%, 130% and 90% respectively, against the corresponding increase of 60% for buses and a meager 27% for railways. Thus, mobility share of private- and para-transit modes[4] increased from 16.2% in 1990-91 to 21.2% in 2000-01, whereas share of both buses and railways declined during the same period (Figure 2).

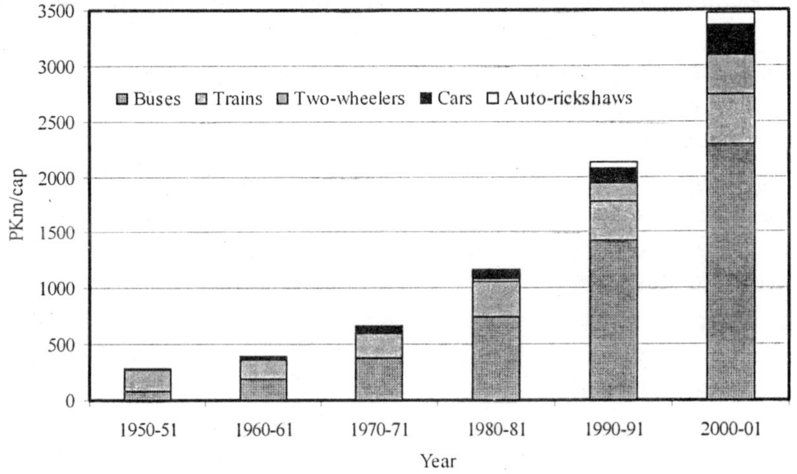

Fig. 1: Mode-wise motorized mobility per capita in India

Although the railways played a dominant role in providing passenger mobility from the second half of the nineteenth century to the early 1950s, the rail-system has been continuously losing its ground from the late 1950s. Between 1950-51 and 2000-01, rail-based passenger mobility increased at the rate of 3.93% per annum against the corresponding annual growth rate of 9.17% for roads. This was largely due to a tremendous increase in the motor vehicle population in the last three decades or so. Currently, motor vehicle population in India is growing at a rate of around 10% per annum. In 1990-91 there were about 21 million vehicles in the country. In 2000-01, this number increased by more than 2.5 fold to 55 million.

The vehicle population in India is growing faster in the category of two-wheelers and three-wheelers (auto-rickshaws). During 1950-51 to 2000-01, the two-wheeler and three-wheeler population grew at an average annual rate of 15.6% and 14.9% respectively. The growth in population of car was relatively modest and in the last five decades, increased at the rate of 7.9% per year. The corresponding figure for buses was 5.7%. If we compare the growth rate in recent years, say from 1995-96 to 2000-01, we find that both cars as well as two-wheelers were growing at the rate of around 10.5% per year, and three-wheelers (auto-rickshaws) increased at the rate of 11.3% per annum. During the same period bus population increased only at the rate of 4.5% per annum, whereas total motor vehicle population increased at the rate of 10.2% per annum. As income of the people increases, demand for personalised modes of transport is expected to increase more rapidly. The modal split indicates that in 1970-71; about 31% of the total vehicles were two-wheelers, which increased to 70% in a span of just three decades. As a result, the percentage share of buses in the total motor vehicle population declined from 4.9% in 1970-71 to 1.0% in 2000-01.

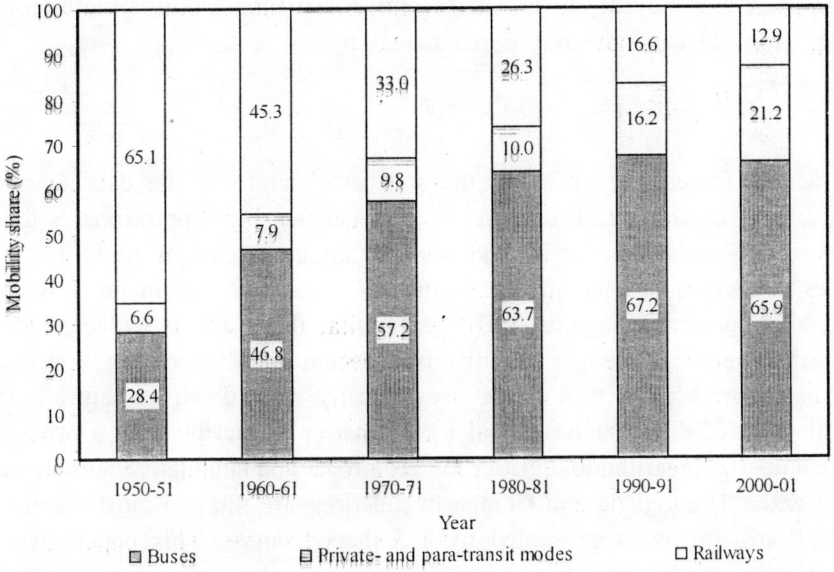

Fig. 2: Share of different modes in providing passenger mobility in India

3. PASSENGER MOBILITY IN INDIA DURING THE NEXT TWO DECADES

3.1 The model

The demand for mobility depends on various socio-economic factors such as age distribution, household composition, employment, educational level, supply of public transport services, infrastructure availability, government policy towards automobiles and transport, prices of different transport services, fuel and vehicle prices, income of the people, etc. At the national level, the relationship between per capita mobility and factors influencing the same can be written as:

$$\frac{PKm}{cap} = f(X) \qquad \text{... (1)}$$

where $\frac{PKm}{cap}$ is passenger-kilometers per capita (representing per capita mobility) and X is a vector of variables influencing the level of per capita mobility.

Using equation **(1)**, it is possible to estimate the future level of mobility if data for each of the variables on the right hand side are available. However, time series data for many of these variables are not readily available for India. In this situation, it is important to find out the key determinants of mobility for which time series data are available. Schafer (1998), Dargay and Gately (1999), Schafer and Victor (2000), Preston (2001) and many others have shown that there is a close relationship between income and demand for mobility. The strong relationship between income and mobility is found for both cross-country as well as time-series data. Figure 3, which presents the relationship between per capita mobility and per capita GDP for India, reiterates the same.[5]

Therefore, in this paper, per capita GDP will be used as the main explanatory variable to project future passenger mobility in India. Assuming that time captures the effects of the omitted variables, equation (1) can now be approximated by

$$\frac{PKm}{cap} = f\left(\frac{GDP}{cap}, time\right) \qquad \text{... (2)}$$

In a practical forecasting problem, the statistical nature of the data-generating process is unknown and the forecaster's task is to select a model that best approximates the 'real life' data generating process. For a time series like the per capita passenger mobility, it is conceivable that the series converges to a maximum as income reaches a certain level. If we plot level of passenger mobility per capita against GDP per capita, the graph is expected to look like some sort of a *S*-shaped curve. Passenger mobility is expected to increase slowly at the lowest income levels, and then more rapidly as income rises, finally slow down as saturation is approached. There are a number of different functional forms that can describe such a process; for example, the logistic, Gompertz, logarithmic logistic, log reciprocal and cumulative normal functions (Dargay and Gately, 1999).[6] The logistic and Gompertz functions are the two most widely used functional forms to describe a process represented by a *S*-shaped curve. This paper also uses these two functions to model and forecast passenger mobility in India.

The logistic model can be written as

$$\left(\frac{PKm}{cap}\right)_t = \frac{\alpha}{1+\gamma\exp(-\beta\left(\frac{GDP}{cap}\right)_t - \lambda(time)_t)} + \varepsilon_t \qquad \text{... (3)}$$

where α is the saturation level and ε_t is an error term at period t. All the parameters α, β, γ and λ are positive.

Similarly, the Gompertz model can be written as

$$\left(\frac{PKm}{cap}\right)_t = \alpha\exp\left[-\gamma\exp\left(-\beta\left(\frac{GDP}{cap}\right)_t - \lambda(time)_t\right)\right] + \varepsilon_t \qquad \text{... (4)}$$

where α is the saturation level and ε_t is an error term at period t. All the parameters α, β, γ and λ are positive. Parameters γ, β and λ define the shape or curvature of the function.

Models **(3)** and **(4)** need to be transformed into a linear form in order to estimate them using Ordinary Least Squares (OLS) method. The logistic model **(3)** can be transformed in a linear form as follows:

$$\ln\left(\frac{\alpha}{\left(\frac{PKm}{cap}\right)_t}-1\right)=\beta_0+\beta_1\left(\frac{GDP}{cap}\right)_t+\beta_2(time)_t+\varepsilon_t \qquad \text{... (5)}$$

where α is the saturation level and ε_t is an error term at period t. Parameter β_0 is positive and both β_1 and β_2 are negative.

Similarly, the Gompertz model (4) can be transformed as

$$\ln\left[\ln\left(\frac{\alpha}{\left(\frac{PKm}{cap}\right)_t}\right)\right]=\beta_0+\beta_1\left(\frac{GDP}{cap}\right)_t+\beta_2(time)_t+\varepsilon_t \qquad \text{... (6)}$$

where α is the saturation level and ε_t is an error term at period t. Parameter β_0 is positive and both β_1 and β_2 are negative.

Models (5) and (6) can be estimated by OLS provided we know the saturation level α.[7] It's possible to get a reliable estimate of the saturation level by making a reasonable assumption about the time spent on travel per person per day (i.e., travel time budget) and average speed of vehicles. For example, if all demands are met at an average speed of 30 km/hour and the travel time budget is fixed at 1.1 hour/capita/day, the total annual distance travel would be around 12000 km/capita.[8] So, if we assume that all demands are met at a maximum possible (average) speed of 30 km/hour, mobility per capita of 12000 will be the saturation level. Considering the socio-economic characteristics of India (such as population density, rapid increase in telephone density, expected boom in information technology, greater reliance on public transport, high fuel prices, etc.) and the level as well as growth in per capita mobility in the developed world, a figure of 12000 PKm per capita appears to be the appropriate saturation level for India.

According to the data published by the ECMT-Eurostat, during the year 2000, land-based PKm per capita in the European Union (EU) countries were around 12000. Although land-based mobility trends differ from country to country, mobility has been relatively stable since 1990 in the United Kingdom and Germany. The saturation level for these two countries may be somewhere around 12000 PKm per capita. Analysis of the data published by the Bureau of Transportation Statistics, USA shows that during the year 2000, passenger-kilometer per capita by rail and road taken together in the United States of America was around 24000. The US is also approaching its saturation level since growth in per capita mobility is slowing down in recent years. The difference in the saturation level between the US and EU is primarily due to the difference in the socio-economic factors. Public transport is far more important for passenger travel in the EU than in the US. The much greater car travel per capita in the US is largely due to far more extensive motorway networks, much cheaper petrol, motor vehicle, and roadway taxes and fees, and the longer trip distances both within and between cities. Since transport availability characteristics in India is more close to the EU, we expect that the saturation level in India would be around

12000 PKm per capita. Singh (2000) estimated that the saturation level for land-based passenger mobility in India will be around 20000 billion PKm. Assuming that the Indian population will saturate at 1.65 billion, saturation level for mobility per capita would be around 12000 Kms. However, both the logistic and Gompertz models will be estimated for three different saturation levels, 12000, 16000 and 20000 PKm/capita to illustrate these alternative paths of per capita passenger mobility in India.

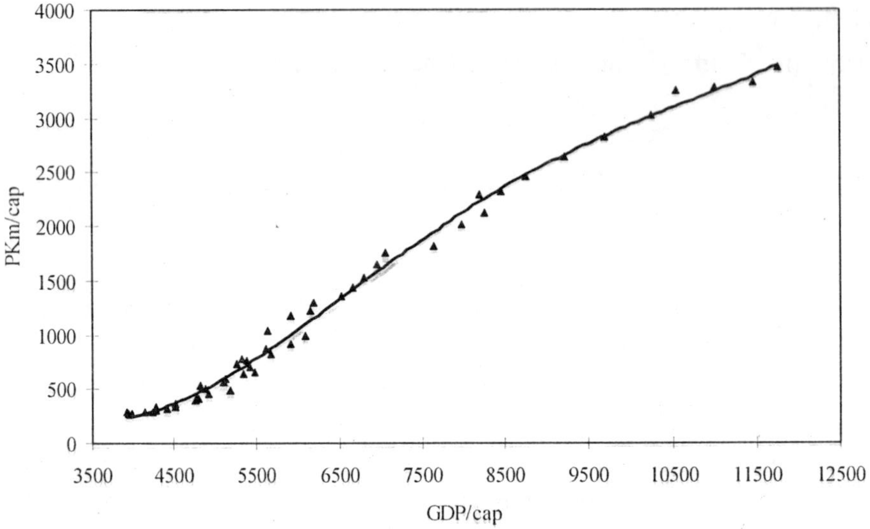

Fig. 3. Motorized mobility (car, two-wheeler, auto-rickshaw, bus, and rail) per capita vs GDP per capita in India between 1950-51 and 2000-01

3.2 Model estimation

The logistic model (5) and the Gompertz model (6) are estimated using the econometric software LIMDEP Version 8.0. Both the models have been estimated for three different saturation levels: 12000, 16000 and 20000 PKm/capita. Annual data of passenger mobility per capita (PKm/capita) and GDP/capita (Rs. in thousand at 1993-94 prices) from 1950-51 to 2000-01 are used for the estimation of the models. The variable *time* takes the following values: 1 for 1950-51, 2 for 1951-52, 3 for 1952-53,......, and so on.

Table 1 reports the estimation results. According to the R^2 values, the models fit the data very well. We also compare the predicted values with the actual values of PKm/capita over the sample period and found the same. The Mean Absolute Percentage Error (MAPE)[9] presented in Table 1, is in the range of 3.86 to 3.93 for the logistic models and 5.77 to 6.08 for the Gompertz models. All the estimated parameters have the expected signs and most are highly significant. To project the future per capita mobility up to the year 2020-21, we have to make reasonable assumptions about the per capita GDP growth rate. Between 1993-94 and 2003-04 (the latest year for which per capita GDP figure is available), per capita GDP in India increased at the rate of around 4.3% per annum. Assuming that GDP/capita will increase at the same rate up to 2020-21, passenger mobility per capita has been projected for the future. Figure 4 presents the future per capita mobility up to 2020-21 for different saturation levels. Since according to MAPE the logistic model is a better model than the Gompertz, and as discussed in the Section 3.1, saturation level is expected to be around 12000 PKm per capita, the next stage of the discussion will be based on the estimated logistic model with saturation level at 12000 PKm per capita.[10]

Table 1: Parameter estimates of the Logistic and Gompertz Models (with t-statistic in parentheses)

Model	*Estimate*			
Saturation level,	α = **12000**			
Logistic (5)	β_0 = 4.29110 (127.9),	β_1 = -0.08260 (8.2),	β_2 = -0.04948 (34.3);	R^2 = 0.996; MAPE = 3.93
Gompertz (6)	β_0 = 1.71227 (101.1),	β_1 = -0.07661 (15.0),	β_2 = -0.01263 (17.3);	R^2 = 0.993; MAPE = 6.08
Saturation level,	α = **16000**			
Logistic (5)	β_0 = 4.52723 (140.0),	β_1 = -0.06914 (7.1),	β_2 = -0.04962 (35.7);	R^2 = 0.996; MAPE = 3.89
Gompertz (6)	β_0 = 1.71740 (115.9),	β_1 = -0.06131 (13.7),	β_2 = -0.01207 (18.9);	R^2 = 0.993; MAPE = 5.90
Saturation level,	α = **20000**			
Logistic (5)	β_0 = 4.72272 (149.4),	β_1 = -0.06189 (6.5),	β_2 = -0.04966 (36.5);	R^2 = 0.996; MAPE = 3.86
Gompertz (6)	β_0 = 1.73150 (128.4),	β_1 = -0.05268 (13.0),	β_2 = -0.01160 (20.0);	R^2 = 0.993; MAPE = 5.77

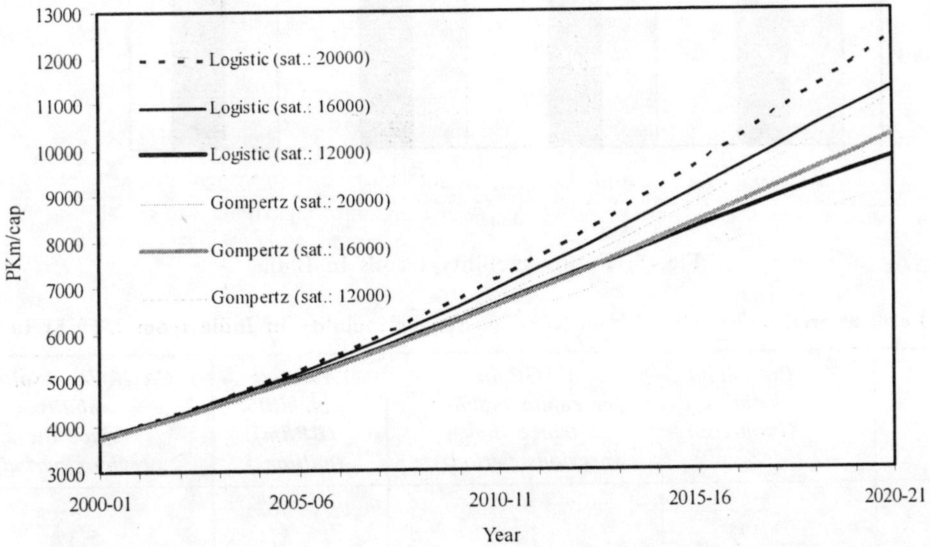

Fig. 4: Assumptions and projections of land-based per capita mobility in India

3.3 Projection of Per Capita as well as Absolute Mobility up to 2020-21

On the basis of the estimated logistic model for 12000 PKm per capita saturation level and assumptions concerning population and GDP, projections of per capita as well as absolute mobility up to 2020-21 are obtained. As stated in the previous section, per capita GDP is assumed to grow at the rate of 4.3% per annum up to 2020-21. Based on *World Population Prospects: The 2004 Revision Population Database* published by the United Nations Population Division, population of India is assumed to grow at the rate of 1.56% per annum from 2000-01 to 2005-06, 1.41% per annum from 2005-06 to 2010-11, 1.27% per annum from 2010-11 to 2015-16, and 1.11% per annum from 2015-16 to 2020-21.

Figure 5 presents the future mobility trends up to 2020-21. It shows that in 2020-21, average Indians will travel about thrice as many kilometers as they traveled in 2000-01. Absolute passenger mobility in India at the end of 2020-21 will virtually touch the mark of 13000 billion PKm. On an average, per capita mobility and absolute traffic volume in India are expected to increase at the rate of 5.31% and 6.72% per annum respectively in the next two decades. However, growth in both mobility per capita and absolute traffic volume are expected to be higher during 2000-11 than 2010-21 (Table 2).

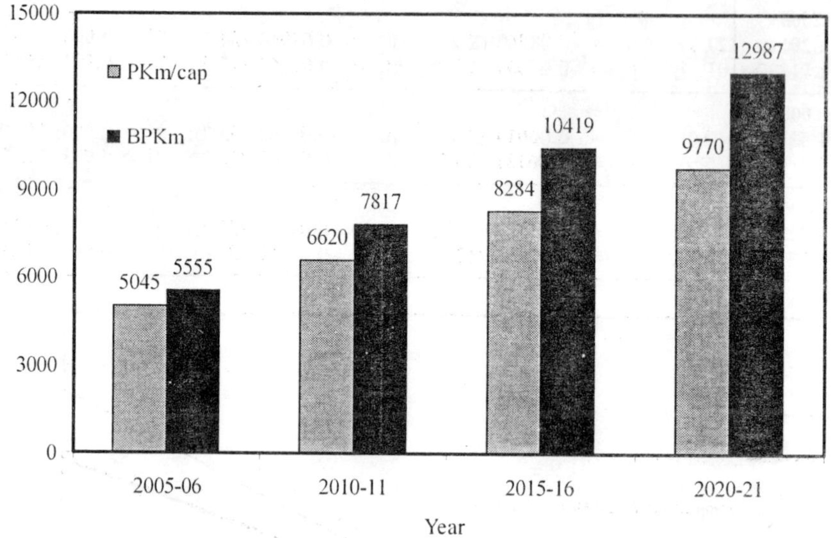

Fig. 5: Future mobility trends in India

Table 2: Level as well as growth of land-based passenger mobility in India from 1950-51 to 2020-21

	Per capita mobility (PKm/cap)	*CAGR in per capita mobility (since the previous period)*	*Absolute mobility (BPKm) (millions)*	*CAGR in absolute mobility (since the previous period)*
1950-51	285	—	102	—
1960-61	395	3.3%	171	5.3%
1970-71	661	5.3%	358	7.6%
1980-81	1169	5.9%	794	8.3%
1990-91	2125	6.2%	1783	8.4%
2000-01	3470	5.0%	3536	7.1%
2010-11	6620	6.7%	7817	8.3%
2020-21	9770	4.0%	12987	5.2%

3.4 Modal Split Changes

As shown in Figure 3, increase in per capita GDP results in rise in per capita motorized mobility. Assuming that an average person spends some fixed time (approximately 1.1 hour per day) on travel, mean travel speed has to increase with the increase in per capita mobility. Because different transport modes operate with different ranges of speed, increase in mobility changes the modal split towards flexible and faster transport modes. Thus, as per capita mobility and per capita GDP increase, traffic share of public transport modes such as buses and trains decrease and share of private- and para-transit modes increase. Figure 6 shows the relationship between mobility and share of low speed public transport. The share of public transport modes went down from 93.4% in 1950-51 to 78.8% in 2000-01 in a linear fashion as per capita mobility increased from 285 Km in 1950-51 to 3470 Km in 2000-01. Similar relationship is found between share of public transport modes and per capita GDP (Figure 7). Both provide somewhat identical future values for the share of public transport modes up to 2020-21.

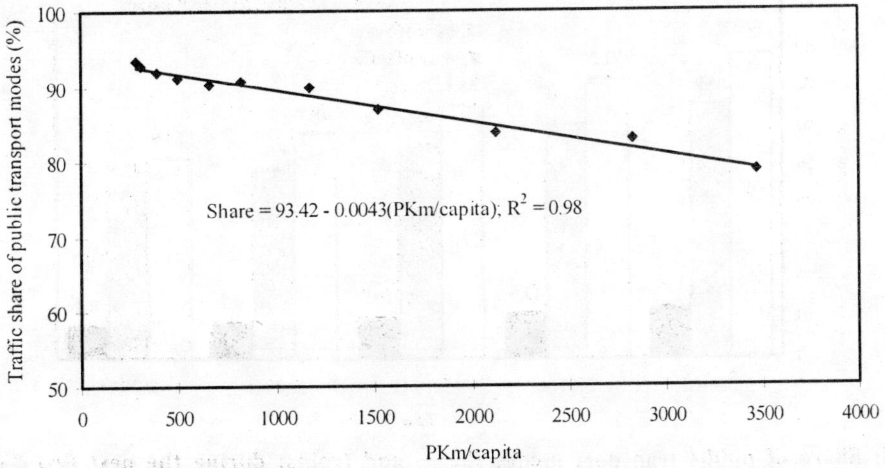

Fig. 6: Traffic share of public transport modes (buses and trains) at different level of per capita mobility between 1950-51 and 2000-01

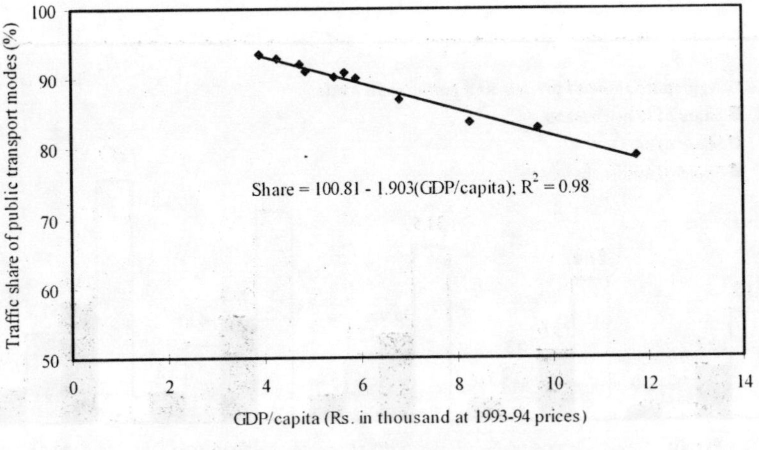

Fig. 7: Traffic share of public transport modes (buses and trains) at different level of income between 1950-51 and 2000-01

It is estimated that the share of low speed public transport (buses and trains) in India will be around 52% during 2020-21 (Figure 8).[11] Since the share of buses and trains in the public transport modes are virtually unchanged from 1993-94 onwards at around 84% and 16% respectively, we assume that the same pattern will be followed up to the year 2020-21. Based on this assumption, the share of buses and trains in meeting the passenger travel demand in future has been projected. It is estimated that 43.6% of traffic mobility in India in 2020-21 will be provided by the buses and 8.3% by the trains (Figure 8).

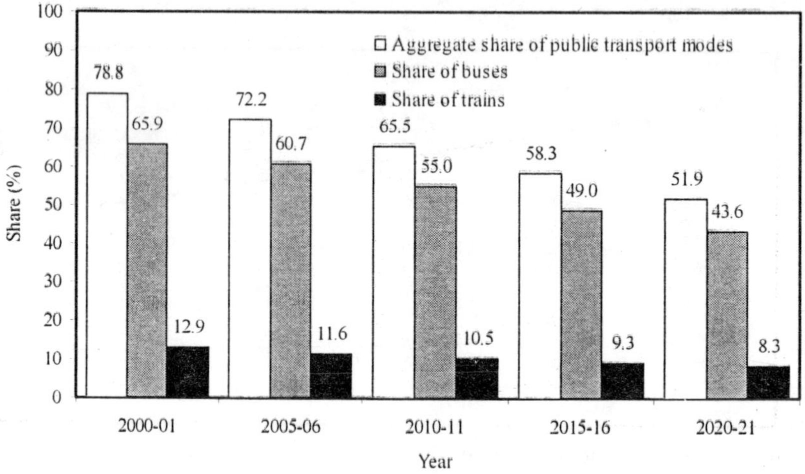

Fig. 8: Share of public transport modes (buses and trains) during the next two decades

Similarly, we projected the share of high speed private- and para-transit modes (cars, two-wheelers, and auto-rickshaws) up to 2020-21. Figure 9 presents the same along with the share of individual modes. It is estimated that the combined share of these modes in India would be around 48% during the year 2020-21.

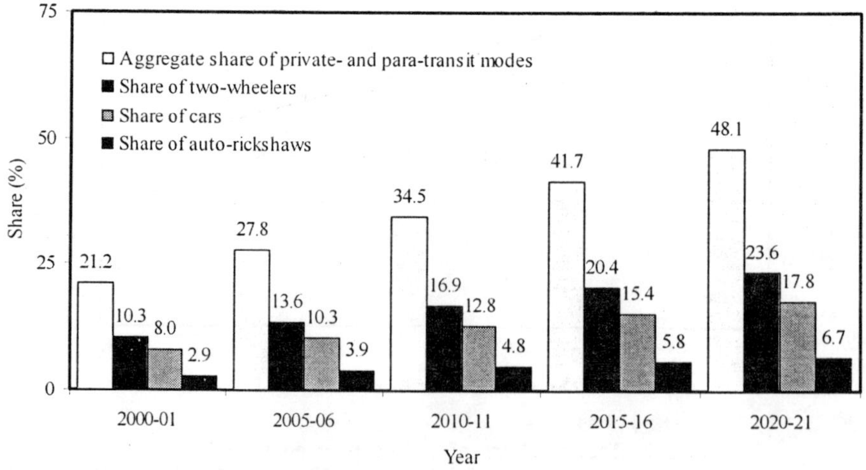

Fig. 9: Share of private- and para-transit modes (cars, two-wheelers, and auto-rickshaws) during the next two decades

Since, in this case also, the share of cars, two-wheelers, and auto-rickshaws within the private- and para-transit modes are virtually unchanged from 1993-94 onwards at 37%, 49%, and 14% respectively, we assume that the same pattern will be followed till 2020-21. This assumption is made because growth rate of car, two-wheeler, and auto-rickshaw population is more or less same from the last seven years or so.[12] This is not expected to change in near future since most of the car owners in India prefers to own a two-wheeler as well. Two-wheelers are perceived to be useful for short distance travel and easy to drive even in congested streets and roads. Also, fuel cost for a two-wheeler in India is hardly 25% of that of a car. Therefore, as income of the people increases, the demand for car and two-wheeler is likely to increase more or less at the same rate. It is unlikely to have crowding out effect of increased car ownership at higher level of income on demand for two-wheeler. One should note that per capita vehicle ownership rate in India is still among the lowest in the world and it can easily sustain the high growth path for these categories of vehicles in the long run. Even if we assume that growth in car ownership may be higher than the two-wheelers at higher levels of income say from 2010-11 to 2020-21, the assumption that the mobility share of cars, two-wheelers, and auto-rickshaws within the private- and para-transit modes will be unchanged is not very strong since the average occupancy of car is expected to decrease with the increase in car ownership. Decrease in average occupancy of two-wheeler and auto-rickshaw is also expected at higher level of ownership but at a lesser rate than that of car when car demand exceeds demand for two-wheeler and auto-rickshaw.[13] Therefore, the assumption that mobility share of cars, two-wheelers, and auto-rickshaws within the private- and para-transit modes will be unchanged from 2000-01 to 2020-21 appears to be plausible. Based on this assumption, the share of individual high speed modes in meeting the passenger travel demand in future has been projected (Figure 9). It is estimated that, during the year 2020-21, 17.8% of the land-based traffic mobility in India will be provided by the cars, 23.6% by the two-wheelers, and 6.7% by the auto-rickshaws. Analysis of changes in modal split reveals that, from 2000-01 to 2020-21 the traffic share of buses and trains will decline whereas the share of cars, two-wheelers and auto-rickshaws will increase substantially. Their rapid pattern of growth in mobility and the resultant energy intensive modal split are expected to have adverse impact on energy demand and CO_2 emission.

4. ENERGY DEMAND AND CO_2 EMISSION FROM PASSENGER TRANSPORT SECTOR

4.1 Energy demand

India's energy consumption has grown rapidly over the last two decades or so. Presently, it accounts for around 3.3% of the world total. Coal (50.9%) and petroleum (34.4%) together account for more than 85% of India's energy consumption, while natural gas (6.5%) and hydroelectricity (6.3%) account for much of the remainder. The transport sector in India is a major energy consuming sector, particularly of petroleum products. About half of the total petroleum products consumption in the country goes into the transport sector in the form of HSD (high speed diesel) and gasoline. India consumes close to 3% of world oil supply and imports around 65% of its requirement. In 2000-01, India consumed 102.5 million tonnes of petroleum products, out of which HSD alone was around 39 million tones (CMIE Energy Database). The transport sector consumes more than 85% of the total HSD consumed in the country.

In India, land-based passenger transport accounts for a significant proportion of energy consumed in the transport sector. The aim of this sub-section is to estimate the present as well as future energy demand in the passenger transport sector in the country. For this, we have to estimate the modal energy intensities of all major transport modes. Table 3 summarises the estimated 2000-01 modal energy intensities and their projected values for 2020-21.[14]

Table 3: Modal share and energy intensities in 2000-01 and projections for 2020-21

Mode of transport	*2000-01*		*2020-21 (Business as Usual Scenario)*		*2020-21 (Efficiency Gain Scenario)*	
	Modal share (%)	*Energy intensity (MJ/PKm)*	*Modal share (%)*	*Energy intensity (MJ/PKm)*	*Modal share (%)*	*Energy intensity (MJ/PKm)*
Car	8.00	0.94	17.80	0.94	17.80	0.77
Two-wheeler	10.30	0.53	23.60	0.53	23.60	0.43
Auto-rickshaw	2.90	0.58	6.70	0.58	6.70	0.47
Bus	65.90	0.19	43.60	0.19	43.60	0.16
Rail (diesel)	7.74	0.24	1.66	0.24	1.66	0.20
Rail (electricity)	5.16	0.12	6.64	0.12	6.64	0.10
Rail (diesel and electricity)	12.90	0.19	8.30	0.14	8.30	0.12
Total (weighted average)	100.00	0.30	100.00	0.43	100.00	0.35

For 2020-21, two scenarios are presented for energy intensities in the sector. First, in the business as usual scenario, the 2020-21 energy intensities of all ground transport modes are assumed to remain at 2000-01 levels. However, rail energy intensity will be different because we assume that the electrified routes will cater to the need of 80% of the rail passenger traffic in 2020-21 rather than the current level of 40%. Although, business as usual scenario may appear optimistic, historically fuel efficiency of automobiles in many countries including OECD countries has not changed significantly during the past 20 years or so. In addition, it is quite likely that average occupancy will decline at higher level of income and mobility. Therefore, even if automobile fuel efficiency improves, energy intensity of individual modes may remain unchanged.

Second, in the efficiency gain scenario, the energy intensities of all ground transport modes are assumed to decline at the rate of 1% per year up to 2020-21 i.e., around 18% reduction in energy intensity of all modes in a span of 20 years. Efficiency gain scenario is also plausible provided government plays active role to achieve the same. Recently, as part of its economic reform programme, the government has tried to change its role in the energy and environment sector. Dismantling price control, reduction in subsidy, opening of the energy sector to private and foreign investment, removing restriction on energy trade, and setting up the independent regulatory commission in energy sector are examples of its changed role in energy sector. The Ministry of Environment and Forests, Government of India, the nodal agency in the administrative structure of the central government, for the planning, promotion, co-ordination and overseeing the implementation of environmental and forestry programmes, has taken a number of measures to tackle environmental issues in the country. As far as environment consciousness in the road transport sector is concerned, the government has tightened vehicle emission standards: making fitting of catalytic converters in new petrol driven passenger cars mandatory, use of unleaded petrol by making it available throughout the country, and extending Bharat-II norms (akin to Euro-II norms) to the entire country with effect from April, 2005. In addition to these, CNG and LPG are permitted to be used as auto fuels. Alternative fuels like di-methyl ether, bio-diesel, hydrogen, electric and fuel cell vehicles, etc. are at various stages of experimentation. Therefore, it is expected that the government will play an active role in promoting energy efficient technology and take measures to improve fuel efficiency.

Measures such as improvement in traffic flow, removal of encroachment on roads, restraint on parking in congested areas, infrastructure improvement, adequate inspection and maintenance program for in-use vehicles, increasing the price of petrol and diesel, tax concession to fuel efficient vehicle, etc. have huge potential to improve fuel efficiency. In general, Indian roads face severe traffic congestion problem. Growing traffic and limited road space have reduced peak-hour speeds to 5-10 kms per hour in the central areas of many major cities in the country (Singh, 2005). Since fuel efficiency is optimum at much higher speed, improvement in traffic flow, removal of encroachment on roads, restraint on parking in congested areas, and road infrastructure improvement will have potential to improve fuel efficiency. Similarly, adequate inspection and maintenance program for in-use vehicles, higher price for fuel, and tax concession for fuel efficient vehicles can significantly improve fuel efficiency. One should note that higher fuel prices induce people to prefer vehicles that are fuel efficient. Demand for fuel efficient vehicles can be increased by providing tax concessions for these vehicles. For example, today, the most efficient car available in the Indian market is about twice as fuel efficient as the least fuel efficient car. Models such as Maruti 800, Maruti Alto, and Maruti Zen have an average petrol consumption of about 5-6 litres per 100 kms whereas Ambassador, once India's most popular car, consumes 8-10 litres of petrol for 100 kms. Similarly, the most efficient two-wheeler (such as Hero-Honda with fuel efficiency of 1 litre per 80 kms) is twice as fuel efficient as the least fuel efficient two-wheeler (such as Bajaj Scooter with fuel efficiency of 1 litre per 40 kms). Similar kind of fuel efficiency differences exist in other categories of vehicles. Therefore, government policy can easily increase the fuel efficiency of the system through pricing and taxation. Although it is beyond the scope of this study to estimate the efficiency gain potential of different policy measures, we assume that the government action can reduce the energy intensities of all modes at the rate of 1% per year up to 2020-21. That is why; energy demand from the land-based passenger transportation in the country is analysed for two different possible modal energy intensities in the future.

4.1.1 Business as usual (BAU) scenario

In this scenario, the average energy intensity in the passenger transport sector in India is expected to increase by around 43% in a span of 20 years from 0.30 mega joules per PKm (MJ/PKm) in 2000-01 to 0.43 MJ/PKm in 2020-21. This is mainly because of increased dependence on automobiles to meet the travel demand in future. Combined with the growth in aggregate transport demand and the projected modal split change, overall land-based passenger transport sector energy use in 2020-21 is projected to be 5584 peta joules (Table 4).[15] Energy demand in the sector is expected to increase at the rate of more than 8% per year from 2000-01 to 2020-21. Table 4 also presents the per capita energy consumption for transport in 2000-01 and 2020-21. Energy consumption per person is projected to rise by a factor of 4 from 1041 mega joules in 2000-01 to 4201 mega joules in 2020-21.

Table 4: Travel and passenger transport energy use in India; business as usual scenario

Mode of transport	*2000-01*				*2020-21 (Business as Usual Scenario)*			
	BPKm	*Energy intensity (MJ/PKm)*	*Energy demand (PJ)*	*Energy use per person (MJ)*	*BPKm*	*Energy intensity (MJ/PKm)*	*Energy demand (PJ)*	*Energy use per person (MJ)*
Car	283	0.94	266.02	261.06	2312	0.94	2172.98	1634.72
Two-wheeler	364	0.53	192.92	189.32	3065	0.53	1624.41	1222.03
Auto-rickshaw	102	0.58	59.16	58.06	870	0.58	504.67	379.66
Bus	2330	0.19	442.70	434.45	5662	0.19	1075.84	809.35
Rail	457	0.19	86.83	85.21	1078	0.14	150.91	113.53
Total	3536	0.30	1060.80	1041.02	12987	0.43	5584.41	4201.10

4.1.2 Efficiency gain scenario

The BAU scenario shows huge increase in energy requirements. Emphasis on efficiency improvements can reduce the energy demand significantly. Hence, in this scenario, it is assumed that there will be continuous efforts to increase the energy efficiency. In particular, we assume that energy intensity of all modes will decrease at the rate of 1% per year from 2000-01 to 2020-21. In this scenario, energy requirement in 2020-21 is estimated to be around 4545 peta joules, around 1000 peta joules less than the BAU scenario.[16] Similarly, per capita energy consumption in 2020-21 will be 3420 mega joules rather than 4201 mega joules (Table 5). Even when there is a reduction in energy intensity of all modes by 1% per year, passenger transport energy demand in India will increase at the rate of 7.5% per year from 2000-01 to 2020-21. This will have huge implications for oil import bills of India. Oil imports, which meet around 65% of India's current demands, will continue to grow due to rapid increase in demand from the transport sector.

Table 5

Mode of transport	*2000-01*				*2020-21 (Business as Usual Scenario)*			
	BPKm	*Energy intensity (MJ/PKm)*	*Energy demand (PJ)*	*Energy use per person (MJ)*	*BPKm*	*Energy intensity (MJ/PKm)*	*Energy demand (PJ)*	*Energy use per person (MJ)*
Car	283	0.94	266.02	261.06	2312	0.77	1780.00	1339.08
Two-wheeler	364	0.53	192.92	189.32	3065	0.43	1317.92	991.46
Auto-rickshaw	102	0.58	59.16	58.06	870	0.47	408.96	307.66
Bus	2330	0.19	442.70	434.45	5662	0.16	905.97	681.56
Rail	457	0.19	86.83	85.21	1078	0.12	129.35	97.31
Total	3536	0.30	1060.80	1041.02	12987	0.35	4545.45	3419.50

4.2 CO_2 emissions

The problem of climatic change is one of the most serious consequences of the emission of large quantities of CO_2 and other greenhouse gases into the atmosphere. Transport in general and road transport in particular constitutes a major share in the CO_2 emissions. Vehicles using fossil fuels (diesel and gasoline) produce CO_2 emissions in quantities that depend on the carbon present in the fuel molecule. Globally, the transport sector now contributes 25% of all the CO_2

emissions released into the atmosphere. Approximately 80% of those emissions are from road transport. Although, currently, India is one of the lowest per capita emitters of CO_2, at 0.27 metric tons of carbon equivalent, energy sector's carbon intensity is high, and the country's total CO_2 emissions rank among the world's highest. In 2002, CO_2 emission in India was around 280 million metric tons of carbon equivalent which was around 4% of the world total (International Energy Annual 2002). Between 1980 and 2002, India's carbon emission increased at an astonishing rate of 5.7% per annum against the world average of 1.26%.

Since land-based passenger transport sector accounts for a significant proportion of energy consumed in the country, its share in CO_2 emission will be equally significant. The aim of this sub-section is to estimate the present as well as future CO_2 emission from the passenger transport sector in India. For this, we have to estimate the CO_2 emission intensities for all the major modes. Table 6 and 7 summarises the estimated 2000-01 CO_2 intensities and their projected values for 2020-21 along with the level of CO_2 emission from the sector.[17] In this case also, two scenarios will be explained in line with the discussion in the previous section.

4.2.1 Business as usual (BAU) scenario

In the BAU scenario, the 2020-21 CO_2 intensities of all ground transport modes except rail are assumed to remain at 2000-01 levels. The rail CO_2 intensity is different because we assume that the electrified routes will cater to the need of 80% of the rail passenger traffic in 2020-21 rather than the current level of 40%. Assuming that refined oil will continuously fuel the passenger transportation sector, CO_2 emissions will grow more or less in proportion to the energy used by the sector. In the BAU scenario, CO_2 emission is projected to increase from 19.80 to 93.25 million metric tons of carbon equivalent in a span of 20 years between 2000-01 and 2020-21 (Table 6).[18] The projected average annual rate of growth in CO_2 emission, around 8%, is somewhat similar to the corresponding growth in energy demand from 2000-01 to 2020-21. Figure 10 presents the per capita CO_2 emission from passenger transportation during the year 2000-01 and 2020-21. In the BAU scenario, CO_2 emission per person is projected to increase at the rate of 6.63% per year from 19.43 kilograms of carbon equivalent in 2000-01 to 70.17 kilograms of carbon equivalent in 2020-21.

4.2.2 Efficiency gain scenario

In the efficiency gain scenario, the CO_2 intensities of all modes decline at the rate of 1% per year up to 2020-21 by assuming that this may happen due to the technological change (fuel efficiency improvements and transportation fuels with lower carbon content), improvement in transportation system management and/or some combination of these two. Emphasis on efficiency improvements is expected to reduce the CO_2 emission significantly. In this scenario, the CO_2 emission in 2020-21 is estimated to be 76.36 million metric tons of carbon equivalent, around 18% less than the emission in the BAU scenario (Table 7).[19] Similarly, per capita CO_2 emission in 2020-21 in this scenario is projected to be 57.41 kilograms of carbon equivalent rather than 70.17 (Figure 10). One should note that even if there is a reduction in CO_2 intensity of all modes by 1% per year, the level of CO_2 emission from passenger transportation in India will increase at the rate of around 7% per year from 2000-01 to 2020-21.

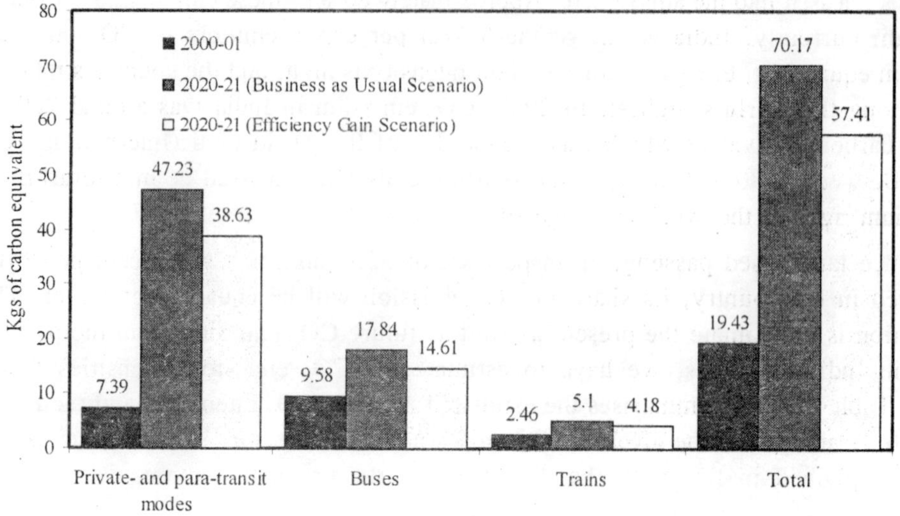

Fig. 10: Per capita CO_2 emission from different modes of transport (kilograms of carbon equivalent)

Table 6: Intensities and the level of CO_2 emission from different modes of transport; business as usual scenario

Mode of Transport	*2000-01*			*2020-21 (Business as Usual Scenario)*		
	BPKm	*CO_2 intensity (grams of carbon equivalent per PKm)*	*CO_2 emission (million metric tons of carbon equivalent)*	*BPKm*	*CO_2 intensity (grams of carbon equivalent per PKm)*	*CO_2 emission (million metric tons of carbon equivalent)*
Private and para-transit modes (car, two-wheeler, and auto-rickshaw)	749	10.05	7.53	6247	10.05	62.78
Bus	2330	4.19	9.76	5662	4.19	23.72
Rail	457	5.50	2.51	1078	6.29	6.78
Total	3536	5.60	19.80	12987	7.18	93.25

Table 7: Intensities and the level of CO_2 emission from different modes of transport; efficiency gain scenario

Mode of Transport	*2000-01*			*2020-21 (Business as Usual Scenario)*		
	BPKm	*CO_2 intensity (grams of carbon equivalent per PKm)*	*CO_2 emission (million metric tons of carbon equivalent)*	*BPKm*	*CO_2 intensity (grams of carbon equivalent per PKm)*	*CO_2 emission (million metric tons of carbon equivalent)*
Private and para-transit modes (car, two-wheeler, and auto-rickshaw)	749	10.05	7.53	6247	8.22	51.35
Bus 2330	4.19	9.76	5662	3.43	19.42	
Rail	457	5.50	2.51	1078	5.15	5.55
Total	3536	5.60	19.80	12987	5.88	76.36

5. CONCLUSIONS

In this study, we projected the level of traffic mobility, energy demand, and CO_2 emission from land-based passenger transportation in India up to 2020-21. The level of land-based passenger traffic in India increased at the rate of 7.75% per year during last two decades from 794 BPKm in 1980-81 to 3536 BPKm in 2000-01 and is expected to increase at the rate of 6.72% per year during the next two decades. Land-based traffic volume in 2020-21 is projected to be nearly 13000 BPKm, out of which, 91.7% will be provided by road and the rest by rail. An average Indian traveled 3470 Kms in 2000-01, out of which, 449 Kms was by rail and 3021 Kms by road. After two decades, in 2020-21, their annual travel figure is projected to be 9770 Kms – 811 Kms by rail and 8959 Kms by road. Analysis of modal split reveals that the share of public transport modes (buses and trains) in providing passenger mobility in India will decline from 78.8% in 2000-01 to 51.9% in 2020-21, whereas share of private- and para-transit modes will increase from 21.2% to 48.1% during the same period. Among the private- and para-transit modes, the share of two-wheelers is expected to increase from 10.3% in 2000-01 to 23.6% in 2020-21, while the corresponding increase for cars and auto-rickshaws will be from 8.0% to 17.8% and from 2.9% to 6.7% respectively. The expected rapid increase in mobility and more energy intensive modal split will have huge implications for energy demand and CO_2 emission from passenger transportation in India.

Assuming that the energy intensity of various transport modes remains unchanged, the energy demand in the passenger transport sector is expected to increase at the rate of more than 8% per year from 1060.8 peta joules in 2000-01 to 5584.4 peta joiles in 2020-21. Similarly, energy consumption per person is expected to rise by a factor of 4 from 1041 mega joules in 2000-01 to 4201 mega joules in 2020-21. Even when we assume a reduction of 1% per year in energy intensity of all modes, passenger transport energy demand is projected to increase at the rate of around 7.5% per year.

Assuming that refined oil will continuously fuel the passenger transportation sector, CO_2 emission will grow more or less in the same proportion as energy demand. In the business as usual scenario (i.e., assuming that the CO_2 intensity of all modes remains unchanged), CO_2 emission is projected to increase from 19.80 to 93.25 million metric tons of carbon equivalent in a span of two decades between 2000-01 and 2020-21. In the efficiency gain scenario (i.e., assuming that the CO_2 intensity of all modes declines at the rate of 1% per year), the CO_2 emission in 2020-21 is projected to be 76.36 million metric tons of carbon equivalent. One should note that even in the efficiency gain scenario, the level of CO_2 emission from passenger transportation in India is expected to increase at the rate of around 7% per year during the next two decades.

Apart from CO_2, substantial amount of local pollutants like carbon monoxide (CO), unburnt hydrocarbons (HC), nitrogen oxides (NO_x), sulphur dioxide (SO_2), lead (Pb), and suspended particulate matters (SPM) are also emitted by the passenger transport sector. The air pollution problem due to vehicular emission in most of the metropolitan cities in India is assuming serious dimension and worsening people's quality of life (Singh, 2005). Pollutants from vehicular emission have various adverse health effects. One of the main pollutants SPM, particularly fine PM, has serious health effects, especially in the form of respiratory diseases. The ambient air pollution in terms of SPM in all metropolitan cities in India exceeds the limit set by World Health Organisation (WHO).

India faces significant challenges in balancing its increased demand for energy with the need to protect its environment from further damage. Population growth and urbanisation make the task all the more difficult. Rapid increase in vehicle ownership will aggravate the already existing air pollution problem and urbanisation will increase the health risks from that pollution. In the absence of coordinated government efforts, including stricter enforcement, air pollution is likely to continue to worsen in the coming years. India's ability to safeguard its environment will depend on its success in promoting policies that keep the economy growing while fulfilling the energy demand in a sustainable manner.

REFERENCES

Bewley, R., and Fiebig, D. (1988), 'Flexible logistic growth model with applications in telecommunications', *International Journal of Forecasting*, Vol. 4, No. 2, pp. 177-192.

CMIE database on Energy and Infrastructure (various issues), Centre for Monitoring Indian Economy (CMIE) Pvt. Ltd., Mumbai, India.

Dargay, J., and Gately, D. (1999), 'Income's effect on car and vehicle ownership, worldwide: 1960-2015', *Transportation Research Part A,* Vol. 33, No.2, pp.101-138.

Franses, P.H. (2002), 'Testing for residual autocorrelation in growth curve models', *Technological Forecasting and Social Change*, Vol. 69, No.2, pp. 195-204.

Heij C. et al. (2004), "Econometric Methods with Applications in Business and Economics", Oxford University Press, New York; p 209.

International Energy Annual 2002, Energy Information Administration, Washington DC, USA. Available on http://www.eia.doe.gov/emeu/iea/carbon.html.

Marchetti, C. (1994), 'Anthropological invariants in travel behavior', *Technological Forecasting and Social Change,* Vol. 47, No.1, pp. 75-88.

Meade, N., and Islam, T. (1998), 'Technological Forecasting - Model Selection, Model Stability, and Combining Models', *Management Science,* Vol. 44, No.8, pp. 1115-1130.

Meade, N., and Islam, T. (1995), 'Forecasting with growth curves: An empirical comparison', *International Journal of Forecasting*, Vol.11, No.2, pp. 199-215.

Mohamed, Z., and Bodger, P. (2005), 'A comparison of Logistic and Harvey models for electricity consumption in New Zealand', *Technological Forecasting and Social Change*, Forthcoming issue.

National Accounts Statistics of India: 1950-51 to 2002-03, EPW Research Foundation, Mumbai, India.

Preston, J. (2001), 'Integrating Transport with Socio-economic Activity - A Research Agenda for the New Millennium', *Journal of Transport Geography,* Vol. 9, No.1, pp.13-24.

Ramanathan, R., and Parikh, J.K. (1999), 'Transport Sector in India: An analysis in the context of sustainable development', *Transport Policy*, Vol. 6, No. 1, pp. 35-45.

Ramanathan, R. (1998), 'Development of Indian Passenger Transport', Energy - *The International Journal*, Vol. 23, No. 5, pp. 429-430.

Schafer, A. (1998), 'The Global Demand for Motorized Mobility', *Transport Research: Part A,* Vol. 32, No. 6, pp. 455-477.

Schafer, A., and Victor, D.G. (2000), 'The Future Mobility of the World Population', *Transport Research: Part A*, Vol.34, No.3, pp. 171-205.

Singh, S.K. (2005), 'Review of Urban Transportation in India', *Journal of Public Transportation,* Vol. 8, No. 1, pp. 79-97.

Singh, S.K. (2000), 'Estimating the Level of Rail- and Road-based Passenger Mobility in India', *Indian Journal of Transport Management,* Vol. 24,No.12, pp. 771-781.

TERI Energy Data Directory & Yearbook (various issues), TERI, New Delhi, India.

World Population Prospects: The 2004 Revision Population Database, United Nations Population Division, United Nations. http://esa.un.org/unpp/index.asp?panel=3.

APPENDIX

Data Descriptions

Although, annual time series data of the level of rail-based passenger mobility in India from 1950-51 to 2000-01 is readily available (e.g., in Statistical Abstract of India published by the Central Statistical Organisation, Ministry of Statistics and Programme Implementation, Government of India, New Delhi), similar series for road-based passenger traffic volume is not offered by any source. Therefore, it is decided to estimate the level of road-based passenger traffic from 1950-51 to 2000-01 on the basis of services provided by the different modes. The estimates are based on the following passenger vehicles: (*i*) Cars (*ii*) Two-wheelers (*iii*) Auto-rickshaws and (*iv*) Buses. Cars include jeeps and taxis as well.

Table A1 reports category-wise motor vehicle population in India for selected years between 1950-51 and 2000-01. This is based on data given in the Motor Transport Statistics published by the Ministry of Road Transport and Highways, Government of India, New Delhi and Statistical Abstract of India published by the Central Statistical Organisation, Ministry of Statistics and Programme Implementation, Government of India, New Delhi. The traffic mobility provided by the different categories of vehicles has been computed after making reasonable assumptions regarding their average annual utilisation and average occupancy. These assumptions are based on studies like National Transport Policy Committee Report (1980), Planning Commission, New Delhi; Road Development Plan 1981-2000 (1984), Indian Road Congress, New Delhi; Estimation of Road Transport Passenger and Freight Demand (1986), Study Report of Ministry of Surface Transport, New Delhi; Report of Steering Group on Transport Planning (1987), Planning Commission, New Delhi; and Singh M. and Kadiyali L. R. (1990) written book on Crisis in Road Transport published by the Konark Publishers Pvt. Ltd., New Delhi. Annual utilisation of cars, two-wheelers, and auto-rickshaws are assumed to be 12600, 6300, and 33500 Kms respectively. Average occupancy of a car, two-wheeler, and auto-rickshaw are assumed to be 3.18, 1.5, and 1.76 respectively. Accordingly, the level of passenger mobility provided by these modes has been computed and presented in Table A2.

Estimation of traffic mobility provided by the buses requires data on bus population, average annual utilisation, occupancy ratio (ratio of number of passengers to the seats offered), and average seating capacity. These data are taken from various sources such as State Transport Undertakings: Profile and Performance (various issues) published by the Central Institute of Road Transport, Pune; TERI Energy Data Directory & Yearbook (various issues) published by the TERI, New Delhi; and Singh M. and Kadiyali L. R. (1990) written book on Crisis in Road Transport published by the Konark Publishers Pvt. Ltd., New Delhi. Table A3 presents these data. Assuming that the average seating capacity is 52, the level of passenger mobility provided by the buses has been computed and presented in both Table A2 and A3. Rail-based passenger mobility data is readily available from 1950-51 onwards. Passenger mobility data for rail, road, and land (aggregate of rail and road) for selected years between 1950-51 and 2000-01 have been reported in Table A4.

Table A1

Motor vehicle population in thousand and its compound annual growth rate in percentage since previous period (in parentheses)

Year	*Cars*	*Two-wheelers*	*Auto-rickshaws*	*Buses*	*Total passenger vehicles*	*Total motor vehicles*
1950-51	159.3 (-)	26.9 (-)	1.7 (-)	34.4 (-)	222.2 (-)	306.3 (-)
1955-56	203.2 (5.0)	41.0 (8.8)	2.5 (8.8)	46.5 (6.2)	293.1 (5.7)	425.6 (6.8)
1960-61	309.6 (8.8)	88.4 (16.6)	6.2 (19.9)	56.8 (4.1)	461.0 (9.5)	664.5 (9.3)
1965-66	455.9 (8.0)	225.6 (20.6)	16.1 (20.8)	73.2 (5.2)	770.8 (10.8)	1099.1 (10.6)
1970-71	682.0 (8.4)	576.0 (20.6)	36.7 (17.9)	91.4 (4.5)	1386.1 (12.5)	1865.0 (11.2)
1975-76	779.0 (2.7)	1057.0 (12.9)	59.4 (10.1)	114.2 (4.6)	2009.6 (7.7)	2720.0 (7.8)
1980-81	1160.0 (8.3)	2618.0 (19.9)	142.1 (19.0)	153.9 (6.2)	4074.0 (15.2)	5391.0 (14.7)
1985-86	1780.0 (8.9)	6245.0 (19.0)	336.9 (18.9)	227.6 (8.1)	8589.5 (16.1)	10577.0 (14.4)
1990-91	2954.0 (10.7)	14200.0 (17.9)	617.4 (12.9)	331.1 (7.8)	18102.5 (16.1)	21374.0 (15.1)
1995-96	4204.0 (7.3)	23252.0 (10.4)	1009.0 (10.3)	449.0 (6.3)	28913.9 (9.8)	33786.0 (9.6)
2000-01	7058.0 (10.9)	38556.0 (10.6)	1725.4 (11.3)	560.0 (4.5)	47899.4 (10.6)	54991.0 (10.2)

Table A2

The level of passenger mobility provided by different modes of road transport during selected years (in BPKm)

Year	*Cars*	*Two-wheelers*	*Auto-rickshaws*	*Buses*	*Road Transport*
1950-51	6.38	0.25	0.10	28.99	35.72
1955-56	8.14	0.39	0.15	50.52	59.19
1960-61	12.40	0.84	0.37	80.15	93.76
1965-66	18.27	2.13	0.95	123.29	144.63
1970-71	27.33	5.44	2.16	204.72	239.65
1975-76	31.21	9.99	4.68	306.88	352.76
1980-81	46.48	24.74	8.38	505.81	585.40
1985-86	71.32	59.02	19.86	757.48	907.68
1990-91	118.36	134.19	36.40	1198.32	1487.27
1995-96	168.45	219.73	59.49	1830.36	2278.03
2000-01	282.80	364.35	101.73	2329.60	3078.49

Table A3

Growth of Indian bus industry; 1950-51 to 2000-01

Year	*Bus population*	*Average annual utilisation (Kms)*	*Occupancy ratio (per cent)*	*BPKm*
1950-51	34411	36000	45	28.988
1955-56	46461	41000	51	50.518
1960-61	56792	46000	59	80.149
1965-66	73175	54000	60	123.285
1970-71	91406	59000	73	204.717
1975-76	114193	68000	76	306.878
1980-81	153909	79000	80	505.807
1985-86	227608	80000	80	757.479
1990-91	331100	87000	80	1198.317
1995-96	448970	98000	80	1830.361
2000-01	560000	100000	80	2329.600

Table A4

Trends in rail, road, and land-based passenger mobility in India

Year	*Rail pass. - km (in billion)*	*CAGR in percentage wrt previous period (Rail)*	*Road pass. - km (in billion)*	*CAGR in percentage wrt previous period (Road)*	*Land pass. - km (in billion)*	*CAGR in percentage wrt previous period (Land)*
1950-51	66.52	—	35.72	—	102.24	—
1955-56	62.90	-1.1	59.19	10.6	122.09	3.6
1960-61	77.67	4.3	93.76	9.6	171.42	7.0
1965-66	96.76	4.5	144.63	9.1	241.39	7.1
1970-71	118.12	4.1	239.65	10.6	357.77	8.2
1975-76	148.76	4.7	352.76	8.0	501.52	7.0
1980-81	208.56	7.0	585.40	10.7	793.96	9.6
1985-86	240.62	2.9	907.68	9.2	1148.30	7.7
1990-91	295.64	4.2	1487.27	10.4	1782.91	9.2
1995-96	342.00	3.0	2278.03	8.9	2620.03	8.0
2000-01	457.02	6.0	3078.49	6.2	3535.51	6.2

Notes:

1. Growth rate is calculated as compound annual growth rate (CAGR) rather than simple annual growth rate. This is followed throughout this paper.
2. Cars include jeeps and taxis. This will be followed throughout the paper.
3. Limited time series data for traffic volume by mode of transport has been compiled and published by the Centre for Monitoring Indian Economy (CMIE), Mumbai, India and TERI Energy Data Directory & Yearbook (TEDDY), New Delhi, India. For example, CMIE provides estimates of road-based passenger-kms from 1950-51 to 1988-89 in 11 data points. It does not present the complete series from 1950-51 to 2000-01 for which motor vehicle population data is readily available. TEDDY provides similar series that seems to be based on CMIE estimates.
4. Private- and para-transit modes include cars (including jeeps and taxis), two-wheelers, and auto-rickshaws.
5. Per capita GDP data, presented in Figure 3, is taken from National Accounts Statistics of India: 1950-51 to 2002-03 published by EPW Research Foundation, Mumbai, India. GDP figures are at factor cost at 1993-94 prices.
6. An overview of such functional forms is given in Meade and Islam (1998); see also Meade and Islam (1995), Bewley and Fiebig (1988), Franses (2002), and Mohamed and Bodger (2005). Application of such functional forms to project the traffic mobility in India can be seen from Ramanathan (1998), Ramanathan and Parikh (1999), and Singh (2000). These studies in the Indian context have used time as the only explanatory variable to project the future mobility in India.
7. Although it is possible to estimate the saturation level, there is no guarantee that the final estimate of the saturation level, a, is close to the global optimum (Heij C. et al., 2004). Therefore, to estimate the models, it is essential to get a reliable estimate of the saturation level of per capita mobility.
8. Schafer (1998) shows that the time spent on travel per person per day are virtually unchanged with respect to per capita income across the countries. Although the reason for travel time budget stability is not very clear, Marchetti (1994) argued that a travel time budget of around one hour per capita per day reflects a basic human instinct. He argued that perhaps security of the home and family, the most durable unit of human organisation, limits exposure to the risk of travel. Also, traveling is naturally limited by other activities such as sleep, leisure, and work. Even when time spent on any of these activities changes, there is evidence that the travel time budget remains constant (Marchetti, 1994). Time-use and travel surveys from numerous cities and countries throughout the world suggest that travel time budget is approximately 1.1 hour per person per day (Schafer and Victor, 2000). It should be noted that the stability of average travel time budget holds only for travel by all modes.
9. The MAPE is commonly used in quantitative forecasting methods because it produces a measure of relative overall fit. The absolute values of all the percentage errors are summed up and the average is computed.
10. One should note that the MAPE values for different saturation levels under the logistic model are very close to each other, hence, it is difficult to choose between them on the basis of their MAPE values.
11. This is somewhat similar to the findings of Schafer and Victor (2000) for high population density countries such as India at per capita mobility level of around 10000 Km.
12. In fact, latest (provisional) figure from the Ministry of Road Transport and Highways, GOI, New Delhi reveals that the growth rate of these vehicles is same from 2000-01 to 2003-04 as well.
13. One should note that modal share of a particular category of vehicle depends on three factors: no. of vehicles, annual utilisation (in km), and average occupancy. For example, in this case, modal share of car = (mobility provided by cars)/(mobility provided by private- and para-transit vehicles) where mobility provided by car = [car population ´ annual utilisation of car (in km) × avg. occupancy of car] and mobility provided by private- and para-transit vehicles = [{car population × annual utilisation of car (in km) × avg. occupancy of car} + {two-wheeler population × annual utilisation of two-wheeler (in km) × avg. occupancy of two-wheeler} + {auto-rickshaw population × annual utilisation of auto-rickshaw (in km) × avg. occupancy of auto-rickshaw}]. It is easy to see that even if car population growth is different than that of two-wheeler and auto-rickshaw say from 2010-11 onwards, modal share of car may be stable since it depends on other factors as well.

14. 2000-01 energy intensities by mode (in Mega Joules per PKm; MJ/PKm) have been estimated by the author. The vehicle mileage for car, two-wheeler, auto-rickshaw, and bus has been assumed to be 12, 45, 35, and 4.5 kilometers per litre of fuel (petrol/diesel) respectively. The average occupancy has been assumed to be 3.18 for cars, 1.5 for two-wheeler, 1.76 for auto-rickshaw, and 41.6 for bus. The energy equivalent value for 1 litre of fuel (petrol/diesel) is taken as 35.85 MJ. The estimates for energy intensities in rail are taken from Ramanathan and Parikh (1999).
15. Sum of modal energy demand may not be equal to the total of the sector since energy intensity figures have been rounded off to 2 decimal places.
16. In the efficiency gain scenario also, sum of modal energy demand may not be equal to the total of the sector since energy intensity figures have been rounded off to 2 decimal places.
17. 2000-01 CO_2 intensities by mode have been estimated by the author based on the data provided by Ramanathan and Parikh (1999).
18. Sum of modal CO_2 emission may not be equal to the total of the sector since intensity figures have been rounded off to 2 decimal places.
19. In the efficiency gain scenario also, sum of modal CO_2 emission may not be equal to the total of the sector since CO_2 intensity figures have been rounded off to 2 decimal places.

29

MISSION 200 MILLION TONNES LOADING FROM STEEL INDUSTRY: POLICY PERSPECTIVES FOR INDIAN RAILWAYS

M. Ravibabu
R. Badri Narayan

ABSTRACT

Indian Railways have targeted the Steel industry as a major potential customer with a plan to increase the loading to 200 million tonnes in five years from an existing level of about 70 million tonnes. The Railways have always been closely associated with the steel industry but with the changing market dynamics, there has been a definite shift towards road. Deregulation in the early nineties combined with the withdrawal of the freight equalisation policy triggered this change. The industry ownership patterns, technology levels and distribution strategies all underwent a major transformation with deregulation. The rationalised movement of steel as a consequence of the withdrawal of the freight equalisation policy led to the loss of a captive market for the Railways. While the steel production grew rapidly from 15.2 million tonnes in 1992 to 49.3 million tonnes in 2007, more noticeable is the diversification of the industry. The industry is more diversified with share of main producers based on blast furnace technology reducing from 63 per cent in 2001 to 52 per cent in 2006, with corresponding increase in share of around 240 secondary producers using varied technologies. Further, other activities of industry usually associated with an integrated plant in one complex are spread out geographically. In 2006, the industry had 37 electric arc furnace units for steel refining, around 1361 re-rolling mills for making end use products, and around 100 units for making a number of value added products. Thus the industry not only grew rapidly, it's structure also is underwent changes with geographical dispersion and changes in ownership pattern. Juxtaposing the rapid growth and diversification of the steel industry with the movement of material from steel industry by the railways presents a picture of contrast. The share of raw material moved by railways fell 58.9 per cent in 1992 to 33.7 per cent in 2006 and that of the finished products from 79.8 per cent to 38.5 per cent. Another dimension of the movement is the focus of railway movement on large plants and negligence of smaller units. In 2007, Out of the18.6 million tonnes of finished steel loaded by the railways,

10 steel plants accounted for 82 per cent of the loading, 87 per cent of the freight and 95 per cent of the net tonne kilometers. Railways remained focused on large integrated plants and were satisfied with year to year incremental growth and did not factor in changes in the industry structure to bring in suitable changes in the marketing strategies.

1. INTRODUCTION

Indian Railways (IR), has targeted to increase its loading from steel industry from the 70 million tonnes in 2005-06 to 200 million tonnes by 2011-12 (Indian Railways, 2007). Designing strategy to achieve this target is a task for the Ministry of Railways. This paper seeks to identify a few key issues that could be kept in mind while designing the strategy. The view here is that IR would have to work in association with Ministry of Steel, State Governments and the private sector in a proactive manner to achieve the ambitious target.

When we look back, 1992-93 emerges as a watershed year for the steel industry logistics as two momentous decisions were made at this time. The first was the deregulation of the steel industry and the second was the withdrawal of the freight equalisation policy by the Government of India (Planning Commission, 2007). Both these changes were in the direction of allowing market forces to dictate economic choices within the industry. Deregulation impacted steel production strategies as it gave rise to new technologies, new strategies of distribution and logistics, and variegated patterns of ownership. The withdrawal of the freight equalisation policy made the movement of finished steel more rational and sensitive to transport costs.

Steel production is generally highly material intensive though the actual material consumed is a function of the state of the technology and quality of inputs. At the aggregate level, the steel industry consumed about 138.6 million tonnes of raw material in 2005-06, including 10 million tonnes of steel scrap, to produce 41.2 million tonnes of finished steel with an average raw material usage of 3.36 tonnes per tonne of finished steel (Planning Commission, 2007). Apart from this there is indirect consumption as the industry consumes around 10,000 million calories equivalent of natural gas and 4100 million units of power. As most of the plants do not use natural gas the average material consumption goes up proportionately. For example, JSW Steel limited, a totally coal based plant, uses 3.5 to 3.9 tonnes of raw material for every tonne of steel produced (RITES, 2007).

The three main materials used in the production of steel are iron ore, coal, and dolomite and limestone. As per JSW Steel data, to produce a tonne of steel, iron ore consumed is 2 to 2.3 tonnes, coal and coke is 1 to 1.1 tonnes, and dolomite and limestone is 0.5 to 0.6 tonnes. By the weight of material consumed, iron ore accounts for around 55 per cent coal accounts for 30 per cent and limestone and dolomite accounts for 15 per cent (RITES, 2007). In a few cases coal is replaced by natural gas. Use of scrap and electricity, used mostly in refining process, reduces the materials required proportionately.

As mentioned earlier because of the large quantity of material used in steel industry, the cost of transportation and material handling is high. For example, in 2006-07, Tata Steel incurred 12 % of its total expenditure on transport and handling of material and this constituted 37 per cent of their raw material cost (Tata Steel, 2007). While data from other companies is not available for comparison, costs of Tata Steel are likely to be lower as its raw material sources are closer to the plant. Even assuming 10 per cent as the industry average, expenditure on transport is clearly a critical component. Given the significance of transport costs, steel plants looking to reduce expenses would place cheaper transport options high on their radar.

To reduce transport costs, the producers can potentially explore a number of options. We classify these into two groups; strategic and tactical. The strategic options are long term and include decisions regarding location of the plants, technologies adopted, feedstock and choice of the market. The tactical options could be decisions relating to investment on handling equipment, the inventory and storage policies, and the modes used for movement of cargo. Our foremost suggestion to the IR policy makers is to rigorously analyse both the strategic and tactical options as a way to increase the market share. All the choices made by the industry in these areas affect the market for rail transport and IR would have to know the factors that affect these choices and devise ways to influence these decisions.

This paper is divided into 5 Sections. The first section spells out the dramatic growth of steel industry since deregulation in 1992. Herein, we also discuss the changes in technology and how that, in turn, affects industry location, firm size and ownership patterns. The impact of change in technology on the segmentation in the industry is also briefly touched upon. The second Section brings out the declining share of IR in moving material from steel industry and how despite recent initiatives the market share has not increased in proportion to the robust growth of the industry. The next Section brings out the new patterns of movement of material that emerged and here some illustrative cases are cited to show how the changed industry structure has led to reduction in rail share in movement of material. Finally, in the last Section, we emphasise the need for a diversified portfolio of actions required for increasing the rail share and conclude by highlighting the need for working out more detailed strategies.

1.1 Changes in steel production process and industry structure

The comparative growth in steel production before and after deregulation indicates rapid acceleration in the growth rates after deregulation (see Table 1). The sector grew at an average of 8.4 per cent after deregulation compared to 5.3 per cent in the ten years preceding the deregulation. The growth in the four year span of the Tenth Plan period at 9.8 per cent is extremely impressive.

Table 1: Growth in production of finished Steel before and after deregulation

Period	*No. of Years*	*Production: million tonne*	*CAGR (%)*
Decade preceding (1982-83 to 1991-92)	10	08.48 to 14.33	5.3
Post deregulation period (1992-93 to 2005-06)	14	15.20 to 44.54	8.4
Eighth Five Year Plan (1992-93 to 1996-97)	5	15.20 to 22.72	9.7
Ninth Five Year Plan (1997-98 to 2001-02)	5	23.37 to 30.64	6.2
Tenth Five Year Plan (20012-03 to 2005-06)	4	33.67 to 44.54	9.8

Source: Joint Plant Committee quoted in Planning Commission (2007).

In addition to increase in growth rates, the sector has seen dramatic changes in the technologies adopted as well as in the composition of the companies. Traditionally Blast Furnace (BF) based integrated plants were predominant. However, deregulation saw the introduction of newer technologies to suit the Indian conditions. This period also saw the successful introduction of Corex technology by the Jindal group and Hot Briquetted Iron Route with Direct Reduction process by the Essar group for setting up their integrated plants at Bellary and Hazira respectively (Wieder, Bohm, Wurn 2005). In addition we witnessed the emergence of Direct Reduced Iron (DRI - sponge iron as popularly referred) as a viable alternative feed stock for production of crude steel. Crude steel produced through different technologies by the various producer groups for the years 2001-02 to 2005-06 is given in the Table 2.

Table 2: Crude steel produced through different technologies and producer groups from the years 2001-02 to 2005-06

(Million Tonnes)

Technology	*2000-01*	*2005-06 rate (%)*	*Growth*	*Remarks*
Main Producers based on Blast furnace: Conventional Integrated steel plants	17.7	21.7	3.8	Consists of Steel Authority of India Company (TISCO) and Rastriya Ispat Limited (SAIL), Tata Iron and Steel Nigam Limited (RINL)
Secondary Producers (based on different DRI technologies)				DRI: Direct reduced iron
Integrated plants	5.9	11.2	15.0	Consist of Jindal, Ispat and Essar
Other secondary producers	4.3	8.7	17.1	Large number of plants distributed across the country
Total	27.9	41.6	8.2	

Source: Joint Plant Committee quoted in Planning Commission (2007).

The Joint Plant Committee (JPC) classifies steel producers into main and secondary producers. Main Producers are conventional integrated steel plants using the traditional Blast Furnace and Basic Oxygen Furnace (BF-BOF) technology comprising of three companies. First, we have the Steel Authority of India Limited (SAIL) with integrated plants at four locations, second is the Tata Iron and Steel Company (TISCO) with an integrated plant, and finally the Rastriya Ispat Nigam Limited (RINL) with an integrated plant. The plants of SAIL and TISCO are near the iron ore and coal mines. RINL plant was located away from the raw material sources on the coast but closer to potential markets for its finished products. All the plants together produced 21.7 million tonnes in 2005-06 growing annually at the rate of 3.8 per cent from 2001-02 to 2005-06.

The secondary producers have opted for Direct Reduced Iron (DRI) technology instead of the conventional blast furnace technology of the main producers. The secondary producers are further classified into integrated plants and other secondary producers. Integrated plants have been set up by three companies. The çompanies use DRI process but even within this group there are different technologies. Jindal uses the Corex-Basic Oxygen Furnace technology at its plant in Bellary of Karnataka. Ispat uses Mini Blast Furnace — Energy Optimising Furnace (MBF-EOF) technology with gas as fuel in its plant located on the west coast in Maharastra. Essar uses Direct Reduction Iron-Electric Arc Furnace (DRI-EAF) technology with gas as fuel on the west coast in Gujarat. All the companies together produced 11.2 milllion tonnes in 2005-06 growing annually at the rate of 15.0 per cent from 2001-02 to 2005-06.

Other secondary producers also use DRI technology but are smaller in size compared to the integrated plants. Though the units are distributed across the country, a large number of plants are located in iron ore-rich states of Jharkhand, Orissa, Chattisgarh, and Karnataka. They produced 8.7 million tonnes in 2005-06 growing annually at the rate of 17.1 per cent from 2001-02 to 2005-06. Growth of other secondary producers has helped in proliferation of a large number of electric arc furnaces and rolling mills across the country.

Looking at the secondary producers the industry suggests a highly dispersed pattern of production. A few secondary producers have production of more than a million tonnes while some small units produce only a few thousand tonnes in a year (Table 3 provides the details).

Table 3: Structure of Producers in Secondary Sector (2005-06)

Industry segments	*Working units*	*Working capacity (in million tonnes)*
Pig Iron	22	9.3
Sponge Iron	218	18.2
Electric Arc Furnace	37	8.7
COREX/MBF	3	3.0
Re-rolling	1361	19.6
HR Sheet/Coil	9	8.4
Cold Rolling	55	6.1
GP/GC sheet	18	3.5
Colour coated	4	0.4
Tin plate	1	.14

Source: Joint Plant Committee quoted in Planning Commission (2007).

In fact, there is a discernible trend towards increased dispersal of production across more producers. The larger role of the private sector is another perceptible change. Production share of primary steel producers reduced from 77% in 1992-93 to 52% in 2005-06. Further, the share of integrated public sector units in crude steel production steadily fell from 63% in 1992-93 to 41% in 2005-06 indicating increased production of steel from privately owned firms.

Clearly, the changes mentioned above have implications for the transportation of raw materials and finished products. The Railways potentially stand to lose from the growth of smaller and more dispersed units since they imply smaller shipments. Railways comparative advantage is in moving train loads rather than wagon loads or piecemeal traffic. The trucking industry is better equipped to deal with the needs of the smaller producers. The actual outcomes in terms of Railways share of the market reflect this perceptible shift. Till 1992-93 railways was the predominant mover of raw materials to steel plants and finished steel. Table 4 shows the share of railways in the movement of finished steel fell dramatically from 79.1 per cent in 1992-93 to 38.5 in 2006-06. The movement of raw material also fell from 62.0 per cent in 1992-93 to 33.7 per cent in 2005-06.

Table 4: Trend of Steel Production and Movement by Railways

(Million tonnes)

Year	*Steel produced*	*Finished steel moved by rail*	*Raw material moved by rail*
1991-92	14.33	11.43 (79.8)	29.53 (58.9)
1992-93	15.20	12.03 (79.1)	32.97 (62.0)
1996-97	22.72	11.81 (52.0)	38.55 (48.5)
2001-02	30.64	12.36 (40.3)	39.35 (36.7)
2005-06	44.54	17.14 (38.5)	52.61 (33.7)

Figures in parenthesis are in percentages. While arriving at percentage of raw material moved quantity required is assumed as 3.5 tonnes per tonne of steel produced.

Source: Column 2 - Joint Plant Committee quoted in Planning Commission (2007), Column 2 and 3 - Annual Statistical Statements of Railways various years.

Deregulation of the steel sector allowed firms to make more market oriented choices on location of the plants, markets to be served, choice of modes of transport while the removal of freight equalisation affected the logistics patterns of the industry. It does appear that the Railways were not prepared to face a liberalised Steel industry and face the consequences.

1.2 Strategic decisions of steel firms and Implications for logistics: A few case studies

In this section each segment of producers is analysed to bring out the diversified strategies of firms while deciding on their choice of transport mode. Focus is on location with respect to raw material sources, markets served, technologies adopted, ownership pattern, and choice of transport mode for inbound and outbound cargo.

Main Producers other than Rastriya Ispat Nigam Limited

Traditionally the main producers used BF-BOF technology and were located closer to the raw material sources of iron ore, coal and limestone and dolomite. They relied heavily on railways to move the raw materials. As they were located either in Eastern India or Central India, they also relied largely on IR for moving their finished product to other parts of the country. The rail share of these plants fell in the nineties, but has recovered in recent years thanks to some focussed marketing initiatives by firms. The main advantage the Railways has vis-à-vis these producers is the rail based infrastructure created in these units. The key element therefore is to encourage utilisation of this infrastructure through appropriate incentives.

Rastriya Ispat Nigam Limited

The Rastriya Ispat Nigam plant was the last of the public sector units set up for steel production and was fully commissioned in the early nineties. Though the company, like other existing integrated plants, used the BF-BOF technology it was located away from the raw material centres in East Coast. The plant is around 260 kilometres from iron ore sources necessitating transport by rail to the plant. Coal was obtained through a sea port and limestone and dolomite by rail from around 500 kilometres. The plant had set up an extensive railway network within the factory to load the finished products, in the same pattern as other public sector plants placing a heavy reliance on rail transport.

Essar Steel Limited

Essar Steel Limited, based in Hazira, Gujarat on the west coast, has revolutionised the logistics of the steel industry by deviating from the conventional rail based transport. Coal the traditional fuel was substituted by natural gas, a resource more easily available on the west coast. The unit's location enables better access by road and rail to markets in Northern India and Western India: Being closer to the coast, it has also benefited from focusing on export markets for its finished products.

More revolutionary is the movement of iron ore. To procure iron ore, Essar Steel commissioned an iron ore pelletisation plant in Visakhapatnam, Andhra Pradesh on the east coast using fines mined 260 kilometers away. To move the fines to the plant it constructed a 267 Kilometer slurry pipeline (the second longest in the world), saving Rs 470 per tonne compared to rail. The pellets are moved from Visakhapatnam to Hazira through the cheaper option of coastal movement thus reducing the transport expenses (Thomas, 2006; Essar Steel 2002).

JSW Steel Limited

JSW Steel Limited has a 4 million tonne plant in Bellary in Karnataka with two downstream rolling mills in the west, one in Gujarat and the other one in Maharastra. The company has plans to expand the plant to 10 million tonnes per annum by 2010. The company sources iron ore from mines close by and transports around 56 % of iron ore by rail and 44 % by road. The plant imports coal at Goa and owns two berths at Goa port. The coal from Goa is moved by rail. Similarly, around 15 % of limestone and dolomite is imported at Goa and moved by rail to the plant. Rest of the limestone is sourced from nearby mines and is moved by rail. The plant adopted direct reduction strategy in the initial phase of production but expansions under progress are based on BF-BOF technologies (RITES, 2007).

Other Segments of the Steel Industry

As commented earlier, the steel industry is more segmented now than in 1992-93. These plants are characterised by their diversity in size, scale, raw materials used, location, and the markets they serve. It is not surprising therefore that each of the industry segments and the firms in these segments follow different strategies in moving their inward and outward cargo. While a detailed analysis of the modes used by each of the firms is not possible due to limitations of data, a brief outline is presented to bring out the preference of the secondary producers for road movement.

First amongst the segments are the sponge iron manufacturers. In 2005-06, India had around 218 sponge iron producers with an aggregate capacity of 18.2 million tonnes. They consisted of plants of different sizes, with the large ones being more than a million tonnes in size, comparable to the integrated Blast Furnace plants. In addition, a large number of small iron plants exist with production levels varying from few lakh tons per annum to a few thousands of tons per annum. The plants are often located closer to iron ore and coal locations especially in Chattisgarh, Orissa,

Jharkhand and West Bengal. Road is the predominant mode for movement of the input material and sponge iron output. In most cases these plants have not developed elaborate rail facilities and are biased towards making modal choices in favour of road.

The other prominent segment in the steel industry is the electric arc furnace refining industry. In 2005-06, India had 37 such units with an annual capacity of 8.7 million tonnes. These plants use sponge iron, scrap and pig iron to produce steel. They either have their rolling facilities or sell refined steel to rolling mills. Electric units also have a lot of variability in size and are dispersed across the country. These plants are mainly dependent on road for moving their cargo and again do not have elaborate rail facilities.

The third segment comprises of the rolling mills which were 1361 in number with an annual capacity of 19.6 million tonnes in 2005-06. The rolling mills are smaller in size and dispersed across the country with concentration in Northern and Western India. They procure refined steel and make finished products for the market or to specific orders. As the firms are small with correspondingly small outward shipment sizes they prefer road for their transport needs. Rail is used rarely, only when there is long distance movement of bulk orders.

Export and import traffic constitutes an important chunk of steel flows. In 2005-06 international trade in steel was 9 million tonnes with exports of 4.8 million tonnes and imports of 4.2 million tonnes. Most of the international trade barring movements from integrated steel plants is predominantly by road.

Analysis of the strategies

A review of strategies by firms indicates great diversity in tackling the logistics issues.

- Though the main producers continued to rely on rail movement, their rail share has reduced and road share gone up since 1992-93.
- Use of natural gas as fuel and availability of imported coal has enabled plants to be located away from coal production centres thus reducing the raw material movement. The plants moved closer to ports.
- Availability of gas and imported coal has made coastal shipping a viable option for moving raw material, especially iron ore, and finished products
- Pipeline as a viable option for moving iron ore fines is now well established and this gives further scope for industry dispersal. As the iron ore mines are not very far from ports in many states, pipeline based movement of fines combined with pelletisation plants in the coast give scope for coastal movement of iron ore. This would enable further dispersal from raw material sources.

Spread of sponge iron plants, electric furnaces, and rolling mills is both an opportunity and a threat for rail transport. These developments have enabled faster growth of the industry, not possible with an industry with only integrated steel plants. However, as these units are smaller, their investment in railway infrastructure is negligible and they rely mostly on road transport.

Another opportunity arises for railways due to dispersal of the production process. In an integrated plant, movement of material for processing of crude steel, pure steel and rolled products was an internal movement undertaken in one integrated complex. With dispersal of production process, transfer of material from one stage to another involved longer distances engaging a transport agency. While the opportunity is clear, the threat for railways emerges as the most of the plants are small in size, and many of the plants may not be able to afford full fledged rail facilities. It is here that railway has to intervene to explore possibilities of aggregating the material.

Further, a striking feature in the firms approach to transporting material is the deviation from using one single mode of transport. As a strategy firms have explored multiple options. More importantly, the mode choice decisions are made part of the strategic or long term decisions influencing the plant location, sources of raw materials and markets to be served. Thus, mode choice decisions for steel producers have to be addressed at strategic levels. This implies that IR should ideally involve itself while companies are deciding to set up their plants.

2. VISION 200 MILLION TONNES: NEW STRATEGIES

While the steel industry was undergoing drastic changes in nineties, IR did not have any plan to tackle these changes. IR's competitive edge was its price. However, cost based pricing was subject to constant upward revision on the plea of increase in costs of operation. Repeated price increases eroded rail competitiveness and rail share fell. Other marketing initiatives like interaction with the customers were sporadic and not focussed, and consequently did not yield the result.

In the late nineties some changes were noticeable when IR either froze most of the prices or reduced them. In addition, the Railways also introduced a number of other steps like lean season discount and volume discount. This strategy did help the railways as the loading from steel industry increased rapidly. In the five year period from 2001-02 to 2005-06, the loading of finished steel increased by 39 per cent and raw material to steel plants increased by 33 per cent. Though the above increase is very impressive and significant, it should be also noted that the overall railway share in moving steel industry products during the five year period fell; share in finished steel went down from 40.3 per cent to 38.5 per cent and that for raw material fell from 36.7 per cent to 33.7 per cent. Juxtaposing these facts, it is seen that though the initiatives taken by IR did help in increased loading from the sector, they were inadequate to increase the market share.

The Railway budget introduced in 2007 targets to increase loading from steel industry to 200 million tonnes by 2011-12. It implies that IR has to increase its loading by 186 per cent over a period of five years. The Eleventh Five Year Plan Working Group report on the Railways assessed that the total loading from steel industry in the year 2011-12 would be 328 million tonnes comprising of 78 million tonnes of finished steel and 250 million tonnes of raw material. This does not include 15,000 million calories of natural gas as it is not loaded by the railways. The numbers suggest that Railways' share has to increase from the current level of 33 per cent to 61 per cent over a period of five years. In other words **the market share has to be nearly doubled within five years.**

The question is: how can IR achieve something as spectacular as this? Is it an unrealistic target or can effective strategies be devised to achieve this? We take the view that while it is a difficult task, the potential does exist. For this to be achieved, IR has to initiate strategic plans with other ministries of the Central Government, State Governments, industry associations and private firms in logistics sector and in steel industry. It would have to integrate rail transport to the strategic initiatives of the manufacturers in the sector. As the sector is segmented, it has to follow a well differentiated strategy to cater to large and small plants.

As plans of large manufacturers are generally well known, Railways should initiate steps to capture as much traffic as possible when the unit is being conceptualised. It has to plan capacity in tune with the plants plans. By this proactive role it should be able to capture as much traffic as possible. The concept of Rail Transport Clearance (RTC) should be reversed. Railways should increase capacity and enter into long term agreements based on commitments. This has already been provided in the railway budget 2007 when the Minister for Railways proclaimed "We have recently signed a 30 year long term Service Level Agreement (SLA) for transportation of coal. Several new cement, steel and mega power plants are being set up in the country. We will provide necessary support services for laying new lines up to their facilities, enhancing capacity of existing lines, making available wagons designed to suit their specific requirements, formulation of pricing policy and in developing loading and unloading terminals. We invite all entrepreneurs to enter into long term SLAs with the Railways."

For smaller units, the strategy would have to be different. The general principle would be to identify centres of production and centres of consumption for raw material and finished product and locate hubs for aggregation and dispersal (Brahma, 2007). The hubs and logistic parks would store and forward raw material and finished products as per industry needs. The hubs can be owned and managed by industry associations or private players. Space can be provided to the industries or traders to store and forward their material to different places. Such hubs as aggregators of raw material and finished products will also provide a signal to the private entrepreneurs to locate the industries closer to these hubs. Without such a strategic initiative to aggregate material the Railways cannot capture cargo of small firms such as sponge iron plants, electric furnaces and rolling mills.

To develop such a policy, active involvement of Planning Commission and the Ministry of Steel would be critical. Cooperation with State Governments is required in locating such hubs and providing the right signals to industry to locate their plants closer to the hubs. Involvement of industry associations and private capital through public-private partnership could expedite the process. The development of Dedicate Freight Corridors (DFC) should provide a positive fillip to these concepts. As DFC routes and feeder routes would have spare line capacity to provide long term commitments, IR should increasingly enter into service level agreements with the steel plants.

Thus a combination of reiteration of existing freight policies and initiation of new policies would be required to achieve 200 million loading by 2011-12.

3. CONCLUSIONS

The paper brings out the segmentation that has happened in the steel industry after deregulation in 1990s. It has also discussed the changes in technology and structure of steel industry, and how it favoured use of alternative modes of transport for moving cargo. It is also shown that IR share in moving steel industry material fell due to lack of understanding of the changes that occurred in the steel industry and repeated increase of freight rates. Finally, the need for a differentiated strategy for large manufacturers and small manufacturers is brought out. The idea is simple. At the economy wide level, the Railways are the best modal choice for the bigger producers — it is energy efficient and environment friendly as compared to the other modes. The Railways would have to take advantage of this basic fact and leverage its strength and credibility to begin long term relationships. For the smaller producers, the comparison between road and rail may not be as stark and road is a key competitor. Here the strategy has to be one that focuses on the needs of the consumer — creation of hubs at various locations that can provide consolidation of the produce of the smaller producers. Thus for large manufacturers railways should match their capacity creation plans in harmony with the industry needs and enter into long term service agreements. For smaller units, Railways should create steel hubs in association with state governments and industry bodies. Capacity created through DFC should be fruitfully used for this purpose.

From the perspective of Railways it would be best to categorise the market into these two categories — the bigger producers with whom there is a need to get into long term agreements and the smaller ones for whom the logistics would have to be altered. In this paper we do not address the details of what would constitute a good long term contract with the big producers. Long term contracting does have its down sides since it is difficult to write a complete contract. However, the historical relationship between the Railways and the big producers could help in designing an efficient contract. The secret of a good contract lies in unravelling this relationship and fully understanding the needs of the industry. We hope to conduct further research in this area. The second category of producers has a natural tendency to prefer road given their economics of size. The suggestion here is to find ways of increasing their size by creating hubs. Another area of research is to evaluate the externality effects of creating such hubs providing a surplus that could then be shared between the Railways and the industry.

The paper discusses a broad outline of action to be taken. A detailed analysis has to be worked for each section of the industry looking at the actual cargo flows to finalise the section capacity enhancements and location of hubs for each group of investors. This should be initiated by IR immediately to realise mission 200 million tonnes.

REFERENCES

Brahma, G. D. (Forthcoming), *The Story of Pilbara Railway in Australia - Seventy Mainline locomotives. 6000 wagons, 4800 employees and loading of 150 million tonnes, RITES Journal.*

Essar Steel (2002), *Iron ore pipeline fo hy grade pellets signed. Construction contract for Rs 300 Crores*, December 4, 2002, www.essar.com/constructions/pr/dec_4_2002.htm.

Indian Railways (2007), *Railway Budget Speech 2007-08,* http://indianrailways.gov.in.

Joint Plant Committee (2007), http://jpcindiansteel.org/ind_profile.asp.

Ministry of Railways (various years) *Indian Railways: Annual Statistical Statements*, Ministry of Railways.

Planning Commission (2007), *Working Group Report on Steel*, available at http://planningcommission.nic.in/aboutus/committee/wrkgrp11/wg11_steel.

RITES Limited (2007), *Study on JSW Steel Limited, Midterm report,* unpublished report

Tata Steel (2007), Annual Report 2006-07,

http://tatasteel.com/investorrelations/an200607/Q4-06-07.

Tata Steel (2007), Annual Report, 2005-06, http://tatasteel.com/investorrelations/an200607/Q4-06-07.

Thomas, P.M. (2006), *Essar Steel starts iron ore slurry pipeline,* Business Standard, March 10, 2006, www.essar.com/steel/new/mar_10_2006.htm.

Wieder, K., C Bohm, J. Wurn (2005), *The COREX and FINEX Processes - reliable, environmental friendly and economical Hot Metal Production,* 28 February' 2005, http://jpcindiansteel.org/corfin.asp.

30

A NOTE ON SOME ASPECTS OF PERFORMANCE ON THE INDIAN RAILWAYS

Sudakshina Gupta

ABSTRACT

The role played by the Indian Railways in the development of the Indian economy has been significant. However, in recent decades, the railways are no longer the dominant mode. Lack of investments for replacements and expansion has hindered provision of adequate services to meet emerging requirements. High level committees including the Rakesh Mohan Committee have pointed out a number of reasons including cross subsidisation, fall in carriage of bulk goods, non-viable investments, etc. More recently, some turn around appears to have been achieved. But demands for long term reform of the system in terms of privatisation, ect. continue. It is against this background that this paper attempts to examine some aspects of performance of the railways with a view to propose some reforms.

1. INTRODUCTION

In India, the railways are the largest mode of transport. The country's vastness and diversity have been connected and coordinated by the largest railway network in Asia. Passengers and goods with equal importance are carried everyday by this mode from one corner of the country to the other. The Indian economy thrives on the Indian Railways. They also happen to be the biggest employer in India.

The British in their own commercial interest started the construction of railways in India. Dalhousie's observation in 1850 stated clearly that the objectives of building the railways were to carry British capital and enterprise to India, bring in the produce to the ports from the interior and to strengthen the military forces. This acted, in fact, as a boon to the Indian Economy. It not only gave an impetus to the Indian Economy but also a sense of nationalism grew among the people of the country. The then isolated villages got connected with each other and with the towns also. The sense of oneness that grew among the Indians ultimately helped them fight for the freedom of the country. In the times of wars and natural calamities also, the railways have served the country quite well.

1.1 Brief History of the Indian Railways

Indian Railways were initiated at the height of capitalism with only British capital being invested, and which was borrowed mainly from the London Money Market. Later, State capital was invested for a brief period and it was reverted to private capital again. The construction and expansion of the railways in the initial period thus followed a very interesting pattern.

The earliest proposal came in 1843-44. The East India Company made contracts with private English companies like the East Indian Railway Company and Great Peninsular Railway Company formed in 1845. The first railway was opened in 1853. Till 1869, the period of the "Old Guarantee System" was in force, where the companies, being under the general control of the Government, were guaranteed annual rate of interest of 5% on all capital raised by them and free land for 99 years by the Government. Half the surplus profit every year had to be paid to the latter. However, because of a lot of wastage and extravagance, the state took over the direct management of the Railways and decided to construct railways through its own agency. The period continued until 1879, when, because of a resource crunch and a hostile feeling towards pure state management in England, the Government resorted to the "New Guarantee System," whereby the rate of interest guaranteed went down to 3½ % and the Government could keep a larger share of the profit, viz. 3/5th. This continued till 1900. Around this time, the Indian States were also invited to open railway lines. Thus, even though privatisation was introduced in the railways, the Government kept a stricter control over them.

In 1853, the "Rebate System" or the grant of subsidy was initiated to open branch or feeder lines, which was replaced by the "Absolute Guarantee System" in 1896. In 1913, as per a modification, capital for branch lines was allowed to be raised partly by the rebate System and partly by the guarantee System.

Because of losses faced during the First World War and a subsequent recommendation made by a Railway Committee, in 1921 the policy of state management was initiated again in 1924, though later, the Government declared that, each case would be considered on its merit regarding the termination of contracts. This policy continued until 1944, after which, except for the lines owned by the princely states and a few remaining under private companies, almost all the lines were nationalised.

1.2 Post-Independence Scenario in India

The entire scenario of the Indian transport sector, however, changed after the independence and the accompanying partition of the country. The government of India took up the policy of a mixed economy, thus nationalising most of the basic sectors, including transport infrastructure. Social return became more important than private return. The vast network of Indian railways was nationalised. The smaller private companies were all merged together. Railway expansion has been one of the main aims and ambitions of the government. A separate ministry has been formed only for the Railways and each year, a separate budget is placed for the Railways.

Both passenger and goods services have increased over time in terms of number and amount respectively, and so has the revenue. Both local and long distance trains have showed the same trend. The route kilometrage also showed an impressive increase.

1.3 Issues as Detected by the Rakesh Mohan Committee

The Rakesh Mohan Committee, a government appointed group chaired by Rakesh Mohan, which submitted its report in 2001, however, found that the Indian Railways, had been plagued by a few problems in recent years. According to this Committee, the rate of growth in revenues had been much less than the rate of increase in costs in the preceding period. These tendencies became accentuated in the 1990s and made the economies of Indian Railways extremely vulnerable. For the first time in 17 years, Indian Railways were not able to pay a dividend to the government on its past investment.

Since the liberalisation of the Indian Economy in 1991 and drop in international transport costs, the railways have seen a slowdown in the rate of growth of freight cargo transportation. The annual growth rate measured in 'net tonne kilometres', averaged 5.33 per cent between 1984 and 1991 but dropped to 1.86 per cent in the next eight years between 1992 and 1999. They were also losing on pricing to other modes.

Investment in unremunerative projects like unigauge projects and unnecessary electrification in places have also escalated during the 1990s. They have not earned any returns. For political reasons, many needless investments have taken place. All these together have caused a heavy burden on the Indian Railways in recent times.

A large workforce, rising employee costs, poor productivity and declining budgetary support have compounded the problem. Staff costs, which accounts for about 50 percent of the total costs is likely to increase even faster with the implementation of the recommendations of the 5th Pay Commission. The pensioners' benefits account for almost 10% of the total costs. The increase in productivity in terms of output is only 82% compared to that in the real wages during 1981-82 to 1998-99. The proportion of expenditure on repairs and maintenance, adequate investments on track renewals and other safety related areas have been declining steadily over the years because of declining resources of the Indian Railways.

1.4 Recommendations of the Rakesh Mohan Committee

The Rakesh Mohan Committee recommended the commercialisation of the Indian Railways rather than privatisation as international experience shows that privatising railways can prove to be difficult and controversial. Commercialisation involves reorganising the rail system into its component parts, spinning off non-core activities, restructuring what remains along business lines and adopting commercial accounting performance management systems with a degree of autonomy being given to the management.

2. OBJECTIVE AND METHODOLOGY OF THE PAPER

In the light of the above discussion, an analysis has been done in the present paper to find out if the expansion in railway route network has in any way, resulted in the benefit of the Indian Railways and the Indian Economy. The data reveals an increase in route-kilometres probably following expansion and branching of the railway network since 1950-51. A rise in passenger kilometres, goods traffic and goods revenue, passenger carried and passenger revenue is also seen (see Appendix 1). The purpose of the paper is to find if the extension in railway network has positively contributed to these factors. With a smaller sample size, relations between route-kilometres and railway net revenue, railway net traffic receipt and railway surplus deficit are also studied.

An attempt is also made to find the relation between railway net revenue and a few variables like passenger earnings and goods earnings, number of passengers carried and tonnage of goods carried with the help of a polynomial equation.

For the study, data has been collected from the official website of the Government of India containing the Economic Survey of India. The information is taken from 1950-51 till recent times. For railway net revenue, net traffic receipts and surplus deficit, however, information could be found from 1980-81 only. Annual data could be collected from 2000-01 and before that, decadal data was available(Appendix 2) The financial variables are suitably deflated with the help of the index numbers published in the above-mentioned website (see Appendix 3).

For the above analysis, the Pearson's Product Moment Formula has been used to find out simple correlation coefficients. The relationships of route-kilometres with the factors like passenger kilometres, goods traffic and goods revenue, passenger carried and passenger revenue have been assessed by the above. For goods traffic, both total originating traffic and total billion tonne kilometres have been considered. Similarly, with a smaller sample size, relation between route-kilometres and railway net revenue, railway net traffic receipt and railway surplus deficit has also been studied. For the first set, the sample size is 10 and the second set, it is 7. Railway net revenue is the summation of railway net traffic receipt and railway net miscellaneous receipts whereas railway net traffic receipt is the difference between gross traffic receipts and working expenses.

A polynomial equation has also been fitted to find out relationships between railway net revenue as the dependent variable, and passenger earnings, goods earnings, number of passengers carried and tonnage of goods carried (revenue earning billion tonne kilometre) as independent variables.

The correlation analysis was done with the help of the Pearson's Product Moment formula used to find out the linear correlation between two variables The formula is:

$$r = \frac{\sum(x-X)(y-X)}{\sqrt{\left[\sum(x-X)^2 \sum(y-Y)^2\right]}} \qquad \ldots (1)$$

where x and y are the two variables with X and Y being their means.

The correlation coefficient or the r-value has its usual characteristics.

For sample size 10, 1% level of significance is 0.765, 5% is 0.632

For sample size 7, 1% level of significance is 0.874, 5% is 0.754

The polynomial is of the following form:

$$Y = \beta_1 + \beta_2 x_2 + \beta_3 x_3 + \beta_4 x_4 + \beta_5 x_5 \quad \dots (2)$$

Using matrix technology the values of the coefficients are found out. Y here stands for railway net revenue as dependent variable and xi's (i = 2, ..., 5) for passenger earnings and goods earnings, tonnage of goods carried and number of passengers carried as independent variables respectively.

3. RESULTS OF CORRELATION ANALYSIS

These results are given below:

Table 1: Coefficients between Route Kilometre and Different Variables

Variable	*Coefficient*	*Significant at*	*Sample Size*
Passenger kilometres	0.8513	1%	10
Goods Carried	0.8780	1%	10
Earnings from Goods Carried	0.8362	1%	10
No. of Passengers	0.9384	1%	10
Earnings from Passengers	-0.7661	1%	10
Railway Net Revenue	0.9067	1%	7
Railway Net Traffic Receipts	0.7804	5%	7
Railway Surplus Deficit	0.7936	5%	7

Route-kilometre is positively and significantly related to each of the following:

1. Passenger kilometres,
2. Goods carried, (same for both total originating traffic and billion tonne kilometre)
3. Passengers carried,
4. Earning from goods carried.

These are expected results. Route-km was, however, found to be significantly but negatively related to earnings to passenger traffic.

With a smaller sample size, route-kilometres was also found to be positively related to railway net revenue, railway net traffic receipt and railway surplus deficit. These results were also as expected.

In a further analysis, the relation between railway net revenue and a few variables are analysed. The polynomial as mentioned above gives the following results:

$$Y = 14174.2768 - 125.9622x_2 + 1.6449x_3 + 36.9529x_4 - 5.1764x_5$$

The coefficients of number of passengers carried and passenger earnings are found to be negative, whereas the others are positive.

3.1 Analysis of Results

The results of the analysis are discussed in the following paragraphs.

1. The positive and significant relation between route kilometres and passenger kilometres is as expected. From 1950-51 to recent times an expansion of the railway network is seen all over the country. A substantial improvement in passenger kilometres is also seen. New passenger trains, both of short and long hauls, have been introduced almost every year. People are travelling distances for work and recreation. It gives a healthy picture of a growing and dynamic economy where more income is generated every day.
2. The goods movement has also increased in tonnage over the years, taking help of the expansion in the railway system. Both raw materials and finished goods of different varieties are regularly carried on trains. Goods trains (mahl gharries) serve the special purpose of extending the markets. Local trains with reserved vendor compartments are used for the daily carriage of eatables for local markets.
3. Earnings from goods carried are an important source of revenue for the Railways. It has increased over the years. Route kilometres and these earnings are positively and significantly related to each other. Apart from the increase in tonnage a possible reason for such a relation may be the difficulty in indulging in free ride of goods.
4. Similarly, a very high positive and significant correlation coefficient is found between route kilometres and number of passengers carried. More people are availing of the trains running with diesel mainly. School, college, office and factory workers take the help of the vast railway system. People travel to reach markets through trains too. The railways help in developing the tourism industry also. This is again a good sign of a thriving economy.

Route kilometres, however, is found to be significantly but negatively related to earnings from passenger traffic over the years.

A smaller sample size gives a positive and significant relation between railway route-kilometres and net railway revenue. It is expected that the net revenue will increase with an increase in the railway route kilometres. The passenger earnings having a negative relation with the route kilometres, it is possible that earnings from goods carried are so high that they make up for the loss in passenger earnings. Similar results are found for net receipts and railway surplus deficits also.

As mentioned earlier, a polynomial equation has been fitted with the railway net revenue as the dependent variable. Among the independent variables as mentioned earlier, tonnage of goods carried and earnings from goods carried show positive coefficients, i.e., the railway revenue increases with an increase in the tonnage of goods carried and earnings there from. This is again an expected result. The railway revenue, however, is found to have a negative relation with the number of passengers carried and earnings from passengers carried. The queer relations of railway route kilometres and railway net revenue with passenger earnings and their numbers are discussed below.

- The number of passengers has increased much more in the low fare sector more than that in the higher fare one. In the latter, the competition with air has made the Railways lose passengers. Therefore, the passenger earnings may not have increased in matching proportion with the number of passengers.
- Again, the cross subsidisation of the low fare passenger segment by the higher fare one and that of the passenger traffic by the goods traffic may be another reason why passenger earnings show a negative relation with both route kilometres and net revenue.
- There has been a traditional practice of the passengers in the Indian Railways to ride for free. So, neither the number of passengers, nor the passenger earnings show a positive reflection in the increase of net revenue and route kilometre.

All these factors together may have caused the relationships between passengers-related variables and route kilometres and net revenue to be negative. Goods carriage, on the other hand, shows positive relation with both route kilometres and revenue. In fact, goods carried make up the bulk of traffic in the Indian Railways. It also earns much more than passenger traffic.

4. CONCLUSIONS

A suggested way out of problems may be decentralisation of the operation of the Indian Railways under private hands. To start with, local operations may be privatised. It may be easier for the private sector to control the local traffic. A rationalisation of the fare structure and a more stringent checking of the fare have the possibility of improving the conditions. A thorough revamping of the staff structure may also be helpful in this regard. Such a reorganisation of operations is recommended for the following reasons.

1. Privatisation of operation of local traffic may bring about efficiency in the railway running. However, competition may lead to lack of discipline and hence breed irregularity and unwanted effects. So, some coordination is needed that may be performed by a railway executive board.
2. For decentralised and private operations, it will be easier to rationalise the fare structure also. Stringent checking will reduce the scope of free ride of passengers too. All these will lead to the proper realisation of revenue, which, in turn, will give the passengers an increased speed, safety and comfort and, obviously, a much regular service.
3. Private operators, in their own interest, may rebuild the staff structure in such a way that more economic expenditure will lead to much better service. The need for subsidy may also become redundant and hence, it may be abolished altogether.

The current system is too vast under the public sector and is bound to lead to inefficiency in operations and other unhealthy practices. Privatisation also has its accompanying evils but small scale operations may be started with so that competition leads to efficiency.

APPENDICES

Appendix 1

Railway Route-Kilometres and Other Values

Year	*Railway Route Km*	*Passenger Km (Bn)*	*Goods Carried (Bn. Tn Km) Total*	*Goods Carried (MT) Total*	*Goods Carried (Bn Tn Km) Rev Erng*	*Earnings from Goods Carried (Rs. Cr)*	*Passenger Originating (Mn. Nos.)*	*Passenger Earnings (Rs. Cr.)*
1950-51	53.6	66.5	44.1	93.0	37.6	139.3	1284	98.2
1960-61	56.2	77.7	87.7	156.2	72.3	280.5	1594	131.6
1970-71	59.8	118.1	127.4	196.5	110.7	600.7	2431	295.5
1980-81	61.2	208.6	158.5	220.0	147.5	1550.9	3613	827.5
1990-91	62.4	295.6	242.7	341.4	235.8	8247.0	3858	3144.7
2000-01	63.0	457.0	315.5	504.2	312.4	23045.4	4833	10515.1
2002-03	63.1	515.0	356.0	542.7	353.2	26231.5	4971	12575.4
2003-04	63.2	541.0	384.0	581.4	381.2	27403.2	5112	13298.3
2004-05	63.5	576.0	411.3	626.2	407.4	30489.2	5378	14113.7
2005-06	63.3	616.0	441.6	682.2	439.5	35554.5	5725	15118.9

Appendix 2

Some Other Financial Values

Year	*Railway Net Revenue (Rs. Cr.)*	*Railway Net Traffic Receipts (Rs. Cr.)*	*Railway Surplus/ Deficit (Rs. Cr.)*
1980-81	127	87	–198
1990-91	1113	942	175
2001-02	2337	1544	1000
2002-03	3830	3042	1115
2003-04	4478	3423	1091
2004-05	5278	4611	2074
2005-06	8005	8918	4338
2006-07	8544	9581	4673

Appendix 3

Index Numbers and Deflated Financial Values

Year	*Index nos.*	*Earnings from Goods Carried (Rs. Cr.) deflated*	*Passenger Earnings (Rs. Cr.) deflated*	*Railway Net Revenue (Rs. Cr.) deflated*	*Railway Net Traffic Receipts (Rs. Cr.) deflated*	*Railway Surplus Deficit (Rs. Cr.) deflated*
1950-51	100.0	139.30	98.20			
1960-61	145.2	193.18	46.92			
1970-71	204.2	294.17	49.91			
1980-81	274.6	564.79	53.36	46.25	31.68	-72.10
1990-91	464.0	1777.37	38.13	239.87	203.01	37.72
2000-01	789.8	2917.96	45.63			
2001-02	835.5			279.7	184.81	119.69
2002-03	865.2	3031.92	47.94	442.68	351.60	128.88
2003-04	941.4	2911.09	48.53	475.71	363.63	115.90
2004-05	1010.6	3016.81	46.29	521.75	456.24	205.22
2005-06	1102.8	3224.04	42.52	725.97	808.67	393.36

REFERENCES

Arkin and Cotton, (1953), Statistical Methods, Barnes and Noble, New York.

Bhattacharya, H.S. (1966), Aspects of Indian Economic History, Progressive Publishers, Calcutta..

Gadgil, D.R. (1924), Industrial Evolution of India in Recent Times, Oxford University Press, Calcutta.

Jathar, G.B. and S.G. Beri. (1942), Indian Economics — A Comprehensive and Critical Survey, Vol.2, 7th Ed., Oxford University Press, Calcutta.

Kumar, D and, T. Roychaudhury (Gen. Ed.) (1983), The Cambridge Economic History of India, Ch viii, Vol. 2, c. 1757-c. 1970, Press Syndicate of the University of Cambridge, New York.

31

A STUDY ON INFRASTRUCTURE ALTERNATIVES WITH SPECIAL REFERENCE TO URBAN TRANSPORTATION

Dinesh S. Hegde
Lakshmikanth Hari

ABSTRACT

This paper analyses some infrastructure alternatives in the context of urban transportation especially the costs, benefits, scope, and barriers associated with the adoption of these alternatives. Alternatives such as Skybus system and Bus Rapid Transit (BRT) system are considered for the study. A BRT system can be a starting point for introduction of alternatives fuels such as hydrogen and bio fuels. It would however, be practically difficult to construct or extend rail based mass transit systems such as underground, surface and elevated railway systems in the existing cities due to constraints and considerations of safety and space requirements in such cases. The Skybus could be a better alternative as it has the capacity of rail based system in addition to being capable of following roadways without occupying the road space.

Yet, it appears that no single alternative by itself would suffice to make a dent on urban transport system. It is imperative that a mix of such viable options such as BRT, Skybus be integrated into a strategic policy shift towards from private to public transportation system. Such a shift in policy strategy has proved to be a major success in cities like Bogota in Colombia and Curitiba in Brazil not only in improving transportation facilities but also in reducing emissions. It is, however, important to note that the success of such a strategy is contingent upon the condition of availability of roads and facilities to pedestrians by way of pathways/footpaths etc. A comparative analysis of a few successful alternatives in other countries is attempted to explore and identify suitable policy strategy for the city of Mumbai.

1. INTRODUCTION

With economic growth and rising urbanisation combined with migration, cities have increasingly been attracting capital, skills and other inputs in addition to opening up new avenues of employment.

This process tends to reinforce itself and gathers further momentum thus boosting investment, output and employment. As a consequence, it gives rise to continued growth in urban regions and poses challenges to economic and social infrastructure. The challenges include the need to create basic infrastructure services and affordable electricity/gas supply, and efficient transportation; social infrastructure, energy and environment being the other challenges. Lack of sufficient urban mass transit infrastructure combined with the growth in income of urban population has driven motorization trends in developing economies like India. As a result, there has been a substantial growth in oil consumption. Similarly, many urban regions face challenges in passenger transport and energy use. Such challenges relate to difficulties in the changing lifestyle of urban dwellers that already depend heavily on passenger vehicles for their mobility. With rising affluence, those living in urban areas travel longer distances by personalised vehicles, which lead to a steady increase in oil consumption, congestion and pollution. Increases in oil demand - driven largely by urban area motorization and heavy dependence on passenger transport in urban areas - have not been met by increases in domestic oil production. In effect, energy security concerns have only risen. So is the concern with environmental degradation and public health.

Urban transportation is one of the critical areas for growth and development with energy and transport being key interrelated inputs. With nearly half the world population living in urban areas and with increasing concerns related to scarcity of fossil fuels and climate change, urban transportation becomes a vital area of concern. The twentieth century has witnessed rapid urbanisation of the world population. The global proportion of urban population increased from a mere 13 per cent in 1900 to 29 percent in 1950 and then to 49 per cent in 2005. This trend is projected to continue and by 2030, 60 per cent of the global population is expected to live in cities(UN, 2006). Further, the urban sector in most developing countries accounts for at least 50 percent of the gross national product and in some countries over 70 percent (World Bank, 2007).

It is seen that transportation is a major energy user worldwide and is overwhelmingly petroleum based. The transportation sector forms a key component of many if not all of the world economies. Often, it is a critical input and a pre-requisite for competitiveness of an economy. Nonetheless, it is a major source of global carbon emissions, and also contributes to air quality concerns, particularly in and around major population centers. (Ortmeyer and Pillay, 2001). Transportation sector consumes more than 27% of the total energy consumption of the world(IEA, 2007). It consumed more than 57.7% of the world oil consumption in 2004. In 2004, Consumption of oil fuels contributed to 39.9 % of the total cabon-dioxide (CO_2) emissions of the world (IEA, 2006), CO_2 is a greenhouse gas and largely contributes to global warming. Over the next 25 years, demand for petroleum and other liquid fuels is expected to increase more rapidly in the transportation sector than in any of the other end-use sectors.(IEA, 2007)

Some recent studies have shown that cities in developing countries often devote 15 percent to 25 percent of their annual expenditures to their transport systems, and sometimes much more. In developing countries, it is common to find that 5 percent to 10 percent of urban household income is spent on transport. In some cases, the figure is 15% or more (WorldBank, 2007). Cities are the major contributors to economic growth, and movement in and between cities is crucial for improved quality of life (Singh, 2005). The transport sector accounts for 28% of the total commercial energy consumption in India. Within this sector, road has the highest share with 81.3% followed by rail with 15.4%, water and air making up the rest. In passenger traffic, road has a share of 77.8% and rail 21%. In the transport sector, urban areas are characterised by huge transportation movements with a chain of interconnected economic activities. Over the years, a rapid increase of private motor vehicles, an inadequate public transport system and congestion have become major problems faced by cities across world. Some of the cities already have metro/suburban railway system, which is the efficient public mass transit system and the cities which don't have are in the process of building it. In spite of this, the problems of congestion on roads have become severe with rapid urbanisation and this may become a constraint for successful functioning of suburban/metro systems as demand would far exceed the supply and thus overcoming the capacity constraint would continue to be a moving target. Therefore, rising population and increase in migration only go to make matters worse for developing countries.

In a city like Mumbai, the problems discussed above are being acutely felt. Besides the gross inadequacy of public transport as can be evidenced by the overcrowded trains and buses, traffic congestion/jams and the snail-like slow movement of vehicles, problems of safety /security, a high degree of discomfort to travelers there are other major concerns on energy wastage and environmental damages. In effect, they have adverse implications for public health, livability of cities and welfare. This is despite the fact that city has a relatively efficient public transportation system with the suburban railway system carrying 80% of total burden of transportation system. There has, thus, arisen a need to look at alternatives.

It is against this backdrop that the present paper explores possible options which would encourage and complement the public transportation system. The paper is structured into seven sections. Section 2 traces the trends in vehicle growth in Indian cities, in general, and Mumbai, in particular. In Section 3, various issues/challenges in urban transportation are discussed after classifying them into three categories related to urban transportation. In Section 4, we describe various strategies for addressing the problem and challenges related to urban transportation. The strategies broadly comprise improved infrastructure & land management, modal shift, efficient energy use and adoption of alternative fuels. The features, merits and implementation experiences of infrastructure alternatives such as BRT system and Skybus system are discussed in Section 5. Scope for these alternatives for implementing in Mumbai along with various other polices so as to improve transportation system are discussed in Section 6. Finally, Section 7 ends with some concluding remarks besides identifying some potential areas for further research.

2. TRENDS IN URBAN TRANSPORTATION IN INDIA

Spurt in the number of private vehicles is a major concern across the world. The number of vehicles in 25 major cities in India increased from 5,109,819 in the year 1989 to 19,869,832 in the year 2003 (Fig.1). It is almost a four-fold increase. During same period (Fig.2), the number of vehicles in Mumbai rose from 588,518 to 1,123,562 i.e., almost doubled. This disproportionately higher growth in the total number of vehicles in major cities in India than that of Mumbai can be attributed to the rapid growth of major cities in other parts of the country during the period and also to the fact that most of the cities apart from Mumbai and Kolkata don't have suburban railway facilities.

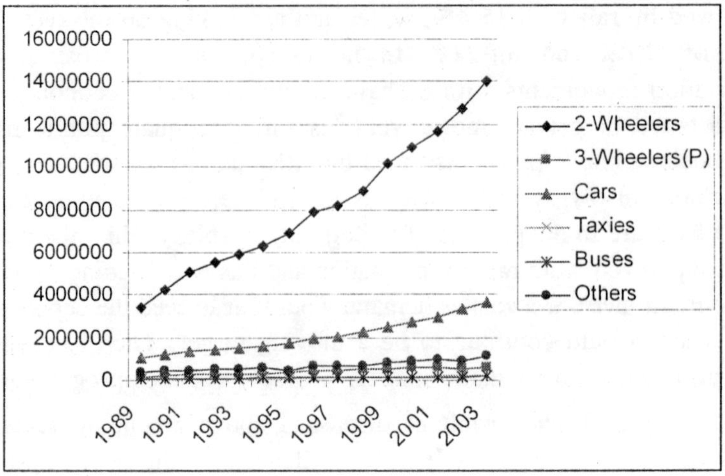

Fig. 1: Vehicle growth in 25 major cities of India*

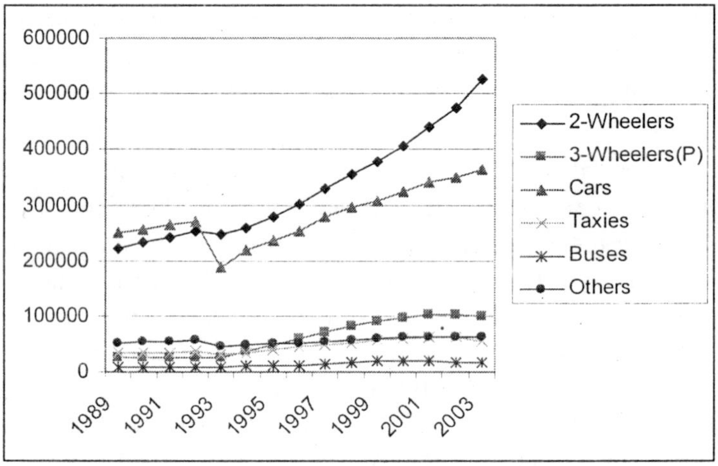

Fig. 2: Vehicle growth in Mumbai*

Source: Ministry of Shipping, Road Transport & Highways, Govt. of India.

The share of two wheelers in all cities of India in the year 1989 was 66% which rose to 70.6% in year 2003. In Mumbai, the shares of two wheelers, and cars was 36.6% and 42.3% respectively as a proportion of total vehicles in 1989. The former jumped to 46.9% in 2003, whereas the latter declined to 32.2% during the same period. From Figure 1, we can observe that 2 wheelers are growing rapidly in the major cities of India. But in the case of Mumbai, both two wheelers and cars are increasing rapidly when compared to other vehicles as shown in Figure 2.

3. ISSUES IN URBAN TRANSPORTATION

Although, issues and problems related to urban transportation system are interlinked with urban planning and development at a broader strategy level, we have confined ourselves to three aspects viz., 1)Problems within the urban transportation system, 2)Problems caused by urban transportation system on other systems (externalities), and 3)Challenges for urban transportation system.

3.1 Problems within Urban Transportation Systems

Major problems within an urban transport system are congestion, inadequate public transportation traffic injuries and accidents. A major cause of these problems is the rapid increase in population of urban areas. Equally important is the increasing number of private vehicles. The present public transport infrastructure is grossly inadequate to meet the demands of rising population. For instance a typical suburban train carries 4200 passengers as against its capacity of 1700, thus resulting in overcrowding far beyond the limit. This inadequacy of the public transportation system combined with increasing incomes of people in urban areas has given rise to a rapid increase in privately owned vehicles. This is a major reason for congestion on the roads. Frequent road extension projects are unable to address these problems as huge numbers of private vehicles are coming on to the road annually. Such massive increases in private vehicles, especially two wheelers are the major sources of accidents on the roads.

3.2 Problems caused by Urban Transportation Systems

Transportation produces noise, emissions and vibration which are the principal sources of annoyance. Automobile transport is the main source of water and soil pollution and green house gases. Poisonous gases which come out of vehicle exhausts and the wear and tear of vehicles go into various lakes and the sea and settle on the soil and plants. Fragments of tyres, huge quantities of carcinogenic bitumen from the wearing down of asphalt, and the waste from automobile garages (which goes through the sewage system and enters human bodies via food and water) thus affect nature as well as public health. Transportation is the principal source of CO which causes heart and circulatory problems, NO_x and SO_2 which affect respiratory and immunological systems, and lead which affects the nervous system and blood production(Reddy, 2000).

3.3 Challenges for Urban Transportation Systems

The major challenges facing urban transportation are to meet the needs increasing population in cities, to find alternatives for reduction in energy consumption and emissions. To address mobility related problems of rising populations in cities, public transportation system need to be improved. Apart from this, non-motorized vehicles use is to be encouraged, as fast depletion of fossil fuels is becoming a major worrying factor for transportation sector, national economy, global economy and from a larger viewpoint of inter-temporal welfare as well. It, therefore, becomes imperative to find alternatives for fossil fuels. Though environmental related issues can be addressed with the adoption of alternative fuels, supply of alternative fuels to meet the huge demand of urban transport is a major challenge. Hence, the need for making concerted efforts to shift to alternative fuels and also simultaneously find ways and means of reducing energy consumption.

4. STRATEGIES FOR SUSTAINABLE URBAN TRANSPORTATION SYSTEMS

4.1 Improving infrastructure and land use management

Energy consumption per automobile in multinuclei cities is less than that of mononuclear cities(Shim et al., 2006). Cities should be planned in such a way that there are more than one Central Business Districts (CBD). If there is only one CBD, it would cause traffic flow in an unidirectional manner and thereby causing traffic jams and congestion on the roads. Again, high density of vehicles also causes increase in energy consumption and environmental emissions(Reddy, 2000). There is, therefore, a need for improved planning and infrastructure & land use management towards addressing the issues in urban transportation. Otherwise, there is always the lurking danger of mushrooming slums in cities which, in turn, impacts tell on the already overstretched infrastructure.

4.2 Shifting the Modal Mix

Modal shift towards public transport and low energy intensity vehicles is seen as a solution to redress problems of congestion and high energy consumption. Such a modal shift towards public transport would result in a reduction of private vehicles on roads thereby minimising congestion, energy consumption and environmental emissions. It is, however, crucial that before encouraging modal shift towards public transport, the adequacy and quality of public transportation system in cities need to be improved substantially to meet the surging demands of the huge population, the income effect and the substitution effect. Alternatives such as BRT and Skybus systems could be adopted which could complement public transportation facilities in the cities. The features, merits and implementation experiences are discussed in the next section.

4.3 Efficient energy use and adoption of alternative fuels

Fuels used in automobile vehicles are the major cause of problem caused by urban transportation systems. Fossil fuels such as petrol and diesel are major sources of pollution and this pollution causes various health effects on the people apart from contributing to global climate change. Hence, there is greater need for efficient utilisation of energy and shifting to cleaner fuels not only to reduce pollution but also address the issue of depleting fossil fuels. Conversion of two wheelers from 2 stroke to 4 stroke, encouraging car pooling for improving vehicle occupancy, efficient pricing of road use and better traffic management are options for reducing energy consumption apart from the modal shift as discussed earlier. Alternative fuels such as CNG, Bio-fuels, Hydrogen and new technology vehicles like Hybrid Electric Vehicles are the other sources of reducing energy consumption and environmental emissions Thus, we need sound transport demand management, supply augmentation and cleaner technologies to evolve appropriate strategies. In a decentralised, democratic set-up, it might be worthwhile to involve the users, media and civil society groups in these efforts.

5. INFRASTRUCTURE ALTERNATIVES

5.1 Mass Transit Systems

Mass transit systems are of two types. One is bus based and the other rail based. A Rail based transit system has a major advantage in terms of passenger carrying capacity, speed and time savings. The major advantage of bus based system is its flexibility to reach all parts of region which is not possible with rail based transit system. The other advantage of a bus based transit system is that its capital cost is half a much and operating cost is 20% of rail based system as revealed by Levinson et.al., (2003).

It is in this cost-benefit context that the present study tries to identify their advantages, disadvantages and scope for implementation of such options. Specific alternatives considered are the BRT system which is bus-based one and the other is Skybus, a rail based mass transit system.

5.2 Bus Rapid Transit (BRT) System

Features of BRT

Bus Rapid Transit (BRT) systems are increasingly receiving attention in cities that are densely populated. Their operating flexibility and their ability to be built quickly, incrementally, and economically underlie their growing popularity. Systems vary in design, operations, usage, and effectiveness.

BRT can be described as a flexible, rubber-tired rapid-transit mode that combines stations, vehicles, services, running ways, and Intelligent Transportation System (ITS) elements into an integrated system with a strong positive identity that evokes a unique image (Levinson et al., 2003). The general idea of BRT is to create a mass transit system using exclusive right of way lanes that mimic the rapidity and performance of metro systems but utilises bus technology rather than rail vehicle technology. BRT systems tend to focus on an array of features that enable a city to transform a standard bus service into a mass transit system (Wright, 2004).

BRT system can be implemented in a variety of environments. The main feature of a BRT System is having dedicated lanes for buses. It enables buses to move at much higher speeds without any traffic jams and thus saves a lot of time. It is estimated that the annual idling time at traffic jams at US was 11 hours per person in 1982 which rose to 36 hours per person in 1999 and the congestion costs are estimated to be around $78 billion (UMBS, 2004). The BRT system, however, entails the construction of separate stations at places where the road width is very large so that halting of one bus does not affect other. Pre-board fare collection and fare verification system are adopted so that rapid boarding and alighting becomes possible. Besides, different types of services are provided in BRT bus with lesser number of stops, express and luxury services to meet the demands of different income groups. Also, an Intelligent Transportation system (ITS) is used to provide location, timings and various other information about bus services at BRT stations. Further, efficient and cleaner fuel technology vehicles are used so that emissions from the buses are minimum. Because of speed of services and travel time saving, ridership of buses is expected to increase. As lanes of private vehicles become more congested, passengers tend to shift from private transport to public transport.

Merits of BRT

In recent years, it has been a matter of concern for transportation and community-planning officials in a large number of countries to explore several alternatives for improved public transportation solutions to mobility issues. Such concerns have led to a re-examination of existing transit technologies and the embrace of new, creative ways of providing transit service and performance. It has been seen that BRT can be an extremely cost-effective way of providing high-quality, high-performance transit. Yet another major reason for implementing BRT systems is lower development costs and greater operating flexibility as compared to rail transit. Moreover, it is found that BRT essentially emulates the performance and amenity characteristics of a modern rail-based transit system but at a fraction of the cost(Wright, 2004). Thus small investments in separate guiding ways can provide rapid transit in cities. In Boston, BRT was selected because of its operational and service benefits, rather than its cost advantages (Levinson et al., 2003). Most BRT systems today are being delivered in the range of US$1–15 million/km, depending upon the capacity requirements and complexity of the project, whereas elevated rail systems and underground metro systems can cost from US$50 million to over US$200 million/km (Wright, 2004).

From the view point of sustainable transportation, a study by Wright and Fulton (2005) showed that fuel-based solutions alone would not achieve cost-effective reductions in greenhouse gas emissions. The most cost-effective means to emission reductions seems to be a diverse and integrated package of measures that promote shifts to lower-emitting modes. Farrell et. al. (2003) argued that cost of introducing hydrogen can be reduced by selecting a mode that uses a small number of relatively large vehicles that are operated by professional crews along a limited number of point-to-point routes or within a small geographic area. In such cases a BRT system can act as a starting point for market introduction of alternative fuels like hydrogen and bio fuels. Cleaner fuel technology buses can be used in BRT vehicles, which can provide the potential demand for alternative fuels at initial stages. Once the infrastructure and demand barriers are removed, these alternative fuels can be used in all other types of vehicles with less cost.

Implementation Experiences

Tracking back its origin, it is found that BRT gained its initial prominence with its application in Curitiba, Brazil in 1974. The system helped Curitiba achieve an average annual ridership gain of 2.3% over the next two decades (Rabinovitch and Hoehn, 1995). This experience together with that of Bogota subsequently has shown that the erosion of public transport mode share is not preordained. Both the cities have demonstrated some innovation with high-quality bus systems and a complementary package of supporting measures, including infrastructure for non-motorized transport and restriction on private cars. In both Bogota and Curitiba, Bus Rapid Transit (BRT) has played a prominent role (Wright and Fulton, 2005).

Other examples of BRT systems in operation are Beijing in China, Jakarta in Indonesia, Leon in Mexico, and Seoul in South Korea. In cities such as Cape Town in South Africa, Dar es Salaam in Tanzania, Hanoi in Vietnam, Lima in Peru, Mexico City in Mexico, and Santiago in Chile, similar projects are underway. Also, visits to Curitiba by US officials have even helped to catalyse a national BRT programme in the USA. However, subsequent projects do not seem to have reached the same level of quality or ambition as Bogota or Curitiba(Wright and Fulton, 2005). The major reason is that, BRT systems of Bogotá and Curitiba have been complemented by new cycle ways, pedestrian upgrades and car-free events. More importantly, both the cities have enjoyed a continuity of transport policy across several political regimes.

As a full BRT system, TransMilenio of Bogota provides several different sources of emission reductions, including the following: (a) Increasing the share of public transport ridership by dramatically improving the quality of service (in terms of travel time, comfort, security, cleanliness, etc.).(b) Requiring the destruction of four to eight older buses for every new articulated vehicle introduced into the system. (c) Managing the fleet through global positioning satellite (GPS) technology and thus allowing the optimisation of demand and supply during peak and non peak periods. (d) Encouraging transit-oriented development around stations and along corridors. (e) Requiring minimum-emission standards for vehicles (Wright and Fulton, 2005)

5.3.7 Skybus

As indicated earlier, the other option for mass rapid transport is a rail based system. For railways, the major alternatives available for improvement are elevated, underground and surface railway system. Elevated railway technically cannot reach truly congested central busy roads where the mass transport is needed. It is also too invasive and may require dislocation of some portions of habitat as well as introduces noise pollution. Underground railway is less invasive on surface but still poses technically challenging risks of fires and evacuations. In addition, it also has to address concerns for foundations of heritage buildings. If road vehicles are involved, in inter-modal transfers, it becomes a weak link in the chain of transport between walking and railway. Both modes suffer from possible derailments thus endangering the safety of commuters. Adding surface railway in an existing city has its own problems.

India has examples of her own suburban systems. The city of Mumbai remains divided by the corridor and it is an eternal noise polluter in the heart of city day in and day out. Sudden rush of heavy loads of commuters at stations creates needless congestion on the roads and causes inconvenience and hardship to people. Almost close to 2000 persons die annually- because of trespassing or falling from suburban trains. Furthermore, there is also the vulnerability to minor vandalism by urchins resulting in grievous injuries like losing one's sight etc. Besides, this mode cannot follow the existing roads and hence the weak link of road vehicles has to be brought in for inter-modal transfers. Derailments, collisions, loss of life are some of the other problems associated with underground, surface and elevated rail systems as experienced in some countries.

Skybus technology, an innovative technology whose patent has been acquired by the India railways in 2001 and 2004 provides a potential urban transport improvement option by way of a railway system. This system appears hanging from the rails instead of passing on the rails. Heavy 52/60 kg/m rails placed at standard gauge floating in elastic medium and damped by inertia of measured mass held in a 8m X 2m box enclosure, supported over a 1m diameter. columns spaced at 15 m and located at 15 m distance from each other, in the divider space in between lanes on a road- way, at a height of 8m above road surface- provides the support and guidance for powered bogies which can run at 100 kmph, with the coach shells suspended below, carry passengers in air conditioned comfort, can follow existing road routes, while existing traffic on roads continue.

Unlike the conventional metro railway system, a Skybus system follows roads but doesn't occupy road space and yet has the capacity of rail based system. This is main encouraging factor for inter-modal shift. The Skybus system is free from derailment and also collision proof. More importantly, this system is very eco-friendly as there will be hardly any noise pollution and air pollution. At present, the Skybus system is not under implementation anywhere in the world. Trial run are being attempted, the Konkan Railway Corporation built a test track of 2 km in Goa for the Skybus project.

6. SCOPE FOR MUMBAI

Mumbai is known for its public transport system. The suburban railway system is largely credited with this followed by Brihanmumbai Electric Supply & Transport (BEST) buses. Suburban railways carry 60% of total burden of transportation in the city. To complement this, Mumbai has BEST bus services providing services round the clock. The major concerns now are an overburdened public transport system and rising number of private vehicles. Government is taking up various projects like construction of new railway tracks, developing business centers in suburbs, expansion of roads etc. Though these measures lessen some of the burden in present public transport system, there is still great concern from the energy and environment points of view. This may require shifting people from using private vehicles to public vehicles. To do this the public transport system must be adequate. The city desperately needs to look for various other options for improving public transport facilities. These new initiatives should be combined with integrated policies.

As discussed earlier, BRT and Skybus are potential alternatives for improving the public transportation system. These initiatives should be combined with other measures to encourage people to use private vehicles less as in the case of Bogota and Curitiba. The government should bring more awareness among people regarding energy and environmental concerns in urban areas and should encourage walking and bicycling for small distance journeys. For this purpose, there should be proper path ways for pedestrians and bicyclers. Moreover, people travelling in public transport sometimes reach the stations/bus stops by walking. Thus providing pathways for walking and bicycling becomes a must for success of public transport improvement initiatives and government should invest in providing these facilities. As we observe daily in Mumbai, movement in the morning hours is towards the south i.e., Central Business Districts (CBD) and in the evening it is in the opposite direction. In these cases, it is seen that one side of the roads are more congested and causing traffic jams and the other side has very less traffic flow. A solution to this problem would be implementing reversible lane system wherein two-third of the road width is used for the vehicles going towards CBDs in the morning hours and in the evening, two-third of the road width is used in opposite direction. This system can be used along with BRT system in places wherever providing separate lanes for buses is very difficult. There should be restriction on use of the private vehicles or heavy vehicles in areas such as the CBD where the density of population during working hours is very high. This will encourage vehicle sharing, car pooling, thereby improving occupancy of vehicles and a shift towards public transport. All the policies and reforms combined with BRT, Skybus and other projects should go together. For implementing BRT, a major requirement is dedication of lanes for buses. Once the lanes are ready, they can be used for the present buses without affecting the traffic. After this, the other feature such as cleaner fuel technology buses, separate station for BRT buses, ITS system, and pre-fare collection methods can be implemented step by step.

7. CONCLUSIONS

In the context of urban transportation system, a few problems, issues are challenges have been discussed in this paper. More specifically, the BRT system and Skybus system have been the focus. After considering the merits and demerits of some of the alternatives, some viable options for the city of Mumbai have been suggested. The BRT and Skybus have the potential of causing a shift from private transport to public transport in addition to bringing about substantial improvements in mobility, energy utilisation, environment and public health. It is however, to be noted that issues of alternative fuel options need to be examined in terms of reduction in energy use, its implementing costs, cleaner environment etc. in the context of the different infrastructure options. Such a comparative analysis would throw further light on the complex and interrelated nature of urban transportation infrastructure.

REFERENCES

Farrell, A., E, Keith, D. W. and Corbett, J.J. (2003). A strategy for introducing hydrogen into transportation. *Energy Policy* , Vol. 31, 1357-1367.

Gulawani, M., Skybus of India: 21st Century innovation in urban public transportation, *Unpublished,* www.ifz.tugraz.at/index_en.php/filemanager/download/300/Gulawani_SA%202004.pdf.

IEA (2006), Key World Energy Statistics (2006). *Energy Information Administration*, U.S. Department of Energy, Washington.

IEA (2007), International Energy Outlook (2007). *Energy Information Administration*, U.S. Department of Energy, Washington.

Levinson, H., Zimmerman, S., Clinger, J., Rutherford, S., Smith. R.L., Cracknell, J. and Soberman, R. (2003), Volume 1: Case studies in Bus Rapid Transit, *Transportation Research Board*, Washington, DC

Ortmeyer T.H. and Pillay, P. (2001), Trends in transportation sector technology energy use and greenhouse gas emissions. *Proceedings of the IEEE 89*, 1837-1847.

Rabinovitch, J and Hoehn, J. (1995), A Sustainable Urban Transportation System: The surface Metro in Curitiba, Brazil, working paper no. 19, *EPAT/MUCIA Research & training, University of Wisconsin-Madison.*

Reddy, B.S. (2000), Urban transportation in India: a tale of two cities. *Energy for Sustainable Development,* 4.

Shim, G.E., Rhee, S.M., Ahn ,K.H., and Chung, S.B. (2006), The relationship between the characteristics of transportation energy consumption and urban form. *The Annals of Regional Science,* 40, 351-367.

Singh S. K. (2005), Review of Urban Transportation in India. *Journal of Public Transportation,* Vol.8, pp. 79-97.

UN (2006),World Urbanisation Prospects - The 2005 Revision. *United Nations.*

World Bank (2007), Urban Transport Overview. *World Bank.*

Wright, L.(2004), Bus Rapid Transit Planning Guide. *GTZ, Eschborn, Germany.*

Wright, L. and Fulton, L. (2005), Climate Change Mitigation and Transport in Developing Nations. *Transport Reviews*, Vol. 25, pp.691-717.

Websites

Konkan Railway, http://www.konkanrailway.com/website/ehtm/sky_bus.htm

UMBS (2004). Sustainable Transportation Special Report. http://www.bus.umich.edu/NewsRoom/SpecialReports/sustainable/mobility-sidebar.htm

32

IMPROVING THE STATE OF MUMBAI'S ROADS: REFORM AGENDA AND STRATEGIC FRAMEWORK

Ramakrishna Nallathiga

ABSTRACT

Mumbai is a rapidly growing city with huge economic growth potential and is vying to emerge as a world class city. However, unlike other world class cities, it does not have good physical infrastructure to support the economic growth and to improve quality of life. Roads are an important constituent of a city infrastructure which need to be of a very good standard to be called as a world class city. Therefore, there is a definite need for improving the way roads are laid down and maintained in Mumbai city. This requires understanding the current scenario of roads and management, causes of shortcomings and charting a reform agenda for improvement, which are presented in this paper. Further, a strategic framework is needed to operationlise the reform agenda, which has been laid down by the Core Group of Bombay First after extensive deliberations. The paper also discusses this model and concludes with some positive comments on recent developments.

1. INTRODUCTION

Infrastructure holds the key to the development of any nation, state or city, as it provides crucial services that are required both to support economic activity and to provide quality services to citizens, which, in turn, enable the realisation of faster economic growth. The converse is also true. Poor infrastructure constrains the level as well as quality of services available for economic activity, thereby impeding the economic growth, and reducing the quality of life of the citizens (India Infrastructure Report 1996). Roads are an important and integral component of urban and rural infrastructure which provide a very crucial service of supporting the movement of goods and people. Their economic function is very vital since they provide the much needed access to markets for the goods and services produced and they provide access for household in order to provide labour service to businesses. Roads already provide great passenger mobility in India to the tune of almost 85 per cent and their share is predicted to reach the level of 95 per cent by the year 2015-16 (Singh 2000). Therefore, laying down the roads connecting various economic activities and human settlement concentrations as well as ensuring their proper maintenance is very important for passenger and freight transport thereby support the economic growth.

Poor road quality, inadequate access, poor maintenance get reflected in the scenario of roads from rural to urban areas and towns to metropolitan cities. While the causes of such state need to be found through a diagnostic assessment, it has been well argued that financial mechanisms have not been well thought of and implemented. As a result, there is always under provision and poor quality of roads due to inadequate finance arising primarily from low user payments which then perpetuates further low returns and poor level and quality of services. Appropriate financial design based on pricing to recover the costs might provide as one instrument of overcoming such 'lower level equilibrium' traps. However, inadequate finances alone are not the problem source. Institutional arrangements for their delivery are equally important (World Bank 2004).

Infrastructure, in general, and roads, in particular, are traditionally provided by public authorities in many parts across the world. Public Works Departments of State and Central governments provide roads and road services in India. However, it is a well known fact that the delivery of these public organisations is well below the requirement in terms of both levels and quality. The institutional structures and incentives available influence the outputs. In the cities, it is further exacerbated by the presence of large utilities - water supply, power and cable lines - which run across the road, rendering the pavement more susceptible to poor performance. These outcomes in most of the cities can be attributed to (Heggie and Vickers 1998) the following factors:

- Wrong institutional framework
- Human Resource Constraints
- Inadequate Financing Arrangements
- Lack of clear responsibilities
- Ineffective management structures

Mumbai is the largest metropolitan city in India and it is the financial and trade capital of India. With the metropolitan population of 17 millions in 2001, it is also the second largest urban centre in the world next to Tokyo. The Mumbai city had a population of 12 million in 2001 within an area of 434 sq km, thereby, standing as one of the densest cities in the world (MCGM 2003). With a large population, robust skill set, strong persistence, Mumbai has always strived hard to position itself on the global map and it would like to transform very much like the other Asia - Pacific cities - Shanghai, Singapore, Hong Kong, Tokyo and Kaulalampur (Bombay First 2003). However, unlike its peers, Mumbai is faced with poor and crippling state of infrastructure which has always been hindering its economic growth and its ability to attract foreign investments. A world-class city needs to have top class infrastructure services, and roads are one such important infrastructure component that provides efficient and effective movement of goods and people. Well- paved roads are vital to speedier and smoother transport of people and goods and, thereby, improve the productivity and efficiency of population as well as economy; above all, they present conspicuously good image of the city to a visitor.

Realising the need for having good roads and finding solution towards achieving it, a 'Core Group' on roads was constituted by the Bombay First, an autonomous city policy research arm of the Bombay Chamber of Commerce and Industry, to discuss the root problems and recommend certain 'systemic' solutions to be pursued by concerning agencies. This 'Core Group' comprised several experts with varied academic and professional backgrounds, who spent time in dovetailing the underlying causes of poor conditions of roads and finding the means of overcoming the situation. The group met on several occasions to deliberate the various issues and solutions and these meetings were coordinated and facilitated by the author. This paper lays down the background to the issues, provides a summary of what has emerged from the group's deliberations and suggests a framework for improving the city road conditions. Besides, it also discusses the proposals laid down by another expert committee by the Municipal Corporation of Greater Mumbai (MCGM) in response to the suggestion made by the Core Group. Lastly, the need for a pragmatic approach towards reform is suggested.

2. STATE OF MUMBAI'S ROADS

Mumbai has a road network length of about 1940 km under Municipal Corporation of Greater Mumbai (MCGM) and also 50 km length State Highways maintained by the Maharashtra State Road Transport Corporation (MSRDC), with most of the road pavement under MCGM control not in good condition. Mumbai Metropolitan Region Development Authority (MMRDA), a planning authority recently began to undertake some infrastructure projects, notably the Mumbai Infrastructure Improvement Project (MUIP). Table 1 provides the road length in major zones of Mumbai. Besides the horizontal roads, the MCGM also owns 11 flyovers, 47 road over bridges (ROBs) and 104 bridges for the movement of vehicles (MCGM 2006). There are also 68 foot-over-bridges and 28 pedestrian subways owned and maintained by the MCGM as civic infrastructure.

Table 1: Sector-wise Coverage of Roads in Mumbai

Type of Road Surface	*Road Length in Major Zones (Km)*			
	Island city	*Western Suburbs*	*Eastern Suburbs*	*Total*
Concrete	115.747	127.663	107.413	350.823
Bitumen	390.721	799.990	399.638	1590.349
Total	506.468	927.653	507.051	1941.172

Source: MCGM (2006).

The total per capita road length in Mumbai is around 0.15 m and the number of vehicles per km is 558, which themselves are very poor given the fact that road transport in the form of buses, cars and autos covers 53 per cent of total city traffic (Atkins study, 1994). The island city has a better coverage of 0.25 m per capita when compared to the levels of 0.11 m and 0.15 m per capita of the western and eastern suburbs respectively (MCGM, 2002). A different picture, however, emerges when it comes to vehicles per km road length, which is1022 in island city, 371 in western suburbs and 260 in eastern suburbs (MCGM, 2002). However, this is not very disturbing given the long historical past of the island city and the presence of relatively affluent community in it. The population densities are also relatively high in the island city at 56 persons per km^2, when compared to 22 and 20 persons per km^2 in the western and eastern suburbs (MCGM 2002).

However, the worrisome feature is the poor condition of roads in terms of: road pavement material and its condition, narrow carriage width and right of way, poor road connectivity and usage, inadequate road network and its maintenance, The condition of roads in Mumbai has to be seen in the backdrop of the vision to become a globally competitive city with comparable infrastructure and quality of life laid down in the Vision Plan of Bombay First (2003) and that of the Government of Maharashtra (GoM, 2004). This is due to the legacy of North-South orientation of city traffic, poor condition of roads and also due to the fact that road traffic has widely varying composition and diverse loading characteristics of incoming and outgoing freight traffic. The old residential developments in the past have also left little room for expanding and improving the roads. Moreover, the state of city's roads becomes even worse during the monsoon rains when rains play havoc with life in Mumbai. The heavy continuous rain deteriorates road surface – particularly, of the bitumen road which most of the city roads are made of – and leads to development of pot holes and deteriorated pavements. Out of the municipal road network under MCGM, only 17 per cent of it is concretized which represents a smaller proportion but that too is a result of the efforts in the last 2-3 years when the MCGM has understood the savings of maintenance costs coming from shift towards concrete pavement and has undertaken it at major junctions (Nallathiga 2002).

3. CAUSES OF POOR ROAD STRUCTURE

The causes of poor road structure in Mumbai city are many but mostly relating to the technical, planning, institutional coordination and management aspects of city roads. Some of the major reasons/causes of poor condition of the city roads are as follows:

(*i*) The condition of roads can be attributed to several technical reasons like poor geometry and alignment, inadequate drainage, inappropriate design, improper road surface, insufficient sub-base material, faulty construction, poor supervision and maintenance, high vehicle/axle loads, road digging by utilities, pavement encroachments, outdated construction methods and inadequate arrangements for immediate repair of potholes.

(*ii*) The poor condition of roads can also be attributed to the problem of multi-agency interference with right of way. It is intercepted by water supply and sanitary pipelines, cable lines, utility works and solid waste transport, all of which are not properly coordinated and done half-heartedly or half-way. Quite often, the roads are dug without any proper leveling and restoration and any such offence is not penalized by the corporation.

(*iii*) The organisational responsibilities are also fragmented. While the MCGM undertakes road construction and maintenance, most of the repair works particularly on highways is undertaken by the Public Works Department (PWD). The Maharashtra State Road Development Corporation (MSRDC) has emerged as a major road organisation after undertaking the construction of over 50 fly overs all across the city with little coordination with MCGM and with the lack of awareness of the city traffic and pavement requirement. The lapses in fly over construction and pavement quality are much debated.

(*iv*) Road space has been used by several people for several purposes, leaving behind little space for the vehicles and people, for example, informal shops, garbage, pavement dwellers, illegal parking, traffic islands and animal movement. It is estimated that about 25 % road space is consumed by encroachments alone, and about 18% of households live on pavements. The scope for road widening is low in several areas.

(*v*) Engineering, technical and planning dimensions are not given adequate attention they require. The sub-surface investigations are not well done and base of pavement is not well prepared in several circumstances. Geometric design is not given adequate importance and so do the order/function of the road in the city. Structural design, road alignment tends to be crude and road construction follows sub-standard and labour intensive methods. Repairs to pavements are made in an ad hoc manner, without a comprehensive understanding of the services rendered by the pavement, material strength of it and the possible life span.

(*vi*) The current road building by MCGM is based upon sub-contracting model of works execution, wherein the supervision of construction and management of roads tends to be very poor and enough checks are not laid down to ascertain the work quality. Construction labourers are paid poor wages, provided poor facilities while supervising staff and agencies do not have adequate incentives for showcasing better performance — indeed incentive exists only for marginal performance.

(*vii*) The current institutional structures for road construction, use and maintenance are highly fragmented. The operational rules for construction supervision, certification and fund release are fraught with many risks and are strong factors of corruption. There are several interested groups on the right of way, but few are interested in a well-coordinated activity. The actors do not have incentives for better performance and there is plenty of room for corruption, scandal, kickbacks, threat, favouritism and nepotism.

4. STRATEGIC DIRECTIONS FOR IMPROVING THE STATE OF ROADS

It is worth reiterating that poor road conditions are prevalent across the cities of developing countries. The poor state of roads calls for several improvements in the current approaches towards road construction and management in order to improve the condition of roads in a city. These improvements need to come through reforms in construction practices, management systems, institutional arrangements and vision planning. An important underlying principle of such reform is to move towards managing the roads in line with the principles guiding the business or commerce so that the compromise on the product quality is not made and technology and financing are well planned to meet the output requirements. These strategic directions are already provided in the past studies, which we shall review hereunder.

The Study of Harral and Faiz (1988) was perhaps the first study to come out with some reform directions to improve roads. It pointed out that road agencies were usually public monopolies and had too many responsibilities, including planning, controlling and executing construction and maintenance programmes. Furthermore, it pointed out that they devoted of staff time, funds and facilities to executing road works and sought separation of planning, controlling and executing of roads with the transfer of execution of roads to the private sector or a specialised autonomous public agency in order to bring about clarity in responsibility, improved incentive structure, and strengthen accountability. The road agencies also needed better management information systems to plan better their investment and maintenance programme. Finally, the study argued that internal accountability had to be improved, perhaps by mobilizing the media and non-governmental organisations to inform public about the high costs of insufficient maintenance.

With increasing infrastructure development across the countries and cities, it is apparent that this is built not by the inefficient processes that lead to the wastage of money. It therefore calls for reforming the road sector in general and that of cities in particular. The four basic building blocks of reforming the roads are (Heggie and Vickers 1998):

- Establishing *responsibility* for managing the roads by clearly assigning roles
- Creating *ownership* of roads by involving road users
- Stabilising road *finance* by securing adequate and continuous flow of funds
- Strengthening *management* of roads by introducing sound business practices and enforcing managerial accountability.

These four building blocks are the core of reform and are interdependent requiring implementation together; otherwise reform may not be successful. The management and financing of roads cannot be reformed without establishing who is responsible for what. The financing problem cannot be solved without the strong support of road users. The support of road users cannot be won without taking steps to ensure that resources are used efficiently. And resource use cannot be improved without controlling monopoly power, constraining road spending, and enforcing managerial accountability. They can move sequentially or in parallel. But, in the end all four building blocks should be in place to ensure that the reform agenda is sustainable and does not drift back to the status quo ante. These building blocks will have to form part of the reform agenda of improving Mumbai's roads, which we will discuss in the next section.

5. SETTING REFORM AGENDA AND LAYING DOWN STRATEGIC FRAMEWORK FOR IMPROVING MUMBAI'S ROADS

5.1 Reform Agenda for Improving Roads in Mumbai

The reform measures to be undertaken include: (*a*) changing the current organisation of road infrastructure management, (*b*) charting new institutional structures, (c) creating financial mechanisms and (*d*) changing the incentive structures, which are discussed below.

Alternative organisation structure

There is need to concentrate on creating a coherent organisational structure for managing different parts of the road network. This requires clearly assigning responsibility among different government departments, different levels of government and individual road agencies. Currently, there are three major agencies — the MCGM, PWD and MSRDC which function with little coordination. The coordination arrangement must be based on an accurate road inventory, functional classification of roads, designation of appropriate agency, formal assignment of responsibility to each road agency and owner/parent ministry. Responsibilities to be assigned include those for operating, maintaining, improving and developing the road network; for traffic management; for handling general accidents and incidents; for road accidents caused by the road agency's own negligence; and for adverse environmental impacts associated with roads and road traffic.

Charting new institutional structures

Major policy reforms in the road sector cannot succeed without the active support of a large and vocal constituency willing to argue for better road management and additional, affordable road financing. The obvious constituents are the stakeholders: road users themselves, the business and trade community e.g., chambers, and other people dependent on a well functioning road network e.g., employers and traders. Given that current financial allocations for roads are erratic and well below the levels needed to keep the network in stable condition over the long term, strong stakeholder support for more road funding must be build up if reform is to succeed. The usual mechanism for winning their support is by involving them in road management. Stakeholders agree to work in partnership with the government to strengthen road management and financing in return for a seat at the table where decisions are made about how roads are to be managed and how funds are to be spent.

Creating financial mechanisms

There is need to establish an adequate and stable flow of funds. Without both, none of the above reforms are sustainable. Budget allocations for road maintenance rarely exceed the requirements, and funds for road improvement are in extremely short supply, particularly in rapidly growing cities like Mumbai, but these are in need of extensive road modernisation. Given the fiscal conditions, financing cannot be done through additional revenues from municipal budget. Additional means of resource mobilisation need to be invented. Levy of road user charges is a proposition that can raise resources to some extent, but there is no guarantee that they will be allocated to roads. Likewise, charges on the utility, cable lines and other services for digging and filling the pavement need to be recouped as it is done in Hyderabad (Mohanty 2003). However, existing financing mechanisms do little to strengthen market discipline either by managing demand or by improving the efficiency of the civic body. Solving the financing problem calls for a radically new approach, hence the concept of commercialisation.

Changing incentive structures

It is essential to focus on creating, commercially oriented road agency by changing incentives. This involves designing the function of road laying and maintenance paying to those who undertake it and to the road users. Moving away from continuous road repair and maintenance contracts (that are awarded to contractors) towards divestiture (integrated road ownership and maintenance). Here, road users need to be involved in the management of roads to ensure that value-for-money services come from spending. Road users expect clear management objectives, an effective management structure, competitive terms and conditions of employment, consolidated budgets, commercial costing systems, and effective management information systems. As production and maintenance by civic authority has become systematic sources of inefficiency in the road sector in several cities, the management structures need to change incentives towards better performance.

5.2 Strategic Framework for Road Improvement in Mumbai

A strategic framework for the overall improvement of the city roads has been laid down by the Core Group is perhaps appropriate to look into, which is shown in Box 1.

Box 1

STRATEGIC FRAMEWORK FOR THE IMPROVEMENT OF ROADS

Vision Mission

Mumbai needs to improve its road infrastructure and bring it on par with other world-class cities like Shanghai. About 20 years ago, Shanghai had more or less similar road conditions to that of Mumbai, but it has improved so much now that it is considered to be the 'New York of Asia'. Mumbai needs to attain this level in the next 10-15 years from now. It needs to be atteinded through a variety of changes in current system of road construction (both material and methods), contract administration, performance criteria and incentives.

Experimental Projects

To demonstrate the success of contracting out the road construction and maintenance work to large private parties, about 4-5 road stretches need to be identified and contracted out on an experimental basis to a reputed construction company with a long standing record and which has a reputation to lose. Such contracts should be given over a period of at least 10-15 years and a variety of the frameworks — BOT, BOO, BOOT and BOLT — can be chosen for this purpose. A detailed study of the scope of work shall be carried out by an independent project management consultant.

Performance Criteria and Standards

For monitoring the performance of the contractor, performance indicators or performance standards of all aspects of construction and management need to be laid down first. These performance criteria and standards have to be laid down with respect to material used, pavement construction and design, and technical specifications, and it has to be done by an independent expert group. The performance indicators include — quality, cost, delivery and safety.

Performance Guarantee and Monitoring

For the successful completion of projects, large contractors/companies need to be made compliant to the commitments made by them in the form of guarantees e.g., smooth and strong pavement, good alignment, and integrating manholes and utilities into the pavement. The enforcement of guarantees has to be monitored by a high-powered committee of experts.

Incentives for better performance

The contractors/companies need to be given adequate incentives in the form of rewards for excellence over and above minimum performance standards laid down in the performance criteria so that he/she will have incentive to show better performance and continue to improve it. This will also make the contractors to show excellence on all aspects of construction and maintenance.

Contract administration

The contract administration has to be improved on all terms — tendering, documentation and awarding of contracts. The current practice of awarding projects to low cost tenders should be given away as it is going against the spirit of high quality pavement with low cost maintenance. Instead, projects with high performance guarantees need to be given preference and contract awarding decisions have to be made by a competent empowered committee.

Source: Author based on the discussions of Core Group.

6. CONCLUSIONS

Mumbai has been rapidly emerging as the most sought after city in Asia. But unlike its peers it does not have a good physical infrastructure to support the city's economic growth and to improve the quality of life of citizens. Roads are an important constituent of city infrastructure which need to be of very good standards to be called as a world class city. However, to the contrary, the roads present a glim picture to the citizens and visitors. Therefore, there is a definite need for improving the way roads are laid down and maintained in Mumbai city. This essentially requires charting a reform agenda which is discussed in this paper. Also, a strategic framework is needed in order to realize the reform agenda, which has been laid down by the Core Group of Bombay First after extensive deliberations. This group also met the Standing Technical Advisory Committee (STAC) and submitted the recommendations.

The STAC has also deliberated the issue at length and came out with the following recommendations (MCGM, 2006):

- Evaluation of existing pavement by carrying out various tests and designing road treatment accordingly.
- Upgradation of road specifications in accordance with Ministry of Road Transport and Highways and incorporating latest techniques, material and machinery.
- Selection of capable contractor by introducing post qualification criteria involving techno-financial capability.
- Appointment of third party quality auditorś in the corporation for the first time to ensure desired quality of road works.
- Preparation of various manuals such as Quality Assurance Manual, Maintenance Manual, Specifications, Quality Audit Manual and Standard bid Document, etc.

While the above recommendations are necessary, they are not adequate to transform the current state of roads in the very near future. The MCGM approach needs to change from the provider of service to facilitator of service provision and it has to focus on long term reform measures outlined earlier using a strategic framework. Moreover, measures such as capital improvement planning (shown in Box 2) are to be in order get a better hold of the road infrastructure management if the MCGM chooses to remain with the current structure. A good step forward is to undertake improving all the roads in a phased manner with concretization plans in 64 roads and improved asphalt roads in 404 roads. However, the coverage is only 48 km and 178 km respectively, whereas the road network is very large to extend further. Therefore, it can chose to award long term contracts to important stretches and focus on the connecting roads.

Box 2

CAPITAL IMPROVEMENT PLANNING

The Capital Improvement Plan (CIP) is a **10-year Plan** that provides a link between the City's long-range plans, the fiscal plan, and its physical development. A capital improvement project is a project for construction, major alteration, remodeling, or repair of streets, storm drainage, sanitary sewers, buildings, parking facilities, and landscaping. **The CIP undergoes a major review and amendment every two years.** Because project requests consistently exceed funds available, not all proposed projects can be funded. Prioritizing capital improvement projects is needed so funds are spent in the most cost-effective manner. The CIP includes projects that can facilitate growth. Examples would be a major road improvement project that would facilitate development near that road or participation in an interceptor sewer extension project needed to facilitate urban development on a tract. These projects may also be necessary for the expansion of services as growth occurs, such as upgrading roads from rural standards to City standards upon annexation of territory, relocating or constructing fire stations to serve growing areas, and new library facilities. The CIP also includes funding for the annual maintenance of all the City's infrastructure systems.

Source: Centre for Good Governance, Hyderabad.

Another interesting and positive development is the MCGM's decision to take a project approach towards the improvement/provision of roads so that roads now include storm water drains, water mains, sewer lines, foot path, lane marking, signage, beautification etc. However, this should not defocus the programme. The Mumbai Urban Infrastructure Project (MUIP) as envisioned by the Mumbai Metropolitan Region Development Authority (MMRDA) appears to show promise by undertaking such a programmatic approach to change the face of Mumbai and its suburbs. The basic aim of MUIP is to improve the road network and implement an efficient traffic dispersal system in Mumbai.

The Mumbai Urban Infrastructure Project was set up with the objective of developing a master plan of road network improvements and efficient traffic dispersal systems in Mumbai. The project work for the same has already started. Mumbai Metropolitan Region Development Authority (MMRDA) has identified 134 roads, 10 elevated roads, 41 flyovers, 16 Rail-Over Bridges (ROB), 10 vehicular subways and 10 pedestrian subways will be taken up for implementation. These critical missing links will facilitate fast and efficient dispersal of traffic. The provisions also include specific measures for pedestrian movement along and across the roads and all major roads will be provided with proper footpaths and pedestrian grade separators at all the essential locations. MUIP also has a provision for Station Area Traffic Improvement Schemes (SATIS), under which the roads and traffic movement around station areas will be improved. It is sure that the changed focus and complementary measure of MUIP will bring about some improvement, but the city needs to have a long term strategy and reform agenda to ensure the sustained and better performance which are still awaited.

REFERENCES

Atkins Study (1994), *Comprehensive Transportation Plan for Bombay Metropolitan Region*, Study prepared by M/s WS Atkins & Co. for the MMRDA

Bombay First (2003), *Vision Mumbai: Transforming Mumbai into a World Class City*, Report submitted to the Government of Maharashtra.

GoM (2004), Transforming Mumbai into a World Class City; Vision 2013, *Report of the Task Force*, Government of Maharashtra, Mumbai.

Harral, C. and A. Faiz (1988), *Road Deterioration in Developing Countries*, The World Bank, Washington DC.

Heggie, I. G. and P. Vickers (1998), Commercial Management and Financing of Roads, *World Bank Technical · Paper No. 498*, The World Bank,Washington DC.

India Infrastructure Report (1996), India Infrastructure Report — Policy Imperatives.

for Growth and Welfare, *Report of Expert Group on Commercialisation of Infrastructure Projects*, Government of India.

MCGM (2002), *Know Your Wards*, A publication of the MCGM, Mumbai.

MCGM (2003), *Environmental Status of Brihan Mumbai*, MCGM, Mumbai.

MCGM (2006), *The Road Ahead*, Retrieved from MCGM website www.mcgm.gov.in

Mohanty, P. K. (2003), Financing Urban Infrastructure: Some Innovative Practices of Resource Mobilisation, *Working Paper*, Centre for Good Governance, Hyderabad.

Nallathiga, R. (2002): Road Concretization in Mumbai, *The CITY* I (3): 44

Singh, Sanjay K. (2000), Estimating the level of rail and road based passenger mobility in India, *Indian Journal of Transport Management Vol.* 24, No.12, pp. 771-781.

World Bank (2004), *Reforming Infrastructure: Privatisation, Regulation and Competition*, The World Bank, Washington DC.